DATE DUE	RETURNED
OCT 0 5 2009	OCT 1 9 2009
Feb.28/17	MAR 0 / 2017 MW
Sep 11/18	

The SAGE Handbook of
Advertising

The SAGE Handbook of
Advertising

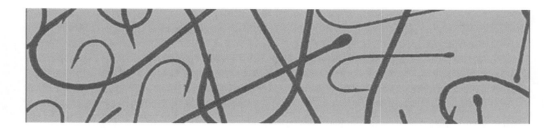

Edited by
Gerard J. Tellis
Tim Ambler

 **SAGE** Publications

Los Angeles • London • New Delhi • Singapore

First published 2007

Apart from any fair dealing for the purposes of research or private
study, or criticism or review, as permitted under the Copyright,
Designs and Patents Act, 1988, this publication may be reproduced,
stored or transmitted in any form, or by any means, only with the
prior permission in writing of the publishers, or in the case of
reprographic reproduction, in accordance with the terms of licences
issued by the Copyright Licensing Agency. Enquiries concerning
reproduction outside those terms should be sent to the publishers.

SAGE Publications Ltd
1 Oliver's Yard
55 City Road
London EC1Y 1SP

SAGE Publications Inc.
2455 Teller Road
Thousand Oaks, California 91320

SAGE Publications India Pvt Ltd
B 1/I 1 Mohan Cooperative Industrial Area
Mathura Road
New Delhi 110 044

SAGE Publications Asia-Pacific Pvt Ltd
33 Pekin Street #02-01
Far East Square
Singapore 048763

Library of Congress Control Number: 2007922745

British Library Cataloguing in Publication data

A catalogue record for this book is available from
the British Library

ISBN 978-1-4129-1886-2
ISBN 978-1-4129-1887-9 (pbk)

Typeset by CEPHA Imaging Pvt. Ltd., Bangalore, India
Printed in Great Britain by The Cronwell Press Ltd., Trowbridge, Wiltshire
Printed on paper from sustainable resources

Contents

Acknowledgements

We are deeply grateful to Jane Scott and Cheryl Tellis who served as assistant editors of the *Handbook* through most of its development. Their dedicated service and attention to detail enhanced the quality, productivity, and timeliness of manuscripts and reviews. We also thank Carolyn van den Haak for her enthusiasm and dedication as assistant editor when the project first started. The Institute of Practitioners in Advertising, and Ann Murray Chatterton in particular, were very helpful.

We are deeply grateful to the many experts who generously served as reviewers of the various chapters: Craig Andrews, Rajeev Batra, Michael Belch, Joel Cohen, Peter Danaher, Marnik Dekimpe, Paul Farris, Winston Fletcher, John B. Ford, Mary Gentile, Guenter Hitsch, Michael Hoefges, Debbie John, Amna Kirmani, Sharmistha Law, Len Lodish, Tina Lowery, Mary Ann McGrath, Edward McQuarrie, Carl Mela, Betsy Moore, Patrick Murphy, Cheryl Nakata, Koen Pauwels, Ross Petty, Leyland Pitt, Joe Priester, Stefano Puntoni, Jef Richards, Don Schultz, S. Siddarth, Dave Stewart, Patti Williams, and Fred Zufryden.

Finally, we thank the authors who agreed to join us in this venture and who have given up a great deal of scarce and valuable time to render such splendid contributions.

Gerard J. Tellis   Tim Ambler
University of Southern California   London Business School
Los Angeles, USA   London, UK

List of Contributors

Tim Ambler is a Senior Fellow at London Business School and researches, mainly, dynamic marketing capabilities, how advertising works and marketing metrics. He is a Chartered Accountant and was Joint Managing Director of International Distillers and Vintners, now part of Diageo. As Marketing Director (CMO), in the UK and internationally, he was involved in the launch of Baileys and other successful drinks brands and the development of Smirnoff vodka worldwide.

Caroline Graham Austin studied history at Mercer University and American studies at the University of Notre Dame before discovering, at the University of Georgia, how much she enjoys marketing and consumer behavior. Her work has been published in the conference proceedings of the European Association of Consumer Research, the American Marketing Association, and the Academy of Marketing Science, as well as in the *Journal of Targeting, Measurement and Analysis for Marketing.*

Carolyn Bonifield is Assistant Professor of Marketing at the University of Vermont School of Business Administration. She received her PhD in 2002 from the Tippie School of Business at the University of Iowa. Her research is concentrated in the area of affect and consumer decision making, with an emphasis on post-purchase decision.

Catherine Cole is Professor of Marketing at the Tippie School of Business at the University of Iowa. She is currently chair of the Marketing Department and a Henry B. Tippie Research Fellow. She received her PhD in 1983 from the University of Wisconsin. Her thesis topic related to age differences in reactions to print and television advertising. She continues to study the older consumer market.

C. Samuel Craig is the Catherine and Peter Kellner Professor and Director of the Entertainment, Media and Technology Program at New York University's Stern School of Business. He received his PhD from the Ohio State University. Along with Susan Douglas, he co-authored *Global Marketing Strategy* and *International Marketing Research,* 3rd edition. His research interests focus on the entertainment industry, global marketing strategy and methodological issues in international marketing research.

Peter Danaher is the Coles Myer Chair of Marketing and Retailing at the Melbourne Business School in Australia. He was previously at the University of Auckland and has had visiting positions at London Business School, The Wharton School and MIT. His primary research interests are media exposure distributions, advertising effectiveness, television audience measurement and behavior, internet usage behavior, customer satisfaction measurement, forecasting and sample surveys.

Marnik G. Dekimpe (PhD, UCLA) is Research Professor of Marketing at Tilburg University (The Netherlands) and Professor of Marketing, Catholic University Leuven (Belgium). His research has been published in journals such as *Marketing Science*, the *Journal of Marketing Research*, the *Journal of Marketing*, the *Journal of Econometrics* and the *International Journal of Research in Marketing*, among others.

Suresh Divakar is Vice President, Global Marketing Intelligence at Avon Products, Inc. Dr. Divakar has extensive business, research and consulting experience in the CPG and Financial Services sectors. He currently works with Avon Products as a VP, having worked with companies such as Kraft, PepsiCo and Citibank before. He has several publications in leading marketing journals and has been invited to make presentations in prestigious marketing conferences. Dr. Divakar holds a PhD and an MBA in Marketing, as well as a BS in Engineering.

Susan P. Douglas is Paganelli-Bull Professor of Marketing and International Business at New York University's Stern School of Business. She received her PhD from the University of Pennsylvania. She is co-author (with C. Samuel Craig) of two books, *Global Marketing Strategy* and *International Marketing Research, third edition* and has published over 60 articles in leading marketing and international business journals. Her research interests focus on global marketing strategy, cross-cultural consumer research and methodological issues in international marketing research.

Minette E. Drumwright's research is in the areas of business and society, business ethics, and marketing for nonprofit organizations. Professor Drumwright is faculty chair of the Bridging Disciplines Program in Ethics and Leadership, and she teaches in the Graduate Portfolio Program in Nonprofit and Philanthropic Studies. She has a PhD in business administration (marketing) from the University of North Carolina at Chapel Hill.

Paul W. Farris is the Landmark Communications Professor of Business at the University of Virginia's Darden Graduate School of Business. Previously, he was a product manager for UNILEVER in Germany, worked in account management for the LINTAS advertising agency, and taught at the Harvard Business School. A recent book, *Marketing Metrics*: *50+ Metrics Every Executive Should Master*, was selected by Strategy + Business, as "2006 Marketing Book of the Year."

Paul Feldwick worked for over 30 years as an Account Planner and Planning Director at Boase Massimi Pollitt, BMP DDB and DDB Worldwide. He has written and lectured extensively on advertising and brands, including the book *What is Brand Equity Anyway?* (WARC 2002). He now works as an independent consultant in the areas of communication, creativity and change. He lives in Bath, England.

Aditi Grover is a third year PhD student in Marketing at the University of Southern California. She earned her Masters in Economics from the State University of New York – Buffalo in 2004, and Bachelors in Economics from University of Delhi in India (1995). She holds an MBA from the FORE School of Management in India. She was formerly a consultant in strategic planning and management with Deloitte Touche Tohmatsu (India). Her research interests lie primarily in exploring effectiveness of health communication messages and rumors in the marketplace.

Dominique M. Hanssens is the Bud Knapp Professor of Marketing at the UCLA Anderson School of Management. His research and teaching focus on strategic marketing problems, in particular the study of marketing productivity, to which he applies his expertise in econometrics and time-series analysis. From 2005–2007 he served as Executive Director of the Marketing Science Institute in Cambridge, Massachusetts. Professor Hanssens' publications may be found at http://www.anderson.ucla.edu/faculty/dominique.hanssens/research.htm.

Robert Heath, MA (Cantab), PhD, FMRS, FCRiAC, FEAA, MCIM, A graduate of Sidney Sussex College, Cambridge, Robert Heath spent 30 years as an advertising practitioner before completing his PhD at Bath School of Management. He is a Fellow of the Market Research Society, a Fellow of the Centre for Research into Advertising and Consumption, a founding member and Fellow of the European Advertising Academy, and has been a Visiting Professor at both Copenhagen and London Business Schools.

Kevin Lane Keller is the E. B. Osborn Professor of Marketing at the Tuck School of Business at Dartmouth College. Keller's academic resume includes degrees from Cornell, Duke, and Carnegie-Mellon universities, award-winning research, and faculty positions at Berkeley, Stanford, and UNC. His textbook, *Strategic Brand Management*, has been adopted at top business schools and leading firms around the world. He is also the co-author with Philip Kotler of the all-time best selling introductory marketing textbook, *Marketing Management.*

Donald Lehmann is the George E. Warren Professor of Business at Columbia University. His research interests include the diffusion of innovations, the value of marketing assets such as brands and customers, and empirical generalizatons. He serves on the editorial boards of several leading journals and is currently co-editor of the *International Journal of Research in Marketing.*

Dara MacCaba is the Managing Director of Mind Research at the TMRC Consultancy in Shanghai, China and a graduate of Yale University. He develops brand strategy for multi-national companies operating in Asia and has been featured in the media for optimizing companies' innovation processes through the use of psychological and biometric techniques.

David Mazursky received his PhD in marketing from the Graduate School of Business Administration at New York University. A Professor at the Hebrew University of Jerusalem, he is the Chair of Marketing Department, and Director of the K-Mart Center for Retailing and International Marketing. Professor Mazursky has published in *Science, Journal of Marketing Research, Journal of Consumer Research, Management Science, Marketing Science, Journal of Applied Psychology, Journal of Experimental Social Psychology*, and others.

Colin McDonald has spent over 45 years in market research and has run his own research consultancy for the last 16 years. With wide experience in advertising and media research, he was a pioneer analyst of single-source data. He has written widely on advertising research, and is on the editorial board of Admap and IJOA. Colin is a Fellow and gold medallist of the Market Research Society and an Associate of the Ehrenberg-Bass Institute, University of South Australia.

Nicole Votolato Montgomery is an Assistant Professor of Marketing at The Mason School of Business, The College of William and Mary. Her research focuses on issues related to consumer behavior and judgement and decision making. In particular, she studies consumer memory and how consumers evaluate experiences overtime.

Elizabeth S. Moore is Associate Professor and Notre Dame Chair of Marketing at the University of Notre Dame. Her research interests are in marketing and society, and marketing to children. She has received recognitions for her teaching and research, including Best Paper Awards at *JCR* and *JPP&M*. She holds an undergraduate degree from Mount Holyoke College and graduate degrees from the University of Florida.

Jon D. Morris, is Professor, in the Department of Advertising, College of Journalism and Communications, and holds a courtesy appointment in the Department of Psychiatry, McKnight Brain Institute, University of Florida. Previously with advertising agencies, including: Nicholson–Morris, Doyle Dane Bernbach and Dancer Fitzgerald Sample, Dr. Morris is the developer of AdSAM, a model for analyzing emotional response to marketing and interpersonal communications and he now uses Functional Magnetic Resonance Imaging (*f*MRI). His papers have been published by, amongst others, the *Journal of Advertising Research, Current Issues in Advertising Research, Journal of Advertising, Journal of Targeting, Journal of Educational Technology, Advances in Consumer Research* and the *Proceedings of the American Academy of Advertising.*

Prasad A. Naik is Professor of Marketing and Chancellor's Fellow at the University of California Davis. He published research in not only Marketing and Advertising (*JMR, Marketing Science, Management Science, JM, JAR*), but also Statistics and Econometrics (*JASA, Biometrika, JRSS-B, JE*). He received *AMS Doctoral Dissertation Award, Frank Bass Award, MSI Young Scholar, Professor of the Year*, and *Marquis' Who's Who in America* and *Who's Who in the World.*

Thomas C. O'Guinn is Professor of Marketing and Executive Director, Center for Brand and Product Management, University of Wisconsin-Madison. Prior to that he was at the University of Illinois at Urbana-Champaign and served as a visiting Scholar at U.C.L.A., Duke, University of Utah, University of Innsbruck, and Dublin City University. His work is often multi-method and truly synthetic of multiple literatures and has been heavily cited and honored several times with best contribution awards (including two Best of *JCR*). He holds consumer research to be truly relevant and important not only to business scholars and practitioners, but to public policy and contemporary society as well. His published work has been reported in such media outlets as *The New York Times, The Wall Street Journal, National Public Radio, Forbes, The Chicago Tribune,* and *Wired*. He is most interested in the sociology of consumption and electronically mediated environments.

Seema Pai is currently a PhD candidate at the Marshall School of Business. Prior to joining the PhD Program, Seema obtained her MBA from the Indian Institute of Management in Lucknow. She also worked for a couple of years as an Assistant Brand Manager with Procter & Gamble in Asia. Her research interests include buzz marketing, advertising, public relations and mass media and econometric modeling.

Richard E. Petty received his PhD from Ohio State University and is currently distinguished University Professor of Psychology there. His research on attitudes and persuasion has resulted in 8 books and over 200 articles. Petty has received research awards from the Society for Personality and Social Psychology and the Society for Consumer Research. He is former editor of the *Personality and Social Psychology Bulletin.*

Rik Pieters is Professor of Marketing at Tilburg University. He holds a PhD in Psychology from the University of Leiden (1989). He was a visiting Professor at the University of Florida,

Auckland and Penn State University, and a Strategy Director at the FCB Advertising Agency (Amsterdam office). His work has appeared in the *Journal of Marketing, Journal of Consumer Research, Marketing Science, Journal of Personality* and *Social Psychology*, and *PINT-news*, among others.

Joseph R. Priester is an Associate Professor of Marketing at the USC – Marshall School of Business. He received his PhD in Social Psychology from the Ohio State University.

Jef I. Richards is Professor of Advertising at The University of Texas at Austin, where he has taught since 1988 and served as Advertising Department Chairman from 1998–2002. His research primarily involves advertising regulation, and he has authored or co-authored two books and numerous articles. He serves on the Advertising Educational Foundation's Board of Directors, and as 2008 President of the American Academy of Advertising.

Derek Rucker is an Assistant Professor of Marketing at the Kellogg School of Management, Northwestern University. Dr. Rucker's primary research focuses on the study of attitudes, persuasion, and social influence. His work aims to better understand how to improve advertising effectiveness by understanding the role of metacognitive processes and emotion in consumer persuasion. He has written and published papers on these topics in a variety of leading journals.

Edith G. Smit holds the Customer Media Chair at the University of Amsterdam, the Netherlands. Prof. Dr. Smit has a background in Marketing, Psychology and Communication, and received her PhD in 1999. Her research focuses on advertising effectiveness, brand communication and relationship media, resulting in various publications in *Journal of Advertising, Journal of Advertising Research* and *Journal of Business Research*.

Ji Hee Song is an Assistant Professor of Marketing and e-Business in the College of Business and Economics at Towson University. She obtained her PhD from the University of Georgia. Her research interest includes interactive marketing and the effect of Web atmosphere on consumer experience online. Her recent article on Web site interactivity has been accepted in *Journal of Marketing*.

David W. Stewart, PhD, is the Dean of the A. Gary Anderson Graduate School of Management at the University of California, Riverside. He has previously served on the faculties of the University of Southern California and Vanderbilt University. Dr. Stewart is a past Editor of the *Journal of Marketing* and is the current Editor of the *Journal of the Academy of Marketing Science*. Dr. Stewart has authored or co-authored more than 200 publications and seven books that have examined a wide range of issues including marketing strategy, the analysis of markets, consumer information search and decision making, effectiveness of marketing communications, public policy issues and research methodology.

Richard Storey is Chief Strategy Officer of M&C Saatchi. A graduate of Cambridge University, he learned his trade at BMP DDB London – "the home of planning" – before joining M&C Saatchi to leading its "brutal simplicity" approach to planning. Richard has won five IPA Effectiveness awards for clients including British Airways, Police Recruitment and Scottish Amicable. Equally passionate about creativity as effectiveness, Richard has also won the very same number of APG Creative Planning awards.

Gerard J. Tellis (http://www-rcf.usc.edu/~tellis/) (PhD Michigan) is Professor of Marketing, Neely Chair of American Enterprise, and Director of Center for Global Innovation, Marshall

School of Business, University of Southern California. He specializes in innovation, market entry, new product growth, advertising, and pricing. He published over 80 papers and books, which have won 15 awards. He is also a Trustee of the Marketing Science Institute and a Senior Research Associate of Judge Business School, Cambridge University.

Rao Unnava is the W. Arthur Cullman Professor of Marketing and Associate Dean of Undergraduate Programs at Fisher College of Business, The Ohio State University. His research is mainly focused on consumer memory and consumer commitment to brands.

Demetrios Vakratsas is Associate Professor of Marketing at McGill University and holds the Tasos Papastratos Research Chair (Visiting) at the Athens Laboratory of Business Administration (ALBA). His research focuses on issues of consumer response to firms' promotional and advertising strategies and strategic market entry decisions. His work has appeared in *Marketing Science, Journal of Marketing, Journal of Retailing, Journal of Applied Econometrics* and *Research Policy* among others. He has won awards in recognition of his research and teaching contributions.

Michel Wedel is the Pepsico Professor of Consumer Research at the Smith School of Business, University of Maryland, and holds an honorary chair at the University of Groningen. Previously head of statistics at the TNO-Nutrition Research Institute, he applies statistical and econometric methods to marketing, notably using eye-tracking to study the effects of visual marketing. With nearly 200 top journal articles, he has been ranked the most productive as well as the third most cited economist in the Netherlands.

Douglas West, PhD, is Professor of Marketing at the University of Birmingham, UK. He has held faculty appointments in the UK and Canada. He sits on several editorial boards and is editor of the *International Journal of Advertising*. Besides budgeting, his research interests include creative marketing, risk and strategic marketing.

David Wethey is the Founder (1988) and Chairman of Agency Assessments International (AAI). AAI is headquartered in London, with partners in the US and globally. David graduated from Oxford University. He was into international management with McCann-Erickson for 11 years. David is leading his own agency for 7 years. He is a frequent speaker at conferences, seminars and workshops – in 20 countries so far. David has authored the *UK Guide to Remuneration*, is a columnist for Marketing Week and also writes for Admap and Market Leader-most read blogger on Brand Republic.

William L. Wilkie is Nathe Professor of Marketing at the University of Notre Dame. He has received the American Marketing Association's highest honor, the Distinguished Marketing Educator Award, Notre Dame's President's Award and BP/Amoco Outstanding Teacher Award, and was elected President of the Association for Consumer Research. One of his articles has been named a "Citation Classic" in the *Social Sciences* by the Institute for Scientific Information. After an undergraduate degree from Notre Dame and graduate degree from Stanford, he served on faculties at Purdue, Harvard, and Florida, as in-house consultant at the Federal Trade Commission, and as Research Professor at the Marketing Science Institute.

Gerald Zaltman is a senior partner in Olson Zaltman Associates, a firm specializing in understanding the mind of the market, and the Joseph C. Wilson Professor of Business Administration Emeritus, Harvard Business School. He is the author of *"How Customers*

Think" and co-author of the forthcoming book, "*Metaphorics: Navigating the Unconscious Mind.*"

George M. Zinkhan (PhD, University of Michigan) is the Coca-Cola Company Professor of Marketing at the University of Georgia. He is past Editor of both the *Journal of Advertising* and the *Journal of the Academy of Marketing Science*.

SECTION I
Overview

Handbook of Advertising

Gerard J. Tellis and Tim Ambler

Advertising is one of the most fascinating phenomena in business. It is pervasive, perplexing, multidimensional, and unfathomably rich. It is seemingly simple, yet full of paradoxes. Lay people and some experts assume they understand well enough how advertising works. Yet research has shown that some simple conclusions are quite wrong. While decades of research have thrown light on how advertising works, even experts disagree about its role, especially when these experts are from differing disciplines.

For example, some economists see advertising as inflating the prices of goods and services because it is unnecessary or anti-competitive. Religious leaders depict advertisers as materialistic because it creates desires for worldly goods and pleasures. Sociologists point to advertising as undermining the values of society and corrupting relationships with commercialism. Some politicians, while turning a blind eye to their own high advertising expenditures, decry advertising as being a waste of scarce resources. Advertisers are naturally enthusiastic about their own ads, but may persist with them past the point that is optimal.

This *Handbook* addresses the whole range of issues that can be called "advertising."

Surprisingly to us, this is the first handbook of advertising which aims to supply a full background resource for practitioners and academics.

The major concern and underlying thread of this *Handbook* is "effectiveness," meaning that advertising meets the goals set for it. These goals may be maintaining or changing awareness, attitudes, or behaviour or increasing sales, market share, or profits. These goals apply to for-profit as much as to not-for-profit advertisers. For example, the army advertises to increase recruits, churches advertise to increase attendance, and politicians advertise for votes. Unless the authors of these chapters have specifically defined it otherwise, the word "effectiveness" in this *Handbook* always means achieving the intended goals. The term "efficiency" refers to the ratio of the benefits from the advertising relative to its costs. Both effectiveness and efficiency have become important criteria in planning advertising and assessing performance.

This introduction first looks at some common perceptions of advertising and suggests that they are wholly or partly flawed. Some are both true and untrue: the paradoxical nature of advertising is part of its charm. Next we review the framework for the book and show

how these chapters address the main concerns of advertising practitioners and academics.

COMMON PERCEPTIONS OF ADVERTISING

We list ten popular views of advertising and then discuss each of them:

1. Advertising powerfully shapes consumer preferences and persuades people to buy what they would not otherwise buy.
2. Advertising simply provides information to assist consumer decision-making.
3. Even if advertising does not work immediately, repetition ensures its ultimate effectiveness.
4. The effects of advertising last for years and even decades.
5. Even if advertising seems ineffective, stopping it could be dangerous.
6. Advertising is highly profitable.
7. Consumers are ultimately rational in making decisions, so ads need to provide at least one logical reason to purchase.
8. Advertising rips off the consumer by causing prices to be higher than they otherwise would be.
9. Sales promotion is more effective than advertising.
10. Advertising alone changes brand equity.

How powerful is advertising?

Some advertisements or some advertising campaigns are very powerful in that they have demonstrable effects. Advertising associations in various countries have awards for advertising effectiveness. The American Marketing Association awards "EFFIEs" for the best ads in various categories. In the UK, the Institute of Practitioners in Advertising (IPA) has had biennial awards since 1980 based on case histories. Those of the winners are published and available from the WARC.com website. These awards are based on creativity or on proven performance.

Many of us have our favourite ads, in the sense that we believe them to have worked. For example, the advertisement for Victoria's Secret in the 1993, Super Bowl

sent millions of people to their website in the first few minutes. The introductory campaign for Altoids propelled this UK brand to prominence in the US market. Thus, some campaigns are successful just as some horses win races. However, when these and many other successes are averaged over billions of dollars of mundane advertising that saturate our media and permeate our lives, the mean effectiveness drops substantially. Estimated advertising elasticities average between 0.05 and 0.1, one-twentieth of corresponding price elasticities (Sethuraman and Tellis, 1991; Tellis, 1989).

How powerful, or effective, are the others? Clearly we do not all respond to all ads. Indeed, if we were to respond immediately to every ad we saw, our lives would be a whirlwind of consumption that would be quite unsustainable, even for a few days! It is not that advertising cannot be powerful. It is just that much advertising gets lost in the noise of competing brands, and some advertising merely adds to the noise. Every creative artist probably hopes to build a winning blockbuster ad. Only a few succeed and these successes are quickly imitated so their edge is dulled. The challenge for advertisers is to know which ads work and when and why they work. These are key topics in this *Handbook*, which Sections 2 and 4 address in depth.

Is advertising merely informative?

Originally ads may have been displays outside commercial premises or small ads in the media. If one were looking for a butcher's shop, signage or an address would help find it. Today most ads are still largely informational. In modern times, ads have resorted to persuasion, i.e., seeking to change consumer attitudes, beliefs, or behaviour. However, most mature products have little need to provide information. Their consumers are familiar with the products, distribution is well nigh universal, and prices are only available from retailers. Nowadays, the most effective ads may rely on emotion more than they do on factual information. Ads may also merely reinforce existing behaviour, rather than seek to change it. Section 2 of this handbook, especially Chapters 2.1 and 2.2 discuss these important aspects of advertising.

Does ultimate effectiveness depend on repetition?

When advertisements do not appear to work right away, advertisers tend to excuse the non-response rather than pull the advertisement. The easy excuse for non-response is that consumers have either not seen the advertisement or need time to think about it and respond to it. When an advertiser and its agency have spent months testing and creating an advertisement, it is tough to call it a failure. Some will spend a little more money to see if repetition might not achieve the elusive effectiveness. This is a problem that decision analysts in other contexts call entrenchment bias, self-involvement bias, or escalation of commitment. Some research shows that if advertising does not work in the reasonably short term (first few weeks), it is unlikely to ever work (Lodish et al., 1995).

Yet, advertising can work in subtle ways. We should be careful not to confuse an inability to *measure* effects with there being no effects. The evidence from certain ads, typically those that do not meet consumer expectations, is indeed that the initial reactions do not match long-term effects, e.g., the UK campaigns for Andrex toilet tissues and Stella Artois beer. The industry belief, that brand managers tend to tire of campaigns before consumers, is not entirely without foundation. This issue is discussed further in Chapter 4.4.

Are the effects of advertising long-lasting?

The belief that the effects of advertising may last years or even decades comes from our ability to remember very old advertising slogans (e.g., AT&T's "reach out and touch someone" or EF Hutton's "When EF Hutton speaks, people listen"). But recalling a campaign does not mean that it was effective: one of these brands is in trouble while the other is dead. Second, economists at one time estimated the effects of advertising with Koyck-type models using annual data. They found that the effects of advertising lasted years or decades. The choice of time periods for aggregating data biases the results (Clarke, 1976; Tellis and Franses, 2006; Vakratsas and Ambler, 1999).

Using more refined (aggregated over shorter periods data), shows the effects of advertising to be short (e.g., Tellis and Weiss, 1995; Tellis et al., 2000). These results by no means imply that "long-term" memory is not involved in advertising response. Indeed, findings from neuroscience suggest that advertising must affect long-term memory or have no effect at all. The reason for this is that short-term memory is quite short, certainly less than a day, so that if an ad on day one affects behaviour some days later, long-term memory must have been involved (Ambler and Burne, 1999). Chapters 2.2 and 4.4 address the memory and long-term effects of advertising respectively.

Anecdotally, one of the editors was responsible for advertising Hennessy cognac in the UK. A famous campaign, involving alpine rescue by a St Bernard dog with a barrel of Hennessy strapped to its neck, had been axed 20 years earlier. Yet current research invariably prompted responses about the dog. This was somewhat aggravating as the dog campaign had been axed because it had been good for the sales of St Bernards but had no effect on Hennessy sales. The advertising was well remembered, even by those too young ever to have seen it, but the brand was not; advertisers care about brand effects, not advertising effects.

Is it dangerous to stop an ineffective campaign?

Even when advertising campaign seems ineffective, advertisers may be loath to suspend it (e.g., Eastlack and Rao, 1989). They may argue that suspension would mean that consumers would be exposed only to the competitors' advertisements, which would then become highly effective. This belief arises from the prisoner's dilemma: advertising may be unprofitable but leaving all advertising to competitors may be even more unprofitable. Furthermore, if advertising is seen as maintenance, then conducting it may not appear to be profitable but failing to do so would be costly in the long run.

One approach is to design a test, one that takes into account sufficiently long periods of non-response, sufficiently deep cuts in advertising, and sufficient exposure to rival brands' advertising. Chapters 4.2, 4.3, and 4.4 focus on the measurement, testing, and tracking of advertising campaigns to help managers make wise decisions about when to stop a campaign.

Is advertising highly profitable?

Advertising may be thought to be highly profitable because there is so much of it or because of expectations that advertising directly leads to increased sales and market share. The perception of the profitability of *advertising* may also be driven by the perceived profitability of some advertisers. The reality can be quite different, not least due to competitive activity. If all brands in a sector are advertising, they cannot all be increasing market share. When competitors get caught up in advertising rivalry, they may overadvertise, i.e., add to costs and not profits (Aaker and Carmen, 1982). Collectively they might well be more profitable if they all stopped, but agreeing to do so is, of course, illegal.

On the other hand, the collective advertising might be raising the sales of the sector as a whole. This is one reason why it is dangerous to measure advertising effectiveness by market share. Effectiveness can be enhanced by careful consideration of the alternative feasible goals and which most helps the overall corporate objectives. Pre-testing works for some advertisers and not others (Ambler and Goldstein, 2003) but almost all advertisers should conduct tracking research to establish whether these goals are likely to be, or have been, met. Such a performance-oriented approach to advertising is important in the current environment with tight budgets and intense competition.

As one might expect, some advertising appears to be highly profitable whereas other advertising may be a waste of money. A central aim of this *Handbook* is to help advertisers and their advisers predict and analyse the reasons for the productivity of their advertising. Section 4 of this handbook addresses how managers can analyse the effects of advertising. Section 5 of the *Handbook* addresses how advertisers can plan advertising profitably.

Are consumers driven solely by rational considerations?

Consumers like to think of themselves as rational decision makers who make the best use of the information they have and the time available. "Cogito ergo sum" said Descartes. He suggested that thinking defined existence and separated man from animals. Reasonable people prefer advertisements that are simple, clear, and informative with a logical reason for purchase. Rosser Reeves (1960) coined the term USP (Unique Selling Proposition) to describe the distinguishing rational claim which every ad should include.

However, research indicates emotional appeals can be more effective than rational appeals. Emotional appeals are more interesting, more easily remembered, more prone to lead to action, and less likely to arouse consumers' defences than rational appeals (Ambler and Burne, 1999; Deighton and Hoch, 1993; Deighton et al., 1989; Tellis, 2004). An analogy is the courtroom. Lay people assume that lawyers argue and juries decide on logic. In reality, emotions play a big and critical part in swaying juries. Indeed Damasio (1994) claims that all human decision-making is linked to feelings: we are not robots. Chapters in Section 2 of this *Handbook* delve into the various aspects of the informative versus emotional routes of persuasion.

Does advertising inflate prices of goods and services?

Interest in the relationship between advertising and pricing has been higher in economics than in the fields of advertising or marketing. Economic research has pursued whether advertising (costs) cause brands to be higher priced, whether advertising reduces price elasticity, and whether advertising encourages niche marketing of premium-priced brands. However, the findings in this field have been limited by fairly old studies, often with aggregate data, and with very strong priors about what should be found. Lind (1998) points out the naiveté of assuming that prices are driven by costs and would be reduced if advertising ceased. Price is set by market forces of which advertising is one, but often not a significant one. Brand leaders may be premium priced but that does not imply that the average price of the market as a whole is higher than it would be without advertising. Sector specific studies, e.g., UK opticians (Office of Fair Trading, 1983), sometimes show that prices declined when advertising was introduced. Research and reviews of research in marketing suggest that the results are contingent on a few factors: informativeness of advertising, content of advertising, and focus on advertising (Farris and Albion, 1980; Kaul and Wittink, 1995).

First, advertisements that provide information about longitudinal price cuts or lower competitive prices may well help to lower prices among competing brands or increase consumers' price elasticity, notably advertising by retailers. The reverse could well hold for advertisements that differentiate brands (Farris and Albion, 1980; Kaul and Wittink, 1995; Sethuraman and Tellis, 1991). Second, retail advertisements that promote availability or sales promotions could help to increase retail price competition and lower retail prices or increase consumers' retail price elasticity (Farris and Albion, 1980; Sethuraman and Tellis, 2002). Manufacturer advertising that focuses on brand uniqueness or superiority relative to competitors could help to sustain high prices or reduce price elasticity (Kaul and Wittink, 1995). Third, mass advertising of new products or new categories could encourage mass adoptions by consumers and enable firms to exploit economies of scale

and lower costs (Golder and Tellis, 1997; Stremersch and Tellis, 2004; Tellis et al., 2003). Similarly, comparative advertising among mature brands could lead to lower brand prices or increased consumers' price elasticity. Fourth, manufacturer advertising could trigger inter-retailer competition as retailers compete to advertise and promote the brand (Steiner, 1973, 1993; Tellis, 1998). This effect could in turn lead to a lowering of retail prices but an increase in manufacturing prices. Thus, generalizations in this area are neither as obvious nor as simple as assumed in some of the economic literature. Section 6 of this *Handbook*, and especially Chapter 6.5 address some of these issues.

Is sales promotion replacing advertising?

Sales promotions have won an increasing share of the marketing budget at the expense of media advertising (e.g., Tellis, 1998). This shift in expenditures has been motivated partly by sales promotions giving more immediate and/or more apparent increases in sales and partly by the increasing negotiating power of large retail chains. The expenditure shift has triggered one of the biggest debates in the field of advertising: whether and when firms should invest in advertising versus sales promotion.

Sales promotion agencies assert that the proof of the pudding is in the sales response. Advertising agencies typically take the view that sales promotions increase short-term sales at the cost of long-term loyalty. A few studies have supported the latter premise (e.g., Mela et al., 1997).

The debate arguably misses the point. The real issue is not whether advertising or sales promotion is the more important but what is the correct balance. The use of both probably increases the overall impact, due to their interactive effect when used jointly (Tellis, 1998). For example, advertising can increase the salience or desirability of promoted brands. Moreover, retailers who see a brand's advertising may pass on more of the brand's trade promotions to consumers as consumer promotions. Similarly, brands purchased on promotion may make users more alert to advertisements from those brands. Alternatively, advertising can help interpret the experience of brands purchased on promotions (Hoch and Ha, 1986). All these effects underscore the importance of the joint use of advertising and sales promotion.

The issue is not, which of advertising or sales promotion to use but how to balance the two creatively and effectively. Unfortunately, research along these lines is currently sparse. Thus, the topic is in need of future research. The debate about advertising versus sales promotion also misses a deeper point about sales promotion. Many reporters assume that the list price of the brand is the competitive price, so that marketers who give discounts off the list price are cheapening their brand image. However, the discount price may well be the competitive price in which case no cheapening of the brand image takes place (Tellis, 1986).

Does advertising alone create brand equity?

An important topic today is the impact of advertising on brand equity. Interest in brand equity has been triggered by the finding that the book value of firms accounts for only a fraction of their market value. Several researchers have sought to link the unexplained market value to advertising. The usual route adopted is to correlate annual aggregate advertising expenditures with R&D expenditures and market value (e.g., Ailawadi et al., 2003; Mizik and Jacobsen, 2003; Simon and Sullivan, 1993). Studies have shown significant effects between advertising and stock market returns (e.g., Agrawal and Kamakura, 1995).

The importance of brand equity has also been triggered by the recognition that successful advertising builds brand equity which can build sales and reduce price elasticity (Ambler, 2003). However, advertising can work without changing brand equity and a number of variables besides advertising drive brand equity. For example, direct response advertising seeks immediate action by the customer rather than leaving memory changes

to impact behaviour at a later date. Among the other drivers of brand equity are the firm's reputation for quality and innovation, consumers' long-term loyalty arising from consumption experience, segmentation, and brand positioning. What researchers have not shown is what role advertising plays in the context of these other variables. Also, they have not shown how advertising's effects at the micro-level of thoughts, attitudes, and behaviours of individuals leads to brand equity at the aggregate level in terms of stock market returns. Two examples are illustrative.

Intel grew from a new brand in the 1970s to be one of the largest firms in terms of capitalization at the peak of the internet boom in 2000. In the 1990s, it ran a major advertising campaign, "intel inside," which is credited for transforming a popular branded product, the personal computer, into a commodity, while transforming an unknown component, the microprocessor, into a recognized and desired brand. This is one of the greatest transfers of wealth and power from retailers and competitors to a manufacturer in the history of advertising. Research has not shown clearly what role advertising, innovation, and reputation have played in that great transformation.

Samsung leapt from being a lowly supplier of cheap electronic products of mediocre quality to a prestigious supplier of high-quality, highly innovative products by massive expenditures in research and development. At the same time, Samsung made a concerted effort through modern marketing and heavy advertising to develop the image of being a high-quality, innovative brand. Indeed, Samsung has surpassed long-term innovative star, Sony, as a manufacturer of state-of-the-art displays and threatens long-term industry leader, Nokia, as a supplier of state-of-the-art cell phones. Both advertising and innovation have played key roles in this transformation. Yet research has not fully unravelled the causal nexus. Chapter 1.4 addresses the knowledge and problems to date in this important and exciting area.

STRUCTURE AND CONTENTS OF CHAPTERS

The main structure moves from theory to practice and then to wider contextual matters as follows:

1. Overview
2. Process
3. Practice
4. Planning
5. Strategy
6. Public policy.

We now provide an hors d'oeuvre for each of these in turn.

Overview

This introductory chapter is followed by Colin McDonald and Jane Scott's brief history of advertising, including content, or "copy," the roles of agencies and the development of media. Most conspicuous is the increasing complexity arising from more specialized agencies offering advertisers multiple choices in an increasing variety of media and increasing outlets within each medium. Thus, practitioners must juggle myriad balls in multiple spaces.

Prasad Naik outlines Integrated Marketing Communications (IMC), a strong and long-lived concept that looks to be here to stay. It shares with Media Neutral Planning the idea that advertising should primarily be seen from the consumer side.[1] The advertiser may have different managers and agencies to deliver different parts of the mix, e.g., advertising, the website, PR and promotions but the same consumer sees all of them. The positioning, packaging, branding, values, and general tone of the brand personality should be consistent. We therefore made the IMC chapter part of the initial overview because advertising needs to be understood, at least by advertisers, within that context.

Kevin Lane Keller brings together the brand equity issues raised earlier by considering advertising forms and functions and providing a model of brand equity for advertising. The model includes brand identity, meaning, responses, and relationships as well as different advertising roles. He then looks at strengthening advertising effects, brand associations, and brand links.

Process

There is a vast body of research on the various ways in which advertising works, or what we here call "process." The two main ways in which advertising works have been called "strong" and "weak" (Vakratsas and Ambler, 1999). The former models advertising as persuasion in the sense that the consumer is encouraged to do something they would not otherwise do, e.g., buy the product. The weak model sees advertising as reinforcing existing habits. The first two chapters in this section address this dichotomy to some extent although neither set of authors accepts the dichotomy as stated here. The argument, made in Chapter 2.1, is not whether the strong or the weak theory is right: both are right much of the time with the balance being dictated by context.

One potential generalization that emerges in the first pair of chapters is that there are multiple routes to persuasion. These routes can be broadly classified as either active or central processing, involving argument and logic, or passive peripheral processing that relies on cues (Petty and Cacioppo, 1986). Various types of visual imagery, music, and emotions could be more important in the latter route than the former. Moreover the latter route of persuasion seems to dominate the advertising media, partly because of the heavy load of competitive advertising and the recipient's limited time. Derek Rucker, Joe Priester, and Richard Petty take an in-depth looks at these two mains routes to persuasion and the various theories, concepts, and findings within each of them.

Robert Heath reviews the work done on reinforcement and low-attention processing. Some would argue that peripheral processing in the first chapter overlaps with low attention in the second but they are not the same. The most interesting observation, made by both Chapters 2.1 and 2.2, is that advertising can work as a weak force even though, or perhaps because, consumers are giving minimal attention to the ads.

The move away from purely rational appeals in advertising has highlighted the importance of emotion. David Stewart, Join Morris, and Aarti Grover identify the underlying theory for the use of emotion. The chapter classifies the differing kinds of emotion. Such appeals vary in intensity, explicitness, and integration with arguments (Deighton et al., 1989). It then describes the use of emotion in advertising, some theories of emotion and the measurement of emotional response.

How ads are received is not as important as their subsequent influence on purchase and consumption. This effect is mediated by memory or how the content of advertising is processed and retained in human memory. Thus we should not be studying the single ad transmission–reception event but the influence of advertising in a chain of events linked by human memory. Nicole Montgomery and H. Rao Unnava focus on the role of memory in advertising communication.

Jerry Zaltman and Dara MacCaba explore a related area, namely the role of metaphor in cognition and in memory so far as advertising is concerned. They suggest that metaphor provides an important way to understand how memory works, or, perhaps, can be tested. This topic is extremely important because memory has a crucial role in advertising in connecting the time when the ad is seen with the time that the relevant decision is made. We know little about how memory actually works and even less about how to measure changes in memory, especially now we have discounted rationality (which people use to report what they can remember) as a key part of the advertising process.

"Metaphor includes all non-literal representations such as the term 'up' to represent an emotional state or other idiomatic expressions such as 'let sleeping dogs lie' to suggest caution about further exploring an issue." Whilst this is just one portrayal of how memory works, it is important because it shows that we need to get away from simplistic views of human memory being verbal, or word-based, or logic like a computer hard drive. How

malleable is memory? And how should metaphor be treated in advertising research?

Many findings in this section are based on experiments, using student subjects, and examining ascertaining contingent or interactive effects of advertising among the consumers' states, the advertisement's message, the advertisement's imagery, and the type of product. We need to address three repeated criticisms of this body of research.

First, critics have asked whether researchers should pursue second-, third-, and fourth-order interactions in experimental situations when field researchers have had difficulty finding the main effects of advertising in the market. The answer may well be, precisely so! The heavy use of advertising by competitors dulls the advantage of standard advertising methods. This fact and the complex ways in which advertising works increases the need for managers to use advertising in precisely the manner and mode in which it is most effective. In competitive scenarios, advertising's advantage may be subtle. Experimental research points the way to take advantage of these subtleties.

Second, critics have assailed the use of student subjects and laboratory settings for most experimental research. Such research is inexpensive and convenient. However, managers cannot assess the validity of research that is done solely in the lab. Moreover, researchers cannot translate findings from the lab to meaningful effects in real markets. Some findings in lab settings may be trivial and some quite important. But when tested only in lab settings, the implications for the field remain unknown. While lab research remains an inexpensive means for testing various theories of advertising and generating a rich body of hypotheses, exclusive research in the lab limits its practical relevance.

Third, the large number of findings from experimental research increases the need for an integrative survey that can unambiguously point to what is known from this body of research and what needs to be known. More importantly, the field of lab research has adopted the paradigm from psychology that seeks counterintuitive results rather integrative commonalities. As a result, the field of lab research is diverging rather than converging in the variety of effects it has identified. This situation increases the need for an integrative framework that can pull together all the experimental findings into a unified whole which is explainable by a single theory.

Practice

The practice section follows the conventional sequence of events from briefing the agency to assessing the performance of the campaign.

David Wethey leads off with an experienced and robust approach to agency–client or client–agency relationships. It takes bravery to tell a couple how they should conduct their marriage and Wethey gets a medal for gallantry. Difficult as it is to cast an objective eye over these very human relationships, ad productivity depends on how well they work. Wethey's experience is summarized in proposals for effective relationships that come from the UK but apply universally.

Richard Storey and Edith Smit explain the creative briefing process. It is arguable that the main reason advertising performance falls short is that practitioners give too little time and energy to briefing both in absolute terms and relative to the other processes. Client and agency are complicit: the client thinks it will know what it wants when it sees it and the agency does not wish its creativity constrained by narrow briefing. As a result, goals are not identified, quantified, or prioritized, they are not matched with realistic budgets, and copy testing cannot be consistent with the objects of the advertising. When the campaign has run, effectiveness cannot be identified. Storey and Smit reflect the current practice, at least in the UK, of encouraging the creative brief to evolve alongside campaign development so that, when the proposed campaign is presented, it will fit the brief and the evolved benchmarks will be most relevant for evaluation. In other words, the brief should not be set in stone. Cynics may read that as licence for agencies to create the ads they want, tailoring the brief accordingly, rather

than meet the original requirement but that depends on the client's strength of purpose.

Paul Feldwick provides a comprehensive review of account planning since its introduction in the 1960s. Curiously, the term was first used simultaneously, but with different meanings, by two independent agencies and understanding has not been helped by a continuing spread of meanings in different agencies to this day. The main driver was the need to provide both client and agency with insights from consumer perspectives and what advertising options were commercially available. Of course clients and agencies have different goals (Devinney et al., 2005) but account planning should provide a bridge. Life is not as simple as that. Feldwick provides an expert tour of the realities.

Peter Field uses the unique resource of the UK database extracted from over 20 years of the winning case histories in the Institute of Practitioners in Advertising to examine best practice. Note the database is UK but some cases are from elsewhere. Field draws nine findings from his analysis of which the most important are the need for formal modelling, e.g., econometric, and a caution on using soft metrics or copy testing for prediction.

Advertising analysis

When the agency is ready, the campaign is presented to the client for approval. The client may well call for pre-testing, or copy testing, to assist this decision. The research may be qualitative, quantitative, or both. Since a great deal of money may be riding on the decision, the need for this research is clear in theory. The question is whether, in practice, pre-testing is predictive and is therefore good value for money. The evidence for the predictiveness of pre-testing is patchy (Ambler and Goldstein, 2003; Lodish et al., 1995) but there are other potent reasons for pre-testing including gaining top-management approval. Rik Pieters and Michel Wedel review pre-testing from a Six Sigma perspective with an emphasis on moment-to-moment measures of advertising processing. They call for systematic application of pre-testing for each and every ad in every campaign. Readers will enjoy their scholarship and enthusiasm even if they do not agree with all their conclusions.

Tracking performance during and/or after the campaign is less controversial. Suresh Divarkar and S. Siddarth explore "Advertising Field Experiments" and "Marketing Mix analysis." Critical aspects of each approach are outlined and major findings about the impact of advertising on sales gained from previous field experiments are summarized. They also provide a packaged goods case study where Marketing Mix analysis was used to evaluate the effectiveness of alternative advertising strategies. A fundamental problem with pre- and post-testing is whether to use the goals established, if they were, in the briefing stage to determine effectiveness or to use the standard metrics employed by the agency as performance benchmarks. In theory one should use both but the practical problem of metric continuity is very considerable.

Marnik Dekimpe and Dominique Hanssens consider econometric models of advertising effects on sales and other tangible performance metrics. They formulate a core advertising response model that accommodates most of phenomena, and extend it for differing advertising media, creative effects, wear-in and wear-out, and other important aspects of advertising practice. A multiple-equation system accommodates potential competitive response, as well as feedback loops within the firm. Finally, insights derived from advertising response models lead to conclusions with implications for decision making.

A large body of research has focused on the effects of advertising on sales or market share, using market or field data. Gerard Tellis reviews this literature and distils many potential generalizations. This body of research has been highly paradigmatic, usually adopting econometric models to analyse the effects of advertising. The many studies and the vast number of models have enabled researchers to carry out some meta-analyses of findings (e.g., Assmus et al., 1984; Clarke, 1976; Lodish et al., 1995; Sethuraman and Tellis, 1991). Some of the premises stated

in the previous section of this introduction come from these reviews. A detailed list of findings is also available in Tellis (2004).

Planning

Each new medium, e.g., the Web, is added to those existing and agency specialities likewise. Consolidation may reduce choice in the future but there is little sign of that occurring at present. Practitioners are evolving various ways to achieve focus or perhaps just to retain sanity. Media and creative considerations, other than Media Neutral Planning which we discussed earlier, are extensively covered in the section in Planning, in which we have six chapters.

We know that creativity is a critical ingredient in advertising. But what exactly do we mean by "creativity?" Some might hold it to be the leap of imagination which solves a problem in an unexpected way. This is primarily why clients, not generally considered to be imaginative, at least by their agencies, employ agencies in the first place. Jacob Goldenberg and David Mazursky decipher the creativity process in advertising. They focus on idea generation or "ideation," which is often viewed as the heart of this process – and then on methods for enhancing creativity. This chapter concludes that creativity has, in essence, two dimensions, namely surprise and regularity. No doubt other authors will label these dimensions in other ways, assuming they reach the same basic conclusions, as we think they will. The paradox that creativity involves simultaneously taking you away from the familiar while remaining relevant is important but does need testing, not least for the strength of its association with ad effectiveness.

The first media chapter (5.2) by Peter Danaher, looks at media planning in a traditional and pragmatic way by following the six steps conventionally used, namely deriving advertising from the overall marketing objectives, including the identification of the target audience. This leads to the selection of media, bearing creative and budget considerations in mind, and the specific media objectives. In that context the appropriate media can be scheduled and purchased. Finally the campaign can be assessed against those objectives.

Paul Farris and Doug West (Chapter 5.3) take a closer look at budgeting. They review many of the traditional approaches to budgeting, which have not changed much over the last 30 years. However, they point to an important middle ground between an extreme of designing *the best* approach and not using any scientific approach at all. The budgeting methods are followed by assessments of company studies with a view to providing insight as to why particular methods were chosen. The final part of the chapter explores a variety of organizational issues that impinge upon setting the advertising budget. The chapter concludes with implications for practitioners and researchers.

The fourth chapter in this section examines the scheduling of ads, i.e., pulsing or duration and spacing of advertising bursts, in more detail. Demetrios Vakratsas and Prasad Naik first outline some pulsing schedules, define the problem, review the empirical literature and identify the questions which are still open. The ad wearout model reveals the main insights and new results. The authors summarize the market conditions where pulsing is superior to even spending. Their concluding section provides directions for researchers and implications for managers.

George Zinkhan, Caroline Austin Graham, and Ji Hee Song (Chapter 5.5) see the modern complexity and diversity of media as leading to consumers being recruited as partners in marketing communications. In other words, the perspective shifts from the practitioner to the consumer. They label this practice as "consumer-based marketing methods" (CBMM). This chapter introduces a schematic representation of CBMM, a group of variables (e.g., risk, visibility, ease of use) that serve to differentiate these emerging promotional methods, and identifies potential problems and opportunities associated with these promotional tools as well as directions for future research.

In the final chapter in this section (5.6), Don Lehmann and Dina Mayzlin briefly describe the new product adoption process and how advertising can influence it. Then they review the key research, which explicitly focuses on advertising for new products. They discuss how advertisers can exploit buzz to launch new products effectively. They conclude with marketing's impact on the new product diffusion process.

Environment

The final section deals with wider public policy implications. So far, authors have been operating within the traditional capitalist paradigm, namely that businesses are there to make money, to do that they have to create demand and advertising is a positive part of that. Not everyone in modern society shares those assumptions.

One way in, which society reconciles these different values is through the regulation of what advertising may and may not do and to ensure that advertising is decent, honest, and truthful. Jeff Richards and Ross Petty (Chapter 6.1) categorize four purposes of regulations as persuasive effects on purchase and non-purchase behaviour, non-persuasive effects, and all other effects on political behaviour.

Society can enforce ethical standards on advertising through government regulation and/or "self-regulation" by industry-financed bodies such as the Advertising Standards Association in the UK. The other option is for individual advertisers to ensure that their own ethical standards are up to the level society expects. Minette Drumwright (Chapter 6.2) sees advertising as at the cutting edge, pushing the boundaries of what is familiar and acceptable. In such an environment, making ethical judgements can be particularly difficult. She uses three levels of ethical analysis – micro, meso, and macro – which are interdependent, each with its own set of issues and dynamics. Solutions to ethical problems in advertising require the micro and the macro levels to be linked through meso-level concepts and approaches. Framing ethical issues in advertising at the meso level, she suggests, enables the possibility of a more integrated approach to research and practice.

International advertisers are faced by both cross-country and also cross-cultural considerations of what is ethical and what is effective. Susan Douglas and Sam Craig (Chapter 6.3) open with a broad review of culture and advertising, before considering the content of cross-cultural advertising in terms of the influence of value orientation, material artefacts and the portrayal of people and the structure of communication. A key issue is whether managers should seek to standardize or adapt advertising to local cultures.

A fourth area in our consideration of ethical standards deals with vulnerable groups, or those deemed to be vulnerable by concerned groups. For example, should foods high in sugar, salt, and/or fats be targeted to young children who have not yet built up their defences to advertising. This area sometimes confuses vulnerable groups with products where excess consumption can be addictive and/or dangerous, e.g., tobacco, alcohol, and gambling. Cathy Cole and Carolyn Bonifield (Chapter 6.4) review research on advertising effects on vulnerable consumers. They suggest that marketers and public policy makers should understand the extent of knowledge that vulnerable consumers bring to consumption decisions and how easily and how willingly consumers retrieve this knowledge.

Tom O'Guinn (Chapter 6.5) considers the overall question of advertising's role in consumption and collective welfare. Is advertising, as a whole, good or bad for society? He does not see compelling evidence that advertising as a singular social agent has made humans any more materialistic than before. Advertising, as a part of a larger affluent consumer culture, probably has contributed to the social construction of a world of things, and consumption-centred solutions both negatively and positively. Advertising has not always been good where it contributed to consumer anxiety, and yet it brought a more honest and open acknowledgement of our relationship with things and an honest striving for a better material existence.

Finally, William Wilkie and Elizabeth Moore (Chapter 6.6) consider advertising in the aggregate and ask whether advertising is really good for society. They explore the key benefits advertising can bring to consumers in market-based systems and significant economic issues about the effects of advertising on overall consumption levels, competition, prices, and product innovation. Then they examine some of the criticisms of advertising by both social critics and consumer advocates, together with assessments of such questions as the utility of information provided by advertising, its persuasive power, and its impacts on consumer values and on vulnerable populations such as children. The chapter concludes with a brief look at the future and the problem of intrusiveness. Advertisers may be creating these problems through the ubiquity and volume of ads ("information overload") but they also have to provide solutions, such as integrated marketing communications, to cut through the noise and encourage consumers to be more active partners in the communications process. The Internet is becoming a major part of this function.

SUMMARY

This introductory chapter set out to highlight some major misperceptions of advertising and to introduce the chapters that constitute the *Handbook*. We encourage readers to immerse themselves in the wealth of scholarship this *Handbook* has brought together. No less than 50 academics and practitioners have provided their expertise and knowledge both in reviewing the extant literature and their own points of view. We have been less restrictive than top journals in confining authors to hard evidence because they have been toiling in these vineyards for decades and their conclusions deserve attention. We value their scholarship and are very grateful to each and every one of them.

We have tried to make this *Handbook* inclusive, with contributions that cover the gamut of advertising. As a result the *Handbook* is quite long. We recognize that few readers will start at the beginning of this *Handbook* and persevere to the end. Readers will vary in their needs and interests. However, whether it is the overview, process or practice, the analysis or planning, or the environment of advertising, we encourage readers to take a section as a whole and not be limited by the contents or thesis of one chapter. Indeed, some chapters disagree with others, while even those which overlap, do so from differing perspectives. That diversity of opinion is part of the fascinating richness of advertising, which we alluded to at the start of this introduction. Advertising is a craft, an art, and a science; it is multidisciplinary and complex; but understanding it makes for an enlightening and rewarding experience.

NOTE

1 Media Neutral Planning waxed and waned rather rapidly in the early 2000s and has therefore not been accorded a chapter in this *Handbook*. The need for the consumer perspective is taken up in IMC but enthusiasts for MNP went much further in suggesting that campaigns should be tailored first to the relevant media for the target market and creative matters considered only after that. Most other practitioners see creative and media considerations as being interactive.

REFERENCES

Aaker, D.A., and J.M. Carmen (1982), "Are You Over Advertising?" *Journal of Advertising Research*, 22, 4: 57–70.

Agrawal, J., and W.A. Kamakura (1995), "The Economic Worth of Celebrity Endorsers: An Event Study Analysis," *Journal of Marketing*, 59, 3: 56–62.

Ailawadi, K.L., D.R. Lehmann, and S.A. Neslin (2003), "Revenue Premium as an Outcome Measure of Brand Equity," *Journal of Marketing*, 67, 4: 1–17.

Ambler, T. (2003), *Marketing and the Bottom Line*, London: FT Prentice Hall, 2nd Edition, (May).

Ambler, T., and T. Burne (1999), "The Impact of Affect on Ad Memory," *Journal of Advertising Research*, 39, 2: 25–34.

Ambler, T., and S. Goldstein (2003), *Pre-testing: Practice and Best Practice*, Advertising Association, Henley on Thames: WARC, April.

Assmus, G., J.U. Farley, and D.R. Lehmann (1984), "How Advertising Affects Sales: Meta-Analysis of Econometric Result," *Journal of Marketing Research*, 21, 1: 65–74.

Chandy, R., G.J. Tellis, D. MacInnis, and P. Thaivanich (2001), "What to Say When: Advertising Appeals in Evolving Markets," *Journal of Marketing Research*, 38, 4: 399–414.

Clarke, D.G. (1976), "Econometric Measurement of the Duration of Advertising Effect on Sale," *Journal of Marketing Research*, 13: 345–57.

Damasio, A.R. (1994), *Descartes' Error: Emotion, Reason and the Human Brain*, London: Papermac (Macmillan).

Deighton, J., and S.J. Hoch (1993), "Teaching Emotion with Drama Advertising," in *Advertising Exposure, Memory, and Choice*, ed. Andrew A. Mitchell, Hillsdale, NJ: Lawrence Erlbaum.

Deighton, J., D. Romer, and J. McQueen (1989), "Using Drama to Persuade," *Journal of Consumer Research*, 16, 3: 335–43.

Devinney, T., G. Dowling, and M. Collins (2005), "Client And Agency Mental Models In Evaluating Advertising," *International Journal of Advertising*, 24, 1: 35–50.

Eastlack, J.O., Jr., and A.G. Rao (1989), "Advertising Experiments at the Campbell Soup Company," *Marketing Science*, 8, 1: 57–71.

Ehrenberg, A.S.C. (1974), "Repetitive Advertising and the Consumer," *Journal of Advertising Research*, 14 (April), 25–34.

Farris, P.W., and M.S. Albion (1980), "The Impact of Advertising on the Price of Consumer Products," *Journal of Marketing*, 44, 3: 17–35.

Golder, P.N., and G.J. Tellis (1997), "Will It Ever Fly? Modeling the Takeoff of New Consumer Durable," *Marketing Science*, 16, 3: 256–70.

Golder, P.N., and G.J. Tellis (2004), "Going, Going, Gone: Cascades, Diffusion, and Turning Points of the Product Life Cycle," *Marketing Science*, 23, 2: 180–91.

Heath, R. (2001), *The Hidden Power of Advertising*, Admap Monograph No.7, Henley on Thames: WARC.

Hoch, S.J., and Y. W. Ha (1986), "Consumer Learning: Advertising and the Ambiguity of Product Experience," *Journal of Consumer Research*, 13, 2: 221–33.

Kaul, A., and D.R. Wittink (1995), "Empirical generalizations about the impact of advertising on price sensitivity and price," *Marketing Science*, 14, 3: G151–2.

Kuhn, T.S. (1996), *The Structure of Scientific Revolutions*, 3rd ed. Chicago, IL: University of Chicago Press.

Lind, H. (1998), *Making Sense of Advertising*, London: The Advertising Association.

Lodish, L.M., M. Abraham, S. Kalmensen, J. Livelsberger, B. Lubetikin, B. Richardson, and M. Stevens (1995), "How T.V. Advertising Works: A Meta-Analysis of 389 Real World Split Cable T.V. Advertising Experiments," *Journal of Marketing Research,* 32, 2: 125–39.

MacInnis, D.J., and B.J. Jaworski (1989), "Information Processing from Advertisements: Toward an Integrated Framework," *Journal of Marketing,* 53, 4: 1–23.

MacInnis, D.J., A.G. Rao, and A.M. Weiss (2002), "Assessing When Increased Media Weight of Real-World Advertisements Helps Sale," *Journal of Marketing Research,* 39, 4: 391–407.

Mela, C.F., S. Gupta, and D.R. Lehmann (1997), "The Long-Term Impact of Promotion and Advertising on Consumer Brand Choice," *Journal of Marketing Research,* 34, 2: 248–61.

Mizik, N., and R. Jacobson (2003), "Trading Off between Value Creation and Value Appropriation: The Financial Implication of Shifts in Strategic Emphasis," *Journal of Marketing,* 67, 1: 63–75.

Office of Fair Trading (1983), *Opticians act, 1958: Opticians and competition: a report ... on sections 21 and 25 of the ... act.* London: HMSO.

Petty, R.E., and J.T. Cacioppo (1986), *Communication and Persuasion,* New York: Springer-Verlag.

Reeves, R. (1960), *Reality in Advertising,* New York: Alfred A. Knopf.

Sethuraman, R., and G.J. Tellis (1991), "An Analysis of the Tradeoff between Advertising and Pricing," *Journal of Marketing Research,* 31, 2: 160–74.

Sethuraman, R., and G.J. Tellis (2002), "Does Manufacturer Advertising Suppress or Stimulate Retail Price Promotion? Analytical Model and Empirical Analysis," *Journal of Retailing,* 78, 4: 253–63.

Simon, C.J., and M.W. Sullivan (1993), "The Measurement and Determinants of Brand Equity: A Financial Approach," *Marketing Science,* 12, 1: 28–52.

Sood, A., and G.J. Tellis (2005), "Technological Evolution and Radical Innovations," *Journal of Marketing,* 69, 3: 152–68.

Steiner, R.L. (1973), "Does Advertising Lower Consumer Prices?" *Journal of Marketing,* 37, 4: 19–26.

Steiner, R.L. (1993), "The Inverse Association Between the Margins of Manufacturer and Retailers," *Review of Industrial Organization,* 8: 717–40.

Stewart, D.W., and S. Koslow (1989), "Executional Factors and Advertising Effectiveness," *Journal of Advertising,* 18, 3: 21–32.

Stremersch, S., and G.J. Tellis (2004), "Managing International Growth of New Products," *International Journal of Research in Marketing,* 21, 4: 421–38.

Tellis, G.J. (1986), "Beyond the Many Faces of Price: An Integration of Pricing Strategies," *Journal of Marketing,* 50, 4: 146–60.

Tellis, G.J. (1988), "Advertising Exposure, Loyalty and Brand Purchase: A Two Stage Model of Choice," *Journal of Marketing Research,* 15, 2: 134–44.

Tellis, G.J. (1989), "Interpreting Advertising and Price Elasticities," *Journal of Advertising Research,* 29, 4: 40–43.

Tellis, G.J. (1998), *Advertising and Sales Promotion Strategy,* Reading, MA: Addison-Wesley.

Tellis, G.J. (2001), *Will and Vision: How Latecomers Grow to Dominate Market,* New York: McGraw Hill.

Tellis, G.J. (2004), *Effective Advertising: How, When, and Why Advertising Works,* Thousand Oaks, CA: Sage Publications.

Tellis, G.J., R. Chandy, and P. Thaivanich (2000), "Decomposing the Effects of Direct Advertising: Which Brand Works, When, Where, and How Long?" *Journal of Marketing Research,* 37, 1: 32–46.

Tellis, G.J., and P. Hans Franses (2006), "Optimal Data Interval for Advertising Response Models," *Marketing Science,* 25, 3, May–June.

Tellis, G.J., S. Stremersch, and E. Yin (2003), "The International Takeoff of New Products: Economics, Culture and Country Innovativeness," *Marketing Science,* 22, 2: 161–87.

Tellis, G.J., and D. Weiss (1995), "Does TV Advertising Really Affect Sales?" *Journal of Advertising,* 24, 3: 1–12.

Vakratsas, D., and T. Ambler (1999), "How Advertising Works: What Do We Really Know?" *Journal of Marketing,* 63, 1: 26–43.

A Brief History of Advertising

Colin McDonald and Jane Scott

> "Studying a subject without an appreciation of its antecedents is like seeing a picture in two dimensions – there is no depth. The study of history gives us this depth as well as an understanding of why things are as they are."
>
> Brink and Kelley (1963)

From as early as the first half of the 19th century, there has been public ambivalence toward advertising (Nevett, 1982). In 1958, Martin Mayer wrote that the advertising man's work "subjects him every day to the worst kind of commercial, social and psychological insecurity." And more recently, William Phillips (1992) wrote: "In less than a hundred years, (British) advertising has run the gamut from the exuberant charlatanism of a cottage industry to the jitters of a world-beating big business which outgrew its financial strength." And yet it is also accepted that it is a key part of keeping us informed, stimulating demand, and thus the economy, and paying for services we enjoy such as newspapers and television.

This chapter seeks to document how today's advertising industry has evolved. We focus on how the advertising agent came to exist, what the early agencies were like and how they developed overtime. We introduce some of the people and agencies that have made a lasting impression on the industry. Finally, this chapter considers how the messages used to communicate to consumers have evolved.

Therefore, the main objectives for this chapter are to:

1. Show how advertising activity has evolved from the early ages to the present day.
2. Describe the development of advertising media.
3. Provide an overview of ad expenditure.
4. Discuss the origins and development of advertising agencies.
5. Describe the changing content and strategies used in advertising message design.
6. Discuss advertising today in the context of its history.

In short, this chapter seeks to show how advertising got to where it is.

HOW ADVERTISING HAS EVOLVED

We have divided the development of advertising into four periods. Advertising began with the earliest forms of commerce, but with the industrial revolution and mass production came the beginnings of mass marketing. The mid 19th century to the beginning of World War II saw the formalization of client, agency and media structures. Finally, modern times have witnessed fragmentation of agencies and media and greater sophistication by marketers and consumers in the uses of advertising.

Those interested in the history of advertising should visit the website of the History of Advertising Trust: www.hatads.org.uk. This remarkable British organization in Norfolk houses acres of archives of advertising through the ages and acts as a repository for clients and agencies to lodge their advertising when they can no longer accommodate it. They also have a substantial library of old and rare books on advertising.

Early civilisations

Advertising began as soon as commerce began. Evidence of outdoor advertising (such as tradesmen's signs and tavern signs) has been found from the early civilizations of Egypt, Mesopotamia, Greece and Rome, as have literary references to services ranging from booksellers to brothels (Nevett, 1982). Similarly, ads for slaves and household goods also occur in the written records of early civilization (Calkins, 1905). Town-criers read public notices aloud and were employed by merchants to shout the praises of their wares. One may consider these people as forerunners to voice-overs in radio or television commercials. Even political advertising is found in ancient times. An example is the *Res Gestae*, in which a carefully edited version of Augustus' deeds was put up in the Roman Forum to help confirm his reputation.

Advertising from its earliest days served to inform, persuade (sell) and remind consumers just as it does today. But it was less pervasive than today because of the limited media and the limited number of goods available for trading (Norris, 1981). Up to the industrial revolution, advertising and production remained primarily a local phenomenon. Items such as land, slaves, and transport (i.e., both goods and services) were advertised, with these messages being usually more akin to classified or outdoor ads than the elaborate electronic advertising of today. Furthermore, it was essentially local.

The Industrial Revolution

Between 1760 and 1830, the Industrial Revolution transformed every aspect of the economy (and indeed, life in general) (Norris, 1981). The huge social and economic changes together with mass transportation resulting from the Industrial Revolution provided the need and means for mass, non-local marketing, which in turn led to mass advertising. People left subsistence farming and moved to the towns and the factories. As town populations rose, a middle class developed to provide government, professional, and business services in the new, more complex environment. For the producer, it meant that mass production, concentrated in a single factory, could produce enough to satisfy a new mass-market spread all over the country, spurred by the increasing urbanization. New transport methods, canals and railroads, could carry this produce to the distributors (directly or through wholesalers) in every town.

Developments in mass printing made it possible to distribute the advertising message more widely, through handbills, posters, and later, newspapers. These national media grew with transportation systems, stimulating growth in mass marketing and communications.

Advertising generated demanding consumers, who began to ask for the brands they knew. Retailers then stocked the advertised brands. Advertisers created economies of scale with pre-packaging giving consumers more confidence in quality compared to products sold loose and packaged by retailers.

The mid-19th century onwards

The American Civil War in the 1860s and the World Wars that followed in the first half of the 20th century created a need for vast amounts of military equipment and uniforms on short notice. This further stimulated the mass production of industrial goods but, perhaps more importantly, it took consumers away from their roots and, to some extent, homogenized societies. Consumers could now please themselves and not just conform to the local provision. This period saw a shift from commerce being dominated by the difficulties of production (supply) to the satisfaction, and perhaps creation of, demand.

Tellis (1998) suggests that military employment meant that women did the shopping, leading to a change in what goods were demanded. Without the men at home to assist with the chores and production of home-made goods, women became more willing to buy ready-made products, such as food and clothes, rather than make them themselves. Innovations in production, combined with the increased responsibilities and independence now felt by women, created demand for new products that made life easier such as sewing machines, cameras, automobiles, and kitchen appliances.

The improving transport infrastructure allowed for transportation of these mass-produced goods to more people. These conditions – low production costs from economies of scale, overcapacity from mass production, markets ready to absorb their offerings, and a still-fragmented distribution system were right for manufacturers to grow into industry leaders. In other words, markets shifted from local to national, and consumers were beginning to enjoy much more choice.

Advertising sought to increase demand to absorb the rapidly increasing output from mechanised production (Nevett, 1977). The manufacturers who benefited most were those for whom variable production costs were low in relation to the fixed costs, or the profit margin per unit was high, or the product was frequently bought by the same customers, or ideally all three. In such conditions, high proportions of sales revenue could be put into advertising. Print media were now more established and perhaps more respectable, and advertising was increasingly cost effective relative to personal selling. Advertising helped increase the demand, the stores passed it back, and the salesmen became part of the distribution channel, selling to wholesalers and retailers rather than end users.

Branding became increasingly important at this time, due to the range of products now competing for consumers. Consumers needed to know which particular item to ask for (based on which one seemed most appealing to them). So each item needed to be branded with a unique name, and its unique advantages communicated to the consumer (although how this was done was fiercely debated, as shall be discussed later in this chapter). Both packaging and advertising were key ways that branding was communicated (Tellis, 1998).

Advertising regulation was triggered by the practices of the patent medicine industry, and the numerous outlandish and untested claims they made (Tellis, 1998). Not only were regulations enforced by the government (for example, the US Pure Food and Drug Act 1906), but advertisers themselves imposed self-regulation, recognizing that the outrageous claims of some medicine makers were giving all advertisers a bad name (Phillips, 1992).

Post World War II

Although World Wars may seem to have little to do with advertising, all forms of commerce ossified while the populace was engaged in hostilities and a surge of development was released when they ceased. The post-WWII economic boom saw consumers making up for postponed purchases, especially in the US and Europe as economies were rebuilt. From an industry perspective, marketing began to be seen as a company function separate from the sales department, and industry was boosted by the arrival of television. Television made access to the mass market much easier, and was particularly beneficial for developing brand names and introducing new products. Furthermore, as shall be discussed later in this chapter, it changed the way advertising messages were structured and delivered.

Technological development accelerated, and new kinds of media created new ways to reach and engage markets. The internet in particular is still evolving as a medium. The TiVo-ing of television has made it possible for viewers to skip commercials entirely, making advertisers justifiably nervous that the interruptive model is broken beyond repair (Samuel, 2004). Fragmentation has made it difficult for a single medium to capture large audiences within a specified target. Even if audiences are reached, media sophistication has increased viewers' beliefs in their own ability to "see through" the tactics of advertisers (Bloxham, 1998).

THE EVOLUTION OF ADVERTISING MEDIA

"It has helped create a vast new audience of magnitude which was never dreamed of … This audience, invisible but attentive, differs not only in size, but in kind from any audience the world has ever known. It is a linking up of millions of homes."

To what new medium does this quote refer? The Internet? Digital television? It was actually radio, with this comment made by the chairman of General Electric in 1929 (cited in Sicart, 2000).

While today, immense interest is centred on the internet, comparable levels of attention were devoted to the introduction of television, radio, telephone, magazines, and newspapers (Leckenby, 2004). History shows that, while each new medium may be proclaimed as a radical transformation in communications leading to the death of existing media, in reality the old adapt to and largely survive in partnership. Since wax tablets, we cannot think of any medium that has disappeared; they merely have a diminishing share of the growing cake. Sometimes the old medium melds into the new, making the new medium something other than it might have been, radio and the web for example (Leckenby, 2004). When a medium is in an early stage of development, it is still dependent on formats derived from earlier technologies instead of exploiting its own extensive power (Murray, 1997).

So, although often they will assume less importance, old media continue to prosper, or at least exist, because they possess unique attributes that satisfy different audience needs (Coffee and Stipp, 1997; Leckenby, 2004). For example, radio did not replace newspapers,

TV did not replace the movies or radio, and satellites and cable did not replace broadcast television (Coffee and Stipp, 1997). Instead, new media have facilitated interpersonal communication to a greater extent than their forerunners (Cathcart and Gumpert, 1983).

The new media disrupted existing patterns and trends, appealing to new social groups (i.e., audiences) and encouraging new uses based on novel technological properties (Leckenby, 2004). The balance of this section considers the main media types, namely, posters or outdoor media which came first, newspapers, magazines, radio, TV, and the internet, the most recent mainstream medium.

Of course, there are other media types such as cinema and sports clothing designed to be seen on TV. Almost anything that moves, and many things that cannot, now carry advertising but we confine ourselves to the main forms noted above.

Outdoor

The early history of outdoor provided here is mostly drawn from Houck (1969), Bernstein (1997) and the US Association of National Advertisers (1952) but see also Nelson and Sykes (1953). The US history of outdoor is also from the Outdoor Advertising Association of America (2006).

Outdoor advertising as a means of mass communication probably began in ancient Egypt when five-foot high basalt tablets were carved with hieroglyphics announcing laws, decrees, and warnings. The Rosetta Stone, held by the British Museum, bears a record of remissions of taxes and other dues owed by the Egyptian people. Priests saw the advantage of circulating these messages to the public and placed copies of the stone in temples along the main highways bearing their desired messages to a wider audience.

The Roman government made its laws known to the public via inscriptions on tablets, buildings, and monuments, often utilizing animals and objects to catch the eye. Soon advertising was circulated with the use of placards at gladiator contests and circuses to promote the event. This is the earliest known form of the sports advertising which now adds colour to professional sports stadia around the globe. Pompeii used almost every available public space to advertise – a goat was the symbol of a dairy, a flagon denoted the wine merchant, while a knife denoted the cutler.

In the 1400s, handbills and poster bills appeared and 200 years later the outdoor sign emerged, dominating London's streets. Many signs became works of art. Saturation bill posting was prevalent as was the competitor's practice of tracking the poster sticker and slapping his own bill over the newly posted one. Bill posters painted their names on areas to make sites their own and eventually erected proprietary "fences" or "hoarding."

The large American outdoor poster (more than 50 square feet) originated in New York when Jared Bell printed circus posters in 1835. Early American roadside advertising was generally local. Merchants painted signs or glued posters on walls and fences to advise travellers of their wares. In 1850, advertising began to be used on streetcars/trams.

Electric signs became possible in 1879, thanks to Thomas Edison, allowing advertising to glow through the night, changing cityscapes for ever. Times Square remains the apotheosis of neon, although some 21st century Asian cities may dispute that.

Michigan formed the first state bill posters' association in 1871 and a number of states followed suit with the Associated Bill Posters' Association for North America created in 1891. Between 1900 and 1912, the billboard structure was standardized for America, allowing for national billboard campaigns. Big brands such as Kellogg, Palmolive, and Coca-Cola began mass-producing posters for use across the country. From 1913, the US industry has allowed public service advertising free use of unsold space.

The prevalence of posters varies greatly by country partly due to regulation and local environmental considerations. Benelux countries, for example, have many small sites but few large ones, whereas Russia, Italy, and Greece have many large sites, but almost no medium-sized ones. Germany has by far the largest number of sites in Europe (355,208), with the UK having the second largest (141,744) (World Advertising Research Centre, 2006).

Nowadays, outdoor advertising is ubiquitous and not necessarily out of doors. It covers massive billboards as well as trains, underground stations, buses, airports, phone boxes, tabletops, public bathrooms, and bus shelters. It may be decorating a tiny car-parking ticket or emblazoned across the sky, towed by a plane. Computer and digital technology has opened up the ability to display moving and still images on any surface. Soon ads will be instantly projectable anywhere in the world along with the ability to change the message at a moment's notice according to current news and other factors.

Newspapers

Throughout the 18th and 19th centuries, the development of advertising and of newspapers went hand in hand. In Europe, newspapers began to emerge in Germany, England, and France in the early 1600s. In 1625, London's *Weekly Relations News* printed one of the first newspaper ads. In 1704, the *Boston Newsletter* was the first US newspaper to carry an ad which offered the reward for the capture of a thief (Wells et al., 2000). Founded in 1785 and published daily in the United Kingdom, *The Times* is a national newspaper which was printed in broadsheet format for over 200 years until it switched to compact size in 2004. It is the original "Times" newspaper, although it does share its name with other papers such as *The New York Times*.

About 400 million people buy a daily newspaper and readership exceeds one billion people per day (World Association of Newspapers, 2005). Some analysts predicted the demise of the newspaper due to the rising popularity of television news and the internet. But this forecast was ill-founded and newspapers adapted with new products (e.g., free dailies), new formats (e.g., downsizing from broadsheet to a more compact size), new titles, and improved distribution, whilst embracing the internet to increase their online presence. In 2004, for example, the audience for newspaper websites grew 32%, and it has grown 350% over the last 5 years (World Association of Newspapers, 2005). Newspapers have, in the process, become less a source for news than comment on the news and entertainment. Advertisers continue to use the medium, with revenues predicted to continue rising and newspapers anticipated to remain the second most popular advertising vehicle behind television, attracting 30% of all main media advertising expenditure (World Association of Newspapers, 2005; ZenithOptimedia, 2006).

These figures, however, combine two rather different types of advertising: display and classified. Display advertising is typically for national brands, whether retail or not, whereas the classified sections deal with the availability of individual opportunities in much the same way as advertising three millennia earlier. Classifieds are local and account for the strength of local and regional newspapers versus nationals. The range of classified advertising is as wide as human needs and wants: property for sale and rental, holidays, jobs, and lonely hearts are just a few popular categories. Classified advertising is usually seen as informational but, as any reader of the lonely hearts columns can testify, emotion and persuasive appeals exist too.

Magazines

By the mid 19th century, a few well-known magazines had launched, for example, *Harper's Illustrated Weekly* in the US and *Punch* in the UK, but these magazines did not then contain advertising – they were primarily literary. Soon however, this untapped revenue opportunity was recognized, and by the end of the 19th century, magazine advertising accounted for two thirds of publisher revenues. Newspaper revenues soon reached a similar proportion, although regional and local newspapers and classified advertising meant that magazines carried a greater proportion of national advertising (Tellis, 1998). This trend has continued.

Magazines were traditionally for the wealthy and well-educated. But in the late 1880s, this situation changed. Firstly, E.C. Allen introduced the *People's Literary Companion* which appealed widely to US general readers. Secondly, Congress lowered postage rates for periodicals so publishers could economically mail their magazines to subscribers (Wells et al., 2000). By 1900, magazines blanketed the United States the way television does now, with 3500 magazines in circulation, reaching 65 million readers (Rothenberg, 2005).

Nowadays, magazines are created for every possible type of audience, with both, mass titles appealing to all (e.g., *Readers Digest*) and niche titles catering to very small audiences (e.g., *Australasian Dirt Bike*). Magazine publishers, like newspapers, are also embracing the web to ensure continued growth.

The reach of the magazine industry can be illustrated by the following:

- The main publishing house in Europe, Axel Springer, has over 150 newspaper titles and magazines in 32 countries and over 10,000 employees (Axel Springer 2006).
- The UK company EMAP (2006) claims to have "over 150 top selling consumer magazines in the UK, France and around the world."
- IPC Media, another UK company, claims to be "the UK's leading consumer magazine publisher," with an unrivalled portfolio of brands, selling over 350 million copies each year, and reaching over 70% of UK women and 50% of UK men (IPC Media, 2006).
- Time Warner, the largest US magazine publisher, claims its 145 or so magazines "are read 340 million times each month worldwide by 173 million adults over 18 years of age, with two out of every three U.S. adults reading a Time Inc. publication every month." (Time Warner, 2006).

Radio

Radio exemplifies the spike which new media types can inject, both causing, and being caused by, significant historical events (Leckenby, 2004). Radio in the US began in the 1920s and almost immediately started to take advertising (Berkman, 1987). During the Great Depression, progress in communication technology made radio available to most American households. Radio was the first national medium for mass marketing, and created a great opportunity for quickly introducing new products and developing brand names (Tellis, 1998). NBC President Merlin Aylesworth said that radio was "an open gateway to national markets, to millions of consumers and thousands of retailers" (Museum of Broadcast Communications, 2005).

In other countries, such as the UK, radio was, for a long time, purely public service broadcasting. The first UK commercial radio station, London Broadcasting Company, was launched on 8 October 1973, 50 years after the BBC (BBC, 2006).

Television

Television broadcasting can be seen as an outgrowth of radio since it used similar technology but with additional visual images. The first US television commercial appeared on 1st July 1941, when the Bulova Watch Company paid $9 to WNBT for a 10-second spot before a baseball game between the Brooklyn Dodgers and Philadelphia Phillies. A Bulova watch was superimposed on a map of the US, with a voiceover of the company's slogan "America runs on Bulova time!" (Bulova, 2006).

The close relationship between television and radio allowed television to draw substantially on the knowledge acquired from the evolution of commercial radio. In its early years, television did not have the same level of penetration as radio because of the high costs associated with producing (and purchasing) the sets.

In the UK, the Television Act established commercial television in 1954 and set up the Independent Television Authority. In 1955, commercial television began, in the London area, with a live transmission from the Guildhall. Since 1936, TV had hitherto been limited to public service broadcasting from the BBC. The first commercial screened was for Gibbs SR toothpaste. The most popular programme was Sunday Night at the London Palladium (ATV) (Office of Communication, 2006).

In 2005, there were an estimated 1.7 billion television sets worldwide (Greene et al., 2005). Television continues to be the largest source of worldwide advertising revenue, accounting for an estimated US$147 billion in 2005 (or 37.2% of all major media expenditure) (ZenithOptimedia, 2005). However, television's dominance of the advertising pie is being threatened by the introduction of new technology such as TiVo which enables the consumer to save programmes and skip advertisements. Product placement, programme sponsorship and advertainment are specific strategies that advertisers are using to reach audiences in light of these technological developments (Scott and Craig-Lees, 2006). Another strategy is designing ads that still work in fast forward mode.

Internet

The Internet is the fastest-growing new medium ever (Leckenby, 2004). Internet advertising began in 1994 and early advertisers included AT&T, MCI, Sprint, Volvo, Saturn, Timex, Jim Beam, and AirWalk (EC[2] @ USC, 2001). It continues to grow 27% each year, and is predicted to overtake outdoor advertising in 2006 (Initiative, 2006; ZenithOptimedia, 2006). From 2005–2008, ZenithOptimedia predicts that it will create US$15.8 billion new ad dollars worldwide and grow 76% (ZenithOptimedia, 2005, 2006).

The web is particularly well suited for search applications such as online local, directory, and classified ads which have been found by the Interactive Advertising Bureau to be efficient in profit terms (Interactive Advertising Bureau, 2006). More surprisingly, they also found significant branding benefits for those same categories.

ADVERTISING EXPENDITURE

One of the major problems in pulling together international advertising expenditure data is that different countries produce different figures at different times and use different methods, definitions, and currencies to measure this expenditure (Dunbar, 1977; Green, 1990). Nevertheless, this section draws some of this research together to demonstrate the growth of advertising expenditure overtime and to identify emerging markets.

Firstly, to provide a historical perspective of media shares of advertising expenditure in the United Kingdom, Dunbar (1977) used data from Taylor (1934) and Kaldor and Silverman (1948) as shown in Table 1.2.1. To limit repetition the table focuses on highs and lows.

These figures compare with more recent UK data in Table 1.2.2 to demonstrate the scale of growth overtime.

The United Kingdom has traditionally been one of the world's top markets, consistently spending, as a percentage of GDP, about 50% more than the other large EU countries (World Advertising Research Centre, 2006). However, the 1980s saw the other European markets grow due to the deregulation of television which helped grow the television

stations' revenues and the number of minutes of commercials shown each day (Green, 1990). By 1990, advertising had exceeded the growth in the economy in 16 European countries every year since 1980 (Green, 1990). However, recent years have seen the more mature markets of Northern America, United Kingdom and Western Europe lose share of worldwide advertising spend, as other markets in Asia and Central and Eastern Europe grow (Initiative, 2006). Indeed, Initiative (2006) predict that 2006 will see Asia overtake Western Europe to become the second largest advertising market in the world. To demonstrate this, Table 1.2.3 shows the changes in worldwide advertising share over the last 10 years, with Table 1.2.4 showing the strength of Japan and Table 1.2.5 showing the development of China (which has now overtaken the United Kingdom).

The scale of advertising in the United States of America can be seen in both Table 1.2.3 and Table 1.2.6. The USA is clearly the largest country in terms of adspend, accounting for just under half the worldwide total (Coen, 2006; Initiative, 2006; WARC, 2006; ZenithOptimedia, 2006). Table 1.2.6 is also useful in highlighting the general pattern of advertising growth since 1990 and even more so, over the last century

Table 1.2.1   Advertising expenditures in the UK, 1907–1956
(All figures include production costs, commission, etc.)

Year	Press £m	Outdoor £m	Cinema £m	Radio £m	Television £m	Total £m
1907	10.5	1.5	–	–	–	12
1912	13	2	1	1	1	15
1922	33	3.5	–	–	–	36.5
1928	25	5	*	–	–	57
1930	48	5	*	–	–	53
1932	40	5	0.4	1	1	45.4
1934	49.5	5.5	0.5	0.3	–	56
1938	51	5.5	0.6	1.7	–	58.8
1948	65	11	2.4	**	–	78.4
1949	78	11	2.3	0.1	–	91.4
1953	119	11.6	3.2	0.7	–	134.5
1956	159	15	5.2	0.8	10.6	190.6

Note: Change in GNP measurement; *not measurable; **less than £0.1m; – no expenditure.
1907–1932: Author's estimates; 1934–1943: based on Kaldor and Silverman; 1947–1956: from Advertising Association Surveys.

Table 1.2.2   Advertisng expenditures in the UK, 1995–2005
Includes classified advertising figures, discounts off rate card and agency commission, but does not include production costs (GB£, million).

Year	Total	Newspapers	Magazine	Television	Radio	Cinema	Outdoor	Internet
1995	8199	3396	1430	2667	271	57	378	–
1996	8839	3571	1600	2873	309	60	426	–
1997	9738	3888	1765	3150	354	72	500	8
1998	10637	4214	1918	3426	418	80	563	19
1999	11280	4474	1922	3672	464	101	595	51
2000	12474	5014	2020	3950	536	105	697	153
2001	11866	4896	1980	3525	487	134	677	166
2002	11908	4808	1873	3690	492	148	702	197
2003	12342	4863	1832	3722	526	148	786	465
2004	13338	5107	1901	3955	545	157	848	825
2005	13836	4909	1891	4097	521	154	897	1366
Change: 05 / 04	**3.7%**	**−3.9%**	**−0.5%**	**3.6%**	**−4.5%**	**−2.1%**	**5.8%**	**65.6%**

Source: The Advertising Association; WARC www.warc.com

Table 1.2.3   Top ten countries by advertising expenditure, 2005.

	1996		2005		96–06
	US$m	Rank	US$m	Rank	% Change
USA	99,095	1	155,252	1	56.7
China*	2,392	17	38,525	2	1510.6
Japan	35,869	2	35,941	3	0.2
UK	13,804	4	25,186	4	82.5
Germany	22,714	13	20,689	5	−8.9
Mexico*	2,419	16	14,268	6	489.8
Brazil*	8,432	6	14,161	7	67.9
France	11,023	5	12,842	8	16.5
Italy	6,621	7	10,753	9	62.4
Canada	4,831	9	8,858	10	83.4

Source: World Advertising Trends 2006, (www.warc.com) IBOPE Media, Nielsen Media Research.
*Data shown are at rate card prices.
Data for remaining countries are shown at discount level.

Table 1.2.4   Advertising expenditures in Japan, 1995–2005
Includes classified advertising figures, discounts off rate card and agency commission, but does not include production costs (¥, billion).

Year	Total	Newspapers	Magazine	Television	Radio	Outdoor	Internet
1995	3643	1078	344	1527	189	504	–
1996	3902	1144	375	1667	198	517	–
1997	4044	1168	404	1747	204	515	5
1998	3883	1089	392	1697	196	499	10
1999	3805	1066	385	1664	186	484	21
2000	4097	1152	402	1809	188	494	52
2001	4028	1111	385	1799	182	487	65
2002	3753	989	373	1684	167	466	74
2003	3751	970	371	1695	164	446	104
2004	3894	976	365	1778	163	452	160
2005	3961	959	363	1776	162	455	247
Change: 05 / 04	**1.7%**	**−1.7%**	**−0.6%**	**−0.1%**	**−0.9%**	**0.7%**	**54.8%**

Source: Dentsu Inc.; WARC www.warc.com

Table 1.2.5 Advertising expenditures in China, 1995–2005
Includes classified advertising figures but does not include agency commission, discounts off rate card or production costs (RMB, million).

Year	Total	Newspapers	Magazine	Television
1995	15480	2028	–	13453
1996	19891	2052	–	17839
1997	30505	8066	164	22274
1998	44142	13920	476	29746
1999	50979	14599	544	35836
2000	80233	21155	1118	57960
2001	98007	24382	1481	72143
2002	139465	33581	2218	103665
2003	198762	44605	3973	150184
2004	261444	57882	5069	198493
2005	315684	61049	6230	248405
Change: 05 / 04	**20.7%**	**5.5%**	**22.9%**	**25.1%**

Source: Nielsen Media Reseach; WARC www.warc.com

Table 1.2.6 Worldwide ad growth: 1990–2006

Year	USA		Overseas		Total	
	US$ Billion	% change	US$ Billion	% change	US$ Billion	% change
1990	130.0	+3.9%	145.9	+11.8%	275.9	+7.9%
1991	128.4	−1.2%	153.9	+5.5%	282.3	+2.3%
1992	133.8	+4.2%	165.4	+7.5%	299.2	+6.0%
1993	141.0	+5.4%	163.2	−1.3%	304.2	+1.7%
1994	153.0	+8.6%	179.0	+9.7%	332.0	+9.1%
1995	165.1	+7.9%	205.9	+15.0%	371.0	+11.7%
1996	178.1	+7.9%	212.1	+3.0%	390.2	+5.2%
1997	191.3	+7.4%	210.0	−1.0%	401.3	+2.8%
1998	206.7	+8.0%	205.2	−2.3%	411.9	+2.6%
1999	222.3	+7.6%	213.8	+4.2%	436.1	+5.9%
2000	247.5	+11.3%	226.8	+6.1%	474.3	+8.8%
2001	231.3	−6.5%	209.6	−8.6%	440.9	−7.9%
2002	236.9	+2.4%	213.6	+1.9%	450.5	+2.2%
2003	245.5	+3.6%	244.4	+14.4%	489.9	+8.7%
2004	263.8	+7.4%	279.8	+14.5%	543.6	+11.0%
2005	271.1	+2.8%	298.0	+6.5%	569.1	+4.7%

Source: Coen (2006)

(when comparing these figures to those in Table 1.2.1).

Since 1964, worldwide ad spending has grown from $23.6 billion (Mandese, 2004) to $600 billion (Coen, 2006). The sectors have shifted their advertising shares. Traditionally, frequently bought grocery and pharmaceutical products accounted for the bulk of consumer advertising. More recently, these products are advertising less while other kinds of advertising have increased, with retail, automotive, telecommunications, and financial products in the top spending categories. Pharmaceuticals still continue to round out this top five (ZenithOptimedia, 2006).

Furthermore, the relative importance of advertising has steadily declined as expenditures on other sales techniques have increased (not only price promotions, but sponsorship, in-store display, product placement, etc). Mayer (1991) comments that whereas in 1980 advertising absorbed approximately two-thirds of all marketing expenditures, by 1990 this share had reduced to one-third.

Dawley (2006) suggests that in the US, the shift to non-media spending is happening faster than average, whereas in Europe and emerging economies, it is slower.

ADVERTISING AGENCIES: THEIR ORIGINS AND DEVELOPMENT

Appearance of the agent

By the mid-nineteenth century, manufacturers could deliver and advertise nationally. Newspapers were proliferating and hungry for advertisements. Manufacturers found that knowing where and how to place ads (especially outside their home location) was difficult. Newspaper circulations were unknown (or kept secret) and advertising rates were uncontrolled and varied. Gathering lists of newspapers in which ads could be placed was time-consuming and costly.

This was responsible for a change in the role of the advertising agent from working primarily for the media to representing the consumer to the brand owner, i.e., working for the client. Agents traditionally represented newspapers (i.e., the media), compiling lists of newspapers and placing ads with them on behalf of advertisers. The newspapers negotiated with the agent to be on his list and the agent contracted with the newspaper for large amounts of advertising space at discount rates before reselling the space to advertisers at a higher rate. Hence, the advertising industry owes its survival to its ability to negotiate between media outlets and manufacturers needing to advertise (Lears, 1994).

Although the advertisers still created the ads themselves, it was more efficient to deal with a single agent (or broker) instead of having to keep track of all the outlets. Because the agent worked explicitly for the media, the media outlet paid him a commission for the advertising he obtained for them. This is the origin of the unique commission system in advertising, in which the agent is paid not by the one who pays for the advertising but by the supplier (the media) – a system which is not yet dead, but is increasingly supplanted by service fees.

The role of Francis Ayer

In Philadelphia in 1841, Volney B. Palmer set up the first US ad agency. In 1869 Francis Ayer bought him out and founded N. W. Ayer & Son. By 1874, Ayer was issuing his own publications, the first of which was the *Ayer and Son's Manual for Advertisers*, an annual publication listing newspapers from which the agency sought its business, the newspapers' rates, and their circulation. The following year they established a printing department which offered typesetting. Other creative services were not offered in these early years, as Ayer believed the client knew its product best (Hower, 1949).

The most significant decision made by this agency was to introduce the radical practice of open contract. This contract guaranteed clients the lowest possible rates the agency could negotiate with publications. Commission was later added and ranged from 8.5% to 15%. By 1909, the open contract became known as "OC +15" by the agency, and the 15% commission later became an industry standard (Hower, 1949; Leiss et al., 1997). This bound the agent and the advertiser for a period of time, usually a year, with the former taking a standard percentage of the billing as his commission. The agent no longer squeezed the advertiser to make a profit, but rather, acted on the latter's behalf in finding the best group of journals for the advertiser's needs. The percentage commission tied the agencies' profits to the gross amount of billings they could win. They would grow only to the degree that new sources of advertising could be channelled through the agencies rather than conducted directly with the newspapers. This new arrangement helped make Ayer the number one agency of the 1890s (Leiss et al., 1997).

Although N.W. Ayer & Son (through Volney Palmer) has been seen as the original

US agency through Volney Palmer, William James Carlton started to sell advertising space in 1864, founding the agency that later became J. Walter Thompson Company, which has also claimed to be the oldest American advertising agency in continuous existence. In the UK, advertising agencies certainly date back to the 18th century when Charles Lamb was a copywriter in England. The Mitchells agency was in business in 1811.

Framework for the modern agency

As middlemen, agents such as N.W. Ayer initially developed great power, since advertisers depended on them for their knowledge of the rates. But soon they could no longer justify their commissions as their insider knowledge of media and purchasing skills were brought into the open. What they could leverage however, was their knowledge of how to do advertising. So as they gained in size and experience, and as manufacturers' needs became more sophisticated, brokers began to offer more services than creating ads. These had always included planning the media mix, but extended to market research, promotions, and overall marketing strategy. In an age where few companies had marketing departments, ad agencies filled the gap and provided a consumer perspective for manufacturers. Thus, they evolved into what were called full service agencies, working on behalf of advertisers rather than publishers. However, their compensation remained the commission system, creating a conflict of interest: agencies worked for advertisers to maximize ad effectiveness, but their earnings were in proportion to the dollars spent on media space and production. However, this was not unusual: architects are still paid pro rata to costs even though they are supposed to be saving costs for their clients. But the commission system was also questionable given that it discouraged advertising agencies from proposing media neutral solutions (Lace, 2000).

By 1990, the long-term pressure on agency rates of commission (the media commissions were shared, legally or not, with major clients)

and the conflict of interest noted above, led to remuneration shifting toward fees. This proved not to be wholly satisfactory: some sharp clients negotiated fees on the basis of spending a certain budget and then, once the fee was final, doubled the budget (and the work for the agency). Conversely, agencies would demand payment of the agreed fees even where the client had been forced to cut the ad budget.

Fees were also promoted as being superior to commission by being fairer and giving agencies more certainty about their cash flows. However, problems soon emerged with this too as it was found that when economic conditions improved, agencies became prisoners of that guaranteed income (Lace, 2000).

The main consequence of this remuneration pressure was to reduce agency headcounts and take them back from full service to simply creating ads. Their media role had already, from the 1980s, gone to specialist media buyers, far fewer in number, who could use their greater buying muscle to secure, allegedly, better deals for clients. We understand that not all clients have been satisfied with the transparency of the distribution of media commissions but the literature is silent on the matter.

A final (so far) twist in the tail has been the introduction of Payment by Results. This has been promoted as "an enhancement in the advertising agency remuneration agreement, based on the achievement of mutually agreed targets or criteria for higher advertiser satisfaction, providing an equitable return to the agency" (ISBA, 1999), i.e., a win–win situation, with the advertiser being more satisfied and the agency receiving higher income and performing better.

The theory of Payment by Results means that both sides can maintain a proper focus on truly important business issues. Objectives have to be quantified and having performance assessed against them, is in theory, good practice. This promotes proactivity, responsibility, efficiency, openness, honesty, accountability, transparency, and better and longer-lasting relationships (Lace, 2000).

There are three types of "results" that can be used for this purpose: business performance such as sales or market share or incremental profit; intermediate (brand equity) metrics such as intention to purchase; and service criteria such as how prompt the agency is in returning phone calls. 2004 estimates suggest that 40% of creative agencies and 46% of media agencies in the US and UK are using this system (Beckett, 2004). Procter & Gamble is one company using this method, announcing in 1999 that they would be treating their ad agencies as partners and sharing the ups and down of profits whether the agency was responsible or not (Waters, 1999).

However, the practical results from Payment by Results have not been as positive as enthusiasts hoped. Agencies are happy to accept bonuses, as they see them, when results are good but not penalties when they are bad because such failures are always the fault of the client – they say. Payment for agency service, particularly favoured in the US, is highly subjective and not "results" anyway.

This section has reviewed the evolution of agency development and remuneration from a historical perspective. For a contemporary overview, we refer you to David Wethey's (2007), Chapter 3.1 covering client–agency relations.

Mergers and acquisitions

We do not have space for a full account of the hundreds if not thousands of major ad agency acquisitions over the last 150 years. This section highlights just a few to give a flavour of the evolution that has taken place.

Whilst we have not seen definitive research, it seems that the aggregate market shares of the three tiers of agency firms by size (i.e., large, medium, and small) remains fairly constant. Given the regular acquisitions of agencies since the earliest times, this seems a little odd. The effect of acquisitions ought to increase the aggregate share of the largest agencies and yet it does not seem to do so. One reason is the departure from the largest agencies of star performers to start their own agencies.

In the UK, the largest 10% of agencies by number represent about 85% of the market by value, and this seems to have been stable along with the market shares by tier. What has, however, changed since the 1960s, in the US, Europe and increasingly round the world is the growth of conglomerates, of which the two largest in 2005 were Omnicom and WPP.[1] The importance of conglomerates is illustrated by the UK market where in 2006, conglomerates had 82% of the billings of the top 30 agencies, whereas in 1996 they had 73%.[2]

In 2004, Omnicom, based in New York, had worldwide revenues of $9.7 bn, of which 53% was in the US, whereas WPP, based in London, had worldwide revenues of $9.4 bn, of which 60% was outside the US. These were followed by Interpublic (New York) ($6.2 bn), Publicis (Paris) ($4.8 bn), and Dentsu (Tokyo) ($2.9 bn). Dentsu as a single agency has a large share of its parent conglomerate's total revenue (68%) and McCann Erickson was 23% of Interpublic, but, for example, J. Walter Thompson and Ogilvy & Mather together were only 22% of WPP.

A major stimulus of the global conglomerate movement was the founding of Saatchi & Saatchi in London in 1970, by brothers with international aspirations. Conglomerates existed before then with Interpublic being the largest at that time and still the largest in the UK in 1996. Conglomerates then saw the merits of multinational campaigns but often struggled with persuading both their local agencies and subsidiary management of multinational businesses to share campaigns. For example, Heublein sought to internationalize Smirnoff vodka advertising at that time but with limited success. The Saatchis saw advertising as a global business and were attracted to, and attractive to, global accounts such as British Airways. Favourable conditions in the London stock market, where the Saatchis listed their company in 1975, and increased cash flow, gave the brothers ready access to the cash needed to buy out the generation of US executives who were looking towards retirement. By 1986, the brothers had turned their original $40,000 stake into a global confederation of 80 companies with capitalized billings of $3.2 billion (Rothenberg, 2005).

Whilst some agencies such as Young and Rubicam and Ogilvy & Mather disagreed with the Saatchis' actions, favouring their own integrated and co-ordinated approach, other agencies believed the Saatchis' approach to expansion was right – or at least a response that was necessary to remain competitive. In late April 1986, three of the most prominent US agencies – BBDO, Needham Harper & Steers, and Doyle Dane Bernbach – announced their own three-way merger under the umbrella of a new company called the Omnicom Group. By mid-May though, Saatchi & Saatchi fought back for dominance, announcing its purchase of the world's third-largest agency, Ted Bates Worldwide (Lears, 1994).

A little more than a year after the Bates buyout, in 1987, Martin Sorrell (who as finance director of Saatchi & Saatchi had helped engineer its spectacular expansion), made a hostile offer for J. Walter Thompson. His successful $566m bid for Thompson and his hostile acquisition of the Ogilvy Group 2 years later in 1989 turned Sorrell's WPP Group into one of the two largest marketing communications conglomerates. It also owned the world's largest public relations agency, the largest direct-marketing specialist and about three dozen other subsidiaries. WPP acquired the other major holdout group, Young and Rubicam, in 2000 (Lears, 1994; Rothenberg, 2005; WPP, 2005).

This world of high finance is a long way from the business of making ads to which we now return.

EVOLUTION OF ADVERTISING CONTENT

Advertising has its roots in providing information

From the 1800s to the early 20th century, advertisements were nearly all classified, un-illustrated offers made to all citizens in order to sell something specific (Phillips, 1992). According to Phillips (1992) nearly all print ads were what we now call informational – what was for sale, the price, and where to find it – although others consider that the distinction between persuasion and pure information may be in the eye of the beholder. What is true is that the classified format of most advertising, then and now, limits the creative opportunities for the ad agency to thumb-nail-size illustrations, small type, and single-column width (Fox, 1984).

Therefore, much advertising at the turn of the 20th century was focused on providing information, with prominent copywriters such as John E. Powers viewing the content as news (Beard, 2005). This approach was often referred to as the "tell" approach, which contrasted to the more persuasive hard sell, "salesmanship in print" approach, which provided the basis for the influential "reason-why" approach (Rowsome, 1970). Advertising agencies sought to disassociate themselves from the showy, aggressive humbug style used by the patent-medicine purveyors in the mid–late 18th century (Laird, 1998).

However, a more artistic soft-sell was established by the early 1900s, following increased calls for enhanced originality and creativity, and the necessity for appealing to emotions (Beard, 2004). Marchand (1985) notes that advertisers increasingly viewed human nature as instinctive and non-rational with growing beliefs that audience members would respond more to emotional appeals than logical arguments and reasons. Advertising increasingly entertained without explicitly selling (Beard, 2005).

In writing this type of history, authors are tempted towards separating evolution into distinct stages, whereas the reality is that they overlap. The rules for devising classified ads in the 17th century apply to classifieds today and the glossy emotional four-colour display ads we associate with the 20th century were in use a hundred years before. The main factors driving differences in content are the changing media discussed above and increasing consumer and advertiser sophistication. Indeed,

Fox (1984) has suggested that hard and soft sell advertising has cycled back and forth throughout the 20th century according to the industry's own rhythms and its perception of the public's boredom level. Furthermore, the recognition that products have life cycles and can die, but brands, properly managed, can last forever (Rothenberg, 2005), coupled with the difficulty of maintaining product differences in an age with high production technology, shifted attention from product to brand differences which by their nature are more subtle.

The creative revolution: Big ideas, big personalities

Bill Bernbach (a founder of Doyle Dane Bernbach, now part of Omnicom), Leo Burnett (founder of the Leo Burnett agency) and David Ogilvy (who worked for Mather & Crowther which became Ogilvy & Mather, now part of WPP) came to prominence in the late 1950s and 1960s. Some of the key personalities of this era were:

- David Ogilvy said it was "brand personality" and not "any trivial product difference" that drew consumers to products. Ogilvy believed in research and copy testing, but also had a tremendous sense of style straddling both the hard and soft approaches to advertising (Wells et al., 2000). His agency created clean, powerful ads marked by graceful, sensible copy and a palpable respect for the consumer's intelligence (Advertising Age, 2005).
- Leo Burnett believed in finding the inherent drama in every product and presenting it as believably as possible through warmth, shared emotions, and experiences (Advertising Age, 2005). The "Chicago-style" of advertising he introduced (i.e., sentimental ads drawn from heartland-rooted values) showed love and respect for the people; it perfectly understood and revolved around the consumer. Using strong, simple, and instinctive imagery, advertising produced at Burnett's talked to people in a friendly manner (Advertising Age, 2005; ciadvertising.org, 1996).
- Bill Bernbach's creative philosophy was simple: "find the simple story in the product and present it in an articulate, intelligent, persuasive way" (Marshall, 1982).
- Theodore F MacManus had a style that was influential, image-oriented, and atmospheric. His elaborate layouts and emotional appeals were a direct contradiction of the rational reason-why appeals, hence his moniker "the father of soft sell" (Beard, 2005; ciadvertising.org, 1999).
- Rosser Reeves picked up where the no-nonsense "advertising must sell" preachings of Claude Hopkins left off, creating the Unique Selling Proposition concept that focused on driving home a central, research-based selling point (Advertising Age, 2005). Reeves believed that a basic dilemma in advertising was that few products were distinctly different. Reeves developed the USP concept in an attempt to distinguish one product from its competitors. The USP was an advancement over previous "reason-why" advertising in that it operated as a part of consumer identity (ciadvertising.org, 2000).
- Jeremy Bullmore was the creative leader of what was arguably JWT's golden era in the UK from the mid 1950s until the 1980s. One of his contributions was that the ad, or stimulus, was unimportant, but it was the consumer's response that mattered (Bullmore, 2003).

By the 1980s, clients increasingly wanted to measure results, meaning short-term financial results. Partly because sales effects were more obvious and partly due to the growing power of mass retailers, companies began shifting their marketing budgets away from television and radio to sales promotion (Belch and Belch, 2001; Coen, 2005; Wells et al., 2000).

ADVERTISING IN THE CONTEXT OF ITS HISTORY

Advertising adapts to current culture, pressures, and conditions. The extent to which advertising mirrors society or creates new culture is considered elsewhere in this handbook but plainly it does both. It is a craft, rather than a science just as it has always been but practitioners now intellectualize to a greater extent. There are awards for advertising creativity and effectiveness. Clients seek to pay only for measurable results.

At the same time, advertising is more regulated and advertisers are expected to respect social goals, such as reducing childhood obesity or excessive consumption of products deemed dangerous.

Advertising remains what it always was: a means of informing, persuading, and reminding customers and potential customers. At the same time, it has become vastly more complex as media and agencies have fragmented. Consumers are bombarded by ever more messages and have built mechanisms to cope.

SUMMARY

The main conclusions from this chapter are:

- Some aspects of advertising are much the same as they always were. Ads seek to gain attention to their brands and, for display advertising, use emotions and entertainment to build brand-consumer relationships.
- Classified advertising, by contrast, seeks to find buyers for specific sales opportunities.
- Media have proliferated bringing new techniques but also more confusion.
- Advertising agencies became the experts from the mid 19th century in the more developed markets but, partly due to complexity, have returned to ad creativity leaving media and other forms of communication to specialist agencies.
- In the last decades of the 20th century, mergers and acquisitions have created a handful of global media and communications giants led by WPP and Omnicom followed by a second tier of worldwide groups and partnerships.
- At the individual agency level, however, the churn of individual talent and the need to avoid brand conflicts has kept the market shares of the large, medium, and small agencies, en bloc, relatively stable.
- Despite the ups and downs, advertising continues to increase as a share of GDP. Traditional packaged goods brands however are less dominant advertisers whereas retailers, including web retailers, and public service advertisers have increased their share.
- Measurement techniques have become more sophisticated partly in response to advertiser demands to see quantified results.
- Ad content has increased in variety with more entertainment and appeals to emotion.
- Regulation, much of it self-regulation, helps to ensure advertising meets the sensitivities of changing cultural demands.

ACKNOWLEDGEMENT

Table 1.2.6 from *Universal McCann's Insider's Report* by Robert J. Coen. The Insider's Report is published periodically by Universal McCann, the global media services operation of McCann Worldgroup, 622 Third Avenue, New York, NY 10017. Ph: (001) 646-865-5000.

NOTES

1 Note that the aforementioned comment about the stability of market shares for the three tiers does not apply to their owning conglomerates whose share has substantially grown. There are also second-tier conglomerates pursuing similar strategies of economies of administrative scale.
2 IPA data provided by personal communication – 28 July 2006.

REFERENCES

Advertising Age (2005), "The Advertising Century: Top 100 People" Available: http://www.adage.com/century/people.html, (accessed 13 December 2005).
Association of National Advertisers (1952), *Essentials of Outdoor Advertising*, New York: Association of National Advertisers Inc.
Axel Springer (2006), "At A Glance" Available: http://www.axelspringer.com/englisch/unterneh/frame.htm, (accessed 18 August 2006).
BBC (2006), "1973: Commercial Radio Joins UK Airwaves" Available: http://news.bbc.co.uk/onthisday/hi/dates/stories/october/8/newsid_2530000/2530721.stm, (accessed 19 July 2006).
Beard, F.K. (2004), "Hard-Sell "Killers" And Soft-Sell "Poets": Modern Advertising's Enduring Message Strategy Debate," *Journalism History*, 30 (3), 141–9.
Beard, F.K. (2005), "One Hundred Years of Humor in American Advertising," *Journal of Macromarketing*, 25 (1), 54–65.
Beckett, G. (2004), "Pricing For Growth," *Admap*, May.
Belch, G.E. and M.A. Belch (2001), *Introduction To Advertising And Promotion: An Integrated Marketing Communications Perspective*, 5th ed. New York: McGraw-Hill.
Berkman, D. (1987), "The Not Quite So Inevitable Origins Of Commercial Broadcasting In America," *Journal of Advertising History*, 10 (1).

Bernstein, D. (1997), *Advertising Outdoors – Watch This Space*! London: Phaidon Press Ltd.

Bloxham, M. (1998), "Brand Affinity And Television Programme Sponsorship," *International Journal of Advertising*, 17 (1), 89–98.

Brink, E. and W. Kelley (1963), *The Management of Promotion*, New Jersey: Prentice-Hall.

Bullmore, J. (2003), *Behind the Scenes in Advertising, Mark III: More Bull More*, 3rd ed. Henley-on-Thames NTC Publications.

Bulova (2006), "About Us" Available: http://www.bulova.com/about/about.aspx, (accessed 19 August 2006).

Calkins, E.E. (1905), "Eliminating the Jobber," *Printer's Ink* (May).

Cathcart, R. and G. Gumpert (1983), "Mediated Interpersonal Communication: Toward A New Typology," *Quarterly Journal of Speech*, 69 (3), 267–77.

ciadvertising.org (1996), "Leo Noble Burnett: The Man Who Caught A Star" Available: http://www.ciadvertising.org/studies/student/96_fall/burnett/burnett.html, (accessed 16 January 2006).

ciadvertising.org (2000), "Rosser Reeves" Available: http://www.ciadvertising.org/student_account/fall_00/adv382j/derrellwilson/p2/index.html, (accessed 16 January 2006).

ciadvertising (1999), "Theodore Francis MacManus: Good Man of Conscience" Available: http://www.ciadvertising.org/studies/student/99_spring/interactive/manzano/mac/start.html, (accessed 16 January 2006).

Coen, R. (2006), *Insider's Report: Robert Coen Presentation on Advertising Expenditures*, June 2006, Universal McCann.

Coen, R.J. (2005), *Insider's Report: Advertising Expenditure Report - December 2005*, New York: Universal McCann.

Coffee, S. and H. Stipp (1997), "The Interactions Between Computer And Television Usage," *Journal of Advertising Research*, 37 (2), 61–6.

Cowlett, M. (2000), "Make It Into The Movies," in *Marketing*.

Dawley, H. (2006), "Worldwide, Advertising Is Losing Share," in *Media Life* 26 (July), 2006 ed.

Dunbar, D. (1977), "Estimates Of Total Advertising Expenditures In The UK Before 1949," *Journal of Advertising History*, 1 (December).

EC[2] @ USC (2001), "Internet Advertising History" Available: http://www.ec2.edu/dccenter/archives/ia/history.html, (accessed 19 July 2006).

EMAP (2006), "About Us" Available: http://www.emap.com/site-search-item.asp?ContentId=2320, (accessed 19 July 2006).

Fox, S. (1984), *The Mirror Makers: A History Of American Advertising And Its Creator*,. New York: Vintage Books.

Green, A. (1990), "International Advertising Expenditure Trends," *International Journal of Advertising*, 9 (2), 181–5.

Greene, J., H. Green, and A. Reinhardt (2005), "Microsoft May Be A TV Star Yet" Available: http://www.businessweek.com/magazine/content/05_06/b3919124_mz063.htm, (accessed 17 January 2006).

Houck, J.W. (1969), *Outdoor Advertising, History and Regulation,* Indiana: University of Notre Dame Press.

Hower, R.M. (1949), *The History of an Advertising Agency: N.W. Ayer & Son at Work*, Cambridge, Mass: Harvard UP.

Initiative (2006), "Spheres of Influence: Global Advertising Expenditure 2006," *Initiative International*.

Interactive Advertising Bureau (2006), "Impacts and ROI of Internet Local, Classifieds, and Directory Advertising" Available: http://www.iab.net/resources/iab_localsearch.asp, (accessed 19 July 2006).

IPC Media (2006), "IPC Media - Home" Available: http://www.ipcmedia.com/, (accessed 19 July 2006).

ISBA (1999), Payment By Results: How To Make It Work In Advertising Agency Remuneration Agreements, London: ISBA/ARC.

Kaldor, N. and R. Silverman (1948), "*A Statistical Analysis Of Advertising Expenditure And The Revenue Of The Press,*" Published for N.I.E.S.R. by Cambridge University Press.

Lace, J.M. (2000), "Payment By Results: Is There A Pot Of Gold At The End Of The Rainbow?," *International Journal of Advertising*, 19 (2), 167–83.

Laird, P.W. (1998), *Advertising Progress: American Business And The Rise Of Consumer Marketing*, Baltimore: John Hopkins University Press.

Lears, J. (1994), *Fables Of Abundance: A Cultural History Of Advertising In America*, New York: BasicBooks.

Leckenby, J.D. (2004), "The Interaction of Traditional and New Media," in *Advertising, Promotion and New Media*, eds. M.R Stafford and R.J. Faber, New York: M.E. Sharpe, Inc.

Leiss, W., S. Kline, and S. Jhally (1997), *Social Communication in Advertising: Persons, Products and Images of Well-being*, 2nd ed. New York: Routledge.

Mandese, J. (2004), "Forty years ago today......" *Admap*, October 2004 (454), 12.

Marchand, R. (1985), *Advertising the American Dream: Making Way for Modernity, 1920–1940*, Berkely: University of California Press.

Marshall, C. (1982), "DDB Founder Bernbach Dead at 71," *Advertising Age* (October 11), 80.

Mayer, M. (1991), *Whatever Happened to Madison Avenue?* Toronto: Little, Brown & Company.

Murray, J.H. (1997), *Hamlet On The Holodeck: The Future Of Narrative In Cyberspace*, New York: Free Press.

Museum of Broadcast Communications (2005), "Advertising Agency" Available: http://www.museum.tv/archives/etv/A/htmlA/advertisinga/advertisinga.htm, (accessed 20 December 2005).

Nelson, R. and A.E. Sykes (1953), *Outdoor Advertising, Its Function In Modern Advertising And Marketing*, London: George Allen and Unwin.

Nevett, T.R. (1977), "London's Early Advertising Agents," *Journal of Advertising*, History, 1 (December).

Nevett, T.R. (1982), *Advertising in Britain: A History*. William Heinemann Ltd.

Norris, V.P. (1981), "Advertising History – According To The Textbooks," *Journal of Advertising History*, (February).

Office of Communication (2006), "An Overview of Television in the UK" Available: http://www.ofcom.org.uk/static/archive/itc/uk_television_sector/overview/key_dates.asp.html, (accessed 19 August 2006).

Phillips, W. (1992), "A Century Of Modern Advertising: From Fin De Siècle To Nervous Nineties," *Admap*, July 1992.

Rothenberg, R. (2005), "The Advertising Century" Available: http://www.adage.com/century/rothenberg.html, (accessed 12 December 2005).

Rowsome, F. (1970), *They Laughed When I Sat Down: An Informal History Of Advertising In Words And Pictures*, New York: McGraw Hill.

Samuel, L.R. (2004), "Advertising Disguised as Entertainment," *Television Quarterly*, 34 (2), 51–5.

Scott, J. and M. Craig-Lees (2006), "Conceptualisation, Consumer And Cognition: The 3 Cs That Will Advance Product Placement Research," in *Asia-Pacific Conference for the Association for Consumer Research*. Sydney, Australia.

Sicart, F. (2000), "AOL, RCA and The Shape of History" Available: http://www.gold-eagle.com/bears_lair/sicart020200.html, (accessed 13 January 2006).

Taylor, F.W. (1934), *The Economics of Advertising*, London: Allen and Unwin.

Tellis, G.J. (1998), *Advertising and Sales Promotion Strategy*, Reading, Massachusetts: Addison-Wesley.

Time Warner (2006), "Time Inc - Overview" Available: http://www.timewarner.com/corp/businesses/detail/time_inc/index.html, (accessed 1 August 2006).

WARC (2006), "World Advertising Research Centre" Available: www.warc.com, (accessed 27 September 2006).

Waters, R. (1999), "P&G Ties Advertising Agency Fees To Sales," *Financial Times* (16 September).

Wells, W., J. Burnett, and S. Moriarty (2000), *Advertising Principles and Practices*, 5th ed. New Jersey: Prentice Hall.

Wethey, David (2007), "Client-Agency Relationships," in *The SAGE Handbook of Advertising*, eds. Gerard J. Tellis and Tim Ambler, London: Sage Publications.

World Advertising Research Centre (2006), *The European Marketing Pocket Book 2006*, London: World Advertising Research Council.

World Association of Newspapers (2005), "World Press Trends."

WPP (2005), "WPP Investor Report - History" Available: http://www.wppinvestor.com/commentary/history.jsp, (accessed 4 January 2006).

ZenithOptimedia (2005), "*Ad Growth Stable With Healthy Hotspots.*"

ZenithOptimedia (2006), "*Promising Outlook For Global Adspend Growth,*" London: ZenithOptimedia.

Integrated Marketing Communications: Provenance, Practice and Principles

Prasad A. Naik

The last 100 years of advertising gave birth to four big ideas: *Scientific Advertising* by Claude Hopkins, *Unique Selling Proposition* (USP) by Rosser Reeves, *Brand Image* by David Ogilvy, and *Integrated Marketing Communications* (IMC) propagated by Don Schultz (for details, see Jones, 2002). Each marks the best response of advertisers and agencies to the then prevailing market conditions. Specifically, advances in print media and direct mail in the first quarter of the twentieth century led Claude Hopkins to master the art of copywriting and to experiment and measure consumers' response, thus ushering science into the craft of advertising. As roadways and railways connected the distant towns, competing manufacturers found opportunities to expand distribution and sales of their products. So Rosser Reeves' USP approach emphasized functional benefits, articulated via a proposition (e.g., Head & Shoulders eliminates dandruff), to not only appeal to

millions of consumers, but also differentiate the advertised product uniquely from other brands. The second half of the last century discovered television and intensified competition, which led David Ogilvy to champion the idea of "building a brand image." Utilizing the strengths of television medium that combines sights, sounds and motion, this idea associates inanimate products with human personalities (e.g., Marlboro conveys masculinity) so that the resulting associations endure for decades because competitors cannot imitate such non-functional brand values (unlike USP-based differentiation via attributes and benefits). During the 1970s through the 1980s, the ideas of USP and brand image fused together and metamorphosed into what is now known as "positioning," where the firm differentiates its brand from competing ones (as in the USP approach) using perceptual dimensions (as created by brand imagery). At the core, however, these three ideas are alike: they decompose advertising into specialized media – print, television, billboards, promotions, direct mail – and manage them individually.

In contrast to this reductionism, Don Schultz at the Northwestern University promoted the IMC perspective, which takes the holistic view of building brands by integrating all marketing communications activities (Schultz, 1989). Such integration, it was felt, would result in synergies, especially given the diminished effectiveness of individual activities due to the proliferation of newspapers and magazines, fragmentation of media via multiple channels, growth of price promotions to concede to powerful retailers, and emergence of the Internet. Advertisers embraced the IMC concept; agencies responded by creating "one-stop-shops" via mergers and acquisitions of related businesses (e.g., database marketing firms). But two fundamental issues surfaced: How can managers measure synergies? How should their decisions differ from those under previous paradigms?

This chapter elucidates not only these issues, but also related principles of IMC. Addressing squarely how managers should act differently, the principle of synergy states that brand managers should *increase* the media budget and allocate *more* than fair share to the *less* effective activity as synergy between activities increases (see Naik and Raman, 2003). I clarify the intuition for these results in propositions 3 and 4. The rest of the chapter proceeds as follows: provenance of the four big ideas, IMC practice, principles of IMC, current trends, and lastly, a prognostic view of the emerging media landscape and areas where research is needed. Finally I provide a chapter summary.

PROVENANCE OF FOUR BIG IDEAS

I briefly sketch these four big ideas that shaped the practice of mass advertising in last century.

Scientific advertising

Claude Hopkins (1866–1932) introduced the scientific method to the practice of advertising. Best known for the "hard sell" approach to copywriting, he believed that the purpose of advertising is to sell and that consumers would buy if an ad copy articulates the "reason why" they should buy the advertised product. He not only implemented this principle, but also measured consumers' response by counting the number of coupons they redeemed, which is a proxy for sales generated by the ad copy. According to Jones (2002: 4), he could demonstrate "differences in effectiveness between media vehicles, between different advertisements, and – most important – between relatively small variations of individual subjects." This application of scientific method to improve advertising sowed the seeds for the formation of market and opinion research companies. Specifically, in 1921, J. Walter Thompson hired John Watson, the father of behavioural research, to understand consumer behaviour; Young and Rubicam hired George Gallup in 1932 to further develop copy and media research.

The big idea in Hopkins' approach that makes it "scientific" is not the hard-selling style per se; rather it is the implicit notions of *measurement* and *accountability*. Companies must use those notions even today; see Schultz's (2005) call for "measure, then budget," urging managers to estimate the effects of advertising so that they could determine the appropriate budget rather than the prevailing practices of either "budget, then measure" approach (i.e., first develop a media plan and then track sales or awareness) or, worse yet, the budget-and-forget approach (i.e., spend budget, collect no measurements, mark-up the budget for media inflation in subsequent years).

Unique selling proposition

Building on Hopkins' research-based hard-sell approach, Rosser Reeves (1910–1984) defined the concept of Unique Selling Proposition (USP), which requires the company to make a proposition to its customers (see Reeves, 1960):

- "Buy *this* product, and you will get *this* specific benefit."
- "The proposition must be one that the competition either cannot, or does not, offer."
- "The proposition must be so strong that it can move the mass millions, i.e., pull over new customers to your product."

The advertisement itself should focus on a single message to be presented repeatedly because "the consumer tends to remember just one thing from advertising – one strong claim or one strong concept."

Another key element of the USP approach is repetitive advertising, i.e., the intensive use of media weight and frequency to "pound the concept into the heads of consumers," as Don Schultz says (personal communication). This combination of USP and repetition increased the sales for such brands as *Anacin*, *Listerine* or *Colgate*. Recent examples of the USP approach include *Oil of Olay*'s campaign, "you get younger-looking skin," or *Head and Shoulders*' slogan, "you get rid of dandruff."

As I noted in the Introduction, the big idea underlying USP was *functional differentiation, mass appeal, and repetitive advertising*, which were driven by intensified competition and increased distribution due to the then prevailing economic milieu. However, functional differentiation is not sustainable because competitors *will* imitate, especially if the advertised benefit succeeds in moving millions of consumers away from their brands!

Brand image

To overcome this drawback of the USP approach, marketers recognized that the advertised benefit need not be "functional" – just something memorable that differentiates the brand from competing ones. David Ogilvy (1911–1999) advocated that, in the long run, advertising can associate a brand with an image or personality.

His advertisements created brands such as Hathaway shirts, American Express, Rolls-Royce and Pepperidge Farm.

The big idea underlying the brand image concept is that clients and/or agencies can *engineer an abstract (i.e., non-functional) differentiation* via associations, personifications, or even imaginary characters. Because an abstract feature cannot be copied by competitors (without evoking ridicule from consumers and trade), it sustains differentiation in the long run (e.g., up to 30 years).

To appreciate the power of this simple idea, consider *Kellogg*'s *Frosted Flakes* brand that enjoys the largest volume share in the US in an intensively advertised category of cereals. In 1952, Leo Burnett agency created *Tony the Tiger*, and this abstract entity has been associated with *Kellogg*'s *Frosted Flakes* for the last five decades consistently. The special centennial issue of *Advertising Age* ranks it as the top 10 icons of the 20th century based on criteria such as effectiveness, longevity, recognizability and cultural impact. Other nine icons include Marlboro Man, Ronald McDonald, Green Giant, Betty Crocker, Energizer Bunny, Pillsbury Doughboy, Aunt Jemima, Michelin Man and Elsie. They all corroborate the hypothesis: strong brand image shields and strengthens the brand's share.

Given that these images stick for decades, managers need to balance the contrasting needs for continuity and for change. As for *Tony the Tiger*, children's book illustrator Martin Provinsen first created an orange cat, which walked on all fours, with black stripes and a blue nose. To keep freshness, combat ad wearout (see Naik et al., 1998 for media spacing strategy), maintain relevance with new cohorts of consumers, Tony experienced dramatic changes, for example, American football-shaped head was replaced with a rounder form; eye colours changed from green to gold; new addition of whisker bones and contours. To maintain continuity, Tony's voice remained unchanged: the sole voiceover and trademark growl – *They're Gr-r-reat!*® – was offered by Thurl Ravenscroft (who passed away recently at the age of 91).

Integrated marketing communications

The IMC concept originated in US business practice in the 1980s and has been forcefully promoted by Don Schultz since then (Schultz, 1989). Many companies embraced this concept in practice not only because mergers and acquisitions led to consolidation of the advertising industry (which resulted in one-stop shopping of communications needs such as media and creative, consumer promotions and direct marketing, PR and product placement), but also because synergies emerged when various communications activities were integrated within the IMC framework. Consequently, academic journals devoted space to deepen the understanding of IMC; see the special issues of *Journal of Advertising Research* (Cook, 2004), *Journal of Marketing Communications* (Schultz, 1996), *Journal of Business Research* (Bearden and Madden, 1996), and numerous textbooks (e.g., Schultz et al., 1993; Belch and Belch, 2003).

The big idea in the IMC concept is *the holistic view* of marketing communications so that brands capitalize synergies among advertising, direct response, sales promotion, and public relations. This creative combination of multiple activities should offer clarity, consistency and impact (Schultz et al., 1993: 6). Raman and Naik (2006) propose a succinct objective:

> An IMC program plans and executes various marketing activities with consistency so that its total impact exceeds the sum of each activity's impact.

PRACTICE OF IMC

The practice of IMC crossed from North America to Asia to Europe to the Pacific Rim and South America. Several studies investigated this rapid diffusion of IMC. Specifically, Schultz and Kitchen (1997) survey the practices of the US agencies; Eagle et al. (1999) and Eagle and Kitchen (2000) review the perceptions among marketers and agencies in New Zealand; Kitchen and Schultz (1999) provide a multi-country comparison, including the UK, Australia and India; Kim et al. (2004) complement these studies conducted in English-speaking countries by surveying managerial practices in South Korea, where marketers tend to operate in-house ad agencies (unlike other countries). Based on this cumulative knowledge, I summarize three conclusions from surveying the practice of IMC.

First, according to 90% of the agencies, communications budgets increase or stay the same when brand managers adopt IMC programmes. This may seem slightly surprising since the realized synergies might prompt some companies to achieve the same results with smaller budgets. Specifically, Table 1.3.1 reports this finding from Schultz and Kitchen (1997: 11), indicating that advertisers are likely to spend more dollars when they adopt IMC programmes. Interestingly, this fits with Proposition 3 (see the section on Multimedia Budgeting in the Presence of Synergy) which suggests that increasing budgets, where IMC has caused them to become more productive, can maximize an advertiser's own profit in the long run.

The second conclusion pertains to the importance of measuring synergy. Schultz and Kitchen (1997: 13) note, "How to measure IMC programs seems to be an issue that most executives are not able to clearly answer, though it is a criteria which is very important to them." In the IMC Framework section, I explain the challenges faced by previous methods, which eluded the estimation of synergy during the past decade,

Table 1.3.1   Impact of IMC on communications budget

	Across all agencies (%)	Across those agencies whose clients practiced IMC (%)
Client budget will increase	73.0	66.6
Client budget will remain the same	19.8	25.4
Client budget will decrease	3.2	4.0

and then describe an implementable approach for estimating synergy using market data readily available to brand managers (also see the section titled "Perils of using regression analysis to estimate synergies," for more recent advances).

Third, some skeptics wondered whether IMC entails anything different from the other three advertising paradigms. In the Principles of IMC section, normative results show that budgeting and allocation behaviours, carryover effects, long-term profitability, and managers' decision-making under uncertainty differ substantively when brand managers adopt the IMC perspective. In addition, empirical evidence from a field study validates some aspects of the IMC concept. Specifically, McGrath's (2005) results show that messages employing an IMC strategy (i.e., those with a common theme executed across multiple media in a visually consistent manner) induce stronger attitude towards the brand than the same messages employing a traditional strategy (i.e., executions with less visual consistency). These empirical results resonate with the emerging IMC principles, which I describe next.

PRINCIPLES OF IMC

Here I review both the standard and IMC models so that I contrast not only their essential difference, but also the consequences for decision-making and profitability. Before presenting the principles, I have extended the IMC framework from communications to marketing-mix activities of various kinds (e.g., sales promotion, displays, customer acquisition and retention, Internet advertising) that potentially increase brand sales and that exhibit synergies amongst them. The IMC model (Naik and Raman, 2003) assumes that the brand sales result from the "efforts" invested in multiple activities in the firm's marketing mix. Although Naik and Raman (2003) *operationalize* "effort" via dollars spent on television and print advertising empirically to validate their model specification, the following propositions hold

true for multiple marketing-mix activities with positive impact on sales and for *all* feasible parameter values (not just the estimated coefficients). So the propositions to be presented below are not empirical generalizations but theoretical generalizations based on an empirically validated model specification. Given this focus on the integration of various kinds of marketing activities, readers interested in advertising budgeting process or media planning and scheduling (i.e., optimal allocation of budget over time) should consult the other chapters (by Farris and West, 2007, Chapter 5.3; Danaher, 2007, Chapter 5.2 and Vakratsas and Naik, 2007, Chapter 5.4).

Traditional advertising (non-IMC) framework

Across the three big ideas in advertising, excluding IMC, the various modes of communications such as television, radio and newspapers exert independent effects on consumers. Given the lack of consideration of joint effects and cross-media complementarities, inconsistencies could arise between the messages carried by disparate communications media from the same organization. This potential for inconsistencies raised questions about how media advertising works. In addition, cognitive psychology shed new light on consumer information processing, suggesting that consumers absorb information about goods and services from a number of sources, not all of which are formal promotional messages. So, no longer can marketers assume that they control the way consumers think about brands via image-building media advertising. Despite these concerns, standard advertising theory offered deep insights by deducing fundamental principles of budgeting and allocation, which I explain in the next two propositions.

For clarity, suppose managers spend u_1 and u_2 dollars on two communications activities with effectiveness β_1 and β_2, respectively; then the total budget is $(u_1 + u_2)$, and the budget allocation is u_1/u_2. Based on Naik and Raman (2003), I state the normative result in the following proposition:

Proposition 1: In multimedia advertising, as the effectiveness of an activity increases, the optimal spending on that activity increases, thus increasing the optimal total media budget. Furthermore, the total budget should be allocated to multiple activities in proportion to their relative effectiveness.

This proposition informs managers that if an ad agency improves the creative copy, thereby increasing the effectiveness of television advertising (say β_1), then they should *increase* the expenditures on TV advertising (i.e., increase u_1). This proposition cautions the managers against the tempting – but incorrect – intuition: "now that we have a better advertising campaign, we should be able to achieve greater impact with less (or the same) budget."

Another insight from this proposition is revealed by the question: Why should managers spend any dollars at all on the less effective media? Because they should not invest in the most effective activity after diminishing returns set in. Rather, they should shift the allocation to the next most effective medium so as to locate the firm on the steep region of the response curve for the less effective medium rather than stay on its flatter portion for the more effective medium. Consequently, as in proposition 1, the eventual budget allocation results in the optimal proportion β_1/β_2 (and not 100% to the most effective activity and zero to the less effective ones).

The standard advertising theory also investigated the role of carryover effects, which capture the long-term effects of advertising. Naik and Raman (2003) showed that not only do managers need a larger total budget when carryover effects are large, but that they should increase spending on each of the communications activities proportionately so that the relative allocation remains *invariant* to the magnitude of the carryover effect. I summarize these findings as follows:

Proposition 2: In multimedia advertising, as the carryover effect increases, the optimal total media budget increases; however, budget allocation does not depend on the carryover effect.

To develop the intuition for this proposition, I observe that *the carryover effect enhances the long-term effectiveness of communications activities*. Specifically, if λ denotes the carryover effect, then the long-term effectiveness of each activity is given by $\beta_i/(1 - \lambda)$, which exceeds the short-term effectiveness β_i (because λ is a positive fraction). Furthermore, the long-term effectiveness of each activity increases *proportionately* by the same factor, $(1 - \lambda)^{-1}$. Hence the *relative* proportion β_1/β_2 must necessarily remain unchanged, keeping the budget allocation invariant to changes in the carryover effect.

IMC framework

Managers should recognize that consumers combine the information they receive from various media whether or not the firm itself integrates those messages across media. To prevent consumers from integrating them inconsistently, they should take charge of this process, and this *proactive* view of IMC represents the new approach to media planning (see the section on "Negative synergies between advertising and promotion in oligopoly markets" for further details). The overriding purpose of IMC is to manage all marketing activities that impact sales, profits, and brand equity.

The IMC model emphasizes the role of joint effects or *synergies* generated due to the orchestration of multiple activities. Consider, for example, the recent launch of F-150 that utilized an IMC campaign. Briggs et al. (2005) report that, in the first two months of this campaign, Ford spent over $60 million in television advertising to target consumers (males, 25 to 49 years), who saw these ads 30 times during the 60-day launch period. Online advertising consisted of page takeovers of major portals and portal "roadblocks," which is a simultaneous ad display across multiple sites. Besides television and online ads, Ford used radio, print, outdoor, and direct mail to support this launch.

One of the goals was to generate synergies between mass media campaigns and online advertising. To this end, Marketing Evolution, a specialist marketing measurement firm, in conjunction with the Advertising Research Foundation (ARF), Association of National Advertisers (ANA) and American Association of Advertising Agencies (AAAA), conducted Cross-Media Optimization Study (XMOS).

Using a model-based approach, Ford measured not only the effectiveness of individual media effects, but also the complementary effects and synergies (for further details, see Briggs et al., 2005). Thus, IMC framework is much more than simply using multiple media concurrently as in the standard multimedia model, where the effectiveness of each activity does *not* depend upon any other activity. In contrast, in an IMC model, the effectiveness of *each* activity depends upon *all other* communications activities used by the firm. Given this IMC framework, a number of fundamental questions arise:

- How to measure synergies using readily available market data?
- How does synergy affect the magnitude of the multimedia budget?
- How should managers alter budget allocations as synergy increases (or decreases)?
- How does synergy moderate the effects of advertising carryover on the budget and its allocation?
- Are there catalytic effects of synergy?
- How should managers make budgeting and allocation decisions under uncertainty?

I address all these issues in turn.

Measurement of synergy

One of the earliest studies attempting to measure media synergy was conducted by a consortium of radio network companies, who sampled 500 adults, ages 20–44, across 10 locations in the United Kingdom. The main findings indicated that 73% of the participants remembered prime visual elements of TV ads upon hearing radio commercials. In addition, 57% re-lived the TV ads while listening to the radio advertisement. Thus, radio ads reinforced the imagery created by TV commercials, resulting in synergy between television and radio advertising (for further details, see Radio Advertising Bureau at www.rab.co.uk).

Although the estimation of cross-media synergy remained elusive, standard advertising models attempted its estimation by specifying brand sales a *response function* of managers' current actions and past outcomes; for example, $S_t = \beta_0 + \beta'_1 u_{1t} + \beta_2 u_{2t} + \lambda S_{t-1} + \varepsilon_t$. Gatignon and Hanssens (1987) pioneered the distinction between a response function and *process functions*, which explain how effectiveness parameters themselves depend on managers' actions. In other words, managerial actions affect not only market outcomes (e.g., sales, share), but also the *effectiveness* of marketing activities. For example, suppose that radio and TV advertising enhance each other's effectiveness. Such effects are captured in the process function (say) $\beta'_1 = \beta_1 + \kappa u_2$, which suggests that the spending level u_2 increases the effectiveness β'_1 in the presence of positive synergy ($\kappa > 0$). When this process function is substituted into the above response function, the resulting IMC model is

$$S_t = \beta_0 + \beta_1 u_{1t} + \beta_2 u_{2t} + \kappa u_{1t} u_{2t} + \lambda S_{t-1} + \varepsilon_t \tag{1}$$

which contains an interaction term that captures the extent of synergy.

This notion of process function is deterministic and static (i.e., without the error terms or lagged βs). Even so, many challenges arise in applying the ordinary least squares (OLS) or related statistical approaches to estimate the parameter for synergy, κ. These challenges arise because OLS and related statistical approaches ignore inter-temporal dependence and non-stationarity in the observed sales process, thereby resulting in biased parameter estimates and incorrect budget determination. I substantiate the perils of using OLS in the section titled "Perils of using regression analysis to estimate synergies."

Advanced estimation techniques overcame these challenges and facilitated the *joint* estimation of both response and process functions. Specifically, applying Wiener-Kalman filtering theory, Naik and Raman (2003) developed an appropriate method and demonstrated its application by analyzing the sales and advertising data for Dockers® brand of Khaki trousers in the fashion apparels market. They furnished strong evidence for the presence of synergy between television and print advertising.

Figure 1.3.1 displays the fit and forecast from Naik and Raman's IMC model. The goodness-of-fit measures in-sample fit with the market data. On the other hand, the quality of forecasts shows how well the model *predicts* out-of-sample observations. To assess this predictive validity, Naik and Raman (2003) conducted a cross-validation study, and these results also are shown in Figure 1.3.1 (see hold-out sample). It indicates that the proposed model, fitted with sub-sample data, predicts the new observations, including the turning points, satisfactorily. Thus, the IMC model not only fits the sample data, but also exhibits strong predictive performance.

They further generalized this approach to estimate a general nonlinear, non-stationary, dynamic and stochastic process functions (for details, see Naik and Raman, 2003: 384). Thus, managers can use this Kalman filtering approach to estimate the magnitudes of synergy for their own brand-specific multimedia advertising (see Schultz, 2004).

In sum, Dockers® brand's advertising furnishes strong support, in terms of both fit and forecast, for the proposed IMC model. Not only the resulting empirical findings contribute to the sparse marketing literature on cross-media synergies, but also the estimation method – based on the Kalman filter for fitting dynamic multi-media advertising models to market data – enables managers to discover empirical insights for their particular brands.

Multimedia budgeting in the presence of synergy

After managers establish the existence of synergy in their markets, how should they determine the multimedia budget? Applying optimal control theory, Naik and Raman (2003) addressed this question by showing that, in dynamic equilibrium, the total budget should be increased to capitalize media synergies. I present this normative result as

Proposition 3: As synergy increases, the optimal total media budget increases.

First, this proposition is consistent with agency beliefs. Table 1.3.1 displays how senior agency personnel think about the impact of IMC on their clients' budgets. A vast majority (73%) believe that the budget will increase when clients adopt the IMC perspective. For agencies whose clients have adopted IMC, their beliefs are informed by their clients' actual use of IMC, and this subset

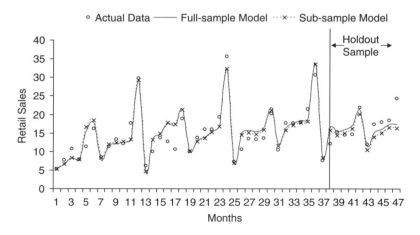

Figure 1.3.1   Actual retail sales versus model forecasts

of agencies also lends support to the above proposition (see the last column of Table 1.3.1).

Second, this proposition addresses the age-old issue of whether or not managers overspend, i.e., actual expenditure exceeds the optimal budget. Overspending is likely to be smaller when the total budget reflects the objectives of orchestrating the communications mix.

Lastly, managers should not simply spend additional money to "do more of the same thing." Rather, the increased budget should be utilized to create synergies between activities. The resulting synergies then enhance both short- and long-term effectiveness of marketing activities.

Multimedia allocation in the presence of synergy

Next I note the important finding that budget allocation is *qualitatively* different in the presence of synergy, requiring managers to act *differently* when implementing IMC. Based on Naik and Raman (2003), synergy alters the budget allocation:

Proposition 4: As synergy increases, the proportion of media budget allocated to the more (less) effective communications activity decreases (increases). If the various activities are equally effective, managers should allocate the media budget equally among them regardless of the magnitude of synergy.

The counter-intuitive nature of this result is its striking feature. To understand the gist of this result, suppose that two activities have unequal effectiveness (say, $\beta_1 > \beta_2$). Then, in the absence of synergy ($\kappa = 0$), the optimal spending on an activity depends only on its own effectiveness; hence, a larger amount is allocated to the more effective activity (see proposition 1). However, in the presence of synergy ($\kappa \neq 0$), optimal spending depends not only on its own effectiveness, but also on the spending level for the *other* activity. Consequently, as synergy increases, marginal spending on an activity increases at a rate proportional to the spending level for the other activity. Hence, optimal spending on the more effective activity increases slowly, relative to

the increase in the optimal spending on the less effective activity. Thus, the proportion of budget allocated to the *more* effective activity *decreases* as synergy increases.

If the two activities are equally effective, then the optimal spending levels on both of them are equal. Furthermore, as synergy increases, marginal spending on each of them increases at the *same* rate. Hence, the optimal allocation ratio remains constant, regardless of the increase or decrease in synergy.

Advertising carryover effects in the presence of synergy

I describe how synergy moderates the carryover effect in the next two propositions:

Proposition 5 (budget): As the carryover effect increases, the optimal total media budget increases; the rate of increase in the media budget increases as synergy increases.

Proposition 6 (allocation): In contrast to proposition 2, budget allocation depends on the carryover effect in the presence of synergy. Furthermore, as carryover increases (decreases), the proportion of budget allocated to the more (less) effective activity decreases (increases).

Based on propositions 2 and 6, managers should act differently: absent synergy, they should allocate the budget to a variety of activities in simple proportion to the relative effectiveness; when synergy is present, the allocation should incorporate the information on the increased magnitude of the carryover effect.

Note that "the carryover effect increases" means the magnitude of λ in equation (1) increases, which can be interpreted as purchase reinforcement or inertia from previous sales (due to loyalty or retention). Although not applicable in the equation (1), if multiple lags were involved (e.g., Tellis et al., 2000), then "the" carryover effect needs to be defined and such a construct would relate to either an average or the total summation of multiple carryover effects across different lagged terms. Future research should investigate how different carryover effects due to multiple lags moderate the effects of synergy within an IMC context.

Catalytic effects of synergy

Does synergy introduce any fundamentally new advertising effect? Yes, since all media are not alike, managers can capitalize on the "catalytic effects" of ancillary activities. This new effect – the *catalytic effect of ancillary activities* – can be defined as follows: a marketing activity is a catalyst if it has negligible direct effect on sales, but exhibits substantial synergies with other activities. For catalytic activities, Raman and Naik (2004) prove the following result:

Proposition 7: Managers should allocate a non-zero budget to catalytic activity even if it is completely ineffective in itself.

Recall that managers should allocate the total budget to various media in proportion to their relative effectiveness (see proposition 1), and so the completely ineffective activity should not even be considered in the communications mix. In contrast to this traditional way of thinking, managers who seek to orchestrate an IMC program benefit from not only the direct effects, but also the indirect effects of various activities. Therefore, they should *not* eliminate spending on an apparently ineffective activity when it enhances the effectiveness of other activities due to its catalytic properties.

In marketing, many activities exert catalytic influence on one another. For example, BMW used product placement in James Bond movies, which may not have increased sales of BMW, but made its TV and print advertising more effective. Or Mini Cooper used the real movie, *The Italian Job*, to build its brand image. More specifically, consider the example from the pharmaceutical industry: product samples or collateral materials may not directly increase sales of prescription medicines, but it may enhance the effectiveness of detailing efforts (Parsons and Vanden Abeele, 1981). Indeed, marketing communications using billboards, publicity, corporate advertising, event marketing, in-transit ads, merchandising, and product placement in movies may not have measurable impacts on sales. Yet, millions of dollars are spent on these activities. Why? Because, these activities, by their

mere presence in the communications mix, may act like catalysts, and enhance the effectiveness of other activities such as broadcast advertising or salesforce effort.

While the above propositions and discussions advanced our understanding of synergy, the impact of marketing effort on sales was assumed to be deterministic. When this assumption is untenable, for instance, in turbulent, volatile markets where uncontrollable factors also may affect sales, managers need to incorporate the role of uncertainty in the analyses. To this end, Raman and Naik (2004) generalized the deterministic IMC model by using the Wiener process to represent uncertainty in their continuous-time dynamic model.

Extending IMC to uncertain environments

Applying stochastic optimal control theory, Raman and Naik (2004) derived the optimal IMC program for uncertain markets. Below I present their main propositions and discuss the substantive implications.

Proposition 8: In uncertain markets, the total media budget increases as synergy increases. Furthermore, the proportion of budget allocated to the more (less) effective medium decreases (increases) as synergy increases.

It is intriguing to find that propositions 3 and 4 in the absence of uncertainty are identical to the above one, seemingly implying that uncertainty plays no role! But jumping to such a conclusion is inaccurate because uncertainty directly affects sales evolution, thereby making the level and growth of sales less predictable in the future. In addition, uncertainty affects the variability in long-term profit, thereby increasing the downside risks of losses and bankruptcies. Thus, uncertainty has serious consequences on both sales and profit.

The proper interpretation of proposition 8, therefore, is that managers should *not alter* their decisions by increasing or decreasing budget in response to the effects of uncertainty on sales and profit. This finding clarifies the conflicting views prevalent in the existing practice. Specifically, advertising agencies advocate that managers should *increase* the media spending in response to demand shocks such as recessions (also see Srinivasan et al., 2005). Whereas an empirical analysis of the national media spending data indicates that managers are likely to *decrease* their media budget during recessions. Resolving these conflicting views, Proposition 8 recommends *neither increasing nor decreasing the media spending, but sticking to the course of action in uncertain times*.

In sum, this proposition highlights the fact that "no action" on budget changes does not imply managerial "inaction," the former requiring knowledge of optimal decision-making under uncertainty, the discipline not to tinker with marketing budgets in the short term, and the commitment to building brands over the long term.

I next describe the effects of uncertainty on the profitability of IMC programs:

Proposition 9: In uncertain markets, the expected value of long-term profitability of the optimal IMC program increases as synergy increases.

Proposition 10: In uncertain markets, the variability of long-term profitability of the optimal IMC program is unaffected by the magnitude of synergy.

According to these propositions, managers should adopt an IMC perspective to increase the brand's profitability. That is, they should think of marketing communications activities not as a set of independent variables, but rather as a set of interconnected activities with potential synergies. By generating synergies, they not only increase the expected profitability in the long run, but they also keep profit variability unaltered. In other words, synergy imposes no tradeoff between profitability and variability. Thus, an IMC perspective raises profit but leaves its variability unaffected, and so it is prudent to build synergies by orchestrating the communications mix.

CURRENT TRENDS

Here I present findings from recent research on marketing synergies.

Simultaneous media usage

Pilotta and Schultz (2004) offer a fresh perspective on how IMC works in the presence of multiplicity of advertising media and scarcity of consumer attention. They posit that consumers multi-task or use various forms of media in combination with each other, a phenomenon they refer to as "simultaneous media exposure." In the presence of cross-media synergy, the impact of advertised messages is not simply additive, but synergistic, so that the overall impact of media advertising may be greater than the sum of its individual parts. They suggest that consumers process multiple media synesthetically, i.e., one source of stimulation evokes the need for information from the other. Consequently, each media pair operates in either foreground or background of consumers' attention.

To validate this conceptualization, Schultz et al. (2005) conduct a large-scale survey-based study. This study reveals that media usage is one of the primary daily activities because consumers devote a substantial part of their life. Table 1.3.2, based on their study, shows that an average respondent devotes 145.6 minutes to television, which represents 10.1% of the total 1,440 minutes

Table 1.3.2   Reported daily media consumption

Media forms	Minutes per day	Percentage per day (Total 1440 minutes = 24 × 60 minutes)
Television	145.6	10.1
Internet	128.6	8.9
Radio	74.6	5.2
Newspaper	36.4	2.5
Magazine	29.0	2.0
Direct mail	20.4	1.4

per day (24 hours × 60 minutes). Television and Internet account for a disproportionate amount of reported media consumption. Radio, Newspaper, and Magazine, together, consume a substantial amount of time.

Furthermore, Schultz, Block and Pilotta (2005) present empirical evidence to support their notion of "foreground" and "background" media. To identify the primacy of media forms, Schultz et al. (2005) asked the respondents, "When you are online, do you watch TV?," and 25.7% of them said they watched TV while online. When the question was reversed, "when you are watching TV, do you go online?" – 21.8% of them reported they went online while watching TV. In other words, consumers clearly considered one medium to be primary and the other as secondary. Schultz et al. (2005, Tables 6 and 7) report the results that suggest consumers do identify "foreground" and "background" media. This distinction of primary-secondary media, together with the catalytic effect explained in Proposition 7, suggests that brand managers and ad agencies should adopt the IMC perspective and allocate more than fair share to the secondary media.

Negative synergies between advertising and promotion in oligopoly markets

Naik et al. (2005) extended the IMC model to dynamic markets with multiple brands. In dynamic competitive markets, brand managers need to account for not only interactions between marketing activities, but also interactions among competing brands. By recognizing interaction effects between activities, managers can consider inter-activity tradeoffs in planning the marketing-mix strategies. On the other hand, by recognizing interactions with competitors, managers can incorporate strategic foresight in their planning, which requires them to look forward and reason backwards in making optimal decisions. Looking forward means that each brand manager anticipates how other competing brands are likely to make future decisions and

then, by reasoning backwards, deduces one's own optimal decisions in response to the best decisions to be made by all other brands.

To operationalize this strategic foresight in practice, for example, brand managers for Ford F-150 truck can build a forecasting model and calibrate it using recent sales and advertising data for their own brand and those for GM, Honda, Nissan and Toyota trucks; then they can simulate various forward-looking scenarios for the plausible *counter-factual* spending plans to be made by all other competing brands. The prediction of spending plans of the competitors for the next quarter can then be compared with the actual spending realized in the marketplace. The resulting discrepancy, or the forecasting errors, between the expected spending and the actual spending can also be used to update the next quarter's forward-looking expectations. This understanding gained from such counter-factual reasoning would allow managers to better anticipate competitors' actions, thereby enhancing their intuition, which can be incorporated in their best response.

Formalizing this notion in a dynamic game-theoretic sense, Naik et al. (2005) investigated the joint consideration of interaction effects and strategic foresight when planning marketing-mix strategies. Consequently, managers can address such questions as: Do advertising and promotion amplify or attenuate their impact on market outcomes (e.g., brand share) when used together? What should be the level of the optimal budget in the presence of strategic foresight? How should managers optimally allocate the total budget to advertising and promotion in the presence of interaction effects? Is own (or competitor's) brand under-advertising or over-promoting (or both)? If brand A's interaction effect increases, should brand B optimally respond with increased advertising or increased promotion?

To enable managers gain insights for their particular brands, Naik et al. (2005) developed two methods: (i) a marketing-mix algorithm to plan optimal marketing-mix strategies, and (ii) an estimation method to determine the effectiveness of marketing activities and their interaction effects for each brand in dynamic competitive markets. Both the methods are general and can be applied to various dynamic oligopoly models used to describe and predict the marketing environment.

Applying the dual methods, Naik et al. (2005) studied dynamic competition among the detergents brands Tide, Wisk, Era, Solo and Bold, where each brand uses advertising and promotion to increase its own market share and reduce or limit the growth of competing brands. Empirically, advertising and promotion have the usual main effects of increasing own brand shares. However, they exert negative interaction effects: *promotion diminishes ad effectiveness and advertising reduces consumers' sensitivity to promotion.*

My summary of the literature is that large brands under-advertise and over-spend on promotion, while small brands under-advertise and under-promote. Besides empirical and normative findings, Naik et al. (2005) furnish evidence that competitive responsiveness is asymmetric. For example, when Tide's negative interaction (between advertising and promotion) increases, it decreases advertising and increases promotion; all other brands' follow Tide's actions. By contrast, when Wisk's negative interaction increases, it increases advertising and decreases promotion (unlike Tide's actions); other brands' follow suit, but not Tide whose best response is to decrease advertising and increase promotion.

In practice, based on this dual methodology, managers can gain insights into how their own brands should respond to changes in a competing brand's situation, whether their own brand experiences synergies, and the budgeting implications of such synergies (for example, whether they are overspending on promotion or under-spending on advertising). In other words, this dual methodology empowers managers to gain valuable and hitherto unavailable insights into their product markets. Thus, the next step for managers is to create PC-based software to implement the dual methodology so that they can incorporate the resulting market-based insights in their mega million dollars budgeting and allocation decisions.

Synergy between tradeshow and personal selling

Does tradeshow activity enhance selling effectiveness? Is there empirical evidence that a trade show, when deployed in conjunction with personal selling, provides a sufficient economic return to justify the investment? Smith et al. (2004) address these managerially relevant – but hard-to-answer questions – by investigating synergies between personal selling and trade shows. They conduct a field study with a group of industrial distributors to show that follow-up sales efforts generate higher sales productivity when firms have already exposed customers to its product at a trade show. They further show that overall profits are greater when firms use the trade show in conjunction with optimal levels of sales effort. Their study not only furnishes strong support for the concept of integrated marketing communications, but also quantifies the productivity of both selling and trade shows activities.

Synergies between DTC advertising and detailing

In pharmaceutical marketing, detailing activities, which refers to the efforts of the sales force to inform and educate medical doctors to buy or prescribe drugs, are an important element of the firm's marketing mix. Narayanan et al. (2004) investigate whether synergies arise between detailing and direct-to-consumer advertising (DTC). Using data from a category of pharmaceutical products (the second-generation prescription antihistamines), they study the impact of synergies between pairs of marketing-mix elements on return on investment. They replicate the empirical analysis for a different pharmaceutical product category (antivirals to treat genital herpes) and lend further support to the key results. Their main findings are as follows: (1) DTC affects category sales, but detailing does not; however, both detailing and DTC affect brand share; (2) detailing has a greater impact on revenues than does DTC; (3) detailing and DTC have long-term effects on revenue that are approximately four to seven times the current-period effects; and (4) synergies between marketing-mix elements (e.g., between price and detailing; between detailing and DTC) do not affect category sales, but influence brand shares. An implicit synergy exists between DTC and detailing because DTC affects category volume and detailing affects brand share. Managers need to consider this implicit synergy when allocating resources between the marketing-mix elements. More generally, resource allocation decisions must also account for explicit marketing-mix interactions. This study identifies several explicit interaction effects; among them is a negative interaction between price and detailing. Because of the negative interaction, greater detailing can exert a downward pressure on prices.

Does impact of synergies vary by brand characteristics?

A national brand may gain more than a private label brand from an end-of-aisle display, while the private label brand may benefit more by combining a display with a price promotion rather than offering the promotions in separate weeks. To understand such issues, Lemon and Nowlis (2002) explore potential synergies among displays, feature, advertising, price promotions, and brands types in different price-quality tiers. Using scanner data and experiments, they find that higher-tier brands benefit more than low-tier brands from price promotions, displays, or feature advertising when these promotional tools are used individually. This advantage disappears, however, when certain promotional tools are used in combination with one another. In particular, price promotions have a stronger effect on low-tier and high-tier brands when these promotions are offered in settings where comparisons are difficult (end-of-aisle displays or feature advertising). Furthermore, the combined effects of displays and price

promotions, or feature advertising and price promotions, are greater on the low-tier brands than on the high-tier brands. For strategic implications of these results for retailers and manufacturers, see Lemon and Nowlis (2002).

Media synergies and marketing–sales coordination

Poor marketing coordination can reduce a firm's profit. Consider a market where consumers' buying decisions involve multiple stages such as impersonal mass communications generate customer inquiries (i.e., contact with the call centre), which are then followed by personal sales calls that culminate in potential sales. For example, a home improvement retailer employs direct mail, radio advertising, newspaper and trade shows to generate leads. In the subsequent stage, the company's salesperson follows up with those leads, but significant delays in making appointments for in-home visits result in a longer wait for prospective customers, thereby risking lost sales opportunities due to declining interest of the prospective customers. Hence, the firm should not generate too many leads that the sales force cannot fulfill given its capacity.

To understand such trade-offs at the marketing-sales interface, Smith et al. (2005) develop a three-stage model that captures the effects of sequential marketing communications on lead generation, appointment conversion, and sales closure. They discover relationships between marketing efforts (multiple media generating leads), delays in subsequent communications (time-lag between inquiry and personal selling follow-up), and the stress placed on sales efficiencies (appointment and sales conversion). More specifically, using household-level data obtained from a national home improvement retailer, they show that each medium (e.g., print advertising, radio advertising, and exhibitions) exerts differential impact across the three buying stages. These findings then serve as inputs to a decision support tool for improving the effectiveness of the entire system through two distinct but interrelated mechanisms: cross-media synergies between lead-generating media, and coordination between marketing and selling activities influenced by capacity-driven delays. Smith et al. (2005) create a user-friendly decision support tool, called *MediaMD*, which empowers the managers to make informed decisions by simulating sales and profit consequences of varying communications budgets and media allocations. Future research should investigate such multi-stage communications by using hidden Markov models (Smith et al., 2006).

Synergy between advertising and sales contest

In financial services or prescription drug sales, a firm's sales depend on both advertising and personal selling efforts (e.g., journal and/or DTC advertising, product sampling). Because of synergies, product advertising can make personal selling more productive and vice versa. Hence, to drive sales, companies like IDS Financial Services utilize a mix of advertising and sales force incentive pro-grammes (e.g., sales contest-based bonuses and memberships in the President's Advisory Council for top financial agents).

To understand trade-offs in allocating a fixed marketing budget to customer-focused advertising and agent-focused sales, Murthy and Mantrala (2005) build a model that takes into account synergy between advertising and selling efforts. They derive the optimal alloca-tion of IMC budget between brand advertising and prizes of a rank-order sales contest for a homogeneous sales force. Their model provides insights into how the optimal budget allocations vary with the synergy between advertising and selling effort, sales force size, salesperson risk-tolerance, perceived cost of effort, selling effectiveness and sales response uncertainty. One of their findings is that sales contest should be designed such that the number of winners is about two-thirds of the sales force size. They also highlight the need for coordination between marketing and sales management when designing a promotion program that involves both advertising and sales force incentives.

Closed-loop IMC

In markets characterized by uncertainty, managers need to adapt marketing budgets in response to changes in market conditions besides taking into account cross-media synergy. To this end, Prasad and Sethi (2005) formulate a stochastic IMC model and derive the closed-loop strategy that depends on a brand's market penetration. One of their insightful findings is that, when brand share drops, managers should spend *more* on IMC activities to offset the share decline.

This result, based on optimality analysis, is in stark contrast with textbook recommen-dation to decrease spending as sales decline. I emphasize that textbook recommendation rests on the percentage-of-sales rule of thumb, which not only lacks theoretical justification, but also initiates the *suicide spiral*: sales decline begets a smaller marketing budget, which in turn drives lower sales and so marketers get to work with still smaller budgets in subsequent years, and so on. To avoid the suicide spiral, following Prasad and Sethi (2005), managers should increase spending when share drops (and vice versa).

They further inquire into an intriguing question, "What would happen if synergy were present in the market, but ignored by managers?" They prove that the total IMC budget would be smaller, brand's profitability diminishes, and the brand attains a lower share in the long run. The smaller IMC budget, however, does not imply that expen-diture on all activities drops proportionately. Consequently, an incorrect allocation to various media sets in when managers ignore synergy present in the marketplace. Hence, it behooves managers to measure synergy using market data and appropriate estimation methods, as I explain next.

Perils of using regression analysis to estimate synergies

Marketers measure a wide variety of metrics ranging from consumer awareness to brand attitudes to dollar sales and market shares. Using these metrics, market research and consulting companies estimate the effects of marketing activities via some marketing-mix model. Based on regression analysis of market data, marketing-mix models would reveal (a) the effect of marketing and communication investments in generating incremental sales and (b) the relative contributions of various marketing activities. Due to increasing availability of single-source data, frequent-shopper programs, consumer panels, and other data gathering methodologies (see Dekimpe and Hanssens, 2000; Koen et al., 2005), marketing mix models have become the "de facto" tools for analysing the effects of marketing investments.

However, the real question is, *are the resulting estimates of marketing effects accurate*? With literally billions of dollars of marketing investments resting on such estimated effects, a more complete review of the methodology and its properties is justified. To this end, Naik et al. (2005) conduct Monte Carlo studies to investigate whether regression analysis yields the true impact of marketing activities accurately.

Despite its popular use, they find an eye-opening result that *regression analysis yields substantially biased parameter estimates because market data contain measurement noise*. This result holds even when a *dependent* variable in dynamic advertising models is noisy. More specifically, the resulting bias in ad effectiveness estimates range from 34% to 41%, whereas both carryover effects and cross-media synergy display downward bias of 13.6% and 27.5%, respectively. Naik and Tsai (2000) also offer similar evidence suggesting that measurement noise causes parameter biases in dynamic models. Empirical analysis based on actual market data also comport with these simulation-based findings. For example, the analyses of Toyota Corolla's multimedia campaign reveal that the estimated effects of magazine and rebate effectiveness are indeed more than twice as large as they should be.

Utilizing such biased estimates in their decision-making, managers would overspend on advertising and rebates because these activities seem more effective than they truly are. In the long run, however, they would commit to a smaller marketing budget than they should because of the under-estimation of carryover effects (which captures the long-term effectiveness of IMC programmes). Furthermore, the under-estimation of cross-media synergy entails the risk of allocating a smaller budget to achieve media integration. Consequently, managers are likely to misallocate a greater proportion of the marketing budget to short-run activities relative to long-term brand-building activities, and this myopic decision-making is driven by the inaccurate estimation of marketing-mix models via regression analysis.

Given the perils of regression analysis, are there alternative approaches that managers can adopt to estimate the effects of marketing activities and synergies? Fortunately, the answer is affirmative – the Wiener-Kalman filter (WKF) estimation approach yields unbiased estimates even in the presence of measurement noise. Naik et al. (2005) compare the performance of WKF with regression analysis under identical conditions, and they show that the WKF yields improved estimates that are much closer to the true effects of multimedia campaign than the corresponding regression estimates.

FUTURE DEVELOPMENTS

Over the last century, advertising evolved and IMC emerged (also see McDonald and Scott, 2006 and Tellis, 1998) in response to the new forms of product distribution and communications media (e.g., railways and roadways, radio and television). I now offer a prognostic view of the media landscape to come.

In the last two decades, a multitude of new forms of distribution and media surfaced; for example, supermarket chains and cable channels in the 1980s; Internet-based companies in the 1990s providing information (Google and Yahoo) and products (Amazon or eBay); and, in this decade, mobile marketing and peer-to-peer communications via social networks on the Internet (Epinions.com). A central distinction between this new class of emerging media and the broadcast media (print, radio, television) is the shift in control from companies to consumers. Specifically, brand information obtained from social network sites, such as epinion.com, provides opinions of other real consumers of the products, whereas the information from broadcast media are controlled by either manufacturers or retailers.

This shift marks a change in the locus of ownership from manufacturers (of advertised images) to consumers (of personal views), raising significant new challenges for managers trying to integrate marketing communications. Not only do they face media proliferation (i.e., many media forms whose effectiveness and synergies need to be assessed) and media fragmentation (i.e., media channels unable to reach large audiences), but they may not even "own" the message content being communicated by consumers and consumed by other consumers. How do consumers, then, combine multiple messages some positive, some negative and other mixed reviews? How should managers, then, integrate their marketing communications strategy to maintain a favorable balance of positive imagery for their brands?

Researchers will also need to look at the effects of IMC across companies. Using IMC to increase synergy, and therefore the budget, sales and profitability should be the case, as indicated above, for a single company but if all companies in a static market adopt IMC, they cannot all increase sales.

Technological innovations will further fragment the media landscape, augmenting the need for IMC. The brand communications that prevail will then consist of both positive and negative messages, from both companies and consumers, giving a new connotation to the old term "communications *mix*." Thus the resulting complexities would necessitate academic researchers and brand managers to deepen their understanding of marketing communications in the emerging media landscape.

SUMMARY

- The objective of Integrated Marketing Communications (IMC) is to assist consumer processing of communications by ensuring consistency of communications and, by extension, of all marketing activities.
- This creates, or increases, synergy between the impacts on the consumer.
- I consider the following eight propositions to hold true:

1. *In multimedia advertising, as the effectiveness of an activity increases, the optimal spending on that activity increases, thus increasing the optimal total media budget. Furthermore, the total budget should be allocated to multiple activities in proportion to their relative effectiveness.*
2. *In multimedia advertising, as the carryover effect increases, the optimal total media budget increases; however, budget allocation does not depend on the carryover effect.*
3. *As synergy increases, the optimal total media budget increases.*
4. *As synergy increases, the proportion of media budget allocated to the more (less) effective communications activity decreases (increases). If the various activities are equally effective, managers should allocate the media budget equally among them regardless of the magnitude of synergy.*
5. *Budget: As the carryover effect increases, the optimal total media budget increases; the rate of increase in the media budget increases as synergy increases.*
6. *Allocation: In contrast to proposition 2, budget allocation depends on the carryover effect in the presence of synergy. Furthermore, as carryover increases (decreases), the proportion of budget allocated to the more (less) effective activity decreases (increases).*
7. *Managers should allocate a non-zero budget to catalytic activity even if it is completely ineffective in itself.*
8. *In uncertain markets, the total media budget increases as synergy increases. Furthermore, the proportion of budget allocated to the more (less) effective medium decreases (increases) as synergy increases.*

- Synergy, which varies by brand, category and media characteristics, therefore needs to be calculated but care should be taken with regression methods.

REFERENCES

Bearden, W.O. and C.S. Madden, Eds. (1996), "Special Issue: A Brief History of the Future of Advertising: Visions and Lessons from Integrated Marketing Communications," *Journal of Business Research*, Vol. 37, Issue 3.

Belch, G.E. and M.A. Belch (2003), *Advertising and Promotion: An Integrated Marketing Communications Perspective*, 6th Ed., New York: McGraw-Hill/Irwin.

Briggs, R., R. Krishnan and N. Borin (2005), "Integrated Multichannel Commuincations Strategies: Evaluating the Return on Marketing Objectives – The Case of the 2004 Ford F-150 Launch," *Journal of Interactive Marketing*, 19 (3), 81–90.

Cook, W.A. Ed. (2004), "Special Issue: IMC's Fuzzy Picture: Breakthrough or Breakdown?" *Journal of Advertising Research*. Vol. 44, Issue 1.

Danaher, P. (2007), "Media Planning," in *The SAGE Handbook of Advertising*, eds. Gerard J. Tellis and Tim Ambler, London: Sage Publications.

Dekimpe, M. and M. Hanssens (2000), "Time-Series Models in Marketing: Past, Present and Future" *International Journal of Research in Marketing*, 17 (2–3), 183–93.

Eagle, L. and P.J. Kitchen (2000), "IMC, Brand Communications, And Corporate Cultures: Client/Advertising Agency Co-Ordination And Cohesion," *European Journal of Marketing*, 34 (5–6), 667–86.

Eagle, L., P.J. Kitchen, K. Hyde, W. Fourie and M. Padisetti (1999), "Perceptions of Integrated Marketing Communications among Markers & Ad Agency Executives in New Zealand," *International Journal of Advertising*, 18 (1), 89–119.

Edell, J.A. and K.L. Keller (1999), "Analyzing Media Interactions: The Effects of Coordinated TV-Print Advertising," *MSI Report No. 99–120*.

Farris, P.W. and D.C. West (2007), "A Fresh View of the Advertising Budgeting Process," in *The SAGE Handbook of Advertising*, eds. Gerard J. Tellis and Tim Ambler, London: Sage Publications.

Gatignon, H. and D.M. Hanssens (1987), "Modeling Marketing Interactions with Application to Salesforce Effectiveness," *Journal of Marketing Research*, 24 (3), 247–57.

Jones, J.P. (2002), *The Ultimate Secrets of Advertising*, Thousand Oaks, CA: Sage Publications.

Kim, I., Dongsub H. and D.E. Schultz (2004), "Understanding the Diffusion of Integrated Marketing Communications," *Journal of Advertising Research*, March, 31–45.

Kitchen, P.J. and D.E. Schultz (1999), "A Multi-Country Comparison of the Drive for IMC," *Journal of Advertising Research*, 39 (1), 21–38.

Koen, P., I. Currim, M.G. Dekimpe, E. Ghysels, D.M. Hanssens, N. Mizik and P. Naik (2005), "Modeling Marketing Dynamics by Time Series Econometrics," *Marketing Letters*, 15 (4), 167–83.

Lemon, K.N. and S.M. Nowlis (2002), "Developing Synergies between Promotions and Brands in Different Price-Quality Tiers," *Journal of Marketing Research*, 39 (2), 171–85.

McDonald, C. and J. Scott (2007), "A Brief History of Advertising," in *The SAGE Handbook of Advertising*, eds. Gerard J. Tellis and Tim Ambler, London: Sage Publications.

McGrath, J.M. (2005), "A Pilot Study Testing Aspects of the Integrated Marketing Communications Concept," *Journal of Marketing Communications*, 11 (3), 191–214.

Murthy, P. and M.K. Mantrala (2005), "Allocating a Promotion Budget between Advertising and Sales Contest Prizes: An Integrated Marketing Communications Perspective," *Marketing Letters*, 16 (1), 19–35.

Naik, P.A. and R. Kalyan (2003), "Understanding the Impact of Synergy in Multimedia Communications," *Journal of Marketing Research*, 40 (4), 375–88.

Naik, P.A., M. Mantrala and A. Sawyer (1998), "Planning Media Schedules in the Presence of Dynamic Advertising Quality," *Marketing Science*, 17 (3), 214–35.

Naik, P.A., K. Raman and R. Winer (2005), "Planning Marketing-Mix Strategies in the Presence of Interactions," *Marketing Science*, 24 (1), 25–34.

Naik, P.A., D.E. Schultz and S. Srinivasan (2005), "Perils of Using OLS to Estimate Multimedia Communication Effects," *working paper*, UC Davis.

Naik, P.A., D.E. Schultz and S. Srinivasan (2008), "Perils of Using OLS to Estimate Multimedia Communications Effects," *Journal of Advertising Research*, forthcoming.

Naik, P.A. and C.L. Tsai (2000), "Controlling Measurement Errors in Models of Advertising Competition," *Journal of Marketing Research*, 37 (1), 113–24.

Narayanan, S., R. Desiraju and P.K. Chintagunta (2004), "Return on Investment Implications for Pharmaceutical Promotional Expenditures: The Role of Marketing-Mix Interactions," *Journal of Marketing*, 68 (4), 90–105.

Pilotta, J.J. and D.E. Schultz (2004), "Developing the Foundation for a New Approach to Understanding How Media Advertising Works," 3rd *Annual ESOMAR / ARF World Audience Measurement Conference*.

Prasad, A. and S.P. Sethi (2005), "Integrated Marketing Communications in Stochastic Monopoly Markets," *working paper*, University of Texas Dallas.

Raman, K. and P.A. Naik (2004a), "Integrated Marketing Communications in Retailing," *Retailing in the 21st Century*, eds M. Kraft and M.K. Mantrala, pp. 381–5.

Raman, K. and P.A. Naik (2004b), "Long-Term Profit Impact of Integrated Marketing Communications Program," *Review of Marketing Science*, Vol. 2, Article 8, http://www.bepress.com/romsjournal/vol2/iss1/art8.

Reeves, R. (1960), *Reality in Advertising*, New York, NY: Alfred Knopf.

Schultz, D.E. (1989), "New Directions for 1992," *Marketing Communications*, 14 (3rd March), 28–30.

Schultz, D.E. Ed. (1996), "Special Issue: Integrated Marketing Communications," *Journal of Marketing Communications*, Vol. 2, Issue 3.

Schultz, D.E. (2004), "Two Profs Prove Real Value of Media Integration," *Marketing News*, Vol. 38, Issue 1, pp. 6–7.

Schultz, D.E. (2005), "Turnaround Strategy: Measure, Then Budget," *Marketing News*, Nov 15 issue, p. 8.

Schultz, D.E., M.P. Block and J.J. Pilotta (2005), "Implementing a Media Consumption Model," 4th *Annual ESOMAR / ARF World Audience Measurement Conference*.

Schultz, D.E. and P.J. Kitchen (1997), "Integrated Marketing Communications in U.S. Advertsing Agencies: An Exploratory Study," *Journal of Advertising Research*, Sept.–Oct., 7–18.

Schultz, D.E., S.I. Tannenbaum and R.F. Lauterborn (1993), *Integrated Marketing Communications: Putting It Together & Making It Work*. NTC Books: Lincolnwood.

Smith, T.M., S. Gopalakrishna, and R. Chatterjee (2005), "A Three-stage Response Model of Integrated Marketing Communications with Dynamic Effects: Investigations at the Marketing-Sales Interface," *forthcoming Journal of Marketing Research.*

Smith, T.M., S. Gopalakrishna and P.M. Smith (2004), "The Complementary Effect of Trade Shows on Personal Selling," *International Journal of Research in Marketing*, 21 (1), 61–76.

Smith, T.M., S. Gopalakrishna and P.M. Smith (2006), "A Three-Stage Model of Integrated Marketing Communications at the Marketing-Sales Interface," *Journal of Marketing Research,* 43 (4), 564–79.

Smith, A., P.A. Naik and C.-L. Tsai (2006), "Markov-switching model selection using Kullback-Leibler divergence," *Journal of Econometrics*, 134 (2), 553–77.

Srinivasan, R., A. Rangaswamy and G.L. Lilien (2005), "Turning Adversity into Advantage: Does Proactive Marketing during a Recession Pay Off?" *International Journal of Research in Marketing*, 22, 109–25.

Tellis, G.J. (1998), *Advertising and Sales Promotion Strategy*, Reading, MA: Addison-Wesley.

Tellis, G.J., R. Chandy and P. Thaivanich (2000), "Decomposing the Effects of Direct Advertising: Which Brand Works, When, Where, and How Long?" *Journal of Marketing Research*, 37 (1), 32–46.

Vakratsas, D. and P. Naik (2007), "Essential of Planning Flighted Media Schedules," in *The SAGE Handbook of Advertising*, eds. Gerard J. Tellis and Tim Ambler, London: Sage Publications.

Advertising and Brand Equity

Kevin Lane Keller

The media environment has changed dramatically in recent years. Traditional advertising media such as TV, radio, magazines, and newspapers are losing their grip on consumers. After the dot-com crash and subsequent hangover in the early 2000s, marketers returned to the Web with vengance, pouring $18 billion into Internet advertising in 2005. While Web advertising jumped 20% during this time, spending for TV ads remained flat.

The prognosis for TV advertising going forward is not necessarily good. With more cable companies building TiVo-like digital video recorders into their digital set boxes, household penetration of DVRs in the US was expected to jump to 33% by 2008. One survey found that almost three-quarters of users of DVRs frequently or always skip over ads when watching recorded programmes. Increased fragmentation from the proliferation of satellite and cable channels has only exacerbated the problem.

Although media rates have continued to climb, viewership and readership with some key demographics such as teenagers continue to slide. The results of a Forrester Research survey of on-line 12–17-year-olds revealed that 94% owned a game console of some kind, two-thirds considered themselves active gamers, and more than 50% of males said they would rather play video games than watch TV.

Paid search services from Yahoo! and Google have exploded to become a $3 billion industry. Consumers are actively creating and sharing content online as consumer communities and blogs have become created on virtually all topics. Seventy-two percent of teens exchange instant messages each day and 64 million Americans use some type of IM application. Cell phones are becoming a critical device for more than phone conversations.

This changing media landscape has forced marketers to re-evaluate how they should best communicate with consumers. As a result, the strategies behind marketing communication programmes have changed fairly dramatically in recent years. In 2004, Procter & Gamble CMO Jim Stengel noted how 90% of P&G's global ad spending was on TV in 1994, but one of its most successful brand launches in history, for Prilosec OTC in 2003, allocated only about one-quarter of its spending to TV. Although there is a strong rationale for such shifts in media spending, the danger is that marketers may overcorrect, failing to take advantage of the important brand-building contributions of advertising that still exist (Duncan, 2002; Keller, 1996).

Towards a better understanding of advertising and brand equity, this chapter has two primary objectives. We first present a detailed model of brand building that helps to provide specific insights into how different types of advertising affect brand equity. The basic theme here is the importance of "mixing and matching" advertising and other communications to create rich and robust brand images (see also Naik, 2007, Chapter 1.3). Second, we address the specific issue of how to devise strategies to improve brand links to communication effects, a major deficiency in most advertising campaigns. We begin our analysis by briefly reviewing the different forms and functions of advertising.

ADVERTISING FORMS AND FUNCTIONS

Advertising comes in many different forms. Five major types of advertising are media (e.g., broadcast and print), direct response (e.g., mail, media, telephone, and internet), on-line (e.g., web sites, search ads, and banner ads), place (e.g., billboards, product placement, and movies), and point of purchase (e.g., shelf-talkers and in-store radio or TV) advertising. Because of its inherent versatility and the control that these different forms afford marketers, advertising can perform many different functions to contribute to brand-building and can accomplish many different objectives.

For example, advertising is a means by which firms can inform, persuade, and remind consumers – directly or indirectly – about the brands that they sell. Advertising represents the voice of the brand and is a means by which the brand can establish a dialogue and build relationships with consumers. Consumers can be told or shown how and why a product or service is used, by what kind of person, and where and when. Consumers can learn about who is behind the product or service and what the company and brand stand for. Consumers can be given an incentive or reward for trial or usage.

Finally, through advertising, brands can be linked to other people, places, events, brands, or experiences. Marketers often find themselves in need of borrowing equity from someone or something else that can help to remedy a brand deficiency or bolster a brand strength. Advertising is often indispensable as a means to leverage that other equity. Thus, although advertising is not the only important means of communication – personal selling, direct response, promotion, events and experiences, and public relations all can contribute to brand equity – it often plays a central role.

The importance of brand equity

Assuming a firm is successful through advertising and other means in building a strong brand with much equity, as Hoeffler and Keller (2003) review, a number of possible benefits may be realised by the firm.

- Improved perceptions of product performance.
- Greater customer loyalty.
- Less vulnerability to competitive marketing actions and marketing crises.
- Larger margins.
- More elastic customer response to price decreases and inelastic customer response to price increases.
- Greater trade or intermediary cooperation and support.
- Increased marketing communication effectiveness.
- Additional licensing and brand extension opportunities.

One key benefit of building a strong brand is increased advertising effectiveness. In a general sense, as a result of the strength and equity of the advertised brand, consumers may be more willing to attend to additional brand advertising, process this advertising more favourably, and have a greater ability to later recall advertising or their accompanying cognitive or affective reactions to that advertising. Brand equity is thus central to the way advertising works, either as a goal in itself or as a mediator to other goals.

Along these lines, academic research has shown a number of communication effects that can be attributed to well-known and liked brands (Sawyer, 1981). For example, consumers are more likely to have a negative reaction to ad repetition with unknown as opposed to strong brands (Calder and Sternthal, 1980; Campbell and Keller, 2003). Familiar brands appear to better withstand competitive ad interference (Kent and Allen, 1994). Similarly, consumers appear to have a more negative reaction with ad tactics such as comparative ads (Belch, 1981) depending on the nature of the brand involved. Humour in ads seems to be more effective for familiar or already favourably evaluated brands than for unfamiliar or less-favourably evaluated brands (Chattopadhyay and Basu, 1990; Stewart and Furse, 1986; Weinberger and Gulas, 1992).

In addition, consumers who are highly loyal to a brand have been shown to increase purchases when advertising for the brand increases (Hsu and Liu, 2000; Raj, 1982). Other advantages associated with more advertising include increased likelihood of being the focus of attention (Dhar and Simonson, 1992, Simonson et al., 1988) and increased "brand interest" (Machleit et al., 1993). Ahluwalia et al. (2000) demonstrated that consumers who have a high level of commitment to a brand are more likely to counter-argue in the presence of negative information (e.g., unflattering claims from a competitor's comparative ad). This may be the reason why strong brands were shown to be better able to weather a product-harm crisis (Dawar and Pillutla, 2000).

These advertising benefits, however, only arise as the result of having a strong brand. Building strong brands is thus a management priority (Aaker, 1991, 1996; Kapferer, 2005). To build a strong brand, the right knowledge structures must exist in the minds of actual or prospective customers so that they respond positively to marketing activities and programmes in these different ways. Advertising can play a crucial role in shaping that knowledge.

A MODEL OF BRAND EQUITY FOR ADVERTISING COMMUNICATIONS

Several different definitions and models of brand equity exist in the academic literature. One well-known model, as developed through a series of books, is from Aaker (Aaker, 1991, 1996, 2004; Aaker and Joachimstahler, 1999). His model, however, is more of an asset-based model and lacks the necessary consumer behaviour perspectives to adequately interpret and provide detailed prescriptive guidance for advertising and communication effects. To do so, a brand equity model is need that would be comprehensive, cohesive, and well-grounded in psychological theory. A model developed with those criteria in mind is the customer-based brand equity model (Keller, 2001, 2003).[1]

According to the customer-based brand equity model, brand equity is fundamentally determined by the brand knowledge created in consumers' minds by marketing programmes and activities. Specifically, *customer-based brand equity* is defined as the differential effect that consumer knowledge about a brand has on their response to marketing for that brand. According to this view, brand knowledge is not the facts about the brand – it is all the thoughts, feelings, perceptions, images, experiences, and so on that become linked to the brand in the minds of consumers (individuals and organizations). All of these types of information can be thought of in terms of a set of associations to the brand in consumer memory. The basic premise of the customer-based brand equity model is that the power of a brand lies in the minds of customers (Janiszewski and van Osselaer, 2000).

Two particularly important components of brand knowledge are brand awareness and brand image. Brand awareness is related to the strength of the brand node or trace in memory as reflected by consumers' ability to recall or recognize the brand under different conditions. Brand image is defined as consumer perceptions of and preferences for a brand, as reflected by the various types of brand associations held in consumers' memories. Strong, favourable, and unique brand associations are essential as sources of brand equity to drive the differential effects and yield the marketing advantages as outlined above.

Although this customer-based brand equity model of brand building has been summarized elsewhere (Keller, 2001, 2003), here we consider its specific advertising communication implications and how it can guide advertising communication development. Building a strong brand, according to the customer-based brand equity model, can be thought of in terms of a sequential series of steps, where each step is contingent upon successfully achieving the previous step. All steps involve accomplishing certain objectives with customers – both existing and potential.

1. **Identity**: Ensure identification of the brand with customers and an association of the brand in customers' minds with a specific product class or customer need or benefit.
2. **Meaning**: Firmly establish the totality of brand meaning in the minds of customers – i.e., by strategically linking a host of tangible and intangible brand associations.
3. **Responses**: Elicit the proper cognitive and affective customer responses to this brand identity and brand meaning.
4. **Relationship**: Convert brand response to create an intense, active loyalty relationship between customers and the brand.

Enacting these four steps is a complicated and difficult process. To provide some structure, it is useful to think of sequentially establishing six "brand building blocks" with customers to accomplish the four steps and create a strong brand. To connote the sequencing involved, these building blocks can be assembled in terms of a brand pyramid (see Figure 1.4.1). Creating significant brand equity involves reaching the top or pinnacle of the pyramid and will only occur if the right brand-building blocks are put into place. The corresponding brand steps represent different levels of the pyramid.

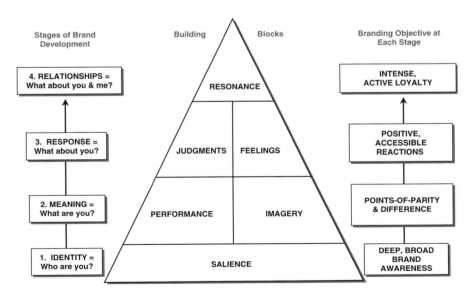

Figure 1.4.1 Customer-based brand equity model pyramid

With the customer-based brand equity model, the most valuable brand building block, brand resonance, occurs when all the other brand-building blocks are completely "in sync" with respect to customers' needs, wants, and desires. *In other words, brand resonance reflects a completely harmonious relationship between customers and the brand.* With true brand resonance, customers have a high degree of loyalty marked by a close relationship with the brand such that customers actively seek means to interact with the brand and share their experiences with others. Firms that are able to achieve resonance and affinity with their customers are more likely to reap the host of valuable benefits that comes from building a strong brand.

Each of these four steps and corresponding brand-building blocks, as well as their implications for advertising development, are examined next.

Brand identity

Achieving the right brand identity involves creating brand salience with customers. *Brand salience* relates to aspects of the awareness of the brand, e.g., how often and easily is the brand evoked under various situations or circumstances. To what extent is the brand top-of-mind and easily recalled or recognized? What types of cues or reminders are necessary? How pervasive is this brand awareness?

Formally, *brand awareness* refers to customers' ability to recall and recognize the brand. Brand awareness is more than just the fact that customers know the brand name and the fact that they have previously seen it, perhaps even many times. Brand awareness also involves linking the brand – the brand name, logo, symbol, etc. – to certain associations in memory. In particular, building brand awareness involves ensuring that customers understand the product or service category in which the brand competes. There must be clear links as to what products or services are sold under the brand name. At a broader, more abstract level, however, it

also means making sure that customers know which of their "needs" the brand – through these products – is designed to satisfy. In other words, what basic functions does the brand provide to customers?

Awareness forms the foundation or base-building block in developing brand equity and provides three important functions. First, awareness influences the formation and strength of brand associations that make up the brand image and gives the brand meaning. Second, creating a high level of brand awareness in terms of category identification and needs satisfied is of crucial importance during possible purchase or consumption consideration opportunities. Third, when customers have "low involvement" with a product category, e.g., because they lack either purchase motivation or ability, they may make choices based on brand awareness alone.

Brand awareness can be distinguished in terms of two key dimensions – depth and breadth. Depth of brand awareness refers to how easily customers can recall or recognize the brand. Breadth of brand awareness refers to the range of purchase and consumption situations where the brand comes to mind. A highly salient brand is one that has both depth and breadth of brand awareness, i.e., such that customers always make sufficient purchases as well as always think of the brand across a variety of settings when it could possibly be employed or consumed. In other words, it is important that the brand not only be "top-of-mind" and have sufficient "mind share" but it must also do so at the right times and right places.

Because of the wide number of settings where advertising can appear – at home, in the store, as well as all places in between – advertising can ensure that the brand stays top-of-mind at the right times and the right places. For example, point-of-purchase advertising can create purchase reminders in a store, whereas media advertising can offer persuasive information or even create consumption reminders in the home. With the "Got Milk?" ad campaign, billboards were placed on homeward-bound commute lanes, radio ads were aired during drive-time, and shelf-takers were strategically placed in food aisles of the store all to remind consumers of the basic message of the TV ads that running out of milk was a pain.

Importantly, the creative content permitted by advertising can help to forge links to the desired purchase or consumption cues. Although sponsorship, product placement, and other forms of promotions are useful to facilitate brand recognition, brand recall requires explicit links to category or needs-based cues. Consequently, more elaborate types of communications as can be found in advertising are often needed to truly shape brand salience in the right way. For example, Campbell Soup's recent reality-base ad campaign themed "Make It Soup Instead" featured Gordon Elliott, television host of "Door Knock Dinners" on the Food Network, intercepting consumers in their home, at work, and on the street and urging them to enjoy a delicious meal featuring soup rather than other meal and snack options. Strategically, the ad could be seen as an attempt to increase brand salience rather than brand image or attitude.

Brand meaning

Brand salience is an important first step in building brand equity, but usually not sufficient. For most customers in most situations, other considerations, such as the meaning or image of the brand, also come into play. Although a myriad of different types of brand associations are possible, brand meaning broadly can be distinguished in terms of more functional, performance-related considerations versus more abstract, imagery-related considerations – with a set of specific dimensions within each.

Brand performance
Brand performance relates to the ways in which the product or service attempts to meet customers' more functional needs. Thus, brand performance refers to the intrinsic properties of the brand in terms of inherent

product or service characteristics. How well does the brand rate on objective assessments of quality? To what extent does the brand satisfy utilitarian, aesthetic, and economic customer needs and wants in the product or service category? In a broad sense, product performance can be related to such dimensions as the primary characteristics and secondary features of a product or service, its reliability, durability, and serviceability, the effectiveness, efficiency and empathy of its service, its style and design, and so on.

The product itself is at the heart of brand equity, as it is the primary influence of what consumers experience with a brand, what they hear about a brand from others, and what the firm can tell customers about the brand in their communications. Designing and delivering a product that fully satisfies consumer needs and wants is a prerequisite for successful marketing, regardless of whether the product is a tangible good, service, organization, etc. To create brand loyalty and resonance, consumers' experiences with the product must at least meet, if not actually surpass, their expectations. Numerous studies have shown that high-quality brands tend to perform better financially, e.g., yielding higher returns on investment.

Despite the fundamental importance of the actual product to brand performance, advertising can still play an important role. First, advertising helps to clarify the actual consumer benefits associated with product performance – i.e., how the product ingredients or features actually create added value for consumers. This translation is often critical to ensure the relevance of product or service features. Second, advertising can actually transform the product experience (Deighton, 1984; Hoch and Deighton, 1989; Hoch and Ha, 1986). Advertising can suggest hypotheses about product performance which consumers may tend to confirm: clothes may fit better, cars may drive more smoothly and service may seem friendlier as a result of well-designed ads communicating those benefits. Finally, advertising can transcend the actual product or service to link intangible brand associations, as discussed next.

Brand imagery

The other main type of brand meaning involves brand imagery. Brand imagery deals with the extrinsic properties of the product or service, including the ways in which the brand attempts to meet customers' more psychological or social needs (Holt, 2004; Levy, 1999; Zaltman, 2003). Brand imagery is how people think about a brand abstractly rather than what they think the brand actually does. Thus, imagery refers to more intangible aspects of the brand. All different kinds of intangibles can be linked to a brand, but four dimensions can be highlighted:

1. *User profiles*. The type of person or organization who actually uses the brand or a more aspirational, idealized user (e.g., VW's iconic "Drivers Wanted" campaign reached out to young adults with a strong sense of activity and adventure).
2. *Purchase and usage situations*. Under what conditions or situations the brand could or should be bought and used (e.g., Corona has run an advertising campaign for years, dubbed by industry experts as "beach in a bottle," that helps to associate the brand with relaxing, timeless beach vacations).
3. *Personality and values*. Personality traits and values similar to people (e.g., Levi's is a brand that may be seen as rugged, whereas Chanel may be seen as sophisticated).
4. *History, heritage, and experiences*. Associations to the past and certain noteworthy events in the brand history – either distinct personal experiences and episodes or more public and broad-based and shared to a large degree across people (e.g., Coca-Cola's strong heritage and persona literally made it impossible to change the product when they attempted to do so with New Coke).

Advertising can play an especially important role shaping imagery and helping to link intangible associations to the brand and its product performance. The types of users and situations depicted in advertising send important signals about brand imagery. The tone or mood of advertising helps to define the brand personality (Aaker, 1997; Aaker et al., 2001). Advertising can also provide information about the character and values of the company behind the brand which in turn can be linked to the brand itself

(Schumann et al., 1991). Corporate image advertising often has the purpose of improving corporate credibility and reputation which has been shown to impact product evaluations (Brown and Dacin, 1997; Keller and Aaker, 1998).

To produce the most positive brand responses, the underpinning of intense and active brand loyalty, it is important that the brand has some strong, favourable, and unique brand associations that serve as points-of-differences, as well as some points-of-parity that negate competitors points-of-difference (Keller et al., 2002).

Brand responses

Brand responses refer to how customers respond to the brand and all its marketing activity and other sources of information, i.e., what customers think or feel about the brand. Brand responses can be distinguished according to brand judgements and brand feelings, i.e., in terms of whether they arise more from the "head" or from the "heart."

Brand judgements

Brand judgements focus upon customers' own personal opinions and evaluations with regard to the brand. Brand judgements involve how customers put together all the different performance and imagery associations for the brand to form different kinds of opinions. Customers may make all types of judgements with respect to a brand (Chaudhuri and Holbrook, 2001), but in terms of creating a strong brand, four dimensions of summary brand judgements are particularly important.

1. *Brand quality*. Perceptions of overall quality, value, satisfaction, and so on.
2. *Brand credibility*. The extent to which the brand as a whole is seen as credible in terms of three dimensions – perceived expertise, trustworthiness, and likeability.
3. *Brand consideration*. The likelihood that customers will actually include the brand in the set of possible options of brands they might buy or use.
4. *Brand superiority*. The extent to which customers view the brand as unique and better than other brands.

Advertising's persuasive appeal can be especially important to elicit positive judgements and create a strong "call to action." By providing engaging product demonstrations or compelling "problem-solution" executions, advertising can create favourable overall brand evaluations and perceptions of quality. As noted above, corporate image or family brand advertising campaigns can create credibility for the corporate brand. Comparative advertising can raise the likelihood of consideration and provide explicit evidence as to brand superiority. These types of advertising appeals can be communicated via direct response, interactive, or media advertising.

Brand feelings

Brand feelings are customers' emotional responses and reactions with respect to the brand. Brand feelings also relate to the social currency evoked by the brand. These feelings can be mild or intense and be positive or negative in nature. Six important types of brand-building feelings are (Kahle et al., 1988):

1. **Warmth**. Warmth refers to more soothing types of feelings – the extent to which the brand makes consumers feel a sense of calm or peacefulness, sentimental, warmhearted, or affectionate about the brand.
2. **Fun**. Feelings of fun are also upbeat types of feelings when the brand makes consumers feel amused, light-hearted, joyous, playful, cheerful, and so on.
3. **Excitement**. Excitement relates to more upbeat types of feelings – the extent to which the brand makes consumers feel energized and a feeling that they are experiencing something special.
4. **Security**. Security feelings occur when the brand produces a feeling of safety, comfort, and self-assurance.
5. **Social approval**. Social approval is when the brand results in consumers having positive feelings about the reactions of others – i.e., when consumers feel others look favourably on their appearance, behaviour, and so on.
6. **Self-respect**. Self-respect occurs when the brand makes consumers feel better about themselves, e.g., when consumers feel a sense of pride, accomplishment, or fulfillment.

The first three are more experiential and immediate, increasing in level of intensity. The latter three are more private and enduring, increasing in level of gravity. In either case, feelings are an area where advertising truly excels, an important consideration given the importance of emotional components to a brand.

Advertising can help to elicit both judgement and feelings responses and may be especially critical in linking feelings to the brand (Aaker et al., 1986; Edell and Moore, 1993; Stewart et al., 2007; Chapter 2.4). Creatively designed advertising can elicit strong emotional responses of all kinds. Brands like Hallmark and Kodak create warmth in their advertising, whereas others such as McDonald's and Coca-Cola create fun or even excitement. Advertising for insurance brands such as Allstate conveys a sense of security for their policy-holders, whereas advertising for fashion brands such as Tommy Hilfiger conveys social approval. Because of the multiple modalities involved of sight, sound, and motion, television advertising is an especially versatile means of evoking emotional responses from consumers.

Brand relationships

Brand resonance refers to the nature of the relationship that customers have with the brand and the extent to which customers feel that they are "in synch" with it (Fournier, 1998, 2000; Fournier et al., 1998). Brand resonance is characterized in terms of intensity or the depth of the psychological bond that customers have with the brand as well as the level of activity engendered by this loyalty (e.g., repeat purchase rates, the extent to which customers seek out brand information, events, other loyal customers, and so on). Specifically, brand resonance can be broken down into four dimensions:

1. **Behavioural loyalty**. How often do customers purchase a brand and how much do they purchase?
2. **Attitudinal attachment**. Do customers state that they "love" the brand, describe it as one of

their favourite possessions, or view it as a "little pleasure" that they look forward to.

3. *Sense of community*. Do customers feel a kinship or affiliation with other people associated with the brand – fellow brand users or customers or employees or representatives of the company?

4. *Active engagement*. Are customers willing to invest time, energy, money, or other resources into the brand beyond those expended during purchase or consumption of the brand?

Brand relationships can be usefully characterized in terms of two factors – intensity and activity. Intensity refers to how strong are the attitudinal attachment and sense of community. In other words, how deeply felt is the loyalty? Activity refers to how frequently the consumer buys and uses the brand, as well as engages in other activities not related to purchase and consumption. In other words, in how many different ways does brand loyalty manifest itself in day-to-day consumer behaviour?

The flexibility of advertising can help to promote resonance in several different ways. Advertising can reinforce the attachment a consumer feels toward a brand. When combined with other forms of communication, advertising can also help to form a sense of community and encourage active engagement. Interactive advertising can be especially helpful in facilitating active engagement. A well-designed website can also foster a strong sense of community by linking brand users to each other.

Different advertising roles

The basic premise of the customer-based brand equity model is that the true measure of the strength of a brand depends on how consumers think, feel, act, etc. with respect to that brand. Achieving brand resonance requires eliciting the proper cognitive appraisals and emotional reactions to the brand from customers. That, in turn, necessitates establishing brand identity and creating brand meaning in terms of brand performance and brand imagery associations.

A brand with the right identity and meaning can result in a customer believing that the brand is relevant and "my kind of product or service." The strongest brands will be those brands for which consumers become so attached and passionate that they, in effect, become evangelists or missionaries and attempt to share their beliefs and "spread the word" about the brand.

Clearly, different target market segments will have different patterns of effects with respect to the six building blocks. It may be difficult with certain segments to achieve sufficiently favourable brand images and positive brand responses to build a large degree of resonance. Different constituents will be even more likely to exhibit different building-block patterns, as brand equity will often differ for channel intermediaries, employees, investors, and so on as compared to consumers.

Regardless of the particular segment or constituency involved, advertising plays a critical role each step of the way, although different forms of advertising will have different degrees of success accomplishing different objectives. Traditional broadcast and print media advertising will be especially useful in the lower two levels of the pyramid, i.e., brand identity and image, by creating brand salience, performance, and imagery. More interactive advertising may be especially advantageous at high levels of the pyramid to help build relationships.

Yet, at the same time, any one form of advertising can have multiple effects on brand equity and the components of the customer-based brand equity model. For example, an advertisement linking a brand with a cause (e.g., Avon's Breast Cancer Crusade) could have multiple effects on brand knowledge: It could build brand awareness via recall and recognition; enhance brand image in terms of attributes such as user imagery (e.g., kind and generous) and brand personality (e.g., sincere); evoke brand feelings (e.g., social approval and self-respect); establish brand attitudes (e.g., credibility judgements such as trustworthy and likeable); and create experiences (e.g., through a sense of community).

Finally, it should also be recognized that the role of advertising is sometimes more than brand-building – it is also designed to generate trial, induce repeat purchases or increase sales volume or profitability in some other way. Some forms of advertising are especially well suited to offer direct financial benefits, e.g., direct response or internet advertising, but even media advertising when combined with other forms of communications (e.g., promotions) may be able to directly drive sales. Even in these cases, however, it is still of interest to understand the longer-term impact on brand equity.

STRENGTHENING ADVERTISING COMMUNICATION EFFECTS

According to a customer-based brand-building perspective, for an advertising exposure of any kind to impact brand equity, it is important that consumer knowledge about the brand change in some way as a result. Brand links to communication effects – performance and imagery associations and judgement and feeling responses – are thus critical to maximize the effects of advertising. Advertising must therefore be carefully designed to maximize the likelihood that the proper communication effects are created.

As noted above, in some cases, communication effects have an immediate impact. Point-of-purchase, interactive, or direct-response advertising often are designed to serve as a reminder of previous advertising or to communicate a simple message in the hopes of resulting in a purchase or the desired consumer brand response at that exact moment. With media advertising, however, exposure and purchase opportunities are typically two distinct points in time and location, often fairly far apart. It is thus important that consumers are able to evoke or access stored brand-related communication effects from past ad exposure in the store or wherever they could make a brand purchase.

Unfortunately, for a number of reasons, media advertising does not always create strong brand links to the communication effects it engenders, especially with television advertising (Keller, 1993, 1996). After reviewing the nature of the problem, several alternative strategies are proposed as solutions.

Factors affecting brand association strength

The strength of brand associations that result from exposure to advertising will depend on the quantity and quality of processing that occurs. The more deeply a consumer processes and responds to an ad and evokes brand-related information in the process, the more likely it will be that strong brand associations are created. The challenge in advertising therefore is to employ message, creative, media, and other strategies such that strong and favourable brand associations result.

Advertisers have a vast range of creative strategies and techniques at their disposal to improve consumer motivation and lead to greater involvement and enhanced ad processing on their part, e.g., through the use of fear, sex, music, and so on. It is crucial, however, that these "borrowed interest" tactics grab consumers' attention for an ad in a way such that the resulting focus of attention and processing is directed in a manner that creates strong brand associations.

Unfortunately, such links are often difficult to create. In particular, TV ads often do not "brand" well. Specifically, weak brand links may exist in memory to the communication effects created by an ad for three main reasons:

1. *Ad content and structure*. In many cases, attention-getting creative strategies may divert processing from the brand itself. For example, advertising using a carefully selected celebrity may still not create the proper brand links in memory if the celebrity dominates the processing of the ad such that consumers fail to assimilate communication effects with brand knowledge. Moreover, when these attention-getting creative tactics are employed, the position and prominence of the brand in the ad are often downplayed,

which may raise processing intensity but also result in attention directed away from the brand. Furthermore, limited brand exposure time in the ad allows little opportunity for elaboration of existing brand knowledge (Baker et al., 2004; Walker and Von Gonten, 1989).

2. *Competitive clutter*. Competing ads in a product category can create interference and consumer confusion as to which ad goes with which brand (Burke and Srull, 1988; Jewell and Unnava, 2003; Keller, 1987, 1991a, 1991b; Kent and Allen, 1994; Kumar and Krishnan, 2004).

3. *Consumer involvement*. In certain circumstances, consumers may not have any inherent interest in the product or service category or may lack knowledge of the specific brand (e.g., in the case of a low-share brand or a new market entry). The resulting decrease in consumer motivation and ability to process translates to weaker brand links. Similarly, a change in advertising strategy to target a new market segment or add a new attribute, benefit, or usage association to the brand image may also fail to produce strong brand links because consumers lack the ability to easily relate this new advertising information to existing brand knowledge (Keller et al., 1998).

Strategies to create stronger brand links

Thus, for a variety of reasons, consumers may fail to correctly identify advertising with the advertised brand or, even worse, incorrectly attribute advertising to a competing brand. In these cases, advertising may have worked in the sense that communication effects – associations to performance and imagery as well as cognitive and affective responses – were stored in memory. Yet, advertising may have failed in the sense that these communication effects were not accessible when critical brand-related decisions were made. As advertisers feel more and more pressure to break through ever-increasing commercial clutter and consumer indifference, they especially run the risk of creating disassociated communication effects inadequately linked to the brand.

Although ad repetition and well-designed media schedules can be employed to some extent to give consumers greater opportunities to link brands and ad effects (Vakratsas and Naik, 2007; Chapter 5.4; Danaher 2007; Chapter 5.2), such approaches can be effective, but expensive. Another tactic to achieve ad and point-of-purchase congruence and improve ad recall is to make the brand name and package information prominent in the ad. Unfortunately, less emphasis as a result can then be placed in the ad on supplying persuasive information and creating positive associations so that consumers have a reason *why* they should purchase the brand.

Three potentially more effective strategies to strengthen brand links that allow for creative freedom in ad execution are brand signatures, ad retrieval cues, and coordinated media, as follows.

Brand signatures

Perhaps the easiest way to increase the strength of brand links to communication effects is to create a more powerful and compelling brand signature. The *brand signature* is the manner by which the brand (name, logo, slogan, etc.) is identified at the conclusion of a TV or radio ad or displayed within a print ad. An effective brand signature must creatively engage the consumer and cause him or her to pay more attention to the brand itself to ensure that communication effects are absorbed in the brand network of associations so that they can add value in subsequent consumer decision-making.

An effective brand signature often dynamically and stylistically provides a seamless connection to the ad as a whole. For example, the famous "Got Milk?" campaign often displayed that brand slogan in a manner fitting the ad (e.g., in flames for the "yuppie in hell" ad or in primary school print for the "school lunchroom bully" ad). As another example, the introductory Intel Inside ad campaign in the early 1990s always ended with a swirling image from which the Intel Inside logo dramatically appeared, in effect stamping the end of the ad with Intel Inside in an "in your face" manner.

In some ways, the key issue is what kind of "punctuation mark" does an advertiser want to employ to sign off its advertising – a period or an exclamation mark? In the absence of such strong ad-induced brand links, however, other strategies may be necessary, as follows.

Ad retrieval cues

An effective tactic to improve consumer's motivation and ability to retrieve communication effects when making a brand-related decision is to use advertising retrieval cues. An *advertising retrieval cue* is visual or verbal information uniquely identified with an ad that is evident when consumers are making a product or service decision (Garretson and Burton, 2005; Keller, 1987, 1991a, 1991b). The purpose is to maximize the probability that consumers who have seen or heard the cued ad will retrieve from long-term memory the communication effects that were stored from earlier processing of that ad.

Ad retrieval cues may consist of a key visual, a catchy slogan, or any unique advertising element that serves as an effective reminder to consumers. For example, in an attempt to remedy the problem they had with mistaken attributions, Quaker Oats placed a photograph of the "Mikey" character from the popular Life cereal ad on the front of the package. More recently, Eveready featured a picture of their pink bunny character on the packages for their Energizer batteries to reduce consumer confusion with Duracell.

Ad retrieval cues can be placed in the store (e.g., on the package or as part of a shelf talker or some other point-of-purchase device), combined with a promotion (e.g., with a free-standing insert (FSI) coupon), included as part of a Yellow Pages directory listing, on a web page, or embedded in any marketing communication option where recall of communication effects can be advantageous to marketers. An ad retrieval cue is most effective when many communication effects are stored in memory but are only weakly associated to the brand because of one or more of the various factors noted above.

Coordinated media

Print and radio reinforcement of TV ads (in which the video and audio components of a TV ad serve as the basis for the respective type of ads) can be an effective means to leverage existing communication effects from TV ad exposure and more strongly link them to the brand (Edell and Keller, 1989, 1999; Naik and Raman, 2003).

For example, a likeable, attention-getting TV ad can be combined with a print ad featuring a key visual from the TV ad as well as including additional product or service information to further elaborate on the relevant brand claims or promise. Such a strategy would capitalize on the unique strengths of each media to compensate for the respective weaknesses of the other media: the limited amount of information that can be conveyed in a TV ad can be overcome by an explicitly linked print ad that has detailed supporting information; and the limited attention-getting properties of a print ad can be overcome by an explicitly linked TV ad that is favourably evaluated and therefore interest-arousing. The self-paced nature of print ad processing would allow consumers the opportunity to consider the ad and brand in more detail, increasing the likelihood that overall evaluations are formed and strengthening the association of the brand with whatever communication effects are created.

Moreover, note that a potentially useful, although rarely employed, media strategy is to run explicitly linked print or radio ads *prior* to the accompanying TV ad. The print and radio ads in this case function as teasers and increase consumer motivation to process the more complete TV ad consisting of both audio and video components. Coordinated print and radio teasers and television ads may be another means to create strong brand name links and associations and brand equity.

Finally, as another strategy, different combinations of TV ad excerpts within a campaign (e.g., 15-second spots consisting of highlights from longer 30- or 60-second spots for those campaigns characterized by only one dominant ad, or umbrella ads consisting of highlights from a pool of ads for those campaigns consisting of multiple ad executions) and across campaigns over time (e.g., including key elements from past ad campaigns that are strongly identified with the brand as part of the current ad campaign) also can be helpful for strengthening dormant associations and facilitating the formation of consumer evaluations of and reactions to the ads and their linkage to the brand.

DISCUSSION

The goal of this chapter was to provide an overview of the various ways by which different types of advertising impact brand equity as well as to suggest strategies to overcome a pervasive advertising problem – weak links or associations in memory from the brand to the communication effects created by advertising for the brand. A key contention of the chapter is that many different forms of advertising exist that can play many different brand-building roles. The customer-based brand equity model and the concept of brand resonance was put forth as a means to help interpret and focus advertising efforts. Given the large number of factors that conspire to produce weak brand name links to communication effects, especially for television advertising, it is also important to consider different strategies to

build stronger communication-infused brand knowledge structures. Brand signatures, ad retrieval cues, and coordinated media were suggested as three possible strategies to overcome that deficiency.

Several broad implications emerged from the above discussion. First, all possible types of marketing communications – different forms of advertising and other non-advertising options – can be evaluated in terms of their ability to affect brand equity. In particular, the customer-based brand equity model provides a common denominator by which the effects of different marketing communications can be evaluated: Each communication can be judged in terms of the effectiveness and efficiency by which it affects the brand building blocks – brand salience, performance, imagery, judgements, feelings, and resonance (see Part 3 for discussion of these topics).

Along those lines, Figure 1.4.2 can be used as a blueprint to help interpret communication effects. Any advertising could be assessed subjectively through expert opinion as well as empirically through marketplace measurement. Using the customer-based brand equity model can also be helpful as

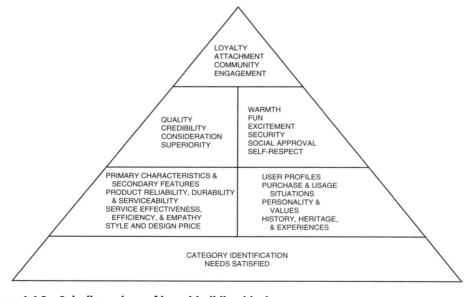

Figure 1.4.2   Sub-dimensions of brand-building blocks

a "big picture" device to assess how well communication programmes are integrated as a whole.

Understanding the broad range of effects engendered by communications helps to explain why prior advertising research may seem to reveal relatively weak or fragile effects. Unless these measures capture the range of proposed potential outcomes, certain effects could be overlooked. In fact, an empirical test of the communication insights proposed above would involve collecting a broad range of measures tapping into all aspects of the building blocks and relating them back to communication activity.

Another important insight that emerges from the above discussion is that advertising often must be explicitly linked (i.e., cued) to allow for the necessary interactions to create a positive brand image and brand equity. Specifically, the key assertion of the chapter is that marketers often should integrate marketing communications by literally taking visual or verbal information from one communication and using it in different ways in another communication. The rationale is that this information can cue or serve as a reminder to related information. By enhancing consumer motivation, ability, and opportunity to process and retrieve brand-related information, these cues can facilitate the formation of strong, favourable, and unique brand associations. Explicitly integrating media in this manner also increases the likelihood that brand knowledge is used in consumer product and service decisions. In these ways, explicitly integrated media can contribute to brand equity.

It should be recognized that the approach espoused here and the basic spirit of this chapter assumes a very linear view of brand-building. Although in most cases such sequences are the conventional route for brand-building, it may also be the case that consumers sometimes will not follow such obvious patterns (Ray et al., 1973). Along those same lines, it should also be noted that this reasoning and model development is designed to capture more conscious consumer processing effects. Certainly there

are examples of non-conscious consumer processing and learning that can result from advertising (Janiszewski, 1990, 1993).

In closing, the basic message of this chapter is simple: marketers need to strategically evaluate advertising to determine how it can contribute to brand equity. To do so, advertisers need some theoretical and managerial guidelines by which they can determine the effectiveness and efficiency of various communication options both singularly and in combination with *other* communication options. Chapter 1.3 (Prasad A. Naik, 2007) of this Handbook provides some additional insight on this latter objective (see also Schultz et al. (1993) and Duncan and Moriarty (1997)).

SUMMARY

- Advertising has several functions. It can inform, persuade, and remind consumers about brands, and it can establish relationships and loyalty between the brand and the consumer.
- High levels of brand equity are advantageous, increasing marketing communication effectiveness (both receptiveness to it, processing it, and acting on it). Improved customer perceptions lead to greater customer loyalty and reduce vulnerability to competitors and price changes. Therefore, brand equity is central to the way advertising works, either as a goal in itself, or as a mediator to other goals. Building strong brands should be a management priority.
- The customer-based brand equity model introduced in this chapter suggests that brand equity is determined by the differential effect of brand knowledge (i.e., all the thoughts, feelings, perceptions, images and experiences that become linked to the brand in the minds of the consumer) on that consumer's response to marketing for the brand. Consumer knowledge about the brand changes as a result of exposure to advertising for that brand.
- There are four steps in building a strong brand – identity, meaning, response, and relationship – with each step only achieved once the one's preceding it are fulfilled. Advertising plays a critical role in each of these steps.
- Brand identity relates to building brand salience and awareness – both depth and breadth – and is

seen when customers can recall and recognize the brand, link the brand to certain associations in memory and/or understand what needs it fulfils.

- Brand meaning can be distinguished in terms of functional, performance-related considerations (e.g., quality) or more abstract, imagery-related considerations (e.g., brand personality, user profiles).
- Brand responses refer to how customers respond to the brand and its marketing activities and can be distinguished according to brand judgements (to do with quality, credibility, consideration, superiority) and brand feelings (e.g., warmth, fun, security, social approval).
- The most important building block is brand resonance, which is characterized by high degrees of loyalty, attachment, engagement, community, and affinity between the customer and the brand – in other words, brand relationships. Advertising should aim to reinforce all these aspects by eliciting in customers the proper cognitive appraisals and emotional reactions to the brand.
- Strategies to create stronger brand links include ad repetition, well-designed media schedules, brand signatures, ad retrieval cues, and media co-ordination.

ACKNOWLEDGEMENT

Thanks are extended to the editors and two reviewers for many helpful suggestions.

NOTE

1 For a review of some other approaches to brand equity based on either consumer psychology, economics, biology, or sociology, see Keller (2002).

REFERENCES

Aaker, D.A. (1991), *Managing Brand Equity,* New York, NY: Free Press.

Aaker, D.A. (1996), *Building Strong Brands,* New York, NY: Free Press.

Aaker, D.A. (2004), *Brand Portfolio Strategy,* New York, NY: Free Press.

Aaker, D.A. and E. Joachimsthaler (2000), *Brand Leadership,* New York, NY: Free Press.

Aaker, D.A., D.M. Stayman and M.R. Hagerty (1986), "Warmth in Advertising: Measurement, Impact and Sequence Effects," *Journal of Consumer Research,* 12 (4), 365–381.

Aaker, J. (1997), "Dimensions of Brand Personality," *Journal of Marketing Research,* 34 (August), 347–356.

Aaker, J.L., V. Benet-Martinez and J.G. Berrocal (2001), "Consumption Symbols as Carriers of Culture: A Study of Japanese and Spanish Brand Personality Constructs," *Journal of Personality and Psychology,* 81 (3), 492–508.

Ahluwalia, R., R.E. Burnkrant and H.R. Unnava (2000), "Consumer Response to Negative Publicity: The Moderating Role of Commitment," *Journal of Marketing Research,* 37 (May), 203–214.

Baker, W.E., H. Honea and C. Antonia Russell (2004), "Do Not Wait to Reveal the Brand Name: The Effect of Brand Name Placement on Television Advertising Effectiveness," *Journal of Advertising,* 33 (Fall), 150–161.

Belch, G.E. (1981), "An Examination of Comparative and Noncomparative Television Commercials: The Effects of Claim Variation and Repetition on Cognitive Response and Message Acceptance," *Journal of Marketing Research,* 18 (August), 333–349.

Brown, T.J. and P.A. Dacin (1997), "The Company and the Product: Corporate Associations and Consumer Product Responses," *Journal of Marketing,* 61 (January), 68–84.

Burke, R.R. and T.K. Srull (1988), "Competitive Interference and Consumer Memory for Advertising," *Journal of Consumer Research* 15 (June): 55–68.

Calder, B.J. and B. Sternthal (1980), "Television Commercial Wearout: An Information Processing View," *Journal of Marketing Research,* 27 (May), 173–186.

Campbell, M. and K. Lane Keller (2003), "Brand Familiarity and Ad Repetition Effects," *Journal of Consumer Research,* September, 30 (2), 292–304.

Chattopadyay, A. and K. Basu (1990), "Humor in Advertising: The Moderating Role of Prior Brand Evaluation," *Journal of Marketing Research,* 27 (November), 466–476.

Chaudhuri, A. and M.B. Holbrook, (2001) 'The Chain of Effects from Brand Trust and Brand Affect to Brand Performance," *Journal of Marketing,* 65 (April): 81–93.

Danaher, P.J. (2007), "Media Planning," in *The SAGE Handbook of Advertising,* eds. G.J. Tellis and T. Ambler, London: Sage Publications.

Dawar, N. and M.M. Pillutla (2000), "Impact of Product-Harm Crises on Brand Equity: The Moderating Role of Consumer Expectations," *Journal of Marketing Research,* 37 (May), 215–226.

Deighton, J. (1984), "The Interaction of Advertising and Evidence," *Journal of Consumer Research,* 11 (December), 763–770.

Dhar, R. and I. Simonson (1992), "The Effect of the Focus of Comparison on Consumer Preferences," *Journal of Marketing Research,* 29 (November), 430–440.

Duncan, T. (2002), IMC: *Using Advertising and Promotion to Build Brands,* Boston, MA: McGraw-Hill.

Duncan, T. and S. Moriarty (1997), *Driving Brand Value: Using Integrated Marketing to Manage Profitable Shareholder Relationships,* New York, NY: McGraw-Hill.

Edell, J.A. and K. Lane Keller (1989), "The Information Processing of Coordinated Media Campaigns," *Journal of Marketing Research,* 26 (May), 149–163.

Edell, J.A. and K. Lane Keller (1999), "Analyzing Media Interactions: The Effects of Coordinated TV-Print Advertising Campaigns," *Marketing Science Institute* report No. 99–120.

Edell, J.A. and M.C. Moore (1993), "The Impact and Memorability of Ad-Induced Feelings: Implications for Brand Equity," in *Brand Equity & Advertising: Advertising's Role in Building Strong Brands,* eds. David A. Aaker and Alec L. Biel, Hillsdale, NJ: Lawrence Erlbaum Associates, 195–211.

Fournier, S. (1998), "Consumers and Their Brands: Developing Relationship Theory in Consumer Research," *Journal of Consumer Research,* 24 (March), 343–373.

Fournier, S.M. (2000), "Dimensioning Brand Relationships Using Brand Relationship Quality," presentation at the *Association for Consumer Research annual conference.*

Fournier, S.M., S. Dobscha and D.G. Mick (1998), "Preventing the Premature Death of Relationship Marketing," *Harvard Business Review,* (January–February): 42–51.

Garretson, J.A. and S. Burton (2005), "The Role of Spokescharacters as Advertisement and Package Cues in Integrated Marketing Communications," *Journal of Marketing,* 69 (October), 118–132.

Hoch, S.J. and J. Deighton (1989), "Managing What Consumers Learn From Experience," *Journal of Marketing,* 53 (April), 1–20.

Hoch, S.J. and Y.-W. Ha (1986), "Consumer Learning: Advertising and the Ambiguity of Product Experience," *Journal of Consumer Research,* 13 (2), 221–233.

Hoeffler, S. and K. Lane Keller (2003), "The Marketing Advantages of Strong Brands," *Journal of Brand Management,* 10 (6), 421–445.

Holt, D. (2004), *How Brands Become Icons: the Principles of Cultural Branding,* Cambridge, MA: Harvard Business School Press.

Hsu, J.L. and G. Shang-Min Liu (2000), "Consumer Perceptions of Fluid Milk Advertising in Taiwan," *International Journal of Advertising,* 19, 471–486.

Janiszewski, C. (1990), "The Influence of Print Advertisement Organization on Affect toward a Brand Name," *Journal of Consumer Research,* 17 (1), 53–65.

Janiszewski, C. (1993), "Preattentive Mere Exposure Effects," *Journal of Consumer Research,* 20 (3), 376–392.

Janiszewski, C. and S. M. J. van Osselaer (2000), "A Connectionist Model of Brand-Quality Associations," *Journal of Marketing Research,* 37 (August), 331–350.

Jewell, R.D. and H.R. Unnava (2003), "When Competitive Interference Can Be Beneficial," *Journal of Consumer Research,* 30 (September), 283–291.

Kahle, L.R., B. Poulos and A. Sukhdial (1988), "Changes in Social Values in the United States During the Past Decade," *Journal of Advertising Research,* February/March 1988, 35–41.

Kapferer, J.-N. (2005), *The New Strategic Brand Management,* London, England: Kogan-Page.

Keller, K.L. (1987), "Memory Factors in Advertising: The Effect of Advertising Retrieval Cues on Brand Evaluations," *Journal of Consumer Research,* 14 (December): 316–333.

Keller, K.L. (1991a), "Cue Compatibility and Framing in Advertising," *Journal of Marketing Research,* 28 (February), 42–57.

Keller, K.L. (1991b), "Memory and Evaluations in Competitive Advertising Environments," *Journal of Consumer Research,* 17 (March): 463–476.

Keller, K.L. (1993), "Memory Retrieval Factors and Advertising Effectiveness" in *Advertising Exposure, Memory, and Choice,* ed., Andrew A. Mitchell, Hillsdale, NJ: Lawrence Erlbaum Associates, 11–48.

Keller, K.L. (1996), "Integrated Marketing Communications and Brand Equity," in *Integrated Marketing Communications,* eds. Jeri Moore and Esther Thorson, Mahwah, NJ: Lawrence Erlbaum Associates, 103–132.

Keller, K.L. (2001), "Building Customer-Based Brand Equity: A Blueprint for Creating Strong Brands," *Marketing Management,* July/August, 15–19.

Keller, K.L. (2002), "Branding and Brand Equity," in *Handbook of Marketing,* eds. Bart Weitz and Robin Wensley, London: Sage Publications, 151–178.

Keller, K.L. (2003), *Strategic Brand Management: Building, Measuring, and Managing Brand Equity,* 2nd ed., Upper Saddle River, NJ: Prentice Hall.

Keller, K.L. and D.A. Aaker (1998), "Corporate-Level Marketing: The Impact of Credibility on a Company's

Brand Extensions," *Corporate Reputation Review*, 1 (August), 356–378.

Keller, K.L., S. Heckler and M.J. Houston (1998), "The Effects of Brand Name Suggestiveness on Advertising Recall," *Journal of Marketing* 62 (January), 48–57.

Keller, K.L., B. Sternthal and A. Tybout (2002), "Three Questions You Need to Ask About Your Brand," *Harvard Business Review,* September, 80 (9), 80–89.

Kent, R.J. and C.T. Allen (1994), "Competitive Interference Effects in Consumer Memory for Advertising: The Role of Brand Familiarity," *Journal of Marketing* 58 (July): 97–105.

Kumar, A. and H.S. Krishnan (2004), "Memory Interference in Advertising: A Replication and Extension," *Journal of Consumer Research,* Vol. 30 (March), 602–611.

Levy, S.J. (1999), Brands, Consumers, Symbols, and Research: Sydney J. Levy on *Marketing*, Thousand Oaks, CA: Sage Publications.

Machleit, K.A., C.T. Allen and T.J. Madden (1993), "The Mature Brand and Brand Interest: An Alternative Consequence of Ad-Evoked Affect," *Journal of Marketing*, 57 (October), 72–82.

Naik, P.A. (2007), "Integrated Marketing Communications: Provenance, Practice and Principles," in *The SAGE Handbook of Advertising*, eds. G.J. Tellis and T. Ambler, London: Sage Publications.

Naik, P.A. and K. Raman (2003), "Understanding the Impact of Synergy in Multimedia Communications," *Journal of Marketing Research,* 40, 375–388.

Raj, S.P. (1982), "The Effects of Advertising on High and Low Loyalty Consumer Segments," *Journal of Consumer Research,* 9 (June), 77–89.

Ray, M.L., A.G. Sawyer, M.L. Rothschild, R.M. Heeler, E.C. Strong and J.B. Reed (1973), "Communication and the Hierarchy of Effects," in *New Models for Mass Communication Research,* ed., P. Clarke, Beverly Hills, CA: Sage Publications, 147–175.

Sawyer, A.G. (1981), "Repetition, Cognitive Response, and Persuasion," in *Cognitive Responses to Persuasion,* eds. R. Petty, T. Ostrum and T. Brock, 237–262.

Schultz, D.E., S.I. Tannenbaum and R.F. Lauterborn (1993), *Integrated Marketing Communications: Putting It Together & Making It Work,* NTC Books: Lincolnwood.

Schumann, D.W., J.M. Hathcote and S. West (1991), "Corporate Advertising in America: A Review of Published Studies on Use, Measurement, and Effectiveness," *Journal of Advertising,* 20 (September), 36–56.

Simonson, I., J. Huber and J. Payne (1988), "The Relationship Between Prior Brand Knowledge and Information Acquisition Order," *Journal of Consumer Research,* 14 (March), 566–578.

Stewart, D.W. and D.H. Furse (1986), *Effective Television Advertising: A Study of 1000 Commercials.* Lexington, MA: D.C. Heath and Co.

Stewart, D.W., J. Morris and A. Grover (2007), "Emotions in Advertising," in *The SAGE Handbook of Advertising,* eds. G.J. Tellis and T. Ambler, London: Sage Publications.

Tellis, G.J. (2004), *Effective Advertising,* Thousand Oaks, CA: Sage Publications.

Vakratsas, D. and P.A. Naik (2007), "Essentials of Planning Flighted Media Schedules," in *The SAGE Handbook of Advertising,* eds. Gerard J. Tellis and Tim Ambler, London: Sage Publications.

Walker, D. and M.J. von Gonten (1989), "Explaining Related Recall Outcomes: New Answers from a Better Model," *Journal of Advertising Research,* 29, 11–21.

Weinberger, M.G. and C.S. Gulas (1992), "The Impact of Humor in Advertising: A Review," *Journal of Advertising,* 21 (4), 35–60.

Zaltman, G. (2003), *How Customers Think: Essential Insights into the Mind of the Market,* Harvard Business School Press.

How Advertising Works

Understanding Advertising Effectiveness from a Psychological Perspective: The Importance of Attitudes and Attitude Strength

Derek D. Rucker, Richard E. Petty and
Joseph R. Priester

"Advertising is persuasion, and persuasion is not a science, but an art. Advertising is the art of persuasion."

William Bernbach, quoted in Stephen Fox,
The Mirror Makers, 1984.

Like Bernbach, one of advertising's greatest pioneers, many have directly linked the study of advertising to the study of persuasion. For instance, previous volumes on advertising have included chapters that integrate work from the persuasion literature (Tellis, 1998, 2004). Indeed, one of the dominant goals of advertising is to persuade the consumer of the benefits of a product or service and to stimulate a purchase. While we are like-minded with Bernbach when it comes to the notion that advertising is tied to persuasion, we diverge markedly from Bernbach in that we believe persuasion, and therefore advertising, is better conceptualized as a science. As a science, we can adopt theoretical perspectives and examine empirical findings to understand factors that contribute to successful advertising. To this end, we draw on the vast scientific literature in psychology to understand some of the underpinnings of successful advertising.

CHAPTER OVERVIEW

This chapter provides a framework for understanding the factors that contribute to advertising effectiveness by attending to two rich literatures in the domain of persuasion. First, we focus on classic and contemporary theoretical approaches to understanding *attitude change*. We discuss conceptualizations and findings that help understand when various elements of advertisements will be successful in promoting favourable attitudes. Second, we focus on work on *attitude strength.* As will be discussed, attitude strength is important for advertising effectiveness as it determines whether attitudes resulting from exposure to advertisements will be persistent, resistant, and likely to influence behaviour.

ATTITUDES AND ATTITUDE CHANGE

The attitude construct

Advertisers are interested in outcomes such as persuasion, product-relevant thoughts and beliefs, cognitive processes, emotions, intentions to buy, and actual purchase behaviour. Attitudes play a unique and important role in relation to each of these constructs. Attitudes have typically been conceptualized as one's overall, global evaluation of an object. That is, attitudes reflect whether individuals like or dislike specific products, brands, advertisements, or spokespersons (Petty and Cacioppo, 1981; Petty and Wegener, 1999). For example, overall, do you like or dislike Pizza Hut Meat Lover's Pizza? You might answer anywhere from extreme liking to extreme disliking, with varying gradations in-between. Your answer would represent your attitude. To more quantitatively measure attitudes, researchers often use a series of semantic differential scales (e.g., good–bad, favourable–unfavourable), with the specific response associated with a number on the scales.[1]

This overall reaction (i.e., one's attitude) has traditionally been conceptualized as encompassing and reflecting three distinct bases; thoughts, emotions and feelings, and one's behaviours. That is, one's overall attitude is the result of and stems from one's affective, cognitive, and behavioural reactions toward that pizza, for example.[2] As such, if an advertisement influences any one of the three components, that change will also be reflected in that individual's overall attitude. For example, if a television

commercial for a greeting card engenders warm feelings in an individual, the extent to which that warmth is transferred to the specific greeting card brand will emerge on measures of the individual's overall attitude toward the brand. Similarly, changes in cognitions and/or behaviours associated with an attitude object will be reflected in the overall attitude.

A veritable bounty of research has demonstrated that one's attitude influences one's behavioural intentions, and that behavioural intentions best predict behaviour (e.g., Fishbein and Ajzen, 1981; Sheppard et al., 1988). Thus, whether people purchase a particular product will be determined, in part, by their attitudes. Studying and identifying consumers' attitudes also has a number of important advantages over studying behaviour itself. An attitude is a global evaluation that can be used to make general predictions about a variety of specific behaviours (e.g., willingness to receive additional information about a product, word-of-mouth, willingness to pay a price premium, purchase behaviour, etc.). Rarely, if ever, is it possible to study all the various behavioural implications of an advertisement. However, by studying global attitudes it is possible to gauge how consumers are likely to act in general across a variety of attitude-relevant situations.

In short, the construct of attitude not only captures the affective, behavioural, and cognitive reactions to products, services, and brands, but also predicts behavioural intentions, and ultimately, behaviour.

Historical approaches

Much contemporary work on persuasion has its roots in the empirical investigations conducted by Carl Hovland and his colleagues at Yale in the 1950s (e.g., Hovland et al., 1953). Importantly, a key emphasis of this work was on the importance of attention, learning and recall processes for message effectiveness, a theme also seen in work on advertising (e.g., Loken and Hoverstad, 1985). Hovland and his colleagues also examined the role of source, message, and recipient factors in persuasion.

Source factors included variables associated with the person delivering the message, such as the credibility or attractiveness of the source (Hovland and Weiss, 1951). Message factors consisted of variables such as the number of arguments (Calder et al., 1974), and whether the message presented arguments that were solely in favour of the position or also disclosed the counterpoints (Hovland et al., 1953). Recipient or audience factors included more stable individual differences in the audience such as intelligence (McGuire, 1968), but also more temporary influences such as the audience's emotional state (Zanna et al., 1970).

A focal aspect of early research was the emphasis on uncovering the single effect of a variable on persuasion; that is, whether a variable, such as source credibility, increased or decreased persuasion. This early work was often accompanied by a focus on a "single-process" perspective where researchers attempted to uncover the single means by which a variable produced its effect (see Petty, 1997). For example, if source credibility increased persuasion, then researchers were interested in identifying the single, and presumably only, process by which it did so (e.g., increasing attention to the message). Initially, work that could be classified into the single effect approach was very fruitful. For instance, regarding the source of the message, credible sources were found to produce greater persuasion than less-credible sources (Hovland and Weiss, 1951). Work on the message itself revealed that more arguments, up to a point, were found to yield greater persuasion (Calder et al., 1974). Work on audience characteristics suggested that associating negative emotions with a message decreased persuasion (Zanna et al., 1970). However, the single-effect approach soon became untenable as research began to produce contradictory findings. For instance, some research indicated that credible sources could be associated with less persuasion (Sternthal et al., 1978), increasing the number of arguments did not always increase persuasion (Norman, 1976), and that negative emotions could actually enhance persuasion (Rogers, 1983).

Contemporary approach: The elaboration likelihood model

The prevalence of conflicting studies posed a serious threat to the field of attitude change and its scholars. Indeed, at one point it seemed as if the field might be destined for oblivion by the perception that there were no reliable or systematic results (e.g., Fishbein and Ajzen, 1972). In response to this pervasive threat the Elaboration Likelihood Model (ELM; Petty and Cacioppo, 1981, 1986) of persuasion was developed to resolve these seemingly incompatible findings under an integrated framework. For over 25 years the ELM has guided many studies of persuasion (see Petty and Wegener, 1999) and we use it as an organizing tool here.[3]

The ELM approaches understanding persuasion by focusing on two routes to attitude change that serve as endpoints along an extent of thinking continuum – a relatively thoughtful route in which people scrutinize the issue-relevant information presented (the central route), and a less thoughtful route in which people rely on simple associations or heuristics to reach decisions (the peripheral route). The route that produces persuasion is determined by the amount of elaboration, or thinking, in which people engage. Furthermore, route selection has implications for the durability and impact (i.e., the strength) of attitudes. Finally, in stark contrast to the "single-effect and single-process" approaches taken in earlier research, the ELM posits that any variable (e.g., source credibility) can have multiple effects on persuasion and do so through a variety of processes in different situations. We next explore the implications of this model in greater detail.

The central route

According to the ELM, the central route to persuasion involves an effortful scrutiny of issue-relevant information in an attempt to determine the central merits of the product or service under consideration. For example, consumers engaged in the central route while receiving a car advertisement would be prone to carefully scrutinize the advertisement for relevant information. In such a situation, consumers would evaluate each piece of information available whether it stems from the source, message, or themselves (e.g., brand, warranty, endorser, their feelings) with respect to whether the information was a relevant favourable or unfavourable piece of evidence. When this occurs, consumers' attitudes towards the advertised product are determined primarily by their cognitive responses or thoughts to the information available (see Cacioppo and Petty, 1981; Petty and Cacioppo, 1986; see also Batra and Ray, 1986 and Wright, 1973, for illustrative examples). If people generate predominantly positive thoughts as a result of scrutinizing the information, a positive attitude will result; if scrutiny leads to predominantly negative thoughts a negative attitude will follow. If people generate a mix of positive and negative thoughts a moderate attitude will result.

Importantly, the notion of cognitive responses deviates from earlier approaches that emphasized message learning and recall (e.g., Hovland et al., 1953). According to the ELM, under high elaboration, it is not necessarily the specific information that consumers can recall about the product that determines their attitudes, but rather it is their idiosyncratic responses to this information. For example, two consumers might both recall that a new plasma television features an integrated DVD player. However, one person might evaluate the integrated DVD feature positively (e.g., "Great, I don't have to buy a DVD player"), but another negatively (e.g., "I already have a great DVD player, and I don't want to pay for a feature I don't need"). Consequently, whereas theories focusing on recall would suggest including this feature would have a similar effect across consumers as long as people attend to and learn the attribute, contemporary theories such as the ELM recognize it is not recall per se, but the idiosyncratic thoughts individuals have about the advertised features. More recent research has stressed that in addition to consumers' cognitive responses, the confidence people have in their thoughts is important. The more confident consumers are

in the thoughts they generate the more these thoughts determine consumers' attitudes (Briñol et al., 2004; Petty et al., 2002).[4]

There are two prerequisites for consumers to engage in the central route to persuasion. First, consumers must have the ability to scrutinize a message carefully. Consumers must be able to understand the message and have the resources to attend to the information present. Factors affecting consumers' ability to *process* a message include, consumers' knowledge (Wood and Lynch, 2002), the amount of distraction present in the environment (Petty et al., 1976), and the number of times the message is repeated (Cacioppo and Petty, 1979b). Some specialized consumer persuasion theories such as the resource matching model (e.g., Anand and Sternthal, 1988; Peracchio and Meyers-Levy, 1997) have focused on the importance of matching the cognitive resources available to the consumer with the resources needed to process the message. According to this approach, persuasion is greatest when available resources match those required to process the message. According to the ELM, this would primarily be true only when the message presents evidence that is compelling when scrutinized. If the message presents weak arguments, then having sufficient resources would allow people to recognize the flaws in the arguments leading to reduced persuasion. When people have too many resources needed for the message, they may become bored and find the message tedious, leading to reduced persuasion, as is the case with excessive message repetition (see Cacioppo and Petty, 1979, 1989). Alternatively, if people have excess resources, they could generate their own unique thoughts that could augment or detract from the message depending on their valence. The latter is most likely under high elaboration conditions when variables in the situation induce a bias to the processing (see discussion of biased processing).

The central route to persuasion not only requires ability, but also *motivation* to process the message. Consumers' motivation to process a message can be influenced by a number of variables, such as the personal relevance of an issue (Petty and Cacioppo, 1979b), people's general enjoyment of thinking (Cacioppo et al., 1983), and being personally responsible for processing the message (Petty et al., 1980). When motivation and ability to process a message are present, advertisers can expect consumers to rely upon the cognitive responses in which they have confidence to determine their reaction to the message. Confidence in one's cognitive responses can also stem from source, message, and recipient factors (see Brinol and Petty, 2004, for a review). For example, people will have more confidence in their thoughts the more easily they come to mind (Tormala et al., 2002).

This conceptualization stresses that what message recipients carry with them under high elaboration conditions: memory of the cognitive responses, rather than memory for the specific executional elements of the ad, is critical (Petty, 1977; see also Mazzocco et al., 2005). Thus, it is not the case that under high elaboration conditions people will necessarily have greater memory for the information in the ad. Rather, when individuals have the motivation and ability to think, it is the thoughts that they have in response to the advertisement (i.e., their cognitive responses) that determine ad effectiveness. This perspective suggests that ad recall and attention may be unrelated to whether the advertisement is effective under high rather than low elaboration. The process of cognitive responses being responsible for the formation and change of attitudes is that hallmark of the central route of persuasion. Under high elaboration, a number of properties of the thoughts themselves are important. The most studied aspects of thoughts are their valence (how favourable or unfavourable they are), their number (how many thoughts are generated), and the confidence with which people hold their thoughts (how valid people believe their thoughts are). Under the central route, the more favourable thoughts people have that seem valid, the more they will be persuaded and the more unfavourable thoughts people

have that seem valid, the more they will resist persuasion.

The peripheral route

When people lack either the motivation or ability to process advertisements, the peripheral route is taken. In the peripheral route, consumers' attitudes are determined primarily by simple decision processes such as classical conditioning (Staats and Staats, 1958), mere exposure (Zajonc, 1968), and use of decision heuristics (Chaiken, 1980). Heuristics represent mental shortcuts that allow for a simple decision based on a rule of thumb. Examples of heuristics are "Experts are usually right," and "Higher prices mean better quality." When relying on heuristics, consumers might be more persuaded by a car advertisement that is accompanied by an attractive model than an advertisement without a model. This might occur because the attractive model creates positive affect that becomes associated with the car. However, to the extent that the attractiveness of the model is serving as a simple cue, including an attractive model in an advertisement would be less likely to persuade consumers who are engaged in central route processing, unless as explained subsequently, attractiveness is serving in some role other than as a simple cue. Other variables that are capable of serving as peripheral cues include the expertise of the message source (Petty et al., 1981), the number of arguments presented (Petty and Cacioppo, 1984), and one's mood (Petty et al., 1993).

To understand the type of psychological process that might be involved in the peripheral route, consider work on classical conditioning. Classical conditioning represents the process whereby an unconditioned stimulus (e.g., a novel product) becomes associated with a conditioned stimulus (e.g., music that elicits happiness). After sufficient pairing of the unconditioned stimulus with the conditioned stimulus, the novel product becomes associated with and elicits the feelings of happiness, even in the absence of the music (a.k.a., conditioned response). Mere exposure represents the process whereby one's liking for an attitude object can be increased by repeated, non-focal exposures. For example, the more one is exposed (albeit out of focal attention) to a melody, the more one likes that melody. Consistent with contemporary theorizing, both of these processes are more influential under conditions of low elaboration likelihood. For example, novel stimuli are easier to classically condition than familiar ones (Cacioppo et al., 1992). Similarly, the mere exposure effect emerges more when the stimuli are perceived without awareness (Bornstein and Dagostino, 1992; Bornstein et al., 1987).

Recall that the hallmark of the central route to persuasion is the specific psychological process whereby thoughtful consideration of the information results in cognitive responses that influence attitudes. Various aspects of this thoughtful process are important such as generation of the thoughts and validation of them. The hallmark of the peripheral route is that variables affect attitudes by serving as simple cues, and there are a variety of more specific mechanisms by which this can occur. Indeed, we have outlined two such processes above, and there are likely even more simple psychological processes that can occur under conditions of low elaboration likelihood. Why this seeming lack of concern with the specific psychological process(es) associated with the peripheral route (e.g., reliance on heuristics versus classical conditioning)? Although there are different psychological processes by which peripheral route attitude change emerges, all of the peripheral processes occur under similar conditions and result in attitudes that are similar in their strength as explained in the next section on "Attitude strength" and elaboration. As such, the peripheral route processes are grouped into the same relatively non-thoughtful category.

ATTITUDE STRENGTH

Conflicting findings in early persuasion research, prior to the advent of the ELM, were not the only challenge faced by scholars of persuasion. Arguably the most fundamental reason for studying attitudes, such as those following advertisements, is that people's evaluations were thought to be instrumental in guiding action and therefore useful in predicting behaviour (Petty and Wegener, 1999). However, as soon as the first serious investigations of attitudes had begun, challenges were raised regarding whether attitudes could predict behaviour (e.g., La Piere, 1934).

In response to this challenge, attitude researchers began to focus on the conditions under which attitudes persist over time, resist attack, and guide behaviour. For example, McGuire's work on inoculation theory (see McGuire, 1964) demonstrated that successfully defending an attitude against a weak attack provided participants with the ability and motivation to defend the attitude against a subsequent challenge. Today, the issue of whether attitudes are consequential or not has been addressed by recognizing that attitudes can vary in their underlying strength (see Petty and Krosnick, 1995). Specifically, strong, relative to weak attitudes, are those that are more likely to influence behaviour, persist over time, and be resistant to change. In addition, objects associated with strongly held positive attitudes are more likely to be chosen over competing alternatives and more likely to be included in a consideration set than weakly held positive attitudes (Priester et al., 2004). Similarly, research suggests that strongly held attitudes are not only more likely to come to mind faster (Priester and Petty, 2003), which makes them more likely to guide behaviour (Fazio, 1995), but that strong attitudes can also influence basic perceptual processes more than weakly held attitudes (Fazio et al., 2000).

Attitude strength has been argued to be a multifaceted construct that has a number of unique and independent inputs (Krosnick and Petty, 1995; Krosnick et al., 1993) with a shared set of identifiable outputs (i.e., influence on behaviour and judgement, persistence, and resistance). Components of attitude strength include both operative and meta-attitudinal features of the attitudes

(Basilli, 1996). Operative features refer to properties of the attitudes that are more structural in nature or observable outcomes, whereas subjective or meta-attitudinal features reflect consumers' perceptions or thoughts about their attitudes. Operative measures include the accessibility of the attitude, the extremity of the attitude, working knowledge, extent of elaboration, and ambivalence of thoughts underlying the attitude. Meta-attitudinal features include factors such as perceived attitude importance, attitude certainty, and perceived thought (for a review of attitude strength features see Petty and Krosnick, 1995). Of course, any property of attitudes that is operative can also be examined in a meta-attitudinal form (e.g., perceived accessibility, ambivalence; see Wegener et al., 1995).

Consequences of central versus peripheral routes

According to the ELM, attitudes formed through the central route, relative to the peripheral route, are more inclined to persist over time, stand resistant to attempts to change them, come to mind quickly, be included in a consideration set prior to choice, and be more likely to influence and predict other judgements and behaviour (for a review see Petty et al., 1995).[5] Thus, when attitude formation and change are the result of thoughtful elaboration, those attitudes are stronger than when attitude formation and change are the result of relatively non-thoughtful processes – regardless of what that specific non-thoughtful process is (e.g., conditioning, mere exposure).

The implications of the attitude strength idea are that consumers with identical attitudes may not behave in the same manner. Specifically, if two consumers hold equally positive attitudes towards a product, but one formed an attitude via greater elaboration than another, it would be expected that the high elaboration attitude would be more directive of behaviour (e.g., purchasing a product), more durable over time, and more resistant to attempts to change it. Thus, advertising

can have an important influence that is not detected by the attitude measures alone, in that the advertising can influence the strength by which an attitude is held without changing the already positive attitude. Because of this, advertising can sometimes work to reinforce an attitude rather than change it (see Heath, this volume). Thus, a consideration of the attitude strength continuum suggests that measures that capture aspects of attitude strength may be as, if not occasionally more, important than traditional attitude measures.

Attitude certainty

At present, one aspect of attitude strength receiving increased research attention is attitude certainty. Attitude certainty typically refers to an individuals' subjective sense of conviction regarding one's attitude and/or the extent to which an individual believes his or her attitude is correct (Festinger, 1954; Gross et al., 1995; see also Petrocelli et al., forthcoming). Increased certainty has been shown to enhance the attitude–behaviour relationship, such that attitudes held with certainty are more likely to predict behaviour (Berger and Mitchell, 1989; Krishnan and Smith, 1998; Rucker and Petty, 2004; Tormala and Petty, 2002) (e.g., Bassili, 1996; Krosnick and Abelson, 1992), and persist across time (Bassili, 1996).

To understand variables that influence attitude certainty, one stream of research has focused on meta-cognitive inferences (see Petty et al., 2007) consumers make about how they reached the attitude. For instance, individuals become more certain of their attitudes after they have successfully defended it against an attack perceived to be strong as opposed to weak (Tormala and Petty, 2002). In such circumstances, consumers are able to infer the validity of their attitude by their perceived ability to defend their position. That is, individuals perceive that their attitude must be valid if they are able to successfully defend it against a strong message. Additional work has shown that when individuals change their attitude, they are more certain of the new attitude when their thinking is directed at considering both their negative and positive reactions to a message than when they focus solely on one side (Rucker and Petty, 2004). This effect is argued to occur because participants perceive that when they have considered both sides, they are better informed. Importantly, in each of these research programmes, attitudes were more likely to predict behaviours when the attitudes were held with greater certainty.

Additional work on attitude certainty has found that attitude certainty can be influenced by repeatedly expressing one's attitude (Holland et al., 2003), the subjective sense of ease associated with listing thoughts in support of one's position (Haddock et al., 1999), whether the attitude is formed in an online or memory-based fashion (Bizer et al., 2006), and whether that attitude is supported by other people (Visser and Mirabile, 2004; Petrocelli et al., 2007). Each of these findings provides initial insights into how advertisers can enhance persuasion by manipulating variables likely to increase the certainty associated with the resulting attitudes.

Summary of attitude strength

As one goal of advertising is not only to foster positive evaluations of a product or service, but evaluations likely to last and impact behaviour, understanding factors contributing to attitude strength is critical in understanding advertising effectiveness. Next we discuss the various roles any given variable can play in attitude change situations.

Disentangling variables from processes

Although the ELM highlights the two routes to persuasion, it is important to note that this does not mean that consumers always process advertisements in either just a central or a peripheral fashion. The central and peripheral routes to persuasion are placed along an elaboration likelihood continuum. Central route processes have a greater impact on attitudes as the extent of elaboration increases and peripheral route processes have a greater impact on attitudes as the extent of elaboration decreases. At most points along the continuum, however, central and peripheral processes operate jointly to influence attitudes (Petty, 1994).

For example, a consumer who receives strong arguments from an attractive model for a new MP3 player might be influenced both by the fact that the arguments are strong and by the incidental affect created by the attractive model. However, as the elaboration likelihood increases, the relative weighting and influence of central route processes (i.e., scrutiny of the arguments) increase while the influence of peripheral route processes (i.e., mood used as a cue to product attractiveness) decrease. As explained next, however, although mood and other variables are less likely to serve as simple cues when elaboration increases, they can affect attitudes in other ways when the motivation and ability to think are high.

Multiple roles for variables

One of the most important features of the ELM is that it recognizes that any variable (e.g., source expertise, recipient mood) can influence persuasion through a finite number of processes depending on the context and the elaboration level. Specifically, variables can influence persuasion by (a) serving as an argument, (b) serving as a simple cue, or (c) influencing aspects of consumers' thoughts (amount, valence, confidence). The ability for any variable to play a variety of roles can explain how the same variable can have different effects and operate through different processes based on the given context and elaboration level.

First, under low elaboration conditions (i.e., when motivation or ability to process is lacking) variables, when they have an impact, are likely to influence attitudes by serving as simple cues. Variables are used as cues under low elaboration because people are not motivated or able to scrutinize the message-relevant information for it relevance and strength. As a result, attitudes are a result of simple associations or inference processes that require little cognitive effort.

For example, as noted earlier, consumers' emotional states might influence whether they like an advertised product in a mood-congruent fashion because the emotional state simply becomes associated with or attached to the attitude object (i.e., "I'm happy right now, so this product must be great!": see Forgas, 1995; Schwarz and Clore, 1983). Similarly, source expertise might be used to determine the quality of a message (i.e., "This movie is endorsed by Roger Ebert, I guess the movie must be good": e.g., Petty et al., 1981). Second, under high elaboration conditions, consumers are inclined to carefully scrutinize all information available and evaluate each piece of information with respect to whether it is a reasonable argument. Because each piece of information is being scrutinized, variables such as a source's expertise or a person's mood are unlikely to influence attitudes as simple cues. Instead, people are likely to consider whether their experienced emotions or the source's expertise provide relevant evidence for the judgement at hand. Thus, when elaboration is high, an advertisement for new tires would be more effective if accompanied by a mechanical expert as opposed to a professional NASCAR sportscaster.

In addition to serving as issue-relevant information, when elaboration is high, a variable can also bias the direction of consumers' thoughts. For example, consumers might be more argumentative towards a message delivered by a non-expert source but more open-minded if the same message is delivered from an expert source (see Chaiken and Maheswaran, 1994). Bias can come from various places. When people think a message is explicitly designed to persuade them, they tend to be motivated to counterargue (Petty and Cacioppo, 1979a). In addition, when a persuasive attempt is masked as simply a question of interest, people may fail to raise defences against it and thus more likely to generate thoughts in favour of the message and thus be more persuaded (e.g., see work on mere-measurement, Williams et al., 2004). Likewise, when elaboration is high, consumers' mood state can colour people's thoughts such that people generate

more positive thoughts when in a good than in a bad mood (e.g., Petty et al., 1993). Similarly, work by Fitzsimmons and Shiv (2001) has found that asking hypothetical questions can lead to a bias or contamination of people's attitudes under high levels of thought. For example, simply asking people how they would feel about a political candidate if they were to hypothetically be convicted of fraud, led to more negative opinions of the candidate even though the negative behaviour itself was hypothetical. Presumably, simply thinking about the possibility of how a politician might commit a nefarious behaviour could bias how people think about the politician (for other biasing effects of accusations see Wegener et al., 1988; Rucker and Petty, 2003).

Another process by which variables can influence persuasion under high elaboration is by affecting the confidence associated with thoughts (Petty et al., 2002). As confidence in one's positive thoughts increases, attitudes become more positive, whereas increasing confidence in negative thoughts reduces persuasion. Recent work examining thought confidence has found that informing participants about the expertise of a source *after* message processing can influence confidence in the thoughts that were generated (Briñol et al., 2004). Specifically, consumers became more confident in their thoughts if they learned a message was presented from a high-credible as opposed to a low-credible source. Emotions following a message have been shown to produce similar effects with positive moods following thought generation enhancing confidence in thoughts and negative moods decreasing confidence (Briñol et al., in press).

Finally, under moderate elaboration conditions (elaboration is not constrained to be high or low by other factors), variables can determine the amount of elaboration in which people engage. Variables can prompt additional processing leading to a reliance on the central route or may discourage additional processing leading to a reliance on the peripheral route. For example, Priester and Petty (1995) found that an untrustworthy expert source solicited more processing than a trust-worthy expert source. Similarly, consumers' emotional states can influence whether people engage in extensive or superficial processing of a message (Wegener and Petty, 1994; Wegener et al., 1995).

One example of how the same variable can influence persuasion differently comes from work on imagery. This research has found that imagery accompanying advertisements can have either a positive or negative effect on persuasion and can operate through various processes. Miniard and colleagues (1991), for example, found that the attractiveness of a picture that accompanied a product, but was not directly relevant to the product, served as a simple cue for persuasion when individuals were not highly motivated to process the message carefully. That is, when people were not motivated to process carefully, the positivity of the picture alone served as a simple cue and led to more liking of the product. However, when people were more highly motivated to process the ad, image positivity was not enough – relevance also mattered. Thus, a picture that was positive and relevant for the product (e.g., a picture of fresh oranges for orange juice) was more effective than an equally positive picture that was irrelevant (e.g., a pretty sunset). Additional work by Smith and Shaffer (2000) showed that message imagery can also influence the amount of message processing. Specifically, imagery that was congruent with the focus of the message elicited greater message pro-cessing (i.e., stronger differentiation between weak and strong arguments) than low-image messages or high-image messages that were incongruent. Finally, recent work has found that the ease with which images can be generated can influence whether imagery has a positive or a negative effect on persuasion (Petrova and Cialdini, 2005). Specifically, when imagery is positive, those who have a natural tendency to struggle generating the mental imagery of the product are more nega-tive towards the product relative to those who can generate the mental imagery more easily.

A second example of how the same variable can influence persuasion by multiple roles is that of positive feelings. For example, suppose that an advertisement evokes positive feelings. From the perspective of the ELM, the crucial question becomes not *whether* positive feelings influenced attitudes, but *by what process* (i.e., how) these feelings influenced attitudes. Petty et al. (1993) found that when individuals are motivated and able to elaborate, their mood influenced their cognitive responses, such that those in a positive mood had more positive cognitive responses than those in a neutral mood, and that these positive cognitive responses led to more positive attitudes. For those individuals who lacked motivation to elaborate, positive mood also influenced attitudes in the same direction. However, under the conditions of low elaboration, the positive mood did not influence cognitive responses, but instead had a direct, non-thoughtful influence on attitudes. Other research demonstrates that under conditions of moderate elaboration-likelihood (viz., when individuals possess the ability but do not possess the motivation), mood can influence the amount of thinking that takes place (Wegener et al., 1995).

In summary, rather than attempt to tie a particular variable to a particular effect or process, the multiple roles logic of the ELM emphasizes that the effectiveness of any given variable cannot be tied to just one particular effect or to one particular process (Petty, 1997). Rather, to understand the role of a given variable in advertising effectiveness, it is important to be aware of both the level of elaboration and the potential roles a variable can play at that level. Importantly, the ELM confines all variables (source expertise, mood, etc.) to a finite set of processes and thus provides a simplifying framework to understand attitude change and from which to analyse new persuasion variables.

Using the ELM to inform other theories and approaches in advertising

Research in the field of advertising has advanced a multitude of theories and approaches to better understand advertising effectiveness. For example, whether advertisements are presented as dramas or arguments (e.g., Deighton et al., 1989), invoke inferences versus passive processing (e.g., Krugman, 1965), rely on explicit versus implicit memory (e.g., Braun, 1999; Heath, 1999), and/or appeal to switching versus reinforcement (e.g., Barnard and Ehrenberg, 1997) have all been advanced as approaches by which to better understand advertising.

We think a key utility of the ELM is that it can be used to further understand or expand upon each of these existing approaches. For example, Deighton and colleagues (1989) discuss how advertisements can be presented along a continuum ranging from "Drama" at one end to "Arguments" at the other. At the extreme end of the "Drama" side of the continuum, advertisements feature a plot and character with no narration. That is, the audience is literally watching a story unfold. At the extreme side of the "Argument" side of the continuum, advertisements are narrated without a character or plot of any sort. Here, the audience is essentially receiving arguments about the product from a narrator. Deighton and colleagues further suggest arguments are more likely to lead to persuasion by evoking positive thoughts or beliefs and failing to lead to strong counterarguments. Dramas, however, are argued to automatically evoke less counterarguments and are more likely to influence persuasion by evoking feelings and verisimilitude of the depicted events.

The ELM can be used to further understand and elaborate upon the "Argument" versus "Dramas" distinction. As but one example, the ELM holds that both arguments and dramas can be evaluated via either the central or the peripheral route. Thus, when consumers are engaged in a high amount of thinking about a drama (i.e., the central route), they will evaluate whether the drama convincingly demonstrates the product's function. However, when engaged in relatively little thinking about the merits of the drama with respect to the product (i.e., the peripheral route), they are more likely to use simple

cues to determine their attitudes such as how cute or funny the drama was rather than scrutinizing whether the drama is a compelling demonstration of the product benefit. Similarly, when an advertisement takes the form of an argument, people might carefully assess the merits of the message arguments when elaboration is high, but simply count the number of arguments when elaboration is low (i.e., Petty and Cacioppo, 1984). Thus, the drama-argument continuum raised by Deighton and colleagues can be examined from an elaboration perspective to advance the theory in new and interesting directions.

To provide a further illustration of the applicability of the ELM to existing advertising theory, consider work on advertising to brand-loyal consumers versus consumers prone to switching. Barnard and Ehrenberg (1997) argue that the consumer population seems to consist of neither completely loyal consumers nor complete brand switchers. Rather, they propose consumers have a number of brands they are favourably predisposed towards that form a general consideration set. As such, they argue advertising should be used to nudge consumers towards a particular brand in the consideration set rather than attempting to create a consumer who is loyal to a single brand. An important question, in this research, would seem to be how to increase the use of one brand over another. The ELM and work on attitude strength can be used as guidance. In particular, the work we have reviewed suggests that in situations where attitudes toward several brands are equally favourable, the brand attitude that is held most confidently (or has other strength features such as accessibility) will be more likely to lead to purchases. The ELM suggests that attitudes can be made stronger by increasing the amount of thought behind them, or using other methods described in the section on attitude certainty. As discussed earlier in this chapter, even if advertising does not appear to further enhance the positivity of an evaluation, it may have the desired impact of leading to attitudes that are stronger and thus more likely to influence behaviour. Thus, the ELM, and the work on attitude strength more generally, could provide an interesting approach with regard to how to "nudge" consumers towards one of many desired brands (see also Priester et al., 2004).

In summary, the ELM is not only a model of persuasion, but it can be used as a framework to build upon and inform other approaches in advertising. We have touched upon two examples, but the potential applicability of the ELM to other theories and approaches in advertising is nearly limitless.

SUMMARY

- This chapter has contributed to understanding factors leading to advertising effectiveness by highlighting past and present advancements in the field of attitude change and attitude strength.
- The study of attitude change and the elaboration likelihood model (ELM) in particular, show that source, message, recipient, and context variables can produce either positive or negative effects on persuasion depending on the role the variable serves in persuasion (e.g., cue, argument, or affecting amount, direction or confidence in thoughts).
- The attitude strength literature shows that some attitudes (e.g., those held with certainty) are more consequential than others. Taken together, the literatures on attitude change and strength can be used by scholars and practitioners of advertising as a roadmap for creating more effective advertisements.
- This chapter focused on the contribution of persuasion to advertising effectiveness. This is not meant to suggest that effective advertising should be equated solely with successful persuasion. In fact, we acknowledge that advertising may be effective even in situations where no persuasion occurs. For example, as reviewed in the work on attitude strength, advertising might be used to reinforce one's attitudes without changing the nature of those evaluations. This is consistent with the general notion of reinforcement discussed in Robert Heath (2007, Chapter 2.2). Thus, while we view persuasion as one component of effective advertising, we also clearly recognize, and endorse the perspective that successful persuasion is not the sole measure of effective advertising.
- The many unanswered questions for researchers include broadening the current subset of the variables that can influence persuasion. In particular, future research could profitably examine the various processes that operate under low levels of elaboration and possible non-thoughtful mechanisms that could increase attitude strength.

In closing, we return to Bernbach's quote a final time. Again, it seems fair to characterize advertising as persuasion, albeit with the caveats above. However, to characterize persuasion as an art suggests there are no verifiable rules or means to anticipate what type of persuasive efforts or techniques will be successful versus unsuccessful – an unsettling thought for practitioners at best. Fortunately, we think it more appropriate to character persuasion, and thus advertising, as a science. As a science, we can develop rules and formulas for predicting what types of persuasive efforts will be effective and are capable of explaining why they are effective. Of course, it would be misleading to say that psychological perspectives on persuasion have produced a single formula for producing successful advertisements. However, we think it is fair to say that, compared to 50 years ago, we have a much better idea of some of the key factors involved.

NOTES

1 Some researchers have also suggested that attitudes can be comprised of deliberative (explicit) reactions to objects as well as more automatic (implicit) associations (for a review see Petty et al., in press). For instance, although former smokers might have negative explicit evaluations towards smoking (e.g., "I think smoking is bad and disgusting."), at an implicit level smoking may be associated with positive evaluations based on past experiences (see Petty et al., 2006).

2 Of course, there are special circumstances when various bases can be in conflict (e.g., Fabrigar and Petty, 1999), or the attitude itself can be composed of both positive and negative reactions (Priester and Petty, 1996; Priester et al., forthcoming).

3 Other dual process models of persuasion and judgement have also been proposed, such as the Heuristic-Systematic Model (e.g., Chaiken et al., 1989). However, these models are in the same spirit as the ELM and points of divergence have relatively minor implications for the issues addressed here.

For additional information on other dual process models the reader is referred to Chaiken and Trope (1999).

4 Consumers' memory is more likely to matter when they do not form an attitude as they are processing a message, but instead are required to do so at some later point in time based upon their memory of the message (Hastie and Park, 1986; Tormala and Petty, 2001). However, even if consumers are retrieving information from memory, their idiosyncratic responses to the retrieved information would still be important in determining attitudes.

5 There are a variety of reasons why high amounts of elaboration are predicted to produce stronger attitudes. These include both operative factors (e.g., thoughtful attitudes are more accessible and likely to come to mind when needed) and meta-cognitive factors (e.g., attitudes about which we have thought a great deal are held with greater certainty and are thus more likely to be viewed as useful guides to action).

REFERENCES

Anand, P. and B. Sternthal (1988), "Strategies for Designing Persuasive Messages: Deductions from the Resources Matching Hypothesis," in *Cognitive and Affective Responses to Advertising*, eds. Patricia Cafferata and Alice Tybout, Lexington, Mass., 135–160.

Basilli, J.N. (1996), "Meta-Judgmental Versus Operative Indexes of Psychological Attributes: The Case of Measures of Attitude Strength," *Journal of Personality and Social Psychology*, 71, 637–653.

Batra, R. and M.L. Ray (1986), "Affective Responses Mediating Acceptance of Advertising," *Journal of Consumer Research*, 13, 234–249.

Berger, I.E. and A.A. Mitchell (1989), "The Effect of Advertising on Attitude Accessibility, Attitude Confidence, and the Attitude-Behavior Relationship," *Journal of Consumer Research*, 16, 269–279.

Bizer, G.Y., Z.L. Tormala, D.D. Rucker and R.E. Petty (2006), "Memory-Based Versus On-Line Processing: Implications for Attitude Strength," *Journal of Experimental Social Psychology*, 42, 646–653.

Breckler, S.J. (1984), "Empirical Validation of Affect, Behavior, and Cognition as Distinct Components of Attitude," *Journal of Personality and Social Psychology*, 47, 1191–1205.

Briñol, P., R.E. Petty and J. Barden (in press), "*The Impact of Mood on Post-Message Processing of Persuasive Messages: An Extension of the Self-Validation Hypothesis*," Unpublished Manuscript, Ohio State University, Columbus.

Briñol, P., R.E. Petty and Z.L. Tormala (2004), "Self-Validation of Cognitive Responses to Advertisements," *Journal of Consumer Research*, 30, 559–573.

Cacioppo, J.T. and R.E. Petty (1979), "The Effects of Message Repetition and Position on Cognitive Responses, Recall, and Persuasion," *Journal of Personality and Social Psychology*, 37, 97–109.

Cacioppo, J.T. and R.E. Petty (1989), "Effects of Message Repetition on Argument Processing, Recall, and Persuasion," *Basic and Applied Social Psychology*, 10, 3–12.

Cacioppo, J.T., R.E. Petty and K. Morris (1983), "Effects of Need for Cognition on Message Evaluation, Recall, and Persuasion," *Journal of Personality and Social Psychology*, 45, 805–818.

Calder, B.J., C.A. Insko and B. Yandell (1974), "The Relation of Cognition and Memorial Processes to Persuasion in a Simulated Jury Trial," *Journal of Applied Social Psychology*, 4, 62–93.

Chaiken, S. (1980), "Heuristic Versus Systematic Information Processing In The Use Of Source Versus Message Cues In Persuasion," *Journal of Personality and Social Psychology*, 39, 752–766.

Chaiken, S., A. Liberman and A.H. Eagly (1989), "Heuristic And Systematic Information Processing Within And Beyond The Persuasion Context," in *Unintended Thought*, eds. J.S. Uleman and J.A. Bargh, New York: Guilford Press, 212–252.

Chaiken, S. and D. Maheswaran (1994), "Heuristic Processing Can Bias Systematic Processing: Effects Of Source Credibility, Argument Ambiguity, And Task Importance On Attitude Judgment," *Journal of Personality and Social Psychology*, 66, 460–473.

Chaiken, S. and Y. Trope (1999), *Dual Process Theories In Social Psychology*, New York: Guilford Press.

Fabrigar, L.R. and R.E. Petty (1999), "Political Persuasion And Attitude Change," *Political Psychology*, 20, 436–439.

Festinger, L. (1954), "A Theory Of Social Comparison Processes," *Human Relations*, 7, 117–140.

Fishbein, M. and I. Ajzen (1972), "Attitudes And Opinions," *Annual Review of Psychology*, 23, 487–544.

Fishbein, M. and I. Ajzen (1981), "Acceptance, Yielding And Impact: Cognitive Processes In Persuasion," in *Cognitive Responses In Persuasion* eds. R.E. Petty, T.M. Ostrom and T.C. Brock, Hillsdale, NJ: Erlbaum, 339–359.

Fitzsimons, G. and B. Shiv (2001), "Nonconscious And Contaminative Effects Of Hypothetical Questions On Subsequent Decision Making," *Journal of Consumer Research*, 28, 224–238.

Forgas, J.P. (1995), "Mood And Judgment: The Affect-Infusion Model (Aim)," *Psychological Bulletin,* 117, 39–66.

Fox, S. (1984), *The Mirror Makers.* Champagne: University of Illinois Press.

Gross, S.R., R. Holtz and N. Miller (1995), "Attitude Certainty," in *Attitude Strength: Antecedents And Consequences,* eds. R.E. Petty and J.A. Krosnick, Mahwah, NJ: Erlbaum, 215–245.

Haddock, G., A.J. Rothman, R. Reber and N. Schwarz (1999), "Forming Judgments Of Attitude Certainty, Intensity, And Importance: The Role Of Subjects Experiences," *Personality and Social Psychology Bulletin,* 25, 771–782.

Hastie, R. and B. Park (1986), "The Relationship Between Memory And Judgment Depends On Whether The Judgment Is Memory-Based Or Online," *Psychological Review,* 93, 258–268.

Heath, R. (2007), "Advertising as Reinforcement," in *The SAGE Handbook of Advertising,* eds. G.J. Tellis and T. Ambler, London: Sage Publications.

Holland, R.W., B. Verplanken and A. van Knippenberg (2003), "From Repetition to Conviction: Attitude Accessibility as a Determinant of Attitude Certainty," *Journal of Experimental Social Psychology,* 39, 594–601.

Hovland, C.I., I. Janis and H.H. Kelley (1953), *Communication And Persuasion.* New Haven, CT: Yale University Press.

Hovland, C.I. and W. Weiss (1951), "The Influence Of Source Credibility On Communication Effectiveness," *Public Opinion Quarterly,* 15, 635–650.

Krishnan, H.S. and R.E. Smith (1998), "The Relative Endurance of Attitudes, Confidence and Attitude-Behavior Consistency: The Role of Information Source and Delay," *Journal of Consumer Psychology,* 7, 273–298.

Krosnick, J.A. and R.P. Abelson (1992), "The Case For Measuring Attitude Strength In Surveys," in *Questions About Questions: Inquiries Into The Cognitive Bases Of Surveys,* ed. J. Tanur, New York: Sage, 177–203.

Krosnick, J.A., D.S. Boninger, Y.C. Chuang, M.K. Berent and C.G. Carnot (1993), "Attitude Strength: One Construct Or Many Related Constructs?" *Journal of Personality and Social Psychology,* 65, 1132–1149.

Krosnick, J.A. and R.E. Petty (1995), "Attitude Strength: An Overview," in *Attitude strength: Antecedents And Consequences,* eds. R.E. Petty and J.A. Krosnick, Mahwah, NJ: Erlbaum, 1–24.

Loken, B. and R. Hoverstad (1985), "Relationships Between Information Recall And Subsequent Attitudes – Some Exploratory Findings," *Journal of Consumer Research,* 12,155–168.

Mazzocco, P.J., D.D. Rucker and T.C. Brock (2005), "Implications For Advertising Effectiveness Of Divergence Among Measured Advertising Effects," in *Applying Social Cognition To Consumer-Focused Strategy,* eds. F. Kardes, P.R. Herr and J. Nantel, Mahwah, NJ: Lawrence Erlbaum Associates.

McGuire, W.J. (1964), "Inducing Resistance To Persuasion: Some Contemporary Approaches," in *Advances in Experimental Social Psychology,* eds. I. Berkowitz, New York: Academic Press, Vol. 1, pp. 191–229.

McGuire, W.J. (1968), "Personality And Susceptibility To Social Influence," in *Handbook Of Personality Theory And Research,* eds. E.F. Borgatta and W.W. Lambert, Chicago: Rand McNally, 1130–1187.

Miniard, P.W., S. Bhatla, K.R. Lord, P.R. Dickson and H.R. Unnava (1991), "Picture-Based Persuasion Processes And The Moderating Role Of Involvement," *Journal of Consumer Research,* 18, 92–107.

Norman, R. (1976), "When What Is Said Is Important. A Comparison Of Expert And Attractive Sources," *Journal of Experimental Social Psychology,* 12, 295–300.

Peracchio, L.A. and J. Meyers-Levy (1997), "Evaluating Persuasion-Enhancing Techniques From A Resource-Matching Perspective," *Journal of Consumer Research,* 24, 178–191.

Petrocelli, J.V., Z.L. Tormala and D.D. Rucker (2007), "Unpacking Attitude Certainty: Attitude Clarity And Attitude Correctness," *Journal of Personality and Social Psychology,* 92, 30–41.

Petrova, P. and R.B. Cialdini (2005), "Fluency of Consumption Imagery and the Backfire Effects of Imagery Appeals," *Journal of Consumer Research,* xx, xxx–xxx.

Petty, R.E. (1977), "The Importance Of Cognitive Responses In Persuasion," *Advances in Consumer Research,* 4, 357–362.

Petty, R.E. (1994), "Two Routes To Persuasion: State Of The Art," in *International Perspectives On Psychological Science,* eds. G. d'Ydewalle, P. Eclen and P. Bertelson, Hillsdale, NJ: Erlbaum, 229–247.

Petty, R.E. (1997), "The Evolution Of Theory And Research In Social Psychology: From Single To Multiple Effect And Process Models," in *The Message Of Social Psychology: Perspectives On Mind In Society,* eds. C. McGarty and S.A. Haslam, Oxford, UK: Blackwell Publishers, Ltd., 268–290.

Petty, R.E., P. Briñol and Z.L. Tormala (2002), "Thought Confidence As A Determinant Of Persuasion: The Self-Validation Hypothesis," *Journal of Personality and Social Psychology,* 82, 722–741.

Petty, R.E., P. Briñol, Z.L. Tormala, and D.T. Wegener, (2007), "The Role Of Meta-Cognition In Social

Judgment," in *Social Psychology: Handbook of Basic Principles* (2nd ed), eds. A.W. Kruglanski and E.T. Higgins, New York: Guilford Press, 254–284.

Petty, R.E. and J.T. Cacioppo (1979a), "Effects Of Forewarning Of Persuasive Intent And Involvement On Cognitive Responses And Persuasion," *Personality and Social Psychology Bulletin*, 5, 173–176.

Petty, R.E. and J.T. Cacioppo, (1979b), "Issue Involvement Can Increase Or Decrease Persuasion By Enhancing Message-Relevant Cognitive Responses," *Journal of Personality and Social Psychology*, 37,1915–1926.

Petty, R.E. and J.T. Cacioppo (1981), *Attitudes And Persuasion: Classic And Contemporary Approaches.* Dubuque, IA: Wm. C. Brown.

Petty, R.E. and J.T. Cacioppo (1984), "The Effects Of Involvement On Response To Argument Quantity And Quality: Central And Peripheral Routes To Persuasion," *Journal of Personality and Social Psychology*, 46, 69–81.

Petty, R.E. and J.T. Cacioppo (1986), *Communication And Persuasion: Central And Peripheral Routes To Attitude Change.* New York: Springer/Verlag.

Petty, R.E., J.T. Cacioppo and R. Goldman (1981), "Personal Involvement As A Determinant Of Argument-Based Persuasion," *Journal of Personality and Social Psychology*, 41, 847–855.

Petty, R.E., R.H. Fazio and P. Briñol, eds. (in press), *Attitudes: Insights From The New Implicit Measures.* Mahwah, NJ: Erlbaum Associates.

Petty, R.E., S.G. Harkins and K.D. Williams (1980),"The Effects Of Group Diffusion Of Cognitive Effort On Attitudes: An Information Processing View," *Journal of Personality and Social Psychology*, 38, 81–92.

Petty, R.E., C.T. Haugtvedt and S.M. Smith (1995), "Elaboration As A Determinant Of Attitude Strength: Creating Attitudes That Are Persistent, Resistant, And Predictive Of Behavior," in R. E. Petty and J. A. Krosnick eds. *Attitude Strength: Antecedents And Consequences* (pp. 93–130), Mahwah, NJ: Lawrence Erlbaum Associates.

Petty, R.E. and J.A. Krosnick (1995), eds. *Attitude Strength: Antecedents And Consequences* (pp. 93–130). Mahwah, NJ: Lawrence Erlbaum Associates.

Petty, R.E., D.W. Schuman, S.A. Richman and A.J. Strathman (1993), "Positive Mood And Persuasion: Different Roles For Affect Under High- And Low-Elaboration Conditions," *Journal of Personality and Social Psychology*, 64, 5–20.

Petty, R.E., Z.L. Tormala, P. Briñol and W.B.G. Jarvis (2006), "Implicit Ambivalence From Attitude Change: An Exploration Of The Past Model," *Journal of Personality and Social Psychology*, 90, 21–41.

Petty, R.E. and D.T. Wegener (1999), "The Elaboration Likelihood Model: Current Status And Controversies," in *Dual Process Theories In Social Psychology*, eds S. Chaiken and Y. Trope, New York: Guilford Press, 41–72.

Petty, R.E., G.L. Wells and T.C. Brock (1976), "Distraction Can Enhance Or Reduce Yielding To Propaganda: Thought Disruption Versus Effort Justification," *Journal of Personality and Social Psychology*, 34, 874–884.

Petty, R.E., S.C. Wheeler and Z.L. Tormala (2003), "Persuasion And Attitude Change," in *Handbook Of Psychology: Volume 5: Personality And Social Psychology*, eds. T. Millon and M.J. Lerner, Hoboken, NJ: John Wiley & Sons, 353–382.

Priester, J.R., D. Nayakankuppam, M.A. Fleming and J. Godek (2004), "The A^2SC^2 Model: The Influence Of Attitudes And Attitude Strength On Consideration And Choice," *Journal of Consumer Research*, 30, 574–587.

Priester, J.R. and R.E. Petty (1995), "Source Attributions And Persuasion: Perceived Honesty As A Determinant Of Message Scrutiny," *Personality and Social Psychology Bulletin*, 21, 637–654.

Priester, J.R. and R.E. Petty (1996), "The Gradual Threshold Model Of Ambivalence: Relating The Positive And Negative Bases Of Attitudes To Subjective Ambivalence," *Journal of Personality and Social Psychology*, 71, 431–449.

Priester, J.R., R.E. Petty and K. Park (forthcoming), "Whence Univalent Ambivalence? From The Anticipation Of Conflicting Reaction," *Journal of Consumer Research*.

Rogers, R.W. (1983), "Cognitive And Physiological Processes In Fear Appeals And Attitude Change: A Revised Theory Of Protection Motivation," in *Social Psychophysiology: A Sourcebook*, eds. J.T. Cacioppo and R.E. Petty, New York: Guildford Press, 153–176.

Rucker, D.D. and R.E. Petty (2003), "Effects Of Accusations On The Accuser: The Moderating Role Of Accuser Culpability," *Personality and Social Psychology Bulletin*, 29, 1259–1271.

Rucker, D.D. and R.E. Petty (2004), "When Resistance Is Futile: Consequences Of Failed Counterarguing For Attitude Certainty," *Journal of Personality and Social Psychology*, 86, 219–235.

Schwarz, N. and G.L. Clore (1983), "Mood, Misattribution, And Judgments Of Well-Being: Informative And Directive Functions Of Affective States," *Journal of Personality and Social Psychology*, 45, 513–523.

Sheppard, B.H., J. Hartwick and P.R. Warshaw (1988), "The Theory Of Reasoned Action – A Meta-Analysis Of Past Research With Recommendations

For Modifications And Future Research," *Journal of Consumer Research,* 15, 325–343.

Smith, S. and D. Shaffer (2000), "Vividness Can Undermine Or Enhance Message Processing: The Moderating Role Of Vividness Congruency," *Personality and Social Psychology Bulletin,* 26, 769–778.

Staats, A.W. and C.K. Staats (1958), "Attitudes Established By Classical Conditioning," *Journal of Abnormal and Social Psychology,* 57, 37–40.

Sternthal, B., R. Dholakia and C. Leavitt (1978), "Persuasive Effect Of Source Credibility – Tests Of Cognitive Response," *Journal of Consumer Research,* 4, 252–260.

Tellis, G.J. (1998), *Advertising And Sales Promotion Strategy,* Reading, MA: Addison-Wesley.

Tellis, G.J. (2004). *Does Advertising Really Work: How, Why, When?* Thousand Oaks: Sage Publications.

Tormala, Z.L. and R.E. Petty (2001), "On-Line Versus Memory Based Processing: The Role Of 'Need To Evaluate,'" *Person Perception, Personality and Social Psychology Bulletin,* 12, 1599–1612.

Tormala, Z.L. and R.E. Petty (2002), "What Doesn't Kill Me Makes Me Stronger: The Effects Of Resisting Persuasion On Attitude Certainty," *Journal of Personality and Social Psychology,* 83, 1298–1313.

Visser, P. and R.R. Mirabile (2004), "Attitudes In The Social Context: The Impact Of Social Network Composition On Individual Level Attitude Strength," *Journal of Personality and Social Psychology,* 87, 779–795.

Wegener, D.T., J. Downing, J.A. Krosnick and R.E. Petty (1995), "Measures And Manipulations Of Strength Related Properties Of Attitudes: Current Practice And Future Directions," in *Attitude strength: Antecedents and Consequences,* eds. R.E. Petty and J.A. Krosnick, Mahwah, NJ: Lawrence Erlbaum Associates, 455–488.

Wegener, D.T. and R.E. Petty (1994), "Mood Management Across Affective States: The Hedonic Contingency Hypothesis," *Journal of Personality and Social Psychology,* 66, 1034–1048.

Wegener, D.T., R.E. Petty and S.M. Smith (1995), "Positive Mood Can Increase Or Decrease Message Scrutiny: The Hedonic Contingency View Of Mood And Message Processing," *Journal of Personality and Social Psychology,* 69, 5–15.

Wegner, M., Wenzlaff, R. M. Kerker and A.E Beattie (1981), "Incrimination Through Innuendo: Can Media Questions Become Public Answers?" *Journal of Personality and Social Psychology,* 40, 822–832.

Williams, P., G. Fitzsimons and L. Block (2004), "When Consumers Do Not Recognize "Benign" Intention Questions As Persuasion Attempts," *Journal of Consumer Research,* 31, 540–550.

Wood, S.L. and J.G. Lynch (2002), "Prior Knowledge And Complacency In Product Learning," *Journal of Consumer Research,* 29, 416–426.

Wright, P.L. (1973), "The Cognitive Processes Mediating Acceptance Of Advertising," *Journal of Marketing Research,* 10, 53–62.

Zanna, M.P., C.A. Kiesler and P.A. Pilkonis (1970), "Positive And Negative Attitudinal Affect Established By Classical Conditioning," *Journal of Personality and Social Psychology,* 14, 321–328.

Reinforcement and Low Attention Processing

Robert Heath

This chapter extends our understanding of advertising theory, by examining how advertising can work without necessarily producing a demonstrable change in attitudes. Section one reviews the "reinforcement model" whereby advertising mostly reinforces prior consumer knowledge and experience. This is in contrast to traditional thinking that advertising has two roles, providing information and/or changing consumer behaviour. This opens the reinforcement model to accusations of being "weak" when compared to the traditional 'strong' persuasion models discussed in Chapter 2.1 by Rucker et al. (2007).

In section two this claim is critically examined and a review of new thinking on decision-making and advertising processing is presented. Decision-making is shown to be less thoughtful and more intuitive than is generally assumed. Affect is found to play an important role in decision-making and can be processed without high levels of attention being paid.

Section three describes a "Low Attention Processing" model which suggests that emotionally competent elements in advertising can be stored at relatively low levels of attention as brand associations, and trigger affective responses which influence intuitive decision-making. Finally, after directions for further research in this area, I provide a summary.

THE REINFORCEMENT MODEL

Advertising working by reinforcement was first noted by Krugman (1965) who suggested that advertising might be '… *merely shifting the relative salience of attitudes, especially when the purchaser is not particularly involved in the message*' *(1965: 21)*. Whilst accepting the economic impact of TV advertising, Krugman pointed out that much of the content of TV advertising was "trivial and sometimes silly," and did not fit the traditional persuasion models prevalent at the time.

Nine years later, Krugman's thoughts on evaluating advertising were expanded into a model of advertising by Andrew Ehrenberg (1974). Ehrenberg proposed that advertising worked not by *changing* attitudes, but by reinforcing attitudes already held by a consumer who had extensive usage experience and knowledge of products. He challenged the traditional notion that advertising "*works by any strong form of persuasion or manipulation*" (1974: 25), and instead asserted that "*advertising's main role is to reinforce feelings of satisfaction with brands already being used*" (1974: 33). His Awareness–Trial–Reinforcement (ATR) theory gained a great deal of popularity amongst advertising agencies, at a time when the sales effects of advertising were seen by many as hard to discern even in hindsight, and virtually impossible to predict. Indeed, "*... the received wisdom (was) that one could seldom if ever read the bottom-line effect of advertising on sales because of the number of intervening variables. Instead, one had to look at intermediate effects ...*" (McDonald, 2000: 9).

At this time models like AIDA and DAGMAR still held sway. Ehrenberg identified four weaknesses in these traditional hierarchy-of-effects models:

- The lack of empirical evidence showing sales increases resulting from advertising.
- The persistence of small and medium brands in the face of massive advertising spend by brand leaders.
- The fact that brands usually survive even when adspend is cut.
- The catastrophic failure rate of new products.

Ehrenberg established that most markets have few 100% loyal buyers as the majority buy more than one brand. He found that brand users held consistently stronger attitudes than non-users, especially evaluative attitudes. But what he could not find was any satisfactory explanation of how attitudes change. This led him to question the core assumption within hierarchy-of-effects models – that attitude change precedes and drives behaviour change. Although Ehrenberg accepted that the traditional idea that "Awareness → Attitudes → Behaviour" made intuitive sense, he found many examples of a sequence in which behaviour leads to "*greater awareness of information to which one is normally exposed ... and to changes in attitude*" (1974: 30). All this challenged the convention that consumers

were rationally persuaded by advertising to change their minds and their brand allegiance.

The ATR model

Ehrenberg's model operates across three stages, with advertising capable of acting in all three of these stages:

1. Awareness of the brand is gained.
2. A trial purchase is made.
3. A repeat purchase decision follows.

He believed that advertising could create, re-awaken or strengthen brand awareness, and it could be one of the factors which facilitate trial purchase. But he also saw a role for advertising as converting trialists into satisfied and lasting customers. And he saw repetitive advertising for established brands as primarily defensive, reinforcing already developed repeat buying habits.

In later work, Barnard and Ehrenberg (1997) refined the model to accommodate split-loyal purchasers, defined as those who regularly purchase more than one brand. Here, the role of advertising was to "nudge" split-loyals towards a greater purchase proportion of one brand or another (ATRN).

Empirical support for reinforcement
Recent experimental work by Braun (1999) confirms the power of advertising as reinforcement in a post-purchase situation. Braun created samples of orange juice of varying quality and gave it to subjects to taste, claiming it was a trial for a new brand. Following a distraction task, half the subjects were exposed to advertising for the brand. It was found that the advertising confounded the subject's ability to accurately judge the quality of the juice, leading to substandard product being highly rated. She concluded that "*... advertising received after a direct product experience altered consumers' recollection of both objective sensory and affective components of that experience*" (Braun, 1999: 332).

Braun's findings are corroborated by a case study of the UK beer brand, Stella Artois.

In 1990 Stella Artois was a highly priced beer brand in the UK, with a well-known but poorly recalled print advertising campaign. The brand owners, Interbrew, planned to rectify this through a TV campaign. However, they had a major problem to overcome before they increased investment in the brand, which was that Stella Artois was very bitter, and many people didn't like its taste compared with other beers. So a number of different recipes were developed, and subjected to sequential testing. The results illustrated the power of the brand that had been created by the print advertising: when blind the beer was rejected by 80% of respondents, but when branded the figures were reversed and it was preferred by 80% of respondents. This branded preference level was the same no matter what recipe was tasted, because the brand and its advertising effectively confounded consumers' judgement (Heath, 1993).

Opposition to the reinforcement theory

The "reinforcement" model generated little enthusiasm among marketers. Jones (1990), characterized it as a "weak" theory compared to the "strong" theory prevalent especially in the USA. Jones described strong theory as "... *a driving force for the engine of demand ... capable of increasing sales not only of brands but also of complete product categories ...*" (1990: 237).

Jones' description of strong theory appears to have much in common with the hierarchy of effects models like AIDA, where consumers must go through a sequence where something is communicated which convinces them, and finally causes them to act. In Jones' view the strong theory "... *increases people's knowledge and changes people's attitudes*" and "... *is capable of persuading people who had not previously bought a brand to buy it once and then repeatedly*" (1990: 237). But it differs from AIDA in that it sees advertising as using creativity to insinuate new information into the minds of "*apathetic and rather stupid consumer (by) the use of psychological techniques that destroy the consumer's defences; in some cases these techniques are not even perceptible to the conscious mind.*" (1990: 237)

Four key differences between Jones' strong theory and Ehrenberg's reinforcement model are.

1. Strong theory sees advertising as working informationally. As we will see, both sides claim emotion as part of their theory but the strong theory implies that persuasion arises from logical analysis of benefits.
2. Strong theory sees advertising as a strongly persuasive dynamic force, driving sales and category growth. Reinforcement identifies an important additional *defensive* role especially for repetitive advertising, which is more subtle.
3. Strong theory sees advertising operating on the blank canvas of an ignorant, rather stupid consumer. Reinforcement sees consumers as far more knowledgeable and intelligent.
4. Strong theory sees advertising working by changing attitudes which leads to changing behaviour. Reinforcement rejects the idea that attitude change must precede purchase.

This suggests that reinforcement advertising is not a form of persuasion at all, since it does not change attitudes. However, persuasion can be defined in more than one way.

Persuasion redefined

The general definition of persuade is "*cause someone to believe, convince*" (Oxford Compact English Dictionary, 1996: 746). More eloquently, it can be defined as "*to move by argument, reasoning, or pleading to a belief, position, or course of action*" (Longman Dictionary, 1984: 1096). The emphasis this definition places on argument reasoning or pleading suggests persuasion under this definition is using "propositional representations" – "... *language-like representations that capture the ideational content of the mind*" (Eysenck and Keane, 2000: 246). This identifies persuasion as an information-processing activity, in which thoughts are actively manipulated to create new beliefs and attitudes.

This definition of persuasion corresponds closely to the Central Route of the ELM

(Petty et al., 1983). As discussed in Rucker et al. (2007), Chapter 2.1, the ELM operationalizes motivation and involvement and develops two routes for persuasion: a more strongly persuasive Central Route and a less strongly persuasive Peripheral Route. A requirement for Central Route processing is the motivation to process the message on the part of the consumer, which leads to a more thoughtful level of processing and more enduring attitude changes. The Central and Peripheral routes differ according to the extent to which the resulting attitude change is due to active thinking (Petty and Cacioppo, 1996).

But this "active thinking" definition is not the only definition of persuasion. The Oxford Dictionary also defines persuasion as "*to induce, lure, attract, entice*" (op. cit.). This does not necessarily imply a verbal or rational process is needed for persuasion to take place, as these words all relate more to feelings and emotions than to thinking. The importance which Ehrenberg places on advertising using an emotional rather than informative tone suggests that this latter definition of persuasion is how he sees advertising working in the reinforcement model.

In modern parlance persuasion is used to encompass both definitions, and is often used to describe *any* activity which changes the attitudes and behaviour of the recipient. Ehrenberg does not deny that advertising works (i.e., influences behaviour), but he does deny that it always has to change attitudes. In similar vein, a characteristic of peripheral processing is that the resulting attitude changes are relatively transient: "*Attitude changes via the Central Route appear to be more persistent, resistant, and predictive of behaviour than changes induced via the peripheral route*" (Petty and Cacioppo, 1986: 191). The peripheral route is also one in which repetition of emotional cue-based advertising is more influential than the informational message. So both models support a role for repetitive advertising that relies less on information than on emotional cues, and fails to achieve a demonstrable or long-lasting change in attitudes.

NEW THINKING ON DECISION-MAKING AND ADVERTISING PROCESSING

If the effectiveness of advertising is defined by its ability to demonstrably change attitudes, then Ehrenberg's model is as "weak" as Jones' claims. However, examination of new thinking in the area of decision-making and the factors which underlie the processing of advertising shows that advertising which operates using the sorts of mechanisms identified in the reinforcement model and the peripheral route of the ELM can in some cases be even more effective than advertising which corresponds to Jones' definition of strong persuasion.

Decision-making and affect

Traditional models suggest that behaviour change is driven by changes in attitudes, and, as discussed in Chapter 2.1 attitudes can vary widely in strength and in how strongly they are changed.

Buying behaviour involves making a decision. Early advertising models saw decision making as driven by 'affect' (i.e., feelings and emotions). For example, the Lavidge Steiner model (1961) identified the role of affect as dealing with liking and preferences. But in the Lavidge Steiner model, cognition preceded affect, which operated only as a consequence of cognition. Zajonc (1980) contradicted this idea, showing that affect is generally pre-cognitive not post-cognitive. In later work, Zajonc and Marcus (1982) confirmed that preferences are primarily affectively based behavioural phenomena, and contested the idea that preferences are cognitive constructs. Although some affective responses can appear post-cognitive, the cognition is always preceded by at least some level of affective response. They also argued that decision-making research overestimated the role of cognition, because people believe they should act rationally and therefore claim rational behaviour in decision-making that they have not actually used.

Zajonc concluded that cognition and affect may depend on separate psychological and biological systems, but only recently has a psychobiological explanation been provided. Damasio (1994), referencing cases where rational decision-making capability is impaired, has shown that cognition is "hard-wired" via the emotions, and that feelings are therefore capable of impeding cognition and even driving decisions in the face of negative cognition. He used this to explain intuitive decision-making, which he believes arises from "somatic markers" – feelings associated with outcomes and embedded in semantic memory by past learning. A negative somatic marker associated with a particular outcome acts as a disincentive, but "... *when a positive somatic marker is juxtaposed, it becomes a beacon of incentive*" (1994: 174).

Although affect has always been seen as involved in decision-making, Damasio's findings identify a far more important role for affect. He finds no evidence for a direct link between "reasoning strategies" and decisions, and shows that emotions operate as a "gatekeeper" which moderates all decision-making. But he also shows that emotions can be responsible for driving decisions on their own. If a prior situation has been experienced which has laid down a marker relevant to the present situation, then this marker can "... *lead to a decision directly, as when a gut feeling impels an immediate response*" (2003: 149). He predicts this sort of behaviour is likely to be enhanced when time is constrained.

The role of affect in time-constrained decision-making has been validated empirically by Shiv and Fedhorikhin (1999). By constraining decision time, they were able to encourage the choice of chocolate cake over fruit salad, showing that a time-poor environment encourages behaviour associated with positive affective responses, even when associated cognitive responses are demonstrably negative. In other words, when time is limited (e.g., busy parents shopping for groceries with their children) our choices are likely to be driven by our feelings rather than by logic or rationality.

Mick et al. (2004) describe the rise in choice coupled with a fall in available time as "hyperchoice." They show that hyperchoice confuses people, and although initially attractive, is "... *ultimately unsatisfying and psychologically draining*" (2004: 207). Heath (2001) attributes a rise in intuitive decision-making to the increase in brand quality. Most categories offer a number of brands, all perfectly capable of satisfying our basic needs. Brand improvements tend either to be trivial, or if important, to be matched with consummate rapidity.

Elliott (1998) presents a conceptual model of emotion-driven choice as an alternative to the information-processing model. He suggests it is possible to "emotionalize" product categories using advertising, citing instant coffee and ice cream as examples of categories that have been repositioned successfully as products with romantic/sexual connotation. Mittal (1994a) empirically confirms the presence of a negative relationship between "information processing mode" and the "affective choice mode" but finds that they are not dichotomous, as both can exist together.

Based on Damasio's findings decision-making, Ambler's Memory-Affect-Cognition (MAC) model proposes three levels of behaviour. At the first level, consumers operate only on memory, buying in a mindlessly habitual manner not dissimilar to that envisaged by Alba (2000). At the second level, choice is strongly influenced by affect, and conscious processing is inhibited. This bears a similarity to the brand conditioning model of Van Osselaer and Alba (2000), where initial brand cues resulted in product information cues being ignored. At the third level cognition is used to rationalise the decision, provided that affect is no obstacle. Ambler's model is supported by experimental research in a separate study (Ambler and Burne, 1999) where affect and cognition in combination were found to be more influential than cognition on its own. In this experiment, advertising with high affective values was better recalled and recognized in the short term, and the application of beta-blockers to suppress emotion significantly reduced the short term recall of ads. This indicates that behaviour is vulnerable to relatively weak influences, especially if they are emotive in nature, and suggests that the strength of attitude, or indeed the strength of *change* in attitude, may not always be an indicator of the effectiveness of advertising.

The role of repetition

Krugman (1984) suggested that three exposures to advertising were enough to achieve persuasion. The first is typified by curiosity, establishing what it is that is being presented. The second establishes relevance of message and allows the "sale" to take place. The third allows completion of the analytical process and initiation of a withdrawal of interest. He points out, however, that these three exposures may not necessarily be sequential, and may be interposed by many non-attentive exposures.

Krugman's three exposure theory, if valid, would seem to undermine Ehrenberg's assertion that repetition is important in reinforcement. On the other hand, Petty and Cacioppo (1986) found that amongst those with low motivation towards a market, repetition of a message from a credible source is more efficacious than the persuasiveness of the message. From this they deduce that repetition is effective in cases where processing is peripheral.

Experimental work by Nordheilm (2002) confirms this view. She finds that repetition when ads are subject to deeper processing causes a downturn (wear-out) in affective responses. But when ads were processed in a shallow fashion, affective responses are enhanced and there is no evidence of a downturn after repetition. In effect, Nordheilm is showing that consumers' natural behaviour of paying less attention to ads they have seen before is likely to greatly extend their acceptability. Indeed, it would seem perhaps that it is only ads which actively *seek* to provoke high levels of attention that are likely to annoy consumers.

Does repetition have a beneficial effect? Manchanda et al. (2006), investigating banner advertising on the internet, found that number of exposures, and the number of web pages and sites had a positive effect on the likelihood of repeat purchase. But they found that increasing the number of creative executions had a negative effect. D'Sousa and Rao (1995) exposed subjects to repeated radio advertising for a mature market in a divided attention situation. They found small but significant increases in top-of-mind brand awareness, predicted brand share, and brand choice, resulting from increased repetition. This directly supports Ehrenberg's reinforcement model, and demonstrates that advertising has a role to maintain the accessibility of brand associations in the consumer's product-brand knowledge structure.

D'Sousa's research took place in a divided attention situation. This leads to another area of importance in understanding reinforcement advertising, which is the role of attention in advertising processing.

Advertising and attention

As already mentioned, the central and peripheral routes differ according to the extent to which the attitude change that results is due to active thinking. Active thinking demands higher levels of attention than passive thinking (Eysenck and Keane, 2000), so although attention does not appear as a construct in the ELM model, the idea that attention is an important property for the central route is clearly implied. Conversely, the peripheral route uses less active thinking, so it follows that advertising processed peripherally is likely to be subjected to lower levels of attention. This is to be expected if the consumer is not involved in the product category.

Attention played an important mediating role in the earliest recorded practitioner models of advertising, AICA (Attention → Interest → Cognition → Action) and AIDA (Attention → Interest → Decision → Action). And although it featured only sporadically in psychology in the first half of the 20th century (Näätänen, 1992), attention continued to be commonplace in advertising models until the mid 1950s, with at least eight different sequential models being recorded by Barry and Howard (1990) as starting with "A" for attention. But from 1960, mentions of attention in advertising models generally ceased (Vakratsas and Ambler, 1999), possibly because of the difficulty attached to the measurement on an ongoing basis of what is effectively an unobservable construct. This conclusion is lent weight by the fact that "A" for Attention is replaced by "A" for Awareness from 1960 onwards (Barry and Howard, 1990), awareness being something which is more easily measured.[1]

The general absence of Attention from post 1960 advertising models does not signify that it has become irrelevant in a practitioner context. What appears to have happened is that high attention has been accepted as *mandatory* to advertising effectiveness. For example, Kotler et al. assert that *"the advertiser has to turn the 'big idea' into an actual ad execution that will capture the target market's attention and their interest"* (1999: 800). Likewise Rossiter and Percy state that *"advertising associations attempt to accomplish three things: attention, brand awareness, and persuasion."* (1998: 279). Even the UK's most celebrated marketing academic, the late Peter Doyle, wrote *"For an advertisement ... to be effective it must achieve first exposure and then attention"* (1994: 240).

Tellis (1998) endorses Doyle's view of the importance of attention as a necessary precursor to the achievement of communication goals. However, he points out that consumers bombarded by advertising use selective attention to simply ignore most messages that reach them. He recommends four strategies (manipulating physical stimuli, providing information, arousing emotions, and offering value) by which attention can be "won and held."

Consumers do not naturally pay much attention to advertising. A survey in 1994 found half of consumers disliked TV advertising, and one third admitted to actively avoiding paying any attention to ads (Mittal, 1994b). Clancey (1992) reveals two thirds of respondents are doing some other activity when watching television, and Soley (1994) quotes various studies which find between 20% and 40% of people leave the room when the advertising breaks are on. Even as long ago as 1989, Gilmore and Secunda quoted sources which found that between 70% and 90% of viewers "zipped" (i.e., fast forwarded) ads in previously recorded material.

So why, in the face of such indifference, do advertisers continue to strive for attention? One reason is that ad research positions attention as synonymous with effectiveness. Pieters and Wedel (2007) in Chapter 4.1, quote Biel's unequivocal statement in a review of pre-testing practice that "... *attention is clearly an element that determines the effectiveness of advertising ...*" (1993: 29) and Table 2 in the same chapter shows that the rational principles of learning (attention, appreciation, and message acceptance) still dominate today's agenda for testing advertising. But a more fundamental reason arises from the tenacious attachment to the idea that attention drives cognition, which drives affect, which drives decision-making (Lavidge and Steiner, 1962; Schachter and Singer, 1962). Although Zajonc (1980) asserted 25 years ago that affect was independent of attention it is only recently that Damasio (2000) has produced hard evidence that emotions and feelings are *always* formed pre-cognitively, and without the need to activate working memory (2000: 55).

Fitzsimmons et al. (2002) identify three types of affective response – evaluations, moods, and emotions – and claim that there is considerable evidence of non-conscious processes within each of these main categories of affective responses. Bornstein (1989) goes further, and provides evidence that affect is *most* effective when it is processed subconsciously. Using a meta-analysis of mere exposure research he demonstrates that conscious processing of affective elements weakens their potency by enabling the subject to counter-argue (i.e., rationally evaluate and contradict the validity of the source.). This implies that the less aware consumers are of affective elements in advertising, the better they will work.

Mere exposure

The importance of affect to advertising became apparent in the 1980s with the arrival of "Mere Exposure" models, a term first used by Zajonc (1968) to refer to the hypothesis that simple unreinforced exposure to a stimulus was sufficient to enhance attitudes. Kunst-Wilson and Zajonc (1980) exposed irregular polygons at time lengths below which they could be physically perceived and showed that subjects could form a preference for shapes that they had only been exposed to for less that one millisecond. This provided sound evidence for the idea of perception without awareness.

Bornstein (1992) explains the mere exposure phenomenon using a *Perceptual Fluency Model*, in which perception takes place without awareness leading to inexplicable familiarity, which in turn raises favourability. An alternative explanation for the mere exposure effect has been put forward by Janiszewski (1993), based on the idea of pre-attentive exposure. Here, perception (which is subconscious because it is non-attentive) stimulates affective responses which in turn influence choice.

What this review suggests is that, in the case of models like reinforcement, it is not so much that attitudes are not changed, but that the attitudes which are changed are deep-seated, emotional, and often hard to measure. But emotional attitudes exert a powerful influence on intuition, which questions the assertion that models like reinforcement are weak.

A LOW ATTENTION PROCESSING MODEL

So far, it has been shown that the following factors underlie advertising processing:

1. Feelings and emotions (affect) are capable of driving decision-making on their own and judgement can be influenced by manipulation of affect, without attention being paid.
2. Intuition tends to drive decisions in crowded markets where product or brand differentiation is low, and time is constrained.

3. Decision-making appears to be vulnerable to be weak influences, especially if they are based on emotions and exposed with relatively high levels of repetition.
4. Affect is processed automatically and pre-cognitive, and may be processed *more* effectively at subconscious levels, when low levels of attention are paid, and counter-argument is inhibited.

This last factor deserves a little more consideration. One argument often levelled at repetition of advertising is that the advertising will become boring and annoy the consumer. If advertising is predominantly emotive, then this allows the viewer to reduce their attention levels and minimise irritation (as in Nordheilm, 2002, discussed earlier). But such a drop in attention does not necessarily detract from the consumer's ability to process the emotive elements in the advertising effectively. This thinking is incorporated into a model which specifically addresses how advertising might work at low levels of attention.

Background to low attention

The idea that advertising can work *without* active attention being paid goes back over a century, when the psychologist Walter Dill Scott quoted a subject who claimed never to have looked at any of the ads in the tramcars she travelled in each day, yet "*knew them all by heart and … held the products they advertised in her highest esteem*" (Scott, 1903). Some 60 years later this debate was re-ignited by Krugman (1965), who asserted that advertising worked at "low involvement" and verified this using eye movement and pupil dilation as measures of interest and involvement (Krugman, 1968). Krugman found anomalies between attention levels and recall, and in 1969 he set up a further experiment in conjunction with the Neuropsychological Laboratory of New York (Krugman, 1971). In this experiment, a subject was connected to a polygraph (a machine for measuring brain activity) in order to measure the type of brain waves emitted when reading a magazine and watching TV advertising.

The relative emissions of slow and fast brain waves signified the level of interest and attention which the subject had when looking at the advertising. A predominance of fast waves indicated attentive processing; a predominance of slow waves inattentive processing. The results showed that more *slow* brain waves were emitted when watching TV advertising than when reading a press advertisement, indicating that processing of TV advertising takes place at lower attention levels than the processing of press advertising. However, due to the predominance of slow brain waves, the results also suggested that processing of TV advertising takes place at low attention per se.

MacInnis and Jaworski (1989) provide the only formal model in which differing levels of attention are considered. Their Ability-Motivation-Opportunity (AMO) model includes a processing stage in which attention interacts with processing capacity (working memory). They hypothesise that motivation focuses attention away from other tasks, utilitarian need focuses attention on problem-solving aspects of the ad, and expressive need focuses attention on symbolic or experiential values in the ad. These types of selective attention are under conscious control, but they concede that stimuli may contain properties that automatically elicit attention. Importantly, the model also includes a very low motivation state in which attention is divided, processing capacity is extremely low, and "*feature analysis*" leads to "*mood-generating affect.*" They see this as an influence of minor importance, stating that because attention is devoted primarily to the secondary task, brand or ad attitudes are unlikely to be formed, and those attitudes that are formed will be weak and confused because consumers do not pay enough attention to the ad to distinguish the ad from the brand.

Low attention is also alluded to in Meyers-Levy and Malaviya's Integrative Framework of Persuasion Theories (1999). They consider three levels of processing, with the first two – systematic and heuristic – sharing similar properties to central and peripheral processing in the ELM. They also add a third processing strategy – experiential processing – in which the amount of cognitive resources that people are willing or able to devote to processing is so meagre that only the most fleeting and scant message processing occurs. Experiential processing plays little, if any role within the information processing context of their model, but they do admit that "*a particularly promising approach which might be taken to advance our understanding of persuasion that occurs through an experiential processing strategy is to follow up on clues offered in the implicit memory literature*" (1999: 55). This is done in the next section.

The psychology of low attention processing

Although attention can be clearly defined, it is not a popular construct in psychology. Psychologists prefer to use the construct of consciousness, although the ongoing debate about what exactly consciousness is indicates that it may be even harder to define than attention. But in simple terms if something is processed at low attention or no attention it is generally categorised as being processed semi-consciously or subconsciously (Eysenck and Keane, 2000).

It is important to note that subconscious is *not* subliminal. The term subliminal applies to stimuli that operates "*below the threshold of sensation or consciousness*" (OCED, 1996: 1030). *Subliminal* advertising refers therefore to things we cannot consciously perceive, for example, frames in film exposed for less than about 1/10th of a second. In contrast, sub*conscious* processing takes place when the advertising is capable of being seen or heard but no active attention is paid to it. Likewise, semiconscious processing takes place when the advertising is capable of being seen or heard but is processed with a low or divided level of attention. Advertising which operates subliminally has been shown by Moore (1982) to be weak at best and generally ineffective, a conclusion supported by a meta-analysis of 23 studies by Trappey (1996) which showed "... *that the effect of subliminal marketing stimuli on influencing* *consumers' choice behaviour or selection process is negligible"* (1996: 528).

Subconscious processing, on the other hand, *has* been shown to influence buying decisions. Shapiro et al. (1997) investigated the effect of low attention exposure of advertising on product consideration, using a computer-controlled magazine in which test material was placed in a column to one side whilst attention was constrained on the centre columns via the performance of two tasks. Their conclusion was that advertising *"has the potential to affect future buying decisions even when subjects … do not process the ad attentively and … do not recollect ever having seen the ad"* (1997: 102).

Implicit learning

Non-attentive learning is defined as Implicit Learning, a fully automatic process (Eysenck and Keane, 2000) which stores information in implicit memory (Berry and Dienes, 1991). The independence of implicit memory from attention has been confirmed by Jacoby et al. (1993) using word fragment completion tests, which are known to reference implicit memory. Their tests were run in both full attention and divided attention environments and found that *"attention at the time of learning may be of crucial importance to subsequent conscious recollection, but is irrelevant to implicit memory"* (Eysenck and Keane, 2000: 190).

A number of experiments carried out in the 1970s and 1980s have established that implicit memory differs from explicit memory in three further ways:

1. Implicit memory is more durable than explicit memory. (Allen and Reber, 1980; Tulving et al., 1982).
2. Implicit memory is more capacious than explicit memory (Standing, 1973).
3. Implicit memory cannot operate cognitively, i.e., analyse and interpret information and develop and store new opinions from it (Berry and Dienes, 1991).

Hunt et al. (1991) have demonstrated the durability of implicit memory in an advertising context using recall and recognition as dependent measures in immediate and delayed time conditions. If recall is facilitated by explicit memory and recognition is facilitated by implicit memory, as is generally posited, then it is to be expected that the former will decay in the delayed time experiment and the latter will not. This is exactly what was seen in the results. Correct recall after two days was more than half the immediate recall, but recognition levels on average hardly changed.

The presence of non-attentive conceptual processing in advertising has also been confirmed by Shapiro (1999). He exposed artificially created advertisements for made-up brands in a variety of permutations (product alone, product + relevant and irrel-evant contextual elements, etc.) in conditions designed to minimize attentive fixation. His findings confirmed that advertising processed incidentally (i.e., implicitly) is able to connect with semantic memory and influence attitudes towards brands.

This indicates that advertising which is capable of being perceived can be processed without active attention and can influence brand attitudes and choice. Alba (2000) claims this sort of inattentive perception is a manifes-tation of *"mindlessness"* by consumers. Bargh (2002), however, identifies such behaviour not as mindless, but as a result of the *"real, noisy, busy world"* where *"deliberate conscious choice processes"* are rejected in favour of automatic choice.

Watzlawick et al. (1967) identify two distinct levels for communication: a content level (communication) and a relationship level (meta-communication). These can be analogized to digital and analogue messages, where the digital "content" communication is rational, unequivocal, recognisable, and easily analysed and classified. In contrast, the analogue "relationship" meta-communication is emotional, subtle, disguised, hard to classify, and sometimes even difficult to identify. But it is this "analogue" relationship-building aspect of communication that is most effective at changing attitudes. Perhaps even more important is that the digital content of a communication fades and vanishes overtime, whereas the subtle patterns evoked by the analogue relationship-building meta-communication endure. This is because the patterns in meta-communication are processed and learned by us automatically, regardless of how much attention we pay. Thus the content communication of the advertising the message may fade, but the relationship forged by the emotional meta-communication – the creativity – endures, even when processed subconsciously.

The low attention processing model

The low attention processing model (Heath, 2000, 2001; Heath and Hyder, 2005; Heath and Nairn, 2005) uses as its starting point the ease with which brands nowadays match each other's performance. This encourages consumers in a time-poor environment to reject considered choice in favour of intuition. This in turn inhibits the desire to seek out information about brands, and minimises the need for consumers to pay attention to advertising. However, as discussed earlier, brand information can be "acquired" at low and even zero attention levels, using passive (semi-automatic low-attention) learning and implicit (fully automatic attention-independent) learning. Processing like this may not establish strong rational brand performance benefits in the consumer's mind, but rather build and reinforce associations over time, with these associations becoming linked to the brand by passive learning. These associations can be extraordinarily enduring. They may be intangible links to emotions, or tangible associations which are *"emotionally competent"* (Damasio, 2003: 91). Both are capable of exerting a powerful influence on decision-making, especially when it is based on intuition more than consideration. A diagram illustrating how this model works is shown in Figure 2.2.1.

One important aspect of the low attention processing model is that passive and implicit learning are semi and fully automatic mental processes, operating every time an ad is

seen or heard. Advertising elements which exploit low attention processing will work better when processed several times at low attention than if processed once or twice at high attention. This offers an explanation for the apparent efficacy of advertising repetition, identified both by Ehrenberg and Petty and Cacioppo. Furthermore, emotive brand associations reinforced by this sort of repetition may remain in memory long after the ad has been forgotten, which accords with the enduring nature of meta-communication as identified by Watzlawick et al.

An example of low attention processing

Because attention facilitates recall (Gardner and Parkin, 1990) it is difficult to isolate and identify the effect of elements processed at *low* attention. People simply tend not to recall them very well. A good example is music, which can initiate a response no matter how little attention is paid to it.

Music sometimes operates simply as a brand recognition device, for example, the Intel jingle. However, we can speculate that the five notes of the Intel jingle are not very likely to trigger much of an emotional response. In contrast, in the late 1980s British Airways introduced a duet from Delibes' opera Lakmé into their advertising. I have found that when the sound track from one of their TV advertisements is played to people, the great majority admit that they visualise a comfortable relaxing environment, and feel they are being well looked after. In other words, the music triggers an emotional response which influences their feelings towards BA. However, when they are played the TV ad in full, with the visuals and sound track, everyone confesses that the visuals take their full attention, and they pay no attention at all to the music. But, if Bornstein (1989) is correct, the music influences their feelings towards British Airways even more, because without attention they cannot counter-argue against it.

This music ran continuously in British Airways advertising until 2006. According to two major IPA Advertising Effectiveness

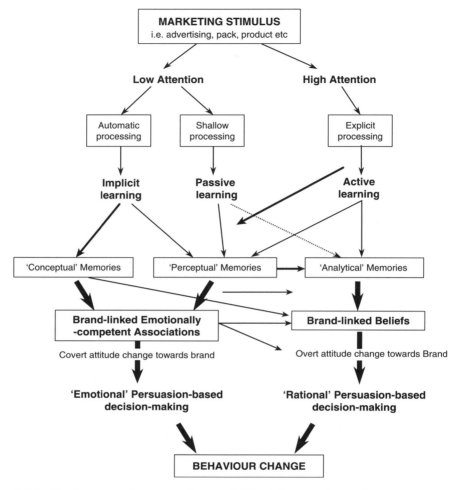

Figure 2.2.1   The low attention processing model (based on Heath, 2001)

Awards (MacGill and Gnoddle, 1995; Day et al., 2005), British Airways advertising has been shown to be a major contributor to their business success. Furthermore, British Airways is the *only* big national carrier in the world which has traded successfully at a profit throughout the onslaught of cut-price air travel. Of course, it has never been possible to show how much the music in their advertising has contributed to this success: it is difficult enough just putting into words the way the music affects us, let alone using these words to frame attitudes, and showing a demonstrable change in those attitudes.

DIRECTIONS FOR FUTURE RESEARCH

This chapter has presented some new ideas in decision-making and advertising processing, and reviewed some alternative models of advertising. Work has been cited which validates reinforcement (Braun, 2004), and implicit memory and attention (Shapiro et al., 1997, 1999). But research into the role of and interaction between emotions and attention remains mostly the province of psychology, and studies are rare even there.

Partly this arises from the continuing dominance of message communication and recall in advertising evaluation. In 1965 Krugman bemoaned the research industry's dependence on the familiar model that assumes high involvement, and as is clear from later chapters, this low involvement/attention model remains a low priority for the advertising industry. Pieters and Wedel in Chapter 4.1 describe many highly sophisticated measurement techniques which allow for the measurement of attention (eye movements, visual attention through fixation speed), affective responses (facial expression coding), and arousal (skin conductivity, cardiovascular response, pupil dilation etc.) Further techniques which scan brain activity itself, such as FMRi scanning, are rapidly being piloted and investigated (Alps, 2005). Yet none of these techniques attempt to operationalize the relaxed low attention conditions in which advertising is nearly always processed by consumers. Nor have any attempts been made to replicate the unpremeditated repeat processing of ads which typify real-life media consumption. Surely these should be areas of priority for those whose task it is to monitor advertising?

Another aspect of the problem is that constructs like attention are hard to measure without introducing high levels of abstraction from reality. Not only do attention levels vary with extraordinary rapidity (James, 1890), but people do not actively monitor what they are paying attention to at any particular moment (Dennett, 1993). Furthermore, if subjects are asked to attempt to monitor their attention levels then their behaviour is invariably affected, and attention generally increases. All this precludes the simplest research methodology, namely post-hoc investigation. As a result, most of the research that has been carried out into attention has used experimental approaches in which attention levels are externally manipulated, thus resulting in high levels of abstraction from reality.

Much work has been done to try to understand emotion in advertising (see Chapter 2.4 and Chapter 2.5). One interesting new development is the CEP™Test, a research technique operated by OTX (Online Testing Exchange) of Los Angeles. This test measures the strength of emotion in advertising compared with the strength of cognition. (Heath et al., 2006) Work on validating the relationship between these two constructs and brand favourability shows that it is emotive strength of advertising which tends to drive favourability towards the brand, and the cognitive strength has little if any influence. This suggests that brand relationships are driven not by the content of advertising, but by the *way* in which the message is delivered. In other words, Watzlawick's findings from interpersonal behaviour research, that it is the creative meta-communication not the message that influences relationships, seems to apply equally to the world of brands and advertising. This opens up an important new area of research into the relationship between emotion and advertising effectiveness.

Another fruitful area of research is the effect of fast-forwarding recorded TV programmes. Goode and Dobbinson (2006) have pioneered research into advertising exposed in fast-forward mode, and shown that elements can still be processed and extracted. Furthermore, Motluk (2006) shows that advertising exposed subliminally can, under certain circumstances, be effective. These studies suggest that our perceptive powers are better than is generally supposed, and should be further researched.

A further development which needs to be researched is the effect of the increasingly popular practice of placing branded products in TV programmes and films. Such products will be far less likely to be attended to when compared to products in advertising, and will effectively be exposed at low attention levels (Scott and Craig-Lees, 2005). Will the effect of this be less than, the same as, or perhaps more than the effect of a traditional advertisement?

SUMMARY

The main findings of this chapter are as follows:

1. The idea that advertising works by reinforcement was advanced both by Krugman and

Ehrenberg, and has much in common with the peripheral persuasion route of the Elaboration Likelihood Model. They suggest that message-based persuasion leading to attitude change is by no means the only way in which advertising works. Indeed, reinforcement advertising works because decision-making is not usually a rational process.

2. The Low Attention Processing Model suggests that ads can work through implicit learning which can have longer lasting effects than conscious rational attention to the information provided by advertising. It is consistent with previous work showing that emotional advertising may well be more effective than that which simply (and unemotionally) presents rational claims. This is especially likely to be the case when such advertising is exposed repeatedly.

3. This area remains poorly researched, perhaps because the industry finds it hard to accept that advertising can work at low levels of attention. Most advertising pre-testing still takes place in high attention situations, and gives priority to message communication and recall.

NOTES

1 However, as Wiles and Cornwell (1990) point out, this approach tends to amplify the importance of cognition and attention and minimize the role of affect: *"Historically, advertising research primarily concentrated on the thinking, or cognitive response to advertising, rather than the affective response"* (1990: 241).

REFERENCES

Alba, J.W. (2000), "Dimensions Of Consumer Expertise ... Or Lack Thereof," *Advances in Consumer Research*, 27 (1), 1–9.

Alps, T. (2005), "Appliance Of Neuroscience Is A Great Leap Forward," *Guardian Newspaper*, 28th (November), Media Section: 10.

Allen, R. and A.S. Reber (1980), "Very Long Term Memory For Tacit Knowledge," *Cognition*, 8, 175–85, cited in Berry and Dienes (1991).

Ambler, T. and T. Burne (1999), "The Impact Of Affect On Memory Of Advertising," *Journal of Advertising Research*, 39 (2), 25–34.

Ambler, T. (2000), "Persuasion, Pride, And Prejudice: How Ads Work," *International Journal of Advertising*, 19 (3), 299–315.

Bargh, J.A. (2002), "Losing Consciousness: Automatic Influences on Consumer Judgement, Behaviour, and Motivation," *Journal of Consumer Research*, 29 (September), 280–4.

Barnard, N. and A.S.C. Ehrenberg (1997), "Advertising: Strongly Persuasive or Nudging?" *Journal of Advertising Research*, 37 (1).

Barry, T.E. and D.J. Howard (1990), "A Review And Critique Of The Hierarchy Of Effects In Advertising," *International Journal of Advertising*, 9 (2).

Berry, D. and Z. Dienes (1991), "The Relationship Between Implicit Memory And Implicit Learning," *British Journal of Psychology*, 82 (3).

Biel, A.L. (1993), "Ad Research in the US; Hurdle or Help? A Brief Review of the State of the Art," *AdMap*, 329 (May), 27–9.

Bornstein, R.F. (1989), "Exposure and Affect: Overview and Meta-Analysis of Research," *Psychological Bulletin*, 1968–1987, 106 (2), 265–89.

Bornstein, R.F.(1992), "Subliminal Mere Exposure Effects," in *Perception Without Awareness: Cognitive, Clinical, And Social Perspectives*," eds. R.F. Bornstein and T.S. Pittman, Guilford, NY. 191–210.

Braun, K.A. (1999), "Postexperience Advertising Effects On Consumer Memory," *Journal of Consumer Research*, 25 (4), 319–34.

Clancey, M. (1994), "The Television Audience Examined," *Journal of Advertising Research*, 34 (4), 76–86.

Damasio, A.R. (1994), *Descartes' Error*, New York: G.P. Putnam's Sons.

Damasio, A.R. (2000), *The Feeling of What Happens*, London: Heinemann.

Damasio, A.R. (2003), *Looking for Spinosa*, London: Heinemann.

Day, R., R. Storey and A. Edwards (2005), "Climbing Above the Turbulence – How British Airways Countered The Budget Airline Threat," in *Advertising Works 13.* ed. A. Hoad, Henley-on-Thames, UK: Admap Publications.

Dennett, D. (1993), *Consciousness Explained*, London: Penguin.

Dickson, P.R. and A.G. Sawyer (1990), "The Price Knowledge and Search of Supermarket Shoppers," *Journal of Marketing*, 54, 42–53.

Doyle, P. (1994), *Marketing Management and Strategy*, Hemel Hempstead, Herts, UK: Prentice-Hall.

D'Sousa, G. (1995), "Can Repeating An Advertisement More Frequently Than The Competition Affect Brand Preference In A Mature Market? *Journal of Marketing*, 59 (2), 32–42.

Ehrenberg, A.S.C. (1974), "Repetitive Advertising and the Consumer," *Journal of Advertising Research*, 14 (2), (April), 25–34.

Elliott, R. (1998), "A Model of Emotion-Driven Choice," *Journal of Marketing Management,* 14, 95–108.

Eysenck, M.W. and M.T. Keane (2000), *Cognitive Psychology,* 4th ed., Hove, UK: Psychology Press Ltd.

Fitzsimons, G.J., J.W. Hitchinson, P. Williams, J.W. Alba, T.L. Chartrand, J. Huber, F.R. Kardes, G. Menon, P. Raghubir, J.E. Russo, B. Shiv and N.T. Tavassoli (2002), "Non-Conscious Influences On Consumer Choice," *Marketing Letters* 13.3, 269–79.

Gardiner, J.M. and A.J. Parkin (1990), "Attention and Recollective Experience in Recognition," *Memory and Cognition,* 18, 579–83.

Gilmore, R.F. and E. Secunda (1993), "Zipped TV Commercials Boost Prior Learning." *Journal of Advertising Research,* 33 (6), 28–38.

Goode, A. and J. Dobinson (2006), "Why Ads Work on Fast Forward and the Implication for Assessing TV Campaigns," *Proceedings of the Market Research Society Conference,* London, (March), Paper 15.

Heath, R.G. (1993), "Reassuringly Expensive – A Case History Of The Stella Artois Press Campaign," in *Advertising Works 7* ed. C. Baker, Henley-on-Thames, UK: NTC Publications.

Heath, R.G. (2000), "Low Involvement Processing- A New Model Of Brands And Advertising," *International Journal of Advertising,* 19 (3), 287–98.

Heath, R.G. (2001), *The Hidden Power of Advertising,* Admap Monograph No. 7, World Advertising Research Centre, Henley-on-Thames, Great Britain.

Heath, R.G. and P. Hyder (2005), "Measuring The Hidden Power Of Emotive Advertising," *International Journal of the Market Research Society,* 47 (5), 467–86.

Heath, R.G. and A.C. Nairn (2005), "Measuring Emotive Advertising – Implications Of Low Attention Processing On Recall" *Journal of Advertising Research,* 45 (2) 269–81.

Heath, R.G., D. Brandt and A.C. Nairn (2006), "Brand Relationships – Strengthened by Emotion, Weakened by Attention," *Journal of Advertising Research,* 46 (4), 410–19.

Hunt, J.M., J.B. Kernan and E.H. Bonfield (1991), "Memory Structure In The Processing Of Advertising Messages: How Is Unusual Information Represented? *The Journal of Psychology,* 126 (4), 343–56.

Jacoby, L.L., J.P. Toth and A.P. Yonelinas (1993), "Separating Conscious And Unconscious Influences Of Memory: Measuring Recollection," *Journal of Experimental Psychology,* General 122, 139–54.

James, W. (1890), *Principles of Psychology,* Dover, New York.

Janisewski, C (1993), "Pre-Attentive Mere Exposure Effects," *Journal of Consumer Research,* 20, (December) 376–92.

Jones, J.P. (1990), "Advertising: Strong Force or Weak Force? Two Views an Ocean Apart," *International Journal of Advertising,* 9 (3), 233–46.

Kotler, P., G. Armstrong, J. Saunders and V. Wong (1999), "*Principles of Marketing,*" 2nd European ed., Europe: Prentice Hall.

Kotler, P. (1991), *Marketing Management,* Englewood Cliffs, New Jersey, USA: Prentice-Hall.

Krugman, H.E. (1965), "The Impact Of Television Advertising: Learning Without Involvement" *Public Opinion Quarterly* 29 (Fall), 349–56.

Krugman, H.E. (1968), "Processes Underlying Exposure To Advertising," *American Psychologist,* (April), 245–53.

Krugman, H.E. (1971), "Brain Wave Measurement Of Media Involvement" *Journal of Advertising Research,* (February), 3–9.

Krugman, H.E. (1984), "Why Three Exposures May Be Enough," *Journal of Advertising Research,* 15–18.

Kunst-Wilson, W.R. and R.B. Zajonc (1980), "Affective Discrimination Of Stimuli That Cannot Be Recognised," *Journal of Experimental Psychology: Learning, Memory, and Cognition,* 13, 646–8.

Lavidge, R.J. and G.A. Steiner (1961), "A Model for Predictive Measurements of Advertising Effectiveness," *Journal of Marketing,* 25 (4), 59–62.

MacGill, F. and K. Gnoddle (1995), "BA – 10 Years Of The World's Favourite Advertising, But How Much Did It Have To Do With The World's Most Profitable Airline?" in *Advertising Works 8.* ed. C. Baker, Henley-on-Thames, UK: Admap Publications.

MacInnis, D.J. and B.J. Jaworski (1989), "Information Processing From Advertisements: Towards An Integrative Framework," *Journal of Marketing,* 53, 1–23.

Manchanda, P., J.P. Dubé, K.Y. Goh and P.K. Chintagunta (2006), "The Effect of Banner Advertising on Internet Purchasing," *Journal of Marketing Research,* 43 (1), 98–108.

McDonald, C.D.P. (2000), *Tracking Advertising and Monitoring Brands,* World Advertising Research Centre, Henley-on-Thames, Great Britain: Admap Monograph No. 6.

Meyers Levy, J. and P. Malaviya (1999), "Consumers' Processing of Persuasive Advertisements: An Integrative Framework of Persuasion Theories," *Journal of Marketing,* 63 (special issue), 45–60.

Mick, D.G., S.M. Broniarczyk and J. Haidt (2004), "Choose, Choose, Choose, Choose, Choose, Choose, Choose: Emerging And Prospective Research On The Deleterious Effect Of Living In Consumer Hyperchoice," *Journal of Business Ethics,* 52, 207–11.

Mittal, B. (1994a), "A Study of the Concept of Affective Choice Mode for Consumer Decisions," *Advances in Consumer Research*, 21 (1), 256–63.

Mittal, B. (1994b), "Public Assessment of TV Advertising: Faint and Harsh Criticism," *Journal of Advertising Research*, 34 (1), 35–53.

Moore, T.E. (1982), "Subliminal Advertising: What You See Is What You Get," *Journal of Marketing*, 46, 38–47.

Motluk, A. (2006), "The Ads You Miss Will Still Get You," *New Scientist,* 29th (April) 16.

Näätänen, R. (1992), *Attention and Brain Function*, Hillsdale, N.J.: Lawrence Erlbaum Associates.

Nordheilm, C.L. (2002), "The Influence of Level of Processing on Advertising Repetition Effects," *Journal of Consumer Research,* 29 (3), 371–82.

Petty, R.E., J.T. Cacioppo, and D. Schumann (1983), "Central and Peripheral Routes to Advertising Effectiveness: The Moderating Role of Involvement," *Journal of Consumer Research,* 10 (September), 135–46.

Petty, R.E. and J.T. Cacioppo (1986), *"Communication and Persuasion: Central and Peripheral Routes to Attitude Change,"* Springer, New York.

Petty, R.E. and J.T. Cacioppo, (1996), *Attitudes and Persuasion: Classic and Contemporary Approaches*, Boulder, Colorado: Westview Press.

Pieters, Rik and Michel Wedel (2007), "Pretesting: Before the Rubber Hits the Road," in *The SAGE Handbook of Advertising,* eds. Gerard J. Tellis and Tim Ambler, London: Sage Publications.

Robson, C. (2002), *Real World Research, a Resource for Social Scientists and Practitioners-Researchers,* Blackwell, 2nd ed.

Rossiter, J. and L. Percy, (1998), *Advertising, Communications, and Promotion Management,* International Editions, Singapore: McGraw Hill.

Rucker, Derek D., Richard E. Petty and Joseph R. Priester (2007), "Understanding Advertising Effectiveness From A Psychological Perspective: The Importance of Attitudes and Attitude Strength," in *The SAGE Handbook of Advertising,* eds. Gerard J. Tellis and Tim Ambler, London: Sage Publications.

Schachter, S. and J.E. Singer (1962), "Cognitive, Social, And Physiological Determinants Of Emotional State" *PsychologicalReview*, 69, 379–99.

Scott, W.D. (1903), *The Theory of Advertising: A Simple Exposition On The Principles Of Psychology In Their Relation To Successful Advertising,* Boston: Small, Maynard and Co.

Scott, J. and M. Craig-Lees (2005), *"Product Placement: Developing Concepts, Constructs and Measures" North American Conference for the Association of Consumer Research 2005, Texas, USA.*

Shapiro, S., D.J. MacInnis, and S.E. Heckler (1997), "The Effects Of Incidental Ad Exposure On The Formation Of Consideration Sets" *Journal of Consumer Research,* 24, 94–104.

Shapiro, S. (1999), "When An Ad's Influence Is Beyond Our Conscious Control: Perceptual And Conceptual Fluency Effects Caused By Incidental Ad Exposure" *Journal of Consumer Research,* 26, 16–36.

Shiv, B. and A. Fedorikhan (1999), "Heart and Mind in Conflict: The Interplay of Affect and Cognition in Consumer Decision Making," *Journal of Consumer Research,* 26 (3), 278–92.

Soley, L.C. (1984), "Factors Affecting Television Attentiveness: A Research Note," *Current Issues and Research in Advertising,* 7 (1), 141–8.

Standing, L. (1973), "Learning 10,000 Pictures," *Quarterly Journal of Experimental Psychology: Learning, Memory, and Cognition,* 19, 582–602.

Stewart, D.W., J. Morris and A. Grover (2007), "Emotions in Advertising," in *The SAGE Handbook of Advertising,* eds. Gerard J. Tellis and Tim Ambler, London: Sage Publications.

Strong, E.K. (1925), "Theories of Selling," *Journal of Applied Psychology,* 9 (February), 75–86.

Tellis, G.J. (1998), *Advertising and Sales promotion Strategy,* Massachusetts, USA: Addison-Wesley.

Trappey, C. (1996), "A Meta-Analysis of Consumer Choice," *Psychology and Marketing,* 13, 517–30.

Vakratsas, D. and T. Ambler (1999), "How Advertising Works: What Do We Really Know?" *Journal of Marketing,* 63, 26–43.

Van Osselaer, S.M.J. and J.W. Alba (2000), "Consumer Learning and Brand Equity," *Journal of Consumer Research,* 27, 1–16.

Watzlawick, P., J.B. Bavelas, and D.D. Jackson (1967), *Pragmatics of Human Communication,* New York: Norton and Co. Inc.

Wiles, J.A. and T.B. Cornwell (1990), "A Review Of Methods Utilized In Measuring Affect, Feelings, And Emotion In Advertising," *Current Issues In Research In Advertising,* 13 (2), 241–74.

Zaltman, G. and D. MacCaba (2007), "Metaphor in Advertising," in *The SAGE Handbook of Advertising,* eds. G.J. Tellis and T. Ambler, London: Sage Publications.

Zajonc, R.B. (1968), "Attitudinal Effects of Mere Exposure," *Journal of Personality and Social Psychology,* Monograph 9.2, part two: 1–27.

Zajonc, R.B. (1980), "Feeling and Thinking: Preferences Need No Inferences," *American Psychologist,* 35, 151–75.

Zajonc, R.B. and H. Markus (1982), "Affective and Cognitive Factors in Preferences," *Journal of Consumer Research,* 9 (September), 123–31.

The Role of Consumer Memory in Advertising

Nicole Votolato Montgomery and
H. Rao Unnava

Since most advertising occurs in a non-purchase context (e.g., watching a television programme, reading a bill board while driving home), the effect of advertising on purchase behaviour should mostly occur through a consumer's memory for the information presented in the advertisement. Consumer researchers have long recognized the critical role played by memory in mediating advertising effects on consumption (e.g., Lavidge and Steiner, 1961), and most information-processing models explicitly recognize the role of encoding and retrieval of brand information in affecting purchase behaviour (e.g., Consumer Information Processing Model, Shimp, 2007). Therefore, memory for an advertisement has important implications for persuasion (see Chapter 2.1) and may be influenced by certain advertisement and consumer characteristics that are discussed at length in other chapters of this book.

In addition to traditional areas of research in memory, more recent investigations have provided greater understanding in areas such as categorization (e.g., Rajagopal and Burnkrant, 2006) and interference (e.g.,

Kumar and Krishnan, 2004). Newer areas such as preconscious processing of advertisements (e.g., Shapiro, 1999) have also received substantial attention. Finally, current research has introduced techniques in cognitive neuroscience to better understand where neural activity occurs in response to advertisements (e.g., Ambler et al., 2000).

In this chapter, we provide marketers with a comprehensive account of the role of memory in advertising by integrating new findings in this area with long-standing research. The first section focuses on the traditional two-store model of memory and examines differences between short-term memory and long-term memory. Next, we look into the factors that affect the encoding of advertising information with a focus on attention, preconscious processing, and elaboration. Thirdly, we explore the storage and organization of information in memory. After that, we discuss the retrieval of advertising information. Several issues are explored in this section including retrieval of information from short-term memory and long-term memory, repetition and spacing effects, interference, the role of cues in retrieval, affect, and reconstructive memory. After discussing cognitive neuroscience underlying memory for advertisements, the last section provides a summary.

LONG-TERM MEMORY VERSUS SHORT-TERM MEMORY

Traditional models of memory have proposed that memory consists of two separate storage systems: short-term memory (STM) and long-term memory (LTM) (Atkinson and Shiffrin, 1968; Waugh and Norman, 1965; Craik and Lockhart, 1972; Raaijmakers and Shiffrin, 1981). LTM is a relatively permanent memory storage system. Once information has been transferred to this storage system, then it may be retrieved at any time if the appropriate retrieval cue is used to access the information from memory. Thus, any errors in accessing information stored in LTM are the result of retrieval error, not encoding error. That is, respondents that are having difficulty remembering a piece of information that is stored in LTM are simply not using the correct accessibility cue; the information is not lost from memory. STM is only a temporary storage system. Information stored in STM is accessible because this information is activated through rehearsal. In the absence of rehearsal, the information will be lost from memory through a process of decay (Nairne, 2002). Thus, any errors in recalling information stored in STM may be attributed to the information no longer being in that storage system as a result of the passage of time.

While the standard model of memory asserts that STM accessibility arises from keeping information activated via rehearsal, a more recent model of memory (i.e., modern model) has proposed that STM may be cue-driven like LTM, with different retrieval cues in effect for each memory store (Nairne, 2002). Thus, the modern model of memory asserts that "people forget with an increasing delay because retrieval cues change with time – not because of spontaneous decay," (p. 74). While there is evidence that STM

may remain constant or even improve after a delay in some cases (e.g., Nairne, 2002; Healy and McNamara, 1996), providing support against the traditional model of memory, there is not enough evidence for the modern model of memory to preclude that rehearsal and decay will play a role in STM (Healy and McNamara, 1996). Therefore, in this chapter we assume that purchase decisions are typically impacted more by advertising information that is stored in LTM because much advertising is temporally removed from the purchase situation. The manner in which advertising information is encoded and later retrieve from LTM will be discussed later in the chapter.

ENCODING OF ADVERTISING INFORMATION

Attention

In addition, to classifying consumer memory into short-term or working memory and long-term memory, researchers have invoked the concept of sensory memory which is charged with the task of forming the interface between a human brain and the environment in which the being operates. The rich array of stimuli that occur in various mediums (i.e., visual, auditory, tactile, olfactory, and taste) are continuously sampled by the five senses, and processed further if more attention is warranted. Thus, one of the critical factors that determines whether advertising information is afforded further processing upon impinging a consumer's senses is the attention that the consumer decides to pay to the advertisement.

The pivotal role played by consumer attention in determining advertising effects has been captured in models of advertising effects, e.g., Greenwald and Leavitt (1984) who develop a framework to outline four major levels of audience involvement and their implications for advertising. From lowest to highest, the four proposed levels are: pre-attention, focal attention, comprehension, and elaboration. At the pre-attentional level, little capacity is used, and only feature representations are sensed and processed. At the focal attention level, moderate capacity levels are required, and category representations are formed (i.e., object, word, or name) using sensory content of the message. At the comprehension level, a propositional representation of the message is formed by using a syntactic analysis. Finally, the elaboration level requires the most capacity to link the propositional codes to existing conceptual knowledge. As the levels of audience involvement increase, the framework presumes that more attentional capacity to the message source is required, and the effects of processing (i.e., cognitive and attitudinal) are more durable. The authors assume serial processing, such that processing occurs at a higher level only after consumers have processed at the levels below that level. A principle of higher-level dominance is also assumed, suggesting that higher level processing effects are dominant to lower level processing effects. In general, consumer researchers accept the notion that for advertising to achieve its intended objectives, a consumer has to pay attention to the information being presented in the ad. Thus, methods like eye-tracking are being utilized to measure consumers' attention to advertisements (see Chapter 4.1). An exception to this basic premise is the recent research on unconscious processing effects (e.g., Janiszewski, 1990; Shapiro, 1999), which will be discussed later in the chapter.

Thus, for information that is presented in the ad to be encoded into memory, a consumer has to pay attention to the information. Factors that affect attention are numerous, and have been studied to a great depth. In general, attention literature proposes that when something is distinctive, it receives greater attention (e.g., Wallace, 1965). For example, bold colours, loud noises, unique smells and such are expected to draw attention because they stand out and pique consumer curiosity. Similarly, something that is unexpected receives greater attention (e.g., Houston et al., 1987). Heckler and Childers (1992) define expectancy as "the degree

to which an item or piece of information falls into some predetermined pattern or structure evoked by the theme," (p. 477). The authors manipulated expectancy in the pictorial versus the verbal components of a set of advertisements, and they found that pictorial information was better recalled and recognized if it was unexpected versus expected. This issue is important because it shows that consumers carry with them some expectations when they encounter any situation. These expectations are based on prior experiences, knowledge, and goals of the consumer (e.g., Huffman and Houston, 1993). For example, Hunt et al. (1992) showed that when an advertising message contained information incongruent with a person's general knowledge structure about a domain (i.e., schema), processing of the entire message was enhanced. Thus, unexpected information not only enhances the memorability of the schema-incongruent information, but to some degree it also enhances recall of the schema-congruent information contained in the message, relative to a message that contains only schema-congruent information. Thus, consumer attention can be gained either through stimulus variables, or by violating their expectations of the information (see Chapter 2.5 for a more detailed treatise on information processing).

Preconscious processing

Interestingly, some recent research has shown that overt attention to information is not a necessary precondition for advertising to affect consumer behavior. Janiszewski (1990) showed that information that occurs outside of normal focal vision gets processed at a preconscious level and has reliable effects on brand choice. Shapiro (1999) showed that preconscious processing of advertisements leads to processing fluency affects (i.e., facilitating decisions when the same stimuli reappear in the decision-making context) and impacts consideration set formation. Consistent with perceptual fluency, the author found that under incidental ad exposure an ad that depicts a product with perceptual features (i.e., novel shape) that match the shape of a product under consideration, will increase the likelihood that the product under consideration will be included in the consideration set. Consistent with the notion of conceptual fluency, the author found that under incidental ad exposure an ad that depicts a product in a given context facilitates the activation of the product schema in memory, resulting in an increased likelihood that the product under consideration will be included in the consideration set, regardless of whether the perceptual features of the product under consideration match the perceptual features of the advertised product. More recently, Lee and Labroo (2004) also showed that preconscious stimuli are registered in memory and lead to processing fluency effects. Specifically, they found that conceptual fluency, resulting from an ad showing a product in a predictive context (i.e., an ad for beer with a picture showing consumers drinking beer in a bar) or an ad showing a presentation of a related construct (i.e., an ad for mayonnaise when the target product is ketchup), leads to enhanced evaluations of a target brand. Thus, while attention plays a major role in long-term encoding and storage of advertising information, one cannot assume that information that is not overtly attended to has no effect on consumer decision-making (see Chapter 2.2 for more information on low-attention learning).

Elaboration

A second important variable that affects the type of encoding of a stimulus is the quality and quantity of processing that the stimulus receives (e.g., Craik and Lockhart, 1972). When consumers pay superficial attention to an advertisement, they may form quick opinions of the advertised product. Neither these quick impressions nor the advertising information are remembered for very long (e.g., Haugtvedt et al., 1994). In order for advertising information to be transferred to long-term memory to be retained for use later, consumers will have to elaborate on the information, making links between the

advertising information and other related concepts that are stored in memory. The more such links are established, the greater is the likelihood that the information will be remembered (e.g., Anderson and Reder, 1979; Meyers-Levy, 1989).

Advertisers have recognized the positive effects of elaboration on learning of information and use several techniques to enhance audience elaboration of advertisements (see Chapter 2.1 for more information on the effects of elaboration). Some of the techniques that have been shown to affect elaboration include the choice of programming and media (e.g., Singh and Cole, 1993), careful targeting of audiences to reach those that have intrinsic interest in the product category (e.g., Brinol et al., 2004), and employing copy writing techniques that enhance elaboration (e.g., self-referencing – Burnkrant and Unnava, 1995; imagery – MacInnis and Price, 1987; use of pictures – Childers and Houston, 1984). For example, Childers et al. (1986) showed that when consumers are presented with ads that contain a pictorial and a verbal component, each with unique information, they are able to recall and recognize more information conveyed in the picture than information conveyed in the verbal copy due to the enhanced elaboration of this component.

The effects of elaboration go beyond superior memory, as discussed in Chapter 2.1. When advertising information undergoes greater elaboration, the attitudes that are formed based on that information are more memorable, more accessible, and held with greater confidence. Such "strength" in the attitude is positively related to how predictive it is of subsequent behaviour.

STORAGE OF ADVERTISING INFORMATION

What happens to the information that consumers glean from an advertisement? While consumers may store information about the advertisement and the brand information contained within the advertisement, we focus on memory for brand information in this section given its relative importance to marketers. Memory researchers are generally comfortable with the idea that brands and attributes (i.e., brand knowledge) are represented in the form of a hierarchical network of nodes and relationships between those nodes. For example, all toothpaste brands might be coded as nodes at a certain level of organization in memory. The attributes of various toothpaste brands, which also are represented as nodes, will be linked with the brand name nodes such that the properties of each brand, and the relationships and shared attributes between various brands, are efficiently represented in memory (e.g., Nedungadi, 1990).

When a consumer is presented information about a brand, and it gets processed to a sufficient depth, that information is integrated into the existing network of nodes and links in memory (e.g., Mandler, 1967). The nature of representation of information has been the subject of research both in consumer behaviour and cognitive psychology literatures.

It is generally accepted that concepts in memory are stored as categories (Rosch, 1975; Loken and Ward, 1990). These categories occur at various levels – subordinate, basic, and superordinate. Thus, oral care products (e.g., toothpaste, toothbrushes, whitening strips, mouthwashes) might be represented as a superordinate category, while toothpaste brands might be represented as a basic category. The various brands that cater to different segments might form the subordinate categories (e.g., children's toothpaste, smokers' toothpaste, toothpaste with whitening properties).

The concept of categorization has two important implications for advertisers. First, it has been shown that consumers are likely to quickly categorize information that is presented to them (e.g., Meyers-Levy and Tybout, 1989). This categorization, in turn, sets up expectations which guide information processing. Advertisements that fit a consumer's expectations of a category member are processed superficially, and the brand information is quickly integrated into existing category knowledge (e.g., Boush and Loken, 1991). When advertising information violates a consumer's expectations of a category member, then the advertising receives greater scrutiny (e.g., Meyers-Levy and Tybout, 1989; Sujan and Bettman, 1989). Thus, if the objective of an advertiser is to quickly reinforce the notion that its brand belongs in a certain category, the ad information should be presented in a manner that facilitates consumer inferencing. On the other hand, if an advertiser was interested in consumers representing its brand separately from existing categories, then the information about its brand should be presented accordingly (e.g., Sujan and Bettman, 1989).

Another important effect of categorization has recently been discussed in consumer research. With an explosion in products that appear to combine product features from different categories (e.g., cell phones and organizers, computers and entertainment systems), marketers should be sensitive to how their product is categorized by consumers. It has been shown that how a complex product is initially categorized has a significant effect on how consumers encode it, and evaluate it (e.g., Moreau et al., 2001; Rajagopal and Burnkrant, 2006). For example, Moreau et al. (2001) showed that when consumers were exposed to a digital camera, which was a relatively new product for most people at the time, exposing consumers to ads for similar products (i.e., film camera and scanner) prior to exposure to the new product influenced categorization of the digital camera. Specifically, presenting an ad for a film camera prior to an ad for a scanner led to more consumers saying the digital camera was like a camera than a scanner.

Information storage has also been studied in the form of schemas and scripts in consumer memory. Schemas and scripts are variations of how knowledge is expected to be represented in memory. They have also been shown to facilitate encoding, storage, and retrieval of information from memory (e.g., Smith and Houston, 1985).

RETRIEVAL OF ADVERTISING INFORMATION

Retrieval of information from LTM versus STM

Once information contained in an advertisement has been encoded in memory, consumers must be able to access the stored information at the appropriate time, a process known as retrieval (Ashcraft, 2002). Researchers have used a variety of tasks to examine retrieval of information from both short-term memory and long-term memory, such as free recall. In *free recall* subjects are provided with a set of information that they may recall in any order, regardless of the order of presentation (Ashcraft, 2002). Free recall findings have consistently shown that subjects have higher accuracy on information presented early and at the end of a to-be-remembered list of information (Crowder, 1976; Ashcraft, 2002), suggesting that consumers will be able to more easily retrieve information presented at the beginning and end of an advertisement. Better memory for items that are presented early in a list of information is known as a *primacy effect*. Better memory for items occurring in the final positions of a list of information is known as a *recency effect*. Past research generally supports the rehearsal explanation for why primacy and recency effects occur (e.g., Craik, 1968; Glanzer and Cunitz, 1966; Raymond, 1969; Rundus and Atkinson, 1970). Specifically, the first items in an advertisement are expected to receive the most rehearsals, which increases the probability that these items will be recalled. As the amount of rehearsal time devoted to early items in an advertisement increases, the likelihood that these initial items will be transferred into LTM increases, making them available for later recall (e.g., Ashcraft, 2002; Crowder, 1976). Recency effects depend on rehearsal in a different manner. Recall performance of the final items in an advertisement is dependent on consumers' ability to retain these items in STM through rehearsal. Once respondents stop rehearsing information in STM, then this information is lost, unless it has been transferred to LTM. When prompted for recall, respondents will recall the most available information first, which is the information that is easily accessible in STM, resulting in enhanced recency effects. If respondents are not able to rehearse items long enough to maintain them in STM until prompted for recall, then recency effects will diminish (e.g., Ashcraft, 2002; Crowder, 1976). As a result, increasing the amount of time between a consumer's exposure to an advertisement and the purchase situation is expected to decrease the amount of information recalled from the end of an ad.

Research has not only found that the temporal location of information contained in a single advertisement is important in determining the impact of this information on subsequent decisions (e.g., Baumgartner et al., 1997), but more recent research has suggested that the location of an advertisement within a set of advertisements may also determine how easily the information contained in a specific ad will be retrieved (Terry, 2005). Specifically, Terry (2005) finds evidence that consumers exhibit better memory for information contained in television advertisements presented at the beginning and end of a set of advertisements, consistent with primacy and recency effects.

Repetition and spacing effects

Additional research has demonstrated the importance of appropriately spacing repeated occurrences of an advertisement in retrieval of advertising information (e.g., Janiszewski et al., 2003). Past research provides evidence that the probability of retrieving information from an advertisement increases by utilizing a distributed presentation schedule rather than a massed presentation schedule (Bahrick, 1979; Janiszewski et al., 2003). The retrieval benefits achieved by spacing occurrences of a repeated advertisement are affected by numerous variables, such as the number of intervening advertisements between the occurrences, the use of words versus pictures in an ad, the complexity of an ad, and the meaningfulness and familiarity of an ad (see Janiszewski et al.,

2003 for a review). From their meta-analysis Janiszewski et al. (2003) suggest that the best advertising repetition strategy may involve one presentation of incidental processing and one presentation of intentional processing because their results are most consistent with the retrieval and reconstruction explanations for spacing effects (see Chapter 5.4 for more information on media scheduling). Retrieval is the idea that the second presentation cues the first presentation, and if they are spaced then the second presentation forces you to retrieve the first presentation from LTM instead of working memory, which facilitates recall. Reconstruction is the idea that spacing forces someone to reconstruct the first presentation upon exposure to the second presentation, which facilitates later recall. If the two presentations occur in close proximity, then the first presentation is still accessible at the second presentation, making reconstruction unnecessary. Encoding variability, the previously supported explanation for spacing effects (e.g., Crowder, 1976), received moderate support as an explanation in the meta-analysis but not as much as retrieval or reconstruction. Encoding variability is the idea that spacing the repetitions allows for more cue-target (i.e., contextual) associations, enhancing overall recall.

Interference

While repeating an advertisement has been shown to increase retrieval ease of information contained within the ad, presenting an advertisement that is similar to other advertisements has been shown to reduce accessibility of ad information stored in long-term memory (e.g., Burke and Srull, 1988; Kumar and Krishnan, 2004). The inhibition of target information by other information has been labeled *interference*. Retrieval of advertising information may be inhibited by the learning of additional information post hoc, a phenomenon known as *retroactive interference* (Bower, 1978; Underwood, 1945), and retrieval of advertising information may be inhibited by previously learned information, a phenomenon termed *proactive*

interference (Whitely, 1927; Whitely and Blankenship, 1936; Postman and Hasher, 1972). An advertisement may be subject to interference effects if consumers view that advertisement in conjunction with an advertisement from a different brand in the same product class (e.g., Burke and Srull, 1988; Keller, 1991). Thus, consumers may not be capable of retrieving information about a particular ad because information from this ad is inhibited by a competitive ad, a phenomenon known as *competitive interference*. More recent research has suggested that interference may also occur if advertisements for two different brands in two different product classes utilize similar pictures in their advertisements, a phenomenon known as *contextual interference* (e.g., Kumar, 2000; Kumar and Krishnan, 2004). Contextual interference may occur for two brands that are not in the same product class. Kumar (2000) demonstrated that similar pictures for two unfamiliar brands may inhibit memory for the brand name, as well as the claims made in the ad. Thus, executions have been shown to cause interference. The inhibitory effects of other similar ads on information from a target ad have been demonstrated for both familiar and unfamiliar brands (Kumar and Krishnan, 2004). Thus, the similarity of advertisements has proven to be a critical factor in assessing how much of an impact an ad will have on a subsequent decision.

Researchers have attempted to uncover underlying mechanisms responsible for interference effects. Interference does not occur because advertising information is unlearned or forgotten; interference occurs because some other information is inhibiting retrieval of stimulus information (i.e., Ashcraft, 2002). Specifically, interference occurs "not just because there have been prior trials, but because these prior trials share some characteristics of the current trial" (Crowder, 1976: 203), suggesting that to enhance the probability that a consumer will retrieve information from an ad, advertisers should attempt to differentiate their ads from competitors' ads and those ads that may be viewed in the same context.

Encoding specificity and the importance of cues

Cues have been shown to play a critical role in the retrieval of advertising information from long-term memory at the purchase situation. Specifically, effective external retrieval cues available at the purchase situation allow for increased accessibility to advertising information (e.g., Ashcraft, 2002). For example, Keller (1987) found that introducing advertising retrieval cues on product packaging (i.e., ad headline and photo) enhances recall of brand claims and evaluative reactions to the ad, and it reduces interference effects. Several brands have utilized the presence of cues in the marketplace to enhance retrieval of ad information. For example, Life cereal's "Mikey" campaign was supported by providing a picture of "Mikey" on the cereal box to facilitate ease of retrieval of information contained in the advertisements when consumers were shopping for cereal at the grocery store (Keller, 1987).

If effective cues facilitate enhanced memory for ad information, then what determines whether a retrieval cue will be effective? According to Tulving and Thomson (1973), "what is stored is determined by what is perceived and how it is encoded, and what is stored determines what retrieval cues are effective in providing access to what is stored." Therefore, recall is impacted by the relationship between the way in which information is encoded and the cues utilized to retrieval information from memory. Specifically, information is more accessible if the way in which information is encoded (i.e., contextual factors) matches the retrieval cues used at recall, a phenomenon termed encoding specificity. Encoding specificity proposes that the picture of "Mikey" was an effective cue for consumers to access advertising information because they encoded information from the Life cereal ads with a picture of "Mikey." Therefore, the encoding contextual cue (i.e., picture of "Mikey") matched the retrieval cue (i.e., packaging with picture of "Mikey") increasing accessibility of the Life ad information.

Encoding specificity has also shown to have important implications for the choice of advertising execution (e.g., Unnava and Burnkrant, 1991; Costley et al., 1997). Unnava and Burnkrant (1991) showed that varying the executions of a brand of shampoo (i.e., different contexts for print ads) resulted in higher recall of the ad message and the advertised brand name than if the same ad was presented the same number of exposures. Thus, using multiple ad executions versus one ad execution allows consumers to encode the information using different contextual cues, resulting in a higher probability that the cues available at retrieval would match one of the cues available at encoding. Costley et al. (1997) further showed that providing retrieval in the same modality as the initial message enhances recall of the message ("modality match hypothesis"). Therefore, recall of advertising information is enhanced when the information is both presented and cued in a visual format or presented and cued in an audio format. Thus, cues for advertising information that are presented in a visual format, such as on the packaging, will be more effective if the initial information is similarly encoded in a visual format (i.e., print ad). Overall, encoding specificity implies the importance of maintaining clarity and consistency across marketing communications (see Chapter 1.3).

While effective retrieval cues are shown to enhance consumers' memory for advertising information, some evidence has suggested that cues may actually inhibit memory in some cases (e.g., Forehand and Keller, 1996). Forehand and Keller (1996) showed that on an initial ad recall attempt, the presence of retrieval cues enhances memory for the ad. However, consumers that receive retrieval cues during initial recall attempts demonstrate a significant decrease in performance on subsequent recall attempts even if subsequent attempts at retrieval also provide cues. The authors suggest that this occurs because initial retrieval is made easier by the presence of cues, requiring less effort at the retrieval task. Thus, subsequent retrieval attempts are hindered because the retrieval route does not receive sufficient reinforcement at initial retrieval attempts. This assertion is supported by the finding that subjects that do not receive retrieval cues during initial recall attempts do not demonstrate a significant drop in recall performance at subsequent recall attempts.

Affect

Another critical factor that impacts retrieval of advertising information is affect (i.e., mood, stimulus valence, and emotional intensity). Evidence for state dependence and mood congruence is prevalent in this stream of literature. *State dependence* is the idea that remembering information in a given mood is partially dependent on what was learned previously in that mood (Blaney, 1986; Bower, 1981). The findings from this area of research suggest that the probability of retrieving information from an advertisement will increase if consumers are exposed to an ad and attempt to make a subsequent decision related to the ad while in the same mood. *Mood congruence* is the idea that information is more likely to be stored and/or recalled when the valence of the information to be stored or recalled is consistent with a person's mood at that time (Blaney, 1986; Bower, 1981). Therefore, the relationship between mood at encoding and recall and the relationship between mood and valence are important in predicting the outcome of a recall task. Thus, consumers may be more likely to recall positive information from an ad when they are in a more positive mood (see Chapter 2.4 for more information on the role of affect emotions in advertising).

More recent research has demonstrated that affect associated with an advertisement can be cued (e.g., Stayman and Batra, 1991). Stayman and Batra (1991) exposed consumers to a television advertisement embedded in a program that yielded similar overall attitudes but either had an affective execution (i.e., likeable music) or an argument execution (i.e., strong arguments). When they were later primed with the brand name, they were faster at retrieving the affect if they were exposed to the affective versus the argument execution ad. Also, the authors showed that positive affect that is experienced upon initial exposure to an advertisement is more likely to be experienced again when brand name is used as a retrieval cue than if a different brand is used as a retrieval cue or positive affect is not experienced upon initial exposure to the ad.

Finally, the emotional intensity of an advertisement has also been shown to have an important influence on retrieval (i.e., Bower, 1981; Baumgartner et al., 1997). In particular, consumers better recall highly emotional ads or emotionally intense components of ads. For example, Ambler and Burne (1999) showed that subjects had better recall and recognition for advertisements that were highly emotional versus cognitive. Thus, emotional ads and ad components have a larger impact on subsequent purchase decisions because of their enhanced accessibility relative to other advertising information.

Reconstructive memory

Several factors, such as interference and retrieval cues, have been shown to impact retrieval of information from LTM, but more recent research demonstrates that even if recall from LTM is possible, there is no guarantee that information will be recalled correctly. Reconstructive memory is a new view of memory that looks at what information is remembered rather than just how much information is accurately remembered (Koriat et al., 2000; Schacter et al., 1998). In this view, "information is not simply deposited into a memory store, but is assimilated and integrated into cognitive structures and later recreated from those structures," (Koriat et al., 2000: 487). Thus, as a result of the constructive processes required at retrieval, memory for information may not always be accurate (Schacter et al., 1998).

In support of this reconstructive view of memory, consumer researchers have demonstrated that advertising can alter consumers' memory for pre-exposure experiences and beliefs (e.g., Braun, 1999; Braun-La Tour and Zaltman, 2006) and consumers' memory for post-exposure experiences (e.g., Braun-La Tour and La Tour, 2005). Specifically, advertising is shown to unconsciously skew beliefs in the direction of the advertising message (Braun-La Tour and Zaltman, 2006). Additional research has even indicated that exposure to an advertisement may substitute for experience as a result of reconstructive memory processes, e.g., Rajagopal and Montgomery (2006) who showed that an ad containing an imagery-laden description of a product experience results in attitudes that are as strong as those formed from actual experience and are as equally capable of predicting future behavior. Despite the impact of reconstructive processes, consumers overwhelmingly believe that advertising does not have an impact relative to their past experience (Braun-La Tour and La Tour, 2005).

Reconstructive processes in memory may also impact consumers' memory for competitive advertisements. Braun-La Tour and La Tour (2004) showed that if a strong brand schema is created through many years of exposure to an existing advertising campaign for a brand (i.e., Snoopy and Charlie Brown for Metlife), then exposure to an ad for another company that has recently employed a similar message strategy (i.e., Hallmark using the Charlie Brown gang) will result in source confusion. Thus, the established brand that originally employed the message strategy will benefit from the other ad in that consumers will be more likely to believe that they saw the company's ad when they had not.

NEUROSCIENCE OF ADVERTISING EFFECTS

Recent research using positron emission tomography (PET) and functional magnetic resonance imaging (fMRI) have allowed marketers to examine the neuroscience underlying consumers' memory for advertisements. The brain consists of an extensive neural network that extends over several lobes, and the PET and the fMRI examine changes in blood flow in the brain to examine where neural activity is occurring (Gabrieli, 1998). Each of the neurons that unites to form the brain is connected to another neuron via the synapse (Ambler et al., 2000). When consumers learn new information via advertising, new neurons or synapses can be created, and when consumers are exposed to previously learned advertising information, old synapses can be reactivated (Ambler et al., 2000). Thus, neural activation occurs by impacting the connection between neurons, or by creating new neurons.

When consumers consciously encode advertising information, research has shown that they exhibit activation in the medial temporal region and the diencephalic region of the brain, particularly in the hippocampus (e.g., Gabrieli, 1998; Schacter et al., 1998; Squire et al., 1993). When an advertisement is encoded in memory, the hippocampus assigns an index to the consumers' memory for the ad. Similar advertising information and encoding episodes may have similar or overlapping neuronal representations in the hippocampus, so memory for a particular piece of information or exposure to a particular ad is dependent upon the extent to which the hippocampus is able to assign a unique (i.e., non-overlapping) representation to that particular episode or piece of information, a process known as pattern separation (e.g., Schacter et al., 1998).

In addition to being responsible for encoding of an episode, the medial temporal region is also partially responsible for the retrieval of an episode. Reconstruction of an advertising exposure episode involves recreating that past episode by linking features together. When a consumer attempts to retrieve information pertaining to a particular advertisement, cues activate the index in the hippocampus, activating all of the features of that ad exposure experience. The "retrieval cues need to be specific enough to activate only a single episode," (Schacter et al., 1998: 312). Otherwise, errors, such as those evident in our review of Reconstructive Memory, may occur. Also, if pattern separation is not successful, consumers may be able to retrieve the gist of the episode (i.e., similar information between episodes), but they may not be able to retrieve specific information about an episode (Schacter et al., 1998; Koriat et al., 2000).

The various features of the ad and the experience are subsequently consolidated into a unified representation of the episode in the neocortex (Schacter et al., 1998; Koriat et al., 2000). "Consolidation is a storage process by which memories become more stable over time," (Phelps, 2006: 34). Once consolidation of the episode has occurred, the hippocampus no longer plays a role in retrieval. Thus, evidence from neuroscience suggests that the hippocampus is responsible for STM for advertising information, while the neocortex is responsible for long-term memory for advertising information (Ambler et al., 2000).

While evidence shows that advertising information seems to be encoded and retrieved through activation of the medial temporal region and the neocortex, memory for emotionally arousing advertising information corresponds to activation of the amygdala and the ventro-medial frontal lobes (VMFL) (Gabrieli, 1998; Ambler et al., 2000; Phelps, 2006). For example, Ambler and Burne (1999) showed that recall and recognition were greater for the high-affect versus low-affect ads. However, giving subjects β-blockers reduced the recall and recognition differences in the high versus low affective ads, demonstrating support for the role of the amygdala in memory for emotional advertisements. The amygdala can also affect encoding of emotional stimuli by focusing attention to the emotional details of a stimulus (Phelps, 2006). Arousal resulting from emotional stimuli, such as ads, can also impact the storage process. Specifically, arousal enhances the consolidation of information from the stimuli in the hippocampus, resulting in enhanced memory for the information (Phelps, 2006).

Evidence from cognitive neuroscience suggests that unconscious processing of ads (i.e., processing fluency) may not activate regions of the brain in the same manner as conscious processing of ads. Specifically, evidence has shown that the neocortex is responsible for preconscious memory processes, such as perceptual and conceptual fluency. However, perceptual and conceptual fluency activate slightly different regions. While conceptual fluency results in activations of the amodal language areas, perceptual fluency results in activation of modality-specific cortical regions (Gabrieli, 1998). Preconscious memory processes depend on the activation of multiple brain regions that are outside of the medial temporal lobe and the diencephalon (Squire et al., 1993).

Principles of neuroscience, as applied to advertising studies, are mostly seen in testing of advertising effects (e.g., Pieters and Wedel 2007, Chapter 4.1). Instead of focusing on presumed cognitive or affective mechanisms, researchers are now able to link physiological changes in people after exposure to advertising to their subsequent opinions and behaviours. In one recent paper, Raju and Unnava (2006) show that highly committed consumers are aroused when their preferred brand is criticized, and arousal was measured using skin conductance.

SUMMARY

In this chapter, we explored the role of memory in advertising effectiveness. Specifically, we examined the way in which consumers encode information contained in an advertisement, store this information, and retrieve this information to utilize in a subsequent consumption decision, and we explored the factors that impact each of these stages of the memory process. Additionally, we examined the role of neural activation in the memory for advertisements.

Our discussion of memory research has provided some insight into the major variables affecting the encoding and storage stages of the memory process. In particular, we have shown that a consumer must pay attention to an advertisement in order for information from the advertisement to be encoded in memory. An exclusion to this rule involves preconscious processing, such as processing fluency effects. Brand choice and consideration set decisions may be facilitated if the same stimuli reappear in the decision-making context. Elaboration is another variable shown to impact encoding of advertising information. Specifically, to retain advertising information for later use, consumers need to make links between the advertising information and other concepts stored in memory. Thus, advertising information that is stored in memory is integrated into an existing memory network of nodes and links, and concepts in memory are generally stored as categories of various levels.

In addition to examining encoding and storage of advertising information, much of this chapter has been devoted to understanding the factors that influence retrieval of information due to the impact that information retrieval can have on subsequent brand decisions. Memory store is one factor that affects the retrieval of information. LTM facilitates memory for the beginning of an advertisement, while STM facilitates memory for the end of an advertisement. However, information stored in LTM remains fairly intact over time, but STM dissipates with time, affecting the retrieval of information retained in the STM store. The spacing of repeated ads also impacts retrieval of advertising information. In particular, retrieval of advertising information is facilitated by a distributed versus a massed advertising schedule. While repeating an ad may facilitate retrieval, past research has shown that presenting an ad that is similar to another ad may reduce the accessibility of advertising information from LTM through a process known as interference. However, when cues presented at the purchase situation match the cues that consumers utilize at encoding, the accessibility of advertising information increases, overcoming the potentially harmful effects of interference. Affect is another variable that may impact retrieval of advertising information. Consumers remember well the emotionally intense components of an ad. Our examination of affect also suggests that the retrieval of advertising information may be enhanced if

a consumer's mood at encoding and retrieval match, or if the valence of the advertising information matches a consumer's mood at retrieval. Finally, retrieval may be impacted by reconstructive memory, the idea that consumers may not always retrieve accurate memories. Instead, the information retrieved from memory may be altered by a consumer's schema or additional information a consumer obtained from another information source.

This chapter also explored the physiological changes that occur in consumers upon exposure to stimuli, such as advertisements, which is one of the most recent advancements in memory research. Our review shows that the medial temporal region of the brain plays a major role in the encoding of advertising information and is partially responsible for the retrieval of information. However, the neocortex is responsible for consolidating information from the advertisement into a unified representation of the advertising exposure episode. The neocortex is also responsible for preconscious memory processes, such as perceptual and conceptual fluency. Finally, our review suggests that the amygdala and the ventro-medial frontal lobes are activated by emotionally arousing advertising information.

Memory plays a critical role in how advertising impacts consumption decisions. Our discussion integrated recent research with long-standing findings in this area to provide a comprehensive account of the role of memory in advertising effectiveness. As a result of the advancements made in memory research, such as understanding preconscious processing and new neurological techniques, marketers today have a greater appreciation for memory and its role in advertising effectiveness.

REFERENCES

Ambler, T. and T. Burne (1999), "The Impact of Affect on Memory of Advertising," *Journal of Advertising Research*, 39 (2), 25–34.

Ambler, T., A. Ioannides and S. Rose (2000), "Brands on the Brain: Neuro-Images of Advertising," *Business Strategy Review*, 11 (3), 17–30.

Anderson, J.R. and L.M. Reder (1979), "An Elaborative Processing Explanation of Depth of Processing," in *Levels of Processing in Human Memory*, eds. L.S. Cermak and F.I.M. Craik, Hillsdale, NJ: Lawrence Erlbaum Associates, 385–403.

Ashcraft, M.H. (2002), *Cognition*, Upper Saddle River, NJ: Prentice Hall.

Atkinson, R.C. and R.M. Shiffrin (1968), "Human Memory: A Proposed System and Its Control Processes" in *The Psychology of Learning and Motivation: Advances in Research and Theory* (Vol. 2), eds. K.W. Spence and J.T. Spence, Oxford, England: Academic Press, 89–195.

Bahrick, H.P. (1979), "Maintenance of Knowledge: Questions About Memory We Forgot to Ask," *Journal of Experimental Psychology: General*, 108 (3), 296–308.

Baumgartner, H., M. Sujan and D. Padgett (1997), "Patterns of Affective Reactions to Advertisements: The Integration of Moment-to-Moment Responses into Overall Judgments," *Journal of Marketing Research*, 34 (May), 219–32.

Blaney, P.H. (1986), "Affect and Memory: A Review," *Psychological Bulletin*, 99 (2), 229–46.

Bousch, D.M. and B. Loken (1991), "A Process-Tracing Study of Brand Extension Evaluation," *Journal of Marketing Research*, 28 (1), 16–28.

Bower, G.H. (1978), "Interference paradigms for meaningful propositional memory," *American Journal of Psychology*, 91 (4), 575–85.

Bower, G.H. (1981), "Mood and Memory," *American Psychologist*, 36 (February), 129–48.

Braun, K. (1999), "Postexperience Advertising Effects on Consumer Memory," *Journal of Consumer Research*, 25 (March), 319–34.

Braun-La Tour, K.A. and M.S. La Tour (2004), "Assessing the Long-Term Impact of a Consistent Advertising Campaign on Consumer Memory," *Journal of Advertising*, 33 (2), 49–61.

Braun-La Tour, K.A. and M.S. La Tour (2005), "Transforming Consumer Experience: When Timing Matters," *Journal of Advertising*, 34 (3), 19–30.

Braun-La Tour, K.A., M.S. La Tour, J.E. Pickrell and E. Loftus (2004), "How and When Advertising Can Influence Memory for Consumer Experience," *Journal of Advertising*, 33 (4), 7–25.

Braun-La Tour, K.A. and G. Zaltman (2006), "Memory Change: An Intimate Measure of Persuasion," *Journal of Advertising Research*, 46 (March), 57–72.

Brinol, P., R.E. Petty and Z.L. Tormala (2004), "Self-Validation of Cognitive Responses to Advertisements," *Journal of Consumer Research*, 30 (March), 559–73.

Burke, R.R. and T.K. Srull (1988), "Competitive Interference and Consumer Memory for Advertising," *Journal of Consumer Research*, 15 (June), 55–68.

Burnkrant, R.E. and H.R. Unnava (1995), "Effects of Self-Referencing on Persuasion," *Journal of Consumer Research*, 22 (June), 17–26.

Childers, T.L., S.E. Heckler and M.J. Houston (1986), "Memory for the Visual and Verbal Components of Print Advertisements," *Psychology and Marketing*, 3 (3), 137–50.

Childers, T.L. and M.J. Houston (1984), "Conditions for a Picture-Superiority Effect on Consumer Memory," *Journal of Consumer Research*, 11 (September), 643–54.

Costley, C., S. Das and M. Brucks (1997), "Presentation Medium and Spontaneous Imaging Effects on Consumer Memory, *Journal of Consumer Psychology*, 6 (3), 211–31.

Craik, F.I. (1968), "Two Components in Free Recall," *Journal of Verbal Learning and Verbal Behavior*, 7 (6), 996–1004.

Craik, F.I. and R.S. Lockhart (1972), "Levels of Processing: A Framework for Memory Research," *Journal of Verbal Learning and Verbal Behavior*, 11 (6), 671–84.

Crowder, Robert G. (1976), *Principles of Learning and Memory*, Hillsdale, NJ: Erlbaum.

Forehand, M.R. and K. Lane Keller (1996), "Initial Retrieval Difficulty and Subsequent Recall in an Advertising Setting," *Journal of Consumer Psychology*, 5 (4), 299–323.

Gabrieli, J.D.E. (1998), "Cognitive Neuroscience of Human Memory," *Annual Review of Psychology*, 49, 87–115.

Glanzer, M. and A.R. Cunitz (1966), "Two Storage Mechanisms in Free Recall," *Journal of Verbal Learning and Verbal Behavior*, 5 (4), 351–60.

Greenwald, A.G. and C. Leavitt (1984), "Audience Involvement in Advertising: Four Levels," *Journal of Consumer Research*, 11 (June), 581–92.

Gregan-Paxton, J. and B. Loken (1997), "Understanding Consumer Memory for Ads: A Process View," in *Measuring Advertising Effectiveness*, eds. W.D. Wells, Mahwah, NJ: Lawrence Erlbaum Associates, 183–202.

Haugtvedt, C.P., D.W. Schumann, W.L. Schneier and W.L. Warren (1994), "Advertising Repetition and Variation Strategies: Implications for Understanding Attitude Strength," *Journal of Consumer Research*, 21 (June), 176–89.

Healy, A.F. and D. McNamara (1996), "Verbal Learning and Memory: Does the Modal Model Still Work?" *Annual Review of Psychology*, 47, 143–72.

Heath, R. (2007), "Advertising as Reinforcement," in *The SAGE Handbook for Advertising*, eds. G.J. Tellis and T. Ambler, London: Sage Publications.

Heckler, S.E. and T.L. Childers (1992), "The Role of Expectancy and Relevancy in Memory for Verbal and Visual Information: What is Incongruency?" *Journal of Consumer Research*, 18 (March), 475–92.

Houston, M.J., T.L. Childers and S.E. Heckler (1987), "Picture-Word Consistency and the Elaborative Processing of Advertisements," *Journal of Marketing Research*, 24 (November), 359–69.

Huffman, C. and M.J. Houston (1993), "Goal-Oriented Experiences and the Development of Knowledge," *Journal of Consumer Research*, 20 (September), 190–207.

Hunt, J.M., J.B. Kernan and E.H. Bonfield (1992), "Memory Structure in the Processing of Advertising Messages: How is Unusual Information Represented?" *Journal of Psychology*, 126 (4), 343–56.

Janiszewski, C. (1990), "The Influence of Nonattended Material on the Processing of Advertising Claims," *Journal of Marketing Research*, 27 (August), 263–78.

Janiszewski, C., H. Noel and A.G. Sawyer (2003), "A Meta-analysis of the Spacing Effect in Verbal Learning: Implications for Research on Advertising Repetition and Consumer Memory," *Journal of Consumer Research*, 30 (June), 138–49.

Keller, K.L. (1987), "Memory Factors in Advertising: The Effect of Advertising Retrieval Cues on Brand Evaluations," *Journal of Consumer Research*, 14 (December), 316–33.

Keller, K.L. (1991), "Memory and Evaluation Effects in Competitive Advertising Environments," *Journal of Consumer Research*, 17 (March), 463–76.

Keller, K.L. (1993), "Memory Retrieval Factors and Advertising Effectiveness," in *Advertising Exposure, Memory, and Choice*, eds. Andrew A. Mitchell, Hillsdale, NJ: Lawrence Erlbaum Associates, 11–48.

Koriat, A., M. Goldsmith and A. Pansky (2000), "Toward a Psychology of Memory Accuracy," *Annual Review of Psychology*, 51, 481–537.

Kumar, A. (2000), "Interference Effects of Contextual Cues in Advertisements on Memory for Ad Content," *Journal of Consumer Psychology*, 9 (3), 155–166.

Kumar, A. and S. Krishnan (2004), "Memory Interference in Advertising: A Replication and Extension," *Journal of Consumer Research*, 30 (March), 602–11.

Lavidge, R.J. and G.A. Steiner (1961), "A Model for Predictive Measurements of Advertising Effectiveness," *Journal of Marketing*, 25 (October), 59–62.

Lee, A.Y. and A.A. Labroo (2004), "The Effect of Conceptual and Perceptual Fluency on Brand Evaluation," *Journal of Marketing Research*, 41 (May), 151–65.

Loken, B. and J. Ward (1990), "Alternative Approaches to Understanding Determinants of Typicality," *Journal of Consumer Research*, 17 (September), 111–26.

MacInnis, D.J. and L.L. Price (1987), "The Role of Imagery in Information Processing: Review and Extensions," *Journal of Consumer Research*, 13 (March), 473–91.

Mandler, G. (1967), "Organization and Memory," in *The Psychology of Learning and Motivation: Advances in Research and Theory (Vol. 1)*, eds. K.W. Spence and J.T. Spence, New York: Academic Press, 327–72.

Meyers-Levy, J. (1989), "The Influence of a Brand Name's Association Set Size and Word Frequency on Brand Memory," *Journal of Consumer Research*, 16 (2), 197–207.

Meyers-Levy, J. and A.M. Tybout (1989), "Schema Congruity as a Basis for Product Evaluation," *Journal of Consumer Research*, 16 (1), 39–54.

Moreau, C.P., A.B. Markman and D.R. Lehmann (2001), "'What Is It?' Categorization Flexibility and Consumers' Responses to Really New Products," *Journal of Consumer Research*, 27 (March), 489–98.

Naik, P.A. (2007), "Integrated Marketing Communications: Provenance, Practice and Principles," in *The SAGE Handbook for Advertising*, eds. G.J. Tellis and T. Ambler, London: Sage Publications.

Nairne, J.S. (2002), "Remembering Over the Short-Term: The Case Against the Standard Model," *Annual Review of Psychology*, 53, 53–81.

Nedungadi, P. (1990), "Recall and Consumer Consideration Sets: Influencing Choice Without Altering Brand Evaluations," *Journal of Consumer Research*, 17 (December), 263–76.

Phelps, E.A. (2006), "Emotion and Cognition: Insights from the Studies of the Human Amygdala," *Annual Review of Psychology*, 57, 27–53.

Pieters, R. and M. Wedel (2007), "Pretesting: Before the Rubber Hits the Road," in *The SAGE Handbook for Advertising*, eds. G.J. Tellis and T. Ambler, London: Sage Publications.

Postman, L. and L. Hasher (1972), "Conditions of Proactive Inhibition in Free Recall," *Journal of Experimental Psychology*, 92 (2), 276–84.

Raaijmakers, J.G. and R.M. Shiffrin (1981), "Search of Associative Memory," *Psychological Review*, 88 (2), 93–134.

Rajagopal, P. and R.E. Burnkrant (2006), "Consumer Categorization and Evaluation of Ambiguous Products," Working Paper.

Rajagopal, P. and N. Votolato Montgomery (2006), "The Effects of Imagery versus Product Experience on Attitude Strength," Working Paper.

Raju, S. and H.R. Unnava (2006), "The Role of Arousal in Commitment: An Explanation for the Number of Counterarguments," *Journal of Consumer Research*, 33 (September), 173–8.

Raymond, B. (1969), "Short-Term and Long-Term Storage in Free Recall," *Journal of Verbal Learning and Verbal Behavior*, 8 (5), 567–74.

Rosch, E. (1975), "Cognitive Representations of Semantic Categories," *Journal of Experimental Psychology: General*, 104, 192–233.

Rucker, D.D., R.E. Petty and J.R. Priester (2007), "Understanding Advertising Effectiveness from Psychological Perspectives: The Importance of Attitudes and Attitude Strength," in *The SAGE Handbook for Advertising*, eds. G.J. Tellis and T. Ambler, London: Sage Publications.

Rundus, D. (1971), "Analysis of Rehearsal Processes in Free Recall," *Journal of Experimental Psychology*, 89 (July), 63–77.

Rundus, D. and R.C. Atkinson (1970), "Rehearsal Processes in Free Recall: A Procedure for Direct Observation," *Journal of Verbal Learning and Verbal Behavior*, 9 (1), 684–8.

Schacter, D.L., K.A. Norman and W. Koustaal (1998), "The Cognitive Neuroscience of Constructive Memory," *Annual Review of Psychology*, 49, 289–318.

Shapiro, S. (1999), "When an Ad's Influence is Beyond Our Conscious Control: Perceptual and Conceptual Fluency Effects Caused by Incidental Ad Exposure," *Journal of Consumer Research*, 26 (June), 16–36.

Shimp, T.A. (2007), *Advertising, Promotion, and Supplemental Aspects of Integrated Marketing Communications* (7th Edition), Cincinnati, Ohio: Thomson Publishing.

Singh, S.N. and C.A. Cole (1993), "The Effects of Length, Content, and Repetition, on Television Commercial Effectiveness," *Journal of Marketing Research*, 30 (1), 91–104.

Smith, R.A. and M.J. Houston (1985), "A Psychometric Assessment of Measures of Scripts in Consumer Memory," *Journal of Consumer Research*, 12 (September), 214–24.

Squire, L.R., B. Knowlton and G. Musen (1993), "The Structure and Organization of Memory," *Annual Review of Psychology*, 44, 453–95.

Stayman, D.M. and R. Batra (1991), "Encoding and Retrieval of Ad Affect in Memory," *Journal of Marketing Research*, 28 (May), 232–9.

Stewart, D.W., J. Morris and A. Grover (2007), "Emotions in Advertising," in *The SAGE Handbook for Advertising*, eds. G.J. Tellis and T. Ambler, London: Sage Publications.

Sujan, M. and J.R. Bettman (1989), "The Effects of Brand Positioning Strategies on Consumers' Brand and Category Perceptions: Some Insights from Schema Research," *Journal of Marketing Research*, 26 (4), 454–67.

Terry, W.S. (2005), "Serial Position Effects in Recall of Television Commercials," *Journal of General Psychology*, 132 (2), 151–63.

Tulving, E. and D.M. Thomson (1973), "Encoding Specificity and Retrieval Processes in Episodic Memory," *Psychological Review*, 80, 352–73.

Unnava, H.R. and R.E. Burnkrant (1991), "Effects of Repeating Varied Ad Executions on Brand Name Memory," *Journal of Marketing Research*, 28 (4), 406–16.

Vakratsas, D. and P.A. Naik (2007), "Essentials of Planning Flighted Media Schedules," in *The SAGE Handbook for Advertising*, eds. G.J. Tellis and T. Ambler, London: Sage Publications.

Wallace, W. (1965), "Review of the Historical, Empirical, and Theoretical Status of the von Restorff Phenomenon," *Psychological Bulletin*, 63 (6), 410–24.

Waugh, N.C. and D.A. Norman (1965), "Primary Memory," *Psychological Review*, 72 (2), 89–104.

Whitely, P.L. (1927), "The Dependence of Learning and Recall Upon Prior Intellectual Activities," *Journal of Experimental Psychology*, 10 (6), 489–508.

Whitely, P.L. and A.B. Blankenship (1936), "The Influence of Certain Conditions Prior to Learning Upon Subsequent Recall," *Journal of Experimental Psychology*, 19 (4), 496–504.

Zaltman, G. and D. MacCaba (2007), "Metaphor in Advertising," in *The SAGE Handbook for Advertising*, eds. G.J. Tellis and T. Ambler, London: Sage Publications.

Emotions in Advertising

David W. Stewart, Jon Morris and
Aditi Grover

Emotional response is seemingly one of life's contradictions. It is ephemeral and long lasting. A well-researched and theoretically supported method for measuring it consists of three dimensions that are orthogonal and related at the same time. Pleasure or the degree of happiness is clearly and scientifically found to be different from arousal or level of involvement. Yet the more pleasing something is the more arousing it tends to be. But the contradictions don't stop with the concepts. Research has shown that an emotional response can occur with or without cognitive processing. Rational thought can either spark or control affect. A fearful reaction, like seeing a snake, can provoke an avoidance response with no rational thought. For a trained snake handler the reaction may be quite different. Thought controls the emotional response to withdraw.

Another incongruity happens to all of us in daily experiences. Most of us have felt happy and sad, confident and apprehensive, or love and hate. Advertisers often hope to stir these kinds of emotions in order to bolster their message and motivate consumers to action, but they only rarely seek to determine if they are successful. In contrast to widely used methods for measuring cognitive and behavioural response to advertising there remains much skepticism about techniques that are used to measure emotional reactions regardless of how well tested or empirically supported.

So then what is emotion and what is an emotional response? This chapter seeks to answer these questions in the context of advertising and response to advertising. It focuses on what creates an emotional response in marketing communications and how can that response be measured. The chapter is organized around five sections. First, emotion is defined and emotions classified. What counts as an emotion and what is a stimulus of emotion or an antecedent of emotion? Section 1 addresses these issues. Section 2 briefly examines the use of emotions in advertising. Section 3 then describes several of the more prominent theories of emotion and Section 4 considers more specific issues related to the measurement of emotional response. Section 5 concludes the chapter by suggesting some opportunities for future research.

WHAT IS EMOTION?: DEFINING EMOTIONS AND RELATED CONSTRUCTS

Emotion is both a very common experience and a remarkably complex phenomenon. Early research and theory described emotions in terms of physiological responses to external stimuli. It is well known that the autonomic nervous system (ANS) of the human body is involved in arousal. The ANS is a collection of neural centers that control most of the normal body functions (breathing, heart beat, etc.) without conscious thought. The ANS has two divisions, the sympathetic nervous system (SNS) and the parasympathetic nervous system (PNS). In simple terms, the SNS acts to arouse emotions, while the PNS slows down most emotional activity. When someone is aroused emotionally, the SNS responds by elevating blood sugar, pumping more blood to the brain, muscles, and sometimes the surface of the skin, changing the rate of breathing, causing the skin to perspire, and dilating the pupils. When the emotion-arousing situation has passed, the PNS operates in the opposite direction to return the body to a resting state. In short, there is a clear, and relatively well-understood physiological reaction associated with emotion.

Unfortunately, a simple physiological definition of emotion fails to capture the richness of the experience and does not account for the fact that the same physiological reaction can be interpreted differently. People commonly talk about feeling anger, love, and sympathy. They will describe television commercials as warm or cold, pleasant or unpleasant, funny or somber. These are labels for some felt internal state. Psychologists Schachter and Singer (1962) suggest that when an external situation elicits an internal state of arousal, people search the environment for a reason for the arousal. They use cues in the environment to interpret and label the internal state. If the situation is one in which anger might be expected to occur, the internal response is interpreted as anger. If the situation is one in which joy might occur, the internal

response is labeled happiness. Thus, there is a strong cognitive component to the emotional experience in addition to the physiological response.

Classifying emotion

There are a number of classification systems for emotions (Osgood et al., 1957; Mehrabian and Russell, 1974; Russell, 1978, 1979, 1980; Plutchik, 1980). Almost all classifications include a general activation or arousal dimension associated with the intensity of what is experienced. A feeling of rage is more arousing than a feeling of irritation. A feeling of joy is less intense than being elated or euphoric. This intensity dimension has strong motivational overtones. The stronger the arousal properties of an emotion, the more likely action will have preceded or will follow the experience.

A second dimension of emotion is pleasantness. Fear is clearly an example of an emotion producing extreme displeasure. Love (at least if requited) may produce extreme pleasure. Some emotions, such as surprise, may be neutral on this dimension. People generally avoid unpleasant emotions, when possible, and seek out pleasant emotions. Most marketers, of course, seek to pair their products, communications, and other relevant stimuli, with pleasant emotions and avoid pairing with unpleasant emotions (although some products may be appropriately paired with the elimination or avoidance of an unpleasant emotion such as embarrassment).

A third dimension of emotion that has frequently been identified is ominance/submission. Submission refers to a lack of control over one's environment and is related to such emotions as anxiety and depression. Dominance, the other pole of this dimension, is associated with feelings of control over one's environment and with feelings of power, potency, or aggressiveness. A final dimension of emotion that has frequently been identified is social orientation, the extent to which the emotion is directed at self or others. Emotions such as affection, defiance, suspicion, and resentment are directed at others, while emotions such as pleased and joyful are directed more at self.

USES OF EMOTION IN ADVERTISING

Advertising is a combination of art and science. After studying the audience, the premises, and the avenues of communication, artistic approaches are devised to convey a selling proposition to sometimes waiting and sometimes skeptical publics. In some cases, the product attributes contain all the necessary elements to stimulate the excitement necessary to stimulate demand. In other situations, specialists, writers and artists must add a twist or turn to propel the features of the product into an inspired madness that creates an accepting mantra. In the world of advertising, executives have long known that elevating an emotional response to the product enhances their chances of successful selling. Transformational advertising, for example, creates a premise that may transport the recipient into a world of imagination by using music, humor, and story telling. This kind of advertising is often seen as more creative and emotion laden.

Regardless of the source, the underlying motivator for selling is emotion. Emotions are direct reactions (see Phillips and LeDoux, 1992) to the stimulating atmosphere that is being created by the artistic execution known as an ad. Feelings from cheerfulness and fascination to cynicism and dissatisfaction are engendered or reinforced by television commercials, magazine ads or point of purchase displays. Emotional appeals have long been used in advertising and personal selling. Examples of the efforts of advertisers to arouse fear, humor, sexual desires, patriotism, and a wide variety of other human emotions are easy to find. Coca-Cola invites consumers to have a "Coke and a Smile." DeBeers suggests to husbands that they "tell her you'd marry her all over again." Kodak produced a long-running advertising campaign with the theme "Preserve the Memories," a theme that played on sentimentality and affection for family. Advertising for fashion products and fragrances frequently uses sex appeal themes. Fears of property loss are a common theme in insurance ads. The range of emotions that may be evoked by advertising is diverse and emotional response play a unique role in bonding a consumer to a product.

A rich literature focuses on the factors that influence the impact of advertising messages on not of individual consumers and the market as a whole (e.g., Stewart and Kamins, 2003). In terms of content, an advertisement is usually defined along two general dimensions: (a) an informational or cognitive dimension, and (b) an emotional or feeling dimension. Both of these two dimensions also have a verbal and a non-verbal component. The informational dimension's verbal component comprises rational and logical arguments; the non-verbal component such as visual imagery, music and language variables, serve to complement, reinforce and clarify the meaning of a verbal message. The emotional or feeling dimension may be verbal but is often non-verbal. The emotional dimension is generally expressed in the form of emotional appeals or messages imbued with content designed to elicit, reinforce and transfer feelings.

Adding appropriate emotional content to a purely information-based advertisement is generally believed to enhance attitude change in audience and audience receptivity. One the other hand, in many mature product categories there are few genuine technological differences that provide a basis for a strong informational claim. Advertisers, therefore, attempt to develop emotional bonds between consumers and the firm or its product(s).

The study of emotional appeals in advertising has most often classified emotional appeals based on valence: some emotions are positive and some are negative. Negative appeals common in advertising content are fear, anger, guilt, disgust and sadness, among others. Common positive appeals include happiness, joy, humour, pride and warmth. Burke and Edell (1989) have offered an alternate classification that further differentiates positive appeals: (1) warmth appeals (e.g., pride and nostalgia), (2) upbeat appeals (e.g., joy, excitement and humour) and (3) negative appeals (e.g., fear and guilt). There is a very substantial empirical research on the effects of emotional appeals in advertising, including anger (e.g., Averill, 1982; Frijda, 1986; Lazarus, 1991; Roseman et al., 1994), empathy (Wells et al., 1971, Bagozzi, 1986; Davis, 1983; Aaker and Williams, 1998), fear (e.g., Brooker, 1981; Mewborn and Rogers, 1979; Witte, 1995; Boster and Mongeau, 1984), happiness (e.g., Lazarus, 1991), hope (DeMello and MacInnis, 2005; Lazarus 1991), humour (Duncan and Nelson 1985; Gelb and Pickett, 1983; Brooker, 1981), irritation (Aaker and Bruzzone, 1985), pride (e.g., Lazarus, 1991), and warmth (Aaker et al., 1986).

Pechmann and Stewart (1988) have drawn another distinction between the types of emotion used in advertising. The product itself may have emotional or experimental benefits. Perfume may offer sex appeal; automobile insurance may reduce fear of property loss. These are emotions that are directly relevant to the product and/or its benefits. A second use of emotion in advertising is unrelated to the product. Rather, the emotional response is evoked to increase the effectiveness of the persuasive communication. It may do this by increasing attention to the ad, by making the ad more memorable, or by suggesting a basis for decision-making. Several researchers have also found that "attitude toward the ad," or the likeability of an ad, i.e., how positively or negatively the viewer regards the ad itself, has an impact on attitudes toward the advertised product (Mitchell and Olson, 1981; Shimp, 1981; Smit et al., 2006).

THEORIES OF EMOTIONS

Although emotion is widely recognized in the study of consumer behaviour, systematic inquiry into the determinants of emotion and its effects on consumer response has been hindered by the lack of a general theory capable of explaining the complex nature of the process and the phenomenology of emotional response (Bagozzi et al., 1999). Though several theories of emotion have been influential in marketing research, no single

theory has captured the complexity of emotional response and its role in consumer behaviour. There are many variants in theories of emotion but most theories fall into one of six broad classes: physiological, arousal, facial expression, basic emotions models, dimensional models and attribution/appraisal process theories.

Physiological theories of emotions

Physiological theories, the oldest theories of emotions, posit that emotional response is characterized by an internal physiological response that is expressed via a specific or nonspecific change in the body's autonomic functions. Emotions, therefore, are manifestations of involuntary physiological or biochemical processes (e.g., changes in skin conductance, blood pressure, skin temperature and heart rate, facial expressions, respiration and pupil dilation, among others).

William James and Carl Lange are credited with independently developing the earliest theory of emotion – the James-Lange Theory of Emotion (James, 1884). This theory suggests that a specific and distinct physiological response produces a unique emotional response. When individuals become aware of this unique physiological response, they infer an emotional state that varies in valence and intensity. The James-Lange theory dominated research on emotion for more than a decade until Walter Cannon (1927), a bio-psychologist, questioned the one-to-one correspondence of the physiological response and emotional response. Cannon asserted that physiological responses are diffuse and that a particular physiological response can correspond to more than one emotional state. Physiological arousal when one is excited by anger, for example, is not much different from when one is excited by elation.

Two contemporary approaches to emotional response trace their roots to the early work on the physiology of emotional response: arousal theory and the theory of facial expressions. Arousal theory focuses on physiological responses, while facial feedback theory suggests that facial expressions (or subtle changes in facial musculature) play a critical role in the experience of emotion (Laird, 1974).

Arousal theory

Arousal theory emphasizes the role of physiological response in an emotional experience, and extends Canon's view that arousal is responsible for not only initiating an emotional response, but also for intensifying this response (Clark, 1982). Furthermore, this theory suggests that physiological arousal arising in response to an event can be transferred to and from one stimulus to another (e.g., Zillman's theory of Excitation Transfer: Zillman, 1978). Although arousal theorists are yet to clearly define the concept of arousal (Stewart, 1984), researchers agree that arousal may be exhibited by way of two responses – an automatic unconditioned response and a learned conditioned response. Each of the two responses can influence a wide range of affective, behavioural and cognitive responses (Corteen and Wood, 1972).

Theory of facial expressions

According to the facial expressions theory, expressions of the face are the primary means by which emotions and feelings are experienced and communicated (Darwin, 1898; Ekman, 1973; Ekman and Freisen, 1982). Facial muscular movements trigger physiological arousal and send sensory feedback to the brain's autonomic nervous system. This feedback then triggers the experience of a subjective emotional response (Tomkins, 1962). In light of the importance of the sensory feedback, the theory of facial expressions is also commonly referred to as the facial feedback hypothesis. The sensitivity of the face also performs a communicative role by influencing and regulating the emotional experience of an observer.

Despite the emotional sensitivity of the face to a stimulus, individuals in the real world learn to mask and control their facial expressions either through a deliberate process of learning (Izard, 1972, 1977) or by imbuing cultural expectations in their responses. Other limitations of the facial feedback theory include an individual's limited ability in judging facial expressions due to his or her own history, immediate situation and cultural background (Ekman and Oster, 1979) and the lack of a corresponding facial expression for every emotional experience. Hope, for example, one of the more pervasive emotional responses, does not have a universal facial expression (MacInnis and DeMello, 2005). Further, not all emotions are articulated nonverbally (e.g., facial musculature), and some emotional experiences may not be communicated at all (Ekman and Davidson, 1994).

Basic emotions approaches

Several scholars have attempted to identify a set of basic emotions that define all subjective emotional experiences. These approaches are based on cross-cultural and developmental research that suggests the existence of a finite set of discrete emotions – such as joy, anger, sadness, and fear – that are innate to all human beings (e.g., Izard, 1992; Plutchik, 1982). The subjective experience of emotion is the result of the particular pattern of responses across these various basic emotions. Thus, in any given situation it is possible to describe emotional response by measuring the extent to which each of the basic emotions is experienced (Richins, 1997). In consumer research, work on hedonic experiences has provided the impetus for moving away from simple dimensional classification to approaches that provide a means for describing more differentiated and subtle emotional states (Hirschman and Holbrook, 1982; Holbrook and Batra, 1987; Holbrook and Hirschman, 1982; Westbrook, 1987).

The basic emotions approach has been criticized as merely labelling without a sound theoretical foundation that explains the experience of emotion (Roseman, 1984). Taken to the extreme, there could be a basic emotion for every emotional response resulting in thousands of such basic emotions. The reliance of basic emotion approaches on labels of the subjective emotional experience is especially problematic. Because the composition of the basic emotion set is derived from evidence that certain emotions are expressed and labelled similarly across cultures, these approaches cannot account for emotional reactions that are not readily labelled in some cultures or for emotional expressions (e.g., facial expressions) that may be similar across a wide range of emotional experiences.

Dimensional theories

Several of the more influential approaches to the study of emotion in the context of consumer behavior fall within a general class of theories that are often referred to as dimensional theories. All dimensional theories attempt to simplify the representation of affective responses by identifying a set of common dimensions that can be used to distinguish specific emotions from one another. Within the context of consumer behaviour, dimensional theories have proven especially useful in predicting consumers' responses to store atmosphere (Donovan et al., 1994), to service experiences (Hui and Bateson, 1991), and to advertising (e.g., Holbrook and Batra, 1987), among others.

Russell and Mehrabian (1977) provide evidence that three independent and bipolar dimensions are need to completely measure the variance of emotional responses: pleasure–displeasure, arousal–calm, and dominance–submissiveness (PAD). There is also strong evidence that the same dimensions of emotion exist across cultures. In contrast to dimensional approaches, circumplex models propose a variety of affective responses based on the relative similarity of emotions and their applicability to a particular target setting or object (Watson and Tellegen, 1985). Circumplex models recognize underlying dimensions of emotion but suggest that these dimensions are combined, much like a colour wheel, to produce subjective experiences of emotion. With circumplex models, however, the full range of emotions and the subjective feelings associated with them may not be captured (Izard, 1971, 1972, 1977, 1992; Plutchik, 1980, 1982).

Though the dimensional and basic emotions approaches have afforded some valuable insights regarding the role of emotions in consumer behaviour, they were not designed to address the process and consequences of emotions. To fill this void, other theories, which more specifically focus on the causes and consequences of emotion, have been proposed and applied in the context of research on consumer behaviour. One theoretical approach in particular, attribution theory, has been used to explain consumer behaviour and has also addressed to some extent the causes and consequences of emotional responses.

Attribution theory

Although developed for a different purpose, attribution theory has frequently been used to predict differentiated emotional responses arising from the distinctions that people make about the cause(s) of an event (Kelley, 1967; Weiner, 1985). Consumers' emotional reactions often vary depending on the perceived cause of a particular outcome. For example, the same product failure may produce anger or regret depending on whether the consumer attributes the failure to the manufacturer or to his or her failure to follow the directions for use (e.g., Folkes, 1984; Maxham and Netemeyer, 2002).

Attribution theory was developed to explain and predict behavior that arises from perceptions of causal factors (Weiner, 1985, 1986; Weiner et al., 1979). Three distinct dimensions of causal attributions have been identified: (1) the locus of the cause (internal versus external to the individual), (2) the stability of the cause (likely versus unlikely to recur), and (3) the controllability of the cause of the outcome of the relevant situation (controllable or not). These dimensions of attribution have been shown to be associated with different patterns of behavior and emotional reactions. For example, as Weiner observes (1985), if an individual attributes the cause of a negative outcome for another person to his or her own actions (i.e., internal, controllable attribution of cause), the person making the attribution of personal responsibility for another's misfortune is likely to feel guilty.

Attribution theory is more properly a theory of the process of identifying and coping with causal factors and outcomes. The empirical research validating attribution theory does provide evidence of a link between cognitive distinctions and differentiated emotional reactions, however, and it suggests a need to more fully consider the relationship between cognitive processing and emotion.

Appraisal theories

Closely related to attribution theory is appraisal theory. Appraisal theories have been credited with providing the most convincing and comprehensive answers to date for key theoretical and practical questions about the nature of emotions (Ekman and Davidson, 1994; Scherer, 2001; Johnson and Stewart, 2004). These theories adopt a unifying approach to the study of emotions and specifically address and make predictions about the degree of arousal, emotional intensity and variation in responses across individuals. Appraisal theories rest on the assumption that it is the unique perception of an individual that is the ultimate determinant of his or her emotional response.

Among the earliest of the appraisal theories was that proposed by Lazarus (1991, 1999) who asserted that an emotional stimulus induces a process of cognitive appraisal that is preceded by both an emotional response and physiological arousal. Lazarus identified three specific appraisal forms: (a) primary appraisals: used for judging the valence or direction (e.g., positive, negative or irrelevant) of an individual's well-being; (b) secondary appraisals: used for judging resources available to an individual to cope with the appraised situation; and (c) re-appraisal: used to monitor and re-evaluate the primary and secondary appraisals with respect to the environment to maximize one's well-being. Lazarus' view explicitly recognized arousal as critical for initiating an emotional state, but also appreciated the vital role of cognition in providing meaning for the experienced arousal state. Appraisal theory is very much a functional theory of emotion because it focuses on the role emotion plays in coping with the environment by examining the antecedents and consequences of emotional response in a specific, goal relevant circumstance.

Each of the several types of theories reviewed here suggests something about how emotion might be used in advertising and how emotional response to advertising might be measured. Unfortunately, there has been a general lack of connection between theories of emotion and emotional response and the use of emotion in advertising. While there is general recognition that emotional appeals in and the evocation of emotional responses by advertising, there has been relatively little effort to use specific theories of emotion to provide normative guidance for the creation of effective advertising. More often the measures of emotional response suggested by various theories have been applied in an attempt to assess the effectiveness of advertising after its creation by tapping into dimensions of consumer response not assessed by other measures. A particularly vexing problem is that each of the several theories of emotion suggests rather different approaches to the use of advertising and different measures of both the subjective experience of emotion and the effects of emotion. As a result, advertising researchers and the managers they inform, often reach quite different conclusions about emotional response specifically and the effectiveness of an advertising execution more generally.

MEASURING EMOTIONAL RESPONSE

The complexity of emotion, the many definitions and theories of the construct, and the many effects that emotion may produce result in a significant challenge for scholars and practitioners interested in the measurement of emotion and emotional response (e.g., Poels and Dewitte, 2006; Stout and Leckenby, 1986; Page et al., 1988). It is also important to recognize that measures of the effects of emotion are not necessarily the same as measures of emotional response. Effects of emotion may be manifest in heightened or lessened attention, greater or lesser recall, and more or less preference, among others. Such measures of response may reveal the effect of emotional content in advertising, as well as other elements of an advertising execution. On the other hand, there are also specific measures of emotional response, which may or may not be related to other measures of response or to the overall effectiveness on an advertising execution.

Emotion can be measured in many different ways that do not always produce consistent results. Emotion in advertising can also produce very different outcomes depending on what is being measured – attention, recall, feelings, attitude or sales. For example, the same emotional response that heightens attention to an advertisement may distract attention from the primary product message. A rich advertising and emotions literature explores the many effects of emotional advertisements on such outcomes as attitude (e.g., Moore et al., 1995; Aylesworth Goodstein and Kalra, 1999), persuasion (e.g., Aaker and Williams, 1998; Burke and Edell, 1986; Holbrook and Batra, 1987; Edell and Burke, 1987), and processing and acceptance of information (Keller et al., 2003; Raghunathan and Trope, 2002). The variety of measures of emotional response is truly staggering. Poels and Dewitte (2006) provide a comprehensive review of specific measures of emotional response to advertising that have been reported in the literature. Most of these measures can be categorized as one of two types: physiological and descriptive (self-report).

Physiological measures

Several physiological techniques have been employed for measuring the level of arousal produced while an individual views an ad. For example, electroencephalographs track electrical activity in the brain and pupillometric studies determine emotional responses based on the change in the size of an eye's pupil. Caution must be exercised when interpreting results from physiological techniques because confounding influences may be present (e.g., transfer of affect from programmes or between advertisements in the same product-category).

A newly emerging field of neuro-marketing combines neuroscience and qualitative methods to study brain responses and processes with respect to feelings produced when an individual views an ad or a product. Neuroscientific techniques such as *f*unctional Magnetic Resonance Imaging techniques (or *f*MRI) are increasingly being used to assess physiological responses (e.g., Kolb and Taylor, 1981; Nakamura et al., 1999; Morris, 2005). Although the *f*MRI is possibly the most promising and reliable method of neuro-marketing most of the current techniques rely on older and less useful technology: EKG (Electrocardiogram), and GSR (Galvanic Skin Response) that measure a single dimension, arousal. Some newer adaptations of these techniques claim to evaluate a combination of heart rhythms and skin conductance to produce a two-dimensional approach similar to the self-report of pleasure and arousal (Hall, 2004). Unfortunately, the validity of these types of measures with respect to purchase behaviour remains to be demonstrated.

Facial expressions, as suggested by the theory of facial expressions, are also important tools because of their ability to effectively communicate internal body states without the use of languages skills (Darwin, 1898; Hazlett and Hazlett, 1999). Various coding systems for facial expressions have been proposed including the Facial Action Coding System or FACS (Ekman and Freisen, 1978) and Marschalk Emotional Expression Deck (Agres, 1984). Each of these coding systems classifies facial expressions based on a select set of dimensions (e.g., pleasantness–unpleasantness and acceptance–rejection). Facial expressions may be captured via cameras or via use of elaborate devices such as electromyographs (EMG), which measure subtle changes in the facial musculature.

Empirical evidence suggests that coding systems are not foolproof in identifying a unique emotional response because individuals can consciously control facial expressions through upbringing or cultural considerations (Izard, 1972, 1977; Scherer and Wallbott, 1994). Skeptics of these types of measures raise doubts about the application of laboratory-based findings to a real-life scenario. Methods are therefore being developed to capture consumers' emotional response in a more typical, real-life scenario (e.g., while using an ATM machine). One such effort is by Teradata, a division of NCR Corporation. NCR, a company that handles several million dollars self-service transactions annually, in collaboration with the University of Southern California's Integrated Media Systems Center is working to develop a system that captures consumers' facial expressions. Analysis of such information, along with customer reported data via surveys is expected to develop a rich database of consumers' emotional responses.

Self-report measures

The various descriptive theories of emotion suggest that the labelling of the subjective experience of emotion provides a means for measuring and distinguishing among emotional states (Hirschmann and Holbrook, 1982; Holbrook and Hirschman, 1982; Holbrook and Batra, 1987; Westbrook, 1987). The marketing and advertising literature is filled with paper and pencil scales for labelling emotional responses (see Bearden et al., 1999, Bruner et al., 1992, 1996, 2000, 2005 for comprehensive listings of these scales). For example, measuring emotional response using the PAD dimensions can be accomplished with two methods. The b-polar PAD scale (Mehrabian, 1980, 1995, 1997) measures emotional responses in terms of three independent dimensions: (a) pleasure (i.e., positive and negative emotional state), (b) arousal (i.e., extent of physical activity and mental alertness associated with the emotional response), and (c) dominance (i.e., degree of control experienced associated with the emotional response).

Alternatively the Self-Assessment Manikin (SAM) (Lang, 1980) has been demonstrated to be better than the verbal checklist for measuring emotional responses because the visual method eliminates cognitive processing (Morris and Waine, 1993). Morris et al. (1995, 1996) developed a measure of emotional response to marketing communications stimuli, AdSAM®, that is based on SAM. ADSAM® uses a graphic character, instead of semantic terms, to represent the three dimensions of the PAD model. Drawing on early work on emotions by psychologists and other social scientists, AdSAM® operates on the theory that all emotions are composed of three underlying dimensions: Pleasure, Arousal, and Dominance. Any emotion can be understood as a unique combination of these fundamental dimensions. Anger, for example, is characterized by low pleasure, high arousal, and high dominance. The same combination of pleasure and arousal with *low* dominance is experienced as fear or anxiety.

AdSAM® has been used to assess responses to television advertising (Morris et al., 1992, 2002), pre-production vs. post-production advertising (Morris and Waine, 1993), and political messages (Morris, 1999). SAM and ADSAM have also been used to measure emotional responses in a variety of studies, including reactions to advertisements (Morris et al., 1992), pictures (International Affective Picture System, IAPS) (Greenwald et al., 1989; Lang et al., 1993), images (Miller et al., 1987), sounds (Bradley, 1994) music (Morris and Boone, 1998) and more. More recently, Morris et al. (2002) showed in a study of over 23 000 responses to 240 advertising messages in a well known copy-testing system, that emotional response – as measured by AdSAM® – explained up to 37% of the variance in purchase intent and brand interest. Cognitive measures, believability and knowledge, explained 0–13%.

In another applied environment, the ARS Group, a well-known copy testing company has shown, using AdSAM®, that responses to successful advertising are a combination of rational and emotional components. The greatest advertising success is achieved when ads have both strong rational and emotional messages. In the ARS study emotional responses were related to significant changes in consumer brand preference and persuasion scores that have been validated as predictors of in-market changes in market share and product trial in the case of new products. An ad that performed well on both measures had ~7 times greater probability of being effective than an ad that is in neither (ARS, 2005). In is interesting to note that this is one of the very few studies to attempt to link measured emotional response to actual sales data. Most studies of emotional response have linked emotion to such intermediate measures of response as attention, recall, and attitude that are themselves not strong and consistent predictors of brand preference and sales. This is a major problem with respect to understanding the influence of emotional response on the effectiveness of advertising.

Verbal versus visual measures

It is difficult to design a verbal based instrument that shares the same meaning when translated from language to language. There is also a general assumption that some dimensions of emotional response are not captured by verbal, self-report measures that are inherently cognitive. Despite this general recognition, most self-report measures reported in the literature are verbal. One exception, AdSAM® (Morris, 1995) is a visual measure. Since AdSAM® uses a graphic character the language bias found in verbal measures (Edell and Burke, 1987) is eliminated (Morris et al., 1996; Morris, 1995; Morris and Waine, 1993). The facial expressions used in AdSAM® have consistent meanings globally and the SAM measure can be effectively interpreted in multiple cultures (Bradley et al., 1992). Furthermore, research by Russell (1983) and his colleagues (Russell et al., 1989) found the Pleasure and Arousal dimensions tapped by AdSAM® to be consistent cross-culturally in Gujarati, Croatian, Japanese, Cantonese Chinese, Greek, Chinese and English.

In contrast to research that has focused on the nonverbal dimensions of emotional response, cognitive theories, such as attribution and the appraisal theories, emphasize the role of knowledge structures in the processing of emotional responses. These constructivist theories largely rely on cognitive measures for emotional response including, written self-reports (e.g., spoken and written words) on rating scales, open-ended questions on surveys and during interviews, responses to projective instruments (e.g., sentence completion tasks, self-assessment tasks and perceptions regarding other peoples behaviour). Attribution and appraisal theories generally employ cognitive responses and dismiss the importance of any immediate affective responses (e.g., Lazarus, 1991). Cognitive responses can be measured, for example, in terms of effect on awareness (e.g., aided and unaided recall), and beliefs generated (e.g., thought-listing surveys). As with other measures of emotional response to advertising, the measures suggested by attribution and appraisal theories have only infrequently been examined in the context of their ability to predict changes in sales or other relevant in-market sales.

SUMMARY: THE FUTURE OF EMOTIONS RESEARCH IN ADVERTISING

Many of the same measures of emotional response used today will continue to be used in the future. Future contributions will come in the form of more sophisticated uses of current measures, i.e., emotional segmentation and identification of drivers of emotions, as well as the further development of physiological techniques, i.e., fMRI. In order for these and other techniques to be adopted and better serve management decision-making, a better understanding of emotion will be required by the marketing community. While there is a rich body of theoretical literature this literature has yet to be systematically linked to normative guidelines for the use of emotion in advertising or well-articulated measures of in-market advertising effectiveness. After a review of measures of various measures of emotional response to advertising Poels and Dewitte (2006) concluded that "[m]uch is still unknown about the predictive validity of different measurement methods. ... We call for studies that investigate how the measurement types relate to external measures such as purchase intention or brand choice behavior" (p. 20).

The present review suggests a similar conclusion but also suggests the need for five other changes in the way research is conducted. First, there is a need for a more explicit link to theory. Second, there is a need to complement research on individual response to aggregate response and the variability within such aggregate response. Third, there is a need to assure that validation involves relevant in-market measures of response, such as changes in sales and market share, in addition to studies of the relationship between emotion and other intermediate outcomes of response to advertising, such as recall, attitude and intention. Fourth, it is important to distinguish between the effects of emotional benefits of products and services depicted in advertising and emotional elements of execution. Finally, knowledge about the effects of emotion will grow as research more clearly distinguishes between emotions represented <u>in</u> the advertising and the emotions evoked in the consumer <u>by</u> the advertising.

Verbal (rational) measures, such as recall, message comprehension and product beliefs, have existed for many years and valid or not are better understood and easier to apply than emotional response techniques. A great deal of research has focused on attempts to link emotional content in advertising to these measures or show how specific measures of emotional response are related to verbal measures. There remains a general lack of attention to and appreciation for the need to establish the validity of measures of advertising with respect to such outcomes as market share and sales. This neglect exists for most measures of advertising effectiveness

but is especially problematic for measures of emotional response.

REFERENCES

Aaker, D.A. and D.E. Bruzzone (1985), "Causes of Irritation in Advertising," *Journal of Marketing*, 49 (2), 47–57.

Aaker, D.A., D.M. Stayman, and M.R. Hagerty (1986), "Warmth in Advertising: Measurement, Impact, and Sequence Effects," *The Journal of Consumer Research*, 12 (4), 365–81.

Aaker, J.L. and P. Williams (1998), "Empathy versus Pride; The Influence of Emotional Appeals Across Cultures," *Journal of Consumer Research*, 25 (December), 241–61.

Agres, S.J. (1984), *The Marschalk Emotional Expression Deck*, Unpublished manuscript, The Marschalk Company, Inc.

ARS (2005), "Superior Performance of Ads in the *Heart Zone* and *Mind Zone* Regions" Unpublished manuscript, RSC the quality measurement company.

Averill, J.R. (1982), *Anger and Aggression. An Essay on Emotion*, New York: Springer.

Aylesworth, A.B., R.C. Goodstein, and A. Kalra (1999), "Effect of Archetypal Embeds on Feelings: An Indirect Route to Affecting Attitudes?" *Journal of Advertising*, 28 (3), 73–81.

Ayelsworth, A.B. and S.B. MacKenzie (1999), "Context is Key: The Effect of Program-Induced Mood on Thoughts about the Ad," *Journal of Advertising*, 27 (2), 17–27.

Bagozzi, R.P. (1986), "Attitude Formation under the Theory of Reasoned Action and a Purposeful Behavior Reformulation," *British Journal of Social Psychology*, 25, 95–107.

Bagozzi, R.P., Mahesh Gopinath, and Prashanth U. Nyer (1999), "The Role of Emotions in Marketing," *Journal of the Academy of Marketing Science*, 27 (2), 184–206.

Bearden, W.O., R.G. Netemeyer, and M.F. Mobley (1999), *Handbook of Marketing Scales: Multi-item Measures for Marketing and Consumer Behavior Research*, 2nd edn, Thousand Oaks, CA: Sage.

Bernstein, D.A., A. Clarke-Stewart, A., L.A. Penner, E.J., Roy, and C.D. Wickens (2000), *Psychology*, 5th edn, Boston, MA: Houghton Mifflin Company.

Boster, F.J., and P. Mongeau (1984), "Fear-arousing Persuasive Messages," in *Communication Yearbook 8*, eds. R.N. Bostrom and B.H. Westley, Newbury Park, CA: Sage, pp. 330–75.

Bradley, M.M. (1994), "Emotional Memory: A Dimensional Analysis," in *The Emotions: Essays on Emotion Theory*, eds. S. Van Groot, N.E. Van dePoll, & J. Sargeant, Hillsdale, NJ: Erlbaum, pp. 97–134.

Bradley, M.M., Greenwald, M.K., and Hamm, A.O. (1993), "Affective Picture Processing," in *The Structure of Emotion: Psychophysiological*, eds. N.Birbaumer & A. Ohman, *Cognitive and Clinical Aspects*, Toronto: Hogrefe & Huber.

Brooker, G. (1981), "A Comparison of the Persuasive Effects of Mild Humor and Mild Fear Appeals," *Journal of Advertising*, 10 (4), 29–40.

Bruner, G. II and P.J. Hensel (1992), *Handbook of Marketing Scales: A Compilation of Multi-Item Measures*, Vol. 1, Mason, OH: Southwestern Publishing.

Bruner, G. II and P.J. Hensel (1996), *Handbook of Marketing Scales: A Compilation of Multi-Item Measures*, Vol. 1I, Mason, OH: Southwestern Publishing.

Bruner, G. II, K. James, and P.J. Hensel (2000), *Handbook of Marketing Scales: A Compilation of Multi-Item Measures*, Vol. 1II, Mason, OH: Southwestern Publishing.

Bruner, G. II, P.J. Hensel, and K. James (2005), *Handbook of Marketing Scales: Vol. 1V: Consumer Behavior*, Mason, OH: Southwestern Publishing.

Bryant, J., P.W. Comisky, and D. Zillmann, (1979), "Teachers' Humor in the College Classroom," *Communication Education*, 28, 110–28.

Burke, M.C. and J.A. Edell (1986), "Ad Reactions Over Time: Capturing Changes in the Real World," *Journal of Consumer Research*, 13 (June), 114–18.

Burke, M.C. and J.A. Edell (1989), "The Impact of Feelings on Ad-Based Affect and Cognition," *Journal of Marketing Research*, 1 (February), 69–83.

Cannon, W.B. (1927), "The James-Lange Theory of Emotions: A Critical Examination and an Alternative Theory," *American Journal of Psychology*, 39, 106–24.

Clark, M.S. (1982), "A Role for Arousal in the Link between Feeling States, Judgments, and Behavior," in *Affect and Cognition: The 17th Annual Carnegie Symposium on Cognition*, eds. M.S. Clark and S.T. Fiske, Hillsdale, N. J.: Erlbaum.

Corteen, R.S. and B. Wood (1972), "Autonomic Responses to Shock Associated Words in an Unattended Channel," *Journal of Experimental Psychology*, 94 (3), 308–13.

Darwin, C. (1898), *The Expression of the Emotions in Man and Animals*, New York: Appleton. (Originally published 1872).

Davis, M.H. (1983), "Measuring Individual Differences in Empathy: Evidence for a Multidimensional Approach," *Journal of Personality and Social Psychology*, 44 (January), 113–26.

de Mello, G.E. and D.J. MacInnis (2005), "Consuming Hope: Motivated Reasoning and the Marketplace as Sources of Hope," in *Inside Consumption: Frontiers of Research on Consumer Motives, Goals, and Desires*, eds. S. Ratneshwar, D. Mick, and C. Huffman, New York: Routledge.

Donovan, R.J., J.R. Rossiter, Gilian Marcoolyn, and Andrew Nesdale (1994), "Store Atmosphere and Purchasing Behavior," *Journal of Retailing*, 70 (3), 283–94.

Duncan, C.P. and J.E. Nelson (1985)," Effects of Humor in a Radio Advertising Experiment," *Journal of Advertising*, 14 (2), 33–40.

Edell, J.A. and M.C. Burke (1987), "The Power of Feeling in Understanding Advertising Effects," *Journal of Consumer Research*, 14 (December), 421–33.

Ekman, P. (1972), *Emotion in the Human Face*, Elmsford, NY: Pergamon.

Ekman, P. and R.J. Davidson (1994), *The Nature of Emotion: Fundamental Questions*, New York: Oxford University Press.

Ekman, P. and W.V. Friesen (1978), *Facial Action Coding System (FACS): A Technique for the Measurement of Facial Action*, Palo Alto, CA: Consulting Psychologists Press.

Ekman, P. and W.V. Friesen (1982), "Felt, False and Miserable Smiles," *Journal of Nonverbal Behavior*, 6, 238–52.

Ekman, P. and H. Oster (1979), "Facial Expression of Emotion," *Annual Review of Psychology*, 30, 527–54.

Folkes, V.S. (1984), "Consumer Reaction to Product Failure: An Attributional Approach," *Journal of Consumer Research*, 10 (4), 398–409.

Frijda, N.H. (1986), *The Emotions*, Cambridge, England: Cambridge University Press.

Gelb, B.D. and C.M. Pickett (1983)," Attitude-toward-the-ad: Links to Humor and to Advertising Effectiveness" *Journal of Advertising*, 12, 39–47.

Greenwald, M.K., E.W. Cook, and P.J. Lang (1989), "Affective Judgment and Psychophysiological Response: Dimensional Covariation in the Evaluation of Pictorial Stimuli," *Journal of Psychophysiology*, 3 (1), 51–64.

Hall, B.F. (2004), "On Measuring the Power of Communications," *Journal of Advertising Research;* 44 (June), 181–7.

Hazlett, R.L. and A.Y. Hazlett (1999), "Emotional Response to Television Commercials: facial EMG vs. Self-Report," *Journal of Advertising Research*, 35 (March/April), pp. 7–23.

Hirschmann, E.C. and M.B. Holbrook (1982), "Hedonic Consumption: Emerging Concepts, Methods and Propositions," *Journal of Marketing*, 46 (3), 92–101.

Holbrook, M.B. and E.C. Hirschmann (1982), "The Experiential Aspects of Consumption: Consumer Fantasies, Feelings, and Fun," *Journal of Consumer Research,* 9 (September), 132–40.

Holbrook, M.B. and R. Batra (1987), "Assessing the Role of Emotions as Mediators of Consumer Responses to Advertising," *Journal of Consumer Research,* 14 (December), 404–20.

Hui, M.K. and J.E. Bateson (1991), "Perceived Control and the Effects of Crowding and Consumer Choice on the Service Experience," *Journal of Consumer Research,* 18 (2), 174–84.

Izard, C.E. (1971). *The Face of Emotion*, New York: Appleton-Century-Crofts.

Izard, C.E. (1972), *Patterns of Emotion,* San Diego, CA, Academic Press.

Izard, C.E. (1977), *Human Emotions,* New York: Plenum.

Izard, C.E. (1992), "Basic Emotions, Relations Among Emotions, and Emotion-Cognition Relations," *Psychological Review*, 99 (3), 561–65.

James, W. (1884), "What is an Emotion?," *Mind*, 9, 188–205.

Johnson, A.R. and D.W. Stewart (2004), "A Re-Appraisal of the Role of Emotion in Consumer Behavior: Traditional and Contemporary Approaches," *Review of Marketing Research*, 1, Armonk, N.Y.: M.E. Sharpe, Inc., pp. 1–33.

Keller, P.A., I.M. Lippus, and B.K. Rimer (2003), "Affect, Framing, and Persuasion," *Journal of Marketing Research,* 40 (February), 54–65.

Kelley, H.H. (1967), "Attribution Theory in Social Psychology," in D. Levine (ed.), *Nebraska Symposium on Motivation,* Vol. 15, Lincoln: University of Nebraska Press, pp. 192–240.

Kolb, B. and L. Taylor (1981), "Affective Behavior in Patients with Localized Cortical Excisions: Role of Lesion Site and Side," *Science*, 214, 89–91.

Lang, P.J. (1980), "Behavioral Treatment and Bio-Behavioral Assessment: Computer Applications in Technology." in *Mental Health Care Delivery Systems,* eds. J.B. Sidowski, J.H. Johnson, and T.A. Williams, Norwood, NJ: Ablex, pp. 119–37.

Lang, P.J., M.K. Greenwald, M.M. Bradley, and A.O., Hamm (1993), "Looking at Pictures: Affective, Facial, Visceral, and Behavioral Reactions," *Psychophysiology*, 30, 261–73.

Lazarus, R.S. (1991), *Emotion and Adaptation*, New York: Oxford University Press.Lazarus, R.S. (1999), *Stress and Emotion: A New Synthesis,* New York, NY: Springer Publisher Co.

Laird, J.D. (1974), "Self-Attribution of Emotion: The Effects of Expressive Behavior on the Quality of Emotional Experience," *Journal of Personality and Social Psychology,* 29, 475–86.

MacInnis, D.J. and G. DeMello (2005), "The Concept of Hope and its Relevance to Product Evaluation and Choice," *Journal of Marketing*, 68 (January), 1–14.

Maxham, J.G. and R.G. Netemeyer (2002), "A Longitudinal Study of Complaining Customers' Evaluations of Multiple Service Failures and Recovery Efforts," *Journal of Marketing*, 66 (October), 57–71.

Mehrabian, A. (1980), *Basic Dimensions for a General Psychological Theory : Implications for Personality, Social, Environmental, and Developmental Studies,* Cambridge, MA: Oelgeschalger, Gunn and Hain.

Mehrabian, A. (1995), "Framework for a Comprehensive Description and Measurement of Emotional States," *Genetic, Social, and General Psychology Monographs,* 121, 339–61.

Mehrabian, A. (1997), "Comparisons of the PAD and PANAS as Models for Describing Emotions and for Differentiating Anxiety from Depression," *Journal of Psychopathology and Behavioral Assessment*, 19, 331–57.

Mehrabian, A. and J.A. Russell (1974), *An Approach to Environmental Psychology,* Cambridge, MA: The MIT Press.

Mehrabian, A. and J.A. Russell (1977), "Evidence of a Three-factor Theory of Emotions," *Journal of Research in Personality,* 11, 273–94.

Mewborn, R.C. and R.W. Rogers (1979), "Effects of Threatening and Reassuring Components of Fear Appeals and the Physiological and Verbal Measures of Emotions and Attitudes," *Journal of Experimental and Social Psychology*, 15, 242–53.

Miller, G.A., D.N. Levin, and M.J. Kozak (1987), "Individual Differences in Imagery and the Psychophysiology of Emotion," *Cognition & Emotion*, 1 (4), 367–90.

Mitchell, A.A. and J.C. Olson (1981), "Are Product Attribute Beliefs the Only Mediator of Advertising Effects on Brands Attitudes?" *Journal of Marketing Research,* 18 (August), 318–32.

Moore, D.J., W.D. Harris, and H.C. Chen (1995), "Affect Intensity: An Individual Difference Response to Advertising Appeals," *Journal of Consumer Research*, 22 (September), 154–64.

Morris, J.D. (1995), "Observations: SAM: The Self-Assessment Manikin: An Efficient Cross-cultural Measurement of Emotional Response," *Journal of Advertising Research,* 35 (6), 63–8.

Morris, J.D. and M.A. Boone (1998), "The Effects of Music on Emotional Response, Brand Attitude, and Purchase Intent in an Emotional Advertising Condition," in *Advances in Consumer Research,* eds. J.W. Alba and J.W. Hutchinson.

Morris, J.D., M.M. Bradley, C.A. Waine and J.B. Lang (1992), "Assessing Affective Reactions to Advertisements with the Self-assessment Manikin (SAM)," *paper was presented at Southern Marketing Association Conference.*

Morris, J.D., K.L., Strausbaugh and M. Nthangeni. (1996), "Emotional Response to Advertisements (or Commercials) across Cultures," in the *Proceedings of the 1996 Conference of the American Academy of Advertising.*

Morris, J.D., M.S. Roberts, and G.F. Baker (1999), "Emotional Responses of African American Voters to Ad Messages," in *The Electronic Election: Perspectives on the 1996 Campaign Communication,* eds. L.L. Kaid and D.G. Bystrom, Mahwah, NJ: Lawrence Erlbaum Associates.

Morris, J.D. and C.A. Waine (1993), "Managing the Creative Effort: Pre- production and Post-production Measures of Emotional," in the *Proceedings of the 1993 Conference of the American Academy of Advertising*, ed. Esther Thorson, Columbia, MO, 158–76.

Morris, J.D., C.A. Waine, and J.B. Lang (1992), "Assessing Emotional Responses to Advertisements with (SAM) the Self-Assessment Manikin," in the *Proceedings of the Allied Southern Business Association, 1993 Annual Meeting.* Allied Southern Business Association.

Morris, J.D., C.M. Woo, J.A. Geason, and J. Kim (2002), "The Power of Affect: Predicting Intention," *Journal of Advertising Research,* 42 (May/June), 7–17.

Nakamura, K., R. Kawashima, K. Ito, et al. (1999), "Activation of the Right Inferior Cortex During Assessment of Facial Emotion," *The American Physiological Society,* 1610–14.

Osgood, C.E., G.J. Suci, and P.H. Tannebaum (1957), *The Measurement of Meaning*, Urbana, Ill: University of Illinois Press.

Page, T.J. Jr., P.J. Daugherty, D. Eroglu, D.E. Hartman, S.D. Johnson, and D.-H. Lee (1988), "Measuring Emotional Response To Advertising: A Comment on Stout and Leckenby," *Journal of Advertising,* 17, 49–52.

Pechmann, C. and D.W. Stewart (1988), "The Multidimensionality of Persuasive Communications: Theoretical and Empirical Foundations," in *Perspectives on the Affective and Cognitive Effects of Advertising,* eds. A. Tybout and P. Caferatta, Lexington, Mass.: Lexington Books.

Phillips, R.G. and J.E. LeDoux (1992), *Behavioral Neuroscience*, 106 (2), 274–85.

Plutchik, R. (1980), *Emotion: A Psycho evolutionary Synthesis,* New York: Harper and Row.

Plutchik, R. (1982), " A Psychoevolutionary Theory of Emotions," *Social Science Information,* 21 (4–5), 529–53.

Poels, K. and S. Dewitte (2006), "How to Capture the Heart? Reviewing 20 Years of Emotion Measurement in Advertising," *Journal of Advertising Research,* 46 (May), 18–37.

Raghunathan, R. and Y. Trope (2002), "Walking the Tightrope Between Feeling Good and Being Accurate: Mood as a Resource in Processing Persuasive Messages," *Journal of Personality and Social Psychology,* 83 (September), 510–25.

Richins, M.L. (1997), "Measuring Emotions in Consumption Experience," *Journal of Consumer Research,* 24 (2), 127–46.

Roseman, I.J. (1984), "Cognitive Determinants of Emotion: A Structural Theory," *Review of Personality and Social Psychology,* 5, 11–36.

Roseman, I.J., C. Wiest, and T.S. Swartz (1994), "Phenomenology, Behaviors, and Goals Differentiate Discrete Emotions," *Journal of Personality and Social Psychology,* 67, 206–21.

Russell, J.A. (1978), "Evidence of Convergent Validity on the Dimensions of Affect," *Journal of Personality and Social Psychology,* 36, 1152–68.

Russell, J.A. (1979), "Affective Space is Bipolar," *Journal of Personality and Social Psychology,* 37, 345–56.

Russell, J.A. (1980), "A Circumplex Model of Affect," *Journal of Personality and Social Psychology*, 39, 1161–78.

Russell, J.A. (1983), "Pancultural Aspects of the Human Conceptual Organization of Emotions," *Journal of Personality and Social Psychology*, 45, 1152–68.

Russell, J.A. and A. Mehrabian (1977), "Evidence for a Three-Factor Theory of Emotions," *Journal of Research in Personality*, 11 (36), 273–94.

Russell, J.A., Lewicka, M. and Niit, T. (1989), "A Cross-cultural Study of a Circumplex Model of Affect," *Journal of Personality and Social Psychology*, 57, 848–56.

Schachter, S. and J.E. Singer (1962), "Cognitive, Social and Physiological Determinants of Emotional State," *Psychological Review,* 69, 379–99.

Scherer, K.R. (2001), "Appraisal Considered as a Process of Multilevel Sequential Checking," in *Appraisal Processes in Emotion: Theory, Methods, Research,* eds. K.R. Scherer and A. Schorr, New York: Oxford University Press.

Scherer, K.R. and H.G. Wallbott (1994), "Evidence for Universality and Cultural Variation of Differential Emotion Response Patterning," *Journal of Personality and Social Psychology,* 66, 310–28.

Shimp, T. (1981), "Attitude Toward the Ad As a Moderator of Consumer Brand Choice," *Journal of Advertising,* 10 (2), 9–15.

Smit, E.G., L. van Meurs, and P.C. Neijens (2006), "Effects of Advertising Likeability: A 10-Year Perspective," *Journal of Advertising Research,* 46 (March), 73–83.

Stewart, D.W. (1984), "Physiological measurements of Advertising Effects: An Unfulfilled Promise," *Psychology and Marketing,* 1 (1), 43–8.

Stewart, D.W. and M.A. Kamins (2003), "Marketing Communications," in B. Weitz (ed.), *Handbook of Marketing,* Thousand Oaks, CA: Sage, pp. 282–309.

Stout, P.A. and J.D. Leckenby (1986), "Measuring Emotional Response to Advertising," *Journal of Advertising,* 15 (4), 35–42.

Tomkins, S.S. (1962), *Affect, Imagery and Consciousness,* Vol. 1, New York: Springer.

Watson, D. and A. Tellegen (1985), "Toward a Consensual Structure of Mood," *Psychological Bulletin,* 98 (2), 219–315.

Weiner, B. (1985), "An Attributional Theory of Achievement Motivation and Emotion," *Psychological Review,* 92 (4), 548–73.

Weiner, B. (1986), An Attributional Theory of Motivation and Emotion, New York: Springer-Verlag.

Weiner, B., D. Russell, and D. Lerman (1979), "The Cognition-Emotion Process in Achievement-Related Contexts," *Journal of Personality and Social Psychology,* 37 (7), 1211–20.

Wells, W.D., C. Leavitt, and M. McConville (1971), "A Reaction Profile for TV Commercials," *Journal of Advertising Research,* 11 (December), 11–17.

Westbrook, R.A. (1987), "Product/Consumption-Based Affective Responses and Post-Purchase Processes," *Journal of Marketing Research,* 24 (3), 258–70.

Witte, K. (1995), "Generating Effective Risk Messages: How Scary Should Your Risk Communication Be?," in *Communication Yearbook,* ed. B.R. Burleson, Vol. 18, Thousand Oaks, CA: Sage, pp. 229–54.

Zillman, D. (1978), "Attribution and Misattribution of Excitatory Reactions," in *New Directions in Attribution Research* eds. J.H. Harvey, W. Ickes and R.F. Kidd, Vol. 2, New York: Wiley.

Metaphor in Advertising

Gerald Zaltman and Dara MacCaba

Recent years have seen many significant advances in the understanding of human cognition and behaviour. Many people have suggested that much current thinking about advertising (and marketing generally) is incomplete or even incorrect since it does not incorporate many of these advances (Schultz, 2005). This chapter provides an overview of important, recent scientific developments about the mind with particular emphasis on the central role of metaphor in cognition and advertising. After all, advertising itself is a representation in one form of what a firm offers in another form. Of course, the idea that metaphor is important in communications including advertising is not new. However, the mechanisms whereby metaphor exerts influence has received relatively little attention in marketing while at the same time there have been important advances in linguistics and the cognitive sciences in understanding metaphor functioning.

Narrowly construed, metaphor is the representation of one thing in terms of another, e.g., the use of a butterfly in a pharmaceutical ad to convey the idea of a gentle, pleasing transformation produced by a branded sleep medication. Broadly construed, which is how the term metaphor is used in this chapter, it includes all non-literal representations such

as use of the term "up" to represent an emotional state or idiomatic expressions such as "let sleeping dogs lie" to suggest caution about further exploring an issue.[1] Many metaphors are described as "dead" since they have become so much a part of everyday conversation. But dead metaphors are very powerful in their afterlife since their effects are more subtle (Lackoff and Johnson, 1999; Kovecses, 2002). It has been suggested elsewhere that only a small proportion of all thought is ever expressed in direct, literal ways (Mithen, 2006).

While metaphors are non-literal expressions it is important to note that they also involve a *re*-presentation. Both a butterfly and a food blender symbolize transformation, but each has special meanings (gentle versus forceful) that carry over or extend beyond the thought being conveyed. As a result of this carry over, the intended thought may be subtly yet significantly changed by virtue of the metaphor used; it is re-presented differently by different metaphors. For example, a particular Ford vehicle is understood very differently when it is represented by a wild horse in its name (Mustang) than when the exact same vehicle is represented by another creature in its name, e.g., the Ford Rhinoceros or Ford Bee.

Thus, in addition to metaphor's role in helping to convey information about a particular product or service's attributes and functions, it also involves the creation of new ideas beyond those unique to the metaphor or to the product or service being advertised. This process whereby new ideas are formed as ideas from two separate domains such as a Ford vehicle and a wild horse are brought together is called conceptual blending. Conceptual blending is central to the use of metaphors in advertising and to the co-creation of meaning (Fauconnier and Turner, 2002). Conceptual blending is part of the imaginative process. This makes it central to the processes in which consumers create meaningful stories using a blend of advertising stimuli and their own knowledge.

The chapter explores the following issues from an advertising perspective:

- The Role of Metaphor in Cognition
- Metaphor and Emotion
- The Role of Metaphor and Memory
- The Use of Metaphor in Advertising Research.

Advertising practitioners and researchers are increasingly aware of the importance of unconscious processes, especially those involving metaphor, and of the limitations of traditional methods in providing insight about these processes. The ideas developed here will be helpful as the industry continues to grapple with these issues. The insights offered should assist in the development of engaging communications and in assessing their impact.

As we shall see, metaphor plays a critical role in cognition or ways of knowing, thinking and representing ideas. While other chapters in this volume address emotion (see especially Chapter 2.4) and ad evaluations in more detail, we also address emotion and the evaluation of advertising from the perspective of metaphor processing. Of special interest is the strong association between memory and emotion. This association is important since for most advertising to be effective, it must have an enduring emotional impact among consumers. Metaphor is critical in mediating between emotion and memory and hence in establishing enduring impact on consumers especially as they create their own meanings or stories based on advertising stimuli. As we shall see, memory itself is often malleable and reconstructive and metaphors (again, broadly construed) are special devices whereby changes in memory can be fostered, partly through conceptual blending. This is especially the case when metaphors introduce or tap into relevant emotions. All of this has important implications for conducting both formative and summative evaluative advertising research.

THE ROLE OF METAPHOR IN COGNITION

The brain is both a representational and connecting organ. Our senses, for instance, acquire information in one form of energy, e.g., light or sound waves, which are then converted and re-presented as other forms of energy by neural systems involving multiple brain sites. Neural associations among these separate sites create yet another representation, e.g., the representation of a face *as if* it were displayed in one place in the brain when in fact different elements of a face are registered in different brain sites. As Antonio Damasio (2003) notes:

> "The neural patterns and the corresponding mental images of the objects and events outside the brain are creations of the brain related to the reality that prompts their creation rather than passive mirror images reflecting that reality."

What the brain records as a foundation for our experience is simply a metaphor, a re-presentation of an external object or event in another form in various regions of the brain. Because people are so biologically similar they construct similar neural patterns. This, in turn, creates the illusion that we have recorded an accurate picture of an external reality rather than a created version of it.

Internal interpretative processes are very active as we create versions of external realities. Interpretative patterns, often called frames, help us process this information and determine which pieces most merit our conscious attention. Frames are very powerful. They determine what information does and does not capture our further attention (both conscious and unconscious), how that information is processed, and how we respond to it (Lakoff, 2004; Lakoff and Jonson, 2004; Velde, 2004). Frames, therefore, determine what we approach and avoid, the stimuli that capture our attention, and the assumptions we automatically generate to give affective meaning to our experiences. Frames are so powerful that facts suggesting a frame is incorrect will tend to be ignored and frames that work to our disadvantage will sometimes prevail over self interest (Lakoff, 2004).

Of special interest here is a type of frame called a "deep metaphor."[2] These are fundamental ways of sensing and representing external realities. For example, some consumers may frame their overall experience as shoppers in terms of a journey while others may frame it in terms of force involving a contest or tug of war between sellers and buyers. These basic frames are automatic, generally unconscious, and yet very important for reasons just noted. In order to communicate effectively, it is necessary to know what frames an audience uses for the topic at hand and which elements of those frames need to be reinforced and which need to be changed. It is also necessary to know what activates the frames in positive and negative ways. For example, having a balanced financial portfolio is particularly important to some investors. A brochure showing a person holding a balancing pole while walking a tightrope across a deep chasm to suggest the protection offered by a balanced financial portfolio indeed activates the deep metaphor of balance. But in one concept test it turned out that for some investors this actually heightened feelings of insecurity and hence activated the deep metaphor in its negative state of imbalance. This produced avoidant tendencies with respect to seeking help from an advisor, just the opposite of the brochure's intent.

In lower mammals, cognitive maps are created by the hippocampus to represent the self in space; in humans, the parietal lobes which evolved from the hippocampus draw on our bodily experiences and use these experiences metaphorically as the basis for understanding. As one neuroscientist explains (Damasio, 1994):

"… our very own organism rather than some absolute external reality is used as the ground reference for the constructions we make about the world around us … our most refined thoughts and best actions, our greatest joys and deepest sorrows, use the body as a yardstick."

Metaphors, then, are not merely convenient devices for describing experience. Every time we use expressions such as "I *see* what you mean," "his words *touched* me" or "let me *walk you* through this problem" we are leveraging shared physical experiences to communicate abstract concepts and ideas not directly related to the sensory or motor systems being employed as metaphors. These physical experiences are key components of deep metaphors which are hardwired through the process of embodied cognition (Gallagher, 2005; Thompson and Rosch, 1991). In this way, metaphors are much like emotions; they determine the way we perceive our world, formulate abstract thoughts, and enable us to communicate experiences through common language and framings often based on shared bodily experiences. Of course, many metaphors such as the reference to a "yardstick" in the above quote do not use the body as a referent.

The power of metaphors in communicating experiences is reflected in the fact that people use them at a rate of about five per minute of speech. For instance, we use the deep metaphor of Resource when we talk about "saving time," "investing time" or "spending time." For a company like Rolex, understanding the metaphors people use to think about time is extremely important. Many of the most successful brands make use of metaphors in their advertising in communicating a brand idea by means of shared physical experiences, real or imagined.

Figure 2.5.1 Running on Air

In Figure 2.5.1, the Nike advertisement invites us to use our associations with running and with air to imagine what it would be like to experience both at the same time using their brand of sneakers. This results in a new idea or blend – the experience of Freedom. (Conceptual blending is discussed further later in this chapter.)

Metaphor and emotion

There has been renewed interest in the role of emotions in advertising (see also Chapter 2.4). An example is The Advertising Research Foundation's project on Emotion in Advertising.[3] This is an ongoing collaborative effort involving leading advertising research companies and national advertisers who are exploring ways of identifying and measuring the emotional content of ads and relating that content to the ad's apparent effectiveness. One unambiguous finding that has emerged in a comparison of ads judged to be especially effective and those judged to be much less so is that the ability of an ad to elicit emotional responses is predictive of its effectiveness.

In fact, the importance of emotion in all human thought including advertising is well established (if often ignored) (Lowenstein and Lerner, 2003). Kovecses (2000) sums up the position of cognitive linguists on this

issue: "… it is impossible to conceptualize most aspects of the emotions in other than metaphorical terms." Metaphor is central to understanding and leveraging emotions and is therefore of special importance in research relating to the development and evaluation of advertising strategies and executions. Emotional language is largely figurative or metaphorical. Figurative speech not only reveals emotions and helps us understand them but can create emotional experiences as well.

Hence, again, the importance of metaphor in conducting research to identify brand and category relevant emotions, in creating specific communications to engage those emotions, and in assessing the emotional impact of communications on consumers. Put differently, we need to understand both how metaphors can activate and represent emotions in order to select the appropriate cues to include in an advertisement. Furthermore, we need to understand whether or not we have been successful in doing so by analysing the metaphors consumers use when expressing how they processed the ad's content. Again, quoting Kovecses (2000),

"Emotion language is largely metaphorical in English (and in all probability in other languages as well) in order to capture the variety of diverse and intangible emotional experiences. Methodologically, then, this language is important in finding out about these experiences. The language, however, is not only a reflection of the experiences but it also creates them. *Simply put, we say what we feel and we feel what we say.* (Italics added)"

Thus, metaphors inform us about emotions, they help transfer emotions from one person to another, and, independently, generate emotions as well. This is consistent with the literature on the impact of behavior on cognition (Damasio, 2002).

There is a general agreement that the basic emotions include joy, fear, surprise, anticipation, disgust, and sadness. (See Chapter 2.4 in this volume for a more detailed treatment of emotions.) Nearly everyone writing on the subject adds other states including social emotions such as shame and guilt. Whatever their number and description, every emotion has a number of functional benefits (Izard, 1993). At a broad level, negative emotions signal problems to be attended to while positive emotions signal rewarding events. Positive and negative affect each contain four families of specific emotions which in turn possess several feelings. (These are shown in Figures 2.5.2a and 2.5.2b.) Fleur J.M. Laros and Jan-Benedict E.M. Steenkamp suggest that most measures of emotion seem to only use the positive and negative affect as basic dimensions (Laros and Steenkamp, 2005). They caution us about the risk of losing important nuances among emotions if we rely only on these two dimensions. Instead we should consider the multiple emotions within both positive and negative affect and how each of these specific emotions contains many nuanced feelings or sub-dimensions. In fact, we often simultaneously experience negative and positive emotion. In order to understand this experience as it relates to a firm's offerings it is necessary to know

the specific emotion or cocktail of emotions involved.

From a marketing perspective, advertisers who understand the specific emotions that underpin a category can identify particular valences that are latent but under-developed and therefore identify new positioning opportunities. For instance, if Victoria Secret's advertising is based on Love, this emotional hierarchy can illustrate whether in addition to Sexy, they have products for a Romantic, Passionate, Loving, Sentimental and Warm-Hearted positioning in their portfolio as well and whether their communications about these products reflect the corresponding nuance about Love. This, in turn, helps identify appropriate signs and symbols – representations – that have the ability to activate these feelings where already present even if dormant or create them where they are absent.

There is often confusion between emotions and feelings with emotions being used

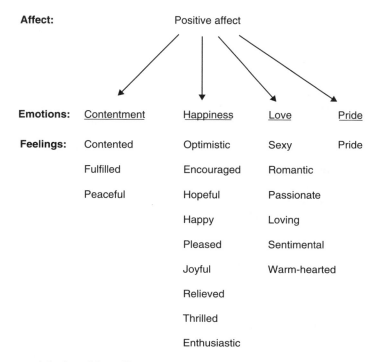

Figure 2.5.2a   Model of positive affect

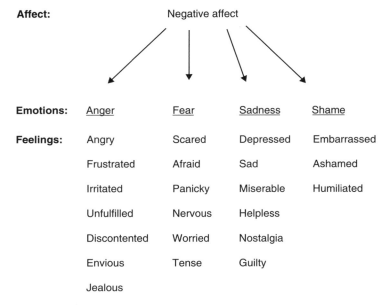

Figure 2.5.2b   Model of negative affect.
Source: **Laros and Steenkamp, 2005: 1441.**

interchangeably with feelings. Sometimes emotion is also used simply to indicate the strength of feeling. Emotions and feelings are related but separate phenomena. An emotion is an unconscious system of detection that receives sensory inputs and produces behavioural, autonomic, and hormonal responses; a feeling is the conscious awareness of the emotional system being activated. Emotions help us to register both what is going on inside our bodies and what is happening in our environment; feelings subsequently occur when the person becomes conscious that emotional changes have occurred. This is a critical distinction for advertising research; someone may feel one way about the advertisement but there may be many more emotions at the unconscious level that are not acknowledged consciously. These underlying emotions may also be affected by the medium in which the advertisement is presented and so relying overly on measures of how consumers feel about an advertisement is likely to paint an incomplete picture of an ad's impact. Media and other contextual dynamics also matter.

The role of metaphor and memory in communications

We have explored the ability of metaphors to re-present one type of thing as an instance of something else. Re-presentation is a fundamental neurological process. For example, as noted earlier, during sensory input the brain re-presents external objects or events in other forms in various regions of the brain. The brain is constantly interpreting these incoming stimuli so it can compare them with its desired internal states and modify its behavioural, autonomic and hormonal activities which we have identified as emotions. In this section we will continue to explore how this sensory input is re-interpreted through the joint filter of emotion and context before finally being re-presented to memory for encoding (see Figure 2.5.3).

It is important for advertisers to understand that a frame is created by the joint filter of context and emotion which consumers use to process information in advertising. This shapes the ultimate brand meaning that is placed in long-term memory. For instance,

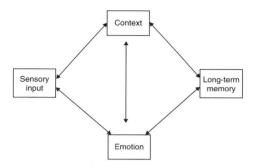

Figure 2.5.3   Interactions among context, input, emotion and long-term memory

research has shown that men are actually more aware of their gender when they are alone in a room of women watching a TV show than when they are in a room with only men. Being more aware of one's gender will mean a different processing of a commercial for, say, Viagra, than when one is more aware of other non-gender self-identities.

Frames are like windows allowing you to look into a room; each window allows you to see certain things but also restricts your perception as well. Frequently, frames need to be identified and adjusted to help people emotionally by re-interpreting the context of an issue. In effect, people often need to look into the same room through a different window. The Holocaust survivor and neurologist Viktor E. Frankl tells of an old man sinking into a deep depression after his wife died. He asked the man what would have happened if the man had died first. The man replied "for her this would have been terrible." Frankl pointed out that the man had spared his wife this suffering and through offering a different context for understanding his wife's death, helped to pull the man out of his depression (Frankl, 1959).

There are many such examples of metaphors as frames being used to re-present ideas "in a new light" or "from a new angle" causing people to have different emotional associations, belief systems, and behaviours.[4] Metaphorical re-framing techniques for instance have been used to help soldiers overcome an ingrained resistance to killing people. The US military started using these techniques after World War II because the non-firing rate was so high: 75–80% of soldiers would not fire their weapons at an exposed enemy. In the Korean War, non-firing rates had decreased to 45% and by the Vietnam War they were down to only 5% (Grossman, 1995). In politics, several metaphorical reframing efforts have been successfully used in political communications; from "compassionate conservatism" to "collateral damage" the power of metaphor has increasingly been used to influence and persuade.

Many advertisers use their understanding of how consumers employ different frames regarding a category and select one (or more) of those frames for creating brand meaning. For instance, automobile drivers use multiple frames of mind for auto tyres. For many years Michelin used the example of a baby contained safely in a Michelin tyre to communicate the idea of safety and the deep metaphor of container. Figure 2.5.4a presents a specific execution of this with a baby in a tyre which also contains pairs of toy animals. The latter brings forth associations with Noah's Ark and the most notorious flood ever. This reinforces the idea of this brand protecting its users from inclement weather. Pirelli, on the other hand, use a different frame also relevant to the tyre category. In Figure 2.5.4b, we see the metaphor of the fist showing the power associated with the Pirelli brand of tires as they grip the road in an aggressive and dominating manner. Whereas the Michelin ad emphasizes the safety dimension of the Container deep metaphor, the Pirelli ad emphasizes two other deep metaphors, namely Force and Connection.

It is also important to understand how the processing of a message is affected by the context of the medium that is selected as well as the context of the outlet where the desired purchase will take place. A commercial for a brand that is received electronically from a friend is different from a branded advergame which is different from a TV commercial and

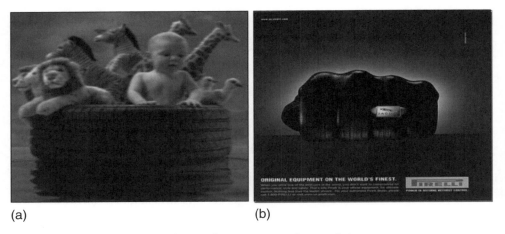

(a)   (b)

**Figure 2.5.4   a) Michelin's use of metaphor to communicate safety.
b) Pirelli's use of metaphor to communicate power.**

so on. For instance, research for Condé Nast revealed that magazine consumers experience a greater sense of "flow" which, in turn, affects how they identify, process, and find personal meaning in advertisements in favoured magazines compared to the intrusive nature of commercials on TV.[5]

Advertising research needs to identify how the context and associated emotions of every media consumption experience influence the ultimate brand meaning created by consumers. It is also important to go beyond the "positive/negative" paradigm often found in biometric and other research measures. For instance, when a viewer watches a heart-wrenching drama is she truly experiencing "negative" emotions? Or is the feeling of poignancy actually being re-interpreted and experienced as something more positive? Or when another viewer sees the same drama but feels it is heavy-handed rather than poignant – having one's "heart strings pulled" – will she re-interpret the emotion more negatively as a feeling of being manipulated? Marketers need to not only understand the emotion being experienced during an advertisement but how these emotions are re-interpreted by consumers as a result of their personal contexts. It is this re-interpretation of emotion that leads to the creation of brand meaning that will help drive purchase and use behaviour.

Long-term memory

Earlier we explored how new metaphors can change people's frames of reference. Now we will explore the system in the opposite direction – how people's existing frames of reference stored in long-term memory influence perception. John J. Ratey (2001) writes:

> "An act of perception is a lot more than capturing an incoming stimulus. It requires a form of expectation, of knowing what is about to confront us and preparing for it ... we automatically and unconsciously fit our sensations into categories that we have learned, *distorting them in the process.*" [Italics added.]

The key issue here is how knowledge becomes distorted during encoding and how this distortion affects our perception of the past, the present and the future.

The nature of memory, the relationship between working memory and long-term memory, and how metaphor can be used to leverage memory's malleability are important issues for advertising (see Figure 2.5.5). As we will see, changes in long-term memory through the use of appropriate metaphors are indicative of new attitudes and beliefs being formed which may lead to changes in behaviour. Measuring these unconscious changes is believed by many to be a more accurate forecaster of future behaviour than self-reported statements of purchase to intent.

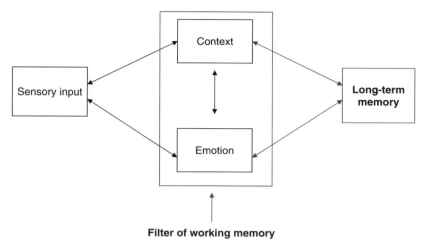

Filter of working memory

Figure 2.5.5   Working memory as a filter

We use working memory to conceptualize events as they occur and long-term memory to orient our plans now and for the future. More specifically, working memory relies on emotion and context in its continuing negotiations with records held in long-term memory to determine what is worth noticing and retaining and what is not. In a nutshell, experience colours perception. The challenge for advertisers is that working memory serves as a bottleneck in this encoding process due to the short duration in which information can be held there. Given the narrow bandwidth of working memory and the challenges of ensuring that sensory input makes it through to long-term memory, advertisers need to develop communications that enable consumers to process information efficiently: minimum necessary stimuli – maximum response. This is where the artful selection of resonant metaphors becomes so critical in the development of advertising and why the assessment of the impact of these metaphors in early stage copy testing is so important.

If a message can break through the clutter in working memory, it can quickly become encoded into long-term memory. To quote John J. Ratey (2001) again:

"studies with amnesiacs have shown that working memory can transfer information to long-term memory within 60 seconds of encoding; the memory is quickly reorganized to minimize dependence on the fleeting short-term memory function, and it is the subjective, interpreted information that is later retrieved for use."

Later we will see an example of a Budweiser commercial which very effectively uses metaphor to help consumers through this process.

Metaphors are excellent devices for coping with the bottleneck. Metaphors are born when a need arises to understand a new experience and we draw on an existing understanding from some other domain to help us classify, comprehend, react to, and store the new experience in another domain in long-term memory. This prior understanding, in effect, imposes clarity and reduces cognitive overload. A given metaphor, then, serves as a zip file to compress large amounts of emotional meaning and quickly transmits it through the bottleneck and into long-term memory. For example, the early advertising for Febreze needed to communicate just how different the mechanism (a patented molecule) for this product was from existing products intended to get rid of malodour. A simple animated ad showing the molecule as an usher surrounding and escorting molecules of malodour out a room captured accurately and simply an otherwise complex process. Consumers could draw on their prior knowledge of what ushers do with unwanted "guests."

Plasticity

Understanding the deep metaphor system is also useful when leveraging the malleable nature of memory. Although people often think of memory as being fixed like a photograph or fingerprint, it is in fact a reconstructive process so that the memory for the same event is different each time it is recalled although the person doing the recalling is unaware of these changes. Of course, the changes involved can be so trivial that for all practical purposes there is no change. This is especially true for frequently rehearsed memories. But sometimes the change can be of consequence, including false memories where a person "remembers" an event that can be demonstrated to have never been experienced (Schacter, 2001).

More specifically, memory is now understood to involve the interaction of three things: data encoded in brain cells (these encodings are called engrams), the cues such as metaphors that active those brain cells, and the reasons or goals being satisfied by recall. Different cues or different reasons for remembering will interact differently with a set of engrams thus producing a different memory. This means we cannot separate the act of retrieval and the memory itself.

The recall of memory pieces from long-term storage and their subsequent formation is influenced by the emotions a person experiences during perception and recall. This can lead to the "Rashomon effect" whereby several people can see the same event, such as a crime, but have very different perceptions, interpretations and recollections of it. For marketers, this phenomenon means that advertising not only engages consumers in forward framing processes, i.e., shaping how they process future consumption experiences, but also in backward framing processes that shape their recall of prior experiences (Braun-la-Tour and Zaltman, 2006). This is particularly valuable in markets where brand switching is common; a better recollection of

a past consumption experience is likely to help increase repeat usage and brand loyalty.

Although the pieces of a single memory are stored in different neural networks, an important question remains: where is memory located once it is reassembled from its constituent pieces? Damasio has proposed that the elements come together at "convergence zones" near the sensory neurons that first registered the event (Damasio, 1994). These zones allow us to automatically conceive of objects, ideas, or interactions as a whole, if the pieces have been put together enough times. The zones also form a hierarchy: "lower" zones link the cues that allow us to understand the general concept of "dog" while "higher" convergence zones allow us to recognize "Oscar" as my neighbour's dog. Research into consumer's unconscious associations using the Response Latency Technique (discussed below) can identify whether brands are successful at activating emotional associations held in consumer's long-term memory and how well these associations are linked with the brand's product cues while other techniques such as ZMET (also discussed below) determine the overall brand meaning in the consumer's mind when the emotional pieces held in memory have been "re-assembled."

Part of the reason for memory's malleability concerns the need to maximize brain efficiency. Instead of storing whole and complete memories, the brain can reconstruct them from a manageable number of reusable elements of experience. The concept of "energize" for instance is one puzzle piece that is available to help complete many different puzzles: coffee, running, sleep, food, vacation. Every puzzle piece is free to interact with other puzzle pieces. This may be one reason why dreams can be similar to life and yet still be so strange as they combine pieces together in unexpected and (hitherto) unimagined ways. These are the same processes that imagination uses during much of our waking hours when we are engaged in "what if" thinking. It is this "what if" thinking that advertisers need to leverage in order to engage consumers in the prospect of a new brand product they have not yet considered.

One of the important developments in recent years in the understanding of memory plasticity is that after learning has occurred there is continued processing and integration of the information into memory (McGaugh, 2003). That is, there is continued elaboration and other processing of an experience after an initial association has been established. This continued processing may last as briefly as a few hours or for a few days and possibly longer. During this period there is a special opportunity to reinforce (and also weaken) a particular judgement or learning that has been established. This represents a potentially important but unexplored area for advertising: what kind of advertising, involving what kind of metaphors, should be used to reinforce a message that has already been learned? To what extent will the reinforcing ad need to differ from the initial ad?

This latest understanding about the workings of memory also raises the important question about how we should best define it: if our memory demonstrates plasticity and therefore can be influenced and changed, are memory and imagination actually different? Is one of these activities "real" and the other "made-up" or are both memory and imagination a form of *storytelling* to oneself? Louis Cozolino (2002) argues that we frequently engage in storytelling in order to keep a stable sense of self, linking our memory of past narratives to our hopes for how they develop in the future:

> "Narratives come to regulate the experience and expression of emotional behavior ... provide an optimistic memory for the future during distress in the present ... Narratives and stories serve as blueprints for behavior and goal attainment. As such, they help to organize moment-to-moment experiences that are required to establish and attain goals. In this way, narratives help us to anchor us in our bodies through time."

Rehearsing this narrative can be a source of comfort and lead to habitual behaviour. However, when advertising successfully activates the deep metaphors underpinning a category, it can encourage consumer imagination and result in new forms of storytelling, referred

to earlier as co-creation. We can consider new ways of seeing ourselves which enable us to renew or redirect our hopes, dream – and aspirations – and the products and brands we use as tools or props to achieve them. When we imagine, that is, when we contemplate that which is missing, we create a variety of potential stories that weave together our multi-sensory emotional, temporal, and memory capabilities so we can fashion new versions of our self-image.

Central to imagination and the way it is encouraged by metaphor is the previously mentioned concept of conceptual blending. So, when Nokia uses the concept of "human" to help highlight certain aspects of its technology by using the phrase "a very human technology," consumers take the concept of privacy (a quality or need activated by the term "human") and the concept of powerful (a product attribute) and imagine yet another quality, either scary or secure. Or, the concept of intelligent (a human quality) and the concept of fast (a product quality) blend to create another thought, intuitive. These blends, e.g., secure and intuitive, become a part of long-term memory; they are knowledge items about a particular cell phone.

Using metaphors in advertising

Learning which deep metaphors underlie thinking about a particular brand, product or experience can help advertisers select a specific metaphor that is likely to produce engagement, comprehension, and recall. In short, a specific metaphor that relates to the fundamental frame(s) or deep metaphors consumers employ when thinking about a product or category will be more effective in conveying a message than one that is not.

An example provided by Margaret Mark and Carol Pearson in *The Hero and the Outlaw,* involves Pepsi Cola which leverages a particular representation, the Rebel, and Coca-Cola which leverages another representation the Innocent (Mark and Pearson, 2001). Although advertising should frame their storylines within the parameters of the metaphors that are uniquely associated with each brand, Coke made the error of trying to combat Pepsi's successful Rebel-style advertising with its own imitation of people throwing tantrums when there was no Coke available. Because both Coke commercials projected a Rebel personality, already owned by Pepsi Cola, which conflicted with its classic Innocent personality, Coke drinkers rejected the campaign. The new ads did not fit the existing frame for Coca Cola and were introduced without a strategic plan to shift to a new frame of reference.

The irony about sculpting a brand and its communications around a single well-chosen metaphor is that consumers will author (or more accurately co-author with the advertiser) multiple meanings; i.e., their unconscious familiarity with the deep metaphor and its association with the brand permits more imaginative engagement with the advertised brand and relate it more clearly to their immediate needs. In short, it enables richer story telling (Coulson, 2001). Conversely, the more ideas advertisers try to explicitly cram into a communication, the more likely it is that the message will falter as it constrains the story telling or co-creation process among consumers. (An example of this involving the beer category is presented shortly.)

McQuarrie and Philips (2005) refer to this phenomenon as weak implicature which "are best thought of as inferences generated as part of an attempt to comprehend advertiser intent." They suggest that it is the openness of indirect metaphorical claims – the lack of constraints on consumer interpretations – that accounts for metaphor's persuasive advantages. Verbal metaphors, anchored visual metaphors (visual ads with a caption) and unanchored visual metaphors (visual ads without a caption) all succeed in stimulating more consumer engagement than literal statements and imagery.

When metaphors are used effectively: Budweiser

A research consortium sponsored by the Advertising Research Foundation (ARF) commissioned a special application of the Zaltman Metaphor Elicitation Technique

(ZMET) (and other methods as well) to assess the impact of emotion in advertising. The specific ads to be evaluated by the different methodologies were chosen by the ARF. The findings highlighted below are some of those emerging from that study. The reader should be made aware that the ZMET methodology requires consumers to self-select images which act as visual metaphors or representations of the thoughts and feelings activated by an advertisement. Respondents see the advertisement one week in advance of the ZMET interview. The respondent's thinking is later probed during a 2-hour, one-on-one in-depth interview using metaphor elicitation and other indirect techniques to access implicit associations with particular cues in the ad and the role of the brand in the advertisement.

The power of deep metaphors is that not only do they implicitly *represent* emotion but they can also *activate* this same emotion in the viewer. In the case of the Budweiser "True" commercial, the deep metaphor of connection is effectively activated through the shared behaviours of the characters who are screaming "Whassup" to each other and holding bottles of Budweiser.

Viewers interpret the "Whassup" as a representation of social ritual which in turn activates the memories of similar rituals and social affiliations in their own lives. As a result, consumers found this funny commercial to have deep personal meaning and relevance. Respondents consistently self-selected images prior to their interview that represented memories of friendship and emotional connection *they experienced themselves* during the ad and that expressed the relevance of this experience in their lives (see Figure 2.5.6).

In addition to activating emotions and memories of social connection through the "Whassup" metaphor (a representation of ritual), the overall context or setting of the ad (guys getting in contact with each other on a lazy Sunday afternoon) also successfully engaged the deep metaphor of connection. Just as it is the context that differentiates the meaning of a love scene in a movie

Figure 2.5.6   Sample images consumers used to represent thoughts and feelings engaged by the True ad

drama from a pornographic film, the context of an ad must be integrated seamlessly with the emotion being generated. (This appears deceptively simple as we will see in the Miller ad in a moment.)

By using the stories that people carry around with them all the time, Budweiser is able to turn a one minute vignette from a Sunday afternoon into a complex story about rituals and the type of brand that can cause great friendships to develop or be readily maintained. In doing so, the Budweiser brand benefits enormously from the deep metaphor of connection. As one respondent said in reference to the True advertisement:

> "The fact that all five guys in this commercial were all drinking the same beer like it kinda gets you to think maybe this is why they became friends, like this particular brand of beer. It might have just been every single Sunday we're going to get Budweiser."

Budweiser has used connection as its deep metaphor time and time again alternatively using frogs, donkeys, clydesdales, people and other animals as different vehicles for delivering the same underlying message. When a brand succeeds in establishing a basic association (literally a neural pathway) in consumers' minds, subsequent activations of this association increase it strength. Eventually an entire neural network develops in consumers' minds implicitly associating Budweiser and connection. The added benefit for any brand that uses metaphor in this way is that through the phenomenon of neural reorganization, it becomes difficult for other brands to use this same association. In effect, the deep metaphor is owned by the advertiser. In this case Budweiser owns connection.

When metaphors are not used consistently: Miller Lite

Although Miller Lite created the light beer category, it lost its once dominant position. A common criticism is that it fails to consistently communicate an emotionally compelling idea. We analysed two 15-second commercials from the "Great Taste, Less Filling" campaign for the ARF project. Both commercials are almost identical and are shown back-to-back. A close-up beauty shot of beer is poured into a glass, followed by a narrator's voice reading the same words that are shown on the screen. In the first advertisement, Miller Lite is touted as a superior beer to Bud Light because Miller Lite "has half the carbs" and has won an event called "The World Beer Cup." In the second advertisement, Miller Lite is said to be a great-tasting beer that has "one-third less carbs than Coors Light."

In both "Great Taste, Less Filling" commercials, the deep metaphor of motion and movement is activated very effectively at the beginning of the ad by the visual image of a wave and a youthful soundtrack (see Figure 2.5.7a for sample frames involving the pouring of beer into a glass). The wave and the music work well together in representing an experience of momentum. This triggered multiple memories, emotional associations and personally relevant meanings for consumers. Some consumers simulated the experience of drinking the beer: "… *you're watching the pour, which gives you the feeling of refreshment. You are practically there holding that beer in your hand and you're drinking it*" while other viewers imagined they were actually in a wave themselves: "… *how fast the beer came down and hit the glass causing that wave. That was energetic. That was definitely exciting to see. It was a good feeling. It was like a thrill. It's that same adrenaline rush that you get if you're under water or you're doing wind-surfing, or you take even a dive into the water.*" Although some people might think of this commercial as being "functional," consumers certainly experienced emotion and

personally relevant meanings at the beginning of the ad through the metaphors of the wave and the music. (See Figure 2.5.7b for examples of how consumers represented their thoughts and feelings about the ad through the collage step of the ZMET process.)

Unfortunately, the remainder of the commercial fails to capitalize on the metaphor that is effectively activated at the beginning. As mentioned earlier, advertising must synchronize the context of the ad with the emotion being generated to motivate consumers' creation of internal schemas about the brand; if consumers' story-telling capabilities are not activated there will be no emotional associations or memories created or enhanced. This does not mean that an advertisement must follow the beginning, middle and end associated with traditional storytelling. It does mean that consumers must find invitations or at least opportunities to bring memories and/or imagination to an advertisement and therefore *find* personal relevance in it.

Participants viewing the Miller ads were frustrated by the experience of starting off with a positive emotional experience and then not being able to integrate this emotion with Miller Lite's compelling slogan "Great Taste. Less Filling." They found the execution too

If in one hand you have 1/2 the carbs of Bud Light

And on the other the gold medal winner of the World Beer Cup

Then you have a Miller Life in each hand. Lucky You.

Miller Life. Great taste. Less filling.

Figure 2.5.7a   Sample frames showing beer pouring into a glass

Figure 2.5.7b   Consumers' visual representations of thoughts and feelings activated by the beginning of the Great Taste Less Filling Ads

packed with ideas rather than having one clear metaphor used consistently throughout the commercial.

The role of metaphor in advertising research

The challenge of traditional research
Emotional framings that underlie thought and behaviour are normally dressed up in rational clothes. Those clothes can be important and provide clues about more significant underlying dynamics. But these outer layers of clothing can also be misleading and incomplete. In fact, it is generally understood that when consumers provide rational explanations of behaviour they are creating largely false if coherent stories about what their unconscious emotional systems have already decided.

"Each of us feels that there is a single "I" in control. But that is an illusion that the brain works hard to produce ... When surgeons cut the corpus callosum joining the cerebral hemispheres, they literally cut the self in two, and each hemisphere can exercise free will without the other one's advice or consent. Even more disconcertingly, the left hemisphere constantly weaves a coherent but false account of the behavior chosen without its knowledge by the right ... The conscious mind – the self or soul – is a spin doctor, not the commander in chief." (Pinker 2002)

Given the difficulties in accurately identifying how the unconscious determines behaviour, the conscious responses given in traditional research methods such as surveys and focus groups are limited in their ability to identify drivers of behaviour operating below awareness.[6] Not all important issues, of course, require or merit going beyond what is readily available in the conscious mind. Often, however, the insights needed to develop engaging communications, i.e., to turn on consumers' minds, do require this deeper understanding. In such cases, tools that tap implicit processes are required to identify the relevant emotional systems and operating frames that drive behaviour. Three tools most familiar to the authors are discussed next. There are, to be sure, additional tools discussed elsewhere which also have great value (ARF, 2005). The reader is particularly encouraged to read Chapter 4.1 in this volume, "Pretesting: 'Before the Rubber Hits the Road," for an excellent treatment of ad pretesting methods.

Developing and testing metaphor communications
Advertisers need to be able to develop communications that engage emotional processes and conscious thought and which produce personally relevant brand stories. This requires using methods that can identify the frames consumers use when thinking about a product and which can help select the metaphors and other advertising cues that will enable consumers to create appropriate meaning about the product. Methods that can determine whether and how well a meaning or message has been integrated into consumer

belief systems are also needed. The following discussion identifies one approach that many firms find helpful in identifying frames or deep metaphors operating among consumers and in developing communications. We also discuss two techniques that show promise in evaluating the nature and degree to which consumers are engaged with advertising information and creating new meanings at an unconscious level.

The Zaltman Metaphor Elicitation Technique (ZMET)

A major challenge in the development and evaluation of advertising is posed by the process of conceptual blending or conceptual integration. Again, this refers to the creative process whereby, for instance, the meaning of "fast" with regard to a computing technology becomes associated through an advertisement with the meaning of "convenient" to create yet an additional or blended meaning of "powerful." By speaking explicitly only about "fast" and "convenient" through the use of metaphor, the communication encourages the audience to also think that something fast and convenient is quite powerful (as a business tool or for satisfying needs quickly). The audience creates the idea of powerful as their existing frames interact with the contents of the ad. This is also referred to as the co-creation of meaning (Zaltman, 2003). In effect, consumers co-author with advertisers the meanings they develop as a result of their ad exposures. This contrasts with what appears to be the dominant model-in-use in advertising described as the hypodermic needle model. That model assumes that a specific meaning can be injected into consumers. This model has little support in the academic literature. It is, however, the primary justification for using various recall measures of advertising effectiveness. Unfortunately, those measures do not capture the personally relevant meanings or stories that advertising does produce and which account for so much of an ad's success or failure.

ZMET analyses the non-literal expressions consumers use to represent their thoughts and feelings about a topic. This technique is widely used now in more than 30 countries by global corporations and others to understand the mental models and deep metaphors or basic frames consumers use when thinking about a need, a product or service category, or a particular brand.[7]

More recently, firms and advertising agencies have been using an adapted form of ZMET to go beyond developing communications strategy and to help in the early assessment of particular advertising executions. In these applications the ZMET interview is a one-on-one discussion that usually takes 90–120 minutes. In preparation for the interview, participants are asked a few days prior to their interview to collect visual images that represent their thoughts and feelings about the product category involved in the advertisement(s) being assessed. Each image is a visual metaphor that the consumer uses to communicate the meaning of a category or particular brands or products in his/her life. Consumers engage in storytelling about the meaning of their self-selected images both with respect to the category and again with respect to the advertising concept or the execution being evaluated. The interviewer probes the meaning and feelings that emerge through these surface metaphors that are associated with each cue to determine the type and degree of emotional affect. Interviews are later analysed to identify which advertising concept is engaging consumers in the richest storytelling and what meanings are emerging through co-creation. Cues that are impeding the communication of the metaphor can be identified and improved. This approach has been effective in identifying unexpected interpretations in response to an ad. Sometimes these are directionally consistent with the ad's intent and sometimes they are counter-productive. This provides considerable guidance for improving the communication.

All methods are compromises with reality, of course, and ZMET is no exception. While it has a number of advantages in developing and evaluating advertising concepts and alternative executions it has certain limitations as well. These limitations also apply to its non-advertising applications. One limitation is that there are occasions when statistical significance is needed as well as substantive significance. ZMET does not provide statistical significance. Put differently, sometimes it is necessary to know the velocity of the wind as well as its direction. ZMET provides direction, not velocity. Additionally, for advertising applications ZMET is most appropriate as a developmental tool to identify relevant options, provide stimuli for creative personnel to use, and to assess concepts and executions in their early stages when corrections are feasible. Despite the examples above involving finished ads, that is not the most cost-effective application unless one needs to know why an ad has or has not been effective. ZMET will not provide a quantitative estimate of likely level of effectiveness. Also, ZMET analyses are labour-intensive and turnaround may require two or more weeks, depending on the particular application. On occasions when these limitations are significant other techniques such as field or laboratory experiments and biometric techniques are important to use. Two relatively novel such alternatives, each based on well-established research traditions are discussed below. There are, however, a number of established quantitative methods available.

Response Latency Testing (RLT)

Response latency is a tool used in cognitive psychology to evaluate a variety of mental processes, such as the effectiveness of a stimulus in activating constructs held in memory. The speed of this activation reveals the associative strength between the stimulus and conceptually related constructs demonstrating the cognitive workload or level of "noise" in processing the new information. The "response latency" is the interval of time between presentation of a stimulus and the resulting response. Measuring these response times to study how the mind works is called mental chronometry. Response times are measured in milliseconds. The data are

analysed using analyses of variance (Mast and Zaltman, 2005).

The Response Latency Test quantifies the ability of metaphors to activate unconscious emotional thinking. One use is in exploring how readily a brand can own a particular metaphor and how this compares to competitors. Frequently two brands will be linked to the same metaphor in qualitative research (e.g., Nike and Under Armor are both associated with "Transformation"). It then becomes important to use RLT in measuring whether one of these brands is particularly associated with this metaphor and therefore whether the brand can more easily activate and "own" that idea than its competitor.

RLT can show the impact of our instinctive reactions and impulses on longer-term belief systems. This has important implications for all types of marketing because these rapid associations become stored in implicit memory systems that drive behaviour. RLT measures have been used to understand voters' perceptions of candidate's faces and how those impressions impact voting behaviour. Voters were asked to judge the "relative competence of recent candidates for U.S. Congress races," based solely on a 1-second view of the candidates' black-and-white head shots. On the basis of only the facial appearances and with no prior knowledge of the person, RLT correctly predicted the election outcomes nearly 70% of the time. This result demonstrates that rapid trait judgements strongly influence voting choices (Science, 2005).

An important goal of advertising is to create empathy which motivates consumer behaviour. Empathy is driven by the activation of mirror neurons. These neurons are in Broca's and the inferior parietal cortex of the brain and some scientists consider mirror neurons to be one of the most important findings of neuroscience in the last decade. A mirror neuron is a neuron which fires when its "owner" observes an action performed by another person. Thus, the neuron "mirrors" the behaviour of the other person, as though the observer were performing the action. When mirror neurons are activated, a consumer not only "knows" what is being experienced by a character in an ad but can feel it as well. Therefore, the advertisement has succeeded in emotionally engaging the consumer through empathy.

One of the requirements for the activation of mirror neurons is that their activity is context-dependent. This means that people not only need to recognize particular movements but can also understand the intention behind them. Due to the importance of context, advertisers can use RLT to identify symbols such as brands and other metaphors that consumers readily associate with one another. Research on consumption constellations for instance strongly suggest that functionally dissimilar yet symbolically related products are used for cognitive organization by consumers and therefore marketers and advertisers should consider the use of RLT for collaborative advertising (Lowry et al., 2001).

Memory integration tests. Having identified the richest advertising concept through ZMET, it is important to measure the extent to which the underlying frame is being adopted by consumers as their new belief system. Memory integration tests enable advertisers to track the enduring impact of reframing on consumer belief systems. These tests are a more accurate indicator of future behaviour than self-reported statements because the implicit nature of the test is measuring emotional thinking at an unconscious level.

The memory integration test measures the degree to which an advertisement has influenced consumers' own memory of their beliefs (Braun-LaTour and Zaltman, 2006). The degree to which an advertisement has caused consumers to remember an earlier reporting of a belief differently and in the direction of the ad's message is an ad that contains information that the consumer has unconsciously adopted as their own and therefore will have an enduring impact on their emotions and behaviour. Measuring this impact is enormously helpful before launching an ad and also to measure its

effectiveness in the marketplace over time. As competitors begin to manoeuvre against it, perhaps by copying the ad's metaphorical framing and style, it is possible to measure when a new set of cues will be needed to effectively reactivate the underlying framing that the marketer seeks to associate with a given brand.

SUMMARY

- A metaphor is a representation of one thing by use of another thing. The "things" involved can be objects or thoughts. The term metaphor is used broadly in this chapter to refer to any non-literal or figurative expression, in effect, any non-literal expression. Whether broadly or narrowly construed, metaphor is a central part of all human thought and communication. It is so central that we are often unaware of its use and its impact.

- Advertising content makes liberal and usually deliberate use of metaphor. It is itself a metaphor for the product, service or practice or other goal it is designed to promote. We have attempted to demonstrate how metaphor works in general as part of the effort to describe its importance in advertising. For this reason we have discussed the importance of metaphor with respect to emotion and memory since one important goal of advertising is to have an enduring (memorable) emotional impact on consumers. This is often best achieved by having communications that engage consumers' own thinking such that they co-author a story or meaning with the advertiser. This is referred to as co-creation in which stimuli in an advertisement interact with existing thinking among consumers to create a story that may vary from consumer to consumer but is directionally consistent with the intent of the advertising. Unless an ad uses emotionally arousing metaphors it is unlikely to engage existing meanings already possessed by consumers (in their existing memory) and hence unlikely to have the intended meaning of the ad ultimately embedded in consumer thought.

- To help consumers co-create a meaning from an ad that makes the ad memorable it is essential that the ad evoke a relevant deep metaphor. A deep metaphor is a basic frame, a kind of archetypical metaphor, that is used unconsciously and automatically by consumers in deciding what information to attend to, whether and how to process that information, and what to do as a result. Deep metaphors are siblings to emotions. In fact, we argue as others do, that metaphor is essentially the language of emotions and therefore central to understanding emotions. Deep metaphors are the stage on which emotions and their corresponding sentiments and feelings play important roles. Advertisers need to identify what that stage is or could be and create advertising with those judgements in mind.

- Since metaphor is so critical to the creation of messages that have enduring emotional impact, it is hardly surprising that an effective way of evaluating advertising copy is to examine the metaphors consumers use when describing how they engage the message. We presented an application of one technique, ZMET, that does this. This application involved two beer commercials. This same technique is also useful in learning what deep metaphors are used for a brand or category and for identifying the kind of surface metaphors that advertisers could use to activate deep metaphors and associated emotions. Other approaches also have been used productively.
- In describing how metaphor works we mentioned the process of conceptual blending. That is, when two different domains are brought together, such as a metaphor as one domain and a product as the other, two things occur. One is that the metaphor helps consumers better understand certain attributes, functions, and emotional consequences of the product or offering being advertised. The second happening which is especially important is that the two domains interact to create a new idea not inherent in either the metaphor or the object being related to it. Thus, the use of metaphor also results in the creation of new thoughts. This is an inevitable consequence of the co-creation of meaning. One implication of this is that when evaluating advertising it is important to identify the additional ideas, intended or not, that are being added by virtue of the metaphors being used. While not discussed here, there are numerous examples of unexpected meanings arising from an advertisement some of which were beneficial and some detrimental to the intended message.

NOTES

1 This broader view of metaphor is also consistent with its treatment in what is perhaps the major journal in the field, *Metaphor and Symbolic Activity.* For a good discussion of the artificial carving between literal and figurative language and the significance of the latter in everyday discourse see, Mark Turner, "The Literal Versus Figurative Dichotomy," in *The Literal and Nonliteral in Language and Thought*, Seana Coulson and Barabara Lewandowsak-Tomaszczyk (eds.), Frankfurt: Peter Lang, 2005, pp. 25–52, Mahwah, NJ: Lawrence Erlbaum Associates, 2005.

2 The term deep metaphor is a trademark of Olson Zaltman Associates.

3 For more information on this initiative contact The Advertising Research Foundation, 641 Lexington Avenue New York, New York 10022.

4 See for example, George Lakoff, *Whose Freedom?: The Battle Over America's Most Important Idea*, NY: Farrar, Straus and Giroux, 2006.

5 This research was conducted by Olson Zaltman Associates for Conde Nast. For further information contact Dr. Scott MacDonald, Direct of Research, at Conde Nast in New York City.

6 For more on this see Daniel Wegner, *The Illusion of Conscious Will,* Cambridge, MA: MIT Press, 2002; and for a different perspective, see Benjamin Libet, *Mind Time: The Temporal Factor in Consciousness*, Cambridge, MA: Harvard University Press, 2004.

7 The intent of discussing ZMET here is simply to introduce one approach that many firms and academics find useful. We can only note in passing for readers unfamiliar with ZMET that various validation studies have been conducted by independent researchers and all have concluded that the technique produces key insights that other techniques miss and which are judged important based on subsequent quantitative research based on ZMET project findings. At the same time these validation studies also yield convergence with findings involving other techniques even while at the same time finding additional relevant constructs not produced by those methods. Over 300 ZMET studies involving diverse issues and cultures have been conducted to date.

REFERENCES

Braun-LaTour, K.A. and G. Zaltman (2006), "Memory Change: An Intimate Measure of Persuasion", *The Journal of Advertising Research*, 46 (1), (March), 57–72.

Coulson, S. (2001), *Semantic Leaps: Frame-Shifting and Conceptual Blending in Meaning Construction*, Cambridge, UK: Cambridge University Press.

Cozolini, L. (2002), *The Neuroscience of Psychotherapy*, NY: W.W. Norton & Company, 166–9.

Damasio, A. (1994), *Descartes' Error*, NY: G.P. Putnam's Sons.

Damasio, A. (2003), *Looking for Spinoza: Joy, Sorrow and the Feeling Brain*, NY: Harcourt Books, 198–9.

Damasio, A. (2002), *The Feeling of What Happens*, New York: Alfred Knopf.

Eaken, P.J. (1999), *How Our Lives Become Stories*, NY: Cornell University Press.

Fauconnier, G. and M. Turner (2002), *The Way We Think: Conceptual Blending and the Mind's Hidden Complexities*, NY: Basic Books.

Frankl, V.E. (1959), *Man's Search For Meaning*, London: Random House.

Freeman, W.J. (2000), *How Brains Make Up Their Minds*, NY: Columbia University Press.

Gallagher, S. (2005), *How the Body Shapes the Mind*, Oxford: Oxford University Press.

Gibbs, Jr., R.W. (1994), *The Poetics of Mind: Figurative Thought, Language, and Understanding*, MA: Cambridge University Press.

Gilbert, D. (2006), *Stumbling on Happiness*, New York: Alfred Knopf.

Grossman, Lt. Col. D. (1995), *On Killing*, NY: Little, Brown, and Company.

Izard, C.E. (1993), "Organizational and Motivational Functions of Discrete Emotions," in *Handbook of Emotions*, eds. M. Lewis and J.M. Haviland, NY: The Guilford Press, 631–41.

Kovecses, Z. (2000), *Metaphor and Emotion: Language, Culture, and Body in Human Feeling*, MA: Cambridge University Press, 17, 191–2.

Kovecses, Z. (2002), *Metaphor: A Practical Introduction*, Oxford: Oxford University Press.

Lakoff, G. (2004), *Don't Think of an Elephant*, Chelsea: Green Publishing Co.

Lakoff, G. (2006), *Whose Freedom?: The Battle Over America's Most Important Idea*, NY: Farrar, Straus and Giroux.

Lakoff, G. and M. Johnson (1999), *Philosophy in the Flesh: The Embodied Mind and its Challenge to the Western Thought*, NY: Basic Books.

Laros, F.J.M. and J.-B.E.M. Steenkamp (2005), "Emotions in Consumer Behavior: A Hierarchical Approach", *Journal of Business Research, (*October), 1441.

Libet, B. (2004), *Mind Time: The Temporal Factor in Consciousness*, MA: Harvard University Press.

Loewenstein, G. and J.S. Lerner (2003), "The Role of Affect in Decision Making," in *Handbook of Affective Sciences*, eds. R.J. Davidson, K.R. Scherer,

and H.H. Goldsmith, Oxford: Oxford University Press, 619–42.

Lowrey, T.M., B.G. Englis, S. Shavitt and M.R. Solomon (2001), "Response Latency Verification of Consumption Constellations: Implications for Advertising Strategy", *Journal of Advertising*[RM1].

Mark, M. and C.S. Pearson (2001), *The Hero and The Outlaw*, NY: McGraw-Hill.

Mast, F.W. and G. Zaltman (2005), *Brain Research Bulletin*, 67, 422–7.

McGaugh, J.L. (2003), *Memory and Emotion: The Making of Lasting Memories*, NY: Columbia University Press.

Mithen, S. (2006), *The Singing Neanderthals: The Origins of Music, Language, Mind, and Body*, MA: Harvard University Press, 2006.

McQuarrie, E.F. and B. Phillips (2005), *Journal of Advertising*, Summer.

Pieters, R. and M. Wedel (2007), "Pretesting: Before the Rubber Hits the Road," in *The SAGE Handbook of Advertising*, eds. G.J. Tellis and T. Ambler, London: Sage Publications.

Pinker, S. (2002), *The Blank Slate: The Modern Denial of Human Nature*, NY: Penguin Books, 42–3.

Prager, J. (1998), *Presenting the Past: The Psychoanalysis and the Sociology of Misremembering*, MA: Harvard University Press.

Ratey, J.J. (2001), *A User's Guide to the Brain*, NY: Random House.

Schacter, D.L. (2001), *The Seven Sins of Memory: How the Mind Forgets and Remembers*, MA: Houghton Mifflin.

Schultz, D. (2005), *Marketing News*, October.

Stewart, D.W., J. Morris and A. Grover (2007), "Emotions in Advertising," in *The SAGE Handbook of Advertising*, eds. G.J. Tellis and T. Ambler, London: Sage Publications.

Turner, M. (2005), "The Literal Versus Figurative Dichotomy," in *The Literal and Nonliteral in Language and Thought*, eds. S. Coulson and B. Lewandowsak-Tomaszczyk, Frankfurt: Peter Lang, 25–52.

Van der Velde, C.D. (2004), *The Mind: Its Nature and Origin*, NY: Prometheus Books.

Varela, P.J., E. Thompson and E. Rosch (1991), *The Embodied Mind: Cognitive Science and Human Experience*, Cambridge, MA: MIT Press.

Wegner, D. (2002), *The Illusion of Conscious Will*, MA: MIT Press.

Zaltman, G. (2003), *How Customers Think*, MA: Harvard Business School Press.

SECTION III
Advertising Practice

Client–Agency Relationships

David Wethey

This chapter provides a blueprint for building and sustaining successful client–agency relationships. It concentrates on the advertising agency – what we now call the creative agency. My employee experience was entirely with such agencies. Although my consulting practice deals with all kinds of communication agencies, the creative agency still looms largest. A missing component from this chapter on the client/agency relationship is the media agency, which is only a small part of our practice area. There are others with more expertise in the field.

Many studies have covered the initiation phase of the client–agency relationship but few have focused on the nuances of nurturing and developing ongoing relationships (Palihawadana and Barnes, 2005). The chapter draws on both the academic literature as well as practical, first-hand experience. Whilst these issues are much the same the world over, the chapter is written from a UK perspective.

In our 18-year consulting practice, we have seen many dysfunctional relationships. In the interest of avoiding a negative orientation, I refrain from focusing on how client–agency relationships can go wrong. Instead, this chapter identifies best practice. First, it explains the evolution of the advertising

agency's role within the marketing function. Second, it outlines the important factors in selecting and evaluating an agency, as well as factors that contribute and inhibit good client–agency relationships. Stemming from this discussion, the chapter then outlines the role of the procurement function in marketing, providing support for such a role. Following this, solutions are offered for both the client and the agency to make their relationships successful. The chapter then summarises advice for client-agency relationships, including multinational relationships, the pitching process, and remuneration techniques.

THE EVOLUTION OF THE AGENCY'S ROLE WITHIN THE MARKETING FUNCTION AND CURRENT TRENDS

From the mid-late 19th century when the first advertising agencies appeared (see Chapter 1.2) until the invention of Account Planning in London almost 100 years later (see Chapter 3.3), advertising focused on designing and sending selling messages, with consumers the passive recipients. By the mid 20th century, advertising had become a sophisticated marketing tool in a world where brands were becoming more important than the companies that made them. The media function was outsourced to specialist companies, with agencies focussing more on creativity. Account handlers were starting to be marginalised, as the internal stars – planners and creatives – took centre stage. But soon things began to change as agencies become less powerful, and the balance within the relationship shifted. Clients were unwittingly expressing their attitudes to the client–agency relationship, advocating that he who pays the piper calls the tune (Fletcher, 1994: 62). Hence, an attitudinal and behavioural shift was taking place whereby clients were asserting their power.

From the agency perspective there is now a more profound change afoot, which gathered momentum in the early 1990s. Everything increasingly has a short-term focus, driven by the finance function, revolving around increasing revenue and tightening margins. Furthermore, agencies continue to lose influence. Dauer (2005) points out that the strength of agencies within the relationship in the 1960s and 1970s was based on the fact that they did far more than just develop and place advertising. They were marketing partners, brand guardians, marketing strategists, marketing researchers, media pioneers, media planners and masters of sales promotion, merchandising, publicity and PR. But today, the client is the brand guardian and there exists a plethora of specialist marketing strategists, researchers, planners, and communications experts. This changed role is exemplified by the move to fees (being paid on a transactional basis for work done) from the commission system (deriving income from a percentage of media spend) as shall be discussed at the end of this chapter.

SELECTING AND EVALUATING AN ADVERTISING AGENCY

Businesses are not totally self-sufficient (Weilbacher, 1991). As Bullmore (1991: 141) stated, "advertising agencies are paid by clients to think of things," thus offering the client a specific skill which is unlikely to be found within the company. Often it is too expensive to employ these top professionals because they command high salaries and prefer to work for specialised firms in order to gain broader experience. But it is useful for the client to be able to hire them on a needs-basis and tap into this breadth of experience. Often this guarantees better solutions to advertising problems than advertisers are likely to get from their own advertising employees.

Research has highlighted several factors that impact on the client's choice of agency. Most are related to the strength of the agency's employees, since an agency is only as good as its people. Cagley and Roberts (1984) highlighted the importance of the quality of people managing the account, the requirement of agency staff to understand the client's business, and the agency's reputation for integrity. White and Dawson (2004) found that advertisers look for a combination of individual and team professionalism, insight (understanding their consumers not just the sector), affinity with the client (enthusiasm, motivation and passion), innovation (ideas the client has not seen before) and dependability. Indeed, personal relationships, compatibility of staff, and the ability for the two teams to work together are very important (Michell, 1988; Verbeke, 1989; Fam and Waller, 2000).

Palihawadana and Barnes (2005) found that advertisers viewed professional and technical skills and quality of advertising service as the most important selection triggers. Henke (1995) also echoed these sentiments, stating that creative skill is the most important factor. Relative to business capabilities, factors identified that should be used as a guide for selecting an agency include transaction costs, offering good value for money, research capabilities, breadth of services on offer, and a proven track record (especially with similar types of business) (Fox, 1984; Michell, 1988; Verbeke, 1989; Henke, 1995). Although much research in this area has been regionally based (e.g., Fam and Waller in New Zealand, Verbeke in Holland, Palihawadana and Barnes in Poland), these common themes still emerge.

WHAT MAKES A GOOD CLIENT–AGENCY RELATIONSHIP?

In every client–agency situation there are actually two relationships: one from the client's standpoint ("what are we trying to achieve with this agency?"), and one from the agency's standpoint ("what are our prospects with this client/brand?"). Of all the changes that have taken place over the last 10–15 years, the most fundamental is the multiplicity of agencies one client will retain. The creative agency will now be in a roster alongside all or most of the following agencies: media buying, media/communications planning, direct marketing, sales promotion, sponsorship, trade marketing, interactive, buzz, guerrilla, content, events and public relations. This is a lot of suppliers to manage, let alone have a relationship with, and the situation is exacerbated by the fact that relationships are often more temporary than they once were. This impacts both businesses, creating a need for more meetings and the establishment of more relationships, more regularly. In the UK for example, the average account stays with its main creative agency for only three years; the Marketing Director who appoints the agency will last an average of only 17 months, and the agency management team is likely to be in a virtually constant state of flux. For example, in 2006, only two of the top 20 UK agencies had the same management teams as eighteen months previously. New relationships are constantly being developed, and knowledge and brand history is often lost without being properly documented as old people leave and new people move into these roles and onto these accounts. But regardless of the age of these relationships, one thing is paramount – aligning the interests of the agency and the client optimizes relationships. The agency should consider the performance of the ad to be as important to them as it is to the client, not only because their reputation and future business relies on it, but also to show their commitment to their client. Strategies for aligning these interests are discussed later in this chapter with regards to agency remuneration.

The key to an effective relationship is widely seen as trust (e.g., Bill Gray of Ogilvy & Mather, 2003; Becky Saeger of Visa, 2004; Roger Adams of General Motors, 2005; Kevin Roberts and Bob Isherwood of Saatchi & Saatchi, 2005) and partnership (e.g., Don Calhoun of Wendy's, 2003; Geralyn Breig of Godiva, 2005; Andy Berlin of Berlin Cameron, 2005) as the cornerstones of constructive client–agency situations. In regard to the importance of partnership, Roberts and Isherwood of Saatchi & Saatchi (2005) say: "It's not a master–servant relationship, it's a marriage of equals. We're climbing the same mountains – together." Similarly, Bill Gray of Ogilvy & Mather (2003) writes: "It's also a relationship in which client and agency understand each other's distinctive capability. They appreciate each other's expertise. They develop a true give-and-take collaboration. When that happens, the results can be truly memorable."

Despite these opinions, experts do not always acknowledge the importance of the relationship, and clients and agencies frequently underestimate the contribution of the other party. It is surprising how often the people who write "how to" books on marketing communications, treat it as just another in-company function like distribution, HR or IT (without an agency in sight), or produce books and learned articles about advertising with little or no mention of the client's role. For example, the otherwise excellent *Advertising, Communications and Promotion Management* (Rossiter and Percy, 1997) has no index entry for "agency" or "advertising agency" in its 600+ pages. The authors mention several agencies and individuals, but there is no attribution of success to the client/agency relationship. It can also happen the other way round, with experts concentrating so hard on the importance of a good relationship, that they fail to mention creativity and strategic contribution (LaBahn, 1996). A good relationship is one that respects the different roles that creative, research and account management play, and that integrates the different processes so they are all working towards a common goal. One is no more important than the other, nor should one necessarily take place before the others (i.e., should research drive the creative, or should a creative concept be developed and then all activities revolve around that?) Rather, they should all work seamlessly together.

The academic literature yields much data on the factors that enhance productive relationships. For example:

- Michell and Sanders (1995) identified seven factors – a stable business environment; large organisational structures; well-defined policies towards suppliers; positive attitudes towards suppliers; effective process involving suppliers; compatible interpersonal characteristics; and actual account performance.
- Palihawadana and Barnes (2005) found that offering an appropriate range of services, good account management, customer care and charging competitive rates are at the heart of a good relationship and retention.
- Delener (1996) suggests that understanding cultural values, developing relationships with clients, having a strategy, developing a full service philosophy and presenting new ideas to clients will strengthen the relationship.
- Davis (2004) found that advertisers want effective campaigns, outstanding ideas and implementation, and strategic counsel and insights from their agency. In contrast, the agency wants respect and trust, fair payment, and good communication (including criticism).

However, it is important to realise that this relationship is not a one-way street. Agencies will also review clients before they take them on board. Roberts and Isherwood (2005) state that their ideal client is one that has passion, loves creativity, is inspirational, ambitious, emotional, adventurous, decisive, realistic, fun, has integrity, treats them as a partner, and can pay their bills!

WHY DO RELATIONSHIPS GO WRONG?

An advertiser should not change agencies simply because the agency has been around for a long time, competitors have recently changed agencies, competitors have larger or better known agencies, or because personnel at the agency or advertiser have changed (Tellis, 1998). However, the constant churn of key people at both ends is bound to destabilise relationships to the point that a review is called. The following reasons have been cited for the disintegration of client–agency relations:

- Unclear relationship expectations – It is the responsibility of both sides to agree on what each party is looking to achieve. However, when there is disappointment, it is far more the agency's problem because the client can easily find another agency. Replacing a valued client is far tougher. Consider writing a "constitution" for the account to minimize such situations (Grant, 2005).
- Ineffectual client reviews and performance appraisals – Ryan and Colley (1967) examined 150 US advertising managers and found that difficulties between clients and agencies did not result from poor work, but from unsystematic performance appraisals. For example, there may be a lack of agreement between the parties over the agency's role (West and Palowoda, 1994). Be brutally thorough in conducting satisfaction surveys, and have third party involvement to ensure objectivity. Evaluation needs to be 360° to work properly, with the client self-evaluating and the agency commenting on the client's contribution to the relationship. In most cases, supplementing the agency's view on its own performance with an objective opinion is indispensable (Grant, 2005).
- Not fixing the fixable – If agencies suspect something is wrong, it is far better to get to the bottom of the problems and engage with the client in a programme to put things right. Both Doyle et al. (1980) and Michell (1986) found that failing to recognize impending client dissatisfaction and crises often led to termination of relationships. Agencies should therefore consider establishing a hierarchy of importance with the client (Grant, 2005). Which issue, if fixed, would have the most impact on the client's view of the agency?
- Letting accounts get stale (Grant, 2005) – There are many ways to minimize this:
  - Remind them about your capabilities and resources, which will probably have expanded since you were appointed
  - Involve agency staffers who do not currently work on the account. Brainstorm. Ask for

honesty as to whether the agency is doing all it could
- ○ Switch teams
- ○ Go offsite
- Poor performance – poor service (DeSouza, 1992); not enough assistance from the client (West and Palowoda, 1994); poor advertising management skills at the client end (West and Palowoda, 1994); the brand has been doing badly and none of the alternatives tried by the agency have worked (Tellis, 1998).
- Changing market conditions – the brand needs a new style that is inconsistent with that of the current agency (Tellis, 1998); there is now a lower priced alternative or one that provides a superior product (DeSouza, 1992); changes in internal or external political considerations (DeSouza, 1992).
- Competitive factors – the current agency has merged with another that serves a competitor (Tellis, 1998); the advertiser has expanded into new regions or counties in which the agency does not have the required expertise (Tellis, 1998).
- People issues – the key personnel responsible for the brand or for past successes have left, and their replacements do not have comparable credentials (West and Paliwoda, 1996; Tellis, 1998); a personality conflict has developed between the account executive and the brand manager (Tellis, 1998).

Procurement: Does it help or hinder the relationship?

Procurement and sourcing organizations now have an increasingly important role in many large corporations. Work in non-traditional areas of spend such as marketing has driven the focus away from mere price reduction and toward strategic partnerships, both internally and externally, thus redefining the entire purchasing process (Stephens, 2004). From requirements definition and supplier selection to ongoing management of the supplier relationships and gathering benchmarking, this approach has focused on the objective of reducing the total cost of ownership in obtaining these services on behalf of the organization (Stephens, 2004; Mirque, 2005). It has evolved from a tactical buying agent function to a strategic partner involved early in the process. Enlightened procurement

has grown to understand that long-term relationships with vendors can yield greater efficiencies and provide more flexibility than churning one-off, lowest-cost provider deals (Krinsky and Marcus, 2004).

In theory, procurement adds value to the business as it allows marketing department to focus on the job of marketing and provides a disciplined approach to executing agreements and securing cost efficiencies. It shifts administrative burdens off marketing's plate and keeps them audit ready, identifying waste in the marketing process so that dollars can be redeployed to value-added activities (Mirque, 2005). Often marketers are resentful of procurement's involvement in the marketing process as they feel that the procurement function is interfering in their established agency relationships. But many procurement people prefer the whole tendering process to be their responsibility as they believe that marketers get too close to their agency colleagues (Melsom, 2004). Marketers on the other hand believe that procurement specialists purely negotiate to get the best cost and do not understand the soft aspects of the function for which they are negotiating (Mirque, 2005).

In companies where the procurement function is well established in the marketing arena, the client has two faces – marketing professionals concerned about developing campaigns, and procurement specialists looking after contracts and terms of business and playing an ongoing role in monitoring existing relationships. Some clients, particularly those who have grown up in a procurement-free environment, have expressed concerns about their influence. But the worry that the influence of procurement will simply result in lowest tender situations and reduced agency margins is over-simplified. The world of marketing has unfortunately shown itself historically to be wasteful and not particularly accountable. The influence of procurement has already been beneficial in pointing the way to increased efficiencies (is process and professionalism delivering value for money, and a return on the agency's fee?) and effectiveness (is the investment in marketing communications working well and cost effectively?).

Procurement is now involved in 50% of agency cost reviews and in 55% of agency negotiations among advertisers that spend over $100 million annually (i.e., it is now common practice with major advertisers) (Melsom, 2004). Education will be a decisive factor in building the procurement/marketing relationship – education for procurement professionals about marketing and advertising, and education for marketing about how procurement's expertise can enhance the advertising process. To facilitate this, the American Association of Advertising Agencies now offers its members courses in communicating in the language of procurement and interacting effectively with client procurement staff (Mirque, 2005).

The first step many organizations take in integrating procurement into the marketing space is to engage the procurement experts in the negotiation of agency contracts (Stephens, 2004). While this can yield some significant benefit in cost and quality of the contractual arrangement, much more significant benefit will be achieved by leveraging the concepts and methods of strategic sourcing in the definition of the agency strategy, selecting potential agencies, and managing the request for proposal and pitch process. Key sourcing techniques that have application in the agency selection process include analysis of current spend and agency relationships/contracts, detailed supply market analysis including labour rates, overhead cost structures, profit margin benchmarking, mapping of existing transaction processes, and assessment of the existing organizational structure against these processes (Stephens, 2004).

Selection and contracting with the agency is only the first level of opportunity. Considering all of the elements required to successfully execute a marketing campaign, and the large percentage of spend that passes through the agency to third parties to manufacture, inventory, distribute, ship these elements, a world-class sourcing organisation will work closely with the production management resources at the agency to ensure these

services are bought in the most advantageous manner. Detailed analysis will be conducted to find key areas of leverage opportunity, process inefficiency, hidden profit, and other types of unnecessary cost. From this work, sourcing strategies can be developed and implemented to capitalise on these opportunities (Stephens, 2004).

Mirque (2005) suggests eight ways to improve the relationship between marketing and procurement:

1. Clearly define the role of procurement versus marketing communications. Procurement should not report to marketing as you would have a "fox guarding a henhouse."
2. Build better partnerships between the groups via regular cross-functional team meetings and correspondence so that all parties understand each other's requirements.
3. Be sure procurement has a seat at the marketing table. Procurement needs to understand the company's real life advertising issues, not what they learn from reading.
4. Involve procurement team earlier in decision making.
5. Marketing needs to understand that strategic sourcing comes to the table with expertise that can facilitate an initiative, not threaten the process.
6. Co-location is clearly productive.
7. Join procurement and marketing at the hip in the management of the agencies form a financial standpoint.
8. Hire strategic sourcing managers who are experts in their commodity and aligning them with the business units.

Far removed from traditional purchasing groups of the past, today's strategic procurement professional is a trusted, strategic partner in achieving business performance. As businesses focus on strategic core competencies, quality, flexibility, and velocity requirements continue to grow and the role of agencies and suppliers in the overall delivery of marketing activities becomes increasingly important. Strengthening these relationships in a fact-based, transparent, and efficient way and demonstrating prudent management of financial resources is vital in ensuring the greatest impact is generated from the client's marketing budget (Stephens, 2004).

What should the agency do to make the relationship work?

Develop distinctive proprietaries (brand differentiation)

In a hyper-competitive market, a distinctive offer is almost certain to produce disproportionate returns. If the technique really works, client satisfaction and marketplace success will follow.

Improve processes and do not concentrate so single-mindedly on personal relationships

A survey of ANA members and AAAA agencies revealed that process improvement was the most frequent action taken by agencies to improve their relationships with their clients (Davis, 2004). A similar stance has been taken by Barwise and Meehan (2004) who argue that improving processes to ensure satisfaction of the basic needs of customers will lead to success and profitability in even the most competitive of markets, since most businesses are now so focussed on differentiating themselves and not delivering the core benefit the customer is after. In coming years, a good process is going to be more durable than a good relationship. Process development is also important because as procurement experts become more skilled at deconstructing agencies' resource package proposals, agencies will have to make their processes more efficient.

Greater commitment to metrics

It is no coincidence that the only growing areas of adspend are the two most obviously measurable – direct marketing and the internet. As pressure grows on marketers to be accountable, agencies have the most obvious incentive to improve the metrics around their product. After all, media is enveloped in numbers and measurement. The creative product of all agencies is bound to be the focus of attention as return on investment becomes more and more of a management consideration.

Be far more selective about pitching

If an agency is spending 20–25% of its time and resources on pitching, its revenue potential is reduced, and its clients will become edgy. Unless an agency wins at least one in three of the accounts it goes after, it has to ask itself whether it is either good enough, or if it is spending its time well. Alternatively, clients who use high-pitch agencies worry during the pitch whether they will ever see these specialist pitchers again or if they are just being used for the pitch. In other words, if the agency wins the account, will these star creative talents stay on the account or be taken away to support new pitches?

When pitching for an account, an agency should ask itself two questions. What went wrong last time? What makes us think we can do better? If the agency does not know the answer to the first question, they should suspend any decision until they have found out. Unless there is a positive answer to the second question, the agency should either devote its efforts to another target, or spend the time on existing clients.

Go for a premium positioning

Premium positioning is a leadership position (founded on outstanding creativity, but not confined to that) which gives an agency licence to achieve two key goals: winning accounts with less effort and by giving less away, and charging more. This position does not come easily, but is worth it. In the UK market, agencies that have established an enviable reputation for excellence have been CDP in the 1970s, BMP and Saatchi & Saatchi in the 1970s and 1980s, AMV and Lowe Howard Spink in the 1980s, HHCL in the 1990s and BBH in both of the last two decades.

Profile clients

Stuart Sanders (www.sandersconsulting.com) put a new spin on Myers Briggs and came up with the four key client personality factors: Headline (hard driving, no nonsense, results focused), Illustration (extrovert, people focused, dominant), Logo (people person, nice, ask-not-tell), and Bodycopy (the often diffident searcher of truth, for whom no research debrief could ever be too long). Clients like working with agency people who share their values and personality.

Get top management involved

This is a frequent response when clients are becoming critical (Davis 2004). A client may be reassured at the appearance of any member of the agency's senior management team (not just the Chairman or CEO). In the international arena, parachuting in experienced agency leaders from the centre or another geography can also frequently solve problems in a market.

What should the client do to make the relationship work?

Davis (2004) found the top three improvement actions taken by clients to improve client–agency relations to be honest feedback, clear precise scope of work, and improved client-briefing process. I have worked with ISBA (the UK advertisers' professional body) for 15 years, devising and running courses on how to be a good and effective client. Our work-shops cover, among other things, managing the agency, motivating the agency, campaign management, and evaluating the agency.

Managing the agency

Clients that manage their agencies well adhere to some basic rules. Firstly, maintain a settled roster of well-resourced agencies, which are committed to our business, and pay them well in order to maintain their loyalty and guaran-tee superior performance. Secondly, produce rules, procedures and toolkits to ensure consistent client management behaviour, and agency adherence. Thirdly, of the many qualities that help clients get the best out of their agencies, patience is important.

Motivating the agency

There is a priceless state for clients, called "being a favourite client." If you are one of ten clients, one of 20 or one of 30, you need to think where you rank in the agency's pecking order. Unless you are one of the clients the agency people wake up thinking about, you will not get the best people on your business, you will not get the best ideas, the fastest turnaround when it matters, or the famous campaigns. Favourite clients get a totally unfair advantage.

Campaign management

Campaign management is the responsibility of the client, just as creative expertise is always going to be vested in the agency.

Evaluating the agency

Agencies need to know how their clients rate the agency's performance. They also need to self-evaluate. Some clients will adopt formal processes, whilst others prefer day-to-day assessments.

A "joint team" mentality

A "joint team" structure is advantageous as it will allow a senior brand manager to work alongside the agency team to shorten lines of communication, and facilitate "selling" up at critical points of the approval process.

Hiring better marketing talent with a feel for getting the best out of agencies – and making the commitment to train and develop that talent

Relationships are only as good as the people on both sides – and the best agency people are going to be wasted if there is not a rich vein of marketing talent to inspire, direct and manage them. A commitment to training is also vital. Consultants can change attitudes and behaviour at the centre of a company. But if you want to change behaviour on the ground (in-market in an international company, or in business units in a matrix organization) you need training.

Accountability and metrics

Whilst agencies should commit to improving metrics, it is certainly not their prime responsibility. The client has the budget and makes the investment and they should be able to measure the results of their investment.

But it is also in the commercial interest of the agency to be more metrics minded and equipped than their rivals.

Budgeting

Each year, $400 billion is spent on marketing communications worldwide – a combined spend of each business' individual marketing budget. Yet how sophisticated is the budgeting process in most companies? (see also Chapter 5.3). Arguably the behavioural change in companies that would make the biggest difference would be transforming the budgeting process. Generally new budgets end up incorporating the flawed logic and practice of previous ones. Moreover, budgets continue to be breeding grounds for unrealistic hopes and aspirations. So in terms of what the client can do to foster the agency relationship and make it more successful, a spring clean of the budgeting process could be a great start.

ISSUES FOR MULTINATIONAL CLIENTS AND THEIR AGENCIES

Relationships between multinational advertisers and agencies are fundamentally different from those for one-country clients. The stakes are bigger, there are far more people involved, and there are many different operating systems. A great deal is written on the subject of international advertising, but much of it comes from the "international campaigns simply do not work" school of thought, citing that an homogenous, blanket campaign will not be effective in reaching audiences of different cultures, preferences, materialism and motives. Each needs to be spoken to in a way that is meaningful and relevant to them, and rarely can this be done through one message the world over. From a relationship perspective, global advertising is difficult for two main reasons, both stemming from that fact that it is no longer a two-party relationship that needs to be managed but rather, a network of relationships.

- Dissatisfied central clients, criticising their agency for having exceeded budget, being behind schedule, and infuriating their in-market colleagues. Often the promise of famous creative work (which settled the outcome of the pitch in favour of the chosen agency) has not been realised at all.
- Frustrated agencies, claiming to be losing money. They are not working well with the clients, and are starting to fall out with their colleagues around the world. These local agency managements much prefer dealing with national clients, who are easier to work with, far more likely to provide opportunities to fill the shop window and win awards, and seen as more profitable.

Despite the perception that a blanket global campaign would be cheaper and easier (one idea, one shoot), such multinational campaign development frequently takes too long and is too expensive, often because too many people are involved and it is too English-focused (in regards to language, culture and markets). So it might not be that local advertising is better, but rather that it is just easier, and in the long run, it often costs far less. For agencies to be successful in developing world-class global advertising, there is no alternative to specialising in international, and giving it the priority and status it deserves. Creative awards for international campaigns should be valued alongside one-market work. Furthermore, career planning needs to be managed so that international jobs are seen as more desirable than staying at home.

But it would be wrong just to blame the agencies. A real problem with advertisers is that during the agency selection process, they frequently take their eye off the ball once the new relationship is under way. Russo, Schoemaker and Russo (1990) explain that groups of capable, intelligent executives often ask and answer the wrong questions, gather the wrong intelligence, fail to learn from history, rush into premature conclusions, fail to assess risk correctly, ultimately making wrong decisions. The client must be careful not to assume that the agency will know best or what development process to follow. For example, it is incorrect to assume that just because a brand is sold all over the world, it should have a global campaign. The client needs to spend as long as it takes to conduct a thorough interrogation of goals and strategy consistent with what it can afford to invest in the campaign, and do so with a long-term focus (e.g., three to five years).

To minimize these aforementioned pitfalls, agency selection specialists have developed a number of tools to help clients and agencies. For example, Agency Assessments International developed a five-stage sequential pathway called DISCO.

Deliverables

What results is the international advertising supposed to achieve? Over what time frame? How will it fit with the rest of the marketing mix? These are the decisions of the client marketing team.

Investment

How much can the client afford to invest to hit those targets? How much should be budgeted for media, production and agency fees? Marketing accountants should lead these decisions with significant upfront input from the media agency. It is worth noting that more campaigns have failed through inadequate levels of spend than creative inadequacies.

Strategy

Once the goals have been established, and the budgetary amount and its allocation decided upon, the next step is to spend time on the marketing and communications strategy, looking in depth at the brand, and digging for insights to inspire the creative process. Brand specialists in the client marketing team, working closely with agency planners, should lead this.

Creative

The central agency creatives and planners should lead this stage, involving colleagues from all key geographies and markets.

Operations

Here the client must ask itself how it will manage their international campaign, whilst the agency team needs to consider how they will resource and operate it. Both teams should work together, led by the central client, considering effectiveness, efficiencies and value.

When a relationship cannot be fixed – back to the pitch [JMS1]

Prior to 1969 any agency reported to the IPA by another member agency for having made an unsolicited approach to the client of another member agency risked being removed from the Institute. But then the rules changed and pitching became the driving force for agencies – a trend accelerated by the emergence of media independents and the replacement of commission by resource package fees as the "gold standard" for agency pay.

If pitching has become a way of life for some advertisers (who clearly are not interested in the long term partnership), the pitch should be recognized as a consulting service which clients demand and agencies offer. In addition, a workshop approach may be a better way to pick an agency than a presentation of speculative creative. Agencies can then charge for the performance, and clients should pay. If it deepens into companionship and a longer association, then that is a separate issue, which should be the subject of a separate negotiation. Alternatively, if the client wants a quick fix or a raft of ideas, it would be better to sign a commercial agreement to buy them.

One approach, starting with the clients, is:

1. Use the DISCO system when clients are planning a review. Do not make any decisions about the operations until absolute clarity has been achieved on deliverables, level of investment, the strategic approach and creative strategy.
2. Look ahead. Do not ask the agencies to simply come up with a better campaign for the autumn. Challenge them to be visionary, and think four or five years into the future. Where and how can we get to from where we are now?
3. Demand an integrated approach by looking at creative and the media environment together, not separately.
4. Make the agencies stakeholders in your success by offering a contract and a remuneration package geared to results.
5. Show the pitching agencies that you are running a fair pitch: clear criteria, not too many agencies, and no unreasonable demands.

And for the agencies:

1. Do not give it all away for free. Leave something to the imagination, and something for when the knot has been tied.
2. Consider the client's point of view by offering them management, not just solutions.
3. Take every opportunity to stand out and be distinctive, to enhance the client's recall of you and their intention to select you.
4. Do not fall for the temptation to pitch too often. Only invest time and money in prospects if (a) you think you've got a good chance of winning, and (b) you can make a difference.
5. Pick change agents for your pitch team to give the client the outcome they want – transformation.

Agency remuneration

How should advertisers pay agencies? How should agencies charge their clients? Paying agencies is no longer straightforward. We have progressed from the age of commission fixed for nearly 100 years at 15% of the gross cost, to the age of fees, to a period of not knowing what method will come next. The client is concerned about cost; the agency about profitability.

From the client standpoint, there are several approaches they can take in responding to agency price proposals. They can either accept the agency's pricing basis and negotiate on detail, establish the company's own pricing criteria, or given that they are in a buyer's market, negotiate from strength.

The agency has several different methods it can adopt in charging clients (IPA, 2006). These range from the traditional commission model (a flat percentage of total media spend) to resource package fees (an agreed upon amount decided on before the activity occurs) to variable fees based on actual hours (where the fee is calculated after the event and based on hours worked) to specific project, concept or licensing fees. Payment by results schemes (which are now being used in 44% of UK creative agency agreements) are an incentive-based concept centred on achieving mutually agreed performance goals, thus creating a win/win situation for both the agency (higher revenues) and the client (measurable outcomes).

The way a remuneration negotiation is conducted will vary between new relationships and existing ones (IPA, 2006). In a new relationship, the client will set out the precise scope of work, and has the opportunity of comparing tenders from pitching agencies. The new agency has the benefit of a newly defined scope of work, and can calculate workload, resource required and desired pricing. The client will be able to benchmark proposed agency cost against what the previous agency charged, and other agency relationships. The agency understands its revenue/cost equation from its relationships with other clients. The client will have a target agency cost in mind, which is likely to be scaled on allocation from the total marketing budget. The agency will probably be balancing its desired revenue (probably based on a resource package fee calculation) against what it anticipates the client will be prepared to pay. The deciding factor may well be downward competitive pressure influenced by bid price from the other pitching agencies.

The annual review of an ongoing situation has a different dynamic. First, the client and agency must analyse qualifying performance for Payment by Results (if applicable), before moving on to negotiate the next year's remuneration. The client must redefine the exact scope of work for the coming year. The agency knows what was needed last year to fulfil the scope of work set for them, and can make necessary adjustments in keeping with any revisions to scope of work. The client marketing team will probably be under pressure to reduce the cost of agency service, whilst the agency will be concerned about account profitability as well as revenue level. The client's hoped for outcome is lower cost (or lower proportional cost if the marketing budget is increasing), and they aim to do this without diminishing the agency's contribution to goals and KPIs, and without demotivating them. Alternatively, the agency's desired outcome is increased account profitability, even if that can only be achieved by reducing resource costs more than revenue reduction. They aim to do this without any measurable effect on service levels, client satisfaction, and most importantly contribution to goals and KPIs.

Regardless of the age of the relationship between agency and client, there is a broad structure that can be offered for arriving at a remuneration deal that both parties are happy with. It is as follows:

1. The scope of work is negotiated – the client defines it, the agency interrogates it. Once agreed upon, each side signs off.
2. The agency anticipates the necessary people hours, writes a work plan and shares it with the client.
3. The client refers back to the marketing budget and relates people hours cost to agency cost provision in the budget.
4. Both sides agree baseline cost at the point where cost provision and people hours (possibly already adjusted) intersect.
5. The client provides the agency with goals and KPIs.
6. The client and agency agree on how much the client is going to pay the agency.
7. Both sides then agree how the agency is to be remunerated (e.g., fees, commission, payment by results).
8. Both sides agree how performance is going to be evaluated and remuneration reviewed in a year's time.
9. Both sides enter definitive discussions on the form of contract to be used.

To help good agreements, the IPA (2006) released a 10-point checklist outlining the qualities shared by best practice remuneration agreements.

1. It should be simple to understand and easy to administer for all involved.
2. It should be fair to both the client and the agency.
3. Client and agency interests and priorities should be aligned so that both parties feel they are working towards a common goal.
4. The agreement should be finalised and understood before work begins and agency resources are committed.
5. The agreement should be recorded in a ratified client-agency contract.
6. The agreement must be flexible enough to accommodate future changes in scope of services, budgets, timing, resource mix, markets, corporate objectives and products.
7. Senior managers should be involved, and accountable for establishing objectives. Principles should be clearly communicated to the teams on both sides.
8. The agreement should be robust to survive both time and changes in management.
9. It should be based on agreed and understood terms and definitions so that everyone is talking the same language.
10. There should be specified tracking and review dates.

SUMMARY

"Words there are not good enough
To match the brilliance of the bluff;
Or adequately to explain
How businessmen of normal brain,
Enter Advertising Houses,
And leave without their shirts and trousers!"
                                    Ramsbottom (1986: 30)

Cynicism is one thing, and agencies criticise clients too. But neither side can ignore the importance of the relationship – especially considering how different the agency and client agendas can be. Diageo have developed the Diageo Way of Building Brands, a toolkit for their marketers (Gladman and Melsom, 2005). Some of their recommendations, which also form my summary of advice, are as follows:

The agency manifesto
- Take risks with the work you generate and present, thereby escaping from the parity of 80% of the advertising that clients and consumers see.
- Benign creativity is not an option; nothing is achieved by being the same; chaos and unpredictability can fuel the creative process.
- Create work that wins accolades for the company. Consider this – "If we win an award we win more business, so that we can win more awards."

The client manifesto
- Do not take risks with the levels of investment involved.
- The work must work, whatever the work is like.

- In the end, judgement will be made on success – the objectives of the business plan, as defined by certain specific metrics, must be met.

In the post-2000 digitally driven world where the consumer decides which selling messages they take notice of, there is no longer one client–agency relationship to manage. The average client now deals with at least five to ten agencies. Agencies juggle numerous relationships, with clients who have different cultures and expectations. There are no rules for managing these relationships, except to maximise the chances of commercial success. Consequently, measurement and accountability rank higher than risk-taking and awards, and both sides will judge their relationship largely, if not wholly, on performance.

REFERENCES

Barwise, P. and S. Meehan (2004), *Simply Better: Winning and Keeping Customers by Delivering What Matters Most*. Bosto: Harvard Business School Press.

Bullmore, J. (1991), *Behind the Scenes in Advertising*. Henley-on-Thames: NTC Publications.

Cagley, J.W. and C.R. Roberts (1984), "Criteria for Advertising Agency Selection: An Objective Appraisal," *Journal of Advertising Research*, 24 (2), 27–31.

Dauer, J. (2005), "The Transactionalization of the Client-Agency Relationship," http://www.sageandyou.com/pdfs/06-30-05-TransactionalizationoftheClient-AgencyRelationship.pdf (accessed: 25 January 2006).

Davis, J. (2004), "Optimising Client agency Relations," *The Advertiser*, (October) (accessed via WARC).

Delener, N. (1996), "Beware of Globalisation: A Comparative Study of Advertising Agency–Client Relationships," *Journal of Professional Services Marketing*, 14 (1), 167–77.

DeSouza, G. (1992), "Designing a Customer Retention Plan," *Journal of Business Strategy*, (March/April), 24–8.

Doyle, P., M. Corstjens, and P.C.N Michell (1980), "Signals of Vulnerability in Agency-Client Relations," *Journal of Marketing*, 44, 18–23.

Fam, K.S. and D.S. Waller (2000), "Attracting New clients: A New Zealand Ad Agency Perspective," *Journal of Promotion Management*, 5 (2), 85–99.

Farris, P. and D.C. West (2007), "A Fresh View of the Advertising Budget Process," in *The SAGE Handbook of Advertising*, eds. G.J. Tellis and T. Ambler, London: Sage Publications.

Feldwick, P. (2007), "Account Planning: Its History and Its Significance for Ad Agencies," in *The SAGE Handbook of Advertising*, eds. G.J. Tellis and T. Ambler, London: Sage Publications.

Fletcher, W. (1994), *How to Capture the Advertising High Ground*, London: Century Business.

Fox, S. (1984), *The Mirror Makers: A History Of American Advertising And Its Creators*, New York: Vintage Books.

Gladman, P. and A. Melsom (2005), "Breakthrough Creativity: A Blend of Art and Science," *Market Leader*, (Winter) (31).

Grant, J. (2005), "The Five Cardinal Sins of Client Relationships," http://www.refresher.com/!jogsins.html (accessed: 12 (January) 2006).

Gray, B. (2003), "Behind Great Client/Agency Relationships," *The Advertiser*, (January) (accessed via WARC).

Henke, L.L. (1995), "A Longitudinal Analysis of the Ad Agency-Client Relationship: Predictors of an Agency Switch," *Journal of Advertising Research*, (March/April), 24–30.

IPA (2006), *Agency Remuneration: A Best Practice Guide On How To Pay Agencies*. Joint Report by the Institute of Practitioners in Advertising, Incorporated Society of British Advertisers, Marketing Communications Consultants Association, and Public Relations Consultants Association, London.

Krinsky, A. and S. Marcus (2004), "How to Involve Procurement in Managing the Advertising Budget," *The Advertiser*, (June).

LaBahn, D.W. (1996), "Advertiser Perceptions of Fair Compensation, Confidentiality and Rapport," *Journal of Advertising Research*, 36 (2), 28–38.

McDonald, C. and J. Scott (2007), "Brief History of Advertising," in *The SAGE Handbook of Adveritising*, eds. G.J. Tellis and T. Ambler, London: Sage Publications.

Melsom, A. (2004), "Marketing and Procurement – A Curious Blend of Art and Science," *Market Leader*, (Summer) (25).

Michell, P.C.N. (1986), "Auditing of Agency–Client Relations," *Journal of Advertising* Research, 26 (6), 29–41.

(1988), "The Influence of Organisational Capability on Account Switching," *Journal of Advertising Research*, (June/July), 33–8.

Michell, P.C.N and N.H. Sanders (1995), "Loyalty in Agency–Client Relations: The Impact of the Organisational Context," *Journal of Advertising Research*, (March/April), 9–22.

Mirque, B.B. (2005), "Procurement – Blessing or Curse," *The Advertiser,* (August).

Palihawadana, D. and B.R. Barnes (2005), "Investigating Agency–Client Relationships in the Polish Advertising Industry," *International Journal of Advertising*, 24 (4), 487–503.

Ramsbottom, B. (1986), *Boardroom Ballads,* Bethesda: Adler & Adler.

Roberts, K. and B. Isherwood (2005), "How An Agency Evaluates A Client," *The Advertiser, (*February) (accessed via WARC).

Russo, J.E., P.J.H. Schoemaker, and E.J. Russo (1990), *Decision Traps: Ten Barriers to Brilliant Decision-Making and How to Overcome Them,* New York: Simon & Schuster.

Ryan, M.P. and R.H. Colley (1967), "Preventative Maintenance in Client-Ad Agency Relations," *Harvard Business Review,* (September/October), 66–74.

Stephens, J. (2004), "Procurement and Marketing: Achieving Value Through Partnership," *The Advertiser,* (October).

Tellis, G.J. (1998), *Advertising and Sales Promotion Strategy*, Reading, Massachusetts: Addison-Wesley.

Verbeke, W. (1989), "Developing an Advertising Agency–Client Relationship In the Netherlands," *Journal of Advertising Research*, 28 (6), 1927.

Weilbacher, W.M. (1991), *Choosing and Working With Your Advertising Agency,* Lincolnwood, Ill: NTC Business Books.

West, D.C. and S.J. Paliwoda (1996), "Advertising Client–Agency Relationships: The Decision-Making Structure of Clients," *European Journal of Marketing*, 30 (8), 22–39.

White, S. and C. Dawson (2004), "Media Snakes, Agency Ladders," *Admap*, December (456).

The Creative Brief and its Strategic Role in the Campaign Development Process

Richard Storey and Edith Smit

"You can't imagine how terrifying the blank sheet is to a creative person obliged to fill it"

(attributed to Peter Souter)

"Oh for the freedom of a restrictive brief"

(attributed to Bill Bernbach)

This chapter examines the creative brief as a key strategic tool within the campaign development process. Together the brand strategy and the marketing plan offer the starting point for developing the communication campaign. Because the brand strategy is too abstract and the marketing plan too broad, these plans are too generic to form the base for developing effective brand communication. It is the creative brief that has the ability to funnel and to translate long-term strategy into short-term activity. Indeed, creating communications to build the bridge between where a brand is and where it wants to be is the key role for the agency. Their response of what they are going to do and who they need to talk to in order to make this happen must be

considered in the context of both the overall marketing strategy and specific campaign strategy.

In this chapter, we discuss key issues emerging from the last decade's literature on creative briefing and outline best practise, as both used and abused by agencies and clients. We conclude by challenging the orthodoxy that a faultless, unchanging, agreed brief must precede the development of effective creative solutions. This chapter is not about creativity per se, but about beginning the creative process. In summary, the process needs to be stimulated by a well-honed creative brief but the brief, and therefore the benchmarks for campaign evaluation, should be allowed to evolve alongside the campaign development.

TYPES OF CREATIVE BRIEFING

One of the great paradoxes of creativity is that it responds well to limitation and constraint when deployed and managed well. It seems that creative minds positively feed off restrictions, boundaries and conventions, frequently using their very existence as fuel to break new ground.

By contrast, the complete removal of all restrictions in an attempt to liberate the creative process often has the opposite effect, either by instilling a kind of "stage fright" on those expected to perform or by producing a highly inefficient "random walk" process that yields fleeting and spasmodic progress.

In most studies on the campaign development process, the brief is identified as the most important part (Fletcher, 1990, 1997). It must simultaneously motivate and inspire, focus and control, expand and control. This is what makes it so difficult. Given this, what forms of briefing are most useful and effective?

Briefing by requirement

If creative people frequently feel anxious or blocked staring down at a blank pad of paper, imagine how Michelangelo might have felt staring up at the blank ceiling of the Sistine Chapel. Where and how did he begin?

Without knowing the answer, it is enlightening to speculate on the kind of brief Pope Julius II might have handed down to the young sculptor in 1506. It is known that the Pope had a somewhat inflexible relationship with Michelangelo and may have strongly coerced him into "accepting" the commission. Given that, it is quite possible that his brief was the firm (and none too polite) instruction "Paint the ceiling."

Whilst this brief has the benefit of brevity and accuracy, it offers little clue or direction for the great artist to begin organising his thoughts. It offers no encouragement or inspiration. What should the artist's theme be? What feelings should he try to evoke? What colours to use? In short, where should he begin?

It may sound absurd to think that any commission is effectively briefed by giving the artist an indication of the space to be filled and instructing them to hurry up and fill it. Nevertheless, the equivalent does happen on a regular basis within the advertising and communications industry – effectively every time an instruction is issued along the lines of "We need a print execution to run in this weekend's press" or "We need a piece to mail to all prospects."

If this simplistic form of "briefing by requirement" is surprisingly common, it is because it is all too easy. It requires little commitment on the part of the commissioner, at least at the initial stage. Ironically it will require commitment from the commissioner at the stage when work is produced, something that may not be so easy to give, without any firm view or expectation of what is to be produced at the outset. It's a lot easier to issue instructions than deal with whatever response they generate.

Briefing by execution

Rather than simply giving Michelangelo the instruction to fill a specific space, Pope Julius would have been more helpful by being more specific on elements of the execution he was expecting. Perhaps something along the lines of "Paint the ceiling using red, green and gold" or the slightly more directional "Paint the ceiling using red, green and *lots of* gold?"

Each of these instructions would have given the artist marginally more guidance. Specifically "lots of gold" is something of a clue that might well have steered the work, perhaps towards a classic, formal style or indeed something ornate and elaborate. It is the kind of clue that creative people seem to discern easily, whether given intentionally or not.

This kind of "briefing by execution" is, once again, not uncommon in our industry. In 1999, a brief was issued for another execution in the long series of highly creative and effective cinema and television adverts for *Stella Artois* in the UK, with the instruction "More of the same, with a bit more reverence for the beer." Given that the idea running throughout the campaign was people's extraordinary reverence for the beer, that is not even as helpful as it sounds. The problem with this kind of brief is that the creative minds charged with responding to the brief need a firm grasp of what their creation should be about, not just how big it should be, what colours it should use or any other executional detail.

A good brief therefore needs to be in some way directional about the content of the work, not just its format.

Briefing by content

Let's imagine that the Pope understood this. He certainly would have cared a great deal about the results achieved in the chapel and would have had some ideas about what he wanted to see. Perhaps then, his instruction was along the lines of "Paint the ceiling using cherubs, angels and mortals."

This brief has merit over the others so far. It limits the scope that the artist can operate in. Previous briefs pretty much allowed anything that was large and ornate. This instruction directs the artist to work with specific content. However, rather than limiting creative potential, it begins to frame and project it. It suggests some interest and drama in the interplay between mere mortals and the angelic hosts. It leaves plenty of scope within the exact depiction of the mortals and cherubs. The equivalent in our industry and our times would be something like "We're looking for a commercial that shows our product along with well dressed young people, trendy urban bars and cock-tails."

The problem with briefing by content is that the more specific you are, the more limiting and unproductive the brief becomes. Mortals, cherubs and angels is reasonably flexible, but start specifying "a cross section of mortals, including all ethnic groups, ages and social backgrounds, a dozen cherubs and the following ten angels" and the creative opportunities start to shrink before your eyes. Again, the real need for creative people is less to be instructed on the content of their work

as the story or message that it is supposed to convey.

Briefing by meaning

The content of the Sistine Chapel suggests that Michelangelo's brief may well have been closer to "Paint the ceiling depicting the creation of the world, man's degradation by sin, the divine wrath of the deluge and the preservation of Noah and his family."

Even the entirely un-creative can begin to appreciate why this is a more useful and inspiring instruction. It gives a narrative and suggests a strong moral conclusion. It invites the artist to research the storyline, to project themselves into it, to think of ways of expressing its drama, and so on. Whilst it is highly specific on the narrative, it is entirely liberating on the specific executional nature of how it best be told.

A brief for police recruitment (APG, 2001) offers a good modern day equivalent. It asked the creative team to dramatise how a police officer has to be able to do things most normal people would struggle to do, such as breaking the news of bereavement to a family, treating a suspected rapist as innocent until proven otherwise or supervising the removal of a child from its parents by social workers. This gave the creatives the scope to dramatise the emotional dilemmas inherent in such circumstances.

Although, not all products immediately suggest quite such powerful themes, it is the responsibility of the teams compiling the briefing to arrive at the most compelling narrative they can identify. "Shifts more stains at low temperature than other non-biological washing powders" may not at first glance sound like the most fruitful subject matter for a gripping story. But add into the mix the drama of how those stains were created (e.g., grass stains from sporting heroics, the pride of a mother in seeing their children smartly dressed, a soccer pitch, and the drama of performing at your personal best) and the potential becomes more visible.

Again, the great danger here is that of being so specific on the subject matter that the latitude for movement becomes negligible. In the previous example, it would take a sizeable creative leap not to write a touching domestic drama about a son's school football final.

So, what brief could Julius possibly have given Michelangelo that would have given both direction and inspiration?

Briefing by creative task

The best way to both guide and inspire the artist would have been to be as clear and challenging as possible in articulating the task his work had to achieve. A directive such as "Paint a tribute to the greater glory of God that inspires devotion in his people" would have issued a powerful and inspiring creative challenge. With this brief, the artist is not just invited to fill the space, but to provoke a certain, very specific and remarkable response in the viewer. He is left in little doubt that just showing a few mortals and a couple of cherubs would not, in itself be enough. He needs to go further to produce the desired response. It is going to require a lot more artistry, sensitivity and creative prowess.

Referring to the real world examples quoted earlier. The brief for Police recruitment asked that the advertising "Make 999 out of every 1,000 people realise they couldn't be a Police Officer, but respect like hell the one who could" – a task that issued a challenge and inspired a thought provoking response. The resulting creative showed well-known celebrities imagining in their mind's eye what a police officer has to be able to cope with, before concluding that they themselves couldn't do it. Likewise, in the soap powder example an instruction to "issue a challenge to stains that no self-respecting mother can refuse" would have been more useful than a simple directive to communicate a low temperature stain removal claim.

The ideal creative briefing

The main argument here is that a good brief should achieve a fine balance of being specific without being entirely restrictive. A good brief closes down options and is directionally precise. Briefs are so called because they are meant to be succinct. Many clients and agencies aim for one single page, sadly a task only the minority achieve in practice.

A good brief is precise in such a way that, at the same time as narrowing the field of play, it opens up inspiring possibilities for the directions and angles that remain. The best briefs turn the description of the task from an instruction into a challenge, and in doing so strikes a balance between direction and inspiration.

However, this is not the only role that the brief is expected to perform within the creative development process.

MULTIPLE ROLES OF THE CREATIVE BRIEF

As part of the bigger picture, it is important that the brief relates to, and follows the thinking of the total marketing and communications strategy and overall corporate business plan, and is consistent with the programs that are already in place. As well as measuring the success of the particular campaign that the brief will conceive, progress towards the bigger and longer-term brand and corporate goals should also be measured (IPA, 2003).

As the platform for the communications campaign, so the better the brief, the better and more accurate the results. Indeed, the better a company's corporate or brand position is defined, and the more thoughtfully its key business issues are described, the more likely the agency's creative and strategic thinkers will be able to produce great solutions.

Most creative development processes involve teams of managers on both client and agency side as well as the team(s) of creatives charged with meeting the brief. In this context, the single briefing document frequently serves three different functions: cementing agreement, aiding judgement and inspiring creative thinking.

Cementing agreement

The brief is the most important information issued by a client to an agency, as it is from the brief that everything else flows. Often, the creative brief fulfils a role as a contract between client and agency. It represents a summary of all current thinking on the task in hand and indicates the kind of response that is expected. It is essential from the agency perspective to ensure that client and creative teams are aligned in understanding the requirement and the rules of engagement on any project. Without it, a great deal of emotionally charged and expensive creative development time can be squandered.

For most agencies, the creative brief is the tool most frequently used by agency managers to both secure and test such agreement. As a result, every single word or phrase is typically interrogated and deliberated over at great length, often with stultifying results. Many agencies have gone as far as to develop systems that supposedly aid the account teams and client teams in completing the various pieces of analysis required to determine the communications strategy (e.g., Davies, 2000; Bech-Larsen, 2001). Whilst these systems often claim to be bespoke to the agency concerned, they essentially involve both parties working together to agree the essential elements of the creative brief. Their value tends to lie as much in the area of cementing agreement as in the strategic insight they generate.

One of the key contracts a brief should establish is the setting of concrete campaign objectives (What do we want to achieve? From what to what?) and success criteria (What will success look like and how will it be measured?). This will help establish accountability and demonstrate the effectiveness of the communications effort. A good brief will leave the agency with a clear understanding of what it is they are trying to achieve and the role that commercial communications will play in this process (IPA, 2003).

Research conducted in the Netherlands on cases nominated (or not) for the EFFIE (meaning Effectiveness) Award found a strong correlation between the proven effectiveness and the setting of clear, numerically stated performance objectives up front (Franzen, 1999; Giling et al., 2001; NieuwsTribune, 2001). In the majority of cases, however, performance objectives have not been stated up front (see also Heuvelman et al., 2002).

Aiding judgement

The brief also fulfils a critical role as an objective touch point to assess creative ideas as they are developed.

The degree to which this process is formalised varies tremendously between different agency and client cultures. In most cases it is best practice for the team to précis the brief and the thinking behind it before any creative solutions are presented or discussed. This then provides a framework for the work to be assessed against (Devinney et al., 2005). In some agency and client cultures it is common to use elements from the brief as a checklist against which the proposed creative solutions are ticked off.

An unspoken assumption behind this role is that the brief does not change in any way between the commencement of creative development and the presentation of possible creative solutions.

Inspiring creative thinking

In the light of all that is involved in securing "sign off" in the process of creative campaign development, it is perhaps not surprising that the brief's role as a catalyst for stimulating creative thinking is frequently overlooked (Langwost, 2004). Nevertheless, as discussed with reference to Michelangelo, that should be the primary function of the brief.

With all three roles bearing heavily on the brief, it is worth examining the specific ingredients of a good, inspiring and directional brief.

WHAT CONSTITUTES A GOOD BRIEF?

There is little published material on creative briefing, the exception being the IPA 2003 study on client briefs and some other studies more specifically focussed on developing creative briefs within agencies (e.g., Barker, 2001; Hill and Johnson, 2004; Tait, 2002; White, 2003). As mentioned before, the brief should be short and fit on one single page. Sometimes additional information is needed, but that should be added as attachment or otherwise. Aside from differences in format, presentation and the wording of headings, the basic structure of a creative brief contains the same six core elements: task, audience, proposition, support, character and requirements.

Creative people working on briefs will often claim that the only one of these that matters is the proposition, to the point that many of them claim that a single statement is the brief. Some write it in large letters, stick it on their wall or find other ways of burning it into their subconscious. Others say they reflect on it and then attempt to forget or "go away from it." Whatever their individual strategies and ways of working, most creative teams use methods that focus their efforts on the proposition.

However, it is manifestly clear from analysing successful case histories that other elements within the brief are of critical importance too (IPA, 2003; White, 2003). We therefore discuss each element of the brief separately, giving guidance on how they best be deployed to improve the chances of creating inspiration.

Task

As we have already discussed, a succinct and directional summary of the task is critical to a good brief. It is the part of the creative brief where the marketing communication objectives are translated into communication solutions ('What should we try to achieve?'). It is also the part of the brief where it becomes clear that the client brief is understood by the agency ('What problem should be solved?').

A common mistake is to describe the task only in terms of interim communications variables, e.g., "Boost awareness of the new variant of X," "Announce the launch of Y" or "Communicate the change in policy for Z."

Although advertising can cause rapid and significant boosts in awareness, that in itself is rarely of direct commercial value. The task of advertising here is not to create awareness of the new variant, but *to change* people's habits and get them to try the new variant. Given this, the task might be much better stated as "to corrupt people's cosy sauce buying habits and dare them to try new spicy variant X." This statement is not only clear in stating the objective as breaking established patterns of behaviour, but it also provides colour and direction on the unchanging, unthinking nature of that behaviour and of the audacity with which this new variety aims to disrupt that routine.

To help direct the task to be more directionally instructive, a simple but useful question that is often worth asking is "what is holding people back?." The more accurately and inventively this can be answered, the more instructive the task definition will become. For example, a 1998 government (DfEE) education campaign was given the task of encouraging parents to read to their young children (APG, 1999). The brief could simply have stated the task as "encourage parents to read to their children," but by examining why parents didn't currently do this, it became clear that knowing what they should be doing was not the issue. Parents were fully aware of their obligations. The problem was observed to be the book at bedtime. With busy lives, parents were frequently getting to that time of the evening feeling they simply didn't have the energy to read a book with their children, they'd much rather relax and perhaps enjoy a glass of wine. The brief therefore described the task much more usefully as "to encourage parents to take advantage of various opportunities throughout the day to read to their children, rather than just at bedtime." This articulate summation of the task explains the strategy better than any snappy proposition.

Audience

A great deal of time and effort goes into determining the target audience for a brand's communications. Whilst this may make for more efficient marketing, often the results of this analysis are expressed in a form that genuinely does not help the creative process. At this point often a lot of miscommunication and conflict exist between apparently totally different professionals (Barker, 2001; Burden, 2003; West, 1993).

The requirement for the creative briefing is to make those receiving the brief feel they both know and empathise with the audience. Overly technical descriptions, such as "BC1C2 emotionally involved mothers" or "men aged 25–45 who are frequent visitors to DIY sheds," do little to bring the audience and their issues to life. Whereas "mums concerned about getting their children to eat well" creates a universally understood picture, not just of the intended target for the message, but of why they might indeed be a willing and grateful recipient of it.

Two descriptions, both applying to the male DIY example above, serve to further illustrate the value of a good audience description:

"Meat and two veg blokes with grime under their finger nails, who smoke Embassy Regal and like to run their thumb down a cupboard doors saying "lovely bit of dovetailing that." They regard themselves as craftsmen, the next best thing to a tradesman."

"Keeping up with the Jones types who believe their humble semi could one day make it into House Beautiful. They care about getting their tones to blend and their contrasts to add accent. They like to host dinner parties to show off the results of their latest project."

Whilst technically fitting the same description of male DIYers aged 25–45, the differences in character and aspiration between the two audiences are abundantly clear. What's more, it is clear that each would respond best to advertising with different creative and strategic approaches. It is imperative therefore for creative people to have a vivid mental picture of the audience and their motivations so they can properly attune what they create. In other words, the audience description needs *consumer insight.*

Proposition

The word "proposition" originated in an age of customer benefits, selling ideas and Unique Selling Propositions (Reeves, 1961). Reeves, of Ted Bates, stated that each advertisement must say to each reader: "buy this product, and you will get this specific benefit" (cited in West, 1993). It embodied the idea that the advertiser was making a strong, unique and relevant offer or proposal directly to the consumer. If he or she took up the offer by buying the product, they would receive the specific benefit articulated in the advertising.

The meaning of "proposition" has softened considerably since then. By the 2000s, the word is more commonly understood to mean a short, succinct and snappy expression that summarizes the message and acts as a focus of the communication (see also Langwost, 2004; White, 2003).

Whilst some briefs do still use propositions based on benefits offered to the consumer, many of the propositions that circulate nowadays are expressions of fact, points of view, commonly admired values, rallying calls, slogans and not strictly offers or benefits. A fairly arbitrary selection of propositions from a generation apart illustrates this shift.

In our opinion, there are two linked reasons for this shift in emphasis. First is the growing advertising literacy of audiences in developed markets (Kover et al., 1997; White and Smith, 2001). It is widely commented that the consumer nowadays understands the conventions of advertising much better. They understand advertisers are trying to offer them some version of a superior performance benefit that only their brand delivers. With that understanding comes a greater cynicism about the nature of the claims, a cynicism compounded in many cases by an erosion of genuine performance differences between competing brands. As a result, advertising has responded by attempting to engage consumers in *the way* it puts its message across, more than the *actual* message it puts across.

In line with this, the creative teams who are effectively the principal users of the brief, have become more marketing literate, and

	'70s/'80s	'00s
Food	*Smash*	*Kit Kat*
	Real mash without the hassle of cooking potatoes	Champions the need for a break
Drink	*Heineken*	*Johnnie Walker*
	Refreshes you when you need it most	Inspires progress
Car	*VW*	*Honda*
	A car you can rely on	Welcome to optimism
Medicine	*Karvol*	*Always*
	Helps children (and their parents) sleep soundly	Experts on women's cycles
Finance	*Bradford & Bingley*	*Privilege*
	Gives you a better deal than any other society	You don't have to be posh to be privileged
Government	*COI*	*COI / HEA*
	Fitting smoke detectors brings you peace of mind	Don't play the sex lottery

(Sources: APG © Data reprinted by kind permission of APG London. www.apg.org.uk; IPA *Advertising Works* Vols. 1–13, WARC www.warc.com)

Figure 3.2.1   Proposition shift

more adept at adding a creative angle to articulate the benefit being sold. Their requirement has shifted from a mere statement of what the benefit is, to a fresh perspective or angle with which to approach the dramatisation of the brand, a need that the Account Planning community has largely fulfilled.

Support

Support refers to the evidence supplied to make the propositional claim more credible. The concept of "supporting evidence" from which the phrase was drawn, supposes that the nature of support is essentially factual, rational and evidential. Classically, support does take this form, as in "no other non-biological powder washes whiter at 40 degrees," "the engine contains no water and so cannot freeze, no matter how cold it gets" or "Sainsbury's strawberry jam contains 20% more strawberries than other supermarket jams costing the same." However, increasingly strategists are finding that broader based forms of expression can also support the new forms of proposition discussed above. These could take the form of surprises, feelings, truths, lines of argument or even pieces of conjecture. The following are all examples:

Surprise:	There is no height requirement to be a police officer (Police)
Feeling:	Business travellers feel no-one understands them when they say that travelling to far off meetings is hard work (United Airlines)
Truth:	Cats are unpredictable (Whiskas)
Line of argument:	If you can see a bus lane enforcement camera, it can see you (Transport for London)
Conjecture:	Of the women who used illegal minicabs last year, we know 18 were attacked. We don't know what happened to all the others (COI)

(Source: APG © Data reprinted by kind permission of APG London. www.apg.org.uk)

Figure 3.2.2   Evidence for the propositional claims

What is important here is that the facts or expressions quoted as support do genuinely help the audience believe or feel more engaged by the proposition. Support is most often abused in practice by becoming the place to record miscellaneous features or messages that don't support the proposition, but are deemed sufficiently interesting or important to warrant a mention somewhere in the briefing documentation.

The *Because Test* is a useful tool for exposing such inappropriate usage. Its form is deceptively simple; reverse the proposition and support expressions to form a sentence, beginning with the word "because." The power of this simple format to reveal expressions that are self-evidently non-supporting is conspicuous. The following examples illustrate: "Because it is easier to swallow, brand x is more effective at fighting migraines," "Because it comes in a range of engine sizes from 1.4 to 3.2 litres, it is the most reliable car ever," "Because you should only drink in moderation, brand y is pure party fuel."

Whilst the role of support is to support the audience's belief in the proposition, it is not the only thing that drives brand differentiation. In an era of more parity products, making similar claims, supported by similar facts, we observe an increased focus on Brand Character to aid engagement, distinctiveness and credibility.

Brand character

Increasingly, the character or tone of voice of the brand's communications is a key element of its effectiveness (see also Chapter 1.4). Some advertising agencies now declare that they spend as much time helping a brand "find its voice" as they do its message (Moore, 2003). Certainly, the much commented on advertising by French Connection UK, that notoriously deployed the acronym "FCUK," was a lesson in attitude before message.

Ironically, for such a crucial element, the "character" section of many creative briefs is sadly lacking in much character. Descriptions like "bold, confident, uncomplicated, modern" are common. The strategist would be well advised to spend more time and find more imaginative ways of describing the brand character they want to reflect.

Adjectives are often part of the problem here. If a novelist wants to evoke a strong sense of scene or character, he does not rely entirely on adjectives. Yet it is often falsely assumed that a short list of adjectives is

the appropriate way to describe the desired character. There are often more other ways of powerfully evoking the desired tone than a tired string of words.

By way of example, the briefing behind a much applauded commercial for a car stated "we'd like to evoke the same effect and feeling as the slow and purposeful opening and closing of an expensive CD player." More colourfully, legend has it that the briefing for a *Kellogg's* commercial consisted of an old fashioned wind up alarm clock placed in a brightly striped cereal bowl. The team could (and probably did) write a brief with the words, colourful, lively, energetic, irresistible, but no-one would have remembered that.

Another part of the problem here is the established practise of determining "brand values." Ever since the value of brands was mooted and ultimately measured, it has become best practise for brand managers to draw a circle, arrow, or other shape and invite members of the team to fill the "brand values" section with adjectives that sum up the brand. Many practitioners could testify to sitting through long sessions debating the finer points of whether the most appropriate word is "bold" or "daring."

As with Support, there is a simple tool here to reveal unhelpful definitions of desired character. The *Opposites Test* simply invites you to ask whether it is useful to state that we would *not* like to reflect the antonyms of the stated tone or character. Thus, for "bold, confident, uncomplicated, modern" it is not exactly a revelation to state that we would not want to reflect a brand that is "timid, unconfident, complex or old fashioned." By contrast, *Guinness* has used a tone of voice that is cryptic, enigmatic and odd. These descriptions do tell us something, because it is unusual to learn that the brand is happy not to be straightforward, easily comprehensible and obvious.

Requirements

We argued at the outset that the requirements were, directionally at least, not the most important element of any creative briefing. Nevertheless, the lack of enough specific guidance here is one of the principal reasons for wasted time and effort in the creative development process (IPA, 2003). In addition, there is still plenty of scope for the requirement section to either limit significantly the potential for creative development or to enhance it. The key is to be specific when the requirements are utterly specific and to invite creative thinking about the format of the output when they are not.

If the communication has to be in black and white, 45 cm by 65 cm or must contain certain elements of legal fly-type, then the creative briefing is the time to say so, not days of weeks later, when large-scale, colour ideas have been developed. Ideally, the reasons behind any strict requirements should be self-evident or should be spelled out, they may themselves spark an idea.

MANAGING THE BRIEFING PROCESS

As mentioned, published research on the role of creative briefs in the process of campaign development is scarce. We identified three key issues in last decade's literature on the creative briefing process: the client agency relationship, the different "languages" within the agency, and the difficult role of research within the process. These issues all deal with managing relationships with the different parties involved: the client, the creative team, account planning and research.

The client–agency relationship

A critical element in a successful client–agency relationship, and the success or failure of any brief, is shared understanding. Advertiser and agency need to agree exactly what the advertising is expected to do for the brand and how the campaign is going to work (White, 2003; see also Chapter 3.1). In reality client and agency often have very different views, caused by the different mental models they use to evaluate creative work (Devinney et al., 2005).

One of the important factors in the client agency relationship is the risk-orientation of

the client and the willingness of agencies to take risks (Belch and Belch, 1995; El-Murad and West, 2003; West, 1993; West et al., 1999). In the end, it is the client who tends to avoid risk.

Another aspect in the client agency relationship is whether client and agency perceive each other as similar or not. A survey on perceived similarity showed its impact on agency performance, communication, the client's intention to remain with the advertising agency, and the client's defection after departure of an agency account member (Crutchfield et al., 2003). In other words, effects of lifestyle variables and social background of the members involved had an overwhelming effect on the outcome variables.

Different "languages" within the agency

Communication problems can arise not only between the client and agency, but within agencies, different "languages" are often spoken as well. This is particularly the case when it comes to the function of brand communications and the purpose and definition of creativity, as shown by studies of Hackley (2003a, 2003b), Young (2000), and Koslow et al. (2003). Creatives for instance are accused of perceiving ads as being more appropriate when they are artistic and original, while account managers tend to perceive ads as more appropriate if they are strategic. Creative individuals are described as being different, smart, intuitive, neurotic, confident, and emotional with a touch of rebelliousness (Ewing et al., 2001), in contrast to their non-creative counterparts within the agency, who operate in a more rational and factual mode, which creatives have difficulty to understand and be inspired of. Goldenberg and Mazursky (Chapter 5.1), elaborate on this issue of creatives being different.

The role of research

The role of research in the creative advertising process is debated. Although research has always been acknowledged as an important part of advertising development in the best agencies (Ogilvy, 1985), creative personnel are often sceptic about its function and purpose (Glen, 2005). Cause of this resistance is the way in which advertising consumer research often is communicated and formulated in creative briefs. The creative requirement is less powerful in shaping research than the marketing one. In place of rationality and evaluation, creativity works by intuition, hunches or unlikely connections (Bayley, 2000). It is the account planner who is involved in distilling insights from research and integrating this into the creative development of advertising and brand communication strategies (Baskin and Coburn, 2001; Davies, 2000; Hackley, 2003a). Bayley (2000) argues that research should much more often be conducted and presented with the sole purpose of providing texture for creatives. Bullmore (2005) summarizes the importance of research as "good insight is like a refrigerator," because as soon as you look into the fridge the light comes on.

SUMMARY

A good brief should be specific without being entirely restrictive. It closes down options, is directionally precise and succinct, i.e., a single page. It should identify the target market and the changes that should result from the campaign.

No brief can be completely right and wholly inspiring at the outset of the creative development process. Furthermore it is very unlikely to remain unchanged in substance and meaning throughout the subsequent development process, if it is to maintain its value as an objective benchmark for the output.

There appears to be little published information regarding the ways in which briefs are actually used within the briefing and creative development process. However, the Account Planning Group in the UK publishes a set of case histories biennially representing "best practice" in creative development from its Creative Planning Awards. A study of

these papers reveals a few notable cases where strategy development, creative briefing and creative development follow a linear sequential process, with a "good" brief providing clear direction to the creative teams in implementing a strategy that remains fixed and consistently defined. However, these examples are in the minority. From the APG papers, it appears to be commonplace in many, if not most, agencies nowadays for creative development and strategic development to be progressed to some degree in tandem, as iterative processes.

The key, from a strategic perspective, seems to be sensitive listening for useful insights, perspectives or changes of approach that warrant a revision or modification to the creative brief. Often insights or observations arise from challenges that creative teams make to existing views about how best to achieve the objective. The traditional model of the strategist as author and sole arbiter of the strategy seems to have been dropped. In its place is an emerging role of the strategist as the collector and assimilator of all differing views and perspectives, whether they be from client, creative, consumer or the strategist's own mother. His skill is less in dictating strategy and more in assimilating it. There are clearly key implications for the way the creative brief is used in these emerging new collaborative creative development processes.

Hopefully, a well articulated brief can have great value in both outlining a clear direction and challenging creative people to pursue that direction as creatively as possible. Nick Worthington of AMV BBDO, London, explained this as "A good Creative Brief sets the basis on which ideas can be sparked off – consciously or subconsciously. It immediately inspires everyone that comes in contact with . In order to achieve this, the Creative Brief reduces the strategy to its essence. This reduction turns the small light of a torch into a kind of focussed 'laser beam', from which many ideas can be sparked off" (cited in Langwost, 2004: 121).

What matters most at the end of this process is that the creative proposals are more likely to be approved and are more likely to work against the defined objective. Being "on brief" is obviously a critical requirement for this. However, the brief can help here by evolving throughout the process, so that it ultimately sets up the creative solution that deserves to get approved because it is the one that is most likely to work.

ACKNOWLEDEGMENT

Figures 3.2.1 and 3.2.2 © Copyright and database rights owned by WARC.

REFERENCES

APG (1999, 2001, 2003, 2005), *Creative Planning Awards*. London: Account Planning Group.

Barker, D. (2001), "How to Write An Inspiring Creative Brief," *Admap*, 419, (July), 14.

Baskin, M. and N. Coburn (2001), "Two Tribes Divided by Common Language? The True Nature of the Divide Between Account Planners and Market Researchers," *International Journal of Market Research*, 43 (3 June), 137–9.

Bayley, G. (2000), "How Creative Is Your Creative Brief," *Admap*, 406 (May), 58.

Bech-Larsen, T. (2001), "Model-Based Development and Testing of Advertising Messages: A Comparative Study of Two Campaign Proposals Based on the MECCAS Model and Conventional Approach," *International Journal of Advertising*, 20, 499–519.

Belch, G.E. and M.A. Belch (1995), *Advertising and Promotion; An Integrated Marketing Communications Perspective* (5th edition). Boston: McGraw-Hill.

Bullmore, J. (2005), "Why Is a Good Insight Like Refrigerator?" *Market Leader*, 29 (Summer), 15–17.

Burden, S. (2003), "Ad Creatives' Relationship With Ad Research." *Admap*, 438 (April), 27.

Crutchfield, T.N., D.F. Spake, G. D'Souza and R.M. Morgan (2003), "Birds of a Feather Flock Together: Strategic Implications for Advertising Agencies," *Journal of Advertising Research*, 43 (4) (December), 361–9.

Davies, M.A.P. (2000), "Using an Analytic Hierarchy Process in Advertising Creativity," *Creativity and Innovation Management*, 9 (2) (June).

Devinney, T., G. Dowling and M. Collins (2005), "Client and Agency Mental Models in Evaluating Advertising," *International Journal of Advertising*, 24 (1), 35–50.

El-Murad, J. and D.C. West (2003), "Risk and Creativity in Advertising," *Journal of Marketing Management*, 19, 657–73.

Ewing, M.T., J. Napoli and D.C. West (2001), "Creative Personalities, Processes, and Agency Philosophies: Implications for Global Advertisers," *Creativity Research Journal*, 13 (2), 161–70.

Fletcher, W. (1990), "The Management of Creativity," *International Journal of Advertising*, 9 (1), 1–37.

Fletcher, W. (1997), "How to Manage Creative People," *Admap* (November), 32–4.

Franzen, G. (1999), *Brands and Advertising. How advertising Effectiveness Influences Brand Equity*, Henley on Thames, UK: Admap Publications.

Giling, A., P. Neijens, B. Van den Putte, and E. Smit (2001), "Welke Kenmerken Maken een Campagne Tot EFFIE Winnaar? (What characteristics Make a Campaign a Real EFFIE Winner?)," In: Effieboek 2001: Bekroonde Voorbeelden van Effectieve Commerciële Communicatie (EFFIE book 2001: Winners of Effective Commercial Communication). Amsterdam: NieuwsTribune Publishing BV, 24–27.

Glen, R. (2005), "No More Talking To the Hand," *MRS Annual Conference*.

Goldenberg, J. and D. Mazursky (2007), "Advertising Creativity: Balancing Surprise and Regularity," in *The SAGE Handbook of Advertising*, eds. Gerard J. Tellis and T. Ambler, London: Sage Publications.

Hackley, C. (2003a), "Account Planning; Current Agency Perspectives On an Advertising Enigma," *Journal of Advertising Research*, 43 (2) (June), 235–45.

Hackley, C. (2003b), "How Divergent Beliefs Cause Account Team Conflict," *International Journal of Advertising*, 22 (3), 313–31.

Heuvelman, E., I. Koppe and A. Van der Lee (2002), *Mediakeuze en Reclamestrategie (Media Selection and Advertising Strategy)*, Amsterdam: SWOCC.

Hill, R. and L.W. Johnson (2004), "Understanding Creative Service: A Qualitative Study of the Advertising Problem Delineation, Communication and Response (APDCR) Process," *International Journal of Advertising*, 23 (3), 285–307.

IPA (2003), *The Client Brief; A Best Practice Guide to Briefing Communications Agencies* (Report from IPA, ISBA, MCCA, PRCA in the UK).

Keller, K.L. (2007), "Advertising and Brand Equity," in *The SAGE Handbook of Advertising*, eds. G.J. Tellis and T. Ambler, London: Sage Publications.

Koslow, S., S.L. Sasser and E.A. Riordan (2003), "What is Creative to Whom and Why? Perceptions of Advertising Agencies," *Journal of Advertising Research*, 43 (1 March), 96–110.

Kover, A.J., W.L. James and B.S. Sonner (1997), "To Whom Do Advertising Creatives Write? An Inferential Answer," *Journal of Advertising Research*, 37 (1 Jan/Feb), 41–53.

Langwost, R. (2004), *How to Catch the Big Idea; The Strategies of Top-Creatives*. Erlangen, Germany: Publicis.

Moore, D.T. (2003), "For Brand's Sake: Partnership Is Everything," *The Advertiser*, (Jan) 20–2.

NieuwsTribune (no author) (2001). "Eerste Resultaten Wetenschappelijke Studie bekend: Wat Maakt een Campagne Tot Effie-Winnaar? (First Results of Scientific Study: What Makes Campaign an EFFIE Winner?)," *NieuwsTribune*, 41 (October), 41, 18–19.

Ogilvy, D. (1985), *Confessions of an Advertising Man*. Random House, Inc.

Reeves, R. (1961), *Reality in Advertising*. New York: Alfred Knopf.

Tait, B. (2002), "The Case for Brand Consultancies," *Admap*, 429 (June), 33–5.

West, D. (1993), "Cross-National Creative Personalities, Processes and Agency Philosophies," *Journal of Advertising Research*, 33 (5 Sep/Oct), 53–62.

West, D., A. Sargeant and A. Miciak (1999), "Advertiser Risk-Orientation & the Opinions & Practices of Advertising Managers," *International Journal of Advertising*, 18 (1), 51–71.

Wethey, D. (2007), "Client–Agency Relationships," in *The SAGE Handbook of Advertising*, eds. G.J. Tellis and T. Ambler, London: Sage Publications.

White, A. and B.L. Smith (2001), "Assessing Advertising Creativity Using the Creative Product Semantic Scale," *Journal of Advertising Research*, 41 (6 Nov/Dec), 27–34.

White, R. (2003), "Best Practice, Briefing Creative Agencies," *Admap*, 440 (June), 12–13.

Young, C.E. (2000), "Creative Differences Between Copywriters and Art Directors," *Journal of Advertising Research*, 40 (3 May/June), 19–26.

Account Planning: Its History and its Significance for Ad Agencies

Paul Feldwick

"'Account Planning' and 'Account Planners' have become part of agency jargon in recent years … unfortunately there is considerable confusion over what the words mean, making discussion of the subject frustrating"

(Pollitt, 1979: 1)

"… it was striking how little substantive agreement there seemed to be on what it is or how it should be done"

(Hackley, 2003b)

What is account planning? Almost from its beginnings, commentators have admitted to some confusion about it, for a number of reasons:

1. As a name adopted simultaneously in two different agencies, account planning in practice never conformed to a single model. As others copied it, the extent of this variation increased.
2. There is often imprecision as to whether "account planning" refers to an agency structure, a process, or a set of principles or beliefs. (It is probably the underlying *principles* of account planning that provide the firmest ground for a definition.)
3. One way account planners differentiated their role from the traditional agency researcher was a focus on "ends" rather than "means," on "objectives

and contribution" rather than "technique." This leads to considerable freedom of interpretation as to what processes, skills, or roles the account planner should utilise in any particular case. (Channon, 1986: 2)

It may be useful to think of account planning as a "movement" continually being reinterpreted, misunderstood, adapted, and evolved into many different forms, some of which end up looking almost antithetical to the founders' ideas. From its beginnings, it proposed radically different ideas about advertising research, advertising models, and agency roles and competences. It questioned beliefs about what kind of evidence has validity in decision making, and challenged traditional agency power structures. Account planning is not change in just one department: it is a blueprint for fundamental change throughout the agency. Some agencies for some periods have moved towards realizing this vision, but taking the industry as a whole, this has not been the case. Traditional epistemologies of research, underlying assumptions about how advertising works, and agency power structures and cultures remain much as they were 40 years ago.

Today, ad agencies face a crisis of culture, role, and practice. Encouragingly, the underlying beliefs of the account planning movement may still offer guidance for changes (for the whole agency, not just the account planners) that are necessary if the agency business is to survive and flourish. But nonetheless, it has provoked criticism, controversy and confusion.

Perhaps the focus on account planning as a separate function has helped agencies to avoid making real change. Forty years' debate about the roles, skills, and legitimacy of account planning departments appear in hindsight as an elaborate projection of unresolved tensions which are the concern of the agency as a whole.

This chapter attempts to get to the heart of many of these issues. What exactly is account planning's significance today? Has the advertising industry really bought into the original principles and beliefs on which account planning was founded? Are these principles still relevant? To offer some answers to these questions, this chapter is structured as follows:

1. A description of the origins of account planning from the UK.
2. A review of the worldwide adoption of account planning.
3. A discussion of the status of account planning in agencies today.
4. A discussion of the significance of the original vision for the future of advertising agencies, and where account planning is headed in the future.

THE ORIGINAL VISION OF ACCOUNT PLANNING FROM LONDON

The original vision 1: Stephen King and J. Walter Thompson

Following World War Two, British ad agencies began to offer both marketing and market research as part of their service to clients. But by 1960 more clients were setting up their own marketing and research departments, and the agency marketing and research people needed a clearer focus for their roles. Account planning emerged as a response to this in London's biggest agency, J Walter Thompson. Under the leadership of John Treasure, an academic economist, who believed that the future of the advertising business lay with the researchers, "the highest level of intellect in the business" – JWT's Marketing Department became more focused on applying strategic thinking and research to make advertising more efficient (Turner and Pearson, 1966: 43; Treasure, 1979). Prominent in this group were researcher Stephen King, creative director Jeremy Bullmore, and Timothy Joyce of JWT's sister company the British Market Research Bureau (Bullmore, 1991; King, 1989).

In 1964, King developed the T-plan (Target-Plan) which was both a formal structure for creating advertising strategy, and a philosophy of advertising. Its opening principle was that "creative strategy ... should be set in terms of the consumer" (Treasure, 1979; Staveley, 1999: 38–9). A research committee, with King as secretary, was set up to improve measurement of advertising effectiveness. It inaugurated the "Advertising Planning Index" (API), an ongoing survey for each brand of awareness, brand imagery, and intention to buy. As Joyce and King studied the API data, they began to query some of the received wisdom about how advertising works (Broadbent, 1999: 115–16), namely models such as Attention – Interest – Desire – Action (AIDA). These models focused on conscious deliberation, rational argument, factual information, and envisaged the advertising process as a one-way, once-off conversion from "prospect" to "sale," concepts which were not overly relevant for JWT's TV advertising for repeat purchase packaged goods (King, 1967: 10).

The fifties in Madison Avenue was a decade of pluralism in research techniques and advertising thinking (Mayer, 1958: *passim*). Ernest Dichter (1964, 1979), Pierre Martineau (1957) and others used Freudian concepts to legitimize the subconscious, the non-verbal, symbol and metaphor, and pioneered qualitative research techniques to understand these levels of response. But this also provoked a backlash among public and clients. After Vance Packard's 1957 best seller, *The Hidden Persuaders*, presented "motivation research" as sinister brainwashing, Rosser Reeves felt obliged to repudiate "the Freudian Hoax:"

> "... there are no hidden persuaders. Advertising works openly, in the bare and pitiless sunlight." (1961: 70)

Reeves' own theory of advertising was simple – "ADVERTISING IS THE ART OF GETTING A UNIQUE SELLING PROPOSITION INTO THE HEADS OF THE MOST PEOPLE AT THE LOWEST POSSIBLE COST." (Reeves, 1961: 70–4, 121, capitals in original). This was hugely influential because it was easy to explain, and easy to measure. The metaphor is of one-way transmission of a message, casting the receiver in a purely passive role. It led to advertising which was often brash, repetitive, single minded: in Reeves' hands it could be brutally effective. But it ignored the possibility that there might be other successful approaches too. Bill Bernbach had built a successful New York agency on principles of treating the audience with respect, charming and entertaining them, valuing "artistry" or "creativity" as a practical means to improve sales (Danzig, 1999). Burleigh Gardner and Sidney Levy wrote in 1955 about the importance of "the brand" as a complex of emotional associations with which the customer developed a relationship.

Based on their own experience, data analysis, and current psychological theories such as gestalt or "cognitive dissonance," the JWT group began to develop their own alternatives to the dominant "sales" or "message transmission" models, picking up particularly on the central importance of the brand. (Broadbent, 1999: 118; Joyce, 1967; King, 1965, 1967, 1970.) King wrote, "Most advertising aims to intensify or lessen people's existing predispositions. It is not trying to drive something new into their brains" (quoted in Treasure, 1985). These "predispositions" were best described in the language of brand imagery rather than rational "propositions," and to understand and work with this, qualitative research was granted a legitimacy that earlier, positivist views of research had denied. For example,

> "Once you have heard people describe Lifebuoy as rather abrupt; Tide as gruff and ex-army; Camay as a bit catty, will you be content to rely solely on the sort of research that gets people to put crosses on a seven-point scale running from 'kind to the hands' to 'not so kind to the hands'?" (King, 1970: 14)

As the interests of the media planning, marketing and research departments were increasingly overlapping in the overall process of understanding and planning advertising for greater effectiveness, King began to imagine a redefinition of departmental roles. In 1968 the departments were united as the account planning department (King, 1989).

The original vision 2: Stanley Pollitt and BMP

Another US-owned London agency during the 1960s was Pritchard Wood and Partners (PWP), part of Interpublic. In 1965, Stanley Pollitt was given responsibility at PWP for research and media, inheriting a situation that in some ways paralleled that at JWT. By the mid-1960s more companies had their own researchers, leaving PWP's agency research department with an unclear role. At the same time, more research relevant to advertising development was becoming available, but Pollitt saw that it was not being effectively used. "It seemed to me that these researchers should be taken out of their back-rooms and converted to being an active part of the group involved with the central issues of advertising strategy" (Pollitt, 1979: 4–5). But Pollitt found the existing agency researchers had grown cosy in their "back-rooms." He decided that "the only way to find this new type of researcher was to breed them ourselves from numerate but broadminded graduates" (Pollitt, 1979).

In 1968 the management board of PWP (including Pollitt and Martin Boase), resigned and set up Boase Massimi Pollitt, offering an opportunity to realize Pollitt's vision of a threefold structure within each account team – account director, creative, and account planner. Each would have equal power and influence, unlike the traditional agency structure where researchers were marginalized as a service department and involved only at the wish of the account director. His specification for the planner's job can be summarized as follows:

1. The planner is an "expert in research" (without the "backroom mentality").
2. The planner uses and understands quantitative research and market data, but accepts qualitative findings with equal validity and importance.
3. The planner *personally* conducts a good deal of qualitative research, thus developing a first hand understanding of the target audiences.
4. The planner is continuously involved in the campaign: in strategic thinking, developing the creative execution, and assessing the results in the market.
5. To make all this possible a high ratio of one account planner to one account manager is recommended.
6. The three parties share responsibility for the creation of effective advertising in a "creative tension" with each standing up for their different points of view.
7. The planner's ultimate commitment is to "get the advertising content right at all costs." Pollitt, as an account director, recognised the pressures to expediency in the job – to meet deadlines, to please the client, to please the creative people. The planner was to be a corrective to this and be "the account man's conscience." For this, account planning needs support from the agency management, and a total agency commitment to effectiveness (Feldwick, 2000: xi).

JWT and BMP – The shared philosophy

Any differences between JWT and BMP were mainly of practical emphasis and implementation rather than of underlying philosophy. Ultimately these are less important than what they had in common. A common "philosophy"

can be summarized in the following five, closely linked propositions:

1. Effectiveness and "getting it right" (defined as benefit to the client's business) is the clear, paramount goal for the whole agency.
2. New, consumer-centred models of how advertising works, based on better understanding of the relevant science and on empirical findings from research, will replace conventional wisdom that has been proven inadequate.
3. The consumer must be put at the centre of the process at all stages of advertising development, through the right use of research. Understanding and representing the response of the consumer is required at all stages of the process. Furthermore, the "consumer representative" must become part of the core team, not merely a service function.
4. There must be a broad and inclusive epistemology of research, with qualitative knowledge and subjective impressions allowed the same significance as what is quantifiable: at the same time applying rigorous methods of inquiry wherever possible.
5. For research to be used in the right way, it must be treated as a core function of the agency, with the consumer and market researcher fully integrated into the account team.

Regarding this final point, an observer of the UK agency business in the 1960s wrote:

"The status of research executives is correspondingly low; typically they are paid less than account executives and copywriters … market researchers languish on the sidelines of advertising. They complain of not meeting clients, not being invited to background meetings, not being properly briefed; they also say that when their research has been done it is often completely ignored." (Tunstall, 1964: 151)

Pollitt's intention was to have "a trained researcher alongside the account man … *as of right*." (Pollitt, 1979: 4 [emphasis added]). This proposition has implications for agency power structures:

"In the all too human context of the advertising agency, the development of a separate account planning function becomes an issue of the relative place, power and (inevitably) monetary rewards of the role of the 'think input' in producing advertising." (Channon, 1986)

While the old research role gained some power through expert skills, it was denied executive power. With the shift to account planning, the value added was defined in terms of "objectives and contribution" rather than of "techniques." Account Planners began to define themselves as users and interpreters of research rather than actual researchers; they came to value plural sources of information and inspiration, not all of which could be classed as "market research" (Stewart, 1986: 23). At the same time, the redefinition of the researcher's role as "making the advertising more effective" posed apparent threats to the power bases of account directors and creative people, which generated resistance to planning in other agencies.

Therefore, as originally conceived, account planning was a coherent agenda for comprehensive change through the whole agency: changes in beliefs about how advertising worked, changes in how research and intellect were valued, a greater commitment to effectiveness as the agency's common goal, a greater emphasis on the agency as strategic partner rather than just a supplier, and a revolution in the underlying power structure within the agency.

THE SPREAD OF ACCOUNT PLANNING WORLDWIDE

By the early 1970s both JWT and BMP had established successful reputations with their new account planning structure. At first there was no eagerness from other agencies to follow – partly due to reluctance to copy competitor's ideas, and partly resistance to the shift of power involved (Newman, 1992: 6). In 1973, John Bartle introduced planning as a core function in the new London office of TBWA (Bartle, 1985). In 1974, Collett Dickenson Pearce, which epitomised the creative revolution in British advertising of the early 1970s, introduced planning, albeit with planners being strictly limited to new business pitches and strategic development. (O'Reilly, 1981). David Stewart-Hunter (1986) looked back on the period from

1977–1983 as "the planning boom years." By 1979 six of the top 20 UK agencies claimed to have planning departments, and by 1985, this rose to 18 (King, 1989; Bartle, 1985).

In 1979 the Account Planning Group (APG) was founded. Its first Chair was Charles Channon, Planning Director of Ayer Barker. Over the following decades, the APG hosted conferences and workshops, debating the future of account planning, and published books on the topic (Cowley, 1989, 1991; Cooper, 1997; Baskin and Earls, 2002). By 1985 the APG had 500 members, with an estimated 300 planners working in the UK (Bartle, 1985; Treasure, 1985).

But the "boom years" of the early 1980s created their own tensions. John Bartle worried that agencies might be adopting the rhetoric of planning, without the investment and skills that it really required. He feared that planners could become "a new breed of well-paid, or over-paid, individuals who assume guru-like status and power, through a sort of intellectual arrogance, a belief in their own monopoly of understanding" (Bartle, 1985). Certainly some saw planners in just that way. More experienced researchers from agency or client-side responded critically to what they saw as the hype of unskilled, inexperienced people, with themselves rejected as "old-style researchers" (Meyers, 1986; Moran, 1988; Reeve, 1992). They argued that the definitions of what planners do (e.g., thinking analytically, thoroughly, and with insight about consumers and brands) did not sound much different from what they thought good researchers did anyway, and that many planners lacked research skills. Whilst these are fair points, the arguments on both sides tended to lose sight of the underlying challenges account planning posed to traditional epistemology, advertising theory, and agency structure.

In 1980 an important development linked with account planning was the launch of the IPA Advertising Effectiveness Awards (see Chapter 3.4 for further detail about these awards). These were the brainchild of Simon Broadbent, a formidably clever and insightful statistician at the Leo Burnett agency, who shared King and Joyce's fascination with questions of how advertising worked and how it could be evaluated. Broadbent became concerned during the 1970s that agencies were not paying enough attention to evaluating advertising, and that without reliable criteria for success, the advertising industry was vulnerable to a "folklore of the ineffectiveness of advertising" (Channon, 1985: x).

Existing methods tended to focus on "intermediate" measures of effect: recall of advertising or its "message," brand awareness or image scales, and (claimed) behaviour. The failure to measure sales effects was not simply negligence: it was actually stated in influential textbooks that there were too many factors involved to relate sales to advertising reliably (Lucas and Britt, 1963: 5; Colley, 1961: 10–12; Reeves, 1961: 3–5). But while intermediate measures had their uses, they were not reliable predictors of business success, sales, revenue or profitability. Therefore, Broadbent persuaded the Institute of Practitioners in Advertising (IPA), the UK trade association of advertising agencies, to sponsor a biennial scheme of awards for case studies that compellingly proved a relationship between advertising and business success. While the cases were expected to include intermediate measures as part of their argument, a convincing link had to be made to business results, and if possible, profit.

The connection with account planning is two-fold. First, account planners have authored the vast majority of papers entered in these awards over the years, and there has been some correlation between the strength of planning in an agency and success in the awards. The awards are a showcase for account planning as the cases exemplify not just the measurement of results, but give detail about the strategic thinking and the research behind successful campaigns. Secondly, the IPA awards increased the focus on effectiveness as a key aspect of account planning (Clemmow, 1992; O'Donoghue, 1994).

In 1982 Jay Chiat, founder of Chiat/Day, visited the UK and was so impressed by account planning that he hired Jane Newman, formerly of BMP, "the only UK planner with a green card and US experience!" (Newman, 1992: 6). This was the beginning of account planning in the US which had initially been an unpromising market, as both agency-client relationships and underlying models of advertising seemed even more unsympathetic to the tenets of account planning than in the UK. In the meantime, Chiat Day had the field to itself for a good six years as larger agencies with established politics and structures found it threatening[1] (Newman, 1992).

Opinions in the US press vacillated between enthusiasm for the exciting, business winning new idea from the UK, and varying degrees of dismissive scepticism along familiar lines – this was merely a "repackaging" of standard research procedures, or a new department whose role was obscure and unnecessary. Even more than the UK, there was resistance from old school account directors, whose power base depended on their monopoly of the client relationship (Feuer, 1985; Madison, 1991; O'Malley, 1999; Sharkey, 1987; Steel, 1998: 57; Walker, 1989).

Despite all this, account planning grew. In 1990 a US Account Planning group was formed, with 30 people meeting in Texas. In 1992, the American Association of Advertising Agencies (AAAA) published a booklet, *What Every Account Executive Should Know About Account Planning* (Newman, 1998; Newman et al., 1992; O'Malley, 1999). By 1992 one third of the 225 largest US agencies claimed to have it (Kendrick and Dee, 1992). Within about ten to fifteen years, a similar growth pattern followed that of the UK.

In 1995, Howard Merrell reported that the proportion of US planning agencies had risen to 56% (quoted in Weichselbaum and Kendrick, 1998). In 2000, attendance at the US APG Conference peaked at over a thousand people, and in 2001 it was estimated there were about 2000 "planners" working in US agencies. Since then the US APG, due to financial problems, has ceased to exist as a separate body, though its annual conference continues under the aegis of the American

Association of Advertising Agencies. Its 2005 conference theme was "Creativity Now," and was attended by 700 people (Broadbent, 2001; www.aaaa.org).

Truth, Lies and Advertising: The Art of Account Planning (Steel, 1998) is the most persuasive explanation of account planning in the US during the 1990s, and its success has enhanced the understanding and the legitimacy of account planning in the United States. Steel argues that advertising is about understanding people – from empathy and first hand experience as well as structured research – and that the positivist model is inappropriate for advertising research. Indeed, he emphasizes that planning in an agency depends on personal relationships: on the personality of the planner, and the willingness of the others in the agency to work constructively with him or her. The successful planner requires certain personal skills, as well as the ability to think both logically and intuitively; these characteristics are more important than a high level of technical expertise in market research or psychology.

ACCOUNT PLANNING TODAY

It is hard to generalize about actual planning practice today. Agencies and individuals interpret the role in different ways, or adapt their practice to circumstances. In a 1998 survey of the US and UK, Weichselbaum and Kendrick categorized agencies into four main clusters of roughly equal size according to their claimed practice:

1. "Traditional Agencies," where marketing and research functions were separate from strategic and creative development;
2. "Full Service Planning Agencies," where the "planners" were fully involved in both strategic and creative development, and conducted their own qualitative research;
3. "Creative Support Agencies," who saw themselves primarily as "a support system for creatives," and tended to conduct their own focus groups; and
4. "Qualitatively Oriented Planning Agencies," rather oddly named in that the main difference

from the "Full Service" group is that the planners tend *not* to conduct their own qualitative research.

5. A few small agencies with no real planning function formed a minor fifth cluster.

The second and third clusters are strongly biased to the US agencies, while the fourth cluster – the ones who do not conduct their own groups – are predominantly in the UK. US agencies are also more likely to involve creative teams directly in the qualitative research. There is little correlation between the clusters and the choice of departmental names – so the "Full Service Planning" cluster are almost equally likely to label the department "research," "planning," or "research and planning." But overall, this study shows that over half of US agencies are doing something recognizable as "account planning" in the original sense, including conducting qualitative research.

Between 1997 and 2001 Christopher Hackley of the University of Birmingham conducted a series of in-depth interviews with senior staff in creative, account management and account planning departments of a number of major agencies in London and in New York. His findings reveal ambiguity about the exact nature of the account planner's role, as well as considerable stress, conflict and tension between the departments.

> "the word 'hate' occurred more than once in interviews with planners in connection with their standing in the agency. Some planners felt that daily working life was a running battle with account executives who excluded the planner from strategic decisions and referred to them for trivial questions" (2003b)

Moreover, creatives, account managers, and planners use fundamentally different epistemologies and models of the consumer, a fact that is intrinsically bound up with the power politics between departments (Hackley, 2003a). There are frequent power games between departments, which account executives and creatives are better placed to win. Planners, however their jobs and titles are specified, remain a minority in agencies, and in the US at least, do not command the top salaries, and continue to lack power and influence. From Hackley's research, it seems as if account planning departments are not much better off than the marginalised research departments of the 1960s they aimed to replace.

Account planning without research

Two surveys presented at the (UK) Market Research Society Conference in 1998 document the emergence of a school of account planning which paradoxically places little value on *any* market research. Cowan and Taylor (1998) found a distinction between "old-style" and "new-style" planners: the new style planners showed little interest in background or contextual issues and often appeared to have made decisions regardless of their relevance or the consumers' view, which they described as a "rear view mirror." It seemed that for them planning was an art which they did not consider should be subjected to scientific testing. Shaw and Edwards (1998) came to a similar conclusion – when their sample of planners was asked which of a list of factors they valued most, "intuition" came top of the list, and "quantitative research" almost bottom.

The (UK) APG has for several years offered awards for cases demonstrating the contribution of account planning to creative campaigns. These take place in alternate years between the biennial IPA Awards. The APG Awards do not consider effectiveness as a criterion, but reward campaigns that are valued by creative directors, who always feature as judges. The winning papers are published in illustrated books, providing a considerable resource of case histories which might be expected to demonstrate in practical detail what account planners do to add value.

What is quite striking in these cases is the general absence of quantitative research or data. Where research is cited it is almost always qualitative. Some papers contain no formal research at all. The planner's contribution is often described as providing "insight" or "inspiration" which may come from anywhere. There is relatively little connection between the ad development process as described here and the business needs or outcomes of the client (Dann, 2001; Neill, 2003).

THE SIGNIFICANCE OF ACCOUNT PLANNING PRINCIPLES FOR THE FUTURE OF THE ADVERTISING AGENCY

To recapitulate the original principles of account planning as summarized earlier:

- **Effectiveness** (defined as benefit to the client's business) is the clear, paramount goal for the whole agency.
- In order to improve effectiveness, new, **consumer-centred models of how advertising works**, based on better understanding of the relevant science and on empirical findings from research, must replace conventional wisdom that has been proven inadequate.
- Following these new models, the **consumer must be put at the centre** of the process at all stages of advertising development, through the right use of research.
- There must be a **broad and inclusive epistemology of research**, with qualitative knowledge and subjective impressions allowed the same significance as what is quantifiable: at the same time applying rigorous methods of inquiry wherever possible.
- For the consumer to be central to the process, **research must be treated as a core function of the agency**, with the research expert fully integrated into the account team.

Within this are two major themes. The first is the significance of account planning as a *philosophy of advertising* and, related to this, as a *philosophy of research*. The other is account planning in the context of *the role and the structure of the advertising agency*.

Account planning as a philosophy of advertising and a philosophy of research

A theme in the history of advertising is whether advertising should be thought of as art or science (Feldwick, 2002: Ch. 8). On the one hand, agencies continue to celebrate and empower their "creative" departments, and some have always argued that intuition and judgment should always be privileged over attempts to make the process measurable and objective: for example Bill Bernbach:

> "There are a lot of great technicians in advertising .... They know all the rules. ... But there's one little rub. *They forget that advertising is persuasion, and persuasion is not a science, but an art.*" (Fox, 1984: 251: emphasis added)

But an opposed tradition, which generally has more appeal to managers, sets up a promise of advertising as something that can be controllable, capable of rationalization and objective measurement, and ultimately freed from risk.

> "The time has come when advertising has in some hands reached the status of a science. It is based on fixed principles and is reasonably exact. The causes and effects have been analysed until they are well understood. The correct methods of procedure have been proved and established. We know what is most effective, and we act on basic laws. Advertising, once a gamble, has thus become, under able direction, one of the safest of business ventures." (Hopkins, 1923: 213)

Hopkins understood that the promise of rules, control, and elimination of risk, appeal more to most managers than any "creative" platform. Supported by a later tradition in marketing (cf. the title of Kotler's (1976) best selling textbook, *Marketing Management: Analysis, Planning and Control*) and by a powerful US-based academic tradition that has attempted for decades to explain and control advertising chiefly through the frame of cognitive psychology, this dream of objectivity and control has created a dominant paradigm of advertising theory which is rational in its assumptions about human behaviour and strongly positivist in its epistemology.

As a result, there has often appeared to be a polarisation between the creative "artists" in the advertising world who are inclined to reject all "research," and the "scientists" who want everything to be measurable. This is a false polarity, based on a traditional view that limits all "science" to a positivist position inspired by the physical sciences (Midgley, 2001; Steel, 1998). The account planning movement was a conscious attempt to bridge this apparent gulf. Pollitt and King wanted to give equal validity to other ways of knowing, most obviously qualitative research, which from the start became one of the signatures of account planning practice. Planning at its best – as in the published volumes of the IPA Effectiveness Awards – has always brought together different kinds of data to build up a rounded picture or story. It aspires to rigour, though the rigour might be the rigour of the historian or the detective, not only that of the physical sciences (Channon, 1987).

From the beginning, account planning tended towards an epistemology that is *humanistic* rather than mechanistic, and *holistic* rather than atomistic. Lannon and Cooper (1983) make explicit the link between one-way, message transmission models of the advertising process ("hammer and nail theories"), and a dehumanizing approach to research – both assume that the consumer/experimental subject is merely a passive object to be influenced, studied, or controlled. To change the question "What does advertising do to people?" into "What do people do with advertising?" leads to new kinds of research practice and new interpretative frameworks.

This shift in human inquiry from treating people as passive objects, to an acceptance of the common humanity of researcher and respondent, could be paralleled generally during the later twentieth century in the human sciences (see for example Reason and Rowan, 1981: xi–xviii; Rogers, 1951: 483–97). Even more broadly, it can be seen as part of a larger reaction against the Cartesian dualisms of mind and matter, reason and emotion, that is dated by Stephen Toulmin as taking place in the mid 1960s – the exact moment when account planning came into being.

There was also a *phenomenological* implication in much of the qualitative research done by account planners. Calder (1979) draws a distinction between three models of qualitative inquiry: *exploratory* (looking for scientific constructs that can later be quantified and tested), *clinical* (implying a detached observer interpreting through some kind of psychoanalytic theory), and *phenomenological*. This last seeks not for abstraction, detachment and interpretation, but for a direct sharing of the other's experience. This fits quite well with much of the language used to describe planning practice. The phrases, "voice of the consumer in the agency" or "surrogate consumer" vividly suggest how the planner was not merely to *report* on what the consumer thought or felt, but to somehow *embody* them. "An account planner isn't just a researcher with insight into the consumer. The planner *is* the consumer, sitting in on the development of ads" (Feuer, 1985).

Account planning, then, was implicitly aiming at a new epistemology for research, which could be described as humanistic and holistic, with aspects of a phenomenological approach. But how widely has this been adopted in marketing departments or agencies?

There remains a huge schism between the worlds of account planning and advertising research, as practised commercially, and as studied and written about by most academics. For example, few, if any, account planners attend the annual conference of the Advertising Research Foundation (ARF) (O'Malley, 1999: 47). Furthermore, advertising decision making and research are still driven to a large degree by the same concepts as in the 1960s: recall, verbal messages, impact, news, persuasion tests, even proposition tests. Standardized quantitative pre-testing techniques, that King and Pollitt found frustrating, are now more dominant throughout the world than ever before, and mandated by many multinational marketing companies. Meanwhile, account planners have done little to build on the theoretical advances made by Joyce and King – agencies have hardly invested in original research and development, and published very little, and on the rare occasions they do it has little impact on their practice. To take one example,

Robert Heath's important 2001 monograph *The Hidden Power of Advertising*, was only written after Heath had left the agency world where he had been an account planner for two decades.

Account planning and the role and structure of advertising agencies

Connected with the failure of account planning to follow through as an intellectual revolution is the failure of agencies to invest time and resource in what Channon called the "think input." Few agencies have approached Pollitt's ideal of one account planner for each account manager. Departments remain small, and the planner's energy is directed towards pleasing other, more powerful departments such as new business or creative in order to maintain their own survival. Hackley's research suggests that the planner's role often appears to be compensating in some way for the weaknesses of other departments, or mediating between them:

> "... From an agency point of view, one dividend of imposing an account planning ethos is that an able exponent might be able to act as a *mediating presence* softening the conflict between creative and account management functions." (Hackley, 2003b [emphasis added])

If it is seen as the planner's responsibility to "translate" between different groups (Steel, 1998: 51), to be the "account man's conscience" (Pollitt, 1979: 4), to be a "mediating presence" in interdepartmental conflict (Hackley, 2003b), to "enthuse" and "unblock" the creatives (Cowley, 1986: 38, 44), and to "take responsibility for the effectiveness of the advertising" (Clemmow, 1992), it obscures the possibility that any of these implied shortcomings might actually be a *shared* responsibility, or that others in the agency might consider changing their own behaviours in order to resolve them. Team collaboration and generosity in personal relationships are good things, but one gets a sense from the literature that the relationship is not expected to be reciprocal, with all the responsibility on the part of the planner to help others in the team. Unfortunately, planners themselves are often eager to collude in taking responsibility for the inadequacy of others: they assume, reasonably, that the more they are needed, the more secure their position. Thus planners have an interest in maintaining a *status quo* that makes others dependent on them, and a corresponding disincentive to promote more fundamental change. This also creates a double bind whereby others resent their dependency on the planners, and so seek to control or exclude them. Indeed, "the striking and occasionally contradictory industry attitudes toward account planning seem indicative of serious and complex issues of advertising agency management" (Hackley, 2003b).

Many debates about account planning, repeated over the years, can be seen as *projections* of more fundamental issues that are not directly discussable – questions about agency strategy, about departmental roles and skills, and ultimately about the role and function of the agency as a whole. Compared to all the agonised debates about the role, competence and legitimacy of account planners over four decades, there have been hardly any about the role definitions of account directors or of creative people.

> "You need creative, media and account people, but if the planners are no good they just wither and die – the planner needs to show his value constantly in order to survive." (Bullmore, quoted in Bartle, 1985)

Such comments only seem self evident if we ignore what they say about power structures in advertising agencies. Presumably if creative or account people fail to "show value" they may eventually be fired; only planners can expect their job to be abolished as well. That all these jobs and their implicit roles are social constructions which could be fundamentally redefined and rearranged hardly seems to have occurred to anyone in the advertising business. But unless agency structures *are* fundamentally redefined and rearranged, it is questionable whether ad agencies will survive at all.

The five basic propositions implicit in the account planning movement invite us to redefine the whole balance and structure of the advertising agency. They imply skills in creating effective communications that should never be concentrated in one, peripheral and under-resourced department, but should represent the core competence of the organisation. Creativity, like effectiveness, should be the concern of everyone in the agency, not just of one department. The conflicts of interest which bedevil agencies today are either based on distorted reward structures (creative awards), or incompatible models of how advertising works (Hackley, 2003a). It would be entirely possible, and the responsibility of management, to eradicate these.

WHERE TO NOW?

In the 1960s, JWT glimpsed a future in which agencies could become all-round experts in effective marketing communications – combining competences in media planning, creativity, strategic thinking and market research, with an enhanced understanding of how advertising works. But in my opinion no agency really took the hard decisions needed to follow through on this. None invested much in research and development; none introduced serious changes in agency structure; none diverted resources towards the new skills and talents that were needed to move the industry on from its old model. Beneath the superficial sideshow of "account planning," agencies continually reverted to and reinforced values and power structures antithetical to it.

Meanwhile, the original foundation of the ad agency, its media broking function, inexorably slipped away into media agencies, and the comfortable system of media commissions was eroded by legislation and client pressure. New competitors, research companies and management consultants, challenged agencies for their role as strategic advisers. Today, all ad agencies face the same crisis: an over-supplied market, forcing desperate new business battles and ever shrinking revenues, and as I see it, a lack of expert credibility. No longer rooted in the media buying business, agencies have to decide if they are going to become merely creators of executions, or if they want to be experts in communications. If the latter, they have a lot of work to do and some hard choices to make.

In this context, the original account planning principles point towards a new kind of advertising agency – one dedicated to effectiveness, and prepared to invest in intellectual as well as creative skills in order to deliver it. Such an agency would develop its own point of view about how advertising works, both in general and in particular cases, and apply this in the interests of the client's business. It would be prepared both to embrace rigour and quantification where it was appropriate (and have the skills and resources to do so), but also to value and reward impressions, intuitions, serendipity, and a humanist respect for the people it set out to communicate with. It would not be afraid to engage intellectually and practically with the huge advances in understanding the mind and brain, and in theories of communication, that have emerged since the 1960s (advances which largely endorse and build on the theories of the early account planners). It would transcend the old dualisms of reason vs. imagination, or research vs. creativity, or art vs. science. Although Gregory Bateson would probably shudder to have his words applied to the business of advertising, this agency would genuinely live by his words: "Rigor alone is paralytic death, but imagination alone is insanity" (Bateson, 1979: 205). This vision implies radical changes in agency structure, in the skills and talents that it values, and in the agency-client relationship. Wherever planning has achieved most, it has begun to influence all of these, but has never gone far enough.

This agency of the future might not have a separate "account planning" department – but its values throughout would be account planning values. The industry now needs to shift away from navel-gazing about the role and skills of account planners, to serious questions about the role, skills and priorities

of the agency as a whole. Unless these questions can be answered, the future for the advertising agency as we know it will be questionable. However, any agency that has the skill, courage, and intelligence to realise such a vision has an opportunity to lead the industry.

SUMMARY

Account planning developed independently and simultaneously in two British in the mid 1960s. What they had in common was taking the consumer's point of view and basing strategy on an intelligent analysis of research. Most British ad agencies went on to develop their own variations on that theme. Account planning spread to the US and other countries but interpretation varied widely and the grounding of strategy in research was abandoned in many cases.

Undoubtedly many account planners make a significant and valuable contribution to agency success. The best are exceptional individuals, inventive, open-minded, good at seeing things in new ways and encouraging others to do so. It is largely thanks to them that many new ideas, from semiotics to improvisation to econometrics, have been applied in the ad business.

Numerically, "account planning" enjoys an apparent success, even in the US, which few would have predicted in the 1990s. But on the other hand, planning departments remain small – no-one has come close to Pollitt's original prescription of matching account managers and planners on a one to one basis, and it is not unusual for one or two planners to service an agency with many accounts. This has inevitable implications for the job that is done. Account planning departments also remain peripheral to the central power bases of the agency, account management and/or creative (Hackley, 2003a).

There is an unacknowledged gap between planning in theory and practice. The "ideal" planner would be involved in strategy, starting with an in-depth understanding of the client's business; in using all kinds of data, including qualitative, conducted personally; in developing communication strategies; in briefing and inspiring creative teams; in working with them and the clients, and using research, to evolve effective executions; to have access to relevant data and the ability to analyse it in depth, in order to monitor marketplace results, and plan for the future. To do all this requires a high ratio of planners with multiple skills. But in reality, few planners give equal effort to all parts of it. Furthermore, while there is wide variation in the amount of research experience that account planners bring to the job, relatively few seem to have the time or skill to make much use of numerical data; some seem to reject research altogether.

Most account planners are stretched in widely differing directions and have to make choices between them. Accordingly, they may take a pragmatic approach, based on what will most effectively "justify their existence." In practice, this may mean spending most time with the creative department, or focusing on new business pitches; it may involve little or no use of research, and little or no evaluation. Hence the tendency for many planners to redefine their role primarily as "inspiring creative people;" words like "insight" and "intuition" become valued, "rigour" and "research" devalued. The intention to inspire creatives is not bad in itself. But if planners adopt the same solipsistic view of creativity as many creative teams do – as an end in itself, defined by peers not consumers – then the fundamental planning values of effectiveness and consumer voice go out the window. Some of the sources cited worryingly suggest that this is happening, that the original vision and values expressed by King and Pollitt have not been realized across the agency business, and that some account planning departments seem to have forgotten or rejected them.

ACKNOWLEDGMENTS

I am indebted to Jeremy Bullmore, Stephen King, and Jon Steel for each taking the time to talk with me while I was writing this paper. I also owe special thanks to Professor Alice Kendrick of Southern Methodist University, who very generously assisted me in accessing a number of important sources, especially to do with the American history and status of Account Planning.

I would like to dedicate this chapter to the memory of Stephen King, who died in February, 2006.

NOTE

1 Though Ogilvy and Mather introduced planning in 1984 (Stewart, 1986). In keeping with its UK origins, most early US planners were ex-pat British.

REFERENCES

Bartle, J. (1985), "Account Planning – Has it a Future?" *Admap*, December.

Baskin, M., and M. Earls (2002), *Brand New Brand Thinking*, London: Kogan Page.

Bateson, G. (1979), *Mind and Nature: A Necessary Unity*, Cresskill NJ: Hampton Press.

Broadbent, S. (1980), *Advertising Works*, London: Holt Rinehart and Winston.

Broadbent, S. (1999), *When to Advertise*, Henley on Thames: Admap.

Broadbent, T. (2001), "Fear and Planning in Las Vegas," *Campaign*, August 3.

Bullmore, J. (1991), *Behind the Scenes in Advertising*, Henley on Thames: NTC Publications.

Channon, C. (1985), *Advertising Works 3: Papers from the IPA Advertising Effectiveness Awards*, London: Holt, Rinehart and Winston.

Channon, C. (1986), [Chairman's Introduction], *Proceedings of Seminar on Account Planning*, Neu Isenberg, Germany, Amsterdam: ESOMAR.

Channon, C. (1987), *Advertising Works 4: Papers from the IPA Advertising Effectiveness Awards*, London: Cassell.

Clemmow, S. (1992), "Towards a new working relationship between planners and researchers," *Proceedings of the Market Research Society Conference*, Birmingham, UK, 37–41.

Colley, R. (1961), *Defining Advertising Goals for Measured Advertising Results*, New York: Association of National Advertisers.

Cooper, A. (1997), *How to Plan Advertising*, Second Edition, London: Cassell/APG.

Cowan, R., and M. Taylor (1998), "Planning in Mid Life Crisis: The love/hate relationship that planners have for researchers," *Proceedings of the Market Research Society Conference*, Birmingham, UK, 207–14.

Cowley, D. (1986), "Working with Creative People" in Channon (1986), 37–45.

Cowley, D. (1989), *How to Plan Advertising*, London: Cassell/APG.

Cowley, D. (1991), *Understanding Brands: by 10 People Who Do*, London: Kogan Page.

Creamer, M. (2004), "Mitchell eschews soft, fuzzy for solid research at Ogilvy," *Advertising Age*, November 29, 18.

Dann, P. (2001), *2001 Creative Planning Awards*, London: Account Planning Group.

Danzig, F. (1999), "Top 100 Advertising People," *The Advertising Century: Advertising Age Special Issue*, 70(13), 51–4.

Dichter, E. (1964), *Handbook of Consumer Motivations: The Psychology of the World of Objects*, New York: McGraw-Hill.

Dichter, E. (1979), *Getting Motivated by Ernest Dichter: The Secret Behind Individual Motivations by the Man Who Was Not Afraid to Ask "Why?"* New York and Oxford: Pergamon Press.

Ehrenberg, A. (1969), "Towards an integrated theory of consumer behaviour," *Journal of the Market Research Society*, 11, 305–37: reprinted as Chapter 6, 'Some Coherent Patterns' in *Consumer Behaviour*, ed. Andrew Ehrenberg and FG Pyatt, Penguin 1971, 67–108.

Feldwick, P. (2000), *Pollitt on Planning*, Henley on Thames: APG/Admap.

Feldwick, P. (2002), *What is Brand Equity, Anyway?* Henley on Thames: WARC Publications.

Feuer, J. (1985), "Account Planners Put Human Face on Statistics," *Adweek*, April 15th, 44.

Fox, S. (1984), *The Mirror Makers: A History of American Advertising and its Creators*, New York, William Morrow and Co Inc.

Gardner, B., and S. Levy (1955), "The Product and the Brand," *Harvard Business Review*, March–April, 33–9.

Gunther, J. (1960), *Taken at the Flood: The Story of Albert D Lasker*, London: Hamish Hamilton.

Hackley, C. (2003a), "How Divergent Beliefs Cause Account Team Conflict," *International Journal of Advertising*, 22(3), 313–31.

Hackley, C. (2003b), "Account Planning: Current Agency perspectives on an advertising enigma," *Journal of Advertising Research*, 43(2), June, 235–45.

Haskins, J. (1964), "Factual recall as a measure of advertising effectiveness," *Journal of Advertising Research*, March.

Heath, R. (2000), *The Hidden Power of Advertising*, Henley on Thames: Admap Monograph.

Hopkins, C.C. (1923, reprinted 1998), *Scientific Advertising*, Lincolnwood, Ill: NTC.

Joyce, T. (1967), "What do we know about how advertising works?" ESOMAR Seminar, *The market researcher looks at the way that advertising works*, Noordwijk aan Zee, Vol 2, 90–127; reprinted as Chapter 10, 'Advertising' in *Consumer Behaviour*, ed. Andrew Ehrenberg and FG Pyatt, London: Penguin, 1971, 151–78.

Kendrick, A., and K. Dee (1992), "Account Planning: A History, Description and Evaluation of its Use in U.S. Agencies," *Proceedings of the 1992 Conference of the American Academy of Advertising*, ed. Leonard N Reid.

King, S. (1965), "How Useful is Proposition testing?" *Advertising Quarterly*, 6 (Winter), 24–34.

King, S. (1967), "Can Research Evaluate the Creative Content of Advertising?" *Admap*, 3, 6 (June), 7–14.

King, S. (1989), "The Anatomy of Account Planning," *Admap*, November.

Kotler, P. (1976), *Marketing Management: Analysis, Planning and Control*, Prentice Hall.

Kravitz, L. (1985), "Shops Worldwide Ask: How do Those British Creatives Do It?" *Adweek*, September 9.

Lannon, J., and P. Cooper (1983), "Humanistic Advertising: A Holistic Cultural Perspective," *Proceedings of ESOMAR Seminar on Effective Advertising*, Monte Carlo, pp. 1–25.

Lucas, D.B., and S. Henderson Britt (1963), *Measuring Advertising Effectiveness*, New York: McGraw-Hill.

Madison, C. (1991), "Rob White: British Account Planning comes to Minneapolis Shop," *Adweek*, January 14.

Martineau, P. (1957), *Motivation in Advertising: Motives that Make People Buy*, New York: McGraw-Hill.

Mayer, M. (1958), *Madison Avenue, USA: the Inside Story of American Advertising*, London: The Bodley Head.

Meyers, B. (1986), "To Plan or not to Plan," *Journal of Advertising Research*, Oct/Nov, 25–6.

Midgley, M. (2001), *Science and Poetry*, London: Routledge.

Moran, J.P. (1988), "Account Planning: a Client View," *Proceedings of the Market Research Society 31st Annual Conference*, Brighton, UK, 89–98.

Neill, M.-L. (2003), *2003 Creative Planning Awards*, London: Account Planning Group.

Newman, J. (1992), "*History of Account Planning*," in Newman et al. (1992), 5–7.

Newman, J. (1998), "Planning 30 years on," *Campaign*, July 10.

Newman, J., C. McAuliffe, C. Wauton, and R. White (1992), *What Every Account Executive Should Know About Account Planning*, New York: American Association of Advertising Agencies.

O'Donoghue, D. (1994), "Account Planning: The State of the Art," *Admap*, January.

O'Malley, D. (1999), "Account Planning: an American Perspective," in John Philip Jones, *The Advertising Business*, Sage Publications, Thousand Oaks, 41–9.

O'Reilly, D. (1981), "Agencies: The Great Leap into Planning," *Campaign*, September 18.

Packard, V. (1957), *The Hidden Persuaders,* London and New York: Longmans, Green & Co.

Pollitt, S. (1969), "Learning from Research in the 1960's," *Admap*, December: reprinted in Feldwick (2000), 11–25.

Pollitt, S. (1971), "Has Anything Gone Wrong with Advertising Research?" *Admap*, May: reprinted in Feldwick (2000), 27–38.

Pollitt, S. (1979), "How I Started Account Planning in Agencies," *Campaign*, April: reprinted in Feldwick (2000), 1–9.

Reason, P., and J. Rowan (1981), *Human Inquiry: A Sourcebook of New Paradigm Research,* Chichester and New York: John Wylie and Sons.

Reeve, B. (1992), "The Future of Advertising Agency Planners," *International Journal of Market Research*, 34(3).

Reeves, R. (1961), *Reality in Advertising,* New York: Alfred A Knopf.

Rogers, C.R. (1951), *Client Centered Therapy: Its Current Practice, Implications and Theory*, London: Constable.

Sharkey, B. (1987), "Do British-style Account Planners have a Future in the US?" *Adweek*, August 10.

Shaw, R., and A. Edwards (1998), "What do planners want from research? Not 'the truth'," *Proceedings of the Market Research Society Conference*, Birmingham, UK, 215–26.

Staveley, N. (1999), "Account Planning: a British perspective" in John Philip Jones, *The Advertising Business*, Sage Publications, Thousand Oaks, 35–40.

Steel, J. (1998), *Truth, Lies and Advertising: The Art of Account Planning*, New York: John Wylie & Sons.

Stewart, J. (1986), "The Role and Evolution of the Agency Planner," *Journal of Advertising Research*, Oct/Nov, 22–26.

Stewart-Hunter, D. (1986), "A Valediction: of Planning," *Admap*, October, 54–5.

Toulmin, S. (1990), *Cosmopolis: The Hidden Agenda of Modernity*, Chicago: University of Chicago Press.

Taylor, F.W. (1913/1980), *The Principles of Scientific Management,* New York: W.W. Norton.

Treasure, J. (1985), "The Origins of Account Planning," *Admap*, March.

Tunstall, J. (1964), *The Advertising Man in London Advertising Agencies*, London: Chapman and Hall.

Turner, G., and J. Pearson (1965), *The Persuasion Industry,* London: Eyre and Spottiswoode.

Walker, D. (1989), "In US, it's Account Planning, *a la cart,*" *Adweek*, October 30.

Weichselbaum, H., and A. Kendrick (1998), "How Agencies Plan Advertising: A Typology of British and American Approaches," *Proceedings of the 3rd Annual Conference of the Global Institute for Corporate and Marketing Communications,* April, Vol 1.

Learning from Case Studies of Effectiveness

Peter Field

This chapter will attempt to identify the "state of the art" of effective communications. It is primarily an examination of an empirical database of practical case studies of advertising effectiveness, not a review of theory or literature. It is intended to illustrate and build upon many of the issues explored in the study reviews of Chapter 3.8.

The primary data source is the UK Institute of Practitioners in Advertising (IPA) Effectiveness dataBANK – a database currently of 820 case studies from 1980 to 2004.[1] The late Simon Broadbent established the IPA effectiveness awards competition in 1980 to encourage a focus on effectiveness amongst UK advertising agencies and to raise their standards of evaluation and proof. The dataBANK is the product of the awards: case studies codified in standard format. As entrants to the IPA awards competition, all case studies have been vetted for accuracy. A judging panel comprised of senior business people, academics and researchers awarded prizes to case studies achieving higher standards of proof (more certain evidence of the contribution made by advertising to the observed effect) or where the effect was

especially evident (and advertising's contribution was consequently similarly evident). The prizes (gold, silver, bronze) awarded to some case studies, therefore principally reflect these standards of proof rather than degrees of effectiveness.

The effectiveness data includes detailed information on the circumstances and nature of the brand and the category at the time of the campaign, as well as a wide-ranging assessment of the changes that resulted.

The IPA DataBank is a unique body of objective, comparable data that observes the conditions of proven effective advertising campaigns. It represents the most complete UK record and definition of practical effectiveness today, as well as a vertical record of the evolution of effectiveness. It has become a major learning tool and reference point for advertisers and researchers. A visit to www.ipa.co.uk will provide more details.

The way in which the data are used is as a "pool" of what works, that can be examined in various ways. So the data are used to look for patterns within the pool of effectiveness: how the natures and circumstances of campaigns influence the outcomes.

Of the many factors at work shaping effectiveness in practice, the data observed here can shed interesting light on the following:

- The dimensions (definitions and measures) of effectiveness used in practice.
- Measures that are associated with successful effectiveness.
- How advertising content (in terms of the strategic advertising mode used) influences effectiveness.
- How media mix and weight correlate with effectiveness.

Finally the chapter ends with a set of actionable recommendations for marketers – a summary of the best practice emerging from analysis of the case study data.

THE DIMENSIONS OF EFFECTIVENESS

It is simplistic to define effectiveness as whether a campaign achieved pre-set objectives, since this takes no account of other valuable effects that may have been achieved but were not envisaged. Case studies reflect this reality and in many cases campaigns are evaluated against wider criteria than those stated as objectives. In practice it is also rare for objectives to be quantified – briefs tend to identify intentions without quantification, so case studies usually attempt to determine the commercial value of the observed effects and to demonstrate a positive return on the money invested in the campaign.

The primary "hard" business objectives set for campaigns are shown in Table 3.4.1 (NB. more than one primary objective is commonplace):

Table 3.4.1 Incidence of "hard" business objectives

Primary "hard" business objectives	Incidence (n = 734)
Sales gain	64.0%
Change attitudes	25.1%
Customer retention/loyalty	24.9%
Market share gain	21.4%
Market share defence	20.7%
Customer recruitment	12.8%
Profit gain	3.8%
Reduction of price sensitivity	1.2%

A sales gain (expressed either as an increase in sales or in share) is the overwhelming primary objective, but defensive objectives (customer retention or market share) also form a significant group. Reduction of price sensitivity is a surprisingly rare objective given its potential contribution to profitability: this may have more to do with the complexity of measurement than disdain for the objective. This hypothesis is supported by the relative lack of reporting of price elasticity (20% of cases) vs. sales gain (77%).

Attitudinal change is seldom sufficient *alone* as a measure of effectiveness in the case of "commercial" (i.e., for-profit) campaigns: these usually need to demonstrate a commercially directly valuable effect *as well* i.e., one of the other "hard" measures listed above.

The primary "soft" response objectives of advertising (intermediate consumer objectives intended to lead to the desired business outcomes) are as follows (Table 3.4.2):

Table 3.4.2 Incidence of "soft" response objectives

Primary "soft" response objectives	Incidence (n = 372)
Brand awareness	51.1%
Brand image	44.6%
Directly influencing behaviour	35.8%
Brand differentiation	33.1%
Brand fame*	21.2%
Brand loyalty (attitudinal)	16.7%
Trust in the brand	8.1%
Beliefs about the brand	6.7%

*Fame in this context is defined as perceptions of strength and/or authority in the category – a sense that the brand *defines* the category, not a measure of awareness. Its relevance is as a reassurance to consumers that the brand is widely esteemed.

There is one revealing time trend in these soft objectives: a shift from building brand awareness to building brand fame (i.e., from actual widespread awareness to the *perception* of widespread awareness amongst the target group). The former is not necessarily a prerequisite for the latter and may be increasingly unaffordable. (In the interests of clarity and brevity, time trends for other soft objectives are omitted from Table 3.4.3, since they reveal little.)

Table 3.4.3   Incidence of awareness vs. fame objectives over time

% of cases with primary advertising objective:	1980–1996 (n = 174)	1998–2004 (n = 198)
Building brand awareness	56.9%	46.0%
Building brand fame	13.8%	27.8%

Given that effectiveness is usually ascertained by "hard" measures, evaluation of progress against these "soft" intermediate objectives is valuable primarily to establish causality rather than effect (i.e., that it was the campaign that led to the observed effects, not other market factors). Whether such measures in practice tend to correlate with effectiveness is examined in the next section of this chapter.

Measures that are associated with successful effectiveness

Without measurement, there can be no reliable learning, but the learning will only be as good as the measures available. The data provides guidance about which advertising measures can be used to provide more convincing and reliable data to general management. This has been a primary objective of the case studies from the outset, the three objectives of which were laid down in 1980:

1. A better understanding of the crucial role advertising plays in marketing.
2. Closer analysis of advertising effectiveness and improved methods of evaluation.
3. A clear demonstration that advertising can be proven to work, against measurable criteria.

The need to improve measurement

In a recent survey of the opinions of investment analysts in London, England (IPA, 2005) 45% said they only consider financial measures of the companies they monitor. Given that the key non-financial measures considered by others were market share, market growth and market position, the level of analyst interest in "soft" measurements (e.g., brand image), is likely to be limited. Only 30% of the sample thought that marketing expenditure was not "a big black hole."

Inevitably, CFOs reflect this wariness of marketing. In a study of 100 UK CFO's

conducted by KPMG in October 1999 (CIA MediaLab/KPMG , 2000), only 46% thought their marketing department set measurable objectives. Moreover they rated their senior marketers 5.4 out of 10 on their ability to measure marketing effectiveness, down from 5.7 three years earlier. This was echoed in a recent qualitative study of CEOs (The Marketing Society and McKinsey and Company, 2004) that reported a view of the marketing function as "undisciplined," "uncommercial" and "not accountable" amongst other criticisms, although there was praise for marketing's passion and energy. It is widely reported e.g., by Ambler (2000) that marketing accountability is an increasing requirement but marketing metrics are evidently judged to be failing to keep up.

This growing pressure for accountability and measurability is reflected in the growth of use of quantitative research-based measures and econometric modelling in case studies over time (Table 3.4.4), as marketers have striven to provide the necessary data.

Table 3.4.4   Incidence of use of quantitative tools in case studies over time

% of cases using:	1980–1996 (n = 609)	1998–2004 (n = 211)
Quantitative Ad pre-tests	28.9%	42.7%
Other Quantitative consumer research measures	19.4%	42.7%
Econometric modelling	23.3%	39.8%

There is however a difference between *practice* and *best practice* and not all measures correlate with effectiveness.

Best practice

The prizes awarded by case study judges (many of whom are senior managers of major advertisers) are a measure of what evidence convinced them most. So conclusions can be drawn about best practice by examining the patterns of evidence used in prize-winning cases.

The most immediate general conclusion drawn from the data is simple: the more measures the better. On average, prize-winning papers used 1.8 times more tools to demonstrate advertising impact than non-awarded papers. They used 4.4 times as many measures of response to advertising and 3.2 times as many "collateral" measures of advertising effect (such as staff productivity and investor stock ratings). Overall it was the greater number of these *different types* of measure that appeared to make the difference to judges: the late Simon Broadbent, father of the IPA Effectiveness Awards used a memorable analogy for this – "spotlights on a statue from different angles." The more we use, the clearer the object. However, winning cases used only 1.2 times as many types of intermediate measures of brand standing (e.g., imagery and awareness) – this issue is examined further shortly.

A corollary of this is that marketers should be wary of single measures of the "effectiveness" of campaigns, such as advertising cut-through. It is appropriate to focus for a moment on cut-through for two reasons:

1. It is quite conspicuously the fastest growing measure used in case studies: it was used in 24% of cases in the period 1980–96 vs. in 60% of cases in the period 1998–2004.
2. Many marketers have developed go/no-go standards based on a single predictive measure of advertising cut-through.

The data suggests that marketers should not rely on advertising cut-through as a single measure, but should broaden their range of criteria to include advertising mode-relevant response measures such as likeability, communication or persuasion (Table 3.4.5).

The data demonstrate that judges were more convinced by response measures alone than by cut-through measures alone. Moreover, analysis of sales effects, suggests that the judges were right to be more interested in response measures (Table 3.4.6). To examine sales effects the data reports the case study author's comparative assessment of whether the effect was Very Large, Large/Substantial, or Small/Negligible. This is clearly not perfect, but it does have the advantage of relating the sales effect to the brand's start-point and to category norms.

The data clearly suggest that the use of response measures (such as likeability) has a much stronger relationship with very large-scale sales effects, than the use of cut-through measures. In this, the data are consistent with many research studies, e.g., the 1991 American Advertising Research Foundation (ARF) copy research project (Haley and Baldinger, 1991), that have shown that likeability of advertising is the best predictor of sales effectiveness.

Measures of advertising cut-through were the most widely provided tracking measure by UK research companies according to Ambler and Goldstein (Ambler and Goldstein, 2003). The widespread use (evidenced above) of measures of advertising cut-through *alone* would appear not to be driven by the

Table 3.4.5   Incidence of prize-winning by cases demonstrating advertising cut-through vs. response measures

Combinations of measures used:	No Cut-through with no response (n = 472)	No Cut-through with response (n = 74)	Cut-through with no response (n = 156)	Cut-through with response (n = 118)
Percentage of cases that were awarded prizes	10.8%	55.4%	43.6%	60.9%

Table 3.4.6   Incidence of very large sales effects by cases demonstrating advertising cut-through vs. response measures

	No Cut-through with no response (n = 87)	No Cut-through with response (n = 64)	Cut-through with no response (n = 66)	Cut-through with response (n = 106)
Percentage of cases achieving "very large" sales effects	19.1%	42.7%	23.3%	60.9%

evidence of their efficacy, but perhaps by their widespread availability. Marketers using advertising cut-through metrics should therefore also introduce other advertising response metrics.

Quantitative advertising pre-testing (taking many forms, but measuring the pre-to-post exposure response of a robust sample of target consumers to the proposed advertising) is widely mandated by general managements, but the data suggests that marketers should not rely entirely on its findings. This was demonstrated using an earlier analysis of this database (Field, 1999): Table 3.4.7 is an update of this analysis showing once again a negative correlation between the level of prize awarded to a case study and the use of quantitative advertising pre-testing.

The data cast some doubt on the ability of quantitative pre-testing to reliably pick winners in the increasingly sophisticated world of modern advertising.

But failure to correlate with well-proven case studies that win awards is perhaps not the same as failure to contribute to advertising effectiveness. To examine the relationship between quantitative pre-testing and the scale and nature of advertising effects, Table 3.4.8 examines the case study author's comparative

Table 3.4.7 Incidence of quantitative ad pre-testing by cases winning prizes

	Non-prize winning (n = 578)	Bronze (n = 93)	Silver (n = 92)	Gold (n = 57)
% cases using quantitative ad pre-tests	32.7%	37.6%	30.4%	24.6%

Table 3.4.8 Incidence of "very large" advertising effects amongst quantitatively pre-tested cases vs. all cases

Nature of effect:	All cases (n = 322)	Cases using Quantitative Ad pre-tests (n = 95)
Awareness	37.3%	34.7%
Commitment	12.4%	17.9%
Trust	4.7%	7.4%
Differentiation	18.3%	22.1%
Esteem	11.8%	13.7%
Fame	16.8%	17.9%
Equity	14.9%	11.6%
Behaviour directly	29.5%	17.9%

assessment of whether a measured effect was Very Large (rather than Large/Substantial, or Small/Negligible).

The use of advertising pre-testing does not generally appear to be associated with increased large-scale advertising effects amongst the sample of case studies, and in some respects appears to be associated with a reduced likelihood of such effects. Perhaps most surprising is the last line of data, suggesting that quantitatively pre-tested advertising is less likely to be associated with campaigns that produced a very large direct behavioural effect (i.e., short term as a direct result of the campaign message). There are many possible interpretations of this, so one should not necessarily jump to conclusions, but in an area where quantitative pre-testing might be expected to deliver real value, this looks contradictory.

Also cautionary is the apparent association between quantitative advertising pre-testing and in-market effects (though clearly other factors might be at play here such as distribution and category pricing, so again one should not jump to conclusions). Table 3.4.9 demonstrates that quantitative pre-testing does not *appear* to be associated more closely with very large-scale in-market effects of advertising (categorized by case study authors in the same way as the intermediate effects of Table 3.4.8). In this the data appear to reinforce the 1991 findings of the American Advertising Research Foundation (Haley and Baldinger, 1991) more fully analysed elsewhere (Eagleson and Rossiter, 1994) that 26 out of the 35 pre-testing measures examined, performed so poorly that they could safely be rejected – and of the 9 that were worthwhile around a half measured advertising likeability in some form or another.

In case doubts about quantitative pre-testing are taken as support for qualitative pre-testing (usually focus groups or one-on-one depth interviews, observing in depth the response of a non-robust sample of target consumers to the proposed advertising), Table 3.4.9 also demonstrates that the latter fared little better in general in terms of association with "very large" in-market effects.

Table 3.4.9 Incidence of "very large" in-market effects amongst pre-tested cases vs. all cases

Nature of "Very Large" effect:	All cases (n = 323)	Cases using Quant pre-tests (n = 88)	Cases using Qual pre-tests (n = 115)
Sales gain	52.9%	38.6%	39.1%
Market share gain	31.6%	34.1%	30.4%
Reduction of price sensitivity	3.1%	2.3%	3.5%
Customer retention/loyalty	7.1%	9.1%	10.4%
Customer recruitment	26.6%	26.1%	21.7%
Profit gain	22.3%	14.8%	20.9%

Both appear unreliable as drivers of effectiveness, though their other roles in the development of advertising and in securing management approval remain unchallenged. This is consistent with Heath (Heath, 2001), who has argued that because many of the impressions of brands held in consumers minds have been stored using "low attention processing" of communications, people cannot reliably answer questions designed to elicit the impact of campaigns on brands. They are not consciously aware of all the messages that have been stored, even when they are triggered at the moment of brand choice.

The broader point the data make is that the very kinds of measures required of marketers in pursuit of accountability, are not always conducive to the pursuit of maximum *efficiency*. Whilst quantitative pre-testing may well reduce the risk of outright failure of advertising (hinted at in Table 3.4.7), the data suggest that "there is no such thing as a free lunch:" the cost of reducing the risk of failure appears to come at the cost of reducing the upside potential of success.

When it comes to the tracking of in-market effects, other studies (e.g., Ambler, 2000) have shown that marketers' areas of interest do not always align with general managements.' "Soft" measures such as brand awareness and brand equity (an ill-defined term, but here meaning measures of brand image and attitudes to the brand) are more highly prized by marketers than by their general management colleagues. These data support the general conclusion that soft measures have become devalued in the eyes of general management: they appeared to make no difference to a case study's chance of award. Clearly there

are situations (e.g., a brand repositioning) when an image shift or an awareness gain might have considerable implications for sales growth, but in general this is not accepted. Again, the data suggests that general management are perhaps right to be wary of "soft measures." "Very large" sales effects were associated with only around 30% of cases using soft measurements (32% for awareness and 35% for image/attitudes measures i.e., no better than the average case at 32%).

General management are more concerned with harder intermediate measures such as brand consideration (e.g., presence within a set of acceptable brands to consumers). This featured about five times as often in prize-winning cases as in non-winners. Cases using this measure were associated with "very large" sales effects in 59% of cases (n = 99). The suggestion is that hard (behaviour-related) intermediate consumer measures are generally more closely associated with sales effect than soft (attitude or awareness-related) ones.

The growing use of econometrics as best practice in accountability is supported: prize-winning cases were almost twice as likely to have used econometrics as non-awarded cases (41% vs. 22%). This is reinforced by a recent survey of UK ad agencies (IPA et al., 2005) that found that 55% used econometric modelling on behalf of their clients for investment decision-making.

How advertising content influences effectiveness

This section will examine the frequency of occurrence of five different advertising modes (plus their use in combination) in various category and brand scenarios. Since all scenarios relate to case studies of success, the assumption is made that where a mode becomes more dominant, it is an indication of the potency of that mode in that scenario. There is of course an in-built assumption here that in the universe of all campaigns from which these cases are drawn, the same dominance does not arise. This is a reasonable assumption given the lack of consistent theory applied in practice.

Taxonomy

The taxonomy of advertising strategies used in the data is essentially based on commercial taxonomies that have achieved significant impact in the UK, and are therefore well understood by case study authors. The taxonomy is not fully comprehensive and some force-fitting of cases is evident in the taxonomy below. The strategic modes are defined in the coding instructions to authors by the following italicised text in quotation marks – the discussion that follows is added here for greater clarity (readers familiar with the source data should note that the names of the categories have been changed to be consistent with international terminology):

- *Information:* "the campaign proved effective simply because of the information it provided." In practice information can be about the brand, the category, the user or their world. This is different from the Rational Persuasion category (below) because although the primary modus operandi of both is informational, no secondary emotional appeal is added in this mode. This category thus includes classic "reason why" advertising, in which a clear functional product benefit (implied or actual) over competing brands is communicated. By providing information about the brand's quality, performance, functionality (and so on) such advertising presents a purely logical rationale for usage or trial. This mode also includes a number of not-for-profit government information campaigns.
- *Rational persuasion:* "the campaign initially gained interest with information and then added emotional appeal." These campaigns primarily used information to persuade consumers by challenging or enhancing existing knowledge or beliefs about the brand, but also used emotional

elements as a secondary tool to persuade and/or make the message more memorable. In practice the emotional content was often low key (note the contrast with the more complex category below). In this mode the process of persuasion to use or try is thus essentially rational.
- *Reinforcement:* "the campaign reinforced existing behaviour rather than changed behaviour (the weak theory)." These campaigns reinforced particular behaviours e.g., usage occasions or usage modes or reinforced linkage with associated events (e.g., telephone call stimulation).
- *Fame:* "the campaign got the brand talked about/made it famous." By generating strong responses in the target group (not necessarily liking) these campaigns caused the brand to stand out distinctly from other brands in the category and be talked about (not in a functional sense but by virtue of the attitudes and point-of-view projected by the brand). Prue (1998) has suggested that this encourages brand usage by creating perceptions that the brand is bigger and more "important" than before. NB this is not the same as advertising designed to raise brand awareness (a constant across all categories) – it is about perceptions of being the brand that is "making waves:" nothing succeeds like success.
- *Emotional involvement:* "the campaign proved effective simply because of the emotions or feelings it touched/how likeable it was." These campaigns achieved their desired effects through feelings generated by, and emotional engagement with the campaign. The intention of such advertising is to transfer these emotions to the brand – consequently to build empathy in the consumer-brand relationship and thereby influence choice. In practice these campaigns do sometimes include information about the brand but it is judged secondary or inconsequential to the success of the campaign.
- *More complex:* "a more complex combination of these or other factors." These campaigns essentially comprised of two or more of the above modes – the overlapping modes included in the "more complex" cases are revealed below (Table 3.4.10). These cases include campaigns where different elements (often media) of the campaign employ a different mode: Vakratsas and Ambler noted this phenomenon in relation to breakfast cereal campaigns that deployed separate modes against parents and their kids (Vakratsas and Ambler, 1999). They also include campaigns where individual elements employ multiple modes.

Table 3.4.10   Modal nature of "more complex" campaigns

Constituent advertising modes comprising "more complex" category:	Incidence amongst all "more complex" cases (n = 61)
Information	44.3%
Rational persuasion	60.7%
Reinforcement	11.5%
Fame	24.6%
Emotional involvement	68.9%

Table 3.4.11   Incidence of advertising modes amongst cases

Advertising Categories:	Incidence amongst all cases% (n = 344)
Information	12.3%
Rational persuasion	32.2%
Reinforcement	3.2%
Fame	9.1%
Emotional Involvement	26.0%
More complex	17.8%

An illustration of both these variants is the twin track British Airways campaign of 2004 (Day et al., 2005). One campaign track redefined some of the "frills" of the service as important (e.g., reserved seats and proximity of airports to city centres) by playing on the emotional disappointments of new low cost airline service. The other track simultaneously evoked the reassuring experiential and emotional values, inherent after long use, of the Delibes Lakme music track, whilst communicating a low cost message (evidenced by sample fares).

The most common combination (24 cases) is Rational Persuasion + Emotional Involvement, essentially a strong emotional platform with a functional competitive advantage, such that neither is judged to be dominant. The next most common combination (13 cases) is Information + Emotional Involvement. This combination is clearly very similar to the previous one and perhaps not importantly different. Authors appear to have categorized cases in this way where the information content is intended to be a statement of fact rather than a comparative claim: the combination includes a disproportionate number of recruitment and retail campaigns, where the information is to do with pay and conditions or price and availability. The key characteristic of "more complex" cases is therefore the combination of rational and emotional platforms in comparatively equal measure.

Advertising mode usage

The overall incidence of usage of each advertising category is shown in Table 3.4.11. A relatively even mix of rational and

emotional modes is revealed, with a slight preponderance of primarily rational ones.

Advertising mode and brand position in market

The data can be used to examine whether a number of different market scenarios appear to favour certain advertising modes in terms of likelihood of being effective. The scenarios examined here are the strength of the brand's position in its market: new-comer versus niche/small brand versus strong challenger brand versus leader. Morgan has observed a number of factors in the success of challenger brands (Morgan, 2000), included amongst which are powerfully emotive brand identities ("lighthouse identities"). The data provide strong evidence to support this (Table 3.4.12).

Emotions-based and more complex modes account for 55.5% of successful challenger brand campaigns, whereas they account for only 37.5% of successful leader brand campaigns. By contrast, effective leader campaigns are more likely to have used rational modes.

Advertising modes and thinking versus feeling categories

The data also shed light on the strength of the relationship between successful advertising mode and the roles of rational consideration (thinking) versus emotions (feeling) in brand choice in the category. Table 3.4.13 reports incidence of advertising modes across four different classifications of market category, depending on whether rational thinking and feeling play a high or low role in brand choice. It clearly does not necessarily follow that a category dominated by thinking in brand

Table 3.4.12   Advertising mode incidence amongst brands categorized by strength of position in market

Advertising Mode:	Launch (n = 63)	Niche/Small (n = 91)	Strong Challenger (n = 63)	Leader (n = 64)
Information	15.9%	9.9%	6.3%	9.4%
Rational Persuasion	27.0%	33.0%	27.0%	34.4%
Reinforcement	0.0%	1.1%	4.8%	7.8%
Fame	15.9%	6.6%	6.3%	10.9%
Emotional Involvement	22.2%	29.7%	36.5%	23.4%
More complex	19.0%	19.8%	19.0%	14.1%

Table 3.4.13   Advertising mode incidence amongst brands categorized by roles of thinking vs. feeling in brand choice

Advertising mode	Low think High feel (n = 109)	High think Low feel (n = 56)	High think High feel (n = 91)	Low think Low feel (n = 11)
Information	0.0%	17.9%	11.0%	9.1%
Rational Persuasion	22.0%	33.9%	33.0%	27.3%
Reinforcement	3.7%	0.0%	2.2%	0.0%
Fame	11.9%	8.9%	9.9%	0.0%
Emotional Involvement	39.4%	19.6%	24.2%	36.4%
More complex	22.9%	19.6%	19.8%	27.3%

choice will also be categorised by rational modes of successful campaigns. The requirement to ensure the message is noticed and remembered cost-effectively argues in favour of an emotional content to communications modes, as Ambler has demonstrated (Ambler et al., 2000). Never-the-less one might expect to observe greater differences than exist in fact.

Whilst the tendency is for the advertising mode to "go with the flow" of choice in the category, it is by no means essential. The data demonstrate that it is possible to have a successful emotional campaign in a thinking-driven category and a successful rational campaign in a feeling-driven category.

Scale of effects of advertising modes

Notwithstanding the above, looking at the scale of measured effects of campaigns suggests some apparent differences in the *principal* effects of the various advertising modes (Table 3.4.14). Here as before, the data reports the case study author's comparative assessment of whether a measured effect was Very Large, Large/Substantial, or Small/Negligible. Data are omitted for advertising modes where the base size was too small for useful analysis.

The data *suggest* that the rational persuasion mode is less strongly associated with customer commitment and brand differentiation in particular, and is in general

Table 3.4.14   Incidence of very large advertising effects amongst advertising modes

Nature of soft effect:	Rational persuasion (n = 89)	Emotional involvement (n = 77)	More complex (n = 60)
Awareness	33.7%	37.7%	28.3%
Commitment	4.5%	22.1%	15.0%
Trust	2.2%	3.9%	10.0%
Differentiation	12.4%	26.0%	25.0%
Esteem	7.9%	16.9%	15.0%
Fame	9.0%	15.6%	21.7%
Equity	6.7%	18.2%	25.0%
Behaviour directly	31.5%	28.6%	25.0%

associated with a lesser scale of effect than the emotional involvement and more complex modes. Rational persuasion's core strength is perhaps directly influencing behaviour (i.e., short term behavioural change) – though the data suggest that this is the case principally in categories where rational consideration plays a strong role in choice (78% of the cases where rational persuasion advertising produced a very large direct behavioural effect were "high think" categories). The data are not suggesting rational persuasion advertising is *ineffective* – quite the reverse, given the number of successful case studies that used it – but they do suggest that such advertising is in general less *efficient* than emotion-based advertising at generating effects.

A further suggestion of these data is that emotion-based advertising is more strongly associated with large shifts in perceived brand differentiation; that it is not sufficient merely to state the rational basis of brand differentiation. To be accepted and remembered most effectively, a brand difference must be emotionally engaging to the consumer (emotion–based advertising). Such a suggestion will not come as a great surprise to marketing professionals – there are after all, many powerfully differentiated iconic brands that have been built in this way, from Apple to Orange and from Nike to Virgin. What the data perhaps begins to achieve is a general proof of this in the world of mere mortal brands.

Another suggestion from these data is that the "more complex" category, making greater use of the potential of integrated communications to tailor the brand message to the moment, is more likely to achieve the widest spectrum of desirable effects. Given that 80% of more complex cases include elements of either emotion or fame (providing the emotional reassurance of being a well-known brand), the data supports another increasingly held belief by marketers: that to achieve the widest range of desirable large-scale effects, brands should use integrated multi-media campaigns with emotional identities at their core.

Extending this analysis to market effects, with the same caveat as before, that this now brings other factors into play (such as distribution and category pricing), also suggests that rational persuasion advertising is less likely to be associated with large effects (Table 3.4.15).

Again, the data are not suggesting that rational persuasion advertising is ineffective; merely that it is perhaps associated with less dramatic sales effects than emotional involvement advertising. But the sceptical observer would be right to suggest that interpretation of the data is being pushed to the very limit here.

Advertising modes in combined circumstances

It will by now have become clear that category and brand circumstances individually, generally have rather weak influences over the likely success of one advertising mode over another. Indeed there are a number of other factors recorded in the data that have been examined and discarded, because individually they exhibit no significant influence.

It is likely that more powerful linkages would be seen to *combinations* of circumstantial factors but the sample sizes rarely support

Table 3.4.15   Incidence of very large in-market effects amongst advertising modes

Nature of hard effect:	Rational persuasion (n = 94)	Emotional involvement (n = 82)	More complex (n = 57)
sales gain	47.9%	57.3%	36.8%
mkt share gain	26.6%	37.8%	31.6%
reduction of price sensitivity	3.2%	2.4%	3.5%
customer retention/loyalty	5.3%	8.5%	10.5%
customer recruitment	25.5%	25.6%	36.8%
profit gain	12.8%	28.0%	24.6%

such multivariate analysis. For example, the number of cases featuring strong challenger brands in "high feel" categories is currently 47. Of these, emotional advertising modes were used in 49% of cases and more complex modes in 19%. Most (two thirds) of these more complex modes featured emotional elements. In a similar situation, any marketer would need a good reason to turn to an advertising mode that was not emotion-based. By contrast, of the 34 cases featuring brand leaders in "high think" categories, 62% used principally rational modes. Again, assuming the brand has a strong functional basis for rational persuasion or information advertising, one would need a good reason not to adopt one of these modes (such as perhaps, a challenger stealing share by using a powerful emotional platform ...).

How media mix and weight correlate with effectiveness

Multi-media effects

The number of media available to marketers is self-evidently an area of massive and rapid change. Much has been written about the proliferation of media in recent years, both off and on-line, so there is no need to add to the pile here. There is widespread familiarity with the fragmentation of audiences and the opportunities created by new media for integrated campaigns. The data reveal how important integrated communications have become amongst effective campaigns (Table 3.4.16).

In this analysis different channels include TV, Press, Radio etc. as well as Internet, Direct Mail, Sales Promotion, Sponsorship and Media couponing.

These data perhaps fail to fully drive home the speed of the shift to integration in contemporary effectiveness: in 2000 just 14% of case studies involved more than six media channels – by 2004 it was 45%. Clearly the

growing use of integrated campaigns is in part a response to the challenge of creating brand cut-through via any one medium, but more importantly it is also a means of tailoring a more sophisticated and richer message to consumers at optimum moments.

The European launch campaign for the Pulse variant of the Lynx deodorant brand (known as Axe in the US) is an example of the power of an integrated multi-channel campaign. The case study (Raillard and Nicholls, 2005) compares the effects of a full multimedia campaign in the UK with a "traditional" advertising-only campaign in France and found the ratio of return on investment to be 2.25 times greater in the UK. The Virgin Trains (O'Bric et al., 2005) and Guardian newspaper (Crawford et al., 2005) campaigns similarly exploited the possibilities of multi-channel communications. As with Lynx, the channels were used differently but consistently to build up much richer brand equities than any one channel could.

The average number of channels used by cases with "more complex" advertising modes was 4.5 – not hugely greater than the 3.1 channels for non-complex modes. It would appear that the use of complex integrated campaigns is driven not only by the availability of new media channels, but also perhaps by a growing belief in the "multiplier effect" of multi-channel campaigns, demonstrated by Lynx. This effect has also been charted by a number of other case studies, notably Cravendale Milk (Edmonds and Donoghugh, 2005) and VW Passat (Butterworth et al., 2003). The Cravendale case study recorded the following sales uplifts, depending on the channels used (Table 3.4.17).

Similar multiplier effects were observed in the VW Passat case study where levels of consumer interest amongst non-VW owners in the new model depended on channel exposure (Table 3.4.18).

Table 3.4.16 Average number of channels used over time

	1980–1996 (n = 195)	1998–2000 (n = 101)	2002–2004 (n = 102)
Average number of channels used in case studies	1.9	3.8	4.9

Table 3.4.17   Cravendale milk case study

Channels used:	Sales uplift
TV only	4.9%
DM (door drop) only	8.6%
Point-of-sale (taste testing) only	0.5%
TV + DM	31.7%
TV + P-o-s	22.5%

Table 3.4.18   VW case study

Channels exposed to:	Consumer Interest
Advertising (TV + Press) only	22%
Advertising + PR	40%
Advertising + DM	42%

It is clear that across the 24-year span of the data, advertising's role has changed considerably from being the sole or dominant element of the communications mix with *total* responsibility for attitudinal and behavioural change, to being merely an important element in a mix where each element is assigned a *partial* role in effecting those consumer changes. Effective communications campaigns are increasingly unlikely to be built around a role for advertising that "clinches a decision" (Krugman, 1972). Yet Krugman's model lingers in the thinking of many of the research tools available to evaluate advertising, rather than the holistic approach to integrated marketing communications that is increasingly necessary. If the role of advertising within an integrated campaign is to direct a prospect to a website rather than to attempt to "clinch the decision," then a very different (but perhaps equally effective) advertising approach might result.

Weight of advertising

If the growth of integrated communications is helping to rewrite many of the rules of brand marketing, it does not appear to have affected one time-honoured truth: the importance of share of voice.

A long-standing PIMS finding (Buzzell and Gale, 1987) from their database of 3000 business units, demonstrates how a brand's market share is strongly correlated with its perceived relative quality. This was refined in a special analysis of the PIMS database in 1998 (Butterfield, 1998). The special analysis

demonstrated that a brand's perceived relative quality is correlated with its relative share of advertising spend (i.e., Share of Voice ÷ Share of Market). The clear implication being that in order to drive up market share, brands need to spend ahead of their position in market (i.e., SOV>SOM).

The data supports this implication by closing the gap between effectiveness and relative spend (albeit with a less commanding sample size than that of PIMS). Of the 101 cases (mostly recent) where full SOV and SOM data is available, SOV was greater than SOM in 78% of cases. The average difference was +12 percentage points. Breaking down the relative position between SOV and SOM reveals the scale of the difference (Table 3.4.19).

Table 3.4.19   Incidence of relative spend levels amongst cases

Relative spend	Difference (percentage points)	% Cases
SOV>SOM	≥30%	15%
	≥20% to 30%	9%
	≥10% to 20%	13%
	>0% to 10%	42%
SOV=SOM	0%	2%
SOV<SOM	<0% to −10%	14%
	≤−10% to −20%	4%
	≤−20%	2%

In many cases then, SOV is less than 10% above SOM, but in more than a third of cases SOV was more than 10% above SOM. A conspicuous factor in the 20% of cases where SOV was less than SOM appears to be the highly fragmented nature of the broad categories concerned: drink, retail and general household goods accounted for over half of these cases. It is possible that the brands operated within a *subcategory* where their relative SOV was actually higher.

Moreover, the data provide more precise support for the PIMS implication by revealing a significant correlation between the relative spend (SOV-SOM) and the growth of market share (Figure 3.4.1).

The data therefore suggest that an average brand targeting more than around 5 share points of growth needs to spend ahead of its market share (i.e., SOV>SOM).

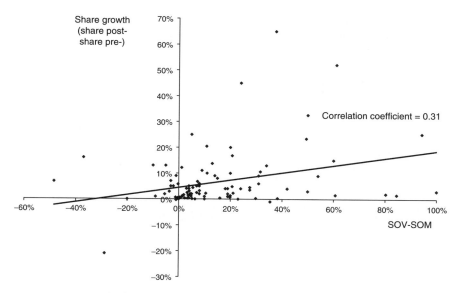

Figure 3.4.1   Share Growth vs. Relative Media Spend

LIMITATIONS AND IMPLICATIONS FOR FURTHER RESEARCH

Although all campaigns included an advertising element (on or off-line), not all included other communications channels. Currently mobile phone based channels and viral marketing are not recorded as separate channels.

Most case studies relate to the UK, but some relate to other European or developed markets. Comparable analysis of case studies from other geographies would enrich the findings.

The data cannot be compared to the wider universe of all marketing campaigns because comparable data for less fully effective campaigns is not available (sadly no-one writes case studies of failure or mediocrity).

Currently, looking for patterns *within* sub-cells (e.g., advertising modes used) yields perilously low sample sizes in some instances. In these situations the apparent implications of the data need to be validated when more data becomes available.[2] The fullest use of the data requires more detailed and multivariate

analyses that will become progressively possible over the next 4–8 years as the dataset expands. In particular, by homing in on combinations of multiple circumstances the data will be able to point more precisely to best practice.

Although the sophistication of the coding has grown over the years, it remains imperfect and not all analysis fields can be followed back before 1998. Since 1998, completion of a common data questionnaire has been a condition of entry for the Advertising Effectiveness Awards and this has resulted in far fewer holes in the data. Prior to this, coding of cases is by expert reader of the case studies, and thus omits fields probed only by the questionnaire. Much of the analysis is therefore only possible for recent case studies and more data are needed for reliability.

Identified improvements needed include:

- A more precise and complete taxonomy of advertising modes.
- More precise definitions of ambiguous terms (e.g., brand equity) provided to authors throughout.

SUMMARY – BEST PRACTICE FOR EFFECTIVENESS

Pulling together the findings from the data leads to the following recommended checklist for marketers:

1. Invest in econometric modelling as a tool to demonstrate effectiveness of communications and as a planning tool for future campaigns.
2. Adopt a proactive and positive approach to measurement and accountability with general management – argue for more measures, not single ones. Set clearly defined objectives for the campaign, but be wary of over-stating the importance of individual channel objectives, in the light of the multiplier effect.
3. Be wary of all pre-testing methodologies (quantitative and qualitative). In particular question the value of predictive measures of advertising cut-though as a single criterion.
4. Include relevant measures of response to advertising, especially likeability, depending on your campaign mode. Measures of advertising cut-through may be relevant but in general are less important than response measures.
5. Recognize that "hard" intermediate brand measures are more predictive of sales success and therefore better suited to target-setting, "soft" ones are more useful for diagnostics.
6. Develop a model of how each channel of your campaign is intended to work and of its role in the whole process. Allow the individual circumstances of the situation to suggest the strategic approach: a variety of strategic modes can work in most situations. However, bear in mind that your chances of success may be improved if you are a challenger and/or in a high feel category using an emotion-based mode. Similarly, if you are a leader and/or in a high think category your chances may be improved with a rational mode.
7. Look to develop an integrated multi-channel campaign for the widest range of desirable effects – especially one that is emotion-based.
8. Evaluate the multiplier effect of multi-channel campaigns to ensure decisions about individual channels are fully informed – you will probably need econometric modelling to do so.
9. If significant share growth is a target, argue for a communications budget that will represent a share of voice that is higher than your share of market. 10 points of share growth will typically require SOV to be over 30 points ahead of SOM.

NOTES

1 More recent data to 2006 has now been added and is reported by Binet and Field (Binet and Field, 2007).
2 This has now been done with the addition of the 2006 data (see Binet and Field, 2007).

REFERENCES

Ambler, T. (2000), "*Marketing And The Bottom Line*," Pearson Education.

Ambler, T., A. Ioannides and S. Rose (2000), "Brands On The Brain: Neuro Images Of Advertising," *Business Strategy Review* 11(3).

Ambler, T. and S. Goldstein (2003), "Copy Testing: Practice And Best Practice," *WARC*.

Binet, L. and P. Field (2007), "Marketing in the Era of Accountability," *IPA dataMINE #2*, WARC.

Butterfield, L. (1998), "How Advertising Impacts On Profitability," *IPA AdValue* issue 1, (Sept).

Butterworth, R., J. Hillhouse and S. Donoghugh (2003), "Beautifully Crafted: Launching The Facelifted Passat In 2001," *Advertising Works 12*, WARC, Chapter 21, 533–58.

Buzzell, R.D. and B.T. Gale (1987), "The PIMS Principles," Free Press CIA MediaLab/KPMG (2000), "*Finance Directors Survey 2000,*" *Institute of Practitioners in Advertising*, London (February).

Crawford, A., A. Perkins, D. Bassett, N. Jones and G. Fowles (2005), "A Fresh Approach To Newspaper Communications," *Advertising Works 13*, WARC, Chapter 17, 431–70.

Day, R., R. Storey and A. Edwards, (2005), "Climbing Above The Turbulence," *Advertising Works 13*, WARC, Chapter 9, 217–41.

Eagleson, G. and J.R. Rossiter (1994), "Conclusions From The ARF's Copy Research Validity Project," *Journal of Advertising Research*, (May/June).

Edmonds, E. and S. Donoghugh (2005), "Cash From Cows," *Advertising Works 13*, WARC, Chapter 3, 59–92.

Field, P. (1999), "Learning From 20 Years of Effectiveness Cases," *Advertising Works 10*, NTC, 513–17.

Haley, R.I. and A.L. Baldinger (1991), "The ARF Copy Research Validity Project," *Journal of Advertising Research*, (April/May).

Heath, R. (2001), "The Hidden Power of Advertising," *Admap Monograph #7*.

IPA (2005), "How Analysts View Marketing," *Institute of Practitioners in Advertising*, London (July).

IPA, ISBA, MCCA and PRCA, (2005), "Evaluation," *Joint Industry Best Practice Guide*, (Aug).

Krugman, H.E. (1972), "Why Three Exposures May be Enough," *Journal of Advertising Research*, 12 (November/December).

The Marketing Society and McKinsey and Company (2004), "The Coming of Age of Marketing," *The Marketing Society*, (Autumn).

Morgan, A. (2000), "*Eating the Big Fish*," Wiley.

O'Bric, G., L. Jenkins and I. Melas (2005), "How A Powerful Idea Fuelled The Engine Room Of Virgin Trains Revenue By Changing Minds And Winning Hearts," *Advertising Works 13*, WARC, Chapter 18, 471–90.

Prue, T. (1998), "An All-Embracing Theory Of How Advertising Works?," *Admap*, (Feb).

Raillard, G. and W. Nicholls (2005), "Proving The Value Of Integration," *Advertising Works 13*, WARC, Chapter 13, 331–60.

Vakratsas, D. and T. Ambler (1999), "How Advertising Works: What Do We Really Know?" *Journal of Marketing*, (January), 26–43.

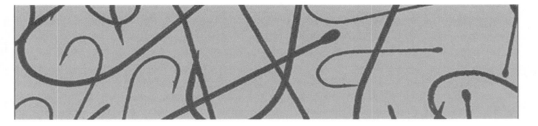

Pretesting: "Before the Rubber Hits the Road"

Rik Pieters and Michel Wedel

Would you have your child continue boarding Flight KX32 if you knew that, although from a trustworthy operator, the airplane has not been inspected for defects? If brands are the firm's most valuable asset, would you let them board a communication campaign under such conditions? This chapter is about pretesting, known in the US as "copy testing," advertising, i.e., researching a campaign before it runs to determine its likely effectiveness and efficiency.

When the above airline operation that carries your brand is at "Six Sigma," it allows only 3.4 defects per million. By contrast, 99.9% perfection would result in 20 domestic airplane crashes each day. Nowadays, most manufacturers adopting Six Sigma achieve levels between three (93.3%) and four Sigma (99.4%). Unfortunately, the advertising industry does not seem to be even there yet. Originally developed at Motorola, Six Sigma is a systematic, data- and statistics-driven approach to process improvement that strives for near-perfection (aiming at six standard deviations – Sigma – between the mean and certain specification limits). It has been credited with having produced billions

of dollars in efficiencies and can be applied to optimize R&D, manufacturing, logistics, sales, but also advertising. The adoption of the philosophy and elements of the Six Sigma framework for enhancing ad-effectiveness, as is advocated here, is not yet standard. But, many of the tools and techniques used with Six Sigma are tried and true pretesting tools and practices that have been available in advertising for many years. The framework organizes and applies these tools in a more disciplined and focused manner. Although it is questionable whether Six Sigma levels of ad effectiveness are currently or ever feasible – its desirability and cost-effectiveness are not entirely undisputed– those of two or three-Sigma would already constitute substantial improvements. Surely, advertising development is a creative process which is fundamentally different from the mass-production of computer chips and cell phones. Yet, advertising as a form of applied creativity is qualitatively different from the "higher arts," because ads need to attain specific communication goals. Thus, whereas the creative process itself may be difficult to penetrate analytically, the creative output, the ads, are aimable to systematic testing in order to assess and improve their likely impact, and pretesting seeks to contribute to this.

Pretesting aims to make advertising expenditure more effective by establishing the likelihood that a specific ad will contribute to attaining the communication goals of the advertising campaign, and by establishing its initial media weight. We advocate pretesting *each and every* advertisement in campaigns to exercise maximal control over the advertising planning process and optimize the effectiveness of advertising. These campaigns include print-ads, television and radio commercials, out-door advertising, retail feature ads, catalog pages, DM letters, and banner ads on web pages, and other visual marketing activities such as package, store and restaurant design. Each of those communication devices deserves consideration of pretesting. Thus, "… the combination of research-based content with creative execution may constitute a powerful basis for effective advertising today" (Tellis, 1998: 91), and pretesting helps to assess and improve on this. The objective of the pretest is to implement a measurement-based strategy that reduces undesirable variability in the outcomes of the ad planning process. In Six Sigma this is accomplished through the DMAIC methodology, a system for improving processes falling below aspired specification limits (Breyfogle, 2003), with the following steps: Define, Measure, Analyse, Improve, Control. Pretesting focuses on the first two steps, Define and Measure. The Analyse step involves the definition of key performance metrics and formal statistical analysis. The "Improve" step involves confronting the metrics with established norms and feeding this back into the ad design and redesign process. Posttesting, campaign evaluation, ad and brand tracking are all done once ads are placed in the media, as part of the "Control" step (see e.g., Chapter 4.2 on advertising tracking).

The next section, discusses advertising and pretesting aims, as part of the "Define" step. Then, separate sections describe pretesting designs and pretesting measures, as the two components of the "Measure" steps. Next, we summarize current pretesting practice, and end with a view on the future of pretesting.

ADVERTISING AND PRETESTING AIMS

The "Define" step involves setting advertising goals and the aims of pretesting itself. In 1982 a group of 21 leading American Advertising Agencies proposed a set of nine general principles to guide pretesting practices, known as PACT (Positioning Advertising Copy Testing) (PACT Agencies, 1982). The principles are summarized in Table 4.1.1.

Each of the nine principles still holds today, with the first and fourth principle focusing on ad and pretesting goals. The first specifies that a pretesting system should be based on measurements which are relevant to the objectives of the advertising. The fourth principle stipulates that a pretesting system should be based on a model of human response to communication. Thus, a pretest should answer questions about the reception, such as "did it catch the consumer's attention," comprehension, such as "was the message identified with the brand," and response, including persuasion and emotion, such as "did the consumer accept the proposition," and "did the consumer think or "feel" differently about the brand after exposure?" (PACT Agencies, 1982: 17). Clearly, these views are inspired by hierarchical models of ad effectiveness, such as the popular AIDA (Attention, Interest, Desire, Action) model and its successors (Starch, 1923; Strong, 1920), which have long served as descriptive models of consumer response to advertising and normative models to guide the advertising planning process. The fourth principle in addition calls for measurements that provide "executional diagnostics," i.e., information about the executional elements of the advertisement that contribute to its performance.

It is useful to distinguish four categories of advertising goals and effects: (1) processing, (2) communication, (3) action, and

Table 4.1.1 PACT principles of pretesting

Principle	Content	Description
1	Ad Objectives	A good pretesting system provides measurements which are relevant to the objectives of the advertising.
2	Decision Criterion	A good pretesting system is one which requires agreement about how the results will be used *in advance* of each specific test.
3	Multiple Measures	A good pretesting system provides multiple measurements – because single measurements are generally inadequate to assess the performance of an advertisement.
4	Model Based	A good pretesting system is based on a model of human response to communication – the *reception* of a stimulus, the *comprehension* of the stimulus and the *response* to the stimulus.
5	Media Weight	A good pretesting system allows for consideration of whether the advertising stimulus should be exposed more than once.
6	Fair Comparison	A good pretesting system recognizes that the more finished a piece of copy is, the more soundly it can be evaluated and requires, as a minimum, that alternative executions be tested in the same degree of finish.
7	Context Control	A good pretesting system provides controls to avoid the biasing effects of the exposure context.
8	Sample Adequacy	A good pretesting system is one that takes into account basic considerations of sample definition.
9	Reliability and Validity	A good pretesting system is one that can demonstrate reliability and validity.

(4) marketing goals. The four categories are ordered from specific and immediate (processing) to aggregate and delayed (marketing), and aim to have specific measurable effects on aspects of the consumer response process. *Processing goals* aim at enhancing immediate desirable consumer responses during ad exposure, essentially comprising (a) ad attention, (b) ad appreciation, such reflected in emotions, and (c) message acceptance, leading to persuasion. Whereas ad appreciation (attitude towards the ad, likeability, warmth) is more pertinent under low-involvement and other low elaboration-likelihood situations, message acceptance (yielding, persuasion), is more important under high-involvement (see Chapter 2.1). *Communication goals* aim at stimulating desirable long-term brand associations by consumers due to ad processing. Two key communication goals are brand awareness and brand attitude improvement. Brand awareness is expressed in strong associations between brand symbols and the product category, and brand attitude in associations between brand symbols and positively valenced attributes, consequences and values. *Action goals* aim at improving overt consumer actions targeted to the brand, including trial and repeat purchase, purchase frequency or quantity, and positive word-of-mouth about the brand. Finally, *marketing goals* aim at enhancing aggregate market response to the brand over time, absolute and relative to competition (including sales, market share, revenue, and profitability). These four categories of goals are central in advertising planning, campaigning and assessment. In advertising planning all four categories are a central part of the creative brief (Chapter 3.2). Actual communication effects are central in brand equity assessment (Chapter 1.4) and advertising tracking (Chapter 4.2), and action and marketing effects are the focus in modeling the sales response to advertising (Chapter 4.3). Pretesting assesses the likelihood that the target ad contributes to the desired processing and communication goals.

PRETESTING DESIGN

Between the moment that a first version of an ad is produced until media placement of the final version, two distinct types of testing are performed: concept testing and pretesting. Although both types are often subsumed under the general heading of pretesting,

Table 4.1.2   Ad testing before media placement

		Typical features	
		Concept testing	Pretesting
1	Main aim	Diagnosis	Prediction
		Select for creative development	Select for media placement
		Fine-tune creative tactics	Determine media weight
2	Stimuli	Concept, rough ads	(Semi-)finished ads
3	Focus	Processing effects, specifically	Processing effects, and
		Ad attention	communication effects:
		Ad appreciation	Brand awareness
		Message acceptance	Brand attitude
4	Design	Non-Experimental	(Quasi-) Experimental
5	Sample size	Small (50 −)	Large (100 +)
6	Measures	Qualitative	Quantitative

we distinguish them in Table 4.1.2, but will focus more on the latter, as explained in the sequel.

Concept testing is done earlier in ad development, using rough versions of the ad (storyboards, sketches, animatics), with qualitative techniques (Morrison et al., 2002), such as focus groups and personal interviews on small samples (usually 50 or less). It targets *processing* effects, consumers' immediate responses during ad exposure, such as the ad's potential to draw attention to the key elements to invoke the desired affective responses, i.e., target feelings and ad appreciation, and to elicit the desired cognitive responses, i.e., support arguments and message acceptance. The goal of concept testing is to diagnose whether the ad is on-strategy (backward looking), and to provide directions for improving the creative direction and tactics (forward looking), and it thus crucial for creative development and fine-tuning.

Pretesting (or pretesting proper) is typically done later in ad development, using (semi-) finished versions of the ad, with experimental design and statistical techniques, on larger samples (usually 100 or more). Next to processing effects, it focuses on communication effects, desirable, learned associations around the brand, specifically brand awareness and brand attitude, as well as on action effects. The goal of pretesting is to provide quality control before an ad is placed (backward looking), and to predict the likelihood that the ad will contribute to

the communication goals (forward looking). Pretests use quantitative measures of processing effects to gain insight into the drivers of the communication effects, but focus on the latter most. Pretesting involves repeated in-context presentation of ads, e.g., presentation of print ads in magazines, feature ads on newspaper pages, blocks of commercials within TV shows or radio programs, banner ads on webpages, and so on. Pretesting is also used to select which ads to run from a set, and to determine the initial media weight of ads, where ads, for example, receive media weight in proportion to their scores on performance metrics for target segments (see Chapter 5.4. for detail on ad scheduling decisions).

The difference in aims between concept testing and pretesting is important in view of principle 2 of PACT (Table 4.1.1), that a pretesting system requires agreement about how the results will be used in advance of each specific test. Using concept testing to predict potential communication effects is less useful, as is using pretesting to guide creative direction. In view of its focus on quality control and prediction, the emphasis of this chapter is on pretesting proper.

In pretesting, the performance of an ad on relevant measures is compared to *norms, benchmarks or specification limits* to allow evaluations and predictions (Lodish et al., 1995). To predict the likelihood that an advertisement contributes to the communication goals and meets the specification limits, pretests use experimental design methods to compare the results to a standard, such as the current version of the ad or a benchmark ad (Kirk, 1968; Tellis, 1998, 2004; Principle 9 of PACT). Common pretesting designs can be characterized according to whether or not they have a control group, and whether or not they involve measurement before the experiment. Four designs are therefore most common in pretesting: (1) One-Group After-Only, (2) One-Group Before-After, (3) After-Only with Control Group, (4) Before-After with Control Group. The first two designs are quasi-experimental which impedes inferences about the causality of advertising effects (Cook and Campbell, 1979). In addition to these, we point to true experimental designs, in particular (5) Factorial Designs.

In the *One-Group After-Only* design, measures of processing and communication effects are collected after a single group of consumers has been exposed to the target ad. Because the design is quasi-experimental in nature, the performance of an ad on the measures can only be compared to norms or benchmarks to allow for evaluations and predictions (see e.g., Lodish et al., 1995; Wells, 2000). Lacking specification limits or a comparison group, valid inferences about the ad's potential communication effects based solely on this design cannot be made.

In the *One-Group Before-After* design, measures of processing and communication are collected before and after consumers are exposed to the target ad. This design is used, e.g., in "theatre" pretests such as those pioneered by Horace Schwerin and Paul Lazarsfeld in the 1950s (Lipstein, 1984). Differences between before-and-after measures are calculated as a "shift" in the performance measure in question. This in turn can be compared to or corrected for norms, to arrive at a normed shift. This design is prone to validity threats such as regression toward the mean (the tendency of extremes to revert toward averages), and test effects (before measures may sensitize consumers for the ads, or consumers guess that they are supposed to change).

In the *After-Only Design with Control Group*, consumers are randomly assigned to one of two groups, one being exposed to the target ad, and the other, the control group, not being exposed to it, or being exposed to a control ad. This can be accomplished in controlled ("laboratory") environments or at home, e.g., through split-cable or web-based ad testing (Henderson Blair, 2000; Lodish et al., 1995; Tellis et al., 2000). Differences between groups in the pretest measures can be validly attributed to the effects of the target ad. Again, differences between groups can be related to general, category, brand, medium, and ad- size/duration norms. If feasible, this design is preferred for pretesting, since it allows for effects on performance to be causally attributed to ad design factors. If sensitization of participants and test effects are (assumed to be) negligible, and assessment of performance shifts is important, initial measurements may be used to render this design a *Before-After Design with Control Group.*

With the Control Group designs enabling causal inference, One Group Designs are still most often used in pretesting, for the following two reasons, in addition to tradition. First, when pretesting emphasizes quality control more so than prediction of future communication performance (Table 4.1.3), a One-Group After-Only design with normed measures may suffice, if (and only if) the predictive validity of the norms has been independently established in prior research. Second, because the same measures are collected before and after with the same consumers in a One-Group Before-After design, it generally requires lower sample sizes, at reduced costs, to find actual shifts (for these reasons the Before-After design with Control Group may be preferable too). There are several ways to limit the inherent validity threats, e.g., adding programme content and distractor ads to hide the true purpose of the research. Without such considerations, control-group designs are optimal for pretesting.

Since Hopkins' (1923) pioneering text on *Scientific Advertising*, marketers have relied on split-run and other (quasi) experimental approaches to ad testing, such as the ones

Table 4.1.3   Focal quantitative pretesting measures

Processing and Communication Objectives	Measures			
	Non-Verbal		Verbal	
	In-process	Post-process	In-process	Post-process
1 Ad attention	(A) Eye-tracking, zapping			(B) Direct memory measures of attention, recall, recognition (Starch-like)
2 Ad appreciation	(C) FACS, Psycho-physiological measures, EDA, EEG, EMG, MRI, pupil dilation	(D) Photosorting, pictorial response formats	(E) Monitoring hedonics, e.g., warmth monitor	(F) Ad response and feelings profiles
3 Message acceptance	(G) FACS, Psycho-physiological measures, EDA, EEG, EMG, MRI, pupil dilation	(H) Photosorting, pictorial response formats	(I) Monitoring instrumentality	(J) Ad response profiles
4 Brand awareness				(K) Direct memory measures, and indirect, fluency-based, measures
5 Brand attitude				(L) Standard response scales and indirect, fluency-based, measures

described above (see also Chapter 1.2). Although as yet less frequenty used in practice, other experimental designs are available and provide powerful alternatives, in particular *Factorial Designs* (Kirk, 1968). In factorial designs, combinations of sets of causal variables (factors) are tested simultaneously. Each observation is thus categorized according to more than one factor, where each factor is defined at several levels. This enables the (lack of) success of the pretested ad to be decomposed into its sources, as systematically varied in the experiment. Then, the main and interaction effects of these variables can be determined in a statistically efficient manner, i.e., with less observations than when studied one at a time. These designs provide insight into optimal ad design in terms of combinations of factors, using for example statistical response surface estimation. Such designs are more costly to implement, given that a range of different concepts needs to be developed and pretested. They can be combined with before-after measurements. Because factorial designs allow unprecedented insight into the drivers of ad effectiveness (Tellis, 1998), they may become more prominent in pretesting than currently.

PRETESTING MEASURES

Measures in pretesting are typically verbal or non-verbal, and post-process or in-process. In verbal measures, consumers are asked questions or exposed to statements, to which they respond by offering or chosing a verbal (self- or predefined) response alternative. Post-process (or: off-line) measures are collected *after* consumers have been exposed to the target ad. In-process (or: on-line) measures, also known as moment-to-moment measures, are collected continuously *during* consumers' exposure to the target ad. As a direct consequence, post-process measures cannot be collected in Before-After Designs.

Moment-to-moment measures hold the great promise of providing diagnostic insights during pretesting into the specific elements of advertisements that contribute or detract from attaining the advertising goals. Moment-to-moment measures also hold promise for advertising postesting and campaign tracking, for instance, by making it possible to establish the exact intensity and duration of advertising carryover effects (Tellis et al., 2000).

Table 4.1.3 presents main quantitative measures (verbal – non-verbal, post-process – in-process) of processing and communication effects in pretesting. Note that the measures, provided in the rows of the table, match directly with the proposed processing and communication goals, and with the preferred testing designs in Table 4.1.2. The general tendency of on-line measures to tap (short-term) processing goals, in the top-left of Table 4.1.3, and off-line measures to tap (long-term) communication goals, in the bottom-left of Table 4.1.3, is evident.

Ad attention: *Nonverbal – In-process*. Eye movements are overt, behavioural measures of the covert visual attention process of prime interest and provide direct measures of visual attention to advertising (Janiszewski, 1998; Krugman et al., 1998; Lohse, 1997; Pieters and Wedel, 2004; Wedel and Pieters, 2000). They are indicated in the top-left, cell A, in Table 4.1.3. Eye movements on stationary scenes such as advertisements comprise of fixations – moments that the eye is relatively stable – and saccades – fast ballistic movements between fixation locations to redirect the gaze. During a fixation, typically lasting around 200–300 milliseconds, a contiguous area in the ad is projected via the line of sight onto the fovea, the small area of the retina with the highest acuity, for detailed visual processing (Rayner, 1998). Eye-tracking continuously assesses that focus of attention during ad exposure, providing information on the duration of exposure to the ad as a whole, to each of the specific elements of the ad, such as the bodytext, pictorial, and brand in the case of print ads, and the moment-to-moment changes in the focus of visual attention, called the "scanpath" of eyes across the ad.

Interest in applying eye-tracking for advertising research and practice has been high since the early 1900s (Nixon, 1924; Poffenberger, 1926). Until recently however, the use of eye-tracking in research for advertising theory and practice remained limited, because it was cumbersome and unnatural for the participants, time consuming for researchers, and expensive. This has changed in recent years due to the new generations of infra-red eyetrackers, which enable eye movement recordings of large amounts of ads and consumers under natural exposure conditions at high precision and low cost.[1] Research has demonstrated how characteristics of advertisements, such as their originality, and the size of their key elements, brand, text, pictorial, reliably influence attention (Janiszewski, 1998; Krugman et al., 1998; Pieters et al., 2002). And, visual attention to advertising systematically contributes to downstream effects such as brand memory, indicating its predictive validity (Wedel and Pieters, 2000). Treistman and Greg (1979) observed that ads looked at longer in an eye-tracking experiment also attained more sales, which is indicative of even further downstream effects. A drawback of eye-tracking measures is that nonattentional ad effects, that have been reported (Janiszewski, 1998), can not be assessed, while less insight is provided into higher-order cognitive, and possibly affective effects. But, pupil dilation has been used as a measure of processing intensity and arousal (Beatty and Lucero-Wagoner, 2000), and is available as a byproduct of infra-red eyetracking.

The detailed information from eye-tracking even under brief ad exposure durations provides insights into consumers' attention patterns that cannot easily be obtained otherwise and facilitates the incorporation of eye-tracking in quantitative pretesting systems. In addition, the reduced costs of eye-tracking systems, and the fact that the ad exposure duration, often a few seconds only, is also the test duration, lowers pretesting costs substantially, allowing virtually each ad in a campaign to be tested. As a consequence, the popularity of eye-tracking in commercial pretesting applications in recent years has grown exponentially.

Ad appreciation and message acceptance: *Non-verbal – In-process.* Observation and psychophysiological measures have not been widely applied in pretesting practice, but may potentially provide unique information into advertising processing. As a consequence of their current lack of popularity, there is little published advertising research to draw from. Therefore, we suffice with a brief mention of some alternatives, see cells C and G in Table 4.1.3.

Affective responses to advertising can be observed and coded by experts, with standardized coding schemes such as FACS (Facial Action Coding System; Ekman and Friesen, 1975). Because the intensity of emotional experiences during ad exposure is often fairly small and difficult to detect, so may be the facial expressions. In a validation study (Derbaix, 1995), verbal post-process affective responses were significantly related to attitudes towards the ad, but FACS scores of consumers' facial expressions during ad exposure were not.

Affective and cognitive responses during ad exposure, in particular their intensity (arousal) may have markers in psychophysiological measures (Stern et al., 2001). Such measures tap observable, physiological responses of the brain and body that accompany unobservable, psychological processes such as consumers' perception, cognition, and emotion. While the list of potential measures is long, responses from the electrodermal, facial muscle, cardiovascular, pupil and central brain systems may hold promise for advertising theory development and perhaps pretesting practice, and thechnological developments make the techniques more accessible.

Electrodermal activity (EDA); as reflected in skin conductance) provides information about people's general states of activation or arousal (tonic) and the significance of specific stimuli (phasic) to them. Although very useful in theory development (LaBarbera and Tucciarone, 1995; VandenAbeele and MacLachlan, 1994), there are some drawbacks of using EDA measurement in

advertising practice. Because the latency of electrodermal activity is about 1–3 seconds (Dawson et al., 2000: 211), this makes them less useful as moment-to-moment measures in pretesting, where cognitive and affective responses may be faster. *Electromyography (EMG)* provides information about the facial muscles, and to the extent that emotions are expressed in the face, they may tap information about ad appreciation during ad exposure. Hazlett and Yassky Hazlett (1999), e.g., presented data that activity in the corrugator muscle (involved in frowning, lowering and contraction of the eyebrows) and in the zygomatic muscle (involved in smiling) during exposure to television commercials were reliably related to subsequent memory for the commercials. *Cardiovascular activity* as reflected in heart rate may indicate, moment-to-moment, the amount of cognitive effort dedicated to advertising processing (Lang, 1994). For instance, heart rate has been shown to go up after switching channels during television newscasts (Lang et al., 2005), which may be of use in advertising zapping studies. *Pupil dilation*, obtained as a corollary of infra-red eye-tracking, has been used as a marker for cognitive load and affective reponses (Beatty and Lucero-Wagoner, 2000), and early work in advertising has suggested (but not uncontestedly so: Loewenfeld, 1999) significant relationships with the emotional content of advertising (Hess, 1965). *Brain activity measurements* (such EEG and MRI) have been applied to gain insights in ad processing, e.g., to examine the influence of visual versus verbal information, and of specific segments in subsequent memory for television commercials (Rossiter and Silberstein, 2001; Rothschild and Hyun, 1990).

In her review of the psychophysiological literature on emotion and motivation measurement, Bradley (2000: 630) described the results of research on picture processing in which verbal measures of hedonic valence and intensity (arousal) were factor analysed with selected physiological measures. The findings show significant associations respectively between verbal measures of hedonic valence and activity of the corrugator muscle, zygomatic muscle, and heart rate, and between verbal measures of hedonic intensity (arousal) and skin conductance and viewing time. These data provide evidence for the convergent and discriminant validity of facial muscle, heart rate and skin conductance measures, and more research along these lines in the context of advertising pretesting is needed. The fairly small sample sizes in psychophysiological measurement that set hurdles to quantitative analyses and the substantial financial investments and processing times before test results become available still present barriers for widescale applications in pretesting practice. Technological advances reduce these barriers further, and the contribution of these measures to advertising theory development is undeniable.

Ad appreciation and message acceptance: *Verbal – In-process.* Moment-to-moment measures of appreciation and acceptance have been applied since the 1930s to monitor movie segments, political debates, and advertising (Peterman, 1940), cells I and J in Table 4.1.3. To this end, consumers apply a key pad, turn dial, joystick, pen, slide or mouse continuously during ad exposure to indicate their (1) momentary liking of ad, i.e., the valence of their current feelings (hedonics: ad appreciation) or "warmth" (Aaker et al., 1986), or (2) the ads informativeness or usefulness (instrumentality: message acceptance) (Woltman Elpers et al., 2003). Although such moment-to-moment verbal measurement of feelings and thoughts might unduly influence the very process that they are trying to assess, there is evidence of their reliability and validity (Fenwick and Rice, 1991; Hughes, 1992). For instance, properties of specific moments in television commercials, such as music and body movements, have been shown to evoke subsequent moment-to-moment emotional responses (VandenAbeele and MacLachlan, 1994). Such (fast) emotional responses during television commercials have been shown to precede and influence (slower) cognitive responses (Pham et al., 2001), and the highest and final level of intensity of the hedonic response (the so-called peak-end rule) during television commercials have been

shown to differentially impact subsequent memory for the television commercials (Baumgartner et al., 1997). Also, high and increasing levels of reported hedonics, but low and decreasing levels of informativeness reduce the likelihood that consumers zap away at any point during a TV commercial (Woltman Elpers et al., 2003), which supports the external validity of these measures.

Ad appreciation, message acceptance, brand awareness and attitude: *Verbal – Post-process.* General and specific verbal response profiles have been proposed to assess consumers' affective (ad appreciation) and cognitive (message acceptance) responses, and the overall attitude towards the ad, after ad exposure. Rather than being based on a strong theory of advertising processing, these profiles are often empirically derived by pruning a large item pool to a manageable set using expert judgment and statistical techniques such as factor analysis. For instance, Wells (1964) proposed an ad response profile containing three main factors, namely vitality, attractiveness, meaningfulness, across 25 semantic differential items. The three factors map directly on the processing goals: ad attention, ad appreciation, and message acceptance, and their predictive validity for attitude toward the advertised brand and purchase intention has been established (Zinkhan and Fornell, 1985). Similar general (Leavitt, 1970; Schlinger, 1979) and specific ad response profiles, e.g., for ad-evoked feelings (Edell and Chapman Burke, 1989), have been proposed.

Because verbal responses are sometimes believed to be less capable of capturing the subtle feelings that consumers experience during ad exposure, or may be prone to social sensitivity biases, non-verbal measures of ad appreciation such as pictorial response formats and photosorts have been used (Young, 2004), see cells D and H in Table 4.1.3. After exposure to the ad, consumers indicate their feeling responses for the commercial as a whole or for key scenes in it by selecting the appropriate pictures, e.g., containing people expressing specific emotions (Ekman and Friesen, 1975), in-door or outdoor scenes, or happy and sad faces. As yet, little validation research has been published, and verbal translation is usually needed to interpret the pictorial data, which attenuates their uniqueness.

To assess brand awareness and brand attitude, verbal (single or multi-item) scales are typically used for direct measurement (see Axelrod, 1968), as shown in cells K and L in Table 4.1.3. Participants are asked to indicate which brands of a particular product they are aware of, and how much they like/dislike them, which are examples of direct verbal measures. Indirect measures on the other hand infer brand attitude and awareness, for instance, from the latency of responding to brand attitude items, or the latency and accuracy of identifying the brand from a perceptually degraded version of the ad (Wedel and Pieters, 2000). The idea behind indirect measures of brand awareness and attitude is that many consumer decisions are influenced by a sense of familiarity, without conscious awareness of the ad exposure episode that gave rise to the familiarity experience (Schwarz, 1998). Thus, feelings of familiarity, the ease of retrieving arguments in favour of a brand, and the overall "fluency" of processing information about a particular alternative may predispose consumer to opt for it, without direct memory for specific situations of being exposed to advertising for the alternative. Such dissociations between direct memory (recall and recognition) and implicit memory, as reflected in fluency effects, are not uncommon, and research has demonstrated convincingly that advertising often functions through implicit, fluency and familiarity-based, "unconscious" routes (reviewed in Krishnan and Chakravarti, 1999; Heath and Nairn, 2005). Indirect measures of brand awareness and attitudes hold promise because they may be more sensitive than direct measures, and less prone to social desirable response tendencies (Greenwald and Banaji, 1995; Lee, 2002). Krishnan and Chakravarti (1999) present a diagnostic template for ad testing based on performance patterns of direct (recognition, recall) and indirect memory tests, which holds much

promise. Even though indirect measures may be both non-verbal (such as response latencies) and verbal (such as word completion tasks), we have chosen to group them with the verbal measures in Table 4.1.3, because of current pretesting practices focusing on the latter.

In addition to these measures of processing and communication effects, memory for advertising itself is often assessed in pretesting practice (Table 4.1.3, right top cell). Advertising memory comprises the explicit recollections and reconstructions by consumers of their prior exposure to advertising, for instance, whether they remember having read half or more of the text of a particular print ad in a magazine. Information about such episodic advertising memory is of interest when (1) the goal is to understand the levels and determinants of ad memorability *per se*, which we argue to be seldom the case in practice, or (2) it is an indicator of the processing or communication effects of main interest. Note that whereas *brand memory* (brand awareness) is a communication goal, *advertising memory* is not (Table 4.1.2), and it thus in general has no natural place in pretesting practice (for a review of applications see Lodish et al., 1995; Singh and Rothschild, 1983). The use of ad memory in pretesting rests on the premise that it is an indirect measure of ad attention and various other constructs. For example, recognition of print ads is considered to reflect "taking a good look and often reading" the ad (Stapel, 1998), interest value (Wells, 2000), comprehension and learning (Finn, 1988), proven recall (recalling specific message elements) and message comprehension and acceptance (Wells, 2000). Recall and recognition of radio and television commercials are measured to assess learning of the ad and its content (Rothschild and Singh, 1983), and the brand's probability of being included in the evoked set (Higie and Sewall, 1991). Ad recognition measures of print ads were pioneered early in the 20th century by Daniel Starch (1923) and others, as an alternative to visual attention measures that were not yet widely available at that time. With direct measures of attention now on hand, there appears to be little reason to use memory-based measures of attention (Biel, 1993: 29), although we are not aware of quantative research on the empirical relationships between attention to advertising and memory for attention to advertising, which is an omission. There is mounting evidence that advertising can contribute to communication effects, such as brand awareness and attitude, without explicit advertising memory as reflected in recognition and recall (Lee, 2002; see also Heath and Nairn, 2005). Partly as a result of this, the predictive validity of advertising memory measures for downstream effects such as actual sales tends to be limited (Higie and Sewall, 1991; Lodish et al., 1995; Tellis, 1998: 330), and not uncontested (Dubow, 1994).

Clearly, the specific designs and measures in pretesting are contingent on the processing and communication goals of the campaign, and these depend on the consumers' decision making processes that the campaign is trying to affect. Thus, the first consideration is whether the campaign mostly targets brand awareness or brand attitude, and in case of the former, whether brand recognition (what category is brand X in?) or brand recall (which brands are in category Y?) is the goal (Rossiter and Percy, 1997). The second consideration is whether message acceptance or message appreciation is the key. Although both of these immediate responses to advertising work in tandem, message acceptance (leading to persuasion) is more important under high involvement and similar high elaboration likelihood conditions, whereas message appreciation (attitude towards the ad, likeability, warmth) plays a larger role under low involvement (Brown and Stayman, 1992). Thus, the content of the specific verbal response profiles to be used, and the emphasis on the specific factors or subscales in them depend on these considerations. The same holds for the precise pretesting designs and exposure conditions. In case of low involvement advertising, in particular for transformational, lifestyle, soft-sell, drama variants (Deighton et al., 1989), where

multiple repetitions of ads are crucial to establish and sustain the associations with the brand, pretesting designs should allow multiple repetitions as well, following PACT principle 5. Conversely, for high-involvement advertising, in particular for informational, problem-solution, hard-sell, lecture, repeated exposures in pretesting may be less important, except when the wear-out sensitivity of the target ads is a major concern. All advertising needs attention, and to establish its success in achieving this, we believe, direct measures of attention should be used in all pretesting systems.

To sum up, implementation of the measurement of ad effectiveness is not hampered by a shortage of measures and metrics, a vast collection being available for pretests. We see a growing role for eye-tracking to assess consumer attention processes, given the increasing levels of attention competiton, that attention is more central than previously believed, and that current technology enables large-scale and precise measurements under close to natural conditions. Advertising memory measures, i.e., memory of prior exposure to ads, are fundamentally problematic and cannot serve as a substitute. But, no method is universally superior, and depending on the targeted advertising goal, measures of Attention, Appreciation, Acceptance, and brand Awareness and Attitudes (the five A's) need to be combined and integrated. Indirect brand awareness and attitude measures hold great promise for detecting changes that consumers may not be able or motivated to report (Krishnan and Chakravarti, 1999). As technology advances further, in-process nonverbal methods such as EDA, EMG, EEG and MRI may find their way to pretesting.

PRETESTING PRACTICE AND FUTURE

Pretesting is not conducted on a systematic basis throughout ad industry, which may be surprising in view of the large stakes involved. It remains a sensitive issue, with clients often in favour and agencies against (Cook and Dunn, 1996). A substantial part of agency researchers and advertising executives does not engage in pretesting at all (Whitehill King et al., 1993), and decisions about pretesting appear to be often made on an *ad hoc* basis (Jones, 2004: 141). If implemented, pretesting predominantly concerns television commercials, the most salient ad stimulus (Ambler and Goldstein, 2003). Moreover, forms of ad testing are often inappropriately applied as well. Market research directors at Top 100 advertisers (Ambler and Goldstein, 2003: 41) predominantly use qualitative pretests only (concept tests), preferring tests of rough rather than finished versions of ads, which hinders precise predictions about potential communication effects. Focus groups are commonly used in testing animatics or storyboards of television commercials (Coe and MacLachlan, 1980; Whitehill King et al., 1993), despite their acknowledged downsides for pretesting (Belch and Belch, 2001: 646). Finally, pretesting results are seldomly used jointly with posttesting and campaign tracking to predict communication, action and marketing effects once the ads run in the media (Ambler and Goldstein, 2003), which prevents learning about advertising effectiveness and improving it (Tellis, 2004).

Current pretesting practices can advance, and Six Sigma thinking has a role to play by showing how to continually analyze each element of the advertising process, its sources of variation and predictability, to determine how it compares in its current state with established norms. There are many reasons to pretest each and every single advertisement in a communication campaign, and few reasons not to. Media costs are often the largest chunk of ad campaign costs, and the media cost of running a good and a bad ad are the same, but the potential revenues of each are not. Pretesting avoids costly mistakes, and improves profitability. Pretesting is mostly inexpensive relative to campaign costs, and fast relative to campaign timing, providing diagnostic and predictive information that cannot be obtained otherwise. Moreover, management judgment of ads, which is sometimes advocated, is not a good substitute for pretesting (Armstrong, 1991; Hoch, 1988).

Will the implementation of systematic pretesting along the lines that we have advocated restrain the creative process and lead to clone ads, pretested to destruction? On the contrary, pretesting tests the creative product but leaves the creative process free. We agree with Heath and Nairn (2005) that effective campaigns may score low on inappropriate pretests (such as transformational advertising tested on ad recall), but also concur that the implication is not that pretesting in general is antithetic to ad creativity and low involvement ad campaigns. On the contrary, creative advertising has been shown to perform well in the right pretests, e.g., by standing out on moment-to-moment measures of attention to advertising, and to contribute to brand memory over and above this attention effect (Pieters et al., 2002). As one creative formulated it: "research does not come up with ideas. You come up with ideas. Research can help you to assess and strengthen them." (Davis, 1979: 42).

New generations of measurement technology and analysis methodologies are commonly accessible, enabling industrialized production of moment-to-moment metrics of advertising processing at unprecedented scale and precision. In spite of its drawbacks and criticisms, the Six Sigma quality initiative affords tools to facilitate that all ads in communication campaigns can be tested both before and after media placement, and their performance tracked over time. One step towards a more systematic use of pretesting is having a common language and agreement between ad agencies, market research companies, and advertisers about appropriate processing and communication goals, and designs and measures and metrics to assess these. Here it can help to have concise specifications, such as those proposed here, of processing and communication goals, and how they relate to marketing objectives, norms/benchmarks derived from those objectives, a focus on the five A's of attention, appreciation, acceptance, (brand) awareness and attitude measures, and powerful experimental designs combined with statistical methods for analyzing, benchmarking and prediction. We emphasized processing and communication goals, because "If you don't know where you are going, any road will take you there," as Lewis Carroll explained in *Alice in Wonderland*.

After more than a century of progress in the theory and practice of advertising and pretesting, the time is ripe for a new PACT with a task force to guide its implementation in industry. It is time to move to the next phase in advertising's evolution, and the advertising industry should make a commitment to enable this. Over and above specifying the requirements for optimal pretesting systems, such as its proven validity and reliability, the new PACT should courageously establish the content of the constructs and measures, and standards, norms and specification limits for such systems. Of course, advertising effectiveness depends on many other factors next to the control variables of the ad or campaign, such as heterogeneity in preferences in the market, other factors in the marketing mix, and competitive dynamics. Pretesting therefore will not predict advertising effectiveness in the market place perfectly, and levels of *Six Sigma* may not be feasible or too costly. It is however in the interest of both companies and consumers to push the envelope on ad quality several Sigma levels. Rather than signaling a lack of trust between clients and agencies, systematically pretesting of advertising expresses the maturity of their relationship, and enhances the professional level of the industry at large.

SUMMARY

This chapter linked the key processing and communication goals of advertising to preferred designs and measures for pretesting, or copy testing, advertising before media placement. In 1982 a group of 21 leading American Advertising Agencies proposed a set of nine general principles to guide pretesting practices: "Positioning Advertising

Copy Testing" (PACT Agencies, 1982). These principles have been integrated with developments in quality control practice.

PACT has two stages: "Define" sets the advertising and pretesting aims and "Measure" deals with the pretest design and measures. Concept testing should be distinguished from pretesting a campaign.

Pretesting is not conducted on a systematic basis throughout ad industry, which may be surprising in view of the large stakes involved. It remains a sensitive issue, with clients often in favour and agencies against (Cook and Dunn, 1996). We believe that pretesting tests the creative product but leaves the creative process free but we agree that inappropriate forms of pretesting can inhibit ad development.

This chapter offers new developments in monitoring the moment-to-moment processing of advertising, among others as related to eyetracking. Pretesting cannot predict campaign results perfectly but, after over 100 years of developing the theory and practice of advertising and pretesting, the time is ripe for a new PACT with experts to guide its implementation.

NOTE

1 See, for example, www.Tobii.com.

REFERENCES

Aaker, D.A., D.M. Stayman, and M. Hagerty (1986), "Warmth in Advertising: Measurement, Impact and Sequence Effects," *Journal of Consumer Research*, 12 (4), 365–81.

Ambler, T., and S. Goldstein (2003), *Copy Testing: Practice and Best Practice: A Review of UK Advertising Research Practice*, Hampshire, UK: The Basingstoke Press.

Armstrong, S. (1991), "Prediction of Consumer Behavior by Experts and Novices," *Journal of Consumer Research*, 18 (September), 251–6.

Axelrod, J. (1968), "Attitude Measures that Predict Purchase," *Journal of Advertising Research*, 8 (1), 3–17.

Baumgartner, H., M. Sujan, and D. Padgett (1997), "Patterns of Affective Reactions to Advertisments: The Integration of Moment-to-Moment Responses into Overall Judgments," *Journal of Marketing Research*, 34, 219–32.

Beatty, J., and B. Lucero-Wagoner (2000), "The Pupillary System," in *Handbook of Psychophysiology*, eds. J. Cacioppo, L.G. Tassinary, and G.G. Berntson, Cambridge, Cambridge University Press, 142–62.

Belch, G.E., and M.A. Belch (2001), *Advertising and Promotion: An Integrated Marketing Communications Perspective*, 5th ed., Boston: McGraw-Hill.

Biel, A.L. (1993), "Ad Research in the US; Hurdle or Help? A Brief Review of the State of the Art," *AdMap*, 329 (May), 27–29.

Bradley, M.M. (2000), "Emotion and Motivation," in *Handbook of Psychophysiology*, eds. J.T. Cacioppo, L.G. Tassinary, and G.G. Berentson Cambridge, UK: Cambridge University Press, 602–42.

Breyfogle, F.W. (2003). *Implementing Six Sigma*. New York: Wiley.

Brown, S.P., and D.M. Stayman (1992), "Antecedents and Consequences of Attitude Toward the Ad: A Meta-Analysis," *Journal of Consumer Research*, 19 (1), 34–51.

Burke, R., and T.K. Srull (1988), "Competitive Interference and Consumer Memory for Advertising," *Journal of Consumer Research*, 15 (June), 55–68.

Coe, B.J., and J. MacLachlan (1980), "How Major TV Advertisers Evaluate Commercials," *Journal of Advertising Research*, 20 (6), 51–4.

Cook, T.D., and D.T. Campbell (1979), *Quasi-Experimentation: Design and Analysis Issues for Field Settings*, Boston: Houghton-Mifflin.

Cook, W.A., and T.F. Dunn (1996), "The Cahnging face of Advertising Research in the Information Age: An ARF Copy Research Council Survey," *Journal of Advertising Research*, 36, (January/February), 55–71.

Davis, H. (1979), "Is It Blasphemy? Creative Director Praises Research?" *Advertising Age* (June 11), 41–2.

Dawson, M.E., A.M. Schell, and D.L. Filion (2000), "The Electrodermal System," in *Handbook of Psychophysiology*, eds. J.T. Cacioppo, L.G. Tassinary, and G.G. Berentson, Cambridge, UK: Cambridge University Press, 200–23.

Deighton, J., D. Romer, and J. McQueen (1989), "Using Drama to Persuade," *Journal of Consumer Research*, 16 (December), 335–43.

Dekimpe, M.G., and D.M. Hanssens (2007), "Advertising Response Models," in *The SAGE Handbook of Advertising*, eds. G.J. Tellis and T. Ambler, London: Sage Publications.

Derbaix, C.M. (1995), "The Impact of Affective Reactions on Attitudes toward The Advertisement and Brand: A Step toward Ecological Validity," *Journal of Marketing Research*, 32 (4), 470–9.

Dudow, J.S. (1994), "Point of View: Recall Revisited: Recall Redux," *Journal of Advertising Research*, (May/June), 92–106.

Edell, J., and M. Chapman Burke (1989), "Ad-Based Emotions, Affect and Cognition," *Journal of Marketing Research*, (February), 69–83.

Ekman, P., and W.V. Friesen (1975), *Unmasking the Face*, Englewood Cliffs, NJ: Prentice Hall.

Finn, A. (1988), "Print Ad Recognition Readership Scores: An Information Processing Perspective," *Journal of Marketing Research*, 25 (May), 168–77.

Greenwald, A.G., and M.R. Banaji (1995), "Implicit Social Cognition: Attitudes, Self-Esteem, and Stereotypes," *Psychological Review*, 102 (1), 4–27.

Hazlett, R.L., and S. Yassky Hazlett (1999), "Emotional Responses to Television Commercials: Facial EMG vs. Self-Report," *Journal of Advertising Research*, (March), 7–23.

Heath, R., and A. Nairn (2005), "Measuring Affective Advertising: Implications of Low Attention Processing on Recall," *Journal of Advertising Research*, (June), 269–81.

Henderson Blair, M. (2000), "An Empirical Investigation of Advertising Wearin and Wearout," *Journal of Advertising Research* (November/December), 95–100.

Hess, E.H. (1965), "Attitude and Pupil Size, *Scientific American*, 212, 46–54.

Higie, R.A., and M.A. Sewall (1991), "Using Recall and Brand Preference to Evaluate Advertising Effectiveness," *Journal of Advertising Research*, (April/May), 56–63.

Hoch, S.J. (1988), "Who Do We Know: Predicting the Interests and Opinions of The American Consumer," *Journal of Consumer Research*, 15, 315–24.

Hopkins, C.C. (1990). *My Life in Advertising and Scientific Advertising*, Two works by Claude C. Hopkins, Lincolnwood, Ill.: NTC Press (original 1923).

Hughes, G.D. (1992), "Realtime Response Measures Redefine Advertising Wearout," *Journal of Advertising Research*, 32 (May/June), 61–77.

Janiszewski, C. (1998), "The Influence of Display Characteristics on Visual Exploratory Search Behavior," *Journal of Consumer Research*, 25 (December), 290–301.

Jones, J.-P. (2004), *Fables, Fashions, and Facts About Advertising*, Thousand Oaks, CA: Sage Publications.

Keller, K.L. (2007), "Advertising and Brand Equity," in *The SAGE Handbook of Advertising*, eds. G.J. Tellis and T. Ambler, London: Sage Publications.

Kirk, R.E. (1968), *Experimental Design Procedures for the Behavioral Sciences*, Belmont, CA: Brooks/Cole Publishing Company.

Krishnan, S., and D. Chakravarti (1999), "Memory Measures for Pretesting Advertisements, An Integrative Conceptual Framework and Diagnostic Template," *Journal of Consumer Psychology*, 8 (1), 1–37.

Krugman, D.M., R.J. Fox, J.E. Fletcher, P.M. Fischer, and T.H. Rojas (1994), "Do Adolescents Attend to Warnings in Cigarette Advertising? An Eye-Tracking Approach," *Journal of Advertising Research*, 34 (6), 39–52.

LaBarbera, P.A., and J.D. Tucciarone (1995), "GSR Reconsidered: A Behavior-Approach to Evaluating and Improving the Sales Potency of Advertising," *Journal of Advertising Research*, 35 (September/ October), 33–53.

Lang, A. Ed (1994), "What Can the Heart Tell Us About Thinking?" *Measuring Psychological Responses to Media Messages*, Hillsdale, NJ: Lawrence Erlbaum Associates, 99–111.

Lang, A., M. Shin, S.D. Bradley, Z. Wang, S. Lee, and D. Potter (2005), "Wait! Don't Turn That Dial! More Excitement to Come! The Effects of Story Length and Production Pacing in Local Television News on Channel Changing Behavior and Information Processing in a Free Choice Environment," *Journal of Broadcasting and Electronic Media*, 49 (1), 3–22.

Lee, A. (2002), "Effects of Implicit Memory on Memory-Based versus Stimulus-Based Brand Choice," *Journal of Marketing Research*, 39, 440–54.

Leavitt, C. (1970), "A Multidimensional Set of Rating Scales for Television Commercials," *Journal of Applied Psychology*, 54, 427–9.

Lipstein, B. (1984), "A Historical Perspective of Copy Research," *Journal of Advertising Research*, 24 (December), 11–15.

Lodish, L.M., M. Abraham, S. Kalmenson, J. Livelsberger, B. Lubetkin, B. Richardson, and M.E. Stevens (1995), "How T.V. Advertising Works: A Meta-Analysis of 389 Real World Split Cable T.V. Advertising Experiments," *Journal of Marketing Research*, 32 (2), 125–39.

Lohse, G.L. (1997), "Consumer Eye Movement Patterns on Yellow Page Advertising," *Journal of Advertising*, 26 (1), 61–73.

Loewenfeld, I.A. (1999), *The Pupil: Anatomy, Physiology, and Clinical Applications*, Boston: Butterworth-Heinemann.

McDonald, C., and J. Scott (2007), "Brief History of Advertising," in *The SAGE Handbook of Advertising*, eds. G.J. Tellis and T. Ambler, London: Sage Publications.

Morrison, M.A., E. Haley, K. Bartel Sheehan, and R.E. Taylor (2002), *Using Qualitative Research in Advertising: Strategies, Techniques, and Applications*, Thousand Oaks, CA.: Sage Publications.

Nixon, H.K. (1924), "Attention and Interest in Advertising," *Archives of Psychology*, 72 (1), 5–67.

PACT Agencies (1982), "PACT: Positioning Advertising Copy Testing," *Journal of Advertising*, 11 (4), 3–29.

Pai, S., S. Siddarth, and S. Divakar (2007), "Advertising Tracking," in *The SAGE Handbook of Advertising*, eds. G.J. Tellis and T. Ambler, London: Sage Publications.

Peterman, J.N. (1940), "The Program Analyzer," *Journal of Applied Psychology*, 24, 728–41.

Petty, R.E., T.M. Ostrom, and T.C. Brock (1981), *Cognitive Responses in Persuasion*, Hillsdale, NJ: Lawrence Erlbaum, Publishers.

Pham, M.T., J.B. Cohen, J.W. Pracejus, and G.D. Hughes (2001), "Affect Monitoring and the Primacy of Information in Judgment," *Journal of Consumer Research*, 28, 167–88.

Pieters, R., L. Warlop, and M. Wedel (2002), "Breaking Through the Clutter: Benefits of Ad Originality and Familiarity on Visual Attention and Brand Memory," *Management Science*, 48 (6), 765–81.

Pieters, R., and M. Wedel (2004), "Attention Capture and Transfer in Advertising: Brand, Pictorial and Text-Size Effects," *Journal of Marketing*, 68 (April), 36–50.

Poffenberger, A.T. (1926), *Psychology in Advertising*, Chicago and New York: A.W. Shaw Company.

Rayner, K. (1998), "Eye Movements in Reading and Information Processing: 20 Years of Research," *Psychological Bulletin*, 124 (3), 372–422.

Rosbergen, E., R. Pieters, and M. Wedel (1997), "Visual Attention to Advertising: A Segment-Level Analysis," *Journal of Consumer Research*, 24 (December), 305–14.

Rossiter, J.R., and L. Percy (1997), *Advertising Communications and Promotion Management*, 2nd ed., New York: The McGraw-Hill Companies.

Rossiter, J.R., and R.B. Silberstein (2001), "Brain-Imaging Detection of Visual Scene Encoding in Long-Term Memory for TV Commercials," *Journal of Advertising Research*, (March/April), 13–21.

Rothschild, M., and Y.J. Hyun (1990), "Predicting Memory for Components of TV Commercials from EEG," *Journal of Consumer Research*, 16, 472–8.

Rucker, D.D., R.E. Petty, and J.R. Priester (2007), "Understanding Advertising Effectiveness from Psychological Perspectives: The Importance of Attitudes and Attitude Strength," in *The SAGE Handbook of Advertising*, eds. G.J. Tellis and T. Ambler, London: Sage Publications.

Schwarz, N. (1998), Accessible Content and Accessible Experiences: The Interplay Between Declarative Content and Experiential Information in Judgment," *Personality and Social Psychology Review*, 2, 87–99.

Shen, F. (2002), "Banner Advertisement Pricing, Measurement, and Pretesting Practices: Perspectives from Interactive Agencies," *Journal of Advertising*, 31 (3), 59–67.

Singh, S.N., and M.L. Rothschild (1983), "Recognition as a Measure of Learning from Television Commercials," *Journal of Marketing Research*, 20 (August), 235–48.

Stapel, J. (1998), "Recall and Recognition: A Very Close Relationship," *Journal of Advertising Research*, (July/August), 41–5.

Starch, D. (1923), *Principles of Advertising*, Chicago: A.W. Shaw Company.

Stern, R.M., W.J. Ray, and K.S. Quigley (2001), *Psychophsiological Recording*, 2nd ed., Oxford: Oxford University Press.

Storey, R., and E. Smit (2007), "Creative Brief and Its Strategic Role in the Campaign Development Process," in *The SAGE Handbook of Advertising*, eds. G.J. Tellis and T. Ambler, London: Sage Publications.

Strong, E.K. (1920), "Theories of Selling," *Journal of Applied Psychology*, 9 (February), 75–86.

Tellis, G.J. (1998), *Advertising and Sales Promotion Strategy*, Reading, Mass.: Addison-Wesley.

Tellis, G.J. (2004), *Effective Advertising: Understanding When, How, and Why Advertising Works*, Thoasand Oaks, Ca.: Sage Publications.

Tellis, G.J., R. Chandy, and P. Thaivanaich (2000), "Decomposing the Effects of Direct Advertising: Which Brand Works, When, Where, and How Long?, *Journal of Marketing Research*, 37 (February), 32–46.

Treistman, J., and J.P. Greg (1979), "Visual, Verbal and Sales Response to Print Ads," *Journal of Advertising Research*, 19 (4), 41–7.

Vakratsas, D., and P.A. Naik (2007), "Essentials of Planning Flighted Media Schedules," in *The SAGE Handbook of Advertising*, eds. G.J. Tellis and T. Ambler, London: Sage Publications.

VandenAbeele, P., and D.L. MacLachlan (1994), "Process Tracing of Emotional Responses to TV Ads: Revisiting the Warmth Monitor," *Journal of Consumer Research*, 20, 586–600.

Wedel, M., and R. Pieters (2000), "Eye Fixations on Advertisements and Memory for Brands: A Model and Findings," *Marketing Science*, 19 (4), 297–312.

Wells, W. (1964), "EQ, Son of EQ, and the Reaction Profile," *Journal of Marketing*, 28 (October), 45–52.

Wells, W. (2000), "Recognition, Recall, and Rating Scales," *Journal of Advertising Research*, (November/December), 14–20.

Whitehill King, K., J.D. Pehrson, and L.N. Reid (1993), "Pretesting TV Commercials: Methods, Measures, and Changing Agency Roles," *Journal of Advertising*, 22 (3), 85–97.

Woltman Elpers, J.L.C.M., M. Wedel, and R. Pieters (2003), "Why Do Consumers Stop Viewing Television Commercials? Two Experiments on the Influence of Moment-to-Moment Entertainment and Information Value," *Journal of Marketing Research*, 40 (November), 437–53.

Young, C.E. (2004), "Capturing the Flow of Emotion in Television Commercials: A New Approach," *Journal of Advertising Research*, (June), 202–9.

Zinkhan, G.M., and C. Fornell (1985), "A Test of Two Consumer Response Scales in Advertising," *Journal of Marketing Research*, 22 (November), 447–52.

Advertising Tracking

Seema Pai, S. Siddarth and
Suresh Divakar

Advertisers and their agencies use a variety of tracking methods to gain insights into what is right or wrong with ongoing ad campaigns. Specifically, tracking studies are used to identify whether ad campaigns work, how they compare to competitors' campaigns and to provide diagnostics that may guide efforts to improve ad effectiveness. Because firms use advertising to achieve a range of goals including informing consumers about a product, attracting attention, increasing brand preference, instilling loyalty, generating trial, increasing purchase frequency and increasing sales and profits, a wide variety of tracking studies, relying on very different metrics, are needed to measure the success of advertising. In a pre-test setting, research provides diagnostic information about a test advertisement's potential for achieving a firm's communication objectives. An implemented ad's actual success in attaining these objectives is measured through post-test tracking of advertising, which is the main focus of this chapter.

Vakratsas and Ambler (1999) identify three dimensions – cognitive, persuasive and behavioural – of how advertising may impact consumers. These categories also represent a useful way to classify tracking methods and their associated metrics. Thus, exposure and awareness measures get at the cognitive impact of advertising, preference and liking measures are based on its affective impact, while sales and other direct response measures such as click-throughs represent the behavioural dimension. The metrics used by each method also have different implications for advertising strategy. Thus, memory-based metrics are more diagnostic in decisions regarding media choice and exposure frequency, persuasion-based measures provide insights into the impact of ad copy and execution, while behavioural measures enable firms to evaluate the return on investment on advertising and to make budget-related decisions.

This chapter provides an overview of the approaches used to track the cognitive, persuasive, affective and behavioural impact of the communication strategies used by a firm. The discussion covers traditional measures used to track the advertising effects of print, radio and television advertising, which currently account for a majority of firms' advertising budgets, as well as tracking methods used to monitor other communication approaches like direct-mail, telemarketing and the Internet, whose use has grown exponentially in recent years.

TRACKING THE COGNITIVE EFFECTS OF ADVERTISING

Exposure and awareness

Contemporary message research traces its roots back to the 19th century when measures of recall and memory were obtained as indicators of the effectiveness of print advertising. Memory phenomena have occupied a central place in thinking about the process and effects of advertising. It is generally believed that exposure to an advertisement leads to a series of events that result in a memory trace. The memory-based approach to measuring advertising effectiveness has largely centred around two concepts, namely recall and recognition. In the rest of this section, we discuss the evolution of memory-based measures in commercial advertising tracking and the key differences between these two concepts.

The first practical measures for advertising tracking were devised in the 1920s by Daniel Starch and George Gallup. In 1922, Starch decided to devise a procedure to measure the readership of advertisements on a continuous basis as they appeared in publications. Starch's procedure was adapted from an advertising pre-testing procedure developed by Walter Dill Scott and Edward K. Strong who interviewed a sample of people regarding recognition of dummy ads to which they had been exposed. Starch's method was engineered to test the recognition of print advertisements that people were exposed to in the course of their regular daily lives. Starch's model led him to devise the Starch Test, a recognition-based system for the measurement of "reading and noting" of press advertising. However, the Starch Test did not take into account the decay in memory resulting from the time gap which elapses between exposure of advertising and actual purchase of the product. George Gallup devised a different intermediate measure known as "Spontaneous Recall" or "Unaided Recall" that allowed for this memory decay.

Recognition measures are obtained by confronting subjects with the original material and asking whether it has been seen or heard before, while recall measures require subjects to be provided a minimal cue and to see if they can retrieve and reconstruct the original information. For instance, in Gallup's Spontaneous recall test, the respondent is asked whether he/she remembers having seen an ad for a particular product category during the past month. On the other hand, in a recognition test, the respondent is shown a series of ads one at a time and is asked to respond "yes" if she remembers seeing the ad and "no" if she does not (Singh and Cole, 1985). Hence, for recall the individual must describe a stimulus which is not present; for recognition the stimulus must merely be identified as having been previously seen or heard (Bettman, 1979). This is a key difference between the two measures.

Later, when TV advertising came into existence in the 1940s, Gallup and Claude Robinson pioneered the popular "Day-after-recall" technique which was the principal measure of communication effectiveness for several years to come. However, it was Gordon Brown who turned recall into the popular and potent metric it has become today. Brown realized that genuine spontaneous recall was going to gradually lose relevance as advertising became increasingly commonplace and therefore devised a more sensitive metric known as ad awareness. Thus, consumers were shown a list of brands and asked the question "which of these brands have you seen advertised on television recently?" The resulting metric known as "ad awareness" led to the development of an "Awareness Index" which provided a single-number score for the amount of claimed ad awareness generated per 100 Gross Rating Points (GRPs) for the campaign. Unlike earlier recall measures, which provided the product category as a cue for consumers to recall advertising, the Awareness Index cued customers with an actual list of brands. This metric gained popularity when Colman and Brown (1986) showed that this Awareness Index was positively correlated to sales.

The Awareness index taps into the most basic level of awareness, i.e., it only measures whether an ad as a whole has been noticed. However, advertisers may also intend for consumers to notice *specific* elements of an ad and associate these features with the advertised brand. This led to the development of more detailed recall measures that go beyond the basic index by capturing elements of consumers' memories for particular advertising information included in the ad.

Several commercial firms provide services that track these metrics. The Starch Readership Service measures reader awareness of magazine advertisements. Advertising indices for each ad are developed by measuring the extent, to which consumers have processed an ad in categories such as "noted," "associated," "read-some" and "read-most." One index compares an advertisement's scores against the average scores for all ads in the magazine issue and the second compares an advertisement's scores against other ads in the same product category as well as the same size and colour classifications. A basic assumption of the Starch procedure is that respondents do in fact remember whether they saw a particular ad in a specific magazine issue. Since these studies have a long history (Starch has been conducting them since the 1920s) an extensive database of norms is available for advertisers and media planners to evaluate the effectiveness of particular advertisements. Millward Brown provides similar awareness measures for television advertising and also has a well-established set of norms against which the effectiveness of a particular television advertisement can be measured. A key strength of the Millward Brown Index is that it measures advertising in more than forty countries around the globe thereby providing international benchmarks on advertising effectiveness.

The Bruzzone Research Company (BRC) provides advertisers with a test of consumer recognition of television commercials. The Bruzzone Company has also performed a large number of tests over time and thus established norms that can be used as a benchmark. BRC has also developed an Advertising Response Model which links consumer responses to 27 descriptive adjectives about the ad to consumer attitudes toward the ad, the brand as well as to purchase intention. Traditionally, the Bruzzone test has involved traditional surface mailing of advertising storyboards to a sample of consumers. However, with the growth of the Internet, these kinds of tests are now performed online as well.

Gallup & Robinson and Mapes & Ross are examples of research firms that provide recall testing of ads placed in print media while Ipsos-ASI and Burke are two firms that test consumer recall of television commercials. Burke reports *claimed recall scores* and *related recall scores* for each tested commercial: *Claimed recall scores* measure the percentage of consumers who recall seeing a particular ad when provided with a product or brand cue (Aided recall) while *Related recall scores* indicate the percentage of consumers who are able to describe elements of the ad execution.

Despite their widespread use, considerable controversy has surrounded both recall and recognition with scholars and practitioners arguing over their relative usefulness (Copland, 1958; Lucas and Britt, 1963; Haskins, 1964; Krugman, 1972; Bagozzi and Silk, 1983). The genesis of this controversy lies in a study by the Advertising Research Foundation (ARF) on "Printed Advertising Rating Methods" (PARM). The PARM study compared recall and recognition scores for a cross-section of ads that had appeared in the same issue of *Life* magazine. Lucas (1960) observed that the mean recognition ratings showed no tendency to drop off with the passage of time while the recall scores dropped substantially over time. Lucas concluded that since memory should decline with the passage of time, recall could be considered a measure of memory while recognition should not. Neu (1961) on the other hand used evidence from the Starch Readership survey to show that recognition scores did actually decline with the passage of time. Wells (1964) showed that reader interest was more strongly associated with recognition than recall. However, an experiment by Appel and Blum (1961) shows that respondents tend to over-report recognition thereby making recognition scores an unreliable measure. This conflict has achieved some level of resolution following studies by Krugman (1972, 1977) that suggest that retention of "verbal content" or print ads can be suitably measured by recall, whereas what is stored in "image memory" is better measured by recognition.

Some research has raised questions about the value of using Day-After Recall as a metric of ad effectiveness. Heath and Hyder (2005) show that Day-After-Recall testing is biased against certain types of advertising content, specifically advertising that is significantly emotive or based on affect-oriented themes. A study conducted by the Foote Cone and Belding advertising agency, comparing three rational or thought-oriented commercials to three emotionally oriented commercials, also supports this finding. Ambler (2000) concludes that it is the "Affective" or "Emotional" content of advertising that drives effectiveness. In 2005, a new project, "Emotional Response to Advertising Study," sponsored by the Advertising Research Foundation and the American Association of Advertising Agencies, was launched to analyze the ability to measure consumers emotional response to advertising (Marketing News, 2005).

Another major criticism of recall as a measure of advertising effectiveness is that it may not link well to sales performance. For example, a meta-analysis of real-world split-cable TV advertising experiments showed a weak relationship between standard recall measures and sales effectiveness (Lodish et al., 1995a) and a later meta-analysis of about 60 sales-analysis studies done by Dyson (1998) at Millward Brown concluded that the correlation between the Awareness Index and sales was close to zero.

TRACKING THE AFFECTIVE IMPACT OF ADVERTISING

Persuasion

Over time, marketers as well as consumer psychologists have become increasingly interested in understanding how consumers' evaluations of issues, products and candidates are affected by media advertising. Almost all of the research in this area is based on the Fishbein-Ajzen's model of the relationship between attitude and behaviour called The Theory of Reasoned Action (Fishbein and Ajzen, 1975, 1980), which posits that a person's behaviour is determined by his/her intention to perform the behaviour and that this intention is, in turn, a function of his/her attitude toward the behaviour The *Affect Transfer Hypothesis* (Gardner, 1985; Mitchell and Olson, 1981; Shimp, 1981) posits a direct one-way causal flow from attitude towards the ad (A_{ad}) to attitude towards the brand (A_b). This theory argues that attitudes can be changed through advertising and created an entirely new approach to evaluating advertising effectiveness based on its ability to "persuade" consumers to change their attitudes or preferences towards brands.

This approach has resulted in several measures of the extent to which advertising changes consumers' attitude or preference for the advertised brand or how it impacts behavioural measures such as purchase intent and purchase frequency. For example, by providing alternate measures of persuasion, the Ipsos-Next*TV method approach allows advertisers to evaluate ads in terms of the specific objectives that the ad hopes to achieve. The Advertising Research Service (ARS) Persuasion method asks respondents to indicate which of a list of pre-specified brands in multiple categories they would prefer to receive if their names were selected in a drawing to win a "basket" of free items (the *premeasure*). After exposure to a television program within which the test commercial is embedded, respondents again indicate what brands they would prefer to receive if their names were selected in a drawing (the *postmeasure*). The ARS Persuasion score represents the postmeasure percentage of respondents preferring the target brand minus the premeasure percentage who prefer the brand. Results of 155 tested commercials from Belgium, Canada, Germany, Mexico, the United Kingdom and the United States have demonstrated that ARS Persuasion scores are valid predictors of in-market performance (Dodd, 1964; Kelly, 1964; Murphy, 1968). A key problem with using measures of persuasion in advertising tracking is that whereas measures of ad exposure are quite sensitive and fluctuate markedly, image measures are usually slow-moving at best. This makes their continuous measurement not just costly, but also frustrating (Heath and Hyder, 2005).

Recently, the "brand commitment" construct has grown in popularity. Brand commitment is defined as the emotional or psychological attachment to a brand within a product class (Lastovicka and Gardner, 1977), reflecting the degree to which a brand is firmly entrenched as the only acceptable choice within such a product class (Traylor, 1981). Although brand commitment implies brand loyalty, the reverse does not hold true as the repeat purchase metrics typically use to measure brand loyalty may merely reflect the consumer's need to reduce effort, simplify decision making or take advantage of promotional prices. Alternative versions of this metric ranging from purchase intent or "first choice brand" to a more complete commitment model have been incorporated into tracking studies, for example via Carat's media/channel focused "cognitive tracking" (White, 2005; Beirne et al., 2003). It may be useful to point out that the persuasion-based advertising metrics described above are an important subset of the many different activities typically used to monitor brand equity and brand-health.

TRACKING THE BEHAVIOURAL IMPACT OF ADVERTISING

Sales, calls and clicks

This section describes some advertising tracking approaches that seek to link advertising and promotional campaigns to key business results, such as volume and dollar sales. Historically, interest in this analysis grew out of the need for marketers to demonstrate the financial impact of marketing as the key driver of marketplace performance. Without the ability to tie marketing activities to the bottom line, marketers face an uphill battle to justify their budgets. Furthermore, without a clear understanding of the effectiveness of different marketing efforts (e.g., good versus bad advertising campaigns) managers are poorly poised to make reallocation decisions when budgets are cut.

Over the past few decades, the use of other forms of communication, such as direct mail and telemarketing has rapidly increased and the growth of the World Wide Web has created a whole new alternate medium for advertising. Both direct marketing and internet advertising are primarily used to drive consumer behaviour (e.g., visiting the company's website or calling the firm that sent the direct mailer), and both approaches generate a host of response variables, such as click-throughs and call backs, which can be directly linked to the advertising that generated them.

Two main approaches traditionally used to quantify the sales response of advertising are Advertising Field Experiments and Econometric analysis. In recent years, Econometric analysis has also been extensively used to analyse response data generated by new communication approaches such as direct marketing, telemarketing and the Internet.

Advertising field experiments

Field experiments expose two (or more) groups of consumers to base and test advertising, respectively and use the differences in sales rates between the groups to measure the impact of the advertising "treatment." Eastlack and Rao (1986) report on the results of some early experiments performed at the Campbell Soup Company that analysed the impact of a new marketing campaign on the sales of V-8 Cocktail Vegetable Juice. The experimental units for the advertising treatment and control groups in these studies were defined by geographical areas defined by Selling Areas Marketing Inc. (SAMI markets) and sales was measured by warehouse withdrawals in these markets over 4 weeks. A set of markets which retained the old, primarily radio, based advertising for the V-8 Cocktail Vegetable Juice served as the control while the treatment groups consisted of a combination of higher budgets, a different media mix and creative execution.

These experiments showed that the new campaign and media mix was significantly better than the existing one and helped management to decide to implement the campaign nationwide. Eastlack and Rao (1989) report on a number of similar follow-up studies that used a similar experimental set-up to examine the impact of advertising budgets, seasonality, changes in the media mix and creative strategy on a variety of different products.

While these experiments were path-breaking in nature, the implementation required significant effort and commitment from the top management at the company to incur the costs required to implement the experiments. These included additional media buys to study the impact of increased media weight (heavy up tests), operational costs of replacing or blacking out nationally aired commercials in specific experimental markets, staff time for monitoring and administering the experiments and, most importantly, the willingness to tolerate the possibly adverse long-term impacts of experimental treatments. Further, the sales response measures used (warehouse withdrawals) had limited accuracy as they assumed a constant store inventory and did not necessarily coincide with market-level consumer demand. Finally, because these experiments relied on comparing sales in two or more relatively large test cities or areas, it was harder to find a match on all of the characteristics of one community with another.

The advent of single-source data, described in greater detail below, addressed many of these shortcomings providing an opportunity to conduct field experiments more economically and with a greater degree of precision than previously possible.

Single-source data: Technological advancements in data capture in three different areas have helped make single source data a reality. These are: (1) optical laser scanning of universal product codes at retail checkouts, (2) electronic television metres to capture household viewing behaviour and (3) split-cable technology, which permits different TV commercials to appear on the same television program within the same geographic region.

Single-source data contains information on a household's brand purchases, based on its shopping behaviour, advertising exposures, based on its TV viewing behaviour, as well as the marketing stimuli that are encountered in the retail store environment. Further, areas with split-cable systems allow two households watching the same program to see two different commercials at the same time by intercepting the network feed and inserting certain commercials in the transmission to specific households. For example, the technology permits one group of households to view different commercials or receive more advertising weight than another group of households. This information is collected from matched groups of households in a representative geographic market who are tracked for a relatively long period for time, typically two or three years.

To test alternative T.V. advertising plans, the split-cable approach splits household panels into two or more sub-groups that are balanced on past purchasing behaviour, demographics and stores shopped over a one-year base period. These samples form different experimental cells or treatment groups and the matching procedure makes it easier to attribute differences in the test period to the effect of the treatment rather than to pre-existing differences between the groups or to an interaction between the test variable and pre-existing differences. Thus, these households, shop in the same set of stores and are therefore exposed to the same set of distribution and marketing mix variables, which rules out alternative explanations of differences between two cells. After a suitable period of time, which is usually a year, the test is ended, and the results are analyzed using analysis of covariance to remove the impact of uncontrolled factors such as competitive and test brand promotions.

The major advantages of the split cable technique over traditional advertising field experiments are the ability to match household samples in different cells and to monitor the elements of the marketing mix. Further because the panels are typically established in small Designated Marketing Areas (DMAs) the cost of testing can often be much lower than using large scale field experiments in which the advertising "buys" have to cover much larger areas and populations.

Lodish and Reibstein (1986) expected these technologies to open the "black box" of consumer response to advertising. Moreover, Jones (1995) states that single-source data offers the most alluring promise of solving the mystery of how advertising works. While this objective may not yet have been achieved, these techniques have provided valuable insights into how advertising works (Blair and Rosenberg, 1994) and provided managers with a powerful tool to track the performance of advertising in the marketplace. IRI's BehaviourScan is the major commercial source for this data. Based on this data, Lodish et al. (1995) report the results of about four hundred different BehaviourScan split cable TV Advertising Experiments that shed insights into the short- and long-term impact of various facets of advertising on sales.

Econometric analysis

Sales response can also be assessed by estimating an econometric model of the impact of advertising on sales. The increasing availability of scanner data led to a rapid growth in the development and use of the so-called Marketing Mix models that analyse historical information on a large set of variables known to impact sales volume such as advertising, promotional events, pricing, and seasonal and market factors. More recently, these models have also been used to track the effectiveness of advertising analyze on other response measures produced by the new emerging media. We discuss each application in turn, next.

Consumer packaged goods

Most applications of these models to consumer packaged goods markets rely on weekly, store or market-level scanner data, though the general approach can also be used with other data sources or time intervals, such as monthly or quarterly data.

As discussed by Dekimpe and Hanssens (Chapter 3.5) a general form of a sales response model is

$$S_t = e^c A_t^\beta X_t^\gamma Z_t^\delta e_t^u,$$

where S_t refers to sales or another performance metric in period t (for example, week t), A_t is a vector of advertising variables in that week, X_t refers to a vector of other marketing mix variables, Z_t is a vector of other environmental factors, u_t is an error term, and c, β, γ and δ are parameters to be estimated.

A sample empirical specification of a typical model used in this analysis appears below and is used to illustrate the methodology. In practice many more variables may be included in the model, especially from the Z vector, so as to obtain the best possible estimates of the "true" impact of advertising on sales volume.

$$
\begin{aligned}
\text{Ln(Volume sales}_t) \\
= c &+ \beta_1 \text{ TV Advertising}_t \\
&+ \beta_2 \text{ Print Advertising}_t \\
&+ \beta_3 \text{ Radio Advertising}_t + \gamma_1 \text{ Price}_t \\
&+ \gamma_2 \text{ Promotion Events}_t \\
&+ \delta_1 \text{ Holiday Dummies}_t \\
&+ \delta_2 \text{ Gas Price}_t + u_t
\end{aligned}
$$

Historical data are used to estimate model parameters. If differences in the effects of the marketing variables across geographical regions are ignored, a common set of parameters can be estimated by pooling data from different markets. This approach increases the number of degrees of freedom available and provides reasonably accurate estimates of the coefficients in practice. An alternative to pooling the data is to estimate separate models for each region (or segment) of interest allowing each region to have a different response. This approach comes at the cost of reducing the degrees of freedom available and can leads to coefficients that are wrongly signed or that have large standard errors. Parameter estimates obtained using Bayesian methods to "shrink" individual region-specific coefficient estimates to the overall mean have been found to be useful in overcoming these problems (Montgomery and Rossi, 1999; Divakar et al., 2005).

The analysis attempts to quantify volume "lifts" caused by marketing activities by decomposing the total sales volume into *base* and *incremental volumes*. The base volume refers to the sales that would have been generated without the extra advertising or marketing activities, while the incremental volume represents the sales that resulted from these activities. In the example above, the baseline sales could be obtained by setting model variables to their "normal" level (or to zero) though sometimes specialized smoothing models are also used (Abraham and Lodish, 1987). The incremental volumes are used to calculate "Effectiveness," "Efficiency" and "Payback" metrics, which are discussed in greater detail below.

Effectiveness: measures a brand's incremental volume per unit of marketing activity e.g., incremental cases per Gross Rating Point. In the example above, if the volume of advertising during the period of analysis was 200 Gross Rating Points and the incremental volume due to the advertising was 5 million units, it would imply that effectiveness was 25 000 units per Gross Rating Point. This standardized metric is comparable across markets and brands, but not across marketing elements, because of differences in how an activity is measured, e.g., Gross Rating Points vs. Circulation dollars.

Efficiency: This metric provides the financial link between spending and the incremental volume generated. It is computed as the ratio of total spending for an activity and the amount of incremental volume that it generates, for example, dollars spent per incremental unit or pound. In the example above, if the 200 Gross Rating Points of advertising cost the company $1 million, then the effectiveness of the advertising is calculated to be $0.20 per unit ($1 million/ 5 million units).

Figure 4.2.1 tracks the efficiency of advertising for a hypothetical brand X year over year and shows that even though higher advertising levels lead to positive increases in volumes, the higher cost of the Gross Rating Points lowered efficiency. By monitoring this metric, a brand manager may be able to identify changes in the advertising campaign that may increase efficiency, for example using more 15 second spots or finding a less expensive show in which to advertise.

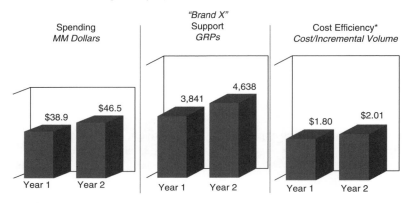

TV advertising support increased in Year 2 behind an increase in expenditures, but became slightly less cost efficient as a result. This was more than likely due to the saturation effect of high weekly support levels.

Figure 4.2.1 Advertising performance summary

Payback: This is the short-term financial return from spending, i.e., the gross contribution of the incremental units divided by the cost of the input expressed in percentage terms. In the example above, if the contribution per unit sold is $0.25 then payback can be calculated as 125% ($0.25 × 5 million/$1 million). This metric captures return on marketing investment and is comparable across brands and activities.

Figure 4.2.2 displays an example of how a multi-product firm may use a brand-level Payback analysis to guide resource allocation. The manager may consider reallocating advertising dollars from brands with low payback to those with high payback. However, such a reallocation typically takes place only after carefully studying the pros and cons of the decision, getting inputs from qualitative studies and incorporating possible diminishing returns to scale.

Direct mail and telemarketing

Sales driven by direct marketing are forecast to have 6.4 percent compound annual growth through 2009, up from 5.3 percent in the period from 1999 to 2004 (Campanelli, 2005) while consumer telemarketing is expected to grow by 7.4% per year (Cerasale and Faley, 2000).

In direct mail campaigns, advertisers frequently include a code (frequently, this is a discount code) within the mailer that the customer is requested to repeat when they respond to the mailer by calling up the firm or visiting the store that sent out the mailer. This enables the marketer to compare the effectiveness of alternate mailings and to calculate the return on investment of the direct mailing campaigns. In telemarketing campaigns, which use "outbound" call centers, tracking is reasonably straightforward since the person making the call can keep track of the customer's response to the call. Most firms categorize response to calls into one of the following categories, namely, "Not available," "Available," "Not Interested," "Need more Information," "Interested" and "Sale."

The availability of "inbound" call centres has allowed firms to combine mass media advertising with direct marketing and obtain response data at a level of temporal disaggregation not available with other approaches. Using data on inquiries for a toll-free referral service generated by different advertising campaigns, Tellis et al. (2000, 2001) estimate an econometric model to evaluate the effectiveness of the campaigns. The model enables the firm to evaluate, among other things, the effects of different advertising

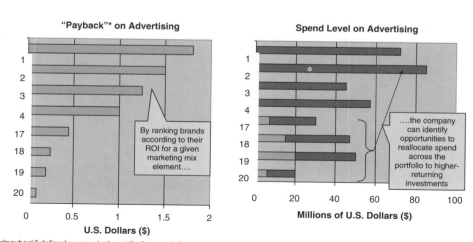

•"payback" defined as marginal contribution per dollar spent, i.e, marginal contribution per pound × incremental pound per dollar spent

Figure 4.2.2   Optimal investment allocation across the portfolio

creatives, the station in which the ad was aired and the number of repetitions.

It is important to point out that the described modeling approach is not limited to the analysis of direct mail or telemarketing data. It can just as easily be applied to other response variables such as sales or clicks, irrespective of whether these are generated by consumer response to traditional (e.g., radio or print) or non-traditional media (e.g., Internet advertising).

Internet advertising

Total online advertising spending reached approximately $12.5 billion in 2005, about 30% over 2004. A study published by Forrester Research in 2005, based on an online survey of 99 of the United States' largest marketers found that 47% would spend more online in the next five years at the expense of traditional channels. A total of 84% of the respondents planned to increase their online budgets by an average of 25% in the coming year. By 2010, online ad spending is expected to reach $26 billion or 8% of all advertising dollars spent.

The current dominant forms of web advertising are "banner advertisements," "paid search advertising" and "affiliate programs." A *banner advertisement* is a small, typically rectangular, graphic image that is linked to a target communication. Target communications, in contrast, may be fairly detailed ranging from a single web page to media-enhanced web pages. A banner advertisement is similar to a traditional print ad to the extent that it also consists of text and an image, but with the added ability to bring a potential customer directly to the advertiser's website. The primary purpose of

a banner advertisement is to get consumers to click it, go to the advertiser's website and eventually make a purchase, while a secondary objective may be to build brand awareness and preference. Different metrics developed to track the effectiveness of banner advertising as measured by these objectives appear in Table 4.2.1.

The second most common form of web advertising is paid search advertising. Advertisers pay a website to allow their links to appear to appear in a separate section of the results page every time a user searches for a particular keyword. The ranking/position of a firm's link among all of the links that appear depends in part on the amount of money the firm is willing to pay per click (the bid). Some of the advantages of pay per click search advertising and the possible reasons behind its rise in popularity are:

- Tracking the effectiveness of pay per click search advertising is simplified by using the click-through rate.
- The ad appears on search engine results only after someone enters a query containing a keyword that matches or relates to the words a firm has bid on. This makes it more likely that the person viewing an ad is proactively searching for something that is related to a firm's products, service or advertising.
- It is easily scalable and can be used by both large corporations as well as small businesses with limited advertising budgets.

Both banner advertisements and pay-per-click search advertising offer only limited visibility to the advertiser, namely, on the websites where the advertiser has purchased banner ad space or on the search engine website. Google revolutionized the world of online advertising by offering advertisers a

Table 4.2.1   Banner advertising metrics

Page views/page impressions	This is the number of times a particular webpage has been requested from the server indicating the number of visitors that could have seen the banner ad. The most common way to sell banner ad space is on a cost per thousand impression or CPM basis
Click-throughs	The number of visitors who click on the banner ad linking to the advertisers' website. Banner ad space is sometimes sold on a cost-per-click basis
Click-through rate (CTR)	This describes the ratio of page views to clicks. It is the percentage of total visitors to a page who actually clicked on the banner ad and is typically under 1%
Cost per sale	This is the dollar value of advertising spent on a single sale at the advertiser's website

third alternative, namely, contextual search advertising. With contextual search advertising, pay-per-click search ads are displayed not only on search engine results pages but on related content pages throughout the World Wide Web. This is accomplished by matching a site's content with the advertisers' keywords. The two largest players in this space are Google with its "Ad Sense" program and Overture with its "Content Match" program. Contextual advertising usually results in an ad being shown on a large number of websites and is very useful for advertisers who are interested in maximizing their reach and frequency across the web in a way that is relevant to the product or service offering.

Some of the metrics tracked by advertisers using keyword search advertising or contextual advertising are:

- Cost per thousand impressions (CPM)
- Cost per click (CPC)
- Conversion rate: The ratio of sales to total visitors arriving by clicking on contextual search results
- Key phrases that bring the most visitors and lead to the most conversions on the advertiser's website
- Key phrases that bring traffic but not conversions.

In general, the cost-per-click models have made it easier to measure advertising effectiveness for web advertising via the click-through rate. However, advertisers cannot focus solely on the click-through rate to evaluate an ad campaign but must consider the overall sales and contribution margins that are generated. For instance, a banner advertisement with a 1% click rate followed by a 50% sales rate is more effective than one with a 5% click rate followed by a 5% sales rate, assuming equal contribution margins across the two products.

The cost-per-click metric does not measure whether or not a customer likes an ad or spends any time viewing it. To assess this impact, advertisers use a variety of interactivity metrics such as the duration of time spent viewing the target communication, the depth or number of pages of the target communication that were accessed or the number of repeat visits to the target communication. Companies such as Comscore and Milward Brown Interactive have developed measurement methods based on a sample of home-based personal computers in the United States (Coffey and Stipp, 1997). The number of panelists required to study Internet surfing behaviour is much larger than what is required to track television channels in order to ensure the representativeness of the samples (Dreze and Zufryden, 1998).

A third category of web advertising is an affiliate marketing program in which online merchants pay commissions on every purchase made at the merchant's site by visitors who are directed there by their partner websites (affiliates). Affiliate programs are usually evaluated with metrics such as the number of sales generated from a particular website, the number of leads generated by a website and the number of impressions provided by the website.

Modeling the impact of web advertising as a part of the overall communication mix poses some unique challenges. Firstly, the amount spent on web advertising is usually a small percentage of the total marketing budget. Without knowing who has or has not been exposed to web advertising, it is impossible to measure the impact of web advertising on sales using regression-based models. Telephone surveys are another commonly used method to measure advertising effectiveness. However, since web advertising typically has a much smaller reach than traditional media, the sample size required to yield a reasonable number of people who have been exposed to an ad is typically very large. Thus, the traditional methods used to track the persuasion-based metrics for television advertising do not work very well with web advertising.

SUMMARY

Firms use advertising campaigns to achieve a variety of communication outcomes ranging from awareness creation to sales generation.

Advertising tracking studies are expressly designed to monitor whether an ad campaign achieves its goals, making them essential tools for assessing and improving the effectiveness of advertising campaigns.

Advertising effects, and the tracking studies that measure them, may be classified into three categories – cognitive, persuasive, or affective, and behavioural. Thus, metrics such as exposure and awareness are based on the cognitive stage of the hierarchy, preference and liking on the affective stage, while sales and clicks tap into the behavioural dimension.

This chapter has provided an overview of the methods and metrics available to track the impact of advertising in traditional media outlets such as print, radio and television as well as in emerging media such as direct mail and internet advertising. Thus the cognitive impact of advertising is measured by memory-based measures like recognition, recall and awareness, while its affective impact is assessed via measures of persuasion and brand commitment. The technological advancements in electronic data capture, the availability of single-source data, and the growing use of other means of communication such as direct mail, telemarketing and the internet has provided data on consumer response in the market in a highly disaggregate form. This has led to new tracking methods such as advertising field experiments and the econometric analysis of sales and other measures of the behavioural impact of advertising.

The emergence of new media vehicles and the increased availability of detailed data on consumer response present new opportunities and challenges that will occupy the attention of researchers and practitioners interested in ad tracking for the foreseeable future.

REFERENCES

Abraham M., and L.M. Lodish (1987), "Promoter: An Automated Promotion Evaluation System," *Marketing Science*, 6 (Spring), 101–123.

Ambler, T. (2000), "Persuasion, Pride and Prejudice: How Ads Work," *International Journal of Advertising*, 19(3).

Appel, V. and M.L. Blum (1961), "Ad Recognition and Respondent Set," *Journal of Advertising Research*, 1 (June), 13–21.

Assael, Henry (1998), *Consumer Behavior and Marketing Action*, Cincinnati, OH: South-Western.

Bagozzi, R.P. and A.J. Silk (1983), "Recall, Recognition and the Measurement of Memory for Print Advertisements," *Marketing Science*, 2(2), 95–134.

Beirne, H., A. Drummond and M. Dodd (2003), "Measuring the Outcome of Marketing Activity," *Admap*, Issue 436.

Bettman, J.R. (1979), "Memory Factors in Consumer Choice: A Review," *Journal of Marketing*, 43(2), 37–53.

Blair, M.H. and K.E. Rosenberg (1994), "Convergent Findings Increase Our Understanding of How Advertising Works," *Journal of Advertising Research*, 34.

Bucklin, R.E. and S. Gupta (1999), "Commercial Use of UPC Scanner Data: Industry and Academic Perspectives," *Marketing Science*, 18(3), 247–73.

Campanelli, M. (2005), "DM Ad Spending Hits $161B, Growth Will Continue," *DM News* (30 September).

Cerasale, G. and P. Faley (2000), "Telemarketing Review-Comment," *http://www.ftc.gov/bcp/rulemaking/tsr/comments/dma.pdf*

Chandy, R.K., G.J. Tellis, D.J. MacInnis and P. Thaivanich (2001), "What to Say When: Advertising Appeals in Evolving Marketing," *Journal of Marketing Research*, 38 (November), 399–414.

Coffey, S. and H. Stipp (1997), "The Interactions between Computer and Television Usage," *Journal of Advertising Research*, 37, 61–7.

Colman, S. and G. Brown (1986) "Advertising Tracking Studies and Sales Effects" *Journal of the Market Research Society*, 25, 2.

Copland, B.D. (1958), *The Study of Attention Value*, London: Business Publications.

Dekimpe, M.G. and D.M. Hanssens (2004), "Persistence Modeling for Assessing Marketing Strategy Performance," in *Assessing Marketing Strategy Performance* eds. D. Lehmann and C. Moorman, Marketing Science Institute, 69–93.

Divakar, S., B.T. Ratchford, and V. Shankar (2005), "CHAN4CAST: A Multichannel, Multiregion, Sales-forecasting Model and Decision Support System for Consumer Packaged Goods," *Marketing Science*, 24(3), 334–50.

Dodd, A.R., Jr. (1964), "New Study Tells TV Advertisers How Advertising Builds Sales and Share of Market," *Printers' Ink*.

Dreze, X. and F. Zufryden (1998), "Is Internet Advertising Ready for Prime Time?" *Journal of Advertising Research*, 38(3), 7–18.

Dyson, P. (1998), "Monitoring Advertising Performance," *Admap Conference*, (January).

Eastlack, J.O. and A.G. Rao (1986), "Modeling Response to Advertising and Pricing Changes for "V-8" Cocktail Vegetable Juice," *Marketing Science*, 5(3), 245–59.

Eastlack, J.O. and A.G. Rao (1989), "Advertising Experiments at the Campbell Soup Company," *Marketing Science*, 8(1), 57–71.

Fishbein, M. and I. Ajzen (1975), *Belief, Attitude, Intention, and Behavior: An Introduction to Theory and Research*, Reading, MA: Addison-Wesley.

Fishbein, M. and I. Ajzen (1980), *Understanding Attitudes and Predicting Social Behavior*, Englewood Cliffs, NJ: Prentice-Hall.

Forrester Research Inc. (2005), "U.S. Online Marketing Forecast: 2005 to 2010."

Gardner, M. (1985), "Does Attitude Toward the Ad Affect Brand Attitude Under a Brand Evaluation Set," *Journal of Marketing Research*, 22 (May), 192–8.

Haskins, J.B. (1964), "Factual Recall as a Measure of Advertising Effectiveness," *Journal of Advertising Research*, 4 (March), 2–8.

Heath, R. (1997), "Brand Commitment as the Predictor of Advertising Effect," *Admap*, 53–7.

Heath, R.G. and P. Hyder (2005), "Measuring the Hidden Power of Emotive Advertising," *Journal of the Market Research Society*, 47(5), 467–86.

Jones, J.P. (1995), "Single-Source Research Begins to Fulfill its Promise," *Journal of Advertising Research*, 35(3), 9–16.

Kelly, P.J. (1964), "The Schwerin Model: How You Can Use It to Build Your Share of Market," *Printers' Ink*.

Krugman, H.E. (1972), "Why Three Exposures may be Enough," *Journal of Advertising Research*, 12 (December), 11–16.

Krugman, H.E. (1977), "Memory without Recall, Exposure without Perception," *Journal of Advertising Research*, 17(4), 7–12.

Lastovicka, J.L. and D.M. Gardner (1977), "Components of Involvement," in *Attitude Research Plays for High Stakes*, eds, J.C. Maloney and B. Silverman, Chicago: American Marketing Association, 53–73.

Lipstein, B. (1985), "An Historical Retrospective of Copy Research," *Journal of Advertising Research*, 24, 11–15.

Lodish, L.M. and D.J. Reibstein (1986), "New Gold Mines and Minefields in Market Research," *Harvard Business Review*, 64(1), (January–February).

Lodish, L.M., M. Abraham, S. Kalmenson, J. Livelsberger, B. Lubetkin, B. Richardson and M.E. Stevens (1995a), "How Advertising Works: A Meta Analysis of 389 Real World Split Cable TV Advertising Experiments," *Journal of Marketing Research*, 32 (May), 125–39.

Lodish, L.M., M. Abraham, S. Kalmenson, J. Livelsberger, B. Lubetkin, B. Richardson and M.E. Stevens (1995b), "A Summary of Fifty-Five In-Market Experimental Estimates of the Long Term Effects of Advertising," *Marketing Science*, 14 (3), G133–40.

Lucas, D.B. (1960), "The ABC's of ARF's PARM," *Journal of Marketing*, 25 (July), 9–20.

Lucas, D.B. and S.H. Britt (1963), *Measuring Advertising Effectiveness*, New York: McGraw Hill.

Marketing News (2005), "ARF Exec Discusses Future of Ad Research," March 15, 2005, 15–17.

Mitchell, A.A. and J. Olson (1981), "Are Product Attribute Beliefs the Only Mediator of Advertising Effects on Brand Attitude?" *Journal of Marketing Research*, 13 (June), 12–24.

Montgomery, A. L. and P.E. Rossi (1999), "Estimating Price Elasticities with Theory-Based Priors," *Journal of Marketing Research*, Vol. 36, (November), 413–23.

Murphy, M.P. (1968), "Empirical Evidence of the Effect of Advertising on Sales," Speech presented in Toronto to the *Professional Marketing Research Society*.

Neu, D.M. (1961), "Measuring Advertisement Recognition," *Journal of Advertising Research*, 1 (December), 17–22.

Penn, D. (2002), "LIP to HIP: Responding to Changing Views," *Admap*, 433.

Schwerin, H.S., and H.H. Newell (1981), *Persuasion in Marketing. The Dynamics of Marketing's Great Untapped Resource*, New York: Wiley.

Shapiro, S., D.J. Macinnis and S.E. Heckler (1997), "The Effects of Incidental Ad Exposure on the Formation of Consideration Sets," *Journal of Consumer Research*, 24, 94–104.

Shimp, T.A. (1981), "Attitude Toward the Ad as a Mediator of Consumer Brand Choice," *Journal of Advertising*, 10(2), 9–15.

Singh, S.N. and C.A. Cole (1985), "Forced-Choice Recognition Tests: A Critical Review," *Journal of Advertising*, 14(3), 52–8.

Tellis, G.J. (1998), "*Advertising and Sales Promotion Strategy*," Reading, MA: Addison-Wesley.

Tellis, G.J., R.K. Chandy and P. Thaivanich (2000), "Which Ad Works, When, Where, and How Often? Modeling the Effects of Direct Television Advertising," *Journal of Marketing Research*, 37 (February), 32–46.

Traylor, M.B. (1981), "Product Involvement and Brand Commitment," *Journal of Advertising Research,* 21, 51–6.

Vakratsas, D. and T. Ambler, (1999), "How Advertising Works: What Do We Really Know?," *Journal of Marketing,* 63(1), 26–43.

Wells, W.D. (1964), "Recognition, Recall and Rating Scales," *Journal of Advertising Research,* 3 (September), 2–8.

White, R. (2005), "Tracking Ads and Communications," *Admap,* Issue 460, 12–15.

Advertising Response Models

Marnik G. Dekimpe and
Dominique M. Hanssens

Advertising is one of the most visible activities of companies and brands. Firms and brands advertise for a variety of reasons, among them to help launch new products, to announce price changes, to increase brand awareness, and to protect the brand franchise against competitive encroachment. These efforts are expensive. In the US alone, advertising expenditures amounted to about $400 billion in 2004. In relative terms, firms' advertising outlays are often of an order of magnitude comparable to that of their profitability, though of course there is considerable variation across firms. For example, in 2004, the US ad spending of Procter & Gamble was about $3 billion, while their worldwide pretax profit was about $6 billion. Thus, knowledge of the economic impact of, and more specifically, the *return* on, advertising spending is of paramount importance to managers and investors alike. As managers are under increasing pressure to be accountable to shareholders, advertising budgets are scrutinized ever more closely (The Wall Street Journal, 2005).

There are several important components to the return on advertising, in particular the choice of performance metrics, the response of that metric to changes in advertising spending, and the market potential and profitability of the products and services being advertised. This chapter focuses on the most challenging of these components, the *response* to advertising, in particular sales response, which has a direct impact on the financial viability of advertising.

Obtaining reliable sales-response estimates is challenging, because so many other factors could also drive sales performance, including swings in the economic environment, the other elements of the marketing mix of the firm or brand, seasonality, competitive moves, etc. Both marketing science and marketing practice have focused on three different methods for obtaining such sales-response estimates: (i) structured judgement, (ii) experimentation, and (iii) advertising-response models.

Structured judgement is a Delphi-type method to collect marketing executives' best guesses about the likely impact of different advertising resource allocations, from which the optimal allocation may be derived analytically (see e.g., Little, 1970). It is very useful when no objective data are available, and/or when there is insufficient time to analyse such data. Its major drawback is that it relies on subjective inputs, which are known to contain several biases. By contrast, advertising experimentation uses objective criteria of randomization, and compares test versus control conditions to infer advertising impact. A well-known example is the series of split-cable TV advertising experiments conducted by Lodish et al. (1995). Advertising experiments are commonplace in *direct marketing*, as it is relatively easy to apply different treatments to different target groups and compare response rates (see e.g., Anderson and Simester, 2004). However, advertising experimentation is often expensive and time-consuming, and is typically limited to the testing of only a few aspects of the brand's advertising strategy.

Our focus is on the third approach, i.e., econometrics-based inference of advertising response. Econometrics, as applied to marketing, uses historical data on performance measures (e.g., sales revenue) and hypothesized determinants of that performance (e.g., marketing-mix expenditures, prices, competitive activity, economic conditions) to isolate the relative impact of each, using statistical methods such as multiple regression analysis (see Hanssens et al., 2001 for an in-depth coverage). That approach is the most complete in that it assesses advertising effects *in conjunction with* other determinants of sales. The price of completeness, however, is a certain amount of complexity relative to straightforward test versus control executions. In addition, the econometric approach also requires high-quality historical databases. Fortunately, continuous advances in information technology make larger and better sales and marketing databases available to companies, and these improvements provide opportunity to gain new and better insights about advertising effectiveness through econometric response modeling.

We organize our discussion of advertising-response models as follows. First, we focus on the basic building block, the single-equation advertising-response model. We discuss, in turn, the shape and the dynamics of advertising response, followed by discussions on data-interval bias and reverse causality. Next we show how this basic structure may be extended to accommodate a variety of phenomena that are often observed in real-world advertising settings, such as the use of multiple media, different copy and creative, and how to model advertising wear-in and wear-out. Finally, we discuss alternative performance metrics, in particular awareness modeling.

Second, we cover the more advanced modeling of advertising effects within a system of consumer response, competitive reactions, and firm decision making. That leads to the derivation of advertising's long-term impact. Finally, we review some known phenomena about advertising response, and discuss how these phenomena can be modeled. After reviewing some major insights that have been obtained through advertising-response modeling, and their implications for effective advertising decision making, we provide a summary.

SINGLE-EQUATION ADVERTISING-RESPONSE MODELS

While the focus of this chapter is on modeling advertising response, it is important to appreciate that virtually all the models we describe *do not* treat advertising in a vacuum. Instead, they assess the impact of advertising, while controlling for the rest of the marketing mix, competition and various environmental factors.

The shape of the advertising-response function

All else equal, higher advertising spending is expected to increase sales for a variety of reasons. Acquiring previously unaware prospects, increasing purchase quantities, increasing brand switching in the direction of the advertised brand, and retaining a larger fraction of the existing customer base are among the major sources. At the same time, we expect *diminishing returns* to these effects, again for several reasons. Consumers cease to be responsive once they have learned the basic message contained in the advertising (saturation effect), markets deplete as successful advertising causes purchasing which then removes the buyers from the market, at least temporarily (market-depletion effects) and, finally, there are natural ceilings to the number or percent of customers that can be targeted or reached (ceiling effect). Diminishing returns imply that, while sales still increase with increases in advertising support, each additional unit of advertising brings less in incremental sales than the previous unit did.

As a consequence, the basic advertising-response function is concave, reflecting diminishing returns. A simple linear specification would not accommodate this, as each additional unit of advertising spending would have the same impact on sales. Instead, we use the following multiplicative model

$$S_t = e^c A_t^\beta X_t^\gamma Z_t^\delta e^u, \qquad (1)$$

where S_t refers to sales or another performance metric in period t (for example, week t), A_t is the advertising support in that week, X_t refers to another element of the marketing mix (e.g., price), Z_t corresponds to an environmental factor (e.g., a macroeconomic indicator), and u_t is an error term. For simplicity of exposition, we list only one X and one Z variable. The base response model may be estimated across time periods t, but could also be specified over cross-sectional units $i = 1, \ldots, I$, or both. We expect $0 < \beta < 1$ in estimation, a condition which results in concavity.

The base model (1) implies that with zero advertising comes zero sales, and with infinite advertising comes infinite sales. Zero-sales is usually unrealistic, and this is addressed by adding a small constant (e.g., $1) to the advertising term in (1). In addition, there is almost always a limit or *ceiling* to sales, usually determined by prevailing market conditions. While there are other ways to represent concavity (see e.g., Hanssens et al., 2001: 100–2), the multiplicative function is particularly appealing as it recognizes that marketing-mix effects interact with each other (i.e., the marginal sales effect of an incremental advertising dollar depends on the other elements in the equation). In addition, taking logarithms linearizes the model:

$$\ln(S_t) = c + \beta \ln(A_t) + \gamma \ln(X_t) \\ + \delta \ln(Z_t) + u_t, \qquad (2)$$

making it more easily estimable. Finally, the response parameters are easily interpreted as response elasticities. An example of an advertising response curve with elasticity $\beta = 0.2$ may be found in Figure 4.3.1a.

In some cases, the response is S-shaped, i.e., there is a minimum or threshold-level of ad spend below which there is little or no impact, followed by a range of advertising spending with rapidly increasing sales response. At even higher spending levels (i.e., past a certain "inflection point"), the usual diminishing returns appear (see Figure 4.3.1b). The base model (1) can readily be extended to an "odds"

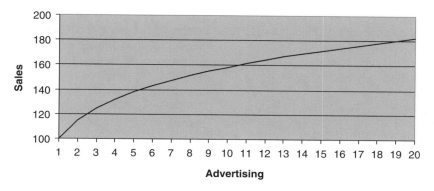

Figure 4.3.1a   Concave response function

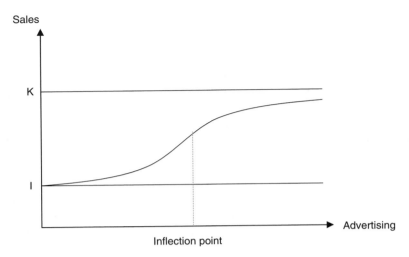

Figure 4.3.1b   S-shaped response function

model that allows for S-shaped response, as demonstrated by Johansson (1979):

$$(S_t - I)/(K - S_t) = cA_t^\beta X_t^\gamma Z_t^\delta e_t^u, \quad (3)$$

where I is the minimum sales level (e.g., the level at zero marketing spend), and K is the ceiling level. For example, if sales is expressed in relative terms (i.e., market shares), I could be set at 0% and K at 100%. For advertising response parameters $0 < \beta < 1$, model (3) is still concave, but for $\beta > 1$, the function is S-shaped. Johansson (1979) discusses the formal estimation of (3) with maximum-likelihood methods, as well as an easy approximation based on ordinary least squares.

For all practical purposes, concavity and S-shape are sufficient functional forms to capture the essence of advertising response.[1] In some cases, the response may be even simpler; if all the advertising spending observations lie in a restricted range of the data, the response function may well be approximated by a linear function. However, since it is tempting and dangerous to extrapolate outside this restricted range, we do not recommend using such overly simplified models. For example, the managerially useful statement "for every dollar in advertising, we generate four extra dollars in revenue," readily obtained from a linear response model, can be very misleading in making future advertising allocation decisions.

Advertising response dynamics

Advertising is communication, which can trigger memory, and thus its impact may easily extend beyond the campaign period. This phenomenon is referred to as the *carryover* effect of advertising. Similarly, customers could be exposed to a given advertising message (e.g., a magazine ad insert) on multiple occasions, which gradually increases the impact of the message because of consumers' increasing familiarity with the campaign. That is referred to as advertising *wearin*. Finally, continued consumer exposure to the advertising campaign past the wearin period may no longer increase its impact, a phenomenon referred to as advertising *wearout*. We refer to Tellis (2004) for a detailed discussion on these phenomena.

The phenomena of wearin, wearout and carryover imply that response models that simply relate current sales to current advertising expenditures are likely to misrepresent advertising's total impact. Wearin and wearout effects are handled by time-varying advertising response parameters, which will be discussed later. Carryover effects may be represented by extending the core model in (1) to a distributed-lag model over time t:

$$S_t = cA_t^{\beta(L)} X_t^{\gamma} Z_t^{\delta} e_t^u, \qquad (4)$$

where $\beta(L) = \beta_0 + \beta_1 L + \beta_2 L^2 + \beta_3 L^3 + \dots$, and with L the lag operator (i.e., $L^2 A_t = A_{t-2}$).

In this model, a one percent increase in advertising spending would increase the sales in the same period by β_0 percent. After the campaign ends, there would be a carryover impact of β_1 percent in the following period, an additional effect of β_2 percent two periods later, etc. Thus, the total or cumulative advertising effect may well differ from the instantaneous effect. The time-delayed effects of advertising captured in the lag-polynomial $\beta(L)$, also referred to as carryover effects (Franses and Vriens, 2004), tend to vary across products, categories and media. For example, in their study of an ethical drug Montgomery and Silk (1972) reported peak effects of direct mail and samples one month after the expenditure, with additional carryover effects of three months. By contrast, journal advertising had a stronger immediate impact and a longer tail in carryover effect, up to six months.

It may be difficult to estimate a large number of β-parameters and/or to define a priori a precise cut-off point for the number of lags to consider. A good alternative is to hypothesize an a-priori decay pattern on the various β-parameters. A popular approach is the geometric decay implied in the Koyck model, in that $\beta_{i+1} = \lambda \beta_i$ (see e.g., Clarke, 1976). Thus in each period after exposure, the impact decays by a constant fraction λ of the previous impact. Another alternative is to use empirical specification methods to determine the functional form of $\beta(L)$, such as the Box-Jenkins transfer-function method (see e.g., Helmer and Johansson, 1977) or the Liu and Hanssens (1982) direct-lag specification method. A technical description of these methods is beyond the scope of this article, but can be found in Hanssens et al. (2001, Chapter 7). Note that the distributed lag-model in (4) is

flexible enough to accommodate a variety of peak-impact and carryover patterns. For example, if it takes two periods for any economic impact to take place, one can specify $\beta(L)$ as $\beta_2 L^2$. If, in addition, advertising effects wear out (decay) at a rate of 10% per period, the lag polynomial $\beta(L)$ can be written as $\beta_2 L^2/(1-0.9L)$. A flexible dynamic specification was used in Tellis et al. (2000) to decompose the effects, at an hourly level, of television advertising for a toll-free referral service.

An alternative approach to assessing the dynamic effects of advertising is ADSTOCK (Broadbent, 1984), which has gained some popularity among practitioners. The Adstock model rests on the assumption that each advertising effort adds to a pre-existing stock of advertising goodwill. Conversely, absent any current advertising, the stock decays at a constant rate. Thus, the empirical specification is

$$ADSTOCK_t = \alpha \, ADSTOCK_{t-1} + (1-\alpha)A_t, \qquad (5)$$

where α is the decay factor $(0 < \alpha < 1)$. Adstock models are elegant in conceptualization and easy to use, as they circumvent the problem of empirical lag specification. However, the decay parameter is often set subjectively, and that may lead to a bias (usually an overestimation) in the advertising impact. Tellis and Weis (1995) present an objective, best-fit method for determining α. Whenever possible, we recommend that decay parameters be estimated from the data. In addition, Adstock does not make the critical distinction between *purchase reinforcement* and *advertising carryover*. Suppose advertising generates trial for a new product, which leads to a positive consumption experience and, therefore, subsequent (repeat) sales. While advertising should be credited with generating the initial sales, it should share that credit with purchase reinforcement for subsequent sales. Givon and Horsky (1990) developed a distributed lag model to disentangle both effects. The econometric approach is relatively simple, and consists of augmenting the Koyck model with additional lagged terms for the dependent variable. Their application in several product categories revealed that the purchase feedback effect dominates the advertising carryover effect.

Data-interval bias

The determination of advertising response dynamics is closely related to the chosen temporal data interval. In the past, data intervals posed a serious econometric problem because they were too coarse to allow for detailed inference. For example, sales and advertising movements sampled annually, or even quarterly, will almost inevitably represent a mixture of consumer response effects, firm decision and competitive reaction effects. Thus, the nature of a *contemporaneous* correlation between advertising and sales is difficult to ascertain. Moreover, marketing researchers have long been puzzled by the empirical observation that estimated carry-offer, and hence, advertising-duration effects, differed depending on whether *dynamic* advertising models were estimated on monthly, quarterly or annual data. Conventional wisdom was then to use as "preferred" data interval the one that most closely resembled the brand's inter-purchase time (see e.g., Leone, 1985, for a review). However, this view was recently challenged by Tellis and Franses (2006), who showed that one can retrieve the correct carryover effects with aggregate data provided one has information about the exact unit-exposure time (defined as the largest interval within which an ad pulse occurs at most once). However, in many instances, applied marketing researchers do not know the ad inter-insertion, let alone the inter-exposure time of consumers. In that case, using data at the lowest level of aggregation was found to be a good heuristic.

Fortunately, advertising databases have become available at much more disaggregate sampling levels. For example, weekly media advertising spending data are routinely collected by Competitive Media Reporting, a division of TNS. When matched with weekly sales numbers, distributed lag models of advertising effects may readily be estimated. Contemporaneous correlations between advertising and sales can then safely be interpreted as consumer response effects, since it would be difficult for most organizations to react to competitive moves and/or to incorporate sales feedback in advertising spending within one week. In some cases, the data interval is reduced even further, for example to hourly measurements in the case of direct-response television campaigns (e.g., Tellis et al., 2000). Overall, it is fair to conclude that advances in data collection technology are gradually obsoleting the problem of temporal data interval bias.

Another form of data aggregation bias is cross-sectional. For example, national data may be used in an advertising response model, even though some regional markets receive different advertising exposures than others. In nonlinear models (as the multiplicative core model (1)), linear aggregation (e.g., when data of the individual regions are summed to a national aggregate) will create biased estimates of advertising's effectiveness if advertising spending differed between the regions across which the summation took place. We refer to Christen et al. (1997) for an in-depth discussion of these issues.

Asymmetric response

The core response model, assumes that advertising effects are symmetric, so if adding 10% to the spending increases sales by 2%, then cutting the spending by 10% implies that sales will decrease by 2%. In reality, however, asymmetries may exist.

Consider the case where a successful new advertising campaign first acquires several new customers quickly, then brings in a lower, but still positive number of new customers. Similarly, at some point a mature brand's sales may have become resistant to further advertising increases, but quite sensitive to advertising reductions (Vakratsas, 2005), a situation many managers may feel applies to their brand. Representing such a process requires that we model, separately, the effects of "starting," "continuing" and "ending" of a campaign. That problem was tackled by Simon (1982), who extends the core response model (with only contemporaneous response effects for simplicity of exposure) as follows:

$$S_t = cA_t^{\beta+\theta I_t} X_t^{\gamma} Z_t^{\delta} e_t^{u}, \qquad (6)$$

where $I_t = 1$ if the period corresponds to the beginning of a campaign, and $I_t = 0$ elsewhere. Similarly, one could add another time-varying dummy variable to denote the ending of the campaign. Thus the start of a campaign has a total positive impact of $(\beta+\theta)$, and the remainder of the campaign has a 'level' impact of β. Simon refers to the asymmetric effect θ as a "differential stimulus" effect. This model was tested by Hanssens and Levien (1982) in the context of Navy advertising for recruits. Their lead generation model showed, for example, that radio advertising had a θ effect of 0.08 added to its level elasticity β of 0.26.

New data sources could provide even better insights into the asymmetric response nature of advertising. For example, in the case of a durable product or service, a company may be able to separate its weekly sales into two components: sales coming from new customers and sales from existing customers. Since we know that advertising has a stronger impact on trial sales than on repeat sales (e.g., Deighton et al., 1994), we may discover the asymmetries by applying the core model (1) separately to both components.

Dealing with reverse causality

Scientists like to make inferences from experimental data, i.e., where the treatment condition is assigned randomly, so that the impact of the treatment is easily isolated from other influences on the dependent variable of interest. Marketing managers, however, would not last long if their allocation decisions were randomized. In the case of advertising spending, for example, some months of the year may be favoured over others, and some

products or regional markets will likewise receive preferential allocation over others. In most cases, these allocations are made based on *ex ante expected sales performance*. For example, in 2000 DreamWorks SKG decided to spend nearly three times as much on advertising one comedy (*Road Trip*) over another (*Small Time Crooks*), most likely because the former was expected to have higher audience potential than the latter.

These well-known managerial conditions create an inference problem called endogeneity, or reverse causality. Econometrically, it means that the error term in (1) may be correlated with some of the explanatory variables, in this case advertising. Ordinary least-squares estimation will then lead to biased estimates of advertising's effects on sales. For example, if management picks successful products to advertise more heavily, an OLS estimator may confuse a true advertising effect with a "popular-product" effect, and thus overestimate the advertising impact.

Endogeneity is most problematic with cross-sectional data, where the modeler lacks the natural passing of time to establish the direction of effects. Standard econometric tests such as the Hausman test are available to diagnose endogeneity, and when detected, alternative estimators such as instrumental-variable methods may be used. We refer to Van Dijk et al. (2004) for an in-depth discussion of these methods. Even so, the most reliable inference of advertising impact on cross-sectional data comes from experimental designs in which some markets or customers are deliberately given different advertising treatments than others. A good example in this context are the V-8 advertising experiments reported in Eastlack and Rao (1986).

On time-series data, endogeneity is a lesser problem provided one has sufficiently short data intervals (e.g., weekly data). It is generally the case that consumers can respond to advertising stimuli a lot faster than companies can adjust their advertising spending to changes in consumer demand. Thus, if an application of core model (1) reveals a

0.2 contemporaneous elasticity of advertising, we can be reasonably confident that this is a true advertising response effect. In addition, any lagged advertising response effects are by definition free of reverse causality effects.

It is important to understand that the presence of decision feedback loops and competitive reactions can create a long-run outcome of an advertising campaign that may be quite different from its short-run impact. In order to assess such long-run effects, we need to replace the single-equation advertising response model by a dynamic system with multiple equations. This approach is discussed in more detail on p. 254.

Media effects

Not all advertising media are created equal, and in many cases a marketer will want to understand the differential impact of spending in different media. The core response model allows for this by including as many explanatory variables in the response model as there are relevant media. For example, a media-mix model may be

$$S_t = e^c \text{TV}_t^{\beta_1(L)} \text{ PRINT}_t^{\beta_2(L)} \text{ DIRECT}_t^{\beta_3(L)} \times X_t^{\gamma} Z_t^{\delta} e_t^u, \qquad (7)$$

where the combined advertising expenditures A_t are now replaced by the respective expenditures in three media (as an illustration): TV, Print and Direct Mail. Each medium has its own response elasticity and lag structure. Provided the database has sufficient degrees of freedom, and provided there is natural variation in the media spending patterns, media-mix models can be used to disentangle the relative contribution of each medium in explaining observed sales variations.

Montgomery and Silk (1972), for example, illustrate such a media-mix model for a pharmaceutical product, showing the differential impact of print advertising, direct mail and sampling and literature. Dekimpe and Hanssens (1995) considered both print and TV advertising for a major home-improvement chain, and found the medium with the lowest

short-run effect (TV) to have the highest long-run impact.

Advertising copy and creative effects

Creativity of communication is an integral part of advertising design and execution, and can have a substantial impact on the persuasive appeal of advertising. From a response modelling perspective, creative impact can be measured in a number of ways. First, one could use categorical variables to distinguish between different creative executions (e.g., campaigns). A simple example with two campaign executions may be

$$S_t = cA_t^{\beta_1(L)+\beta_2(L)E_t} X_t^{\gamma} Z_t^{\delta} e_t^u, \qquad (8)$$

where $E_t = 0$ for the base execution, and $E_t = 1$ for the new execution. Insofar as the new copy had a different impact on sales than the previous execution, the terms in $\beta_2(L)$ will be different from zero. Alternatively, one could try to directly import creative-quality metrics into the market-response model. For example, suppose a panel of experts rate the creative execution of each advertising campaign on a 5-point scale. Then the basic advertising response model may be extended to distinguish between spending elasticities and creative-execution elasticities as follows:

$$S_t = cA_t^{\beta_1(L)+\beta_2(L)Q_t} X_t^{\gamma} Z_t^{\delta} e_t^u, \qquad (9)$$

where the $\beta_1(L)$ terms now measure the pure spending effects of advertising, and the $\beta_2(L)$ terms measure how these effects increase with higher-quality creative, measured by Q_t. This approach was used in a Bayesian framework for measuring advertising copy effects by Gatignon (1984) and Chandy et al. (2001).

Attitudinal response models

In our discussion thus far, we have chosen a behavioural metric of advertising response, such as sales, because it is intrinsically related to the firm's business objectives, and because it allows us to study advertising effects in conjunction with other important elements of marketing strategy. Nevertheless, in some cases, firms will want to measure advertising impact on attitudinal constructs, in particular, brand awareness. For example, when new products are launched in either existing or new markets, raising consumer awareness of these products through advertising (i.e., a "pull strategy") may be an important element of the firm's launch strategy. Mahajan et al. (1984) conducted an extensive comparison of the leading awareness forecasting models in marketing, including "Tracker," "News" and "Litmus." The authors' overall conclusion is that the existing models perform about equally well in estimating advertising impact on awareness and predicting future awareness levels.

Attitudinal response models are similar to the base response model (1), with two special provisions: (1) awareness is by definition constrained between 0 and 100% of the target market; and (2) awareness level are more inert than sales, i.e., once established, consumers can remain aware of brands for a long time even if they never purchase or use them. These conditions are reflected in currently available awareness tracking models, such as the "News" model (Pringle et al., 1982). Franses and Vriens (2004) go one step further, and consider whether there is a hierarchy in advertising's effects on, respectively, awareness, consideration and brand choice. For the category studied, they found that most advertising effects existed for awareness, however they also noted some direct impact on choice.

SYSTEM'S MODELING OF LONG-RUN ADVERTISING RESPONSE

We have argued earlier that advertising impact is determined not only by response, but also by performance feedback (e.g., the firm's advertising decision rules) and competitive reactions. Together, these forces shape the total, long-run sales response of advertising,

and we will need a systems (multiple-equation) approach to adequately capture the various channels of influence that lead to this ultimate effect. A flexible way to do this is the Vector Autoregressive Specification (VAR). To explain this approach, consider the following VAR extension of Equation (2), where A denotes the own advertising spending, and CA competitive advertising spending. Rather than having one dependent variable, we now have three variables whose over-time evolution is explained by the model, i.e., the *Vector* $[\ln(S_t)\ln(A_t)\ln(CA_t)]'$. The explanatory variables are these variables' own past; hence the term *Auto-Regressive*. For ease of exposition, the intercepts (c), other marketing-mix instruments (X) and environmental factors (Z) have been omitted from (10).

$$
\begin{bmatrix} \ln(S_t) \\ \ln(A_t) \\ \ln(CA_t) \end{bmatrix} = \begin{bmatrix} \pi_{11}^1 & \pi_{12}^1 & \pi_{13}^1 \\ \pi_{21}^1 & \pi_{22}^1 & \pi_{23}^1 \\ \pi_{31}^1 & \pi_{32}^1 & \pi_{33}^1 \end{bmatrix} \begin{bmatrix} \ln(S_{t-1}) \\ \ln(A_{t-1}) \\ \ln(CA_{t-1}) \end{bmatrix}
$$

$$
+ \cdots + \begin{bmatrix} \pi_{11}^J & \pi_{12}^J & \pi_{13}^J \\ \pi_{21}^J & \pi_{22}^J & \pi_{23}^J \\ \pi_{31}^J & \pi_{32}^J & \pi_{33}^J \end{bmatrix}
$$

$$
\times \begin{bmatrix} \ln(S_{t-j}) \\ \ln(A_{t-J}) \\ \ln(CA_{t-J}) \end{bmatrix} + \begin{bmatrix} u_{S,t} \\ u_{A,t} \\ u_{CA,t} \end{bmatrix},
$$

$$ (10) $$

J is the order of the model, and $\vec{u} = [u_{S,t}\ u_{A,t}\ u_{CA,t}]' \sim N(0, \Sigma)$. This specification is very flexible, and reflects various forces or channels of influence: delayed response $(\pi_{12}^j, j = 1, \ldots, J)$, purchase reinforcement (π_{11}^j), performance feedback (π_{21}^j), inertia in decision making (π_{22}^j) and competitive reactions (π_{32}^j). Only instantaneous effects are not included directly, but these are reflected in the variance-covariance matrix of the residuals (Σ). Estimation of these models remains straightforward: (1) all explanatory variables are predetermined, so there is no concern over the identification issues that are often encountered when specifying structural multiple-equation models, and (2) all equations in the system have the same explanatory variables so that OLS estimation can be applied without loss of efficiency.

However, this flexibility comes at a certain cost. First, the number of parameters may become very large. For $J = 8$, for example, the VAR model in equation (10) will estimate $9 \times 8 = 72$ autoregressive parameters. If, however, one considers a system with 5 dependent variables, this number increases to $25 \times 8 = 200$. Several authors (see e.g., Dekimpe and Hanssens, 1995) have therefore restricted all parameters with $|t| < 1$ to zero.[2] While this may alleviate the problem of estimating and interpreting so many parameters, it is unlikely to fully eliminate it. As a consequence, one typically does not interpret the individual parameters of the VAR models, but one focuses instead on the impulse-response functions (IRFs) derived from these parameters. IRFs trace, over time, the incremental performance and spending implications of an initial one-period change in advertising support. In so doing, they provide a concise summary of the information contained in this multitude of parameters, a summary that lends itself well to a graphical and easy-to-interpret representation. In Appendix A, we briefly outline how such an impulse-response function can be derived for the simple case of a first-order VAR model.

Note, however, that Equation 10 (or Equation A.1 in Appendix A) provides no direct estimate of the instantaneous effects. The residual correlation matrix can be used to establish the presence of such an effect, but not its direction. Various procedures have been used in the marketing literature to deal with this issue, such as an an a priori imposition of a certain causal ordering on the variables (i.e., imposing that an instantaneous effect can occur in one, but not the other, direction) as in Dekimpe and Hanssens (1995), a sensitivity analysis of various causal orderings (see e.g., Dekimpe et al., 1999), or accounting for expected instantaneous effects in the other variables when deriving the impulse-response functions, which are then referred to as "generalized" impulse response functions (Peasarn and Shin, 1998). We refer to Dekimpe and Hanssens (2004) for a more detailed discussion on these issues.

A graphical illustration of some IRFs, taken from Dekimpe and Hanssens (1995), is given in Figure 4.3.2. It shows the IRF tracing the incremental performance (top line) and advertising-spending (bottom line) impact of a $1000 shock (unexpected increase) in the advertising allocation of a large home-improvement chain. Because of the chain reaction of events (consumer response, purchase reinforcement, competitive reactions, …) reflected in this IRF, we see various fluctuations overtime. Interestingly, neither of the two IRFs depicted in Figure 4.3.2 converge to zero, which demonstrates that the initial $1000 shock sets into motion various forces that result in a *continued*

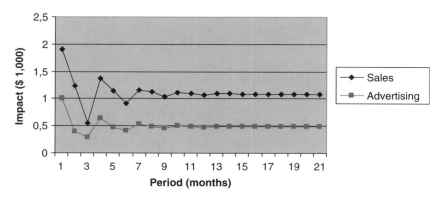

Figure 4.3.2   Impulse response functions

(or *persistent*) effect on the firm's sales and spending levels. A behavioural explanation for the increased sales level could be the fact that the advertising campaign attracted new customers to the firm or brand who also generate an ongoing revenue stream of repeat purchases. Alternatively, existing customers could have increased their purchase rate after the ad campaign. The continued increase in advertising spending, in turn, could be attributed to a firm-specific budget rule which specifies that a fraction of the (incremental) sales revenue is reinvested in maintenance advertising.

While impulse-response functions are useful summary devices, the multitude of numbers (periods) involved still makes them somewhat awkward to compare across brands, markets, or marketing-mix instruments. To reduce this set of numbers to a more manageable size, various summary statistics may be derived from the IRFs (see Pauwels et al., 2002):

(i) the *immediate* performance impact of the advertising increase;
(ii) the *long-run* or permanent (persistent) impact, which is the value to which the IRF converges; and
(iii) the cumulative effect before this convergence level is obtained. This cumulative effect is often called the total *short-run* effect. If the IRFs converge to zero, this reflects the area under the curve. In case of a persistent effect, one can compute the combined (cumulative effect) over the time span it takes before the persistent effect is obtained. The time interval before convergence is obtained is often referred to as the dust-settling period (Dekimpe and Hanssens, 1999; Nijs et al., 2001).

A technical discussion of the various modeling decisions to be made in the specification of VAR models and the subsequent derivation of the impulse-response functions is beyond the scope of the current chapter, and may be found in Dekimpe and Hanssens (2004). Early applications of this approach have revealed (see e.g., Steenkamp et al., 2005), among other things:

(i) that substantial differences may exist between the short- and long-run impact of advertising;

(ii) that a firm's own reaction to its past advertising helps determine its future spending and long-run sales impact;
(iii) that it typically takes a sustained advertising effort rather than a temporary investment in order to create meaningful long-term impact; and
(iv) that consumer response is more important than competitive reaction in determining the total advertising effect.

RESPONSE MODELS, ADVERTISING PHENOMENA, AND ADVERTISING DECISION MAKING

We conclude the chapter by summarizing various empirical regularities that have been obtained by applying the models described above to a multitude of real-life datasets, reviewing the substantive advertising phenomena proposed by John Little, and summarizing how response models have dealt with them. We then extend our models to important performance metrics other than attitudes or sales, and we discuss the impact of advertising response modelling on advertising decision making.

Summary of quantitative advertising effects

Over 25 years ago, John Little (1979) wrote a seminal paper proposing that advertising response was characterized by the following five phenomena:

- The steady-state response of sales to advertising is concave or S-shaped;
- Upward response is fast; downward response is slow;
- Competitive spending matters;
- Advertising effectiveness changes over time;
- Response can tail off even under constant spending.

Advertising response research in the last 25 years has put these findings in a sharper perspective:

- The predominant response function is concave. S-shaped response functions, i.e., threshold effects, may exist, but are the exception (e.g., Rao and Miller, 1975). In terms of overall sales sensitivity, advertising elasticity is 0.1 on average. That makes it the weakest of the marketing-mix instruments (see, e.g., Hanssens et al., (2001) for details). That does not imply, however, that advertising is the least profitable instrument (Jones, 1990).

- Advertising elasticities are demonstrably higher for new products (about 0.3) than for established products (about 0.01) (Assmus et al., 1984).
- Visible short-term lifts are a *condition* for the existence of long-term effects. For example, an extensive experimental study by Lodish et al. (1995) showed that about *one-third* of television commercials showed a significant effect on sales in the first year. The long-term impact of these *effective* commercials is about twice the short-run effect.
- While competitive spending matters, the ultimate effects of advertising are more influenced by the nature of consumer response itself than by the vigilance of competitors' reactions (Steenkamp et al., 2005).
- Smaller competitors tend to have higher advertising-to-sales (A/S) ratios than market leaders (e.g., Tellis, 2004).
- Advertising wear-in and wear-out patterns help explain why ad response can tail off even under constant spending. After nearly half a century, Zielske's (1959) experimental result that 3 to 4 exposures is best, still holds.

Interpreting the findings

In understanding the rationale behind Little's phenomena, it is helpful to make a distinction between advertising for durables and advertising for consumables (products and services). For durables, *market rejuvenation* is a key concept. Effective advertising for a durable reduces the untapped market (buyers remaining), resulting in a loss of aggregate effectiveness. After some time has elapsed, the market is rejuvenated with new prospects, and a new campaign can once again be effective. For consumables, we know that people "learn faster than they forget," which helps explain the different rise/decay rates in ad response. By the same token, we know that advertising has a stronger effect on trial rates than on repeat rates (Deighton et al., 1994).

For both durables and consumables, we know that advertising is stronger in creating awareness than in fostering preference. The performance feedback loop (i.e., product usage experience or purchase reinforcement) is much stronger than advertising in determining future consumer choices. Hence, while advertising can be used to initiate trial, it alone is not sufficient to sustain repeat purchase without a favourable product evaluation. This, too, helps explain the declining role of advertising over the life cycle.

Many studies have focused on various qualitative aspects of advertising (see Vakratsas, 2005, for a review of recent contributions). Among the most promising is recent work on eye movements that has revealed which aspects of a print ad (e.g., text, pictures, brand name, relative position on the page, etc.) are the most impactful (Pieters et al., 1999). Their results could well lead to a new, improved practice of copy writing. On the other hand, we know little about the *relative importance* of advertising quality and advertising quantity, e.g., can higher spending make up for poorer advertising quality?

Other response metrics

Last, but not least, we must recognize that sales revenue is not the only performance metric against which advertising effectiveness should be judged. We list below a number of important alternative performance metrics, and we make some observations about how advertising is known to affect them. Note that the response models for these alternative metrics are generally similar in nature to the models we have discussed in this chapter.

- Protecting or enhancing *price premiums.* There is evidence that, ceteris paribus, nonprice advertising leads to lower price sensitivity, and hence the ability to charge higher prices (e.g., Farris and Albion, 1980). Note that, by the same token, price advertising may *increase* price sensitivity (see also Kaul and Wittink, 1995).
- Enhancing sales-call effectiveness. Advertising support may pre-educate a prospect so that subsequent sales calls have a higher chance

of success. For example, Gatignon and Hanssens (1987) found this to be the case in military recruitment.

- Building distribution. When the trade makes stocking decisions based on anticipated consumer demand, and when they perceive that demand to be influenced by advertising, higher distribution levels may be obtained (e.g., Parsons, 1974).
- Motivating employees. Advertising may have an "internal" audience in addition to its usual external audience (e.g., Gilly and Wolfinbarger, 1998).
- Lifting stock price. Investors are exposed to advertising much as consumers are. Evidence from the PC industry suggests that advertising may increase stock prices above and beyond the effect expected from an increase in sales and profits (Joshi and Hanssens, 2005).
- Reducing earnings volatility. Advertising spending is relatively easily manipulated and is fully amortized in the period in which it occurs. That makes it a convenient expenditure category to expand in times of strong earnings, and reduce in times of weak earnings, thereby reducing the firm's earnings volatility and its cost of capital. This strategic use of advertising is supported by the finding that, over long time periods, higher marketing expenditures are associated with lower firm risk (Kim et al., 2005).
- Signalling intentions to competitors. As an example, large-budget motion pictures under-development may advertise a release date to the public up to one year in advance, in order to discourage competitive entry in their chosen launch week.
- Building a brand (see Chapter 1.4). Although brand-building is often claimed as an intangible (and, ergo, difficult-to-measure) effect of advertising, we are not aware of any scientific evidence that advertising impacts brand equity *above and beyond* its direct effects on sales, price premiums, etc. On the other hand, advertising is often argued to be a powerful instrument to keep private labels at bay (Steenkamp and Dekimpe, 1997), and to lessen the negative impact of competitive price promotions (Nijs et al., 2001; Steenkamp et al., 2005).

Advertising response and advertising decision making

A critical question is whether firms' actual advertising decisions are *in line* with observed response patterns. Although, there is no clear-cut answer to this question, several components suggest that advertising decisions (especially spending decisions) are *not* necessarily made with market response in mind (see Chapter 5.3). In particular:

- There is a clear feedback loop between sales performance and advertising spending (this is one of the early empirical findings of the marketing science literature, e.g., Bass, 1969).
- Likewise, at the macroeconomic level, higher consumption leads to more advertising (see, e.g., Ashley et al., 1980) and a strong determinant of advertising spending at the firm level is corporate profitability: As profits rise, so do advertising budgets, and vice versa. Interestingly, the advent of new media makes little difference. In the U.S., for example, relative advertising spending has been a *mean-reverting time series*, fluctuating around 3% of GNP, for many decades, regardless of technological breakthroughs in communications.
- Advertising levels are also determined by competitive spending; i.e., firms strive to match or exceed their competitors' A/S ratios. This practice can lead to advertising spending escalations that have negative consequences for profitability (e.g., Metwally, 1978).

As a result, a complete measurement of advertising effectiveness needs to account for the fact that budget allocations are made from within the system of study, and not necessarily exogenously determined. In some instances, expenditures are made and resources are allocated to maximize return on investment; in other instances, expenditures are made because of last year's sales. In either case, the amount of expenditure cannot always be treated as an independent variable. For example, we rarely observe a *reduction* in advertising spending as successful products march through their life cycles. Instead, advertising is generally treated as an *expense* rather than an investment (see e.g., Ambler, 2003), and its key determinant is availability of discretionary funds. When this occurs, the system's modelling discussed in Section 2 becomes necessary if we want to describe not only advertising's impact on sales, but also draw meaningful recommendations that improve the practice of advertising. Further research, however, is needed on how to best use the estimated response parameters to make managerial recommendations for change. Indeed, under what conditions can inferences on advertising effectiveness, derived from historically observed response patterns and decision rules (both within-firm and competitive), be used to make predictions of the impact of radically different allocation schemes (see e.g., Franses, 2005; Van Heerde et al., 2005)? While this is a challenging task, it is a necessary one to move from the more descriptive uses of most currently-available response models to sound normative recommendations.

SUMMARY

This chapter focused on econometric models of advertising effects on sales and other tangible performance metrics. We formulated a core advertising response model that accommodates most of the fundamental advertising response phenomena, and extended this model to account for different advertising media, creative effects, wear-in and wear-out, and other important aspects of advertising practice. We then expanded the model to a multiple-equation system to accommodate potential competitive response, as well as feedback loops within the firm.

Increasing sales is not the only goal for advertising, but response models for these alternative metrics below are generally similar in nature to the models we have discussed in this chapter. Examples in this respect could be:

- Protecting or enhancing *price premiums.*
- Enhancing sales-call effectiveness.
- Building distribution.
- Motivating employees.
- Lifting stock price.
- Reducing earnings volatility.
- Signaling intentions to competitors.
- Building the brand.

NOTES

1 We refer to Hanssens et al. (2001) for a review of other functional specifications that have been used in the literature.

2 Note that this may necessitate the use of SUR, rather than OLS, estimation, as the equations may now have a different set of explanatory variables.

REFERENCES

Ambler, T. (2003), *Marketing and the Bottom Line.* London, U.K.: FT Prentice Hall.

Anderson, E. and D. Simester (2004), "Long-run Effects of Promotion Depth on New versus Established Customers: Three Field Studies," *Marketing Science,* 23 (1), 3–20.

Ashley, R., C.W.J. Granger and R. Schmalensee (1980), "Advertising and Aggregate Consumption: An Analysis of Causality," *Econometrica,* 48 (July), 1149–67.

Assmus, G., J.U. Farley and D.R. Lehmann (1984), "How Advertising Affects Sales: Meta-Analysis of Econometric Results," *Journal of Marketing Research,* 21 (February), 65–74.

Bass, F.M. (1969), "A Simultaneous Equation Regression Study of Advertising and Sales of Cigarettes," *Journal of Marketing Research,* 6 (August), 291–300.

Broadbent, S. (1984), "Modeling with Adstock," *Journal of the Market Research Society,* 26 (October), 295–312.

Chandy, R., G.J. Tellis, D. MacInnis and P. Thaivanich (2001), "What to Say When: Advertising Appeals in Evolving Markets," *Journal of Marketing Research,* 38, 4 (November), 399–414.

Christen, M., S. Gupta, J.C. Porter, R. Staelin and D.R. Wittink (1997), "Using Market Level Data to Understand Promotional Effects in a Nonlinear Model," *Journal of Marketing Research,* 34 (3), 322–34.

Clarke, D.G. (1976), "Econometric Measurement of the Duration of Advertising Effect on Sales," *Journal of Marketing Research,* 16 (May), 286–9.

Deighton, J., C. Henderson and S. Neslin (1994), "The Effects of Advertising on Brand Switching and Repeat Purchasing," *Journal of Marketing Research,* 31 (February), 28–42.

Dekimpe, M. and D. Hanssens (1995), "The Persistence of Marketing Effects on Sales," *Marketing Science,* 14 (Winter), 1–21.

Dekimpe, M.G. and D.M. Hanssens (1999), "Sustained Spending and Persistent Response: A New Look at Long-Term Marketing Profitability," *Journal of Marketing Research,* 36 (November), 1–31.

Dekimpe, M.G., D.M. Hanssens and J.M. Silva-Risso (1999), "Long-run Effects of Price Promotions in Scanner Markets," *Journal of Econometrics,* 89 (1–2), 269–91.

Dekimpe, M.G. and D.M. Hanssens (2004), "Persistence Modeling for Assessing Marketing Strategy Performance," in *Assessing Marketing Strategy Performance*, eds. D. Lehmann and C. Moorman, Marketing Science Institute, 2004.

Eastlack, J.O. Jr. and A.G. Rao (1986), "Modeling Response to Advertising and Pricing Changes for 'V-8' Cocktail Vegetable Juice," *Marketing Science*, 5 (Summer), 245–59.

Farris, P.W. and D.C. West (2007), "A Fresh View of the Advertising Budget Process," in *The SAGE Handbook of Advertising*, eds. G.J. Tellis and T. Ambler, London: Sage Publications.

Farris, P.W. and M.S. Albion (1980), "The Impact of Advertising on the Price of Consumer Products," *Journal of Advertising Research*, 44 (Summer), 17–35.

Franses, P.H. (2005), "On the Use of Econometric Models for Policy Simulations in Marketing," *Journal of Marketing Research*, 42 (February), 4–14.

Franses, P.H. and M. Vriens (2004), "Advertising Effects on Awareness, Consideration and Brand Choice Using Tracking Data," *Working Paper*, Erasmus University Rotterdam.

Gatignon, H. (1984), "Toward a Methodology for Measuring Advertising Copy Effects," *Marketing Science*, 3, 4 (Fall), 308–26.

Gatignon, H. and D.M. Hanssens (1987), "Modeling Marketing Interactions with Application to Salesforce Effectiveness," *Journal of Marketing Research*, 24 (August), 247–57.

Gilly, M. and M. Wolfinbarger (1998), "Advertising's Internal Audience," *Journal of Marketing*, 62 (January), 69–88.

Givon, M. and D. Horsky (1990), "Untangling the Effects of Purchase Reinforcement and Advertising Carryover," *Marketing Science*, 9 (2), 171–87.

Hanssens, D.M. and H.A. Levien (1983), "An Econometric Study of Recruitment Marketing in the U.S. Navy," *Management Science*, 29 (October), 1167–84.

Hanssens, D.M., L.J. Parsons and R.L. Schultz (2001), *Market Response Models*, 2nd ed. Boston, Mass.: Kluwer Academic Publishers.

Helmer, R.M. and J.K. Johansson (1977), "An Exposition of the Box-Jenkins Transfer Function Analysis with Application to the Advertising-Sales Relationship," *Journal of Marketing Research*, 14 (May), 227–39.

Johansson, J.K. (1979), "Advertising and the S-Curve: A New Approach," *Journal of Marketing Research*, 16 (August), 346–54.

Jones, J.P. (1990), "The Double Jeopardy of Sales Promotions," *Harvard Business Review*, 68 (5), 145–52.

Joshi, A. and D.M. Hanssens (2005), "Advertising Spending and Market Capitalization," *Working Paper*, Los Angeles, Calif.: UCLA Marketing Studies Center.

Kaul, A. and D.R. Wittink (1995), "Empirical Generalizations About the Impact of Advertising on Price Sensitivity and Price," *Marketing Science*, 14 (3), G151–60.

Keller, K.L. (2007), "Advertising and Brand Equity," in *The SAGE Handbook of Advertising*, eds. G.J. Tellis and T. Ambler, London: Sage Publications.

Kim, M., L. McAlister and R. Srinivasan (2005), "Marketing and Systematic Risk of the Firm," *Working Paper*, University of Texas at Austin, September.

Leone, R.P. (1995), "Generalizing What is Known of Temporal Aggregation and Advertising Carryover," *Marketing Science*, 14 (3), G141–50.

Little, J.D.C. (1970), "Models and Managers: The Concept of a Decision Calculus," *Management Science*, 16 (April), 466–85.

Little, J.D.C. (1979), "Aggregate Advertising Models: The State of the Art," *Operations Research*, 27 (July–August), 629–67.

Liu, L.-M. and D.M. Hanssens (1982), "Identification of Multiple-Input Transfer Function Models," *Communication in Statistics Theory and Methods*, 11 (3), 297–314.

Lodish, L.M., M. Abraham, S. Kalmenson, J. Livelsberger, B. Lubetkin, B. Richardson and M.E. Stevens (1995), "How TV Advertising Works: A Meta-Analysis of 389 Real World Split Cable TV Advertising Experiments," *Journal of Marketing Research*, 32 (May), 125–39.

Mahajan, V., E. Muller and S. Sharma (1984), "An Empirical Comparison of Awareness Forecasting Models of New product Introduction," *Marketing Science*, 3, 3 (Summer), 179–97.

Metwally, M.M. (1978), "Escalation Tendencies of Advertising," *Oxford Bulletin of Economics and Statistics*, 40 (May), 153–63.

Montgomery, D.B. and A.J. Silk (1972), "Estimating Dynamic Effects of Marketing Communication Expenditures," *Management Science*, 18, B485–501.

Naik, P.A. and K. Raman (2003), "Understanding the Impact of Synergy in Multimedia Communications," *Journal of Marketing Research*, 40 (November), 375–88.

Nijs, V.R., M.G. Dekimpe, J.-B.E.M. Steenkamp and D.M. Hanssens (2001), "The Category-Demand Effects of Price Promotions," *Marketing Science*, 20 (1), 1–22.

Parsons, L.J. (1974), "An Econometric Analysis of Advertising, Retail Availability and Sales of a New Brand," *Management Science*, 20 (February), 938–47.

Pauwels, K., D.M. Hanssens and S. Siddarth (2002), "The Long-term Effects of Price Promotions on Category Incidence, Brand Choice and Purchase Quantity,"

Journal of Marketing Research, 39 (November), 421–39.

Pesaran H.H. and Y. Shin (1998), "Generalized Impulse Response Analysis in Linear Multivariate Models," *Economic Letters*, 17–29.

Pieters, R., E. Rosbergen and M. Wedel (1999), "Visual Attention to Repeated Print Advertising: A Test of Scanpath Theory," *Journal of Marketing Research*, 36 (November), 424–38.

Pringle, L., R. Wilson and E. Brody, (1982), "NEWS: A Decision Oriented Model for New Product Analysis and Forecasting," *Marketing Science*, 1 (1), 1–39.

Rao, A. and P.B. Miller (1975), "Advertising/Sales Response Functions," *Journal of Advertising Research*, 15 (April), 7–15.

Simon, H. (1982), "ADPULS: An Advertising Model with Wearout and Pulsation," *Journal of Marketing Research*, 19 (August), 352–63.

Steenkamp, J.-B.E.M. and M.G. Dekimpe (1997), "The Increasing Power of Store Brands: Building Loyalty and Market Share," *Long Range Planning*, 30 (December), 917–30.

Steenkamp, J.-B.E.M., V.R. Nijs, D.M. Hanssens and M.G. Dekimpe (2005), "Competitive Reactions and the Cross-Sales Effects of Advertising and Promotion," *Marketing Science*, 24, 1 (Winter), 35–54.

Tellis, G.J. (2004), *Effective Advertising: How, When, and Why Advertising Works*, Thousand Oaks, CA: Sage Publications.

Tellis, G., R.K. Chandy and P. Thaivanich (2000), "Which Ads Work, When, Where, and How Often? Modeling the Effects of Direct Television Advertising," *Journal of Marketing Research*, 37 (February), 32–46.

Tellis, G. and P.H. Franses (2006), "Optimal Data Interval for Econometric Models of Advertising Carryover," *Marketing Science*, 25 (May/June), 217–29.

Tellis, G.J. and D. Weiss (1995), "Does TV Advertising Really Affect Sales?" *Journal of Advertising*, 24 (3), 1–12.

The Wall Street Journal (2005), "Econometrics Buzzes Ad World As a Way of Measuring Results," August 16.

Vakratsas, D. (2005), "Advertising Response Models with Managerial Impact: An Agenda for the Future," *Applied Stochastic Models in Business and Industry*, 21 (4–5), 351–61.

Van Dijk, A., H.J. Van Heerde, P.S.H. Leeflang and D.R. Wittink (2004), "Similarity-Based Spatial Methods to Estimate Shelf-Space Elasticities," *Quantitative Marketing and Economics*, 2, 257–77.

Van Heerde, H.J., M.G. Dekimpe and W.P. Putsis Jr. (2005), "Marketing Models and the Lucas Critique," *Journal of Marketing Research*, 42 (February), 15–21.

Zielske, H. (1959), "The Remembering and Forgetting of Advertising," *Journal of Marketing*, 23 (January), 239–43.

APPENDIX A: IMPULSE-RESPONSE FUNCTIONS: MATHEMATICAL DERIVATION

$$
\begin{bmatrix} \ln(S_t) \\ \ln(A_t) \\ \ln(CA_t) \end{bmatrix} = \begin{bmatrix} \pi_{11} & \pi_{12} & \pi_{13} \\ \pi_{21} & \pi_{22} & \pi_{23} \\ \pi_{31} & \pi_{32} & \pi_{33} \end{bmatrix} \begin{bmatrix} \ln(S_{t-1}) \\ \ln(A_{t-1}) \\ \ln(CA_{t-1}) \end{bmatrix}
$$

$$
+ \begin{bmatrix} u_{S,t} \\ u_{A,t} \\ u_{CA,t} \end{bmatrix}, \qquad (A.1)
$$

one sets $[u_S, u_A, u_{CA}] = [0,0,0]$ prior to t

$\qquad\qquad\qquad [0,1,0]$ at time t

$\qquad\qquad\qquad [0,0,0]$ after t

and computes (simulates) the future values for the various dependent variables, i.e.,

$$
\begin{bmatrix} \ln(S_t) \\ \ln(A_t) \\ \ln(CA_t) \end{bmatrix} = \begin{bmatrix} \pi_{11} & \pi_{12} & \pi_{13} \\ \pi_{21} & \pi_{22} & \pi_{23} \\ \pi_{31} & \pi_{32} & \pi_{33} \end{bmatrix} \begin{bmatrix} 0 \\ 0 \\ 0 \end{bmatrix} + \begin{bmatrix} 0 \\ 1 \\ 0 \end{bmatrix}
$$

$$
= \begin{bmatrix} 0 \\ 1 \\ 0 \end{bmatrix},
$$

$$
\begin{bmatrix} \ln(S_{t+1}) \\ \ln(A_{t+1}) \\ \ln(CA_{t+1}) \end{bmatrix} = \begin{bmatrix} \pi_{11} & \pi_{12} & \pi_{13} \\ \pi_{21} & \pi_{22} & \pi_{23} \\ \pi_{31} & \pi_{32} & \pi_{33} \end{bmatrix} \begin{bmatrix} 0 \\ 1 \\ 0 \end{bmatrix} + \begin{bmatrix} 0 \\ 0 \\ 0 \end{bmatrix}
$$

$$
= \begin{bmatrix} \pi_{12} \\ \pi_{22} \\ \pi_{32} \end{bmatrix},
$$

$$
\begin{bmatrix} \ln(S_{t+2}) \\ \ln(A_{t+2}) \\ \ln(CA_{t+2}) \end{bmatrix} = \begin{bmatrix} \pi_{11} & \pi_{12} & \pi_{13} \\ \pi_{21} & \pi_{22} & \pi_{23} \\ \pi_{31} & \pi_{32} & \pi_{33} \end{bmatrix} \begin{bmatrix} \pi_{12} \\ \pi_{22} \\ \pi_{32} \end{bmatrix} + \begin{bmatrix} 0 \\ 0 \\ 0 \end{bmatrix}
$$

$$
= \begin{bmatrix} \pi_{11}\pi_{12} + \pi_{12}\pi_{22} + \pi_{13}\pi_{32} \\ \pi_{21}\pi_{12} + \pi_{22}\pi_{22} + \pi_{23}\pi_{32} \\ \pi_{31}\pi_{12} + \pi_{32}\pi_{22} + \pi_{33}\pi_{32} \end{bmatrix},
$$

$$
\text{Etc}\ldots
$$

Advertising Effectiveness in Contemporary Markets

Gerard J. Tellis

How effective is advertising in real markets?

Researchers have been studying the effectiveness of advertising in real markets, since managers started using advertising to influence consumer behaviour. However, knowledge about advertising's effects in real markets has grown rapidly in the last 50 years, after researchers began to combine scientific methods of experimentation with econometric and statistical analyses of real market data. Researchers have published their findings in journals of advertising, consumer behaviour, marketing, management, psychology, and economics. As such, they have spawned a vast, rich body of knowledge of how advertising works.

What have we learnt from this vast body of research?

Actually, we have learned quite a bit. Some of this learning has been replicated again and again, so that we can claim to have some generalization or even precise metrics about the effects of advertising. On other issues, we have a growing consensus but no clear metrics. On a third set of issues, because of limited research and little or no consensus, we have only a preliminary understanding.

Two paradigms have researched the effects of advertising: the behavioural paradigm and the modelling paradigm. The behavioural paradigm has primarily examined the effects of advertising content on mental processes (such as recognition, recall, attitude, persuasion, brand liking, or brand equity). This paradigm has predominantly used laboratory experiments or theatre tests. Because an experiment involves a careful design of variables in an artificial environment, it provides a strong test of causality but is low on relevance to real markets. Section 2 of this handbook reviews the major findings from this research paradigm.

The modeling paradigm has primarily examined the effects of advertising intensity on market behaviour. Advertising intensity has been measured by a brand's advertising expenditures, gross ratings points, or ad exposures delivered to the market. Market behaviour has been measured by a brand's unit sales, revenues, choices, or market share (in units or revenues). The method of analysis has been field experiments (Chapter 4.1) or econometric models (Chapter 4.2 and Chapter 4.3). Because econometric models typically use real market data, which may not be easily controlled, they are strong on relevance but weak on ascertaining causality.

Neither the laboratory experiment nor the econometric approach is universally superior by itself. However, the market experiment represents a nice hybrid. If properly designed, it can combine the strengths of the laboratory experiment and the econometric model without being straddled with their limitations. A hybrid approach also has the strength of determining advertising's impact on the mental processes (to help copy design) and on sales (to help budgeting).

This chapter reviews the findings from studies that have used econometric models or market experiments and have all been carried out in real markets. It presents the learning from published market studies that used the tools and methods explained in Chapter 4.1, Chapter 4.2, and Chapter 4.3. However, it does not cover the study of the unique database of award-wining ads described in Chapter 3.4. It also does not cover those studies that assess the effect of advertising on price or brand equity as an end in itself (see Chapter 1.4; Ambler, 2004; Ambler and Hollier, 2005).

The chapter is divided in to three parts. Part A deals with the effects of advertising intensity. Part B deals with the dynamic effects of Advertising. Part C deals with the content effects of advertising. The chapter does not cover the effects of advertising reach (Vakratsas and Ambler, 1999). At the end, the chapter summarizes what we have learnt in each of these areas.[1]

PART A: EFFECTS OF ADVERTISING INTENSITY IN MARKETS

Classification of studies

Researchers have carried out a vast number and variety of studies on this topic. To meaningfully organize this body of research and summarize the main findings, we need some basis by which to classify them. The focus of various studies provides such a basis. Most of these studies focus on one or more of three aspects of advertising intensity: weight, elasticity, or frequency (see Table 4.4.1).

Weight studies examine the effects of *differences in the advertising* across time periods or across regions. **Elasticity studies** examine the effects of *changes in advertising* from period to period within a region. **Frequency studies** examine the effects of *changes in ad exposures* targeted to consumers from period to period within a region.

These three aspects of advertising effectiveness are related. The total advertising budget in a time frame determines how much can be applied from period to period in that time frame. The period budget determines how many exposures are targeted to individual consumers in that period. However, they differ in three important ways. Frequency studies provide the best understanding of how advertising works in persuading consumers to act. Elasticity studies provide less understanding than frequency studies on this dimension, while weight studies provide the least understanding. On the other hand, the implications of weight studies are transparent in terms of actionable guidelines

Table 4.4.1   Description of studies on advertising intensity

Type of study	Ad weight	Ad elasticity	Ad frequency
Independent variable	Increase or decrease in total ad budget	Variation of ad budget from period to period	Variation of ad exposures from period to period
Target	Total market or segment	Total market or segment	Consumer or household
Response (dependent variable)	Sales, Revenues, or market share	Sales, Revenues, or market share	Sales or choices
Metric of Effectiveness	Change in response if any	Elasticity of response to advertising	Effective frequency at which response peaks

Source: Adapted from Tellis (2004).

for managers. The implications of elasticity studies are less transparent than those of weight studies. The implications of frequency studies are the least transparent of the three.

Ideally, these three aspects of advertising should be examined simultaneously in one study. However, because response to advertising is complex, researchers have focused on only one or at most two of these aspects at a time. On each of these aspects, we have a stream of research and a small body of findings. To compare studies within a stream and arrive at potential generalizations, this chapter summarizes the findings separately by these three types of studies.

Studies of advertising weight

Explanation of terms and studies

Several studies sought to determine whether increases or decreases in advertising weight have any effect on sales and market share (Tellis, 2004). If increases in advertising weight lead to increases in sales and profits that more than compensate for the additional cost of advertising, then the brand needs to stay with that increase. Similarly, if decreases in advertising weight do not lead to decreases in sales and profits that exceed the savings from the lower weight, then the brand needs to stay with the lower weight. Studies that have researched this issue have done so through various market tests.

We need to define some commonly used terms in such market experiments: weight, copy, media, schedule, and audience tests. The word **test** means a specific experiment. A **weight test** is a market experiment in which the researcher compares the effect of advertising between two or more markets, each at a different level of intensity of advertising. Typically, one of these test markets has the level of advertising that the firm currently uses. This market is called the control condition. The other markets are called the test conditions. In the spirit of good experimentation (see Chapter 4.1), *all other factors are kept as similar as possible between the conditions.*

The dependent variable in these tests typically is sales (or market share). The goal of a weight test is to see whether the increase or decrease in the level of advertising *alone* has any effect at all on sales. In addition to weight, other aspects of advertising that researchers also test are copy, media, audience, and schedule. When testing the effect of any other aspect of advertising, the researcher must keep all other factors constant between the test conditions. Researchers can vary two or more variables (e.g., weight and copy) at a time. However, to obtain a valid experiment, the number of conditions rapidly goes up as the product of the levels of the factors. For example, to validly test two levels of weights with 3 levels of copy, the researcher will need $2 \times 3 = 6$ conditions. The term copy, in this section, refers broadly to any changes in the content of the ad.

Researchers have carried out over 450 market experiments to assess the effectiveness of advertising. Six sets of experiments are especially instructive about the effects of advertising on sales. These experiments were associated with Anheuser-Busch, Grey and D'Arcy Advertising, AdTel, Campbell Soup, and Information Resource Inc. In addition, two advertising researchers (Aaker and Carmen, 1982) review the first three of these studies as well as several smaller experiments. The following subsections describe key features of these studies and summarize their main findings.

Ackoff and Emshoff (1975) describe an interesting set of experiments at Anheuser-Busch, Inc, for the Budweiser brand of beer, in the mid 1960s. The experiments varied advertising levels, pulsing patterns, media, and other promotional activity. The most elaborate of these experiments involved changes in advertising weight of -100%, -50%, -25%, 0%, $+50\%$, $+100\%$, $+200\%$ relative to current expenditures. Each level was tried over six areas for greater confidence in the results. The experiments showed that in the short term decreasing the level of advertising had no negative impact on sales. The authors attributed the response pattern to the over saturation of primary segments with past advertising of the brand. They found that suspension for more than a year led to some deterioration in sales. In these situations, the sales levels and sales growth could be restored with just the previous (normal) advertising level. These results suggest the use of scheduling, in which a firm staggers normal levels of advertising with periods of complete suspension of all advertising (also called flighting, see Chapter 5.4). Cost for advertising can be lower with the suspension, while advertising can be re-started as soon as sales seem to erode.

As regards the effectiveness of different media, they found no significant difference between radio, magazines, and newspapers. However, they found that television was slightly superior to the other media, while billboards were slightly inferior. They also found that promotional expenditures were close to the optimum. Careful implementation of their recommendations led to a decrease in advertising expenditures from $1.89/barrel to $.8/barrel with a corresponding sales increase from 7.5 million to 14.5 million barrels.

Review of field experiments

Aaker and Carman (1982) summarized the results of 120 AdTel experiments in three cities during the 1960s and 1970s, in which AdTel controlled advertising by varying either ad-levels or ad-content to subgroups in each city. Of the 120 tests, 48 were weight tests and 36 were copy tests. Six of the 48 weight tests involved lower levels of advertising. However, none of these six tests showed any decline in sales. Of the 42 remaining tests (involving increased advertising), 30% showed sales changes that were different from the control groups. Most of the latter tests were for new products. In contrast, 47% of the copy tests showed significant differences in sales between test and control groups.

Aaker and Carmen (1982) report on a total of 11 experiments conducted by Grey Advertising and D'Arcy Advertising. Overall, this set of experiments showed that advertising increases were effective in about half the experiments, while an advertising decrease

had no deleterious effect in sales in the one place it was tested.

Aaker and Carmen (1982) also analysed a total of 69 other experiments. Eleven of these tests involved a reduction in advertising, some for 2 years or more. Almost all (10 of 11) of these experiments indicated that such reductions in advertising had no deleterious effects on sales. Of the remaining 58 experiments, only a minority of the experiments showed that increases in advertising were sufficiently effective in increasing sales so as to justify an increase in the advertising budget for the tested brand.

Eastlack and Rao (1989) reported a series of 19 advertising experiments on the sales of six brands of the Campbell Soup Company in the mid 1970s. The experiments varied factors such as advertising weight (−50% to +50%), scheduling, media, copy, and target market. The experiments show that changes in advertising weight had little or no impact on sales. However, changes in copy, media, and target markets did result in sales increases in some situations. Whenever sales increased significantly, the increase occurred early on rather than after prolonged repetition.

Magid and Lodish (1989) and Lodish et al. (1995a, 1995b) summarized over 389 advertising tests conducted over the last 10 years of BehaviourScan Advertising Tests at Information Resources Inc. (IRI) (see Chapter 4.3). For 49% of the weight tests, increased advertising yielded significantly higher sales at the 80% level of significance. The number of test results that would be significant at the 95% level is likely to be substantially lower, but the authors do not report that number. Even when the advertising was effective at this level of significance, it was found to be profitable (within the medium term of one year) in only 20% of the cases. An important finding, which echoes that from prior studies, was that massive increases in advertising weight were not more likely to yield better sales responsiveness than moderate increases. Increases in advertising were more likely to lead to increase in sales when the copy strategy is changed or the brand is in a growth stage. Advertising was much more effective for new products than for mature or established products. Most importantly, if advertising were not effective early on, then it would never be effective, even if it were repeated.

Implications

The review of experiments is important because of its scope. It covers 450 experiments, by numerous investigators, using a variety of brands, contexts, and time periods. The review indicates that for many mature brands, advertising weight, or the level of TV advertising per se is not critical in influencing sales. More than half the time, increases in weight alone do not lead to an increase in sales. However, neither do decreases in weight lead to sales decline, at least in the short to medium term. On the other hand, changes in other factors (media, copy, product, segments, or scheduling) could influence the effectiveness of advertising. In general, novelty in any of these factors may lead to an increase in sales.

Tests that involve a reduction in advertising, do not typically lead to a decrease in sales immediately. That could mean that past advertising has some carryover effect that does not decline immediately. Alternatively, it could mean that firms are overadvertising, so that the recent advertising was not effective at all. Prolonged cessation of advertising seems to have deleterious effects in some tests but no negative effects in other tests. What has not been studied is whether deleterious effects from cessation can be quickly corrected by fresh advertising. Thus, firms should be very careful about complete cessation of all advertising for prolonged periods of time. If they do so, they need to monitor the effects of such changes closely for a long period of time.

Thus the overall message from these studies is that advertisers may be overadvertising, at least in targeting the same segments with the same copy, media, schedule, and product. This situation would be exacerbated if advertisers resorted to further increases in advertising weight alone in these conditions.

The experiments indicate that advertising may have carryover effects, though there is less unanimity about the pattern of these effects. Most importantly, if advertising has any effect, that effect is visible early on. If it has no effect early on, then it is unlikely to have an effect with further repetition. On the other hand, when advertising is effective and maintained over a period of a year, its effects could last at least for two more years. In these cases, the effect in the latter two years could equal that in the first year.

While experiments provide a strong, clear test of causality, they suffer from the limitation of not being carried out in an entirely natural setting or taking into account other competitive activities. The following set of market studies compensates for this weakness in experiments.

Studies of advertising elasticity

Explanation of terms and studies

Advertising elasticity is the percentage change in sales (or market share) for a 1% change in the level of advertising. Because the numerator and denominator are in percentages, elasticity is units free (i.e., independent of the units of sales or advertising). It can also be called the **elasticity of sales to advertising**. Researchers estimate advertising elasticity by analysing the differences in sales or market share due to differences in advertising budget from period to period within a time frame.

Like weight tests, studies on advertising elasticity also focus on the advertising budget. However, studies of advertising elasticity go beyond the weight tests in that they determine the shape and strength of the advertising response function. Typically, researchers express this shape as a particular mathematical function (see Chapter 4.3) and the strength as an elasticity. To do so, researchers use some econometric model of the effect of advertising on sales or market share.

Researchers have conducted a vast number of studies of advertising elasticity. Most of these studies have used naturally occurring market data from research firms or advertisers themselves. However, some of the studies have also generated data through market experiments of the type described above.

Various reviews and meta-analyses have tried to summarize the findings from the original econometric models of advertising response. A literature review briefly describes each original study and summarizes the results across studies. In contrast, a meta-analysis is a study that treats the findings from original studies as dependent observations, which are then pooled together and analysed by the characteristics of those original studies.

Review of studies

There are at least two major reviews and two major meta-analyses of the effects of advertising on sales. We review only the two meta-analyses, for one important reason.[2] The two meta-analyses are comprehensive enough that they encompass the scope and findings of the two reviews. We first provide a brief explanation of the meta-analytic approach and then present the results of the meta-analyses.

The common mean of advertising elasticity across all the studies gives the best estimate of the effect of advertising in the population, i.e., across all contexts and research designs. Indeed, by the early 1990s, a variety of primary studies yielded over 400 estimates of the advertising elasticity. One formal approach for analyzing these estimates is **meta-analysis.**

The meta-analytic approach determines the mean of these elasticities and its systematic variation, if any, due to differences in design or contexts of the primary studies. Assmus et al. (1984) conducted a meta-analysis of 128 econometric models from primary studies that analysed the impact of advertising on sales or market share. Their major findings were the following:

- The grand mean for the advertising elasticity was 0.2.
- The grand mean for the carryover elasticity of advertising was 0.5.
- Short-term elasticities were much lower in models that incorporated a carryover coefficient (a lagged dependent variable) than in models without one.
- Models that contained exogenous variables had smaller short-term elasticities than those that did not.

- Elasticities in linear additive models were higher than those in multiplicative models (see Chapter 4.3) for different types of models).
- Pooled data involving cross-sectional observations in addition to time series observations, yielded higher elasticities.
- Food products have an elasticity that is .1 higher than other products.
- Elasticities were significantly higher for Europe relative to the US.
- Elasticities did not differ by measure of the dependent variable (sales or market share), by product or brand, by type of estimation method.

Sethuraman and Tellis (1991) and Tellis (1988b) carried out a more recent meta-analysis of advertising elasticities than the one above. Their study covered 260 primary estimates of the elasticity of sales or market share to advertising. Their major finding is that the average elasticity across all 260 estimates is 0.11. This estimate is half that of Assmus et al. (1984). The authors attributed the differences to their larger and more recent sample.

What does this number of 0.1 mean? Strictly, an elasticity of 0.1 means that a 1% increase in the level of advertising results in only about a 0.1% increase in sales. Empirically, the authors also compare this advertising elasticity with the corresponding price elasticity obtained from primary studies that estimated *both* elasticities. The price elasticity is -1.6 (Tellis, 1988b). Thus, the results of the empirical analysis show that the average price elasticity is almost *15 times* the average advertising elasticity. Because the average can be influenced by outliers, the authors also compared the advertising and price elasticities based on medians. They found the median price elasticity was almost 20 times that of the median advertising elasticity. For durable goods, the median price elasticity is 25 times the median advertising elasticity, whereas this ratio is just 5 for nondurable goods.

This result suggests that in the case of nondurable goods, price discounting *could* be more profitable than an advertising increase. The actual profitability would depend on margins, pass-through of promotions, and consumer switching. Based on estimated levels of pass-through and of consumers switching brands for a better deal, the authors make a rough estimate of the optimality of the advertising in durables and non-durables. They suspect that marketers of non-durables are probably over-advertising while those of durables are probably under advertising.

Another important finding is that the advertising elasticity is almost half as high in the US as it is for Europe. The reason may be that advertisers in the US tend to over advertise or that those in Europe are not advertising as much as they should. In terms of the ratio of the median price elasticity to advertising elasticity, the ratio is three times higher for the US (19.5 versus 6.2). This difference may suggest consumers are much more price sensitive than advertising sensitive in the US relative to Europe. One reason, again, may be that the level of advertising is too high in the US. Another reason may be that there is less scope and correspondingly less sensitivity for price discounting in Europe than in the US.

The authors also report that products in the early stages of their life cycle have a median ratio of price to advertising elasticity of 17.7 whereas those in the later stages have a significantly higher median ratio of 22.2. This result indicates that price discounts would be more effective in promoting sales in the later stages of the product's life cycle whereas in the early stages advertising would be more effective in promoting sales in the early stages of the product's life cycle.

Studies of ad frequency

Explanation of terms and studies

Advertising normally works through its effects on individual consumers. Thus the advertising budget in a time period ultimately translates into a sequence of individual exposures targeted to one or more consumers. Similarly, sales may be considered an aggregate of consumers' choices about individual brands. The term, **frequency**, refers to the number of ad exposures each consumer receives in a particular time period. **Effective frequency** refers to the optimum frequency

that maximizes the outcome designed by the advertisers, such as sales, profits, or price level.

Databases that record consumers' choices of brands, sometimes record the delivery of advertising in the form of advertising exposures. The analysis of consumers' choices presents unique problems and opportunities for understanding the effects of advertising. The major problem is that, since each consumer has a large number of purchases, the size and complexity of the data base quickly increases with the sample size. However, a focus on choice provides a large number of advantages. The key advantages are greater insight into how advertising works and a freedom from bias that occurs if one aggregates data over consumers or exposures.

Like studies on advertising elasticity, studies on frequency also determine the effectiveness of advertising in terms of the shape of the response function. However, studies on advertising elasticity capture the response function of aggregate sales to aggregate advertising expenditure. In contrast, studies on advertising frequency capture the response function of disaggregate consumers' choices to disaggregate advertising exposures. Thus such studies are far more specific in details and insight. At the same time, they are not immediately practical. Even if a manager knows the effective frequency, he or she still needs to know what advertising budget and scheduling will deliver that frequency to the appropriate consumers. So this stream of research by itself is insufficient to understanding how to use advertising.

Review of studies

We review the findings from five of these studies of the effect of ad exposures on consumer choice.

McDonald (1971) analysed the diary records of a sample of 266 panelists in nine product categories for 13 weeks. He took great care to avoid spurious causality when analysing the data. In particular, he made sure that he did not interpret the pattern of loyal consumers of a brand being targeted with more ads, as one of response to advertising. First, McDonald (1971) found that panelists were 5% more likely to switch to than from a brand, when, in the interval between two purchases, they had seen two or more ads for the brand. Second, the above effect was stronger for ads seen less than four days before the purchase than for ads seen more than four days before the purchase. Third, subjecting panelists to three or more exposures did not seem to have a stronger effect than doing so with two exposures.

Tellis (1988a) did a choice analysis of panelists' purchases of toilet tissue in single source data. Despite the almost commodity status of this category, total advertising in the category amounted to about a hundred millions dollars. First, the effects of advertising were small and quite difficult to identify. In contrast, the effects of sales promotions were strong, immediate, and hard to miss. Second, brand loyalty moderated the effects of ad exposure. Buyers responded more strongly to brands to which they were more loyal. Third, the response to ad exposure seemed non-linear. However, brand loyalty strongly moderated this non-linearity. The response for brands to which the consumer was loyal, occurred rapidly and peaked at two to thre exposures. However, brands with which the consumer was not familiar, required many more exposures per week, but could achieve a higher peak. Fourth, advertising had a small effect in winning new buyers but a little stronger effect in reinforcing preference.

Pedrick and Zufryden (1991) studied the effectiveness of advertising in the yogurt category using single source data. Three of the results that Pedrick and Zufryden (1991) obtained are similar to those of Tellis (1988): the effects of advertising are relatively small, the effects of promotions are much stronger than those of advertising, and the response to ad exposure is non-linear. The most important result they obtained is that market share increases were much more responsive to increases in reach than to increases in frequency.

Deighton and Neslin (1994) carried out analysis of single source data using econometric models similar to the two prior studies described in this sub-section. The authors studied the effect of exposure frequency on brand choice of the advertised brand. As in the prior two studies, the authors found that the effects of other promotional variables were much stronger than that of advertising. The effect of advertising was significantly different from 0 for two of the three categories. The authors' most important finding was that probability of a consumer buying a brand increased steadily with the number of exposures, even going up to exposure levels of 20. However, this effect went up at a declining rate. Also, the biggest increase occurred when going from an exposure level of 0 to 1.

Jones (1995) analysed single source data for 142 brands in 12 categories for 1991. All 12 were from packaged grocery products and included markets that were competitive and heavily advertised. He focused on the short-term effect of advertising that occurred in the 7 days just prior to purchase. Jones (1995) found that advertising does have short-term effects on household purchases of the advertised brands. However, the direction of the effect is not universal. About 50% of the brands have ad effects that are moderate to strong. About 30% have effects that are not clearly distinguishable, while 20% strangely have negative effects. Some fraction of the brands that have a short-term effect, also have long-term effects on sales. But long-term effects are much less pronounced than the short-term effects. The most important result from the Jones' (1995) study is about advertising repetition. He found that in the 7 days just prior to purchase, the first exposure gets the most response. Additional exposures do not add much. Thus the conclusion from this study is that "one exposure is enough."

A marketing consultant, Gibson (1996) found similar results from analysing TRI-NET market experiments of 60 commercials at General Mills. He found that just one exposure of an ad was adequate to achieve big changes in attitude and coupon usage for that brand; multiple exposures were not necessary.

This last result, stated as above, has created some controversy and has led some researchers to question Jones' (1995) analysis and interpretation. Two issues that are most pertinent are the formation of the baseline sample and the identification of the 7-day period. First, the results of the study are only valid if advertisers do not target households, who buy their brands with heavier advertising. If that is the case, then Jones (1995) might pick up an effect of advertising that is merely due to targeting. McDonald (1971) took great pains to ensure that his analysis is free from such a spurious correlation. Second, Jones' (1995) analysis excludes households that may have received ads earlier than the 7-day period. Thus any increase in response from those unmeasured exposures remains unaccounted.

In conclusion, Jones (1995) obtained some very important results. However, the validity and generalizability of the findings must await replication that is assuredly free of the above two problems.

PART B: ADVERTISING'S DYNAMIC EFFECTS IN MARKETS

Besides intensity, market studies on advertising effectiveness have focused on three dynamic aspects of advertising, carryover effects, wearin, and wearout. This section reviews studies on each of these three topics.

Studies about advertising carryover

Explanation of terms and studies

The analysis of advertising carryover is important for several reasons. First, the total effect of advertising depends on the instantaneous effect plus any carryover. If the carryover is substantial, then ignoring this component can grossly underestimate the true effect of advertising. Second, if a pulse of advertising has some carryover effect, it may suggest that the next pulse need not be scheduled until the effect of the first pulse decays. Third, the duration of the effects of advertising may have implications for whether firms should treat advertising as

an expense or an investment and whether the government should allow it to be tax-deductible or not.

A large number of primary econometric studies have attempted to estimate the size and duration of the carryover effect of advertising. We have two meta-analyses of these primary studies. This section summarizes what we have learned about advertising carryover from the two meta-analyses and from four important primary studies after these meta-analyses.

Review of studies

Clarke (1976) carried out a meta-analysis of the carryover effect of advertising on sales or market share. Clarke (1976) surveyed the results of 28 studies that analysed the effects of advertising on sales or market share. From those, he found 69 estimates of the carryover effects of advertising. He found that these estimates gave widely different estimates of how long it took for most (90%) of advertising's effects to last or dissipate. Estimates varied from a low of 0.8 of a month to a high of 1368 months, or 113 years! On closer analysis, he found that a key factor, that affected the estimates of the duration of advertising carryover, was the level of **data aggregation**. Now this term refers to the level at which data on sales and advertising is collected and analysed. In the sample of original studies Clarke (1976) surveyed, this aggregation could be in weeks, months, quarters, or years. His major finding was that the higher the data aggregation, the longer the *estimated* (but not necessarily true) duration of advertising's carryover. So which data interval is the right one?

Clarke (1976) assumed that the appropriate data interval was the *purchase frequency* – the average frequency with which consumers purchase the product being studied. Based on that, he estimated that the duration of the effects of advertising on sales for the sample of categories he surveyed was between 3 and 15 months. Clarke's (1976) major assumption – the appropriate data interval is the purchase frequency – is probably not warranted. Tellis and Franses (2006) argue that the appropriate data interval is the unit – exposure time – the largest period in which advertising exposure occurs at most only once and then at the same time every period. This interval is probably in days, hours, or minutes. Thus, the duration of advertising's effects would probably be much shorter than that estimated by Clarke (1976).

Leone (1995) computed the duration of the carryover effect from past studies. In particular, he used as input the 114 estimates of the carryover effect of advertising collected by Assmus et al. (reviewed above). To compute the duration of the carryover effect, Leone (1995) used the principle established by Clarke (1976). Leone (1995) found that the average carryover effect of advertising was 0.69. Based on this figure, he found that 90% of the effect of advertising would last 6 months. This time period is a little shorter than that determined by Clarke (1976) but also based on an erroneous assumption about the true data interval.

Tellis et al. (2000) tried to answer this question, with a model of advertising response at a highly disaggregate level of hours in the day when advertising occurred. They used a distributed lag model such as that described in Chapter 4.3. A key feature of the model is that it captured the effects of individual ads, channels, and times of the day. Data for the empirical testing was gathered for five markets in the US. In contrast to most past studies, the authors found that the carryover effect of advertising was fairly short. Over the five markets studied, the average carryover effect was 8 hours. While this number might seem unreasonably long, consider that consumers receive hundreds of messages a day. The new messages could well erase the effect of the old messages. Another important result of the study was the advertising carryover varied across cities and across times of the day. For example, there is a slight delay in the response to advertising, especially in the mornings when consumers are very busy. This variation over time of the day and cities suggests that managers need to carryover out their analyses by specific markets and time periods.

Mela et al. (1997) examined the "long-term" effects of promotion and advertising on consumer's brand choice. This study is probably one that focused on the longest time horizon – 8¼ years. As such, the title of "long-term" is probably justified. The authors analysed single source data in one product category – a frequently purchased non-food packaged product. During the time period of the study, the authors found that advertising had declined while promotions had increased. The author's most important finding was that advertising reduces consumers' price sensitivity while promotion increases consumers' price and promotion sensitivity. They found that these effects were significantly larger for a price-sensitive segment than for a loyal segment. Subsequent analysis of profitability on the same data set indicated that advertising could be more profitable than promotions or price discounting (Jedidi et al., 1999).

Lodish et al. (1995) found that in general, the effects of advertising did not die out immediately after a campaign stopped. When advertising was effective, 76% of the initial increase persisted for a year later, *after the campaign ended*, and another 28% persisting for a third year. So the total carryover effect could equal the current effect (computed in the first year). In these cases, there was also a small (about 6%) carryover effect in category volume. Advertising effectiveness was also more persistent over time for new products than for mature products. Note, that the findings of this study seem to conflict sharply with those of Clarke (1976) who found that advertising carryover is from 3 to 9 months, and those of Tellis et al. (2000) who found that advertising carryover last only about 8 hours. One solution to this conflict comes from considering the time frame. Lodish's (1995) finding about advertising carryover is different from that computed in all prior studies reviewed above. The prior studies try to estimate the average carryover effects of advertising in separate time periods or separate ads while the campaign is progressing. In contrast, Lodish and his associates (1995) estimated the carryover effect of an *entire campaign after it ends*. Thus, even though many authors have tried to compare the two types of findings and draw generalization, no simple comparison is valid. The two sets of findings must be treated as complementary findings about the carryover effects of advertising.

Dekimpe and Hanssens (1995) sought to determine the long-term or persistent impact of advertising. They tested their model on monthly sales of a chain of home improvement stores from 1980 to 1986. The authors found that sales and total advertising spending have a long-run or evolving component, for two reasons: (1) repeat purchases from those who bought due to advertising and (2) purchases from those who heard about the product from those who saw the advertising. They argued that these higher sales feed back into higher advertising as managers set ad budgets based on sales figures. They suspected that the evolving pattern they found is due to such a chain reaction. The authors' most important and ambitious claim was that while some of the effect of advertising dissipates in the short term, some of it lasts or persists, even when the advertising is stopped. They estimated that an extra dollar in advertising updates the long run sales forecast by $1.09 and the long run advertising forecast by $0.49. On the other hand, the authors found that even though advertising has a positive persistent effect, it does not have a positive persistent profit impact.

Studies about wearin and wearout

Explanation of terms and studies

Wearin and wearout are phenomena that refer to ad campaigns. Strictly speaking, a **campaign** is a series of ad exposures during a particular time period. The campaign could use just one ad or a series of differing ads so long as they have a common theme. A good recent example is the various executions of the Master Card "There are some things money can't buy …" campaign, which ran successfully for over 5 years.

Wearin is the increasing response to an ad with increasing repetition of exposures

of the ad (see Table 4.4.1). This effect typically happens in the early stages of a campaign. In contrast, **wearout** refers to the decreasing response to an ad with increasing repetition of exposures of the ad. This effect typically occurs in the latter part of a campaign (see Figure 4.4.1). Thus, by their very definition, the phenomena of wearin and wearout typically refer to the effectiveness of an ad campaign. Two reviews of the literature and three studies address the wearin and wearout of ad campaigns.

Review of studies

Greenberg and Sutton carried out an early, important review of published studies on wearout. Most of their review focused on market studies, or quasi-market studies. Their review suggested the following major conclusions. All ad campaigns ultimately wearout. More effective campaigns might take longer to wearout than those that are less effective. A creative may wearout more slowly for product categories where purchase occurs infrequently than for those where it occurs frequently. Wearout occurs more slowly for campaigns in which exposures are spaced apart than for those in which they are positioned together. If a worn out creative is reintroduced after a break, it might be effective once more. However, it will wearout even faster a second time around. Wearout of an ad campaign occurs faster among heavy TV viewers than among light TV viewers, assuming that the heavy TV viewers see the campaign more often than the light viewers. A creative, which is simple or unambiguous, wears out faster than one that is more complex or ambiguous. At the extreme, a creative that involves only a single punch line or point of humor wears out relatively fast. The use of a variety of creative executions in an ad campaign can delay wearout. Wearout is further delayed, the more these individual executions differ from each other. In contrast, campaigns with just a single creative wearout relatively fast.

Pechmann and Stewart (1992), Sawyer (1981), and Sawyer and Ward (1976) carefully reviewed all studies that included wearin

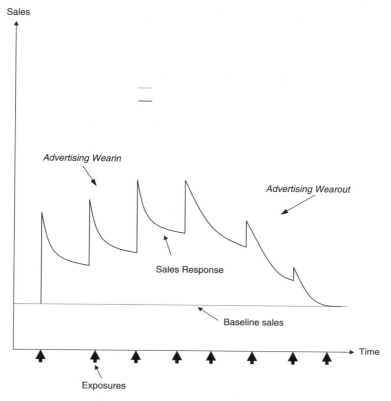

Figure 4.4.1   Wearin and wearout in advertising effectiveness
Source: Adapted from Tellis (2004).

and wearout. None of their conclusions contradict those of Greenberg and Sutton. However, some of their conclusions complement those of the previous review, especially on wearout. Here are their main conclusions. Wearin either does not exist or occurs quite rapidly. Wearin may take a little longer in the field than it does in the laboratory. The reason is that in the field all consumers may not see an ad every time it is released. In addition, even if they were to see the ad, consumers' exposure in the field tends to be voluntary, while that in the laboratory tends to be forced. Wearin may also occur more slowly when ads are scheduled apart rather than when they are scheduled together. Ads that use emotional appeals wearout more slowly than those that use arguments. Wearin and wearout occur faster for consumers who are highly motivated and actively process the message in the ads,

than for those consumers who are not so motivated and active.

Tellis et al. (2000) examined the wearin and wearout of the creative. The advertiser in that study retained all its old creative executions, which it used in old and new markets. Thus the authors had access to a bank of over 60 creative executions, which were aired over a variety of cities, time periods, and durations. Indeed, this study is probably the largest field study that rigorously examined the wearin and wearout of ads. Here are the main conclusions. Behavioural response of a creative declined steadily with use. The strongest response occurred in the first week in which the creative was aired. That is, wearin is immediate. Wearout occurred from the second week of use of a creative. That is, wearout starts quite early in the life of a creative. Wearout is steepest in the first few weeks of the airing of a creative. Thus, consistent with the results of Jones and others, ads did not seem to have much of a wearin. On the contrary, they began to wearout pretty soon after being used, and the wearout was fairly rapid early on in its use.

Blair (2000) analysed the effects of 20 split-cable copy tests for wearin and wearout. She measured response in terms of awareness and trial. She is one of the few authors to report substantial wearin. Her major findings are the following. Ads show both wearin and wearout. Ads with higher persuasion scores show stronger wearin with increasing delivery of GRPs in the market than those with lower persuasion scores. Totally ineffective ads show neither wearin nor wearout.

Some other studies find other complementary results about wearin and wearout. An article reports on 168 studies involving 58 product categories and 111 brands in 5 countries of North America and Europe (Masterson, 1999). The results suggest that wearout does occur internationally, as in the Blair (2000) study above. A recent study about attention (Pieters et al., 1999) suggests no wearin and immediate wearout as in the Tellis et al. (2000) study above. The study found that that attention to an ad decreased almost 50% from the first to the third repetition, in both natural and artificial conditions. The immediate decline in attention with repetition may be one reason for early wearout of a creative.

PART C: MARKET EFFECTS OF ADVERTISING CONTENT

Explanation of terms and studies

There are a vast number of market studies on advertising effectiveness. Almost all of these studies have focused on either on advertising weight, elasticity, or frequency. Only two of these studies have considered the role of individual ads and especially the content or creative of these ads. In contrast, a vast literature in consumer behaviour has addressed how the content of an ad must be configured to make the ad effective. However, most of these studies have been laboratory experiments conducted in highly artificial environments (Tellis, 2004; Vakratsas and Ambler, 1999). An emerging effort in market studies is to integrate these two streams of research by determining the effect of the content of ads on sales in real markets. There are only two major studies in this stream of research.

Review of studies

Chandy et al. (2001) sought to determine the effectiveness of various ad appeals in real market situations. Their study was an extension of the one reported above for the referral service. The service started initially in only one city (market). Over a decade, it gradually expanded to cover over 23 markets. Thus, the markets varied in age from a few months to over 10 years. During that time, the service developed a set of 72 ads that it used with varying frequency and intensity over the various cities.

One important finding was that the effects of advertising on sales and profits varied substantially over markets, TV channels, and especially creative. Many creative executions were not effective in increasing sales while most were not profitable. A valuable part of the analysis was its specific findings about creative executions, media, and time slots that worked. The analysis pinpointed which creative executions the advertiser should pursue and those it should drop, the channels it should use and those it should drop, and the time slots in which media buys would be most productive.

The ads themselves used a variety of appeals. The authors measured these appeals on a rich set of behavioural variables. In particular, they assessed to what extent the ads used argument, emotion, or endorsement, how the message was framed, and how long the key message was on. With these measures, the authors were able to assess the effectiveness of various ad appeals depending on whether they were used in new versus old markets. A general finding was that advertising response was stronger in younger markets. The results of the study indicate that argument-based appeals, expert sources, and negatively framed messages are particularly effective in new markets. Emotion-based appeals and positively framed messages are more effective in old markets.

MacInnis et al. (2002) report on a set of multistage experiments conducted in the 1990s. The authors developed a database of TV commercials that had been used in advertising weight tests for frequently purchased products. The database contained 47 ads, each tested in a different market experiment. Twenty-five of these ads produced statistically significant increases in sales, while 22 did not do so. The authors then recruited and trained a set of 22 paid judges to evaluate these ads on a scale of emotional to rational appeals. The results showed that emotional ads were significantly more likely to have produced increases in sales in the weight tests. On the other hand, ads that used heuristic-based or rational appeals were more likely to have not produced increases in sales in the weight tests. In a further experiment, the authors pursued whether these ads affected subjects in laboratory conditions. They found that ads that produced positive feeling and limited negative feelings were more likely to have produced increases in sales in the weight tests.

The message from these set of experiments, is that in frequently purchased mature product categories, emotional ads that create positive feelings and limit negative feelings can benefit from increased advertising.

SUMMARY

This section summarizes the findings about the markets effects of advertising.

Findings about advertising weight
The review of weight studies lead to the following common findings:

- Weight alone is not critical. Increases in weight alone do not necessarily lead to an increase in sales. Decreases in weight alone do not lead to sales decline, at least in the short to medium term.
- Prolonged cessation of advertising shows deleterious effects in some tests but no negative effects in

other tests. These results reiterate the importance for determining if firms are over-advertising in the short term.
- If advertising has any effect, that effect is visible early on. If it has no effect early on, then it is unlikely to have an effect with further repetition.
- Changes in media, copy, product, segments, or scheduling are much more likely to lead to changes in sales than do changes in weight.

Findings about advertising elasticity
The review of elasticity studies leads to the following major substantive findings:

- The grand mean of the advertising elasticity is 0.1. In comparison price elasticity is at least sixteen times higher in magnitude but opposite in direction.
- Advertising elasticity is higher in the early stages of the product life cycle than in the latter stages.
- Food products have an elasticity that is 0.1 higher than other products.
- Elasticities in the US are almost half those in Europe.
- The ratio of the median price to advertising elasticity for non-durables is five times that for durables.
- Short-term elasticities are much lower in models that incorporated a carryover coefficient (a lagged dependent variable) than in models without one.
- Models that contained exogenous variables had smaller short-term elasticities than those that did not.
- Elasticities in additive models were higher than those in multiplicative models.
- Pooled data involving cross-sectional observations in addition to time series observations, yielded higher elasticities.
- Elasticities did not differ by the measure of the dependent variable in the original study, whether sales or market share.
- Elasticities did not differ by the subject of the original study, whether product or brand.
- Elasticities also did not differ by type of estimation in the original studies.

Findings about advertising frequency
The studies on frequency suggest some convergence on the following main findings:

- The effects of ad exposure on choice are much less prominent than those for price and sales promotions.

- Higher frequency of ad exposures leads to increased probability of purchase.
- Purchase probability exhibits a concave response to higher ad frequency. That is, the probability of purchase increases but at a decreasing rate.
- For mature, frequently purchased products, the optimum level of exposure tends to be relatively small, ranging from 1 to 3 exposures a week.

Some important but unique findings, not replicated across studies, are:

- Brand familiarity or loyalty moderate response to ad exposures. That is, more established brands have a different response to ad exposures than newer brands. In particular, older established brands have an earlier and lower peak response to ad exposures than newer brands.
- Purchase probability may be more responsive to reach than to frequency.

Findings about advertising carryover

The following effects of advertising were very general:

- The effects of advertising are non-instantaneous. That is, advertising has some carryover effect.
- Advertising's carryover needs to be modeled very carefully with appropriate data. The estimated duration of advertising's carryover increases with the level of data aggregation. In particular, two contrasting recent studies how that:
  - In terms of total weight of a one-year ad campaign, advertising carryover may last as long as another two years.
  - In terms of individual ads analysed in very small time periods such as hours, advertising carryover may be quite short, lasting just about 8 hours.

The following effects are important although they have been confirmed by only one study.

- Advertising seems to have an indirect long-term positive brand effect in terms of reducing consumers' price and promotion sensitivity.
- In some situations, advertising shows some hysterisis. That is, it can cause some permanent or persistent increase in sales.
- Within a product category, advertising carryover of the same ad varies somewhat across cities and across times of the day.

Findings about wearin
- Wearin either does not exist or occurs quite rapidly.
- Wearin occurs more slowly:
  - When exposures are schedule apart
  - Attention is not forced
  - For emotional appeals relative to arguments
  - For consumers who are not highly motivated or active in processing ad messages
  - In field situations relative to laboratory settings.

Wearin might be stronger with ads that have higher persuasion scores.

Findings about wearout
- All ad campaigns ultimately wearout.
- Wearout may occur more slowly:
  - For a creative that is complex, uses an emotional appeal, or is ambiguous
  - For ads that are less effective than those that are more effective
  - For product categories where purchase occurs infrequently than for those where it occurs frequently
  - For campaigns in which exposures are scheduled apart than for those in which they are scheduled together
  - For light viewers of TV than for heavy viewers
  - For campaigns that use a variety of creative executions relative to those that use a single creative.
- If a worn out creative is reintroduced after a break, it might be effective once more. However, it will wearout even faster a second time around.

Findings about advertising content
- Changes in the creative, medium, target segment, or product itself sometimes lead to changes in sales, even though increases in the level of advertising by itself does not.

NOTES

1 This review is based on Tellis, G.J (1998), *Advertising and Sales Promotion Strategy,* Reading, MA: Addison Wesley, and Tellis, Gerard J. (2004), *Effective Advertising: How, When, and Why Advertising Works*, Thousand Oaks, CA: Sage Publications.
2 The two reviews of econometric studies that are not covered here are Aaker and Carmen (1982) op cit, and Leone and Schultz (1980), "A study of Marketing Generalization," *Journal of Marketing*, 44 (Winter), 10–18.

REFERENCES

Aaker, D.A. and J.M. Carmen (1982) op cit, and Leone and Schultz (1980), "A study of Marketing Generalization," *Journal of Marketing*, 44 (Winter), 10–18.

Aaker, D.A. and J.M. Carman (1982), "Are You Over Advertising?" *Journal of Advertising Research*, 22, 4 (August/September), 57–70.

Abraham, M. and L. Lodish, "*Advertising Works: A Study of Advertising Effectiveness and the Resulting Strategic and Tactical Implications.*" Chicago: Information Resources, Inc., 1989.

Ackoff, R.L. and J.R. Emshoff, "Advertising at Anheuser-Busch, Inc. (1963–68)," *Sloan Management Review*, 16, 2, Winter 1975, 1–16.

Ambler, T. (2004), *Marketing and the Bottom Line, 2nd* ed., London: Financial Time Prentice Hall.

Ambler, T. and E.A. Hollier (2005), "The Waste in Advertising Is the Part That Works," *Journal of Advertising Research*, 44, 4 (March), 1–15.

Assmus, G., J.U. Farley and D.R. Lehmann (1984), "How Advertising Affects Sales: Meta Analysis of Econometric Results," *Journal of Marketing Research*, 21 (February), 65–74.

Blair, H. (2000), "An Empirical Investigation of Advertising Wearin and Wearout," *Journal of Advertising Research*, (November/December), 95–100.

Chandy, R., G.J. Tellis, D. MacInnis and P. Thaivanich (2001), "What to Say When: Advertising Appeals in Evolving Markets," *Journal of Marketing Research*, 38, 4 (November), 399–414.

Clarke, D.G. (1976). "Econometric Measurement of the Duration of Advertising Effect on Sales," *Journal of Marketing Research*, 13 (November), 345–57.

Deighton, J., C. Henderson and S. Neslin (1994), "The Effects of Advertising on Brand Switching and Repeat Purchasing," *Journal of Marketing Research*, 31 (February), 28–43.

Dekimpe, M.G. and D.M. Hanssens (1995), "The Persistence of Marketing Effects on Sales," *Marketing Science*, 14 (1), 1–21.

Dekimpe, M.G. and D.M. Hanssens (2007), "Advertising Response Models," in *The SAGE Handbook of Advertising*, eds. G.J. Tellis and T. Ambler, London: Sage Publications.

Eastlack, J.O. Jr. and A.G. Rao (1989), "Advertising Experiments at the Campbell Soup Company." *Marketing Science*, Vol. 8, (Winter), 57–71.

Field, P. (2007), "Learning from Case Studies of Effectiveness," in *The SAGE Handbook of Advertising*, eds. G.J. Tellis and T. Ambler, London: Sage Publications.

Gibson, L. (1996), "What Can One Exposure Do?" *Journal of Advertising Research*, (March/April), 9–18.

Jedidi, K., C.F. Mela and S. Gupta (1999), "Managing Advertising and promotion for Long-Run Profitability," *Marketing Science*, 18 (1), 1–22.

Jones, J.P. (1995), "Single-Source Research begins to Fulfill Its promise," *Journal of Advertising Research*, (May/June), 9–15.

Keller, K.L. (2007), "Advertising and Brand Equity," in *The SAGE Handbook of Advertising*, eds. G.J. Tellis and T. Ambler, London: Sage Publications.

Leone, R.P. (1995), "Generalizing What is Known About Temporal Aggregation and Advertising Carryover," *Marketing Science*, 14 (3), Part 2 of 2, G141–9.

Lodish, L.M. et al (1995a), "How T.V. Advertising Works: A Meta-Analysis of 389 Real World Split Cable T.V. Advertising," *Journal of Marketing Research*, 32 (May), 125–39.

Lodish, L.M. et al (1995b), "A Summary of Fifty-Five In-Market Experimental Estimates of the Long-Term Effect of TV Advertising," *Marketing Science*, 14, 3, Part 2 of 2, G133–9.

MacInnis, D., A.G. Rao and A.M. Weiss (2002), "Assessing When Increased Media Weight Helps Sales of Real World Brands," *Journal of Marketing Research*, forthcoming [update].

Masterson, P. (1999), "The Wearout Phenomenon," *Marketing Research*, 11, 3, (Fall), 26–31.

McDonald, C. (1971), "What is the Short-Term Effect of Advertising?" *Marketing Science Institute Report No. 71–142* (Cambridge, Mass.: Marketing Science Institute).

Mela, C.F., S. Gupta. and D.R. Lehmann (1997), The Long-term Impact of Promotion and Advertising on Consumer Brand Choice," *Journal of Marketing Research*, 34 (May), 248–61.

Pai, S., S. Siddarth and S. Divakar (2007), " Advertising Tracking," in *The SAGE Handbook of Advertising*, eds. G.J. Tellis and T. Ambler, London: Sage Publications.

Pechmann, C. and D.W. Stewart (1992), "Advertising Repetition: A Critical Review of Wearin and Wearout," *Current Issues and Research in Advertising*, 11 (2), 285–330.

Pedrick, J.H. and F.S. Zufryden (1991), "Evaluating the Impact of Advertising Media Plans: A Model of Consumer Purchase Dynamics using Single Source Data," *Marketing Science*, 10, 2 (Spring), 111–130.

Pieters, R., E. Rosbergen, and M. Wedel (1999), "Visual Attention to Repeated Print Advertising: A Test of Scanpath Theory," *Journal of Marketing Research*, 36, 4 (Nov) 1999, 424–38.

Pieters, R. and M. Wedel (2007), "Pretesting: Before the Rubber Hits the Road," in *The SAGE Handbook of Advertising*, eds. G.J. Tellis and T. Ambler, London: Sage Publications.

Chandy, R., G.J. Tellis, D. MacInnis and P. Thaivanich (2001), "What to Say When: Advertising Appeals in Evolving Markets," *Journal of Marketing Research*, 38, 4 (November), 399–414

Sawyer, A. (1981), "Repetition, Cognitive Responses and Persuasion," in *Cognitive Responses in Persuasion*, ed. by R.E. Petty, T.M. Ostrom and T.C. Brock, Hillsdale, New Jersey: Lawrence Erlbaum Associates.

Sawyer, A. and S. Ward (1976), "*Carry-Over Effects In Advertising Communication: Evidence And Hypotheses From Behavioral Science*," Cambridge, MA: Marketing Science Institute.

Sethuraman, R. and G.J. Tellis (1991), "An Analysis of the Tradeoff Between Advertising and Pricing," *Journal of Marketing Research*, 31, 2 (May), 160–74.

Tellis, G.J. (1988a), "Advertising Exposure, Loyalty and Brand Purchase: A Two Stage Model of Choice," *Journal of Marketing Research*, 15, 2 (May), 134–144.

Tellis, G.J. (1988b), "The Price Elasticity of Selective Demand," *Journal of Marketing Research*, 25 (November), 331–41.

Tellis, G.J. (2004), *Effective Advertising: How, When, and Why Advertising Works*, Thousand Oaks, CA: Sage Publications.

Tellis, G.J., R. Chandy and P. Thaivanich, "Decomposing the Effects of Direct Advertising: Which Brand Works, When, Where, and How Long? (2000)," *Journal of Marketing Research*, 37 (February), 32–46.

Tellis, G.J. and P.H. Franses (2006), "Optimal Data Interval for Advertising Response Models," *Marketing Science*, 25, 3, May–June.

Vakratsas, D. and T. Ambler (1999), "How Advertising Works: What Do We Really Know?" *Journal of Marketing*, 63, 1 (January), 26–43.

Vakratsas, D. and P.A. Naik (2007), "Essentials of Planning Flighted Media Schedules," in *The SAGE Handbook of Advertising*, eds. G.J. Tellis and T. Ambler, London: Sage Publications.

Advertising Creativity: Balancing Surprise and Regularity

Jacob Goldenberg and David Mazursky[1]

Creativity is considered the ultimate of human qualities, central to people from all walks of life, and even one of the measures of intelligence. Our ability to create is believed to be Godlike – "a gift from the gods," as the author of *Amadeus* says of Mozart.

Successful *creativity management* is the hallmark of a vital and prosperous advertising agency: "The most important function of an agency is designing creative ads" (Tellis, 1998: 93). It is the only organizational instance in which *Creativity* is the name of a department headed by a *Creative Director*. Creative thought is so valuable in advertising agencies that entire business structures are sometimes designed around the talents of one "creative genius" (Cummings, 1984).

Creativity in general and the creative department in particular represent important criteria in selecting advertising agencies. It is an important predictor of overall satisfaction with an agency (Halinen, 1997: 28; West, 1993), and is also central to agency–client relations in advertising (Michell, 1984).

Overall, few advertising and promotion executives would question the centrality of

good creative strategy and execution (Martin, 1995). "Creativity is the heart and soul of advertising services" (Halinen, 1997: 28). "The word 'creative' is the currency with which ad agencies operate; without it there are no agencies" (Arden, 2004: 105).

And yet:

Perhaps surprisingly, creativity has remained a rare topic in consumer research (Burroughs and Mick, 2004: 402), although the undisputed success of many products may be attributed to consumer creativity (von Hippel, 1986). Likewise, creativity has remained almost unexplored in the area of advertising (Kover, 1995; Stewart, 1992). Zinkhan (1993) surveyed the previous 15 years of the *Journal of Advertising* and found only five published papers that dealt explicitly with *creativity*. Besides analyses of advertising content and tests of execution effectiveness, only a handful of empirical studies about advertising creativity have appeared in research literature (Reid et al., 1998). Moreover, most advertising textbooks say relatively little about it (O'Guinn et al., 2000: 308). This constitutes a gap in the literature, highlighting the current lack of development of theories and practices of advertising creativity – resulting in a state of knowledge that is highly tentative and disconnected (Smith and Yang, 2004: 32).

We review the literature and bridge this gap by combining two steps. First, since insufficient systematic empirical knowledge is available in the field of advertising creativity, we have derived a framework of the creativity process by borrowing from other fields. These approaches often suggest that creativity emerges from the basic elements of *surprise* and *regularity*. An appropriate balance between the two elements underlies creative ads, though whether ads that win awards are also necessarily *effective* in the marketplace, has also been debated in previous research. Second, in implementing these views, methods of creativity enhancement are subsequently reviewed. They can be divided into methods that advocate a *random* process, based on the assumption that there is a high degree of *chance* in coming up with a winning creative idea, and methods advocating *bounded regularity* that are analytical and focused rather than random or blind. Thus this chapter is structured around *surprise and regularity* which have been found to sustain a constructive tension in the creativity process and therefore should guide the development of conceptual thinking and methods for designing creative ads.

DEFINING THE CREATIVITY PRODUCT

Creativity is an enigmatic phenomenon. Like intelligence, it represents a highly complex and diffuse construct (Sternberg, 1985). Although, one may argue that there is no universally accepted definition of *creativity* (Ackoff and Vergara, 1981), a review of literature soon reveals that the *creativity product* is conceived of as a conceptual space abounded with *dualities*.

Arguably, such dualities fall into two major types: those denoting two components of the internal workings of the "system" of advertising creativity (e.g., familiarity – surprise, Boden, 1995; likeness – hidden, Bronowski, 1956; familiarity – unrecognized, Goldenberg and Mazursky, 2002), and those denoting one component of the internal workings of the "system" and one component of the external relations of the "system" with the surrounding environment (e.g., novelty or originality) – and usefulness (or appropriateness, Amabile, 1983; Martindale, 1999).

Creativity is thus often defined as useful novelty – "not novelty for its own sake, but novelty that can be applied and add value" (Oldham and Cummings, 1996). Amabile proposes that a product will be judged creative to the extent that it is a novel and appropriate, useful, correct, or valuable response to the task at hand (Amabile, 1997). Leo Burnett defines advertising creativity in a similar manner: "The art of establishing new and meaningful relationships between previously unrelated things in a manner that is relevant, believable and in good taste" (cited in Blasko and Mokwa, 1986: 43).

In the following discussion, we shall focus on the first set of dual components, which we shall term – for reasons of convenience and applicability – *surprise* and *regularity*. This approach may balance the overemphasis found in the literature on concepts such as *novelty, uniqueness, divergence, difference* or *originality* (i.e., *surprise*). All the latter concepts are usually represented as one-dimensional constructs with little conceptual difference (Smith and Yang, 2004: 36). Following this survey, we shall briefly focus on the final measure of advertising – its effectiveness.

THE CREATIVITY PROCESS

Creativity in advertising may consist of overcoming the *banal* (sheer *regularity*) on the one hand and the *bizarre* (sheer *surprise*) on the other; thus achieving a middle way between *normativity* and (to use de Bono's term) *crazitivity*, and enhancing *effectiveness*.

The basic elements of *surprise* and *regularity* have intrigued many scholars, some putting their trust in the former and others in the latter. Not many, however, have entertained the notion that both *surprise* and *regularity* may coexist and nourish each other in creativity. The common understanding of this issue is: "At present, there is considerable disagreement about the psychological process involved in creative thought, with one camp claiming it represents a sudden, holistic view of relationships between previously unconnected elements … – and the other camp claiming that it is the result of considerable information gathering and extended problem solving" (Durgee, 1985: 30).

Surprise and regularity

Some people have explained creativity in terms of divine inspiration, and many others in terms of some romantic intuition, or insight. Boden (1991) suggests that "if we take seriously the dictionary-definition of creation, "to bring into being or form out of nothing," creativity seems to be not only beyond any scientific understanding, but even impossible to define." Popper claimed that creativity is a divine spark that may not be dismantled and examined through the use of scientific tools (Popper, 1959). Peters (1997) linked creativity to surprise, and equated surprise with grace, excitement, and "bending the rules and going the extra mile" (White and Smith, 2001: 27). It may therefore be concluded that the psychologist who insists that creativity can be studied scientifically must bear the burden of proof, in the face of centuries of testimony by mystics, artists and others who claim that at least in their moments of inspiration human beings are not subject to the laws of nature.

This sense of a leap is manifested by frequent descriptions of creativity as emerging from "thin air," or even from an apparently complete "void." Sinnott argues that it is common for a new idea to arise almost spontaneously in the mind, often seemingly out of nothing and at a time when a person may be thinking of something different (Sinnott, 1959). Poincaré (1952) describes his work on a mathematical problem in the same vein and in a casual manner: "One day, as I was crossing the street, the solution of the difficulty which had brought me to a standstill came to me all at once." Mozart likewise accounts: "When I am, as it were, completely myself, entirely alone, and of good cheer – say, traveling in a carriage, or walking after a good meal, or during the night when I cannot sleep; it is on such occasions that my ideas flow best and most abundantly" (Mozart, 1954: 34).

Other thinkers and researchers conclude that the secret of creativity is concealed in the rather vague notion of *rule-transcending* rather than *rule-following*. *Rule-transcending* was formulated as *total freedom*, achieved by the elimination of directional guidance, constraints, criticism and thinking within bounded scopes (Csikszentmihalyi, 1996). Such elimination of constraints is expected to enhance the accessibility of ideas drawn and contemplated from a virtually infinite space of ideas (Grossman et al., 1988).

Tellis summarizes these views in the context of advertising, observing that creative ideas flourish in an environment of *freedom from rules*. The simple truth about *rules* is that they promote *conformity* and suppress *diversity* – one of the prerequisites of creativity (Tellis, 1998: 84–5). Aaker et al. (1992) note along the same line, albeit in a more tentative manner, that the best ads are *sometimes* those that break all the rules. However, this does not mean that we should avoid learning from the experience of the great practitioners of the art. "Great practitioners" – associated for instance with the "creative revolution" of the 1960s – are such mythological figures as Leo Burnett, David Ogilvy, and Bill Bernbach. What exactly should we learn from these larger-than-life authorities?

Many scholars hold that the creative process is qualitatively different from ordinary, day-to-day conventional thinking (e.g., Guilford, 1950; Wallas, 1926). Guilford has shown that most of the aptitude factors identifiable as belonging in the category of creativity may be classified as a group of *divergent-thinking* abilities. These abilities (evaluated by such tests as the "unusual uses"), in contrast to regular *convergent-thinking* abilities, emphasize searching activities with freedom to go in different directions, if not a necessity to do so in order to achieve excellent performance (Guilford, 1959: 161).

Some researchers stress that creativity involves special cognitive processes. Thus, they emphasize the importance of insight and productive thinking in creative processes. Also, that in contrast to regular analytical problem-solving operations, the processes underlying insight in creative mechanisms of thought are not verbalizable (Smith et al., 1995: 328). In this context, one has only to mention Einstein's remark: "The words or the language, as they are written or spoken, do not seem to play any role in my mechanism of thought. The psychical entities which seem to serve as elements in thought are certain signs and more or less clear images which can be 'voluntarily' reproduced and combined" (Einstein, 1954: 32). Ogilvy echoes this, noting in regard to advertising creativity that most original thinking isn't even verbal and requires a groping experimentation with ideas, governed by intuitive hunches and inspired by the unconscious (Ogilvy, 1976).

Advertising industry interviews on the creative process have tended to describe the activity in such terms as "the ultimate leap of the imagination," or "a stroke of genius" (Sederberg, 1979) – semantic expressions of *originality* (Michell, 1984: 11). The path of *surprise* is illustrated in the literature on *advertising creativity* by a decisive stress on *novelty* and *diversity*. Tellis (2004: 22) states that "novelty is the key to effective advertising," and that creativity thrives on *difference* while precognitive commitment is bound to *sameness* (Tellis, 1998: 84). Others observe that creative ads involve *newness*, *risk*, *divergent thinking*, and *a sense of humor* (Jewler and Drewniany, 1998; Marra, 1990). Ang and Low (2000: 837) conclude their review of literature by pointing out that across the various definitions of *creativity*, one finds a

stress on *divergence* from the norm along with a sense of *uniqueness* and *originality*. Higgins maintains that the most important aspect of advertising is "to be fresh, to be original" (Higgins, 1965: 14).

The creative department in advertising agencies is often seen as staffed by brilliant yet eccentric people (Wells et al., 1992: 114). Ogilvy believed that in the advertising industry to be successful one must accumulate a group of creative people. This probably means a fairly high percentage of high-strung, brilliant, eccentric nonconformists (Ogilvy, 1976). Such a notion is echoed by the blatant saying of George Lois: "If you're not a bad boy, if you're not a big pain in the ass, then you are in some mush in this business" (see Rothenberg, 1994: 135). Should all copywriters and art directors, then, be mad or at least somewhat disturbed?

Csikszentmihalyi concludes his study of creativity (1996: 1) by noting that "a genuinely creative accomplishment is almost never the result of a sudden insight, a lightbulb flashing on in the dark, but comes after years of hard work." Perkins (1981, 1988) and Weisberg (1986, 1992), among others, suggest that creativity is the outcome of regular thinking but only quantitatively different from it, and does not necessarily require a qualitative leap or a creative spark. Weisberg (1986) summarizes this issue by commenting that Creative thinking is not an extraordinary form of thinking. Rather, it becomes extraordinary because of what the thinker produces, not because of the *way* in which the thinker produces it. Attempts to define the regularities within the phenomenon of *creativity* have produced several schemes developed in various disciplines, such as linguistics (Chomsky, 1957; Eco, 1986), anthropology (Levi-Strauss, 1974), random graphics (Palmer, 1985), venture and transitional management (Kauffman, 1995), psychology (Simon, 1966) and artificial intelligence (Minsky, 1988).

A creative person is expected to deviate from accepted social norms, and even exhibit mental disturbance and mood disorders (e.g., Post, 1994). Jamison (1989) noted that extremes in mood, thought and behaviour – including psychosis – have been linked with artistic creativity for as long as man has observed and written about those who write, paint, sculpt or compose. Thus, creative artists have often been described as suffering from disequilibrium in their personal lives and reflecting deviations in their work (Runco, 1994).

The study of creativity began to some extent with the study of genius (Becker, 1995; Isaksen and Murdock, 1993). However, the claim that creativity is restricted to high IQ "geniuses" was debunked long before, in studies conducted by Terman (1947, 1959). According to Simonton (1984) there just isn't any correlation between creativity and IQ. At best, only average intelligence is necessary as a resource of creative behaviour (Barron and Harrington, 1981; Sternberg, 1985). It is thus concluded that creative ability is not necessarily related to intelligence (although a minimum level of intelligence is required) (Fletcher, 1990); rather, it may be related to such obscure factors as "style or modes of experiencing" (Barron, 1971). These findings stand in contrast to West's claim that personal intelligence is a personal characteristic, second only to originality – valued by senior directors when hiring advertising creatives (West, 1994).

Meyer (1991) concludes that creative behaviour is a learned pattern of habits and attitudes, not related to IQ, basic ability or aptitude; and that with training, an individual can reach creative achievement from almost any aptitude level. When creativity is considered surprising and irregular, the suggestion that it can be taught or trained seems indeed odd (Maltzman, 1960). It is difficult to train someone to think in an unexpected manner, as the outcome is not known in advance (Pickard, 1990).

In a more recent study, White (2006) notes that brain scans suggest ways in which the mental activity of creative people physically differs from that of the less creative, in the ways that connections are made as well as the parts of the brain in which activity is concentrated. However, he adds the reservation that it does not mean that not everyone can be creative; just that some people will be more reliably and regularly creative than others.

Whether or not creativity is associated with mental ability, it seems to entail a stable set of core *personal characteristics*. Creative individuals exhibit broad interests, attraction to complexity, intuition, aesthetic sensibility, toleration of ambiguity and self-confidence. They convey concentrated effort, persistence, high levels of energy in their work, and commitment to the creative endeavor. This all leads to an intensive absorption in their work, high aspirations, and an excessive willingness to grow, take risks, surmount obstacles and persevere (Amabile, 1983; Barron and Harrington, 1981; Cummings and Oldham, 1997; Golann, 1963; Helson, 1996; Helson et al., 1995; Martindale, 1989; Sternberg and Lubart, 1991; Tardif and Sternberg, 1988). One more identified form of regularity in the practice of advertising creativity – related, among other factors, to differences in tastes and personalities – is known as *creative styles*. It is based on the assumption that the creativity process is not entirely random: hence, advertising creatives have distinctive styles that permeate their work (Tellis, 1998: 87).

Cognitively speaking, it is plausible that not all creative thinking follows the same pattern. Whereas some classic discoveries appear to have resulted from surprising flashes of insight, others seem to have come about through more regular incremental applications of prior knowledge. The evidence that special processes such as insight, incubation, and activation of disparate elements may be discerned in noncreative tasks also helps to resolve the "surprise versus regularity" dilemma. Whether or not a particular cognitive process is deemed special, it is clear that no such processes are encountered uniquely in creative thinking (Smith et al., 1995: 328–9).

When referring to creativity, most researchers of cognitive style note complementary contradictions corresponding to *regular* (*systematic*) and *random* (*intuitive*) thinking (e.g., reflective-impulsive, Kagan,

1966; analytical-intuitive, Allison and Hayes, 1996; rational-intuitive, Harren, 1979). The *regular* style refers to the tendency to analyse a situation logically and intentionally. In contrast, the *random* style refers to the tendency to capture a pattern (e.g., meaning, structure) without conscious thinking and without being able to account for the source of the knowledge or information.

An important part of being creative is to know the "rules of the game" and to become skilled at applying them (Perkins, 1981). Simonton (1984, 2003) states that the creative genius is an expert in a given domain, well acquainted with its rules and regularities. However, even in the exact sciences one cannot apply fixed rules mechanically. The creative genius Poincaré noted that mathematical work is not simply mechanical; that it cannot be carried out by a machine, however perfect. It is not merely a question of applying rules, of making the most possible combinations according to certain fixed laws – the combinations so obtained would be exceedingly numerous, useless, and cumbersome. The true work of the innovator consists in choosing among these combinations so as to eliminate the useless ones or rather to avoid the trouble of making them; and the rules that must guide this choice are extremely fine and delicate. It is almost impossible to state them precisely; they are (tacitly) felt rather than (explicitly) formulated (Poincaré, 1929).

Finke et al. (1992) note the existence of two distinct processing phases of creative thinking: a *generative* phase, followed by an *exploratory* one. In Kelly's terms, there is a *creative cycle* of *loosening* and *tightening*. When being creative, we first *loosen* our constructions; then, finding a novel construction that seems to have some potential, we focus on it and *tighten* it, giving it substance or form (Kelly, 1955). An apparently similar rationale drives Barron (1968) to conclude that the essence of creativity is the ability to experience the extreme of psychological states – *crazy* and yet *sane* – and the use of both primitive and structured experiences and modes of thought. Thus we constantly oscillate between *surprise* and *regularity*.

Although these and other scholars are somewhat cognizant of the notion of *complementary contradictions* inherent in creativity, they neither fully acknowledge nor explicitly resolve the workings of this notion and its practical implications. At most, they tackle it in a general, descriptive sense. Some of this unexplored theoretical and practical potential will be briefly illustrated below, following the discussion of the resulting advertising *effectiveness*.

THE ROLE OF EFFECTIVENESS

Creativity is at the heart of every advertising campaign; but does it really sell? We are all familiar with so-called *original* creative ads that do not sell successfully. While these ads may win awards, they are not effective in the marketplace. A case in point is Nissan's "Mr. K" campaign. The creative community loved the campaign, but the Nissan dealers were sitting on an unmoving inventory (O'Guinn et al., 2000: 306). Such cases are difficult to analyse because they do not offer any controlling condition (e.g., advertising vs. non advertising simultaneously to the *same* target audience), and therefore leave us with more questions than answers. In a rather simplistic manner, many advertising professionals believe that an ad is effective if it meets the sponsor's objectives (such as increasing sales or market share). The philosophy of one worldwide agency states: "It isn't creative unless it sells" (Wells et al., 1992: 389).

The vast external, social and cultural *effect* of advertising occupies the mind of many social scientists. Cronin (2000) points out that in societies increasingly dominated by consumerism, advertising plays a key role in mediating identities, power and rights. A survey of 20 of the largest advertising clients in the United States found that failure to produce effective advertisements was the single unforgivable shortcoming an agency was considered to have (Kingman, 1981). Yet one may wonder what is concealed behind this opaque concept of *effective advertising*, how it can be evaluated, and how it is related to the complexity of the internal components of *surprise-regularity*.

Tellis (2004: 5) notes that despite its importance and wide implications, evaluation of the effectiveness of advertising is very difficult, as it depends intrinsically on response to communication. Lautman and Hsieh (1993: 18) claim more conclusively that "it is unlikely that a single executional formula for communicating messages simply will be discovered."

Some advertising researchers and practitioners feel that effective advertising can indeed have a tremendous impact on public taste, making a positive aesthetic contribution as well as ringing up sales on the cash register (Wells et al., 1992: 389). Watkins concludes in his *The 100 Greatest Advertisements* (1959: V) that as an instrument of sales, advertising has fulfilled its first glowing promise fabulously. West (1999: 39) claims that "a 'winning creative idea', one that stands out from the crowd and is memorable, can have enormous impact on sales." Researchers have estimated that a winning creative idea can generate a sales increase of up to five times, controlling for the same budget, product, distribution, and other marketing efforts (Buzzell, 1964; Blair, 1988; Rossiter and Percy, 1997).

However, advertisers today are aware that sales and effectiveness are subject to many variables, of which advertising is only one. "The sales of a product are determined by the mix of marketing variables: the product, the price, the package, the public relations, the merchandising, the sales force and the distribution. No element of the mix taken in isolation can be a unique determinant of sales ... all the elements must pull together in combination" (Evans, 1988: 6). Ogilvy and Raphaelson (1982: 15) concluded that for nearly half a century, Gallup, Starch, and other research firms have measured the noting and relationship of tens of thousands of advertisements; nobody has been able to correlate these measurements with sales.

It appears that the defining audience for creatives is other advertising professionals,

and creatives in particular (Kover et al., 1997). This is one of the reasons why the judgement of creative award shows appears to be held in much higher esteem by most advertising creatives than by researches demonstrating the effectiveness of the advertisements they create (Young, 2000: 19). Advertising managers, on the other hand, claim that creative advertising may win awards but may have little to do with effectiveness. The resolution of this struggle must by now be obvious: compounding *surprise* and *regularity* by way of an "effective Wow!," both creatives and advertising managers may achieve their desired goals and approach the hall of fame.

DEVISING CREATIVITY-ENHANCEMENT METHODS

Creativity-enhancement methods are numerous and diversified. Smith (1998) provides an analysis of 172 idea-generation techniques used by organizations and creative consultants. However, when the notion of *surprise* or *novelty* is polarized, there might be less methods or techniques. El-Murad and West (2004) conclude, for instance, that despite attempts to apply the most *systematic* and scientific methods toward developing creative ideas, the evidence suggests that it is a *random* process, because there is a high degree of *chance* in coming up with a winning creative idea. *Random* creativity is, accordingly, important (Gross, 1972).

It is however clear that while experimentation without any pattern of inference may supply many new facts for contemplation, it is not a *method* (Blachowicz, 1998: 11). Trusting sheer *randomness* or pure *chance*, with complete sacrifice of rationality and better judgement, is obviously not a preferred path toward stable and continuous advertising creativity. Some methodological frameworks should be devised and implemented. The essential question remains: what method should be adopted?

Parallel to the mode in which the *creativity process* is deciphered, scholars, researchers, and practitioners have devised different *creativity-enhancement methods* hopefully leading to the much-aspired Holy Grail of a *creativity product*.

In general terms, we suggest classifying the prevalent creativity methods into two ideal types: *unbounded randomness*, emphasizing the element of *surprise,* proceeding *from divergence to convergence*; and *bounded regularity*, proceeding *from convergence to divergence*. Let us review each of them.

Methods advocating unbounded randomness

Working most often in teams, copywriters and art directors try to come up with creative ideas that set their advertising apart. Such idea-generation is an extremely challenging task, and various methods have been developed to facilitate the process (Aaker et al., 1992: 403).

The *creation stage* of advertising encompasses the *idea-generation* process, the generation of written copy (*copywriting*), artwork of various kinds (*illustrating*), and a preliminary or comprehensive version of the advertisement (*layout*). Aaker et al. (1992: 372) view the initial phase of *idea-generation* as the "heart" or "key" of the creativity process.

Most methods for the enhancement of *idea-generation* devised over the last decades have been based on the belief that in order to "ignite the creative spark," all we have to do is break away from existing (sound) mind-frames and search for the *surprising* and the *irregular*, reaching the aspired goal of "generating a large quantity of ideas" (Aaker et al., 1992: 372). The implicit assumption behind such methods is that the greater the number of ideas, the greater the probability of achieving a set of quality ideas after filtering. Nobel Prize winner Jonas Pulling said, "The best way to get a good idea is to get a lot of ideas."

Ideation is therefore measured often in *quantitative* rather than *qualitative* terms, and is directed in a *random* manner. Alex Osborn, founder of Batten, Barton, Durstine & Osborn (BBDO) – one of the largest advertising agencies in the United States – tells of a successful copywriter at his agency who starts a job by clearing his mind, sitting at a typewriter and simply writing down everything that comes to him. He even includes silly and worthless phrases, with the thought that they will block others if they are not written down (Osborn, 1948: 135).

Aaker et al. (1992) note that it is somewhat ironic that in refining decision theory very sophisticated methods have been developed to choose among alternatives, although we still have only the crudest notion of how to generate these alternatives. They find no available means to solve this predicament, except to fall back upon the age-old technique of *brainstorming* – probably the most widely recognized and used method for creativity-enhancement.

Developed by Osborn (1948, 1958) and used regularly at most advertising agencies, *brainstorming* features a group of six to ten people who focus on a problem. The cardinal rule is that judgement is deferred and criticism prohibited. "No line of inquiry should be ruled out." The wilder the ideas that survive the better, for they may stimulate a new association that will trigger more useful ideas. The participants are encouraged to build upon ideas as they appear, combine and improve them. The atmosphere is positive. The objective is quantity, with the assumption that it leads to quality.

Following a first stage of *divergence* (*conceptual brainstorming*) – or what was termed by De Bono "messing around with ideas" – the method proceeds with an attempt at *convergence* (*screening*). During the second stage, the ideas (tens or sometimes hundreds) are filtered to produce a smaller set, which is subsequently examined and tested for economic feasibility and value (*usefulness* along with *novelty*).

Another method, developed by Gordon, is known as *synectics* (from the Greek, the joining together of different and apparently irrelevant elements). *Synectics* applies to the integration of diverse individuals into a purposeful group. This is an operational theory for the conscious use of the pre-conscious mechanisms present in human creative activity, and aims at increasing the probability of success in problem-stating, problem-solving situations (Gordon, 1961).

Additional methods include *lateral thinking* (DeBono, 1971), which proceeds in discontinuities, jumping about from idea to idea without structure; *divergent thinking* (Guilford, 1973), in which thoughts flow in all directions from one starting point, even if the path seems illogical; *associative thinking* (Young, 1975), in which one puts together unrelated ideas; *soft thinking* (Von Oech, 1983), which includes metaphorical, paradoxical, ambiguous and fantasy thinking (giving the following direction, among others: "be foolish and silly"); as well as other methods, such as *mind mapping* that calls for free association and flow of thoughts, and *random stimulation* that posits that a remote analogy may sometimes stimulate a chain-reaction of new thoughts and loosen a fixation (for further details, see Goldenberg and Mazursky, 2002).

All these methods are based on the requirement that judgement be suspended and divergent ideas emerge by associative thinking in an unconstrained space (e.g., Grossman et al., 1988). Therefore, the resultant *idea-generation* process is mostly *random*, or at least *blind* and *haphazard* (Campbell and Paller, 1989; Simonton, 1994).

Methods based on *unbounded randomness* are still often used in general management (e.g., Kiely, 1993; Rickards, 1998) as well as in advertising (e.g., O'Guinn et al., 2000). It is our contention that such methods have, by and large, directed advertising creativity into non-fruitful and inhibiting avenues. Notwithstanding the popularity of these methods, they have been questioned in numerous studies (Bouchard, 1969; Diehl and Stoebe, 1987, 1991; Paulus et al., 1993; Weisberg, 1992). Proponents of methods advocating *randomness* have provided no research evidence based on systematic assessment of their efficiency. In particular, they have not offered a way of controlling and discarding failed trials, thus dooming all trials and responses to qualitative commensurateness (see Blachowicz, 1998). A study testing the performance of a group of problem-solvers instructed to randomly "break the rules, get out of the square and shift paradigms," showed no significant differences between the ideas generated by this group and those generated by problem-solvers given no instructions. Moreover, the study showed that while such methods may increase the apparent *novelty* of ideation, they decrease the *appropriateness*, *usefulness* or *effectiveness* of the ideas produced.

It was further observed that people frequently asked to come up with new ideas sometimes try to find their own regulated means of becoming more productive at ideation tasks. They may, for instance, identify patterns common across different contexts and apply them on an *ad hoc* basis within a certain category. Such patterns will be less transient than the random extrication of thought (e.g., Boden, 1991; Dasgupta, 1994; Weisberg, 1992).

As to the *synergetic effect* – commonly identified with such unbounded randomness methods and presupposing that a group of people thinking together is superior to a "nominal group" in which individuals think alone – at least one study asserted that this plays only a minor role in creativity ideation. In a controlled experiment, ideas suggested by individuals working alone were even evaluated as superior to those raised in brainstorming sessions (Weisberg, 1992). It was repeatedly and conclusively shown by investigators that the most prevalent method of *brainstorming* does not generate more ideas or greater creativity than do nominal groups (Diehl and Stoebe, 1987, 1991). All in all, groups were shown to be suppressive of individual productivity, and the quality and originality of ideas generated by them to be inferior (Sutton and Hargadon, 1996). Grimes (2005) concludes that without a specific problem to solve, the *brainstorming* session and the ideas will be aimless. Without a good balance of people, the session will be one-sided. The more people in the room with preconceptions about a subject, the harder it will be to break free.

Often, the reason we don't see the source of our problems is that the means by which we try to solve them are the source (Bohm, 1992). The main conclusion of such studies is that an excess of ideas obscures the *ideation process*, and *randomness* and *irregularity* impede creativity. It has finally been realized that *total freedom* in idea-generation is inadequate (Paulus et al., 1993; Stroebe et al., 1992).

In addition, techniques for idea-generation such as *lateral thinking*; *divergent thinking*; *associative thinking*, *soft thinking*, *mind mapping* and *random stimulation* are phrased in vague generalities or prescriptions rather than in terms of measurable cognitive operations. Thus, for instance, even if we are convinced that *lateral thinking* can promote creativity, we would wish to identify the specific kinds of cognitive processes that give rise to or constitute this kind of thinking, and then provide an explicit account of the way in which they may be extended to different situations or contexts (Finke et al., 1992: 6).

Compared to methods advocating *unbounded randomness*, methods advocating *bounded regularity* – briefly reviewed below – manage cognitive processes rather than ideation sessions; are analytical and focused rather than random or blind, and are specific rather than general in applicability.

We may conclude that while the notion of *randomness* stresses the *quantity* of ideas, the notion of *regularity* stresses their *originality*. However, in order to achieve *creativity*, both these notions must be combined: both *quantity* and *originality* are needed in order to ignite the "spark."

Methods advocating bounded regularity

Assuming we would like to set rules and regularity in creative ideation what form should we look for? In an empirical study conducted by Johar et al. (2001) five real-world creative teams from an advertising agency were given a strategic brief for a new beverage product and asked to design the layout for a print ad. Think-aloud concurrent protocols obtained from each team's copywriter, art director, and the two working together were analysed to examine the creative process and its relationship to the created advertisement. Interpretive analyses of the protocols revealed four of the five teams chose to pursue a single mythic structure to the apparent detriment of their final product. Only one team engaged in fully diversified idea generation involving a wide range of alternative scenarios. However, this more flexible team produced the ad judged most successful by advertising professionals. Could it be that this team has found the optimal path?

An ambitious attempt at creating an "exact science of creativity" was made during the 1940s by a chemical engineer named Genrich Altschuller. He postulated that there must be discernable, measurable and learnable patterns or formulas underlying successful creative ideas. By backward analysis of more than 200 000 patents and technological inventions, he succeeded in defining more than 40 patterns of invention which he labelled "standards." Those non-intuitive patterns could be described, predicted and controlled independently of external influences. They consisted of system dynamics determined solely by the intrinsic features of the products – a revolutionary idea in the field of creativity analysis (Altschuller, 1985, 1986).

More recent creativity research has shown certain fundamental patterns or formulas underlying creative designs (e.g., Blasko and Mokwa, 1986; Goldenberg et al., 1999a; Scott, 1994). It has further indicated that some identifiable patterns may serve to enhance creativeness (Goldenberg et al., 1999a, 1999b; Moreau et al., 2001). In a recent paper McQuarrie and Phillips' (2005) study focused on certain regularities (e.g., pictorial metaphors), and it was found that when consumers are presented with an indirect metaphorical claim, they become more receptive to multiple positive inferences about the advertised brand. When the indirect metaphorical claim takes the form of a picture, consumers are more likely to spontaneously generate positive inferences at the time of ad exposure. If correct, why not aim the ideation to such design structures whose effectiveness is already measured and known? Would it be possible to impose certain regularities and bound the processes effectively?

The concept of *bounded regularity* is embedded in a number of current ideation methods; for example in marketing consider *morphological analysis*. This cluster of methods, among them one known as HIT (Heuristic Ideation Technique), breaks down a system, outcome or process into essential sub-concepts, each representing one dimension in a multi-dimensional matrix. Ideas are created by searching the matrix for new, previously non-existent combinations of attributes (Tauber, 1972). The major shortcoming of this cluster of methods is its lack of definition of specific guidelines for combining the attributes, and its lack of a prescribed reduction mechanism facilitating the process of selecting the best ideas.

Design structures in creativity

The study of design structures in creativity has systematically developed in two main directions. The first focuses on *rhetorical figures*, defined as stylistic variations that appear to enhance effectiveness. McQuarrie and Mick (1996) relate to *rhetorical figure* as an artful deviation from audience expectation in the form taken by a statement. As an aspect of advertising style, such figures include rhyme, antithesis, pun, and metaphor, among others (McQuarrie and Mick, 2003: 579). Such figures are independent of the specifics of the site of its occurrence, or of the occasion on which it occurs. The promise of rhetoric is that there is a system for identifying the most effective form of expression in any given case.

An alternative research direction was developed by Goldenberg et al. (e.g., 1999a). In their studies, *templates* are identified as simple structures that can be uniquely formulated schematically. The use of *creativity-templates* assures the generation of unique creative ideas (Hayes, 1978). Experiments show that individuals trained in the *creativity-template* technique are able to generate new ideas superior to those generated by untrained individuals or people using rival techniques – as judged by experts who were blind to

the existence of *templates*. Moreover, most of those template-fostered ideas are not replicable by any other ideation technique (Goldenberg and Mazursky, 2002: xi–xii). Finally, *creativity-templates* enable the repetition of messages, greatly contributing to awareness and recall without risking the loss of the customers' attention or the ill effects of boredom.

As to the focal region of mind of advertising creativity the *creativity-templates paradigm* assures superior creativity management because it facilitates the focused cognitive effort involved in generating new ideas and the capacity to access relevant information, as well as recognition (Goldenberg and Mazursky, 2002: 148, 165). This taxonomy eventually promotes the generation of superior ad ideas in creativity judgements, brand attitudes and recall (Goldenberg et al., 1999a, 1999b). The last point is essential, as "some 85 percent of magazine readers do not remember seeing the average advertisement, and 75 percent of viewers cannot recall the average television commercial the day after they have seen it" (Ogilvy and Raphaelson, 1982: 14).

The *creativity-templates paradigm* extends the view of common patterns by deriving universal *templates* characterizing the evolution of successful ideas. They were initially defined through backward analysis of product innovations. The history of a product was traced through its former versions. By portraying the configuration of each product version and subsequently examining the stepwise changes between versions, common patterns of change were observed, which were later classified into *creativity-templates*. Only five templates were found to cover the majority of successful new product innovations (Goldenberg and Mazursky, 2002: 179ff). The use of templates can lead to even more effective ads than reliance on simple norms or rules such as "be remarkable!" or even the use of divergent, lateral, associative, soft thinking and the like. Indeed, Tellis noted that "Research indicates that being *different* is neither the only nor a sufficient key to effective ads. On the contrary, effective ads can emerge from *templates*" (Tellis, 2004: 24).

The two research directions of structures in advertising creativity indicate the type of cognitive processes and strategies that lead to creativity, demystifying it while avoiding circularity. Creative performance is no longer explained simply in terms of "creative thinking," but with reference to the particular, deeply embedded types of cognitive structures that one employs (Finke et al., 1992: 7); and especially in terms of the characteristics (components and attributes), links, configurations and operators defining these structures (Goldenberg and Mazursky, 2002: 168ff). Under these disciplined conditions one may enjoy the benefits of a constrained, yet more fruitful and effective search for ideation. As observed by Boden (1991), "constraints – far from being opposed to creativity – make creativity possible. To throw away all constraints would be to destroy the capacity for creative thinking. Random processes alone, if they happen to produce anything interesting at all, can result only in first-time curiosities, not radical surprises."

In this context of "constrained creativity," design structures *can* play the role of *attractors*: paths that the self-organized mind tends to follow, assisting the individual to process and organize information by using favorable processing routes proven in the past to lead to productive ideas (see Kelso, 1997). The small number of paved routes (i.e., basic mental operations or mechanisms) avoids spending "a lot of time going down blind alleys" typical to brainstorming (Otnes et al., 1995), and offers the much demanded "escape from freedom" which reduces anxiety (Fromm, 1971), thus maintaining – in Einstein's words – the "joy in creative expression and knowledge," and sustaining the "courage to create" (May, 1975).

SUMMARY

As we cluster together the metaphor-like juxtapositions of *coherence* and *relevance*, we achieve a new sense of what is *similar*

(*regular*) and what is *different* (*surprising*) in the human *process of creativity* in general and in its very "heart" of *idea-generation* or *ideation* in particular. Thus we could suggest a new *ecology of mind* that points toward a new resolution of such intriguing questions as how ideas interact; is there some sort of natural selection that determines the survival of some ideas and the extinction of others; what sort of economics limits the multiplicity of ideas in the region of mind of *creativity*; what conditions are necessary for stability or survival of this region, and the like.

In a broad generalization, we may now propose that *creative ads* are those that by maintaining *coherent* relationships between the internal components of *surprise-regularity* – while sustaining their *constructive tension* (see Jung, 1943: par. 34) – are more *effective* at achieving their external goal than others, and are therefore more *relevant* to the *consumers* (the people who buy or use the *creativity product*). It thus seems that while the *creativity-templates paradigm* gives the process of ideation its much needed *operational regularities* and sustains its *surprising novelty*, it should also enhance its *effectiveness* to the consumer. This remains to be tested.

This approach overcomes some of the inherent shortcomings of available *creativity-enhancement methods*, many of which rely on sheer *randomness* rather than on the complementary contradictions between *randomness* (*surprise*) and *regularity*. Such methods are based on a false assumption, insisting that "despite even the most systematic and scientific approaches toward developing winning creative ideas, the evidence suggests it is a random process" (West, 1999: 40); that "[an inherent difficulty is] the lack of procedural guidelines to validate the creative process given its prelogical and preconscious nature" (Martineau, 1957); or that "the literature tends to support the … view that creativity cannot be programmed or regularized" (Michell, 1984: 21). On the contrary, in promoting a specified and restricted *theoretical coherence* instead of an *unbounded divergence*, we may gain the benefits of discernable, measurable and learnable *regularities* assuring *effective surprises*.

NOTE

1 The authors would like to thank Idan Yaron for his suggestions and editing of this chapter.

REFERENCES

Aaker, D.A., R. Batra, and J.G. Myers (1992), *Advertising Management*, London: Prentice-Hall International.

Ackoff, R.L. and E. Vergara (1981), "Creativity in Problem-Solving and Planning: A Review," *European Journal of Operational Research*, 7: 1–13.

Allison, C.W. and J. Hayes (1996), "The Cognitive Style Index: A Measure of Intuition-Analysis for Organizational Research," *Journal of Management Studies*, 33: 119–35.

Altschuller, G.S. (1985), *Creativity as an Exact Science*, New York: Gordon and Breach.

Altschuller, G.S. (1986), *To Find an Idea: Introduction to the Theory of Solving Problems of Inventions*, Novosibirsk, USSR: Nauka.

Amabile, T.M. (1983), *The Social Psychology of Creativity*, New York: Springer-Verlag.

Amabile, T.M. (1997), "Entrepreneurial Creativity Through Motivational Synergy," *Journal of Creative Behavior*, 31 (1): 18–26.

Ang, S.H. and S.Y. Low (2000), "Exploring the Dimensions of Ad Creativity," *Psychology & Marketing*, 17 (10): 835–54.

Arden, P. (2004), *It's Not How Good You Are, It's How Good You Want To Be*, New York: Phaidon.

Barron, F. (1968), *Creativity and the Creative Process*, New York: Holt, Rinehart & Winston.

Barron, F. (1971), "An Eye More Fantastical," in *Training Creative Thinking*, eds. G.A. Davis, and J.A. Scott, New York: Holt, Rinehart and Winston.

Barron, F. and D.M. Harrington (1981), "Creativity, Intelligence, and Personality," *Annual Review of Psychology*, 32: 439–79.

Becker, M. (1995), "Nineteenth Century Foundations of Creativity Research," *Creativity Research Journal*, 8: 219–29.

Blachowicz, J. (1998), *Of Two Minds: The Nature of Inquiry*, Albany, New York: State University of New York Press.

Blair, M.H. (1988), "An Empirical Investigation of Advertising Wearin and Wearout," *Journal of Advertising Research*, 28 (6): 45–50.

Blasko, V.J. and M.P. Mokwa (1986), "Creativity in Advertising: A Janusian Perspective," *Journal of Advertising*, 15 (4): 43–50.

Boden, M.A. (1991), *The Creative Mind: Myths and Mechanisms*, London: Abacus.

Boden, M.A. (1995), "Creativity and Unpredictability," *SEHR*, 4 (2).

Bohm, D. (1992), *Thought as a System*, London: Routledge.

Bouchard, T.K. (1969), "Personality, Problem Solving Procedures, and Performance in Small Groups," *Journal of Applied Psychology*, 53: 1–29.

Bronowski, J. (1956), *Science and Human Values*, New York: Harper & Row.

Burroughs, J.E. and D.G. Mick (2004), "Exploring Antecedents and Consequences of Consumer Creativity in a Problem-Solving Context," *Journal of Consumer Research*, 31 (September), 402–11.

Buzzell, R.D. (1964), "Predicting Short-Term Changes in Market Share as a Function of Advertising Strategy," *Journal of Marketing Research*, 1 (3): 27–31.

Campbell, D.T. and B. Paller (1989), "Extending Evolutionary Epistemology to 'Justifying' Scientific Beliefs," in *Issues in Evolutionary Epistemology*, eds. K. Hahlweg, and C. A. Hooker, Albany: SUNY Press, 231–57.

Chomsky, N. (1957), *Syntactic Structures*, S-Gravenhage: Mouton.

Cronin, A.M. (2000), *Advertising and Consumer Citizenship: Gender, Images and Rights*, London: Routledge.

Csikszentmihalyi, M. (1996), *Creativity*, New York: Harper, Collins Publishers.

Cummings, B.A. (1984), *The Benevolent Dictators: Interviews with the Advertising Greats*, Chicago, IL: Crain.

Cummings, A. and G.R. Oldham (1997), "Enhancing Creativity: Managing Work Contexts for the High Potential Employee," *California Management Review*, 40 (1): 22–38.

Dasgupta, S. (1994), *Creativity in Invention and Design: Computational Cognitive Explorations of Technological Originality*, Cambridge: Cambridge University Press.

De Bono, E. (1971), *Lateral Thinking for Management*, Chicago: American Management Association.

Diehl, M. and W. Stroebe (1987), "Productivity Loss in Brainstorming Groups: Toward the Solution of the Riddle," *Journal of Personality and Social Psychology*, 53: 497–509.

Diehl, M. and W. Stroebe (1991), "Productivity Loss in Idea-Generation Groups: Tracking Down the Blocking Effect," *Journal of Personality and Social Psychology*, 61: 392–403.

Durgee, J.F. (1985), "Depth-Interview Techniques for Creative Advertising," *Journal of Advertising Research*, 25 (6) (December), 29–38.

Eco, U. (1986), "On Symbols," in *Frontiers in Semiotics*, eds. J. Deely, B. Williams, and F.E. Kruse, Bloomington, IN: Indiana University Press.

Einstein, A. (1954), "Letter to Jacques Hadamard," in *The Creative Process: A Symposium*, eds. Ghiselin, Brewster, Berkeley and Los Angeles: University of California Press, 32–33.

El-Murad, J. and D.C. West (2004), "The Definition and Measurement of Creativity: What Do We Know?" *Journal of Advertising Research*, (June), 188–201.

Evans, R.B. (1988), *Production and Creativity in Advertising*, London: Pitman.

Finke, R.A., T.B. Ward, and S.M. Smith (1992), *Creative Cognition: Theory, Research, and Applications*, Cambridge, MA: The MIT Press.

Fletcher, W. (1990), "The Management of Creativity," *International Journal of Advertising*, 9 (Spring), 1–11.

Fromm, E. (1971), *Escape from Freedom*, New York: Avon Books.

Golann, S.E. (1963), "Psychological Study of Creativity," *Psychological Bulletin*, 60: 548–65.

Goldenberg, J. and D. Mazursky (2002), *Creativity in Product Innovation*, Cambridge: Cambridge University Press.

Goldenberg, J. D. Mazursky, and S. Solomon (1999a), "Creativity Templates: Towards Identifying the Fundamental Schemes of Quality Advertisements," *Marketing Science*, 18 (Summer), 333–51.

Goldenberg, J., D. Mazursky, and S. Solomon (1999b), "Creative Sparks," *Science*, 285 (September), 1495–6.

Gordon, W.J.J. (1961), *Synectics: The Development of Creative Capacity*, New York: Harper & Row.

Grimes, J. (2005), "How to Run a Better Brainstorming Session," *Admap*, (November), 25–28.

Gross, I. (1972), "The Creative Aspects of Advertising," *Sloan Management Review*, 14 (1): 83–109.

Grossman, S.R., B.E. Rodgers, and B.R. Moore (1988), *Innovation, Inc.: Unlocking Creativity in the Workplace*, New York: Wordware Publishing.

Guilford, J.P. (1950), "Creativity," *American Psychologist*, 5.

Guilford, J.P. (1959), "Traits of Creativity," in *Creativity and Its Cultivation*, ed. H.H. Anderson, New York: Harper & Row, 142–61.

Guilford, J.P. (1973), "Creativity – Retrospect and Prospect," *Journal of Creative Behavior*, 7 (4): 247–52.

Halinen, A. (1997), *Relationship Marketing in Professional Services: A Study of Agency–Client Dynamics in the Advertising Sector*, London: Routledge.

Harren, V.A. (1979), "A Model of Career Decision-Making for College Students," *Journal of Vocational Behavior*, 14: 119–33.

Hayes, J.R. (1978), *Cognitive Psychology: Thinking and Creating*, New York: Dorsey Press.

Helson, R. (1996), "In Search of the Creative Personality," *Creativity Research Journal*, 9: 295–306.

Helson, R., B. Roberts, and G. Agronick (1995), "Enduringness and Change in Creative Personality and the Prediction of Occupational Creativity," *Journal of Personality and Social Psychology*, 69: 1173–83.

Higgins, D. (1965), *The Art of Writing Advertising: Conversations with Masters of the Craft*, Lincolnwood, IL.: NTC Business Books.

Isaksen, S.G. and M.C. Murdock (1993), "The Emergence of a Discipline: Issues and Approaches to the Study of Creativity," in *Understanding Creativity: The Emergence of a Discipline*, eds. S.G. Isaksen et al., Norwood, NJ: Ablex, 13–47.

Jamison, K.-R. (1989), "Mood Disorders and Patterns of Creativity in British Writers and Artists," *Psychiatry*, 52: 125–34.

Jewler, A.J. and B.L Drewniany (1998), *Creative Strategy in Advertising*, Belmont: CA: Wadsworth.

Johar, V.G., B.M. Holbrook, and B.B. Stern (2001), "The Role Of Myth In Creative Advertising Design: Theory, Process And Outcome," *Journal of Advertising*, 30 (Summer), 2, 1–25.

Jung, C.G. (1943), "On the Psychology of the Unconscious," in *Two Essays on Analytical Psychology*, idem, Princeton, NJ: Princeton University Press, 1–119.

Kagan, J. (1966), "Reflection-Impulsivity: The Generality and Dynamics of Conceptual Tempo," *Journal of Abnormal Psychology*, 71: 17–24.

Kauffman, S. (1995), *At Home in the Universe*, Oxford University Press.

Kelly, G. (1955), *The Psychology of Personal Constructs*, New York: W. W. Norton.

Kelso, J.A.S. (1997), *Dynamic Patterns: The Self-Organization of Brain and Behavior*, Cambridge: MIT Press.

Kiely, T. (1993), "The Idea Makers," *Technology Review*, 96: 32–40.

Kingman, M. (1981), "A Profile of a Bad Advertising Agency," *Advertising Age*, (November 23), 53–4.

Kover, A.J. (1995), "Copywriters' Implicit Theories of Communication: An Exploration," *Journal of Consumer Research*, 21 (March), 596–611.

Kover, A.J., W. James, and B. Sooner (1997), "To Whom Do Advertising Creatives Write?" *Journal of Advertising Research*, 37 (1): 41–53.

Lautman, M. and S. Hsieh (1993), "Creative Tactics and the Communication of a 'Good Taste' Message," *Journal of Advertising Research*, (July/August), 11–19.

Levi-Strauss, C. (1974), *Structural Anthropology*, New York: Basic Books.

Maltzman, I. (1960), "On the Training of Originality," *Psychological Review*, 67: 229–42.

Marra, J.L. (1990), *Advertising Creativity*, Englewood Cliffs, NJ: Prentice Hall.

Martin, M. (1995), "Do Creative Commercials Sell?" *Campaign*, 22 (September), 34–5.

Martindale, C. (1989), "Personality, Situation, and Creativity," in *Handbook of Creativity*, eds. J.A.Glover, R.R. Ronning, and C.R. Reynolds, New York: Plenum, 211–32.

Martindale, C. (1999), "Biological Bases of Creativity," in *Handbook of Creativity*, ed. R.J. Sternberg, Cambridge: Cambridge University Press, 137–52.

Martineau, P. (1957), *Motivation in Advertising*, New York: McGraw Hill.

May, R. (1975), *The Courage to Create*, New York: W. W. Norton.

McQuarrie, E.F. and D.G. Mick (1996), "Figures of Rhetoric in Advertising Language," *Journal of Consumer Research*, 22 (4): 424–38.

McQuarrie, E.F. and D.G. Mick (2003), "Visual and Verbal Rhetorical Figures under Directed Processing versus Incidental Exposure to Advertising," *Journal of Consumer Research*, 29 (March), 579–87.

McQuarrie, E.F. and B.J. Phillip (2005), "Indirect Persuasion in Advertising: How Consumers Process Metaphors Presented in Pictures and Words," *Journal of Advertising* 34 (2) (Summer), 7–20.

Meyer, J.K. (1991), "On a Simple Minded Definition of Creativity," *Creativity Research Journal*, 4: 300–2.

Michell, P.C.N. (1984), "Accord and Discord in Agency–Client Perceptions of Creativity," *Journal of Advertising Research*, 24 (5): 9–23.

Minsky, M. (1988), *The Society of Man*. New York: Simon and Schuster.

Moreau, C.P., A.B. Markman, and D.R. Lehmann (2001), "What Is It?" Categorization Flexibility and Consumer's Responses to Really New Products," *Journal of Consumer Research*, 27 (March), 489–98.

Mozart, W.A. (1954), "A Letter," in *The Creative Process: A Symposium*, ed. Brewster Ghiselin, Berkeley and Los Angeles: University of California Press, 34–5.

Ogilvy, D. (1976), *Confessions of an Advertising Man*. New York: Atheneum.

Ogilvy, D. and J. Raphaelson (1982), "Research on Advertising Techniques that Work – and Don't Work," *Harvard Business Review*, (July–August), 14–18.

O'Guinn, T.C., C.T. Allen, and R.J. Semenik (2000), *Advertising*, Cincinnati, OH: South Western College Publishing.

Oldham, G.R. and A. Cummings (1996), "Employee Creativity: Personal and Contextual Factors," *Academy of Management Journal*, 39 (3): 607–35.

Osborn, A.F. (1948), *Your Creative Advertising*, New York: Dell.

Osborn, A.F. (1958), *Applied Imagination: Principles and Procedures of Creative Thinking*, New York: C. Scribner.

Otnes, C., A.A. Oviatt, and D.M. Treise (1995), "Views on Advertising Curricula from Experienced 'Creatives'," *Journalism Education*, 49: 21–30.

Palmer, E.M. (1985), *Graphical Evolution: An Introduction to Random Graphic*, New York: Wiley and Sons.

Paulus, B.P. and M.T. Dzindolet (1993), "Perception of Performance in Group Brainstorming: The Illusion of Group Productivity," *Personality and Social Psychology Bulletin*, 19: 78–89.

Perkins, D.N. (1981), *The Mind's Best Work*, Cambridge, MA: Harvard University Press.

Perkins, D.N. (1988), "The Possibility of Invention," in *The Nature of Creativity*, ed. R.J. Sternberg, Cambridge: Cambridge University Press, 362–85.

Peters, T. (1997), *The Circle of Innovation: You Can't Shrink Your Way to Greatness*, New York, NY: Knopf.

Pickard, E. (1990), "Toward a Theory of Creative Potential," *Journal of Creative Behavior*, 24: 1–9.

Poincaré, R. (1929), *The Foundations of Science: Science and Hypothesis, the Value of Science, Science and Method*, New York: The Science Press.

Poincaré, R. (1952), *Science and Method*, New York: Dover.

Popper, K. (1959), *The Logic of Scientific Discovery*, New York: Basic Books.

Post, F. (1994), "Creativity and Psychopathology: A Study of 291 World-Famous Men," *British Journal of Psychiatry* ,165: 22–4.

Reid, L., K. King, and D. DeLeorme (1998), "Top-Level Creatives Look at Advertising Creativity Then and Now," *Journal of Advertising*, 27 (2): 1–16.

Rickards, T. (1998), "Assessing Organizational Creativity: An Innovation Benchmarking Approach," *International Journal of Innovation Management*, 2 (3): 367–82.

Rossiter, J.R. and L. Percy (1997), *Advertising Communications & Promotion Management*, New York: McGraw-Hill.

Rothenberg, R. (1994), *Where the Suckers Moon*, New York: Knopf.

Runco, M.A. (1994), "Creativity and its Discontents," in *Creativity and Affect*, eds. M.P. Show, and M.A. Runco, Norwood, NJ: Ablex, 102–26.

Scott, L.M. (1994), "Images in Advertising: The Need for a Theory of Visual Rhetoric," *Journal of Consumer Research*, 21 (September), 252–73.

Sederberg, K. (1979), "Top Agency Creatives Take A Closer Look at Creativity," *Advertising Age*, (June 4).

Simon, H.A. (1966), "Scientific Discovery and the Psychology of Problem Solving," in *Mind and Cosmos: Essays in Contemporary Science and Philosophy*, ed. R.G. Colodny, Pittsburgh: University of Pittsburgh Press.

Simonton, D.K. (1984), *Genius, Creativity and Leadership: Historiometric Inquiries*, Cambridge, MA: Harvard University Press.

Simonton, D.K. (1994), "Individual Differences, Developmental Changes and Social Context," *Behavioral and Brain Sciences*, 17: 552–3.

Simonton, D.K. (2003), "Scientific Creativity as Constrained Stochastic Behavior: The Integration of Product, Process, and Person Perspectives," *Psychological Bulletin*, 129: 475–94.

Sinnott, E.W. (1959), "The Creativeness of Life," in *Creativity and Its Cultivation*, ed. H.H. Anderson, New York: Harper & Row, 12–29.

Smith, G.F. (1998), "Idea-Generation Techniques: A Formulary of Active Ingredients," *Journal of Creative Behavior*, 32 (2): 107–33.

Smith, R.E. and X. Yang (2004), "Toward a General Theory of Creativity in Advertising: Examining the Role of Divergence," *Marketing Theory*, 4 (1/2): 31–58.

Smith, S.M., T.B. Ward, and R.A. Finke eds. (1995), *The Creative Cognition Approach*. Cambridge, MA: The MIT Press.

Sternberg, R.J. (1985), *Beyond IQ: A Triarchic Theory of Human Intelligence*, Cambridge, England: Cambridge University Press.

Sternberg, R.J. and T. Lubart (1991), "Creating Creative Minds," *Phi Delta Kappan*, 72 (8) (April), 608–14.

Stewart, D.W. (1992), "Speculations on the Future of Advertising Research," *Journal of Advertising*, 21 (3): 1–18.

Stroebe, W., M. Diehl, and G. Abakoumkin (1992), "The Illusion of Group Productivity," *Personality and Social Psychology Bulletin*, 18 (5): 643–50.

Sutton, R.I. and A. Hargadon (1996), "Brainstorming Groups in Context: Effectiveness in a Product Design Firm," *Administrative Science Quarterly*, 41: 685–718.

Tardif, T.Z. and R.J. Sternberg (1988), "What Do We Know about Creativity?" in *The Nature of Creativity*, ed. R.J. Sternberg, New York: Cambridge University Press, 429–40.

Tauber, E.M. (1972), "HIT: Heuristic Ideation Technique: A Systematic Procedure for New Product Search," *Journal of Marketing*, 36 (January) 58–61.

Tellis, G.J. (1998), *Advertising and Sales Promotion Strategy*, Massachusetts: Addison-Wesley.

Tellis, G.J. (2004), *Effective Advertising: Understanding When, How, and Why Advertising Works*, Thousand Oaks, California: Sage.

Terman, L.M. (1947), *Psychological Approaches to the Biography of Genius*, London: Eugenics Society.

Terman, L.M. (ed.) (1959), *Genetic Studies of Genius*, Stanford: Stanford University Press.

Von Hippel, E. (1986), "Lead Users: A Source of Novel Product Concepts," *Management Science*, 32 (July), 791–805.

Von Oech, R. (1983), *A Whack on the Side of the Head: How to Unlock Your Mind for Innovation*, New York: Warner Books.

Wallas, G. (1926), *The Art of Thought*. New York: Harcourt Brace.

Watkins, J.L. (1959), *The 100 Greatest Advertisements: Who Wrote them and What They Did*, New York: Dover.

Weisberg, R.W. (1986), *Creativity: Genius and Other Myths*, New York: W. H. Freeman.

Weisberg, R.W. (1992), *Creativity Beyond The Myth of Genius*, New York: W. H. Freeman.

Wells, W., J. Burnett, and S. Moriarty (1992), *Advertising: Principles and Practice*, New Jersey: Prentice Hall.

West, D.C. (1993), "Cross-National Creative Personalities, Processes, and Agency Philosophies," *Journal of Advertising Research*, 33 (5) (September–October), 53–62.

West, D.C. (1994), "Restricted Creativity: Advertising Agency Work Practices in the U.S., Canada and the U.K.," *Journal of Creative Behavior*, 27 (3): 200–13.

West, D.C. (1999), "360° Creative Risk," *Journal of Advertising Research* (January–February), 39–50.

White, A. and B.L. Smith (2001), "Assessing Advertising Creativity Using the Creative Product Semantic Scale," *Journal of Advertising Research* (November–December), 27–34.

White, R. (2006), "Creativity Unconfined?," *Admap* (January), 3.

Young, C.E. (2000), "Creative Differences between Copywriters and Art Directors," *Journal of Advertising Research* (May–June), 19–26.

Young, J.W. (1975), *A Technique for Producing Ideas*, Chicago: Crain Books.

Zinkhan, G.M. (1993), "Creativity in Advertising: Creativity in the Journal of Advertising," *Jou* (June).

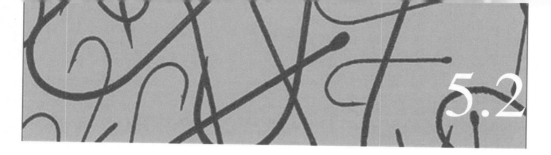

Media Planning

Peter J. Danaher

The topic of Media Planning has consumed whole books, let alone book chapters. Nevertheless, we will attempt in this chapter to give an overview of the key media planning concepts and definitions. Media planning is mostly about the placement and timing of advertising messages. In their daily lives media planners must define a target audience, decide which media (TV, radio, online, etc.) are appropriate and stipulate the dates and times for the advertisements. All this must be done while trying to achieve an audience exposure target and keep within a budget. Since media planning is a very practical and structured component of advertising, we also discuss the key steps and decisions that arise in the media planning process. Table 5.2.1 lists the key steps in media planning in sequential order and outlines the structure of this chapter and how it relates to other chapters.

This chapter is organized according to the steps listed in Table 5.2.1. In addition, we also define a number of key media planning terms and briefly discuss some media data sources. We also introduce and discuss some basic models used for estimating media exposure. After an example of a media plan, the chapter concludes with a summary.

Media planning is an important and sophisticated component of advertising management, but we have space here for only a brief introduction. More detailed discussion of the key topics can be found in a number of classic books and articles, including Aaker and Myers (1987), Barban et al. (1993), Katz (1995), Little (1979), Little and Lodish (1969), Rossiter and Danaher (1998), Rust (1986), Surmanek (1985) and Sissors and Baron (2002). More recent texts on media planning have been written by Brierley (2002) and Kelley and Jugenheimer (2004).

MARKETING OBJECTIVES

Media planning objectives can be divided into the categories of marketing, advertising and media objectives. In this section we primarily discuss marketing and advertising objectives. Marketing objectives are "higher level" objectives, which determine the advertising objectives and the strategy and tactics necessary to achieve the objectives. A common marketing objective is the attainment of increased sales or market share. Kelley and Jugenheimer (2004: 47) note that good marketing objectives are those with goals that are quantifiable, such as increasing sales by 2% in the next year. Simply stating that the objective is to increase sales is too vague and

Table 5.2.1   Steps in media planning

Step	Explanation
Set Marketing Objectives	Sets sales or market share targets
Define Target Audience	Decide on who to aim the advertising at and find out their media consumption habits
Media Selection	Decide which media (TV, radio, print, internet, etc.) are appropriate for your objectives and your budget
Media Objectives	Is the intention to expose a lot of people just once to the campaign or a smaller group many times, i.e., breadth versus depth
Media Scheduling	Considers the timing, placement and size/length of advertising
Media Buying & Budgeting	Addresses issues like total advertising budget and how it might be spread over different media. Also covers media buying discounts and negotiation
Assessing Campaign Effectiveness	Evaluation of the success of the campaign after it is executed. Measures of effectiveness include ad awareness, recall and likeability. Other measures are brand attitude, sales and market share. Attainment of media objectives within budget are also relevant

does not help set the downstream advertising and media objectives. Another marketing objective might be the repositioning of a product via advertising of brand attributes, such as price and nutrition for a breakfast cereal.

Advertising objectives are tailored to the marketing objectives, but are specific to the domain, as opposed to another element of the marketing mix. For example, if the marketing objectives is to increase sales, and it is known that brand awareness is a precursor to sales, then an appropriate advertising objective may be to increase brand awareness. However, if awareness is already high, a more appropriate marketing objective might be to increase brand preference, in which case a suitable advertising objective is to enhance attitude towards the brand (Katz, 1995: 41). Other chapters in this book deal with advertising awareness (Chapter 4.2), response modelling, i.e., the effects of advertising on sales (Chapter 4.3), budgeting (Chapter 5.3) and ad scheduling (Chapter 5.4). For this reason we will not go into any detail on such advertising objectives.

Decisions on the marketing objectives have a downstream effect on media planning. For example, if a firm is pursuing a "push strategy" to achieve its marketing objective of increasing sales, then advertising effort should be directed at channel partners. Hence,

advertising messages are more appropriate in trade publications rather than mass appeal consumer magazines. Barban et al. (1993: 16) illustrate this for a packaged good, where a push strategy results in print ads in *Progressive Grocer*, *Supermarket Business* and *Grocery Marketing*, while a 'pull strategy' fits better with advertisements in *Family Circle*, *Woman's Day* and *Good Housekeeping*. Push and pull strategies also differ markedly in their relative allocation of expenditures to personal selling, consumer sales promotion and dealer promotions. For a fixed total promotion budget, when a large proportion of the funds are allocated to "below the line" spend to the trade, this necessarily reduces the 'above the line' spend on consumer advertising. In turn, this might leave insufficient funds for a successful TV ad campaign, resulting in advertising in newspapers and radio, which are cheaper than television. Even for this simple example it is apparent that the initial marketing objectives have a large impact on later decisions about media and therefore media objectives. Hence, we cannot emphasize enough the importance of setting marketing objectives first.

Media objectives include targets for the proportion of the target audience exposed to the advertising campaign or perhaps the number of times target audience members are exposed. Before discussing media objectives in detail, we need to define several key terms that are commonplace in media planning.

MEDIA PLANNING TERMINOLOGY

There are several terms that are commonly used in the context of media planning (see Sissors and Baron, 2002; Surmanek, 1985; and Rust, 1986, for extensive glossaries). Unfortunately, these terms have not always been defined consistently in the past. To remove any ambiguity, we use a simple illustration based on the viewing of two television sitcoms that enjoyed enormous success over the past decade, *Friends* and *Seinfeld*. Neither show is still in production, but at their peak they both attracted large audiences. For the purposes of this illustration, suppose the target audience is all US households with a TV set. A *household rating* is the percentage of households with TVs that tune into the program.[1] Suppose that in a particular week *Friends* rates a 15, while *Seinfeld* rates a 10. This means that 15% and 10%, respectively, of households tune into *Friends* and *Seinfeld*. As both shows are prime time comedies, they will have some overlap in audience, with say 5% of households watching both programs in a week. This 5% of households is common to both shows and is called the *duplicated* audience.

The ratings and the duplication are depicted in Figure 5.2.1.

The rating for *Friends* is comprised of two parts, the 10% of households that view just *Friends* and a further 5% that view both shows, making a combined rating of $10 + 5 = 15$ for *Friends*. *Seinfeld*'s total rating is 10, comprised in a similar way, being $5 + 5$ for the exclusive and duplicated viewers.

So far we have discussed only the viewing of programs, but not advertisements. It is very common for media audience suppliers to provide program ratings, with advertising ratings assumed to be equal to those of the program. Of course, this is unlikely to be true in reality, since there is evidence of people switching channels during commercial breaks (Danaher, 1995; Yorke and Kitchen, 1985). Some countries, such as the UK, use commercial break ratings rather than program ratings, but even this is not an exact advertising exposure measure. The conventional way around this complex issue of ad exposure versus program exposure is to describe a viewer of a program (or reader of a magazine or newspaper) as having an *opportunity to see* (OTS) when they are exposed to a *media vehicle*. A media vehicle is a generic term for the delivery channel for a media message and could any one of television, radio, newspaper, magazine, outdoor or the internet. Hence, when someone watches a program, they have an opportunity to see all of the commercials that are broadcast during that program. The true advertising exposure is anywhere from 50 to 95% of those watching a program (Danaher, 1995; Kneale, 1988; Yorke and Kitchen, 1985).

Returning to the example in Figure 5.2.1, suppose that an advertiser places a single 30 second commercial in *Friends* and also places this commercial into *Seinfeld* in the same week. In media planning parlance, commercials or ads are often called *insertions*. We say that an insertion has been placed in *Friends* and another in *Seinfeld*, making a two insertion ad campaign.

We are now ready to define some key media planning terms.

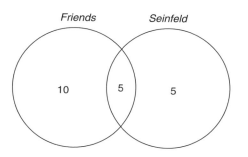

Figure 5.2.1   Household ratings for *Friends* and *Seinfeld*

Reach

Reach is defined as the percentage of the target audience exposed to the advertising campaign at least once in a specified time period. In the UK, reach is called coverage, a term which nicely conveys the meaning of reach. That is, it is a measure that counts all the unique households (or people) that are covered by the campaign. In the packaged goods industry an equivalent term is penetration, being the percentage of households that have purchased a product in a certain time period. For the example in Figure 5.2.1, the reach of the campaign is $10 + 5 + 5 = 20\%$. This is the sum of the percentage of people exclusively exposed to Friends or Seinfeld, plus those exposed to both programs. Notice that those households exposed to both programs are counted only once in the reach calculation. For this reason, choosing two media vehicles with high duplication in audience is not a good way to increase reach (we illustrate this in the section on Models for Estimating the Exposure Distribution).

Notice that reach can also be calculated from the *nonreach*, i.e., from those not seeing either vehicle. Figure 5.2.1 shows that 80% of households see neither program. Hence, the percentage seeing at least one program is $100 - 80 = 20\%$.

Gross Rating Points

Gross Rating Points are defined as the sum of the ratings for the ads placed in all the media vehicles, ignoring any duplication across media vehicles.[2] For the example in Figure 5.2.1, the Gross Rating Points for the two-insertion advertising schedule are $15 + 10 = 25$. If there had been two insertions in *Friends* and three in *Seinfeld*, the Gross Rating Points would be $2 \times 15 + 3 \times 10 = 60$. Therefore, Gross Rating Points are simply the sum of the ratings across all of the insertions in an advertising campaign, or a particular time period, such as a week. Often advertisers set GRP norms for ad campaigns, expecting, for instance, 200 Gross Rating Points per week for a TV campaign. A "heavy" advertising weight would be 300–400 Gross Rating Points per week.

Since Gross Rating Points are very easy to calculate, they are commonly used to gauge the strength of an ad campaign, and are generally considered to be the "currency" of media planning. This is in part due to their portability across different media types. The concept of the sum of ratings applies equally well to newspapers, radio and magazines. However, part of the reason the internet has struggled to gain acceptance as a mainstream advertising medium is the difficulty of defining a GRP for the internet (Smith, 2003).

As might be expected, Gross Rating Points and reach are related, but not linearly. Generally, reach increases as Gross Rating Points increase, but at diminishing return levels. This gives rise to "reach curves," which are charts that relate Gross Rating Points to reach (Surmanek, 1985: 34; Wood, 1998). There is another link between Gross Rating Points and reach, which we now discuss.

Frequency

The term frequency goes hand-in-hand with reach. Unfortunately, frequency has not been consistently defined in the literature (Dixon, 1991; Kelley and Jugenheimer, 2004; Rust, 1986) and this had led to a number of misconceptions about what frequency actually is. The term frequency is intended to convey how *often* someone is exposed to an ad campaign. We define frequency, or more precisely, average frequency, as the average number of exposures among those reached by the advertising campaign (Barban et al., 1993: 54; Surmanek, 1985: 29).

Returning to the example in Figure 5.2.1, only 20% of households are reached by the campaign that has single insertions in each of *Friends* and *Seinfeld*. Of those households reached, 10% see *Friends* only and 5% see *Seinfeld* only. These households have just one exposure each. There are a further 5% of households exposed twice to the campaign. Hence the average number of exposures among those seeing any ads is

$$[1 \times (0.1 + 0.05) + 2 \times (0.05)]/0.2$$
$$= 0.25/0.2 = 1.25.$$

Therefore, the average frequency, or frequency as it is popularly known, is 1.25 exposures. Notice in the calculation that the average number of exposures is divided by the reach. This is because frequency is calculated among the subset of households or people that are reached by the campaign. This seems reasonable, as those who are not reached by the campaign see no ads (Sissors and Baron, 2002: 99).

Although there is no formal link between Gross Rating Points and reach, there is a formula that links reach, frequency and GRPs. It is

$$\text{Reach} \times \text{Frequency} = \text{GRPs.} \quad (1)$$

This formula only makes sense when frequency is defined as the average number of exposures among those reached. For the example in Figure 5.2.1, Reach × Frequency = 20 × 1.25 = 25, which equals the Gross Rating Points we calculated earlier.

The reach/frequency formula in equation (1) illustrates an important trade-off between reach and frequency. For a fixed level of GRPs, when reach increases, frequency must decrease, and vice versa. This has big implications for media planning and scheduling. For instance, a straightforward way to get a high reach is to choose popular media that do not overlap much in audience. This lack of overlap results in fewer households or people being exposed multiple times, thereby lowering the average frequency of exposure. Conversely, an easy way to increase frequency is to have multiple insertions in the same TV program, magazine or radio station. Due to audience loyalty to a particular TV program or magazine, this results in multiple exposures to the same households or people. This increases the average frequency of exposure, but does little to increase the reach, since few new unique households are exposed.

Exposure distribution

A less well known, but very important concept in media planning, is the exposure distribution, sometimes known as the frequency

Table 5.2.2 Exposure distribution for the example in Figure 5.2.1

Number of exposures	0	1	2
Percent of households	80	15	5

distribution (Barban et al., 1993; Rossiter and Danaher, 1998). The exposure distribution is the percentage of the target audience exposed no times, just once, just twice and so on. The exposure distribution for the example in Figure 5.2.1 is given in Table 5.2.2.

The reason the exposure distribution is so useful is that all three audience measures of reach, frequency and Gross Rating Points can be calculated directly from the exposure distribution, as we now demonstrate.

Firstly, reach is the percentage exposed to the ad at least once, being either one or two exposures in this case. Table 5.2.2 shows that the reach is 15 + 5 = 20%. Alternatively, reach is 100 − nonreach = 100 − 80 = 20%, as before. Secondly, the Gross Rating Points in Table 5.2.2 are the total ratings, being 1 × 15 + 2 × 5 = 25. Notice that the duplicated audience (5%) is multiplied by 2, as each of households receives 2 exposures. Thirdly, the frequency, or more precisely the average frequency among those reached, is (1 × 15 + 2 × 5)/20 = 1.25.

The calculation of these three audience measures gives some insight into how the reach/frequency formula in equation (1) is derived. Multiplying reach by frequency results in 20 × (1 × 15 + 2 × 5)/20 = 25, which equals the 25 Gross Rating Points calculated earlier. This shows that Gross Rating Points are the average exposures (multiplied by 100) among the *entire target group*, not just those reached. Hence, an alternative way to write equation (1) is

$$\text{Reach} \times \left[\frac{\text{Average Exposures}}{\text{Reach}} \right] = \text{GRPs.}$$

$$(2)$$

Equation (2) highlights two things. First, average frequency is, by definition, the average number of exposures divided by the reach. Second, that Gross Rating Points can also be thought of as the average number of exposures among the entire target group, not just those reached. In our example, GRPs = 25, but this is in percent form, meaning that the average number of exposures among *all* households is $25/100 = 0.25$. Contrast this with average frequency, which is 1.25, being the average number of exposures among just those reached. Hence, the reason that Gross Rating Points and frequency are linked is not due to some magical law of media planning. It is a linkage that results from the (correct) definition of frequency. By definition, frequency is Gross Rating Points divided by reach and this, in turn, gives rise to equation (1).

We have belaboured the definition of reach, frequency and Gross Rating Points as there have been a number of erroneous discussions of frequency and the formula in equation (1). See, for example, Kelley and Jugenheimer (2004: 19) who appear to define frequency as the total number of insertions in the campaign. See also Dixon (1991) who defines the average frequency among the entire target group rather than just those reached. He effectively defines average frequency to be the same as GRPs, as also noted by Farris and Parry (1991) and Cook (1991). The definitions stated here are consistent with the intended meaning of frequency, as illustrated in the authoritative texts of Barban et al. (1993: 57), Sissors and Baron (2002: 99) and Surmanek (1985: 29).

Another reason the exposure distribution is important is that for more complex ad campaigns than depicted in Figure 5.2.1, an exposure distribution can either be compiled from the raw data or estimated by a mathematical model (Chandon, 1976; Rust, 1986; Danaher, 1992) and media exposure measures can be calculated directly from the empirical or estimated exposure distribution. Moreover, the exposure distribution is the basis for calculating other media effectiveness measures, such as the proportion of the target audience exposed to at least 3 ads, often called effective frequency (Krugman, 1972; Naples, 1979). Effective frequency at the 3+ level was the cornerstone of advertising media planning for almost three decades, but Jones (1995) has questioned its importance, and has advocated a preference for reach (1+) as a desirable criterion for an ad campaign. Either of these criteria can be obtained with ease from the exposure distribution.

Cost per thousand

Until now, our media terminology has addressed audience size and frequency of exposure, but not advertising cost. Generally speaking, the larger the audience for a media vehicle, the higher the cost, particularly within a single medium such as television. To enable cost comparisons across alternative media vehicles, a common measure is the cost per thousand, conventionally abbreviated as CPM, where the M designates the Latin word for one thousand, mille. For example, in Figure 5.2.1, suppose there are 100,000,000 households in the US with a TV set. Then a household rating of 15 for *Friends* means that 15 million homes watch this show, while 10 million tune into *Seinfeld*. If a 30 second commercial on national television costs $350,000 for *Friends*, while a *Seinfeld* commercial costs $280,000, then the respective CPMs are $350,000 \times 1000/15,000,000 = \$23.33$ and $280,000 \times 1000/10,000,000 = \$28.00$. In words, this means that the cost of reaching 1000 households by broadcasting a commercial on *Friends* is $23.33. Since the CPM for *Friends* is lower than that for *Seinfeld* in this hypothetical example, *Friends* is better financial deal. An appealing feature of CPMs is that they are "portable" across different media, being easy to calculate for magazines and radio, for instance. Since all ad campaigns operate within a budget, CPMs provide a simple way to compare both across different media types, such as television and radio and within a single medium, such as comparing *Seinfeld* and *Friends*.

A related cost efficiency measure is cost per rating point (CPRP), which is the ratio of the insertion cost to the rating (in percent). Hence for *Seinfeld*, the CPRP is $280,000/10 = $28,000.

SOURCES OF MEDIA DATA

All media planning requires the analysis of data from the respective media types. Detailed descriptions of how media data are collected for traditional media ranging from TV to cinemas are given in the book by Kent (1994). The methodology behind comScore Media Metrix measurement of internet audiences is given by Coffey (2001). Some of the larger media measurement suppliers provide details of their methodology on their websites (see, for example, www.agbnielsen.net and www.tns-global.com). We give just a short outline of how media audiences are measured for some key media.

Television

In many countries, television ratings are determined by a peoplemeter panel of homes. The USA and UK, have about 6000 peoplemeter panel homes. Many other countries operate smaller panels, ranging from 300 to 600 homes. Panels are normally designed to represent the country with respect to region, level of TV viewing, size of household, number of TVs in the home, age of main household shopper, presence of children, and several other demographic variables, via a stratification system known as control matrices (Kent, 1994).

A peoplemeter is literally a "black box" that sits on top of the TV set and continually monitors all the television activity. To ensure that the peoplemeter records what the people in the house are watching and not just what the TV is doing, all eligible householders use a remote control to "log in" when they are watching TV. Data are collected in real time, but generally the data are sent to a central processor in the early hours of the morning. Ratings for the previous day are available to clients the following morning, usually in the form of minute-by-minute ratings. Peoplemeters are relatively sophisticated but

they depend on compliance by panelists. Non-compliance occurs when someone is watching TV but has not logged in or is logged in but not watching. Most countries check for this with "coincidental surveys" (Danaher and Beed, 1993). In these surveys, panelists are called by telephone and asked if they were watching television at the time the phone rang. Their verbal response is compared with the actual peoplemeter records at that time instant. Danaher and Beed (1993) report that over 90% of panelists pass this test of compliance.

Another popular method for measuring TV ratings is via a diary panel. Here, booklets which list each channel and quarter-hour for a week (sometimes longer) are left in the home to be completed every day by each eligible person living in the home. The diary method has shown a bias towards reporting viewing of TV shows which might be considered socially acceptable. As a result, programs like evening news shows usually have higher ratings by the diary method because people think they "always watch the news" or "should watch" when, in fact, they often miss one or two nights (Beed, 1992). A further problem with diaries is that people often under-record their viewing to daytime and late-night television and small (often cable) channels. With the rapid profusion of small channels in the past 15 years, this is clearly a problem for the TV diary method.

Print

As print survey questionnaires often use show-cards, print media surveys are usually accomplished with face-to-face interviews of people aged 10 years or older. Telephone surveys are also common. The samples tend to be large and fully national, being spread evenly over a year. The survey asks each respondent which vehicles he or she has recently read or looked at from a long list of magazines and newspapers. Two question formats commonly used for weekly magazines are the "reading habit" and "recent reading" methods, which asks about the number of issues read in recent past. The primary format used in the U.S. is the recent reading method, particularly by SMRB (Simmons) and MRI (Mediamark).

For daily and suburban newspapers, respondents are asked to recall their reading behaviour over the last seven days. For instance, if they are interviewed on a Wednesday, they'll be asked if they read a particular newspaper on the previous Wednesday through Tuesday. Days when the newspaper is not published are omitted from the questioning.

Print media audience measurement worldwide is therefore mostly based on recalled vehicles read (reach) and recalled reading occasions (frequency).

Radio

Radio-listening audiences are typically measured by the diary method (similar to that used in some countries for television). Diaries are dropped off in randomly selected homes for later pickup. Respondents tick (check off) the appropriate station box in the diary for every quarter-hour of radio they listen to. A relatively recent technology has been developed by Arbitron (www.arbitron.com) that can handle both radio and television audience measurement. It is called the "portable peoplemeter" and consists of a small device about the size of a pager (there is also a wristwatch version) that is worn by a panelist throughout the day and evening. It has the capability to detect an inaudible signal from a TV or radio station. Each station has a unique identifier that is captured whenever the panelist is within earshot of a TV or radio station. Trials have been conducted in Philadelphia, Manchester, UK and currently Houston, which show that the technology is steadily improving.

TARGET MARKET DEFINITION

One of the cornerstones of marketing is segmentation. Products and services do not appeal to everyone equally and this gives rise to clusters of people, households or firms that have a higher than average uptake or potential uptake of an advertising offer. Target markets can be set in many ways, based on any or all of personal demographics, geographic location, users of a product and buyers or nonbuyers of a product.

Traditionally, demographic factors have been the predominant method for defining a target. For example, a popular target group among television advertisers is women aged 18–49, as this group is often the grocery buyer in a household. Such demographic targets are usually based on market research that profiles buyers or users of a product by an array of demographic variables such as age, gender, income, occupation, family size, presence of children and socio economic status. For instance, a soda brand may find that their product has a higher than average consumption rate for high-income men aged 25–34. The media planner then sets about finding media that appeal to this target group. That is, an attempt is made to match a product's users with the appropriate media, with demographic factors acting as an intermediary. This method of targeting is called "indirect matching" (Assael and Poltrack, 1991) and is extremely common in the advertising industry. An alternative is "direct matching," where a database of users or buyers of a product is scrutinized to see which TV programs or magazines these users/buyers watch the most. Assael and Poltrack (1991, 1994) argue strongly in favor of direct matching over indirect matching, as using demographics as an intermediary dilutes the strength of the relationship between product user and their media consumption.

While it is hard to fault this logic, the barrier to direct matching is a lack of "single-source" data that directly link buying behaviour to media consumption. It is much more common to have separate databases, one on buying behaviour and a separate one for media consumption (such as Nielsen's peoplemeter panel data). Attempts at nationwide single source data have proven financially costly and burdensome for sample respondents (Rossiter and Danaher, 1998: 64–6). Some notable exceptions are MediaMark Research's (MRI's) nation-wide sample of magazine readership that also asks about the usage of 500 categories and 6000 brands (Kelley and Jugenheimer, 2004: 53). The clear limitation here is that the MRI service is primarily aimed at magazine media planning, rather than say, television. In the UK, Taylor Nelson produce the TGI service that links product consumption and media consumption, but in that case data fusion is used to link two separate databases, with demographics being one of the factors used in making the linkage. Therefore, there is still an element of indirect matching in the TGI method.

At the heart of indirect matching is a technique called "indexing." Indexing is a simple and intuitive way to help select particular vehicles within a media type, such as television. Staying with the target group of high income men aged 25–34 for a soda brand, Table 5.2.3a lists the TV ratings for five programs, among all people aged 5 or more and among the target group. The index is the ratio of the rating among the target group to the rating among all people. A higher index number indicates that viewing a program correlates well with membership of the target group. Programs with the highest index numbers are candidates for advertising, subject to budget constraints of course.

Clearly, *Monday Night Football* and *David Letterman* have high indices and should be considered as suitable television programs for targeting high income men aged 25–34.

In contrast, direct matching uses data on program viewing and product consumption without referring to demographic

Table 5.2.3b   Example of direct matching

Program	Percent of viewers that are high soda consumers
CSI Miami	8%
Monday Night Football	16%
Lost	14%
Desperate Housewives	3%
David Letterman	9%

intermediary variables (Assael and Poltrack, 1991, 1994). For example, Table 5.2.3b gives typical data on soda consumption among viewers of the same five television shows in Table 5.2.3a. A "high soda consumer" is defined to be someone who consumes 50% more than the average person in a week. Table 5.2.3b shows that 8% of viewers of *CSI Miami* are classified as high soda consumers. This time, the top-ranked shows for reaching high soda consumers are *Monday Night Football* and *Lost*. Assael and Poltrack (1991, 1994) report that such differences in program selection between indirect and direct matching are common. They favor direct matching because it properly captures product or service usage with the most relevant potential advertising viewers. Nonetheless, indirect matching is still commonly used due to the lack of widely available single source data.

MEDIA TYPE SELECTION

Kelley and Jugenheimer (2004: 36–42) list the advantages and disadvantages of ten different media types, ranging from newspapers, radio, outdoor and the internet. The selection of media types for a campaign is subjective, but depends very much on the advertising media objectives and the budget. The choice of media will also depend on the media objectives. For example, a campaign that demands a high reach but moderate frequency should concentrate on television and newspaper insertions. However, if high frequency is required and lower reach is acceptable then outdoor and radio advertising are appropriate (Brierley, 2002: 108).

Table 5.2.3a   Example of program indices

Program	Rating for ...		Index
	Those aged 5+	High income men aged 25–34	
CSI Miami	5.5	5.7	104%
Monday Night Football	8.9	15.2	171%
Lost	4.3	4.2	98%
Desperate Housewives	10.2	8.3	81%
David Letterman	3.6	4.7	131%

Rossiter and Danaher (1998, Chapter 5) and Tellis (1998: 357–60) discuss many of the issues that are germane to media selection. These include the "fit" of the creative execution with the proposed media, the intended length of time to attain the audience goals, the appeal of interaction (as offered by the internet), whether the ad is informational or transformational, the consumer's involvement with the product or service, the geographic coverage of each media, potential frequency of repeated exposures, the speed of message delivery, the location where the media is consumed and the relative cost of each media.

Decisions about which media to select are linked to the copy or content of the advertisement. For example, if the ad is to be strongly visual or convey and emotional message, it is natural to choose television as the medium. However, television is an expensive medium, so magazines might be the only affordable channel, in which case, the ad copy is likely to be informational (Rossiter and Danaher, 1998). Hence, the decision of which comes first, copy (creative, content) or media choice is not straightforward. Tellis (1998: 88–93) and Aaker and Myers (1987: 460–3) discuss this issue. Rossiter and Danaher (1998: 51–5) discuss how the creative elements of visual appeal, memorability and attitude formation help to drive decisions on media selection. Furthermore, the advertising budget often has a large influence on the choice of media as we now illustrate.

A reasonable starting point for media selection, suggested by David Fletcher of Media Edge in London, is to prioritize each media type, then ask yourself what you can achieve with your number one choice. For example, it would typically cost $4 million for an effective national television advertising campaign in the UK comprising about 500 GRPs. By contrast a newspaper campaign starts to be effective with a $1 million ad spend. Moreover, Fletcher commented that media such as print and outdoor are scalable, meaning that doubling the expenditures generally doubles

the effectiveness and vice versa for half the expenditure. Scalability of ad spend is not a feature of television advertising effectiveness, however. Since television needs a threshold level of expenditure before becoming effective, a total advertising budget of $6 million could be divided to have the minimum of $4 million on TV, with the balance being split between newspapers and perhaps an experimental medium like the internet or text messages. There is also an implicit, but underresearched, belief that television is the most effective medium, once the minimum level of expenditure is achieved.

MEDIA OBJECTIVES

Media objectives can now be set using the media audience definitions in the section on Media Planning Terminology. Common media objectives are based on reach, frequency and/or GRPs, such as setting a goal of reaching 35% of the target market within a one week period (Jones, 2004: 107). It might take 60 Gross Rating Points to achieve this reach target. Notice the use of a time span in this objective. This is important, as achieving a reach of 35% reach is more demanding in a one-week period than a four-week period. Rossiter and Danaher (1998) formalize this by setting objectives such as the "minimum effective frequency per advertising cycle," where the advertising cycle is typically 4 weeks.

Brierley (2002: 108) suggests that reach targets should be around 75–80% of the target population over the course of the campaign, rather than just a week. A common practitioners' rule of thumb is that a TV campaign should attain about 200 Gross Rating Points per week. Kelley and Jugenheimer (2004: 94) state that "Most brands rarely set their reach goals less than 50 percent for the purchase cycle. Most stay in the two-thirds to four-fifths range." That is, they set reach targets between 66% and 80% of the target audience. Brierley (2002: 108) makes the observation that, as the number ads in the campaign becomes large, the reach increases at a decreasing rate (diminishing returns). Hence, it is common for an advertiser to accept that once a high reach target is attained, further insertions largely serve to increase just the average frequency of exposure. Such practice leads to the accumulation of effective frequency or effective reach (Naples, 1979), whereby a media planner might want to achieve a "reach of 50% at the 3+ level," meaning that half of the target audience is exposed to the campaign at least three times. In doing so, the usual reach (i.e., reach at the 1+ exposure level) must be higher than 50% and is likely to be of the order 70–90% in order to achieve a 3+ reach of 50%.

A further important consideration when setting media objectives is to assess the advertising of one's competitors. Since many advertisers appear to set annual media budgets in accordance with their market share (Schroer, 1990) and there are demonstrated effects of interference effects of competitor advertising (D'Souza and Rao, 1995; Kent and Allen, 1994), it is imperative that an advertiser makes allowance for current and future advertising patterns of their competitors (Lodish, 1971).

ASSESSING CAMPAIGN EFFECTIVENESS

Since media purchases are based on historical data (often for the comparable time period in the previous year), media planners must work with forecasts of audience measures in future time periods. For this reason, the actual audience achieved (measured by reach or GRPs, for instance) may differ from the forecast audience. For example, suppose that media purchases are made with the intention to achieve 400 television Gross Rating Points over a 3 week period among the target audience. Media planning software would typically be used to access historical ACNielsen ratings data to obtain a mix of programs and time slots that result in the required 400 GRPs, while keeping within the

time period and budget constraints. Planning might be done anywhere between one year and one week ahead of the time the ads actually go to air.[3] Shortly after the conclusion of the campaign it is possible to get the actual ratings data and compare this with the forecasts, a process known as post-analysis. If the actual audience delivered is 400 Gross Rating Points or higher then the advertiser is happy with their purchase. If not, and the actual audience is only 350 GRPs, then the advertiser may request a "make good" from the media supplier. This practice is very common in the television industry. In the example presented here, the advertiser is 50 Gross Rating Points short of their target, which would be made up with spare ad inventory that is available at the stations who delivered the original campaign.

Evaluation of media effectiveness is not limited to GRPs. It could involve a comparison of sales, market share or ad awareness targets with what was actually achieved. The UK-based firm, Millward Brown (www.millwardbrown.com) specialize in advertising awareness tracking and provide examples where Gross Rating Points correlate well with ad awareness (Brown, 1985, 1991). This enables them to give advice about the required number of Gross Rating Points needed to achieve an awareness target. In turn, awareness can be linked to more tangible marketing objectives like sales or market share via an econometric model (Hanssens et al., 1990; Leeflang et al., 2000).

MODELS FOR ESTIMATING THE EXPOSURE DISTRIBUTION

There is a long history of probability models being used for estimating the exposure distribution. Such models are required when a media planner requires media effectiveness estimates, such as reach, that are outside the exposure range available from survey data, collected via the methods mentioned in the section on Sources of Media Data. Exposure distribution models fall into three classes, *ad hoc*, simulation and stochastic. Excellent literature reviews of the historical development of exposure distribution models are given by Chandon (1986) (who compared 47 different models), Rust (1986) and Danaher (1992). Danaher (1989a) discusses several simulation methods. Some new model-based methods are reviewed by Danaher (1992) and we will look at these in more detail below. In this section we discuss some modeling ideas for univariate through to multivariate exposure distributions.

To motivate the modeling issues, consider the observed exposure distribution for two popular weekly magazines, *TV Guide* and *People* based on a sample of 5000 people over a four week period. Let X_1 and X_2, respectively, denote the exposures each person has to *TV Guide* and *People*, and $X = X_1 + X_2$ is the total exposures each person has to both these magazines. The bar chart in Figure 5.2.2 shows a count of the number of people in the sample with X exposures, X ranging from 0 to 8. It is apparent that this is an extremely 'lumpy' distribution. This is because although X is a simple sum of random variables, two non-ignorable correlations make modeling it difficult (Danaher, 1989b, 1992). One is the intra-vehicle correlation due to repeat reading/viewing to the same media vehicle (Danaher, 1989b; Morrison, 1979) and the other is inter-vehicle correlation, where there

might be an overlap (i.e., duplication) in exposure to two vehicles, as illustrated earlier in the Media Planning Terminology section. The example in Figure 5.2.2 has spikes at 4 and 8 exposures. The 4 exposure spike is comprised of people that persistently read just one of the two magazines. Hence, in a four week period, they read all four issues. The 8 exposure spike corresponds to those people that consistently read *both* magazines.

Suppose a media planner now decides to have five insertions in *People* instead of four. If the survey data asks respondents about their reading habits over the past four weeks we can no longer obtain the observed distribution of X so a model is needed. The question now is, how much data do we use? Traditionally only the observed frequencies for the marginal distributions of X_i and the observed bivariate distribution for all pairs of magazines are stored either in tabulated books (e.g., Simmons or Telmar) or on computer files (Chandon, 1986; Leckenby and Kishi, 1982; Rust, 1986). It is this data limitation, particularly for the print media, which makes modeling necessary.

Despite the lumpiness of many observed print media exposure distributions, the most popular model used to estimate total exposures is one based on a smooth beta-binomial distribution, commonly attributed to Metheringham (1964). The mass function of

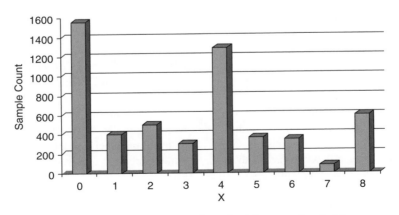

Figure 5.2.2   Observed exposures distribution for schedule comprised of four insertions in *TV Guide* and *People*

the beta-binomial distribution is

$$f(X = x) = \binom{k}{x} \frac{\Gamma(\alpha + \beta)}{\Gamma(\alpha + \beta + k)} \frac{\Gamma(\alpha + x)}{\Gamma(\alpha)}$$
$$\times \frac{\Gamma(k - x + \beta)}{\Gamma(\beta)},$$

where $X = 0, \ldots, k$ and α and β are parameters to be estimated. The advantages of the beta-binomial model are that it is relatively simple to estimate and requires only readily available survey data for model fitting. While it is an excellent model for one media vehicle (Chandon, 1986; Rust, 1986), Danaher (1992) demonstrates its limitations for two or more magazines due to the lumpiness seen in Figure 5.2.2.

Now generalizing to a multivariate setting, a formal statement of the exposure distribution set-up is as follows. Let X_i be the number of exposures a person has to media vehicle i, $X_i = 0, 1, 2, \ldots k_i, i = 1, \ldots, m$, where m is the number of different vehicles. The exposure random variable to be modeled is $X = \sum_{i=1}^{m} X_i$, the total number of exposures to an advertising schedule.

As seen in Figure 5.2.2, in the case of print media, observed empirical exposure distributions are known to be particularly lumpy due to strong intra-vehicle correlation. As a consequence, Danaher (1988, 1989b, 1991) shows that it is necessary to firstly model the joint multivariate distribution of $(X_1, X_2, \ldots, X_m)$, from which the distribution of total exposures, $X = \sum_{i=1}^{m} X_i$, can be derived. This is less of a problem with television exposure distributions (Rust, 1986) where loyalty from episode to episode is generally moderate, with intra-exposure duplication factors of the order 0.28 (Ehrenberg and Wakshlag, 1987). In addition, for the television environment there are more vehicle choices than for the print medium (Krugman and Rust, 1993) and this helps to reduce both intra- and inter-vehicle correlation. As a result, models for just X, like the beta-binomial, rather than the full multivariate $(X_1, X_2, \ldots, X_m)$ are often adequate for television exposure distributions, which tend to be smooth (Rust and Klompmaker, 1981).

A reasonably robust model for multivariate exposure distributions that captures both the intra- and inter-vehicle correlations is Danaher's (1991) canonical expansion model. It is a generalization of Goodhardt and Ehrenberg's (1969) 'duplication of viewing law.' The mass function for the canonical expansion model is

$$f(X_1, X_2, \ldots, X_m) = \left\{ \prod_{i=1}^{m} f_i(X_i) \right\}$$
$$\times \left[1 + \sum_{j_1 < j_2} \rho_{j_1, j_2} \frac{(x_{j_1} - \mu_{j_1})(x_{j_2} - \mu_{j_2})}{\sigma_{j_1} \sigma_{j_2}} \right],$$

where $f_i(X_i)$ is the univariate distribution for vehicle i, which could be a beta-binomial distribution, ρ_{j_1, j_2} is the correlation between any pair of vehicles, and μ_j and σ_j are the mean and standard deviation of the number of exposures for vehicle j. The final model for the total number of exposures is obtained from the multivariate model in the following way:

$$f_X(x) = \sum_{\{(x_1, \ldots, x_m): x_1 + \cdots + x_m = x\}} f(X_1, X_2, \ldots, X_m),$$
$$x = 0, 1, 2, \ldots, k_T.$$

Danaher (1991) demonstrates that the canonical expansion model predicts better than all other models across a range of media vehicles. It can also accommodate cross-media situations, whereby an advertising campaign may combine, print, television and outdoor advertising, for example. Video Research International in Japan have successfully used the canonical expansion model for this purpose (Video Research Limited, 2006).

To date very few models have been developed for online media. Leckenby and Hong (1998) adapted the beta-binomial model to internet media planning, but they had to artificially aggregate panel-based website exposure data in such a way so as to force it into the same format as that used in offline media. Rather than restricting the number of exposures to coincide with a pre-specified time period, as done by Leckenby and Hong (1998), Danaher's (2007) internet media exposure model allows each person's exposure level to range from zero to infinity. This is more appropriate for the internet, where there is varying exposure opportunity per website visitor. For a single website the appropriate model is the negative binomial distribution. For many websites, Danaher (2006) uses a Sarmanov distribution (Park and Fader, 2004) to create a multivariate negative binomial distribution. In a rigorous validation exercise, this multivariate negative binomial distribution performs extremely well, doing better than proprietary commercial models.

AN EXAMPLE MEDIA PLAN

We conclude this chapter with a short example of a media plan.[4] A common target demographic for packaged goods is the household shopper, defined to be the person who does the majority of the grocery buying in a home. Suppose the advertiser is Folgers coffee and they have a budget of $350,000 to spend in the St Louis network television market over a four week period. An initial comparison of the television ratings among all people and those who are household shoppers created indices, as discussed in the section on Target Market Definition. All of the ten programs in Table 5.2.4 have indices above 130%, indicating they are suitable for the target audience.

Table 5.2.4   Audience and cost information for the example media plan*

Program	Rating, %	Cost/Ins, $	CPM
Will & Grace	9.1	22 000	2.4
The Apprentice	8.0	31 000	3.9
Desperate Housewives	14.7	43 000	2.9
American Idol	12.1	37 000	3.1
Lost	7.6	28 000	3.7
ER	14.9	38 000	2.6
West Wing	12.2	29 500	2.4
CSI	12.5	33 000	2.6
House	8.6	28 000	3.3
Bones	4.0	15 000	3.8

*These are realistic but not actual ratings and costs – they are for illustration only.

Table 5.2.4 shows that *ER* is the top-rating program among those eligible for advertising, with *Desperate Housewives* a close second. We also give costs per 30 second commercial slot for each of these programs, from which the cost per thousand (CPM) can be calculated. On a CPM basis, *Will and Grace* and *West Wing* are the most cost efficient programs, having the lowest CPM. Table 5.2.4 does not show the duplications among each of the programs, but we can report that many of the pairs of programs do have overlapping audiences, such as *Desperate Housewives* and *ER*. Such pairwise duplications have important implications for determining schedules with high reach or frequency. For instance, higher reach is achieved by selecting vehicles that do not overlap much and vice versa for high frequency schedules (Rossiter and Danaher, 1998).

Having selected the initial set of programs it is now necessary to find the mix of programs that maximizes reach or frequency, while keeping within the total budget. For this example we use a simple media model software package, called Media Mania, which is reported in more detail in Rossiter and Danaher (1998). It uses the rating for one episode and the reach over two episodes for each program, plus the pairwise duplications as input to Danaher's (1991) Canonical Expansion model described above.

In this example we employ a feature of the Media Mania software which maximizes the reach or the effective frequency at the 3+ level, while staying within the budget. Table 5.2.5 shows the number of insertions that should be in each program to maximize either reach or frequency at the 3+ level (sometimes referred to as effective reach). The difference between the two media plans is very apparent. The reach strategy spreads the commercials over 8 different shows, with no program having more than 2 insertions. By contrast, the frequency strategy concentrates its commercials into just two programs, with each having 5 insertions.

Figure 5.2.3 shows a bar chart of the full frequency distribution resulting from the media plans in Table 5.2.5. It clearly shows

Table 5.2.5 Optimal media plans for reach and frequency strategies

Program	Reach strategy insertions	Frequency strategy insertions
Will & Grace	2	0
The Apprentice	0	0
Desperate Housewives	1	0
American Idol	1	0
Lost	1	0
ER	1	5
West Wing	2	5
CSI	2	0
House	0	0
Bones	1	0
Reach at 1+	72.5%	52.3%
Reach at 3+	11.2%	22.7%
Total Cost	$333,000	$337,500
GRPs	121	136

that the reach strategy has a much higher 1+ reach, but this switches over at the 3+ frequency level, where the frequency strategy then has a higher audience. The choice between these two media plans depends on the marketing and media objectives. High reach would be desired when the intention is to expose a lot of people just once or twice, with a view to increasing or maintaining awareness. High frequency might be more suitable when the objective is to counter a competitor who is advertising heavily or when the goal is to induce brand switching among those presently loyal to another brand (Rossiter and Danaher, 1998).

SUMMARY

This chapter provided an overview of the media planning process, terminology and how it fits into other components of advertising management. Planning is critical and accounts for much of the total media budget. Fortunately, this stage of advertising decision making has ample support from large databases, accurate forecasting models and a great deal of documentation.

The chapter, covered the setting of marketing objectives and defining the target audience, media selection and objectives, scheduling, buying and budgeting and assessing campaign effectiveness primarily for Gross Rating Points (see Pai et al., 2007 for a broader view of advertising tracking). Models for estimating the exposure distribution were followed by an example of a media plan. Exposure distribution models are required when a media planner requires media effectiveness estimates, such as reach, that are outside the range available from conventional sources. Exposure distribution models fall into three classes, ad hoc, simulation and stochastic.

NOTES

1 Technically the definition of a television rating is a little more complicated than this and depends on the number of minutes viewed by household in a large sample panel.

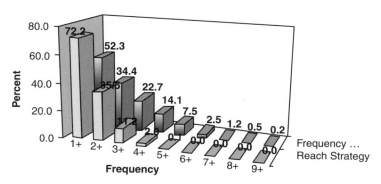

Figure 5.2.3 Frequency distribution for reach and frequency strategies

2 In the UK, Gross Rating Points for television are called TVRs (TV ratings), while in Australia and New Zealand they are called TARPs (Target Audience Rating Points).

3 Network TV sells its advertising time well in advance of the actual broadcast date. Spot TV has a shorter lead time, while cable TV would be shorter again (Katz, 2003).

4 Additional case examples for Levi Men's Dockers, Samsonite and Sun Microsystems can be found in Barban et al. (1992).

REFERENCES

Aaker, D. and J.G. Myers (1987), *Advertising Management*, 3rd ed. Englewood Cliffs, NJ: Prentice-Hall.

Assael, H. and D.F. Poltrack (1991), "Using Single Source Data to Select TV Programs Based on Purchasing Behavior," *Journal of Advertising Research*, 31, 4, 9–17.

Assael, H. and D.F. Poltrack (1994), "Can Demographic Profiles of Heavy Users Serve as a Surrogate for Purchase Behavior in Selecting TV Programs," *Journal of Advertising Research*, 34, 1 (January/February), 11–17.

Barban, A.M., S.M. Cristol, and F.J. Kopec (1993), *Essentials of Media Planning: A Marketing Viewpoint*, 3rd ed., Lincolnwood, IL: NTC Business Books.

Beed, T.W. (1992), "An Overview of the Transition from Diary-Based Television Audience Measurement to People Meters in Australia and New Zealand," *Proceedings of the ARF/ESOMAR Worldwide Audience Broadcast Research Symposium*, Toronto, Canada, 139–62.

Brown, G. (1985), "Tracking Studies and Sales Effects: A U.K. Perspective," *Journal of the Advertising Research*, 25, 1, 52–64.

Brown, G. (1991), "Modelling Advertising Awareness," *ADMAP*, 1 (April), 25–29.

Brierley, S. (2002), *The Advertising Handbook*, 2nd ed., London, UK: Routledge.

Chandon, J-L.J. (1986), *A Comparative Study of Media Exposure Models*, New York, NY: Garland.

Coffey, S. (2001), "Internet Audience Measurement: A Practitioner's View," *Journal of Interactive Advertising*, 1, 2, (http://jiad.org/vol1/no2/coffey/index.html).

Cook, W.A. (1991), "Erratum:'GRP: A Case of a Mistaken Identity'," *Journal of Advertising Research*, December, 72–4.

Danaher, P.J. (1988), "A Log-linear Model for Predicting Magazine Audiences," *Journal of Marketing Research*, 25, 4 (November), 356–62.

Danaher, P.J. (1989a), "Simulating Media Exposure Distributions," *Communications in Statistics: Simulation and Computation*, B18, 4, 1381–92.

Danaher, P.J. (1989b). "An Approximate Log-linear Model for Predicting Magazine Audiences," *Journal of Marketing Research*, 26, 4 (November), 473–9.

Danaher, P.J. (1991), "A Canonical Expansion Model for Multivariate Media Exposure Distributions: A Generalization of the Duplication of Viewing Law," *Journal of Marketing Research*, (August), 28, 3, 361–7.

Danaher, P.J. (1992), "Some Statistical Modeling Problems in the Advertising Industry: A Look at Media Exposure Distributions," *The American Statistician*, 46, 4, 254–60.

Danaher, P.J. (1995), "What Happens to Television Ratings During Commercial Breaks?" *Journal of Advertising Research*, 35, 1, 37–47.

Danaher, P.J. and T.W. Beed (1993), "A Coincidental Survey of Peoplemeter Panelists: Comparing What People Say with What They Do." *Journal of Advertising Research*, 33, 1, 86–92.

Danaher, P.J. (2007), "Modeling Page Views Across Multiple Websites With An Application to Internet Reach and Frequency Prediction," *Marketing Science*, 26, 4 (July/August), 278–91.

Dekimpe, M.G. and D.M. Hanssens (2007), "Advertising Response Models," in *The SAGE Handbook of Advertising*, eds. G.J. Tellis and T. Ambler, London: Sage Publications.

Dixon, P.R. (1991), "GRP: A Case of a Mistaken Identity," *Journal of Advertising Research*, Feb/Mar, 55–9.

D'Souza, G. and R.C. Rao (1995), "Can Repeating an Advertisement More Frequently than the Competition Affect Brand Preference in a Mature Market," *Journal of Marketing*, 59 (April), 32–42.

East, R. (2003), *The Effect of Advertising and Display: Assessing the Evidence*, Boston, MA: Kluwer Academic Press.

Ehrenberg, A.S.C. and J. Wakshlag (1987), "Repeat-viewing with People-Meters," *Journal of Advertising Research*, February, 9–13.

Farris, P.W. and M.E. Parry (1991), "Clarifying Some Ambiguities Regarding GRP and Average Frequency – A Comment on 'GRP: A Case of a Mistaken Identity,'" *Journal of Advertising Research*, December, 75–7.

Farris, P.W. and D.C. West (2007), "A Fresh View do the Advertising Budget Process," in *The SAGE Handbook of Advertising*, eds. G.J. Tellis and T. Ambler, London: Sage Publications.

Goodhardt, G.J and A.S.C. Ehrenberg (1969), "Duplication of Television Viewing Between and Within Channels," *Journal of Marketing Research*, 6 (May), 169–78.

Hanssens, D.M., L.J. Parsons and R.L. Schultz (1990), *Market Response Models: Econometric and Time-Series Analysis*, Boston, MA: Kluwer Academic Press.

Jones, J.P. (1995), *When Ads Work: New Proof that Advertising Triggers Sales*, New York: NY: Lexington Books.

Jones, J.P. (2004), *Fables, Fashions, and Facts About Advertising: A Study of 28 Enduring Myths*, Thousand Oaks, CA: Sage Publications.

Katz, H. (1995), *The Media Handbook: A Complete Guide to Advertising Media Selection, Planning, Research and Buying*, Lincolnwood, IL: NTC Business Books.

Katz, H. (2003), *The Media Handbook: A Complete Guide to Advertising, Media Selection, Planning, Research and Buying*, 2nd ed., Mahwah, N.J.: Lawrence Erlbaum Associates, Inc.

Kelley, L.D. and D.W. Jugenheimer (2004), *Advertising Media Planning: A Brand Management Approach*, Armonk, NY: M. E. Sharpe.

Kent, R.A. (1994), *Measuring Media Audiences*, London, UK: Routledge.

Kent, R.J. and C.T. Allen (1994), "Competitive Interference Effects in Consumer Memory for Advertising: The Role of Brand Familiarity," *Journal of Marketing*, 58 (July), 97–105.

Kneale, D. (1988), "Zapping of TV Ads Appears Pervasive: Study Details Viewing Habits to the Second," *Wall Street Journal*, April 25.

Krugman, D.M. and R.T. Rust (1993), "The Impact of Cable and VCR Penetration on Network Viewing: Assessing the Decade," *Journal of Advertising Research*, 33 (January), 67–73.

Krugman, H.E. (1972), "Why Three Exposures May Be Enough," *Journal of Advertising Research*, 11–14.

Leckenby, J.D. and S. Kishi (1982), "How Media Directors View Reach/Frequency Estimation," *Journal of Advertising Research*, 22 (June), 64–9.

Leckenby, J.D. and J. Hong (1998), "Using Reach/Frequency for Web Media Planning," *Journal of Advertising Research*, 38 (January), 7–20.

Leeflang, P.S.H., D.R. Wittink, M. Wedel and P.A. Naert (2000), *Building Models for Marketing Decisions*, Boston, MA: Kluwer Academic Publishers.

Little, J.D.C. (1979), "Aggregate Advertising Models: the State of the Art," *Operations Research*, 27(4), July–August, 629–67.

Little, J.D.C. and L.M. Lodish (1969), "A Media Planning Calculus," *Operations Research*, 17(1) (Jan–Feb), 1–35.

Lodish, L.M. (1971), "Considering Competition in Media Planning," *Management Science*, 17(6), B293–306.

Metheringham, R.A. (1964), "Measuring the Net Cumulative Coverage of a Print Campaign," *Journal of Advertising Research*, 4 (December), 23–8.

Morrison, D.G. (1979), "Purchase Intentions and Purchasing Behavior," *Journal of Marketing*, 43 (Spring), 65–74.

Naples, M.J. (1979), *Effective Frequency: The Relationship Between Frequency and Advertising Effectiveness*, New York, NY: Association of National Advertisers.

Pai, S., S. Siddarth and S. Divakar (2007), "Advertising Tracking," Chapter 4.2 in *The SAGE Handbook of Advertising*, eds. Gerard J. Tellis and Tim Ambler, London: Sage Publications.

Park, Y-H and P.S. Fader (2004), "Modeling Browsing Behavior at Multiple Websites," *Marketing Science*, 23, 3 (Summer), 280–303.

Rossiter, J.R. and P.J. Danaher (1998), *Advanced Media Planning*, Norwell, MA: Kluwer Academic Publishers.

Rust, R.T. (1986), *Advertising Media Models: A Practical Guide*. Lexington, MA: Lexington Books.

Rust, R.T. and J.E. Klompmaker (1981), "Improving the Estimation Procedure for the Beta Binomial TV Exposure Model," *Journal of Marketing Research*, 18, (November), 442–8.

Schroer, J.C. (1990), "Ad Spending: Growing Market Share," *Harvard Business Review*, (January), 44–8.

Sissors, J.Z. and R.B. Baron (2002), *Advertising Media Planning*, 6th ed., Chicago, IL: McGraw-Hill.

Surmanek, J. (1985), *Media Planning: A Practical Guide*, Lincolnwood IL: NTC Publishing Group.

Tellis, G.J. (1998), *Advertising and Sales Promotion Strategy*, Reading, MA: Addison-Wesley.

Vakratsas, D. and P.A. Naik (2007), "Essentials of Planning Flighted Media Schedules," in *The SAGE Handbook of Advertising*, eds. G.J. Tellis and T. Ambler, London: Sage Publications.

Video Research Limited (2006), "Service and Products," http://www.videor.co.jp/eng/products/index.html#analysis.

Yorke, D.A. and P.J. Kitchen (1985), "Channel Flickers and Video Speeders," *Journal of Advertising Research*, 25, 2, 21–5.

A Fresh View of the Advertising Budget Process

Paul W. Farris and Douglas C. West

Advertising budgeting is an important and controversial topic as $Billions are spent on advertising every year, and yet there is an increasing discussion of "marketing productivity," i.e., of how effective (or ineffective) advertising spending is, and the need to provide adequate justification for marketing investments (Rust et al., 2004). However, setting advertising budgets rarely involves a single approach or procedure, such as matching competition or setting budgets as a percentage of sales. Instead, models, rules of thumb, and judgements constitute multiple stakes in the ground (using a combination of methods) that guide the marketer, who, when all is said and done, must decide upon a single dollar amount. Exactly, how the recommendations of various approaches are (should be) combined to determine a single dollar figure is, unfortunately, not clear.

Many modelers espouse implementing a profit maximizing method of budgets. On the other hand, few practitioners adopt that or any other scientific approach. If response models are used to generate a single budget amount, it is frequently assumed that the single amount would be the advertising budget that maximizes profit. Further, there is an unspoken assumption that the profit-optimal budget estimate would be expected to trump budgets generated with other budgeting approaches. However, management surveys and our experience do not support these conclusions. Instead, even relatively robust models (based on direct response advertising and grounded in specific media vehicles) rarely play a role more influential than providing one more "stake in the ground." As with Tellis et al. (2000), the management process is more akin to incremental adjustments based on eliminating unprofitable media buys and expanding profitable ones.

Indeed, surveys (e.g., Piercy, 1987a/b; Hung and West, 1991; Miles et al., 1997), interviews with managers (e.g., Hooley and Lynch, 1985; Low and Mohr, 1999) indicate that models are rarely used to estimate and recommend profit-optimal budgets. A much more frequent application is to use models to reallocate funds among media or marketing mix elements to increase productivity of marketing spending. With respect to overall marketing budget levels, the role of models is most frequently limited to motivating incremental, step-changes in the direction of profit-optimal budgets. The results of these step-changes are subject to review in the next budget cycle.

Such step-changes are consistent with current thinking on continuous improvement processes such as "lean thinking," "kaizen," "six sigma" and "Voice of the Customer (VoC)." These and similar process improvement procedures and techniques are growing in importance. Like manufacturing and distribution, marketing organizations will increasingly be expected to apply these principles whenever and wherever possible. Accordingly, the application of continuous improvement processes principles will require a revised view of the advertising budgeting process. That revised description must include far more detail than has historically been available or possible. For example, descriptions will need to specify sub-processes that make up the overall process and for each sub-process, the inputs and outputs of sub-processes, responsible "owners," and advertising-related efficiency and effectiveness metrics identified.

If the current budgeting practice is viewed as the rote application of simplistic rules of thumb, there will be little interest in describing such well-defined processes. On the other hand, if existing processes are totally lacking in structure, it will be difficult or impossible to describe the budgeting process in the kind of detail needed to apply process improvement techniques. The view suggested here is that the current process (in relatively sophisticated companies) is somewhere in the middle; not so simple as to be "un-improvable" and not so complicated so as to be "un-modelable."

This chapter is organized into four sections. The first briefly reviews the marketing literature on advertising budgeting. We then discuss five classic budgeting methods, e.g., market response models versus rules-of-thumb. The third section addresses the organizational processes that underlie the budgeting decision, including a review of the specific steps in the budgeting process. This review discusses the evolution of process

improvement technologies, emphasizing the detailed requirements for process descriptions that have to be met in order to apply continuous improvement processes techniques such as six sigma or "lean" thinking. In the light of that we present a revised view of the budgeting setting process that has the potential for systematic improvement through continuous improvement processes. The concluding section makes some suggestions for future research on the budgeting process, draws management implications and provides a summary.

PAST RESEARCH

Advertiser's budgeting methods have received a great deal of academic and practitioner attention since Neil Borden (1942) indicated that advertisers' budgeting methods in the US were generally unsophisticated given the preponderance of what he considered simplistic rule of thumb methods in his survey. Before examining the five types of categories and methods within, bear in mind that organizations generally combine a variety of methods with studies showing between 2–3 methods are used on average (West and Hung, 1993).

There is a summary of the advertising budgeting studies in Table 5.3.1 highlighting the year of the study, the authors, their sample and main findings. Two strands of research are evident examining methods used and organizational structures. Method studies started with the basic and necessary question of what methods are companies using. It can be seen in the table that the effects of market type, size, performance and country remain unclear on method. There are signs that B2C advertisers, larger companies, better performers and those within more highly developed economies are more sophisticated, but it is by no means proven. Authors have struggled to reach definitive conclusions without the advantage of laboratory conditions and have been unable to isolate the myriad of factors at play. As such the organizational strand developed, beginning with the work

Table 5.3.1   Leading studies of budgetary methods

Year	Authors	Sample	Main findings
1975	San Augustine & Foley	Top 25 B2C & Top 25 B2B	B2C more sophisticated/Finance & marketing execs disagree on many budgeting issues
1977	Gilligan	92 Large & SME's	Majority unsophisticated
1977	Permut	Top 50 B2C & Top 50 B2B	B2C more sophisticated/Marketing execs in Europe have more control than the US
1981	Patti & Blasko	54 Top Advertisers	Large firms are sophisticated
1981	Hanmer-Lloyd & Kennedy	17 Large companies	Information manipulated to alter budgets
1983	Lancaster & Stern	60 Marketing Executives	Methods poorly applied
1984	Piercy	12 Marketing Executives	Budgets are function of politics and power
1985	Hooley & Lynch	1,775 Marketing Executives	Larger & better performers are more sophisticated
1987	Lynch & Hooley	560 B2B Advertisers	Larger B2B advertisers more sophisticated than small
1987	Piercy (JA)	130 Marketing Executives (medium-sized companies)	Budget size related to power of marketing department
1987	Piercy (JM)	140 Marketing Executives (medium-sized companies)	Budget method and size related to direction of process
1989	Lynch and Hooley	536 B2B Advertisers	B2B increasingly sophisticated
1989	Synodinos, Keown & Jacobs	484 Advertisers in durable/non-durable markets	Different methods used in different countries
1990	Lynch & Hooley	1,380 companies	Generally an improvement. Top performers more likely to use objective & task
1990	Ramaseshan	126 Retailers	Generally ad hoc and unsophisticated
1991	Hung & West	100 Top Advertisers	Larger firms are more sophisticated
1991	Parry et al.	130 Nonprofit Hospitals	Process has no effect on method
1993	West & Hung	100 Top Advertisers	Type of process (bottom-up/top-down) affects method chosen
1995	West	310 Marketing Executives	Large companies more likely to set their marketing budgets after their sales forecasts rather than prior/simultaneously
1996	Fairhurst et al.	74 Service companies	Predominant use of of sales
1997	Miles et al.	43 Farm cooperatives	Generally sophisticated sector
1999	Low and Mohr	21 B2C Managers	Institutional pressures affect media allocations
2002	Kissan & Richardson	2,763 companies from Compustat	Level of managerial ownership of firm affects use of affordability method (agency cost theory)
2003	Yoo and Mandhachitara	2 Scotch brands	Competitive spends need not be matched
2005	Supanvanij	198 companies	Executive compensation linked to advertising expenditures

of Hanmer-Lloyd and Kennedy (1981) and Piercy (1986), to examine the factors that underpin chosen methods. Organizational studies have been able to use this work as a basis and branch out to explore the functions and processes involved. Bear in mind that many of the methods are intuitive, historic and have not been taught so much as observed and classified by researchers. To a great extent a messy business reality has been formalized and compartmentalized by researchers and it is best to keep this in mind in reviewing the table and in the following discussion.

BUDGETING METHODS

Judgemental

These consist of three primary methods: *arbitrary, affordable,* and *decision calculus.* The arbitrary is a naive approach, being based solely on what is "felt" to be necessary for advertising. The affordable is also a simple method, but represents an improvement in that the company determines what it can spend on areas such as production and operations and then decides how much it can then afford for advertising. The issue is whether such a simple approach should be used alone, given affordability is often not linked to any objectives. Decision calculus approaches can range from simply breakeven estimates to Little's (1970) ADBUDG. In essence these approaches employ quantitative models that are calibrated with subjective judgements about outcomes of the process (e.g., market share or sales of a firm) under a variety of hypothetical scenarios (e.g., advertising spending level, promotion expenditures). Once the model linking process outcomes to marketing decision variables has been made, the next stage in the process is to derive an optimal marketing recommendation (e.g., Little, 1970; Little and Lodish, 1981). Judgemental methods are often criticized because of the lack of analysis. Nevertheless, there is a fundamental truth to the point that all budgets need to be affordable and this is a judgement based on estimates of future cash flow and earning estimates as well as current performance.

Objective and task

Spending is set in accordance with what *tasks* are required to meet the advertising *objective(s)*. The way it works is that:

1. Objectives are set, ranked by importance.
2. Tasks are agreed on to meet these objectives.
3. Costs are estimated (e.g., it will require $4m for TV and $2m for billboards).
4. If the final campaign cannot be afforded, lower importance objective(s) are eliminated until the budget can be afforded.

Often objectives are set in terms of sales, share, or profits. Tasks then become the corresponding reach and frequency of the media plan among target groups that would (estimated) be needed to achieve these objectives. The campaign cost would be derived from the media purchases required to obtain the reach and frequency. This is the most strategic method given it links the budget to what the organization is hoping to achieve with its advertising. However, it is an "advertising literate" process. That is, it would be difficult

for an organization to go through the steps if they had little idea about advertising effects on stages of the customer decision process (without contacting an advertising agency or similar for advice). For direct-response advertising it may be possible to identify particular campaigns and media buys that meet profitability objectives without setting reach-frequency objectives (e.g., Tellis, 1998; Tellis et al., 2005).

Percentage of sales

There are three methods to implement the percentage of sales approach: *% last year's sales, % anticipated sales* and *unit sales.* Furthermore if you hold it at 10% the allocation of resources will rise when business is good and fall when bad, despite whatever might be the appropriate allocation (e.g., it might be appropriate to increase the spend when business is bad). Occasionally, these guidelines are extended to unit sales (e.g., case rates) and the cost of customer acquisition. Regardless of the problems with using the percentage of sales method to set budgets, it remains a widely accepted metric for benchmarking (and reviewing) advertising intensity. See, for example, Farris and Buzzell (1979); Farris and Albion, (1981) and Fairhurst et al. (1996). Work by Nerlove and Arrow (1962) has shown that with constant advertising and price elasticities, advertising/sales ratios should remain constant. The percentage of sales method provides a "comfort zone" for managers given it establishes resource norms over time. Setting a specific dollar advertising budget that is calculated using an estimate (record) of future (past) sales does not reflect the same logic. Even if the organization does not see it this way, setting advertising budgets as a function of sales rather than vice versa is usually a fundamental flaw. However, using the forecast of sales and advertising budget to calculate and evaluate advertising as a percentage of sales may be a convenient and justifiable method for assessing the mutual consistency of sales goals and advertising budgets.

Competitive

There are two methods based on competitive spends. The competitive *absolute (match competition)* is where a budget is set roughly in line with the closest rival. Competitive spending estimates can be purchased from research organizations such as AC Nielson that monitor media spends (TV, press, radio, posters and cinema). However these surveys are notoriously inaccurate, especially in tracking spending for non-mainstream media. Another problem is that a rival may have completely different objectives to you. An alternative approach is the *competitive relative (share of voice)* where all the competitors in the market tend to spend in line with their market share. Thus, if you have 5% market share you spend about 5% of the overall total. Logically this is akin to the percentage-of-sales method, as each company will proportionately spend in line with their market share. Share of voice benchmarks have been the focus of research for many years. Jones (1992) also provides strategic advice on budgeting couched in these terms.

Yoo and Mandhachitara (2003) examined different kinds of competitive markets based upon two Scotch whisky brands in Thailand from the perspective of the best budgeting strategies for the maximum performance. They developed a 2 × 2 matrix on four advertising budgetary strategies based on whether your company affected a competitor's sales or whether a competitor affected your sales each offering budgetary spending advice. They found that in the "zero-sum" quadrant, where brands are strong substitutes and the market is not growing, increasing advertising will negatively affect both you and your rival. Conversely, in "symbiotic competition," where both brands are strong and the market is growing, it is best to maintain a modest increase in your advertising budget.

Data-based and modeling methods

These methods attempt to use data and models in estimating sales response functions to determine the budget level at which some measures of profits are optimized. For example, one might use a combination of different budgets in separate tests with links to sales established through barcode data. Four broadly equivalent geographic test areas might have budget levels based on:

1. target spending levels in one test area,
2. slightly (but, measurably different) less in another,
3. slightly more in the third, and
4. no advertising at all in the fourth test area.

Ceteris paribus, this should indicate whether better results could be achieved by spending the same, more or less and the control area hopefully provides some insight into the general effect (carryover) of past advertising. It offers an option for some companies to gauge the effect of their advertising outside of laboratory experiments. However, as a method, it does require additional resources and planning beyond the campaign effort and its test options are limited by media use (depending up whether split-cable facilities are available). However, even with direct-response advertising, some modeling will be required to interpret the results and generate generalized response functions for the evaluation of different budgets including the evaluation long-term effects (e.g., brand equity).

Understanding the construction and calibration of models has become more difficult in many cases. Models tend to become increasingly complex as they attempt to deal with complications such as interactions among media or mix element, carryover effects, feedback among competitors and the trade (how will competitors and customers react to our changed budgets?), and uncertainties regarding message quality, media costs, and general economic conditions. Even carefully controlled, split-cable, experiments have been criticized for their inability to assess long-term effects of advertising on distribution channel reactions that moderate advertising direct effects on consumers (Farris and Reibstein, 1984).

Decision calculus models that are calibrated with market response data might also be included in the category of data-based and modeling methods. For models and associated response function estimates to be capable of generating profit-optimal budgets the response functions must be non-linear, exhibiting diminishing returns to spending. A variety of methods and data have been used to estimate these response functions. Little (1970) documents many of the choices concerning response functions and model formulations that must be made. Here, our focus is on the role of these models in making budgeting decisions. Almost all "rational" methods of budgeting are tied to non-linear response functions, exhibiting diminishing returns that allow derivation of the budget levels at which marginal returns just equal marginal costs of advertising.

The evidence that managers do not use these models as trump cards in the budgeting process seems clear (see for example, West, 1995; Fairhurst et al., 1996; Low and Mohr, 1999). Farris et al. (1998) confirmed this overall finding in two studies sponsored by the Marketing Science Institute and American Association of Advertising Agencies (see Appendix 1 and 2 for more detail). Why do managers choose to regard the recommendations of models as merely one input? There are several reasons. Although he wrote this more than 30 years ago, Little's (1970) observations is still relevant today:

> "People tend to reject what they do not understand. The manager carries responsibilities for outcomes. We should not be surprised if he prefers a simple analysis that he can grasp, even though it may have a qualitative structure, broad assumptions, and only a little relevant data, to a complex model whose assumptions may be partially hidden or couched in jargon and whose parameters could be the result of obscure statistical manipulation." p. 1842

Another problem with many models is that there is no clear recommendation possible. For example, with a simple elasticity function (e.g., Sales = Advertising$^\varepsilon$), there may be a wide range of dollar budgets that return virtually equivalent profits. For example, should we prefer a higher budget that delivers higher sales for a modest profit decrease compared to the profit-optimal budget? Or, should managers opt for a risking a lower budget in case the estimation process was flawed or competitors react in ways unanticipated by the model? Figure 5.3.1 and Table 5.3.2 illustrate this "flat maximum" property for an hypothetical advertising response with an elasticity of 0.2. Guidelines for historic advertising-sales ratios, desired share of voice, changes versus historical budgets, might easily carry the day in arguments for one budget or another in such

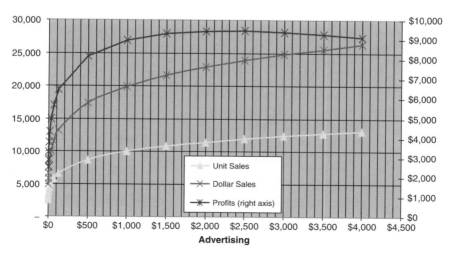

Figure 5.3.1 Flat maximum principle

Table 5.3.2 Flat maximum principle

Advertising ($)	Unit sales ($)	Dollar sales ($)	Profit ($)	A/S ($)	ROMI ($)
1,350	10,568	21,137	9,218	6.4	683
1,600	10,934	21,867	9,334	7.3	583
1,850	11,256	22,511	9,406	8.2	508
2,100	11,545	23,089	9,445	9.1	450
2,350	11,807	23,615	9,457	10.0	402
2,600	12,049	24,097	9,449	10.8	363
2,850	12,272	24,544	9,422	11.6	331
3,100	12,480	24,960	9,380	12.4	303
3,350	12,675	25,350	9,325	13.2	278
3,600	12,859	25,718	9,259	14.0	257

Notes:
1. Sales $= 10,000 * (\text{Adv}^{.2})(\text{Price}^{-2}) *$ Price, where price $= 2$ and COGS (cost of goods sold) $= 1$, A/S $=$ Advertising/Sales, Profit $= \{$Sales $* ($Price-COGS /Price$) -$ Advertising and ROMI (Return On Marketing Investment) $=$ Profit/Advertising
2. See also Chintagunta (1993) and Tull et al. 1986

an instance. Figure 5.3.1 portrays a situation in which current advertising has relatively high leverage, because in this example there are no carryover effects. Although the inclusion of carryover effects would not affect the flat maximum property, it might further complicate the choice of a single budget number. Even more sophisticated approaches would involve the trade-off among advertising media spending, promotional pricing, pass-through percentages, and targeting price promotions to price sensitive segments (Sethuraman and Tellis, 1991).

Two relatively recent developments in modelling the response to marketing communications are the use of customer lifetime value metrics and the increased use of search engine advertising. Each will be briefly addressed in the following section.

Customer lifetime value approaches to budgeting will bring significant improvements in our ability to account for some types of "carryover effects" (Johnson et al., 2006). Even if we are unable to completely separate budgets into "acquisition" and "retention" spending, customer lifetime value helps marketers retain the focus on customer behaviour in the budgeting process (Venkatesan and Kumar, 2004). The focus on individual customers will help improve advertising efficiency through more appropriate targeting. Carryover effects of advertising estimated with market response models are grounded in loyalty of individual

customers. Modelling individual customer behaviour increased management comfort and trust of long-term effects that otherwise may be too abstract a concept to affect budget decisions.

The rapid growth in search engine advertising, like other direct response media, similarly have brought increased desired for accountability in other marketing spending. It shows, we believe, that managers are not averse to measuring advertising responses when the data are reliable and the connections between advertising spending and sales results clear.

While, acknowledging the power of these conceptual and technological breakthroughs in evaluating the efficiency and effectiveness of marketing spending, the strategic issues of budgeting remain as organizational challenges to be managed with improved decision processes, not merely mathematical problems to be solved.

ORGANIZATION

Studies have confirmed that marketers are largely responsible for drafting the advertising budget and top management primarily approves (or revises) the proposed amounts (San Augustine and Foley, 1975; Permut, 1977; Piercy, 1987a; West and Hung, 1993). Widening to the other phases of the budgetary process (scrutinize, allocate and report) it has also been found that the marketers were the most strongly represented throughout save for approval. Beyond approval, top-management's role is generally more limited to scrutiny and to a lesser extent, drafting and allocating. The finance department's main role is in allocating, but has also been found important in scrutinizing, in budget approval and in reporting. Links between function and method were investigated by West and Hung (1993) who indicated that highest sophistication was when top-management was involved in scrutinizing the budget, the finance department oversees its allocation, and advertising agencies helped plan the budget. Marketers were forced to justify their decisions and raised their game. Furthermore, the greater the authority and discretion delegated to marketing personnel, the greater the likelihood of high budgetary sophistication.

Piercy (1986/7a,b) applied Hanmer-Lloyd's and Kennedy's organizational processes to his study of power and politics in marketing budgeting in 141 manufacturing companies in the UK. He concluded that the type of budgetary process affected the method of advertising budgeting. Where top management power was preeminent in the process (i.e., in top-down and top-down/ bottom-up processes), the budgeting method was least sophisticated and the affordable method was most often used. Conversely, where the marketing executive power was stronger (i.e., in bottom-up and bottom-up/ top-down processes) the budgeting method was relatively more sophisticated, and the objective-task method more popular. His explanation was that marketing executives were usually required to justify their allocation of resources and to give details of their targets and tasks, whereas top management would simply allocate according to what it believed the company could afford. Parry et al. (1991) also examined the influence of power and politics and processes in budget setting amongst 130 nonprofit hospitals in the US. However, they found no difference between bottom-up or top-down processes

and the sophistication of budgetary method used or any links to power and politics. Whereas, West and Hung's (1993) findings were compatible with Piercy's in that the degree of budgetary sophistication was higher when top-management was involved in scrutiny and the finance department in budget allocation and when the process was initiated by the marketing executives, that is: "bottom-up" from the marketing department to top management.

Taking a wider perspective, there are clearly a number of organizational pressures and stresses which larger organizations are prone to in setting advertising budgets. Such pressures were investigated in a series of in-depth interviews conducted by Low and Mohr (1999). The found three categories of factors which they termed, the "good," the "bad" and the "ugly:"

- *Good* factors are when organizations enable marketing executives to take risks; allow them to combine quantitative research with gut instincts; and when organizations focus on brand equity and take a longer-term view.
- *Bad* factors are when retailers extort rather than act as partners; when you have to deliver in the short-run (or lose your job); and when the budget is set from the top-down with little discussion at the market level.
- The really *ugly* factors were the political influence of the sales force on the total marketing budget as they generally favor sales promotions over advertising for short-term results, and when there is inertia which results in doing what was done last year despite clear evidence for a change.

Gathering momentum for process improvement

"What is Six Sigma? It is a business process that allows companies to drastically improve their bottom line by designing and monitoring every-day business activities in a way that minimizes waste. ... It provides methods to re-create the process so that defects and errors never arise in the first place." (Harry and Schroeder, 2000: vii)

Many "seasoned" marketing academics may believe that the last thing the field needs is one more management fad. Undoubtedly, much of the skepticism about how much is really new is justified.[1] However, in many businesses, process improvement (e.g., 'six sigma') is seen as the primary force driving increased productivity. For example, Quality Function Deployment (QFD) was one of the first process improvement processes developed at Mitsubishi's Kobe shipyards in 1972 and later adopted by Toyota in the 1970s and introduced into the US in the mid 1980s. QFD was one of the first processes to force functional areas other than marketing to conduct marketing research. Building on QFD Griffin and Hauser (1993) have argued that companies need to fuse strategic and operational decisions to develop the Voice of the Customer (VoC) – "a hierarchical set of 'customer needs' where each need … has assigned to it a priority which indicates its importance to the customer. Developing products based on the voice of the customer became a key criterion in total quality management" (1993: 2). Six Sigma relies upon VoC and objective data to underpin the DMAIC process (define, measure, analyse, improve and control). However, to apply these techniques, detailed descriptions of the actual or desired processes are needed.

The MAX project (Farris et al., 1998) set out to understand the processes used in companies that were regarded as using "state-of-the-art" budgeting practices for their industries. Interviews were conducted with senior managers responsible for the budgeting process with the goal of understanding the actual process used. They concluded that the budgeting process for marketing communications expenditures in these firms was more complicated and, perhaps, more sophisticated than previously suggested. Instead of a budgeting process in which managers apply one of several possible rules of thumb, managers tend to simultaneously consider several "stakes in the ground," looking to improve efficiency and effectiveness, while considering risks. While this research contributed to a more realistic and complete description of the budgeting process used at many companies, much remains to be done. For example, sub-processes should have input, outputs, and process owners identified.

Further, metrics that reflect the process efficiency and performance level are required.

Figure 5.3.2 depicts a proposed approach for systematizing and improving marketing processes. While it is tempting to say that this approach would be more appropriate for tasks that are repeated often (say, generating price quotes), it will be difficult to improve budgeting processes without a clear idea of what these processes entail.

A revised view of budgeting methods: PROBE

This section proposes a revised view of formulating advertising budgets that incorporates five discrete stages. The work combines the authors' perspectives from their individual interviews with managers along with work done separately by Low and Mohr (1999) and Broadbent (1988), among others and has links to the Six Sigma approach to projects. This view of advertising budgeting may be a step toward developing and describing a process with sufficient detail (precision) that it can be improved. The "PROBE Process" can be seen in Figure 5.3.2 and is largely self-explanatory. It is an iterative process with each stage referring back to the previous one. It begins with defining the Problem to be addressed. Next, the Reference (stakes in the ground) is established by reviewing and assessing current and baseline performance data (bearing in mind the expected nature of competitive response). It is here, with the application of form and informal budgeting techniques that the different guideposts for advertising budgets would be established. Objectives are then set and rank-ordered in terms of importance. Following this, the Budget stage sets the amount to be spent by territory and over what time period. If the final budget is unaffordable, you need to revisit the objectives and eliminate lesser order ones until it can. Finally, the Execution stage is where the media and creative plans are implemented, monitored and evaluated with a certain percentage set aside for a contingency.

Throughout the PROBE process metrics are required to assess the performance and

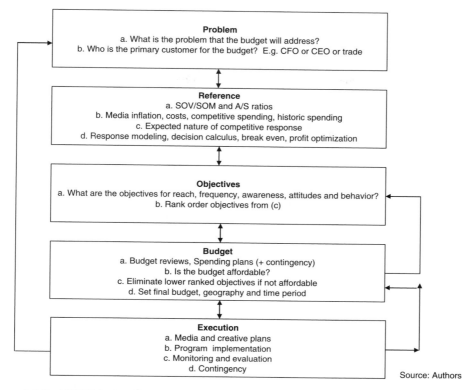

Problem
a. What is the problem that the budget will address?
b. Who is the primary customer for the budget? E.g. CFO or CEO or trade

Reference
a. SOV/SOM and A/S ratios
b. Media inflation, costs, competitive spending, historic spending
c. Expected nature of competitive response
d. Response modeling, decision calculus, break even, profit optimization

Objectives
a. What are the objectives for reach, frequency, awareness, attitudes and behavior?
b. Rank order objectives from (c)

Budget
a. Budget reviews, Spending plans (+ contingency)
b. Is the budget affordable?
c. Eliminate lower ranked objectives if not affordable
d. Set final budget, geography and time period

Execution
a. Media and creative plans
b. Program implementation
c. Monitoring and evaluation
d. Contingency

Source: Authors

Figure 5.3.2   PROBE budgeting process

efficiency of the sub-processes. Increasingly, the availability of real-time data on market response is shortening the learning cycle. The lead-lag effects in market communications response are not only problems for modeling, but learning and decision-making (e.g., Forrester, 1959). Further specificity as suggested by Albers (1998) in differentiating among expected-actual gaps according to whether they represent errors in predicting consumer response, competitive actions/reactions, or failure to implement planned programs will also improve the quality of the learning feedback loops.

AREAS FOR FUTURE RESEARCH

The large number of papers published on budgeting over the years in the academic and trade press denoting the high degree of attention devoted to the subject. The diligent analysis of

the theory and practice of budgeting methods has significantly improved our understanding of the problems and issues involved. It is recognized that the selection of advertising budgeting method is a complex issue not easily distilled to a few factors. Company history, personalities, company politics and organization and specific market conditions are all noticeable factors that will play a role.

One discernable research trend is an increasing fusion between methods used and organizational factors. This is particularly noticeable with the work in the past few years linking agency theory and the use of the affordable budgeting method. Here are some suggestions for future work.

Over- or under-advertising?

Do some types of advertising budgeting process lead to over-advertising. For example any oil company using the percentage of sales method will significantly increase their spend to little likely effect. Do others lead to under-advertising? For example, a company using the objective and task might set too limited objectives. Some senior advertising agency managers believe that vague, ill-defined budgeting approaches reduce the willingness of senior managers to invest in advertising and thus, they are "under-advertising." On the other hand, many researchers appear to believe that firms are "over-advertising" and have questioned why managers continue to spend large sums of advertising in industries where measures of advertising's effects on sales are minimal (Aaker and Carman, 1982; Abraham and Lodish, 1990; Tellis and Weiss, 1995). We need to find out if academics and managers even agree on what might constitute "under-" or "over-advertising?"

Agency theory?

There is a relatively recent stream of advertising budgeting research based upon the application of agency theory examining over-or under-advertising. Agency theory examines risk relationships between "agents" (managers) who have different perspectives from "principals" (owners). Managers and owners often have varying risk preferences. The implication for advertising budgeting is that if companies have excess cash, they might spend too much of it on advertising given managers are motivated by increasing sales for personal and short-term gains. Kissan and Richardson (2002) have suggested the relationship is non-monotonic in that as ownership increases the overspending first declines, then increases and then declines (an inverted "U" relationship). The reasoning is that a small degree of ownership initially aligns managers with owners. However, as managers increase their ownership the more they find they can act without fear of the market. Finally, as ownership increases further, managers begin to merge their objectives with the owners again (see also Supanvanij, 2005). Further studies examining overspending and company practice (in-depth interviews, cases

and/or surveys) are needed to confirm these database studies.

Competitive action and reactions?

In some businesses there appears to be a cycle of spending that is affected by competitive advertising or new product initiatives. When competitive actions are anticipated, the usual reaction is to increase the business unit's own spending to preserve "share of voice." The hope seems to be that other competitors will suffer the market share loss or the new entrant will fail. Following the competitive action, a new (reduced?) level of market share and business unit profitability is recorded. Modelling and understanding these "punctuated equilibria" will be more challenging.

Brand equity?

Compelling arguments have been made that brand advertising is that should be considered a two-stage process involving (1) advertising effects on brand equity and then (2) brand equity effects on sales, prices, and profits (Ambler and Styles, 1997). Understanding the effects marketing actions (especially advertising) on brand equity is clearly an important, but poorly understood aspect of evaluating budgets. We believe that progress in this area will require a deeper understanding of how brand equity metrics are the same or different from customer relationship metrics and other long-term measures of marketing productivity (e.g., "goodwill" or "advertising stock"). Formal measurement of brand equity before and after the campaign should be part of the budgeting process (as suggested in the PROBE process in Figure 5.3.2).

Organizational influences?

Studies have confirmed that marketers are largely responsible for drafting the advertising budget and top management primarily approve. The finance department's main role is in allocating, but has also been found important in scrutinizing, in budget approval and in reporting. How has this changed with the declining power of marketers (Vargo and Lusch, 2004) and the rise of the retail power? Studies have also found that where the marketing executive power was stronger (i.e., in bottom-up and bottom-up/top-down processes) the budgeting method was relatively more sophisticated, and the objective-task method more popular (Piercy, 1984/7a,b). Is this still a factor? With the increasing use of flat organizational structures does the distinction between top-down and bottom-up stand up today.

Does practice lag theory or does theory lag practice?

There are gaps between budgeting theory and practice, but it is not clear whether these gaps exist because practice lags theory or vice versa. The perception that many managers use rules of thumb to set budgets reinforces the notion that practice lags theory. Budgeting is different from measurement. Budgeting involves planning for the future and is oriented toward what might be. Measurement, by its very nature, is historical. Even the staunchest defenders of modern measurement techniques are reluctant to claim the ability to project advertising effects into the future. We need better measures and better models. However, better measures and models may not be the best way to improve budgeting in the short-term. Improved measurement and modelling techniques that do not deal with the fundamental uncertainties that loom large in the managers' mind will continue to be rejected. Better data is still historical. The effects of advertising depend on the following uncertain assumptions about the future: (1) quality of message execution; (2) media vehicle costs; (3) actions and reactions of competitors and resellers; (4) own firm changes in marketing mix (product, price, promotion); (5) trends in demand and supply of related categories. Budgeting techniques should, whenever possible, reflect the risks perceived by managers.

Detailed research of the criteria that managers and academics use to judge which are leading- and are trailing-edge practices would be helpful in identifying and analysing the theory practice gaps.

IMPLICATIONS FOR MANAGERS

Some managers and academics regard the quest to improve advertising budget as a fool's errand – that the problem is too complicated and that it is a waste of time to work on it. Others seem to believe that we already have good budgeting techniques and tools; we just need to use them. Unfortunately, neither of these attitudes is likely to foster the kind of careful review and classification of budgeting processes that are required to improve them. The early work on advertising budgeting led several studies examining organizational issues perhaps out of a frustration that organizations were not adopting more sophisticated methods. At the same time as this work was being published, surveys of methods used began to indicate the wider use of more sophisticated methods such as the objective and task. However, recent studies involving agency theory, however flawed in method, have suggested that for many companies still use the affordable. The problems in reviewing and drawing conclusions from budgeting studies are that: (1) There is no universally accepted definition of advertising budgeting sophistication; (2) Few of the studies used the same methods in their surveys making comparisons beyond categories extremely difficult if not impossible; (3) Each survey has used a different population and within this studies have been both cross-sectional and quota in nature; (4) Studies have been unsystematic in their comparisons to previous work (there are few replicative studies); (5) The problem of isolating the effect of advertising in the marketplace has made all attempts at more scientific approaches difficult to implement. Marketers have to set budgets while responding to routines, precedents, various social and political pressures and dilemmas that allow little opportunity to reflect on best practice.

The advertising budgeting process is distrusted. There is strong suspicion that it could be improved. Exactly how it could be improved is not so clear. Indeed, it is not even clear how CEOs and CFOs can know that reasonable diligence has been exercised in proposing a specific marketing communications budget. Although it is widely accepted that the advertising budgeting process is flawed, we still do not have a program for improving the process. Without knowing more about the budgeting process, it may be naive to assume that better measures of advertising effects, more data, or more sophisticated models will improve the budgeting decision.

The challenge for top management in advertising budgeting is to reconcile market-orientated approaches and inter-group conflict over resource allocations, without imposing top-down solutions. On the "input" side of the marketing productivity equation, marketing's spending has often been driven by incrementalism (adjustments to the previous year's spending levels) and parity with competitors (Sheth and Sisodia, 2002). The affordable and arbitrary approaches to budgeting often function as top-down processes for setting the budget, while the objective and task method is an example of a bottom-up process. Are bottom-up processes superior? Companies, which rely on marketing managers close to the customer interface for bottom-up decision-making, recognize the importance of this familiarity in marketing. Best practice planning is generally participative. Closely related to this is the concept of market orientation, which, among other things, stresses the importance of generating (at a market level) information, which is then shared. The opposite (i.e., authoritarian withholding of information and non-participative decision making) is considered counter-productive. Bottom-up approaches are a more logical approach to budgeting, and recognize that budgeting is an interactive process. In contrast, top-down approaches have no theoretical basis and have no overall strategy to guide them. Such approaches are not always linked to objectives and strategies. It is generally agreed that budgeting methods that are more interactive and more bottom-up in process lead to allocations that are better linked to objectives and strategies and often, consequently, more "sophisticated." As concluded by Low and Mohr (1999), to successfully develop and implement an advertising budget, managers must have a comprehensive strategy to guide the process rather than a piecemeal non-interactive and non-theoretical approach.

SUMMARY

Many authors have been careful to point out that they do not agree with the depiction of the advertising budgeting process as the "automatic" application of rules-of-thumb, such as "match competition" or spend % of anticipated sales. Permut (1977) argues that "simple rules do not clearly define the budgeting process" and Piercy (1987a) acknowledged that, "a major gap in our understanding of how advertising budgets are really determined relates to the organizational influences." Low and Mohr (1997) described a process that involved communication up and down the organization that is anything but simple that remain relevant today. However, this leads to the question why certain heuristic models have emerged as accepted descriptions of the budgeting process?

(a) For long periods of time, firms may spend at levels that are consistent with fixed percentages of sales or other measures. See, for example, the Nerlove and Arrow (1962) conclusion that constant advertising/sales ratios should persist if advertising elasticities and price elasticities (margins) do not change.

(b) The processes to set budgets are largely unknown. Researchers have generated a language and possible rationales (advertising/sales ratios, objective and task, competitive parity) for organizational processes that have little formal structure. Indeed, event the inputs, outputs, and metrics for evaluating the effectiveness and efficiency of the budgeting process need to be specified.

(c) Without well-specified input, output, and process metrics, feedback is slow and unclear." In such situations, "an organization is likely to repeat decisions simply because it has made them before" (March et al., 1989).

This chapter has argued that rules of thumb, formal advertising response modeling, and management judgements (including decisions calculus approaches) are often used to produce multiple "stakes in the ground." Each of these "stakes" can serve as a different reference point from which to evaluate marketing communications budgets. While it is consideration of budgets from different reference points may make the budgeting decision more robust, it makes the budgeting process very difficult to formalize, systematize, and improve. The proposed PROBE budgeting framework provides an iterative process that addresses the need to reduce waste, improve accountability and meet their advertising objectives.

NOTE

1 Consider, for example, the role of supermarkets as source or inspiration or late adopter of "lean" techniques. Keller (1993: 155–6) writes that Taiichi Ohno, the acknowledged father of Toyota's lean manufacturing system was inspired *"by his observation of an American supermarket. In essence, his thinking went this way: in a supermarket the shelves were restocked when they needed to be, as goods were sold to customers. The stock on the shelves was not controlled by the producer of goods, but by the shelf stocker and the end user. … in effect, final demand pulled goods through the system rather than the manufacturer pushing them through."* More recently, James Womack, author of Lean Manufacturing, was asked, other than Toyota, how have companies done generally in implementing lean, in their supply chain? He responded, *"Tesco, the UK-based grocer is an example of a success story. They asked, 'How would Toyota run a grocery business?' … What Tesco is doing is really just a Toyota knock-off: Small amounts frequently replenished, and let the customer be the trigger point at the scanner."* (Quinn, 2005: 33).

REFERENCES

Ambler, T. and C. Styles (1997), "Brand Equity: Measuring What Matters," *Australasian Journal of Market Research,* 5 (1), 3–9.

Borden, N.H. (1942), *The Economic Effects of Advertising,* Chicago: Irwin.

Broadbent, S. (1988), *The Advertiser's Handbook for Budget Determination,* Association of National Advertisers: Lexington Books.

Chintagunta, P.K. (1993), "Investigating the Sensitivity of Equilibrium Profits to Advertising Dynamics and Competitive Effects," *Management Science,* 39 (9), 1146–62.

Fairhurst, A. and M. Gable (1996), "Determining Advertising Budgets for Service Enterprises," *Journal of Services Marketing,* 10 (6), 18–33.

Farris, P.W. and D.J. Reibstein, (1984), "Over Control in Advertising Experiments," *Journal of Advertising Research,* 24 (3), 37–42.

Farris, P. and R.D. Buzzell (1979), "Why Advertising and Promotion Costs Vary: Some Cross-Sectional Analyses," *Journal of Marketing,* 43 (4), 112–22.

Farris, P.W. and M.S. Albion (1981), "Determinants of the Advertising-to-Sales Ratio," *Journal of Advertising Research,* 21 (1), 19–28.

Farris, P., D. Reibstein and E. Shames (1998), *Advertising Budgeting: A Report from the Field,* American Association of Advertising Agencies.

Forrester, J.W. (1959), "Advertising: A Problem in Industrial Dynamics," *Harvard Business Review* (April), 37 (2) 100–10.

Gilligan, C. (1977), "How British Advertisers Set Budgets," *Journal of Advertising Research,* 17, 47–9.

Hanmer-Lloyd, S. and S. Kennedy (1981), *Setting and Allocating the Marketing Communications Budget: A Review of Current Practice,* Cranfield: Marketing Communications Research Centre.

Harry, M. and R. Schroeder. 2000, *Six Sigma: The Breakthrough Management Strategy Revolutionizing the World's Top Corporations,* Random House, Inc.

Hooley, G.J. and J.E. Lynch (1985), "How UK Advertisers Set Budgets," *International Journal of Advertising,* 4, 223–31.

Hung, C.L. and D.C. West (1991), "Advertising Budgeting Methods in Canada, the UK and the US," *International Journal of Advertising,* 10 (3), 239–50.

Johnson, M., A. Herrmann and F. Huber (2006), "The Evolution of Loyalty Intentions," *Journal of Marketing,* 70 (2), 122–32.

Jones, J.P. (1992), *How Much Is Enough,* Lexington Books.

Keller, M. (1993), *Collision: GM, Toyota, Volkswagen and the Race to Own the 21st Century,* Doubleday, New York.

Kissan, J. and V.J. Richardson (2002), "Free Cash Flow, Agency Costs and the Affordability Method of Advertising Budgeting," *Journal of Marketing,* 66 (1), 94–108.

Lancaster, K.M. and J.A. Stern (1983), "Computer-Based Advertising Budgeting Practices of Leading

U.S. Consumer Advertisers," *Journal of Advertising*, 12 (4), 4–9.

Little, J. (1979), "Aggregate Advertising Models: the State of the Art," *Operations Research*, 27 (4), 629–67.

Little, J.D.C. and L.M. Lodish (1981), "Commentary On 'Judgement Based Marketing Decision Models," *Journal of Marketing*, 45 (4), 24–9.

Little, J.D.C. (1970), "Models and Managers: The Concept of a Decision Calculus," *Management Science*, 16, No. 8, b-466–84.

Low, G.S. and J.J. Mohr (1997), *"Marketing Communications Budget Allocations: Antecedents and Outcomes,"* Cambridge, MA: Marketing Science Institute.

Low, G.S. and J.J. Mohr (1999), "Setting Advertising and Promotion Budgets in Multi-Brand Companies," *Journal of Advertising Research*, 39 (1), 67–79.

Lynch, J.E. and G.J. Hooley (1985), "International Journal of Advertising," *International Journal of Advertising*, 4 (3), 223–31.

Lynch, J.E. and G.J. Hooley (1987), "Advertising Budgeting Practices of Industrial Advertisers," *Industrial Marketing Management*, 16, 63–9.

Lynch, J.E. and G.J. Hooley (1989), "Industrial Advertising Budget Approaches in the U.K.," *Industrial Marketing Management*, 18, 265–70.

Lynch, J.E. and G.J. Hooley (1990), "Increased Sophistication in Advertising Budget Setting," *Journal of Advertising Research*, 30 (1), 67–76.

March, J.G., L.S. Sproull and M. Tamuz (1989), "Learning from Samples of One or Fewer," *Organizational Science*, 2 (1 February), 1–12.

Milch, R.A. (1980), "Product-Market Differentiation: A Strategic Planning Model for Community Hospitals," *Health Care Management Review* (Spring), 7–16.

Miles, M.P., J.B. White and L.S. Munilla (1997), "Advertising Budgeting Practices in Agribusiness: The Case of Farmer Cooperatives," *Industrial Marketing Management*, 26 (4), 31–40.

Nerlove, M. and K. Arrow (1962), "Optimal advertising policy under dynamic conditions," *Economica*, 29 (May), 129–42.

Parry, M., A.E. Parry and P.W. Farris (1991), "Marketing Budgeting in Nonprofit Hospitals," *Journal of Health Care Marketing*, 11 (2), 2–24.

Patti, C.H. and V.J. Blasko (1981), "Budgeting Practices of Big Advertisers," *Journal of Advertising Research*, 21, 23–9.

Permut, S.E. (1977), "How European Managers Set Advertising Budgets," *Journal of Advertising Research*, 17, 75–9.

Piercy, N. (1986), "The Politics of Setting an Advertising Budget," *International Journal of Advertising*, 5, 281–305.

Piercy, N.F. (1987a), "The Marketing Budgeting Process: Marketing Management Implications," *Journal of Marketing*, 51 (4), 45–59.

Piercy, N.F. (1987b), "Advertising budgeting: process and structure as explanatory variables," *Journal of Advertising*, 16, 34–44.

Quinn, F.J. (2005), 'The Lion of Lean: An Interview with James Womack,' *Supply Chain Management Review*, July/August, 9 (5), 28–33.

Ramaseshan, B. (1990), "Research Note: Marketing Budgeting Practices of Retailers," *European Journal of Marketing*, 24 (8), 40–5.

Robinson, P.J., H.M. Dalbey, I. Gross and Y. Wind (1968), *Measurement and Decision Making*, Allyn & Bacon, Inc.

Rust, R.T., T. Ambler, G. Carpenter, V. Kumar and R.K. Srivastava (2004), "Measuring Marketing Productivity: Current Knowledge and Future Directions," *Journal of Marketing* (October), 68 (4), 76–89.

San Augustine, A.J. and W.F. Foley (1975), "How Large Advertisers Set Budgets," *Journal of Advertising Research*, 15, 11–16.

Sethuraman, R. and G.J. Tellis (1991), "An Analysis of the Trade-off Between Advertising and Pricing," *Journal of Marketing Research*, 31, 2 (May), 160–74.

Supanvanij, J. (2005), "Does the Composition of CEO Compensation Influence The Firm's Advertising Budgeting?" *Journal of American Academy of Business*, 7 (2), 117–23.

Synodinos, N.E., Keown, C.F and Jacobs, L.W. (1989) "Transnational Advertising Practices: A Survey of Leading Brand Advertisers in Fifteen Countries," *Journal of Advertising Research*, 29, 43–50.

Tellis, G.J. and D.L. Weiss (1995), "Does TV Advertising Really Affect Sales? The Role of Measures, Models, and Data Aggregation," *Journal of Advertising*, 24 (3), 1–13.

Tellis, G.J. (1998), *Advertising and Sales Promotion Strategy*, Reading, MA: Addison-Wesley.

Tellis, G.J., R. Chandy and P. Thaivanich (2000), "Decomposing the Effects of Direct Advertising: Which Brand Works, When, Where, and How Long?" *Journal of Marketing Research*, 37 (February), 32–46.

Tull, D.S., V.R. Wood, D. Duhan, T. Gillpatrick, K.R. Robertson and J.G. Helgeson (1986), "'Leveraged' Decision Making in Advertising: The Flat Maximum Principle and its Implications," *Journal of Marketing Research*, 23 (1), 25–32.

Vargo, S.L. and R.F. Lusch (2004), "Evolving to a New Dominant Logic for Marketing," *Journal of Marketing*, 68 (1), 1–17.

Venkatesan, R. and V. Kumar (2004), "A Customer Lifetime Value Framework for Customer Selection and Resource Allocation Strategy," *Journal of Marketing*, 68 (4), October, 106–25.

West, D.C. and C.L. Hung (1993), "The Organizational Budgeting Processes of Top Advertisers in Canada, the U.K. and the U.S.A.," *Journal of Euromarketing*, 2 (3), 7–22.

West, D.C. (1995), "Advertising Budgeting and Sales Forecasting: the Timing Relationship," *International Journal of Advertising*, 14 (1), 65–77.

Yoo, B. and R. Mandhachitara (2003), "Estimating Advertising Effects on Sales in a Competitive Setting," *Journal of Advertising Research*, 43 (3), 310–21.

APPENDIX 1: MAX I INTERVIEWS (FARRIS, REIBSTEIN, SHAMES, 1998)

A series of interviews were conducted with 20 managers in 14 different companies. These managers were questioned about their approaches to proposing and reviewing advertising and marketing communications budgets. Industries represented included consumer non-durables, pharmaceuticals, consumer durables, chemicals, and financial services. Company considered to have leading-edge budgeting practices were selected and included Johnson & Johnson, Procter & Gamble, Shell Oil, TIAA/CREF, IBM, BAT, DuPont, among others. The goal of the interviews was to understand (and report) these procedures in enough detail, that, given the same starting information, a different manager could use the procedures to arrive at (at least approximately) the same dollar budget. Interview questions included these:

How was the initial request for (insert type of expenditures) determined? Note: we expect to probe for detail to understand the exact procedure used to establish the dollar amount of the proposal.

1. What information was assembled and used to establish the proposal? How was this information used?
2. What were the key assumptions used to project the financial impacts of the budget?
3. If the initial budget request was reviewed, who conducted this review? What procedure was used for the review? What information is required to conduct the review?
4. Did the review result in a revised amount? What procedures were used to establish this revised amount?

See Farris et al. (1998) for a full report. The authors reported that, in not a single instance were they able to discover a budgeting process or procedure that could be sufficiently well-specified as to allow someone else to duplicate the budgeting decision. Instead, the overall finding, was that managers used multiple "stakes in the ground" to gauge the reasonableness of a budget number. Historical budgets, new productions, anticipated competitive reactions, share-of-voice, advertising/sales ratios, and marketing mix models were in various measures, seen as inputs to the process or reference points by which to gauge a budget. Importantly, among this sample of senior managers with profit-loss responsibility, models were seen as "blunt instruments" that could inform and guide shifts in allocation to improve marketing efficiency, but could not be trusted to justify major changes in marketing budget levels.

Following this report a Web-based budgeting questionnaire was developed (MAX II). A limited, convenience sample of consumer packaged goods companies were recruited to respond to that survey.

APPENDIX 2: SELECTED FINDINGS FROM MAX II: SURVEY OF CONSUMER PACKAGED GOODS

$N = 29$, 28 managers with profit/loss account-ability, experience range 3–20+ years

1. Thinking about [decrease/increase] in your budget, what were the causes of this specific [decrease/increase] please check up to three that apply.

	[Increase, Decrease]
a. Our new product introduction	10/2
b. Competitive product introductions	4/1
c. Competitive spending increases	3/1
d. Competitive spending decreases	1/2
e. Better than expected copy quality	–/–
f. Worse than expected copy quality	–/–
g. Inventory, capacity problems	1/5
h. Price increases or decreases	2/8
i. This brand/business profits	2/8
j. Corporate Operating Profit	2/14

2. Thinking about the last significant [decrease/increase] in your ad budgets, when projecting sales [decrease/increase] that are expected to result from significantly [lower/higher] ad spending, the highest likely danger that these [decrease/increase] will not be predicted accurately are:
   (4) Inaccurate market research (6) Competitive reactions (1) Inadequate inventory, production or operating capacity (1) Unexpected events (economy, weather, …)

3. **Budgeting Procedures**

| | 1. How important a role does this procedure play in your reaching your recommendation? | | | | 2. How important a role does this procedure play in convincing your CEO/CFO to approve your recommended budget level? | | | |
	High	Medium	Low	Don't Use	High	Medium	Low	Don't Use
A. Percentage of Sales:	2	7	8	8	5	8	6	4
B. Share of Competitive Spending (Voice):	-	3	7	12	5	7	5	6
C. Models, Test Markets and Profit Maximization Models	-	3	7	12	1	3	2	14
D. Task Method	10	1	9	3	6	7	8	4
E. Historical Budgets + Media Inflation	13	10	2	2	10	12	2	2

Essentials of Planning Media Schedules

Demetrios Vakratsas and
Prasad A. Naik

How should an advertiser schedule its advertising messages over time given a certain advertising budget? More specifically, should the budget be concentrated over a short period (i.e., a blitz schedule) or spread uniformly over the entire planning horizon (i.e., the even schedule)? Such questions arise when brand managers or media planners allocate gross rating points (GRPs)[1] worth hundreds of millions of dollars so that a few concentrated pulses of weekly advertising are interspersed with silent periods of no advertising over the annual planning horizon. The resulting on and off media spending patterns over time are called pulsing (or flighted) media schedules. The practical significance of the difference between pulsing and even schedules boils down to making a "big impact periodically" versus maintaining a "continuous presence."

Figure 5.4.1 illustrates pulsing schedules used by a major telecommunications company in the United Kingdom (see Bass et al., 2005). It shows GRPs over time for five different advertising themes and other competitors' advertising (aggregated). Such pulsing schedules are universally used by managers across brands and countries, and academic research, at least in most cases, tends to suggest that pulsing is the optimal scheduling strategy.

The optimal allocation of advertising money over time and the various types of advertising schedules managers have at their disposal will be the main theme of this chapter. We will present insights and results from the scheduling academic literature that finds its roots in the classic study by Zielske (1959) and, over the last four decades, it attracted both scholars (e.g., Sasieni, 1971; Mahajan and Muller, 1986; Feinberg, 1992) and managers (e.g., Strong, 1977; Zielske and Henry, 1980; Jones, 1995). In addition, we will also address the following managerially important questions: If a blitz schedule is used, then what should be the level or intensity of spending and how long should

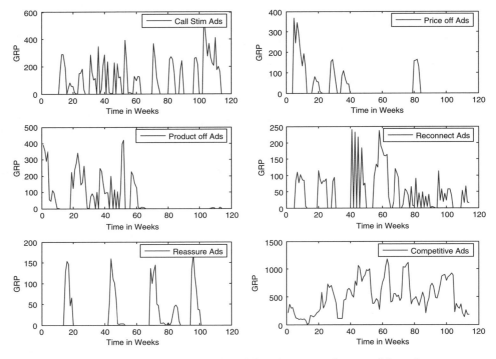

Figure 5.4.1   Pulsing schedules for five advertising themes and competitive ads

this burst last? More generally, for multi-pulse schedules, how long should each pulse last? Or should they be equally long? What should be the spacing between pulses? These questions – simple to state, but hard to answer – have remained open for a long time (see, e.g., Corkindale and Newall, 1978; Simon, 1982; and Table 8.1 in Hanssens et al., 1998: 254).

We organize this chapter as follows. We first define a few salient pulsing schedules, review the empirical pulsing studies and identify the long-standing open questions on duration and spacing of advertising pulses. To understand the issues of duration and spacing, we then describe the ad wearout model, which reveals the main insights and new results via the blitz, two-pulse, multi-pulse and multi-campaign schedules. Next, we summarize various other factors that justify the use of pulsing schedules. Finally, we provide a chapter summary in the form of "scheduling prescriptions," which should be useful for practitioners. Also, for the

interested reader, we elucidate the S-shaped response theory of pulsing in a Technical Appendix.

DEFINING MEDIA SCHEDULES

The total number of media schedules from which managers can consider a few good ones to implement an annual media plan is over one thousand trillions (see the section on Optimal Multi-Pulse Schedule for details), thus here we define a few prominent types of schedules.

- *Blitz (or massing)*. A one-pulse media schedule in which an advertiser concentrates its entire efforts (i.e., GRPs, dollar budget) in some initial period of the planning horizon.
- *Flighting (or bursting)*. An advertiser uses irregularly scheduled "bursts" of spending for short periods, separated by long periods of no advertising.
- *Pulsing*. An advertiser regularly alternates the spending rate between high and zero levels.

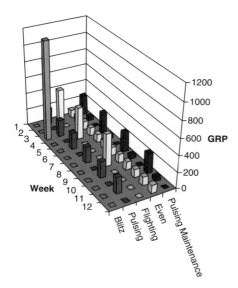

Figure 5.4.2 Examples of media schedules

- *Pulsing-maintenance.* A special case of pulsing with a minimum non-zero level of advertising, usually the maintenance level.
- *Even.* An advertiser expends its effort at some constant level throughout the planning horizon.

Figure 5.4.2 illustrates the previously defined media schedules.

The definition of the pulsing schedule above is the "standard" one, but it can be extended to include pulses of unequal length and size, which would also yield flighting schedules (Naik et al., 1998). We thus use the terms "flighting" and "pulsing" interchangeably. While we defined a few media schedules, in practice managers implement media plans via a combination of such schedules. For example, they expend budgets on blitz campaigns for pre-release advertising of movies or launch of new products. Mature consumer brands utilize pulsing schedules with several weeks of no advertising. Pulsing-maintenance schedules find applications when managers combine general advertising with specific communication goals, for example, to announce corporate name change or limited time promotional offers (say, Memorial Day rebates on cars). No one technique is better to achieve all marketing goals; i.e., each has its own role in marketing communications.

EMPIRICAL STUDIES ON MEDIA SCHEDULING

Here we first describe field experiments and econometric studies, and then identify open questions that directed further research inquiry.

Field experiments

Zielske (1959) designed a field experiment to measure recall and forgetting of advertisements. Two randomly selected groups of women were exposed to thirteen print advertisement messages for a food ingredient product. One group was exposed at a frequency of once every week for thirteen weeks and nothing for the rest of the year (i.e., a blitz schedule). The other group received the same thirteen advertisements at a frequency of once every four weeks over the year (i.e., a 13-pulse schedule). Advertising recall was measured in both groups by telephone interview. Table 5.4.1 reports the results, showing that the pulsed schedule is superior to the blitz schedule based on total awareness as the measure of performance.

Strong (1974, 1977) noted that the better performance of the "even" schedule versus a blitz one does not necessarily imply that it is optimal. In fact, Zielske's even schedule can once again be interpreted as pulsing since advertising does not take place every single week of the year. Strong then conducted similar field experiments, but with three scheduling conditions: weekly, biweekly, and monthly. He concluded that "... schedules with flights should be considered as practical alternatives ... that a schedule with flights

Table 5.4.1 Empirical performance of blitz and pulsing schedules

Schedule	Cost $	% Recall[a]	Recall per dollar[b]
Blitz (weekly)	650	21.0	4.2
Pulsing (monthly)	650	29.0	5.8

a. Percentage of housewives who remembered the advertised message (averaged over 52 weeks).
b. Number of housewives who remembered the advertised message per advertising dollar cost (averaged over 52 weeks).

obtains greater average annual recall in the audience than an even spaced schedule …" Strong (1977: 377).

Econometric studies

Given the superiority of some pulsing schedules, it is natural to ask the question: Which scheduling option is the best one? Hubert Zielkse, as the national director of Foote, Cone & Belding advertising agency, was interested in knowing the answer to this central issue, and so he extensively studied the effects of gross rating points (a measure of media budget) on unaided recall (a measure for awareness). Zielske and Henry (1980) reported the findings based on the econometric analysis of data from seventeen tracking studies, where the budget varied from 1600 to 4000 GRPs across six products and services, and the GRP allocation patterns were pulsing schedules with the pulse duration of 8–20 weeks. To gain insights, they specified an awareness formation model,

$$A_t - A_{t-1} = \beta u_t - \delta A_{t-1}, \qquad (1)$$

where $(A_t, u_t, \beta, \delta)$ denote percentage awareness, weekly GRPs, advertising effectiveness, and the forgetting rate, respectively. Equation (1) says that the growth in awareness, ΔA_t, is driven by GRPs, and the loss in awareness is due to forgetting, which is proportional to the prevailing awareness level. Regression analysis of tracking data using model (1) revealed that the ad effectiveness $\hat{\beta} = 0.03$ and the forgetting rate $\hat{\delta} = 0.092$.

Next, using the best fitted model $A_t = 0.03u_t + (1 - 0.092)A_{t-1}$, Zielske and Henry (1980) proceeded to determine the best pulsing policy. They considered the allocation of 1300 GRPs over 52 weeks via the following five pulsing schedules:

- Plan A: Blitz Schedule. 100 rating points per week for 13 consecutive weeks.
- Plan B: Blitz Schedule. 50 rating points per week for 26 consecutive weeks.
- Plan C: Even Schedule. 25 rating points per week for 52 consecutive weeks.
- Plan D: 13-pulse Schedule. 100 rating points at four week interval.

- Plan E: 2-pulse Schedule. 100 rating points per week for the first seven weeks, a nineteen-week hiatus, 100 rating points per week for the next six weeks, and no advertising for the remaining period.

Note that Plan A mimics the field experiment of mailing prints ads over 13 weeks; Plan B is twice as long and half as intense as Plan A; Plan C is the even schedule; Plans E and D are 2-pulse and multi-pulse schedules, respectively.

Figure 5.4.3 displays the awareness generated by the five pulsing schedules. We sum the awareness generated in each period and the terminal value to obtain the total awareness, which equals $\sum_{t=1}^{51} A_t + \frac{A_{52}}{0.092}$. Table 5.4.2 presents the resulting total awareness due to these plans. Based on those results, Zielske and Henry (1980) concluded that "… there are many recall patterns that can be achieved within the same budget … some patterns will be more productive than others … but it will not, in itself, answer the question: Which scheduling option is the best?" This conclusion is intriguing because the best scheduling option can be determined. Indeed, Table 5.4.2 shows that the best option is the even schedule via Plan C! In other words, this empirical study furnishes support for Sasieni's (1971) result that no pulsing schedule can outperform the even schedule.[2]

Nonetheless, practitioners' preference for pulsing schedules persisted. For example, J. Walter Thompson Company, a major advertising agency, continued the development of a media planning software, named SESAME, which stands for the System of Evaluating, Setting & Allocating Media Expenditure. Ms. Lilia Barroso, media director for Latin America, says that "… with SESAME, you have more flexibility in how you spread your advertising throughout the year" (Malkin, 1993: I-14). The flexibility comes from scenario analysis that brand managers can conduct to assess the impact of alternative schedules and then decide the spending patterns and budget amount.

Finally, in a large-scale econometric analysis of TV advertising, Lodish and colleagues

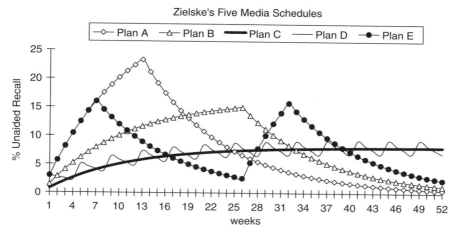

Figure 5.4.3 on the chart: "Zielske's Five Media Schedules" with legend Plan A, Plan B, Plan C, Plan D, Plan E.

Figure 5.4.3   Awareness generated by five pulsing schedules using total budget of 1300 GRPs

Table 5.4.2   Performance of the five pulsing schedules

Pulsing Schedule	Plan A Blitz	Plan B Blitz	**Plan C Even**	Plan D 13 Pulses	Plan E 2 Pulses
Total Awareness	424.45	425.13	**432.01**	430.88	426.2

(1995) noted that "standard" pulsing schedules are not effective and that weight added either to the front or back of media plans would help generate increased sales. This does not necessarily contradict the optimality of pulsing schedules; in fact it is consistent with Strong's conclusion, and it rather suggests that the bigger the difference between the "high" and "low" levels in a schedule, the more effective the plan.

Early academic studies have assumed standard response functions (concave or S-shaped), ignored competition, wearout, and typically assume allocation of budget in a single medium. For example, the extant models ignored an empirical feature: *advertising wearout*, i.e., a decline in the effectiveness of advertisements. The resulting implicit assumption of the constancy of ad effectiveness may have led to the smoothing of media spending patterns over time, suggesting uniform spending as the optimal strategy. Next we review factors such as wearout, restoration, competition and flexible advertising response

that may influence the advertising scheduling decision.

ADVERTISING WEAROUT

Empirical evidence on ad wearout

Grass and Wallace (1969) conducted several laboratory and field experiments to learn about wearout characteristics of advertisements. In one such study, as reported in Greenberg and Suttoni (1973), he exposed a group of consumers to television advertisement for three months at varying exposure intensity: low (1–3 ads/month), medium (4–6 ads/month), and heavy exposure (7–12 ads/month). In addition, he tracked a matched sample of control group who did not see any advertisements. He measured brand awareness at the beginning and at the end of each of the three months. During this period, the awareness level of the control group remained constant at 2.9% (due to other marketing activities). Figure 5.4.4 plots brand awareness over time

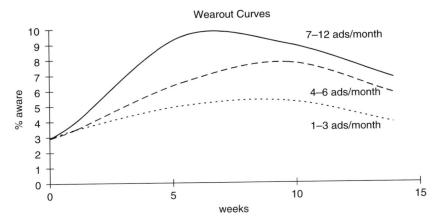

Figure 5.4.4   Awareness over time under constant exposure to television advertisements

under constant exposure to television ads at three levels of intensity. These wearout curves clearly show that continued exposure to advertising drives the decline in brand awareness.

Other empirical studies comport with these findings. For example, in the comprehensive review article, Pechman and Stewart (1990: 14) state that "... as the exposure rate increases and the exposures become increasingly massed, wearout becomes increasingly likely even under ordinary viewing conditions. More specifically, advertising at a high rate may be *no more* effective – or even *less* effective – than advertising at a low rate." For further evidence, see Blair and Rabuck (1998). The extant literature further identifies two kinds of wearout: copy wearout and repetition wearout. Copy wearout is due to the passage of time, while repetition wearout is due to the frequency of exposure. We briefly describe these phenomena.

Copy wearout

Ad copy provides information when it is new, while over time consumers acquire experience with the brand, and so the impact of advertising dilutes (Lodish et al., 1995). Sometimes advertising style gets imitated, resulting in lower perceived contrast between ads (Groenhaug et al., 1991: 44). For example, several brands in a single month came up with the "copy-catting"

claims: "All fiber is not created equal" (Metamucil), "All calories are not created equal" (Campbell's Soup), "All gold is not created equal" (Visa), and "All cigarettes are not created equal" (Kool). Copy-catting interferes with consumers' memory, thus reducing ad effectiveness. Other reasons for copy wearout include decline in novelty of ads (Axelrod, 1980), diminished message persuasiveness (Blair, 1988), and drop in celebrity's popularity (e.g., O. J. Simpson, Michael Jackson, Kobe Bryant).

Repetition wearout

Cacioppo and Petty (1979) suggest that increase in repetition from low to moderate enhances agreement with message advocacy, whereas additional exposures result in a decline in agreement because negative thoughts exceed the positive ones. Other explanations for repetition wearout include irritation and inattention. Greyser (1973) notes that irritation in advertising is positively related to frequency of repetition, intensity of spending, similarity of ad executions and is negatively related to number of ad copies in a campaign. Ads wear out due to inattention of the audience to repeated exposure; for example, Craig et al. (1976) show experimentally that brand name recall declines when exposures exceeds the number needed to learn brand names. Naik (1996) and Naik et al. (1998) provide mathematical models of the dynamics of advertising wearout and we refer the interested reader to these studies for details. Next we discuss scheduling optimality issues in the presence of advertising wearout.

Optimal blitz schedule

Given the ad wearout dynamics, the multi-million dollar question is, "Should managers concentrate resources or spread them evenly?" To this end, Naik (1996: 93) shows that, in the presence of wearout, blitz schedules can be superior to the even schedule. Figure 5.4.5 illustrates the total awareness $R(l)$ generated by spending fixed amount of budget via blitz schedules of duration l weeks, where $l = 1, 2, ..., 52$. In this example, several blitz schedules with varying durations (say, $10 < l < 50$) are superior to the even schedule ($l = 52$ weeks), yielding total awareness $R(l) > 9000$ units. Furthermore, blitz schedules do not uniformly dominate the even schedule; for example, some highly concentrated blitz schedules ($l < 6$ in the left-hand region of Figure 5.4.5) are worse than the simple even schedule. Finally, *there exists one best blitz schedule*, which in this example, lasts for 19 weeks and generates the maximum total awareness of 11,359 units.

The intuition for the superiority of blitz over the even schedule is as follows. Copy and repetition wearout are two opposing forces. Because ad effectiveness declines due to copy wearout, advertisers should spend the media budget at the beginning (rather than spread it over the year) when ad effectiveness is still high. Now suppose an advertiser spends its entire budget in the first few nanoseconds; the spending intensity of this schedule will be too high, resulting in severe repetition wearout. To counteract repetition wearout, media budget needs to be spread out. But, to mitigate copy wearout, media budget needs to be concentrated. These opposing forces drive the optimal duration, l^*, so that budget is neither too concentrated, nor too spread out. In other words, the best blitz schedule avoids both the extremes of $l = 0$ (the nanosecond plan) and $l = T$ (the even schedule). Thus, in the presence of advertising wearout, *media resources should be optimally concentrated rather than spread evenly*.

In sum, an answer to the open question, raised originally by Little (1979) – why not make the duration of pulses half as long and twice as intense, or twice as long and half as intense? – is that increasing the spending level intensifies repetition wearout, whereas extending the duration induces copy wearout.

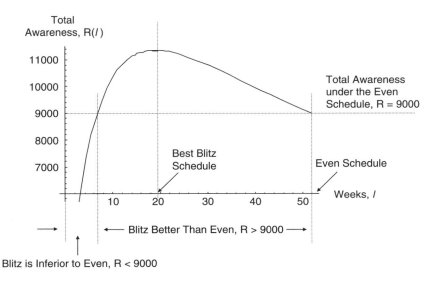

Figure 5.4.5   Total awareness as a function of the duration of blitz schedules

To offset these two countervailing forces, managers need to discover the best blitz schedule.

Optimal two-pulse schedule

Any two-pulse schedule differs conceptually from blitz schedules because of the presence of media hiatus, i.e., spacing between advertising pulses. This hiatus introduces silence, and "silence is golden" because spacing enhances attention. Below we discuss the existence of ad restoration phenomenon during hiatus, and present new results on how copy and repetition wear out affect the planning of pulsing schedules.

Ad restoration phenomenon

To forestall ad wearout after an intense blitz schedule, managers can introduce hiatus or spacing before commencing the next pulse. Grass and Wallace (1969: 8) observe that "regeneration of attention or interest level is possible after commercials have passed the satiation point if they are removed from the air." Greenberg and Suttoni (1973: 53) state that "a commercial that is running for a while can be removed and reintroduced after a time and take on a sense of newness." Corkindale and Newall (1978: 334) explains that ad effectiveness restores because people forget the advertisement messages and, hence, the greater the forgetting, the more the enhancement.

Figure 5.4.6 illustrates a two-pulse schedule and the corresponding dynamics of ad effectiveness, which declines due to wearout and restores due to hiatus. Based on the ad wearout and restoration dynamics, managers can determine the optimal duration and spacing of two-pulse schedules (for details, see Chapter 4 in Naik, 1996). Thus, advertisers should not only concentrate spending (as shown in the section on Optimal blitz schedule), but also wait and restart advertising for the second time. The benefit of waiting lies in the restoration of ad effectiveness due to forgetting effects during the hiatus.

Optimal multi-pulse schedule

The general problem of determining the best multi-pulse schedule is challenging. Indeed, managers *cannot* allocate budget optimally across a 52-week planning horizon by experience and judgment alone. To appreciate this point, consider whether a brand should advertise or not in a given week, then the next week, the subsequent week, and so on for 52 weeks. This apparently simple task generates 2^{52} possibilities of various pulsing schedules, an astronomical number that exceeds $(2^{10})^5 > (10^3)^5 > 10^{15}$, which equals one thousand trillion pulsing schedules from which to choose one best plan. It is humanly impossible for a brand manager to eye-ball these thousands of trillions of pulsing schedules even with the aid of sophisticated

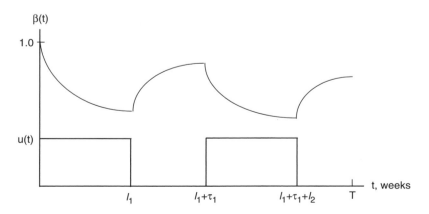

Figure 5.4.6   Ad effectiveness dynamics under the two-pulse media schedule

spreadsheets in modern computers. *Even if each pulsing plan requires just 1 second of managerial attention, this brand manger would have to live a long life of 30,000 millennia to find the best pulsing schedule!*

To solve this planning problem efficiently, Naik et al. (1998: 228) develop an implementable algorithm that searches a large number of alternative pulsing schedules and identifies a handful of "good candidates" for further managerial consideration. Their algorithm is based on the combination of Genetic Algorithm and the Kalman Filter; the former scans the decision space of 52 dimensional binary vector (with unity when ads are on, and zero otherwise), and the latter evaluates the total awareness generated by any candidate pulsing schedule, accounting for awareness formation dynamics, ad wearout dynamics, and ad restoration dynamics. They demonstrate this approach via two case studies for major cereal and milk chocolate brands in the United Kingdom. In both the cases, their algorithm discovers pulsing schedules, and not the even schedule, that were not only similar to the ones used in practice, but also superior to them in building total awareness.

To maintain focus on substantive issues, we do not elaborate here on the estimation of dynamic models or the development of decision-support systems. However, for model estimation, we refer interested readers to the review chapter by Dekimpe et al. (2007) and Dekimpe and Hanssens (2007). For the five-step algorithm to find good pulsing schedules, see section 5.2 in Naik et al. (1998). If managers seek to determine optimal unequal spending levels in different weeks when advertising is on, then the decision task becomes even more complicated and requires some modifications to the algorithm given in Naik et al. (1998).

Optimal multi-campaign schedules

The above analyses assume that an advertiser is using a single creative theme. In practice, however, advertisers concurrently run multiple campaigns. Hence, Bass et al. (2005) further extend the above ad wearout

model by incorporating differential wearout and restoration effects across various themes. Specifically, they study advertising conducted in the UK by a major telecommunication company, who classifies its advertising into five themes: product offer, price offer, reconnection, reassurance, and call stimulation. Figure 5.4.1 shows the GRPs over time for each theme and competitive advertising. They develop an estimation approach and analyze the impact of budget re-allocation across the portfolio of themes. Their results indicate that copy wearout for price offer theme is faster than that for reassurance ads, furnishing new market-based evidence to support the notion that "hard sell" ads (e.g., informative) wear out faster than "soft sell" ads (e.g., emotional appeals). Interestingly, estimated values of the wearout parameter w were negative, indicating empirical support for the phenomenon of wear-in. It seems the rotation of ads across different themes keeps the ads fresh and induces the wear-in effect. In other words, although ad repetition causes wearout, the use of varied executions mitigate such wearout effects and can even reverse it to manifest wear-in effects. Comparing the optimal versus actual allocation of the total GRPs across the five different themes, they investigate the policy implications for re-allocating the same level of total budget – see Figure 5.4.7 for recommendations. The optimal re-allocation suggests that the company should increase spending on reconnect and reassurance ads at the expense of the other three themes, and it would generate an additional 35.82 million hours of calling time, which represents about 2% increase in demand.

COMPETITION

A notable omission from standard models considering the optimality of advertising scheduling strategies is competition. Yet, advertising does not work in isolation and competitive activity may have a detrimental effect on a brand's advertising efficacy (Vakratsas et al., 2004). Research has shown that accounting for competition in standard

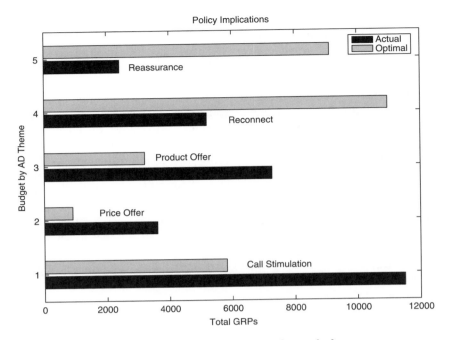

Figure 5.4.7   Actual versus optimal reallocation of GRPs for each theme

advertising response models, leads to pulsing as the optimal scheduling strategy.

More specifically, Park and Hahn (1991), in one of the first theoretical advertising models accounting for competition, concluded that pulsing is the optimal policy even if market share change is a concave function of advertising. Thus, it is more beneficial for a firm to advertise "out of phase." A similar conclusion was drawn by Villas-Boas (1993), who investigated the oligopoly case using an S-shaped advertising response function. He concluded that firms should advertise "out of phase" and verified empirically his proposition by examining network TV advertising data on eight consumer product categories and one service category.

The issue of competition is also addressed by Dube et al. (2005), who consider a flexible advertising response function (see more details below), estimate it and then take their results to the supply side to derive optimal advertising strategies. They also find pulsing to be the optimal strategy. Although the optimality of pulsing is driven by the response function (S-shaped), it also holds

under competition. Thus consideration of competition in advertising response models appears to suggest pulsing as the optimal advertising strategy.

FLEXIBLE ADVERTISING EFFECTS

A prominent feature of the debate whether pulsing is preferred to even schedules, has been the existence of increasing returns to advertising. In other words, since the optimality of pulsing schedules typically relied on an S-shaped function, such a response should be empirically observed for pulsing schedules to be a realistic possibility. Yet, early on, the overwhelming evidence on the shape of advertising response functions pointed to the lack of increasing returns (e.g., Simon and Arndt, 1980). Hanssens et al. (1998) point out that "the S-shaped response function cannot be used to justify a pulsing policy." However, since then, studies have suggested that advertising effects are frequently more complex than assumed by a concave shaped function (e.g., Vakratsas, 2005; Vakratsas et al., 2004).

Table 5.4.3   Optimal advertising policies under different conditions

Condition	Optimal policy	Related studies
Competition	*Pulsing* even if advertising response is concave	Park and Hahn (1991), Villas-Boas (1993)
Ad wearout	*Pulsing*	Naik et al. (1998)
Carryover effects	*Pulsing*	Dube et al. (2005)
Threshold effects (including S-shaped response)	*Pulsing*	Sasieni (1971), Mahajan and Muller (1986), Dube et al. (2005)
Budget constraints	No budget constraints: *even*	Sasieni (1989)
	Budget constraints-*even* or *pulsing* depending on the response and the rest of the conditions	
Hysteresis	*Pulsing*	Simon (1982)
Brand switching or repurchasing	*Pulsing* (short pulses) when advertising affects switching	Bronnenberg (1998)
	Long pulses (*sustained*) when advertising affects re-purchasing	

This intricacy of advertising effects influences the optimality of media schedules. In a seminal work, Simon (1982) suggested that advertising may exhibit hysteresis effects, where advertising increases may have stronger effects than corresponding decreases. This phenomenon, in turn, will lead to a pulsing optimal advertising policy. One shortcoming of Simon's paper is that the proposed advertising model can only yield pulsing as the optimal policy and does not include the even schedule as a possibility under any conditions.

Bronnenberg (1998), in a discrete Markov process framework, distinguishes between advertising effects on switching versus repurchasing. Similarly to Park and Hahn (1991) and Villas-Boas (1993), he finds that pulsing is the optimal policy despite the concavity of the response functions. Interestingly, he also finds out that long pulses (closer to a sustained or even schedule) are preferable if advertising affects predominantly repurchasing whereas short pulses, similarly to Sasieni and Mahajan and Muller, are preferable when advertising predominantly affects switching. These results can be explained in terms of the advertising effects on the untapped market: when advertising affects switching, it influences the untapped market which becomes increasingly smaller. Therefore, sustained advertising would generate less and less response. When advertising affects predominantly repurchasing, it influences the tapped market and sustained advertising

can generate cumulative responses. Dube et al. (2005), similarly to Vakratsas et al. (2004), accommodate advertising threshold effects by employing a flexible (spline) sales response function. They apply their model to GRP data for frozen entrees and, using the estimates of their empirical model, derive pulsing as the optimal advertising strategy. Table 5.4.3 summarizes the conditions under which pulsing schedules are desirable.

OTHER FACTORS

Other factors could drive pulsing patterns; for example, seasonality in sales, advertising goal, carryover effects, and media buying practices. Here we discuss issues related to the influence of such factors on scheduling decisions.

Advertising goals

Vakratsas and Ambler (1999) identify goals as a major driver of advertising strategy, and scheduling is no exception. If the goal of the advertiser is to gain attention or inform consumers, especially in the case of a new product, blitz would be the appropriate schedule. If the goal is persuasion, then pulsing is preferred since it represents a more persistent schedule and allows brands to advertise "out-of-phase" and thus avoid clutter and stand out in consumer memory during a pulse. Finally, when the goal is to simply remind consumers (e.g., established brands or corporate advertising), an even schedule is preferable.

Sales patterns/seasonality

Sales patterns also dictate scheduling strategies such as asynchronous (for market expansion) or synchronous (for catching-the-wave). Variation in sales due to seasonality may induce advertisers to employ a pulsing or flighting schedule and also advertise at the same time as competitors do, engaging in advertising wars. For example, the shoe retailing (and manufacturing) market is characterized by two peak (Spring, Fall) and two off-seasons (Winter, Summer), essentially dictating a pulsing or a pulsing-maintenance schedule. Similarly, lawn-mower manufacturers may use a flighting schedule for attracting new buyers in their peak-season and clearing inventory in the off-season. Villas-Boas (1993) discusses how "out-of-phase" advertising may not work for seasonal products (e.g., cough medicines) that need to advertise during peak seasons.

Carryover effects

The role of carryover effects is also important. Tellis (1998) identifies four causes of delayed advertising effects: (a) Long-term memory, (b) delayed purchasing decisions, (c) purchase deliberation leading to delayed persuasion, and (d) word-of-mouth diffusion of the advertising message. All these factors can justify the presence of advertising effects long after advertising stops, suggesting that pulsing should be better than even scheduling and that a new pulse should occur after the bulk of the effects of the previous pulse has been realized.

Buying tactics

Buying tactics of media buyers and the availability of advertising time by the networks may drive pulsing patterns. Television network companies control the sale of advertising time and they may implicitly or explicitly force advertisers to pulse depending on the advertising inventory that is available. Thus, an observed pulse may be the result of excess commercial time or advertising space availability. This issue is interesting and additional research is needed in order to investigate to what extent schedules are media-driven.

Multi-media scheduling

Scheduling research has focused on either a single medium or total aggregate expenditures. However, recent research suggests that advertisers may benefit from synergies across multiple media (e.g., Naik and Raman, 2003) or messages that vary in the levels of involvement; for example, television commercials with less involving media such as billboards or product placements, or complex versus simple messages, long copy versus short copy, or hard sell versus soft sell (see Janiszewski et al., 2003). It would be interesting to investigate whether the optimal combination of all media schedules is pulsing or whether optimal pulsing schedules for each medium result in an even schedule for all media combined.

Additional issues

Naik et al.'s (1998) ad wearout model shows that pulsing practices are justifiable, for example, when ad effectiveness declines under constant exposure (due to wearout effects) and restores during a media hiatus (due to the forgetting effect). Such waxing and waning of ad effectiveness, and thereby the induced duration and spacing of pulses, depend on the parameters reflecting ad wearout and restoration dynamics, which can be estimated using market data. Because various advertisements would yield different parameter estimates, future researchers can investigate the characteristics of advertisements that influence the magnitudes of wearout and restoration rates. For example, emotional ads wearout slower than ads based on non-emotional (or rational) appeals (e.g., Ray and Sawyer, 1971; Bass et al., 2005), possibly because emotional ads elicit imagery processing while verbal arguments elicit cognitive processing (MacInnis and Price, 1987). Similarly, different wearout patterns across domestic versus international markets (China, South America) need further investigation.

Do pulsing principles apply across different time-scales (e.g., hourly, weekly, quarterly)? To derive the principles that remain invariant to the time-scale issue, pulsing models are formulated in continuous-time (e.g., Sasieni, 1971, 1989 or Naik et al., 1998). The "time" variable in a continuous-time model has no units, and so the principles apply generally regardless of the unit of measurement (time-scale). The issue of time-scale effects arises only when actual data are used (i.e., hourly, weekly, quarterly) to estimate the model. The different time scales lead to different estimated values of the model parameters. For example, if one estimates a model $y_t = a + by_{t-1}$ using weekly data, one will get different estimates from those obtained from using monthly data (or hourly or annual data). The size of the estimated coefficients reflects the time-scale of the data; specifically, $\hat{b}$ would increase as the time-scale becomes coarser (e.g., hourly to weekly to monthly to quarterly to annual). We encourage further research to shed light on this topic.

Finally, the influence of usage rate or purchase cycle or business cycles (Smith et al., 2005) on the optimal policy is an issue of practical import. Of particular significance is the scheduling of media for durable goods where purchase cycles are long but there are always consumers in the market at any given time. Given advertising's carryover effects, advertising should also influence consumers that are not currently in the market and this may eventually affect the optimal policy.

SUMMARY

Based on our discussion of academic studies, but also on practitioner experience with scheduling, media executives and brand managers should consider the following points:

- The objective of using pulsing media schedules is to make a big impact periodically rather than

maintain a continuous presence via the use of even schedule.

- In using a blitz schedule, managers spend their entire media budget in the first few months rather than spread it out over the year. While this strategy mitigates the copy wearout over time, they should not concentrate the spending in too short a time (e.g., a week) because that intensifies repetition wearout. To maximize impact, balance the trade-off between copy wearout and repetition wearout.

- In two-pulse schedules, managers can introduce a hiatus between two spending pulses. The benefit of the hiatus is to forestall ad wearout and restore ad effectiveness because people forget advertised messages when advertising is not on. The duration of the two pulses and the inter-pulse spacing can be unequal; they depend upon the magnitude of ad effectiveness, forgetting rate, and copy and repetition wearouts. To plan better pulsing schedules, managers need to estimate these effects using awareness and GRP data for their particular brands.

- For multi-pulse schedules, managers have an option to choose from over a trillion pulsing schedules. To select good schedules, they need to develop software (e.g., "dashboard") that deploys the algorithms mentioned in this chapter for planning multi-pulse schedules and re-allocating budget across multiple themes.

- In the presence of competition, managers should advertise out-of-phase (i.e., advertise own brands when competitors don't) to place own brands in consumers consideration set. Hence pulsing is preferred over even schedules.

- In the presence of carryover effects, pulsing is preferred over even schedules. A new pulse should begin after the effects of the previous pulse dissipate.

- In the presence of thresholds effects, pulsing schedules are recommended because managers can benefit from the increasing returns to media spending.

- In case of hysteresis, increased media spending leads to sales gains that exceed the decline in sales for the same amount of a media spending decrease; thus managers can alternate between high and low spending to ratchet up their sales over time.

- In the case of brand-switching (repurchasing), pulsing schedules with short (long) duration are recommended.

- Other factors to consider when planning pulsing schedules include seasonality, advertising goals, and media buying practices. For example, if the goal is to remind, an even schedule is preferred, blitz is better for gaining attention, and persuasion can be achieved via pulsing. Seasonality may induce competitors to advertise at the same time, at the risk of causing clutter. Buying tactics of media buyers and the availability of advertising time by the networks may result in observed pulsing patterns.

NOTES

1 GRPs are defined as the product of reach and frequency, where reach is the percentage of the target audience exposed to the campaign and frequency-the average number of exposures among those reached (Danaher, 2007).
2 The interested reader may refer to the Technical Appendix for a background on the S-shaped theory of pulsing schedules, related to the seminal work of Sasieni (1971).

REFERENCES

Axelrod, J.N. (1980), "Advertising Wearout," *Journal of Advertising Research*, 20 (October), 13–18.

Bass, F., N. Bruce, S. Majumdar and B.P.S. Murthi (2005), "A Dynamic Bayesian Model of Advertising Copy Effectiveness in the Telecommunications Sector," *Working Paper*, University of Texas Dallas.

Blair, M.H. (1988), "An Empirical Investigation of Advertising Wearin and Wearout," *Journal of Advertising Research*, 27 (December–January), 45–50.

Blair, M.H. and M.J. Rabuck (1998), "Advertising Wearin and Wearout: Ten Years Later – More Empirical Evidence and Successful Practice," *Journal of Advertising Research*, 38 (September/October), 7–18.

Bronnenberg, B.J. (1998), "Advertising Frequency Decisions in a Discrete Markov Process under a Budget Constraint," *Journal of Marketing Research*, 35 (August), 399–406.

Cacioppo, J.T. and R.E. Petty (1979), "Effects of Message Repetition and Position on Cognitive Response, Recall, and Persuasion," *Journal of Personality and Social Psychology*, 37 (January), 97–109.

Corkindale, D. and J. Newall (1978), *Advertising Threshold and Wearout*, MCB Publications: Bradford, England.

Craig, S., B. Stemthal and C. Leavitt (1976), "Advertising Wearout: An Experimental Analysis," *Journal of Marketing Research*, 13 (November), 15–22.

Danaher, P. (2007), "Media Planning," in *The SAGE Handbook of Advertising*, eds. Gerry Tellis and Tim Ambler, London: Sage Publications.

Dekimpe, M., P.H. Franses, M. Hanssens and P.A. Naik (2007), "Time Series Models in Marketing," *Handbook of Decision-Modes*, Editor Berend Wierenga, forthcoming.

Dekimpe, M. and M. Hanssens (2007), "Advertising Response Models," in *The SAGE Handbook of Advertising*, eds. Gerry Tellis and Tim Ambler, London: Sage Publications.

Dubé, J.-P., G. Hitsch and P. Manchanda (2005), "An Empirical Model of Advertising Dynamics," *Quantitative Marketing and Economics*, 3, 107–44.

Feinberg, F. (1992), "Pulsing Policies for Aggregate Advertising Models," *Marketing Science*, 11 (Summer), 221–34.

Grass, R. and W.H. Wallace (1969), "Satiation Effects of TV Commercials," *Journal of Advertising Research*, 9 (September), 3–8.

Greenberg, A. and C. Suttoni (1973), "Television Commercial Wearout," *Journal of Advertising Research*, 13 (October), 47–54.

Greyser, S.A. (1973), "Irritation in Advertising," *Journal of Advertising Research*, 13 (February), 3–10.

Groenhaug, K., O. Kvitastein and S. Gronmo (1991), "Factors Moderating Advertising Effectiveness as Reflected in 333 Tested Advertisements," *Journal of Advertising Research*, 30 (October–November), 42–50.

Hanssens, D., L. Parsons and R. Schultz (1998), *Market Response Models: Econometric and Time Series Analysis*, 5th Printing, Kluwer Academic Publishers: Boston, MA.

Janiszewski, C., N. Hayden and A.G. Sawyer (2003), "A Meta-analysis of the Spacing Effect in Verbal Learning: Implications for Research on Advertising Repetition and Consumer Memory," *Journal of Consumer Research*, 30 (June), 138–49.

Jones, J.P. (1995). *When Ads Work: New Proof that Advertising Triggers Sales*, New York : Lexington Books. *Journal of Advertising Research*, 20 (August), 11–28.

Little, J.D.C. (1979), "Aggregate Advertising Models: The State of the Art," *Operations Research*, 27 (July–August), 629–67.

Lodish, L.M., M. Abraham, S. Kalmenson, J. Livelsberger, B. Lubetkin, B. Richardson and M.E. Stevens (1995), "How T.V. Advertising Works: A Meta-Analysis of 389 Real World Split Cable T.V. Advertising Experiments," *Journal of Marketing Research*, 32 (May), 125–39.

MacInnis, D. and L.L. Price (1987), "The Role of Imagery in Information Processing: Review and Extensions,"

Journal of Consumer Research, 13 (March), 473–91.

Mahajan, V. and E. Muller (1986), "Advertising Pulsing Policies for Generating Awareness for New Products," *Marketing Science*, 5 (2), 89–111.

Malkin, E. (1993), *Advertising Age*, Jan.18, Vol. 64, No.3, I-14.

Naik, P.A. (1996), *Optimal Advertising Scheduling Strategies in the Presence of Advertising Wearout*. Dissertation UMI Nos. 9709284, Bell & Howell Company: Ann Arbor, MI.

Naik, P.A. (1999), "Estimating the Half-life of Advertisements," *Marketing Letters*, 10 (4), 351–62.

Naik, P.A. and K. Raman (2003), "Understanding the Impact of Synergy in Multimedia Communications," *Journal of Marketing Research*, 40 (November), 375–88.

Naik, P.A., M.K. Mantrala and A.G. Sawyer (1998), "Planning Media Schedules in the Presence of Dynamic Advertising Quality," *Marketing Science*, 17 (3), 214–35.

Park, S. and M. Hahn (1991), "Pulsing in a Discrete Model of Advertising Competition," *Journal of Marketing Research*, 28 (November), 397–405.

Pechmann, C. and D. Stewart (1990), *Advertising Repetition: A Critical Review of Wearin and Wearout*, MSI Working Paper, No. 90-106, Cambridge, MA.

Ray, M.L. and A.G. Sawyer (1971), "Behavioral Measurement for Marketing Models: Estimating the Effects of Advertising Repetition for Media Planning," *Management Science*, 18 (December), P73–P89.

Sasieni, M. (1971), "Optimal Advertising Expenditure," *Management Science*, 18 (December), 64–72.

Sasieni, M. (1989), "Optimal Advertising Strategies," *Marketing Science*, 8 (December), 358–70.

Simon, H. (1982), "ADPULS: An Advertising Model with Wearout and Pulsation," *Journal of Marketing Research*, 19 (August), 352–63.

Simon, J.L. and J. Arndt (1980), "The Shape of the Advertising Response Function," *Journal of Advertising Research*, 20(4), 11–28.

Smith, A., P.A. Naik and C.L. Tsai (2005), "Markov-Switching Model Selection Using Kullback-Leibler Divergence," *Journal of Econometrics*, forthcoming[update].

Strong, E.C. (1974), "The Use of Field Experimental Observations in Estimating Advertising Recall," *Journal of Marketing Research*, 11 (November), 369–78.

Strong, E.C. (1977), "The Spacing and Timing of Advertising," *Journal of Advertising Research*, 17 (December), 25–31.

Tellis, G.J. (1998), *Advertising and Sales Promotion Strategy*, Reading, MA: Addison-Wesley.

Vakratsas, D. and T. Ambler (1999), "How Advertising Works: What Do We Really Know?" *Journal of Marketing*, 63 (January), 26–43.

Vakratsas, D. (2005), "Advertising Response Models with Managerial Impact: An Agenda for the Future," *Applied Stochastic Models in Business and Industry*, 21 (4–5), 351–61.

Vakratsas, D., F.M. Feinberg, F.M. Bass and G. Kalyanaram (2004), "The Shape of Advertising Response Functions Revisited: A Model of Dynamic Probabilistic Thresholds," *Marketing Science*, 23 (1), 109–19.

Vidale, M.L. and H.B. Wolfe (1957), "An Operations-Research Study of Sales Response to Advertising," *Operations Research*, 5 (June), 370–81.

Villas-Boas, M. (1993), "Predicting Advertising Pulsing Policies in Oligopoly: A Model and Empirical Test," *Marketing Science*, 12 (1), 88–102.

Zielske, H.A. (1959), "The Remembering and Forgetting of Advertising," *Journal of Marketing*, 23 (January), 239–43.

Zielske, H. and W. Henry (1980), "Remembering and Forgetting of Television Ads," *Journal of Advertising Research*, 20 (April), 7–13.

APPENDIX: S-SHAPED RESPONSE THEORY OF PULSING SCHEDULES

Let sales response to advertising be an S-shaped function as shown below:

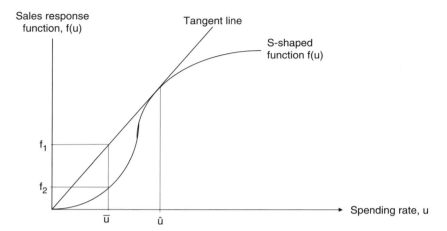

When the sales response function has a convex region, an advertiser should alternate the spending rate between the minimum spending $u = 0$ (origin) and the maximum spending $u = \hat{u}$. By alternating *infinitely* often, the convex region gets linearized by the tangent line, in theory, leading to *chattering*. The resulting response under such a chattering policy is f_1, which is always larger than f_2 that would be achieved by spending uniformly at an average spending rate $\bar{u}$. Further, when pulsing frequency is finite, shorter cycle times (i.e., more number of pulses per planning horizon) perform better than the longer ones (Theorem 2, Sasieni, 1989). Mahajan and Muller (1986) suggest that three to four pulses can achieve 90% of the theoretical maximum attained by the chattering policy.

Peer-to-Peer Media Opportunities

Caroline Graham Austin,
George M. Zinkhan and Ji Hee Song

Various defining characteristics of late 20th and early 21st century life (e.g., limited "free time," dedifferentiation, fragmentation, the ubiquity of marketing messages) have resulted in consumers' ignoring or resisting much of the advertising that is targeted to them. Marketing managers recognize this fact, but some of their counter strategies (e.g., turning up the volume, using larger, more shocking or flamboyant ads) sometimes serve to bolster consumers' defences against such "noise" (Rumbo, 2002; Kozinets, 2002; Holt, 2002; Austin et al., 2005; Godin, 1999). In the midst of this cacophony, old-fashioned word-of-mouth – consumer information passed directly from one person to another – is one communication device that still has impact in a complicated and fragmented marketplace.

Consumers highly value the purchasing advice they receive from a mentor, trusted expert, colleague, friend, family member, or neighbour (Dye, 2000; Phelps et al., 2004; Carl, 2006). The popular press is filled with titles on interpersonal, i.e., peer-to-peer influences on marketing and consumer choices (e.g., Gladwell, 2000; Rosen, 2000).

Not surprisingly, marketing managers look for ways to use these conduits to advance their own messages. When managers successfully recruit consumers to further advance their marketing activities, we label this practice as consumer-based promotion. Informal communication among consumers is the crux of consumer-based promotional methods. In this paper, we use the terms "consumer-based promotions" and "peer-to-peer promotions" interchangeably. However, it is important to note the distinction between peer-to-peer *communication* and peer-to-peer *promotion*: While not all peer-to-peer communication is a form of consumer-based (or peer-to-peer) promotion, all consumer-based promotions *are* a form of peer-to-peer communication.

In consumer-based promotional techniques, the distinction softens between buyers and sellers. Although, many contemporary marketing managers are excited about the creative and promotional horizons that new technologies (e.g., the Internet) have opened for consumer-brand interactions, most of these methods have been around in some form, for a century or more. In a peer-to-peer promotional environment, a woman sends a "wish you were here" postcard to her sister; an amateur athlete's sports- and leisurewear are splashed with logos; a child proudly shows off a temporary tattoo of his favourite cartoon character to his classmates; a blogger extols the virtues of her new favourite toothpaste. Some consumers may not even be aware that they are participating in marketing campaigns or acting as corporate spokespersons at the street level. However, through buying and using certain products, they become the marketer's promotional ally. Consumers' assumption of this role is volitional, as marketers lack the power to coerce consumption of their branded products and services.

A major theme in this chapter is to explore ways in which marketers have taken a postmodern perspective on this blending of promotions, mass communication, and word-of-mouth communication, and attempted to revamp old marketing forms that use this power, as well as initiate new ones. Along these lines, our main objectives are three-fold: (1) to introduce a schematic representation of peer-to-peer promotional techniques, (2) to introduce a group of variables (e.g., risk, visibility, ease of use) that serve to differentiate both ancient and emerging promotional methods, and (3) to identify potential problems and opportunities associated with these promotional tools and offer promising directions for future research.

We first provide a conceptual framework for how consumer-based promotion fits in with a developing understanding of the postmodern new-tech marketplace (see, e.g., Arnould and Thompson, 2005; Arias and Acebron, 2001; Watson et al., 2000; Firat and Venkatesh, 1995). We also discuss consumers' use of brands as a form of interpersonal communication. Next, we present a classification of consumer-based promotional methods and provide definitions and rationales for its use. This scheme is designed to illuminate similarities and differences, trends and themes in consumer-based promotion for both researchers and managers. After suggestions for future research, we conclude with a summary.

It is important to note that this chapter offers neither a comprehensive history of promotional creativity, nor predictions about what new marketing techniques will be invented in the future. Rather, our aim is to sort out and illuminate the ways that marketers' and consumers' use of word-of-mouth promotions is evolving with the introduction of new technologies and media.

CONCEPTUAL BACKGROUND

Two conceptual backgrounds are employed to identify and examine different consumer-based promotional methods: (1) Postmodernism and (2) Self-brand connection. Each approach is discussed in following section.

Postmodernism and marketing

The modernist places the human being at the centre, as the subject of the action. Modernity promotes order and the establishment of proper ways, means, places, times, and reasons for doing things. The modern view of marketing has always promoted consumption: value is created in production and destroyed in consumption, so consumption is regarded as secondary to production in a modernist business and marketing paradigm (Trist, 1973; Ramirez, 1999).

In contrast, the characteristics of a postmodern society are reflected in current marketing practices, as well as in the challenges organizations face in an increasingly complex, global marketplace. We explore three important themes related to consumer-based promotion: (1) dedifferentiation, (2) fragmentation, and (3) hyperreality.

Dedifferentiation
One postmodern theme that conspicuously influences contemporary marketing strategy is dedifferentiation, where the identities of individuals and institutions become blurred, shared and mixed (Arias and Acebron, 2001), as when an independent consumer creates an advertisement such as George Masters' online commercial for the iPod mini (Kahney, 2004).

Thomas (1997) provides such examples of dedifferentiation as advertorials (advertising editorials), infomercials (information-heavy commercials), and shopping centres that also act as theme parks, such as ESPN Zone (see e.g., Kozinets et al., 2002). Other marketing practices provide additional examples of the blurring of traditional categorizations and illustrate another characteristic of postmodern society, that of paradoxical juxtapositions, where apparent opposites become simultaneously possible (Arias and Acebron, 2001). For example, Converse Chuck Taylor All-Star tennis shoes carry an independent, iconoclastic brand meaning for their wearers, despite being iconic themselves (en.wikipedia.org). Furthermore, they are often viewed as being an anti-Nike sportswear choice, even though Nike bought Converse in 2003 (Watson, 2003).

In a postmodern age, consumption has become a process where individuals define themselves and their images in contemporary society (Bourdieu, 1984). As a result, marketing managers have designed means through which this consumption and identity-creation process can be simultaneously harnessed to accomplish organizational objectives. Thomas (1997) specifically notes that postmodern marketing openly challenges the axiom of buyer-seller separation. Consumer-based promotion focuses on this lack of separation. In this chapter, we describe several promotional practices in which the consumer assumes the role of a marketer. Some examples include: temporary and permanent tattoos; temporary and permanent graffiti; consumer-generated and -mediated web pages, blogs, and email; and paper and electronic postcards.

Marketing managers have a long history of attempting to generate positive word-of-mouth about branded products, but consumers today have become far more integral to the marketing process. Under this model, the consumer is both consumer and marketer. Not only are consumers disseminating marketing communications, but they are also developing new products, new media, new content and new marketing materials on their own, using pre-existing technologies, techniques, and materials to connect with each other and the firm. These re-combinations of media and content are called "mashups." One early example comes from amateur and professional DJs, who digitally remixed music by two or more artists into a new song, and subsequently released it online for free. Other forms of web-based, interactive social media have arisen in fields such as "psychogeography" (e.g., www.platial.com), real estate (e.g.,, www.zillow.com), and advertising (e.g., www.thespecspot.com). New media mavens, such as Google's Vint Cerf, embrace these consumer-based forms of marketing.

"There are creative people all around the world, hundreds of millions of them, and they are going to think of things to do with our basic platform that we didn't think of. So the mashup stuff is a wonderful way of allowing people to find new ways of applying the basic infrastructures we're propagating." (Perez, 2005)

It is important to note that the assignment of symbolic meanings in material culture may occur with little or no input from marketing managers. In the modernist industrial value-creation system, customers are seen as "destroying the value which producers had created for them" (Ramirez, 1999). Under the postmodern view, customers do not destroy value; they create it. Value is not simply 'added,' but is mutually 'created' and 're-created' among actors with different values. Nonetheless, a distinct boundary often remains between the firm and the consumers/users (e.g., Bosman, 2006). In many cases, consumers still may display disinterest, suspicion, or antipathy towards marketing managers and their branding efforts. From an investment perspective, many venture capitalists see mashed-up businesses such as Zillow as interesting and socially useful, but unworthy of their support, mainly due to how open and available their source materials are. In other words, mashed-up websites may be fun, but are so easy to copy that they occupy no long-term defensible position in the consumer's or the investor's mind (Hafner, 2006).

Fragmentation

In the 21st century, mass communication (e.g., advertising, broadcasting) is still largely effective as a means of reaching audiences of considerable size. Nonetheless, technological advances have led to increasingly fragmented audiences across nearly infinite channels of communication and influence, as new media have always provided finer segmentation alternatives to older media. Compare TiVo to TV to cinema; Podcasts (or Skypecasts) to radio broadcasts; blogs to newspapers; email to telephones to face-to-face conversations. With respect to media, individual consumers in the 21st century choose what they want to consume, and when, where and how they want to consume it. Beginning in the early 20th century, technology has promoted an increasing fragmentation of media outlets, mass culture, and individual consumer behaviour.

Peer-to-peer promotions try to fill in the gaps, to target the niches that are resistant to traditional means of advertising, as well as to reach those audiences that commercial "noise" has desensitized to traditional marketing techniques (Muniz and O'Guinn, 2001; Firat and Venkatesh, 1993; Irvine, 1998; Close and Zinkhan, 2005). Fragmentation dictates distinct strategies for each targeted segment, and in extreme cases, a strategy can be tailored to an individual consumer. Moreover, postmodernism abandons the notion of a single, unified, consistent self-image or lifestyle and even encourages the fragmentation of the self, increasing the potential for choice, not only among brands but also among a myriad of assumed identities and projected images (Firat and Venkatesh, 1993). It is now quite common for scholars to write about the notion of "constructed self" – the idea that each person possesses a unique combination of innate and adopted attributes and characteristics that changes overtime (Elliot and Wattanasuwan, 1998; Dittmar, 1992; Gabriel and Lang, 1995; Giddens, 1991; Thompson, 1995).

Hyperreality

Under modernist accounts, people have control over their lives, and humans are seen as the masters of their domains (i.e., masters of nature). Postmodern individuals find themselves objects as often as subjects in their interactions with their culture. For this reason, objects in a postmodern society, including people, are commodified. Therefore, no aspect of life, including anti-corporate rebellion, is exempt from being used as a marketing message (Firat and Venkatesh, 1993). Anti-branding advocates such as Naomi Klein, Michael Moore, and *Adbusters* magazine are brands unto themselves (e.g., Walker, 2006).

As a result of this merging of consumerism and culture, there is a new phenomenon, "metamarketing," in which marketing is seamlessly incorporated into mass media, and media into marketing, so that the whole activity of marketing becomes an end unto itself (Firat and Venkatesh, 1993). Consumer-based promotion plays into the idea of metamarketing by integrating purchasing behaviours, cultural norms, personal styles, and day-to-day communications. Culture is consumed; consumption is culture (Firat and Venkatesh, 1993).

This mingling of commerce and culture can present obstacles for marketers; the "clutter" it creates in people's minds makes it increasingly difficult for any single marketing message to stand out (Godin, 1999). However, the union also offers solutions in the form of peer-to-peer promotions. Americans, especially young people, are used to being sold to, and to having their lives constantly market-tested.

> "[Kids] are extremely aware of how valuable they are," says Jeff Kaufman, vice president of research and planning at MTV. "You can't pull the wool over their eyes .... In fact, sometimes, when we're testing a show, we'll say, 'What do you think?' And they'll say, 'Well, I can see what MTV is trying to do here. If they air it in the right time slot, after the right lead-in, they'll probably get the target demographic they're going after.'" (Dunn, 2001: 106)

Postmodern consumers are educated, savvy, and skeptical. Brand managers who understand such consumers see an opportunity to employ consumer-based marketing techniques, and have consequently revived interest in word-of-mouth promotions.

The self–brand connection

Consumer-based marketing relies on consumer investment in a product, a brand, a parent company, or an ideal related to one or more of these three. (We will use the word "brand" to stand for any of these terms, unless otherwise noted.) The strength of the investment depends on the consumer's attitudes and is linked to the symbolic meaning of the brand.

Sirgy (1982) provides an excellent overview of the research literature on the subject, of how self-image and brand image are intertwined, the main points being:

- Brands leverage symbolic as well as concrete value for consumers; and
- Consumption behaviour is generally predicated on the synergy between consumer self-concept (either actual or ideal) and symbolic value of a brand.

Without the investment of one's self into a brand's symbolic value, a consumer is far less likely to purchase, or even consider purchasing, that brand. Conversely, loyal users have been shown to identify very strongly with certain products, firms and brands (see Belk, 1988; Fournier, 1998; Muniz and O'Guinn, 2001).

In consumer-based marketing, no actual purchase is required (in most cases) for the transmission of the marketing message to occur. Consumer *use* of the marketing materials, however, is imperative. The content of the peer-to-peer message, its mechanism of distribution, and the person initiating its transmission are in most cases enough to imbue the brand with co-created symbolic meaning – a kind of street-level cachet. As long as this cachet is passed along from consumer-communicators to others who *do* purchase the brand, street-level marketing is successful. This follows the classic two-step flow model

of communication effects first postulated by Lazarsfeld et al. (1944), in which media-savvy early adopters pass on their knowledge of what is "new and improved" to the later-adopting public at large. This ripple or "viral" effect is at the heart of peer-to-peer marketing techniques.

In the initial stages of consumer-based new product launches, samples and giveaways to influential and visible consumers are commonplace. These senders of the message (early adopters) must feel some level of self-brand connection, but this connection does not necessarily arise from, or result in, their making a purchase. For example BzzAgent (www.bzzagent.com), a word-of-mouth marketing agency, not only sends its volunteer "worker bees" samples of the products they have been hired to create buzz about, but also has a reward system in place for those agents who buzz the best. Peer-to-peer communication becomes a means to an end in quite a different way for BzzAgents than for consumers who simply discuss products as part of their everyday interactions with their friends, family and colleagues (Carl, 2006). Thus, the level of commitment required by the first person transmitting a message is, in many cases, lower than it would be for a person who chooses to purchase and use the relevant brand. The risk for early communicators is also relatively low, so managers are quite willing to experiment with consumer-based innovations. In many cases, it is relatively easy to observe the immediate impact on performance (e.g., in terms of sales).

From an organizational perspective, there is a possibility that managers lose some control of their brands' images. Since consumers decide how to use the message, they have the option to put their own "twist" on the brand if they choose (Aubert-Gamet and Cove, 1997). In early 2006, Chevrolet invited patrons of its website to create and post 30-second spots for its 2007 model Tahoe SUV because it didn't want to miss the "gold rush fever" of excitement surrounding consumer-generated advertising and viral blogging (Huba, 2006).

The most talked-about (i.e., buzz-inducing) ads were those that were sharply critical of the Tahoe's poor fuel economy. These ads were ironic because they used glossy, gorgeous images of the Tahoe in the wild (provided gratis by Chevrolet), overlaid with stark text about the environmental irresponsibility of driving an SUV (Bosman, 2006). Clearly, the ultimate impact of the consumer-based promotional message depends on the direction and strength of the customer's connection to the brand.

CONSUMER-BASED PROMOTIONAL METHODS

Our classification of consumer-based promotions is shown in Table 5.5.1. In the left column, we identify the major methods of consumer-based promotion. Note that some methods (e.g., tattoos) have a number of alternative forms (e.g., temporary, semi-permanent, permanent). In the remaining seven columns, we identify key elements or features that distinguish the communication

Table 5.5.1 Elements of consumer-based promotional methods

Medium	Consumer commitment	Consumer risk	Visibility	Ease of use	Initiation	Who pays?	Recruitment method
Word-of-Mouth	Low	Very Low	Low	Very High	Hybrid	NA	Conversion
Postcards	Medium				Brand	Brand	
Paper		Low	Very Low	Medium			Passive
Electronic		Medium	Low	High			Conversion
Tattoos			High			Consumer	
Temporary	Medium	Low		High	Brand		Conversion
Semi-Permanent	High	Low		Medium	Hybrid	(Brand)*	Active/Conv
Permanent	Very High	Very High		Low	Consumer		Conversion
Graffiti	High		Very High			Brand	
Temporary		Medium		Medium	Hybrid		
Permanent		High		Low	Hybrid		
Auto Wraps	Very High	High	Very High	Very Low	Brand	Brand	Passive/Conv
Stickers					Brand		Passive
Giveaway	Low	Low	High	Very High		Brand	(Active)
Purchase	Medium	Low	High	Very High		Consumer	
Bumper Stickers	High	Medium	Very High	High		Consumer	
Clothing						Consumer	Conversion
Brand-name	High	Very Low	Medium	Very High	Brand		
"Message"	High	Low	High	Very High	Hybrid		Active
Branded gift- or purchase-with-purchase			Low		Brand	Consumer	Active
Concurrent Acquisition	Low	Low		High			
Subsequent Acquisition	Medium	Medium		Low			
Logo-bearing Products	Variable	Very Low	Medium	Very High	Brand	Consumer	Active/Conv
Internet					Hybrid	NA	NA
Email	High	Low	Low	High	Either		(Active)
Chat Rooms	High	Medium	High	High	Either		
User-Rating Systems	Very High	Medium	Very High	Medium	Hybrid		(Passive)
Product-Related Sites			(Very) High				
Official	Low	Low		Very High	Brand		(Active)
Consumer-run	(Very) High	Med./High		Low	Consumer		(Passive)
Online Graffiti	Medium	High		High	Consumer		(Conversion)
Weblogs ("Blogs")	High	Medium	Variable	Medium	Consumer		(Conversion)
Podcasts/Skypecasts	High	Medium	Variable	Low	Either		
Consumer-generated media							
Online	High	High	High	Low	Brand	Brand	Active
Offline		(Medium)	(Medium)		(Either)		(Conversion)

*Parentheses designate notable exceptions to categorical generalizations, e.g., brands recruiting professional athletes to wear semi-permanent advertising tattoos, with tattooing being a category that is, on the whole, consumer-mediated.

methods one another. For the purpose of illustration, we use the labels "Consumer 1" (to refer to the sender of a message) and "Consumer 2" (to refer to the message receiver). Our focus here is to understand consumer-mediated marketing techniques from the perspective of Consumer 1. How well Consumer 2 receives, understands, or acts upon the message is not under consideration for this particular analysis. Each method is discussed in next section, followed by a section to discuss key features that distinguish the methods.

Consumer-based promotional media

Word-of-mouth

Word-of-mouth communication is defined as the transfer of information from one consumer to another. Word-of-mouth is especially influential in industries such as toys, motion pictures, fashion, and recreation services (Dye, 2000). As we noted earlier, there is increasing interest in trying to stimulate positive word of mouth, and more methods are now available for monitoring what users are saying or writing about brands. For instance, managers can read blogs or critical reviews online.

Postcards

Along with graffiti and branding, paper postcards are an extremely durable method. They have been in use for generations and still thrive today. Introduced worldwide during the 1860s and 1870s as a paper-conserving means of communication, postcards were quickly recognized to have mass marketing potential for alerting people to a sale or to an escaped convict, or promoting the attractiveness of a town (Doster, 1991). Today, advertisers use them as a means of building general brand awareness and image, and to promote specific events.

Generally, advertising postcards are seeded in restaurants and bars, and their design indicates that most people picking them up will be drawn by the graphic image on the front, not bothering to read the fine print on the reverse until they get home (or somewhere else with better light and fewer distractions). Most are meant to be used in the traditional sense, being mailed from Consumer 1 to Consumer 2, although a few attempt to build brand loyalty by capturing consumer information from mail-in offer.

Tattoos

Tattoos are used by advertisers both *in* ads and *as* ads, to promote products as diverse as motorcycles, beer, Pokemon and the Girl Scouts. Casa Sanchez, a San Francisco restaurant offers a free lunch for life to anyone who gets a permanent tattoo showing the restaurant's "Corn Man" logo (Wells, 1999). In March, 2001, Fifty Rubies, a New York-based marketing firm, attempted to sell NBA players as billboards, leasing their bare skin for temporarily-tattooed corporate logos. The NBA nixed the idea, citing its own policy of not allowing any corporate advertising on its uniforms (Robinson, 2001). The Black Star Brewery ran a promotion promising to give away a Harley-Davidson motorcycle to the person who presented the largest tattoo of the Black Star logo. The brewery discontinued the promotion after receiving a significant amount of criticism (Wells, 1999).

Indeed, tattooing draws considerable criticism, whether it is virtual (in the case of the Girl Scouts' ads), temporary or permanent. The body, in critics' opinions, is sanctified, private space, and they sometimes refer to commercialized tattooing as shocking, outrageous and sinister, defacing the body (Wells, 1999; Robinson, 2001; Rubin, 2001; Wutz, 2000).

Because permanent tattoos require such a high level of commitment from their bearers, they can be a litmus test for consumer-based promotions in terms of brand loyalty. For example, there are two major classes of Harley-Davidson aficionados: riders and bikers. Riders probably do not sport logo tattoos, while bikers invariably do (Hill and Rifkin, 1999). Harley-Davidson has leveraged this difference by expanding its product line, offering everything from apparel to playing cards to cigarettes, so that anyone interested in the brand may display the logo in some form.

Nonetheless, the tattoo still stands as a symbol of the highest level of commitment to the brand, and the lifestyle.

Graffiti

With graffiti and other consumer-based initiatives, established companies are using "cool" cultural artifacts to build their own brand identities, hoping to tap into a jaded and overstimulated consumer market. For instance, IBM implemented a multi-million-dollar campaign for its Linux operating system in April, 2001 that included several street-level components, including spray-painting the iconic message "Peace, Love and Linux" (a peace symbol, a heart, and the Linux penguin) on sidewalks in Chicago and San Francisco. Unfortunately, Ogilvy & Mather's original idea – to use biodegradable chalk for the stencils in lieu of spraypaint – was not properly conveyed to the street teams who executed the stenciling, and IBM was fined by both cities for defacing public property (Niccolai, 2001).

People have used graffiti as a medium for public discourse since antiquity. Until recently, these messages have been transmitted virally at the grass-roots level, rather than from the top down (Gonnerman, 1999). The local "writers" of such viral graffiti are generally anonymous, and the messages conveyed are meant to be public service announcements of a sort. IBM and other large corporations that have adopted graffiti as an advertising medium, such as Reebok, are trying to bypass consumers' advertising radar by using the same kind of subversive methods that activists have employed in the past (Kenigsberg, 2001).

Graffiti, whether chalked or painted, generates controversy as a consumer-based marketing tool. Michael Jacobson of the Center for Science in the Public Interest says of graffiti and tattoos in particular, and of consumer-based methods in general, "Many of these things will come and go, but the sum total is the added invasion of previously ad-free space. It's an annoyance to the public and completely inappropriate" (Wells, 1999).

Auto wrapping

Auto wrapping is the only consumer-based method included in the table where consumers are paid cash for their services as street-level marketers. Drivers of wrapped cars have the option of either driving a new car for free (excluding gas and insurance charges), or of receiving a monthly check, with the amount depending upon the extent of wrapping.

Wrapping, which may be the most visible form of non-electronic consumer-based promotion, is the least easy to use from Consumer 1's standpoint. Wrapping an entire car takes approximately eight hours, and the driver must submit to a semi-weekly or monthly car inspection in order to receive payment. This check-up includes an odometer reading, a global positioning system (GPS) check, and a cleanliness review. In a standard agreement, drivers must log at least 1000 miles a month, and must keep the GPS unit turned on at all times.

In most cases, drivers are selected from a pool of applicants based on the fit between their driving habits and the communications needs of the sponsors. Therefore, car owners have little or no say about which ads they would like to place on their vehicles, indicating that commitment to the brand is far less important to them than financial reward they receive for participation. However, most auto wrappers are now offering their services to nonprofit organizations as public service announcements, which drivers may request.

Branding methods: Stickers, clothing, branded gifts, purchase-with-purchase, and logo-bearing products

The bottom half of Table 5.5.1 includes assorted branding methods. When a teenage boy puts a band's logo sticker on his skateboard, this practice is not fundamentally different from a debutante's wearing a designer suit to a lunch date. One result of branding is that consumers identify with their peer group.

"Many products, for example house furnishings and clothes, are highly visible and regarded as indicative of the owner's values. Such visible purchases are intended to communicate a favorable image. They cater to such life goals as wanting to be admired, beautiful, socially accepted, and so on." (O'Shaughnessy 1987: 10–11; see also Lascu and Zinkhan, 1999)

The Internet

In the 21st century marketplace, a consumer can widely disseminate word-of-mouth information, both positive and negative, via various Internet outlets (e.g., email, blogs, chat rooms, spoof sites) as well as through more traditional means (Pitt et al., 2002). According to Forrester Research, the average household receives nine email marketing messages each day and tends to ignore such messages. In contrast, Internet users pay more attention to email messages that emanate from their family members, friends, or relatives (Phelps et al., 2004).

Some e-commerce firms, such as Epinions. com, include Web features to highlight customers' word-of-mouth communications. For example, customers can rate products and services and, at the same time, review products. In this way, word-of-mouth communication can be a cost-effective way to transform customers into a marketing force.

The Internet offers the greatest opportunity for a firm to leverage networking and consumer-based initiatives. Almost all of the more traditional consumer-based promotional campaigns also have an online component (e.g., IBM's Linux campaign). Many consumer-based promotional initiatives exist solely in cyberspace and may belong entirely to consumers without any input, authorization, or oversight from a brand's official managers. This creates interesting, and potentially outrageous, possibilities for consumers taking marketing into their own hands.

Nader Traders was an email-based grass-roots campaign designed to garner 5% of the national vote for Green Party candidate (and one-man brand) Ralph Nader in the 2000 Presidential election (Harris, 2000). Although, it was not ultimately successful, it generated considerable publicity. Vote swapping was

considered so dangerous to the democratic process that several swap-facilitation sites were shut down by government order. Subsequently, California and New York orders were upheld in Federal court (Zaret, 2000). Information regarding Nader Traders traveled through the voting population via email, without any overarching or centralized architecture provided by Nader or the Green Party.

Viral marketing may be the next "killer application" of the Internet. Certainly media financiers are banking on its networking capacity to generate revenues in virtual marketspaces that have not yet seen any profits, as evidenced by Rupert Murdoch's acquisition of MySpace and Accel Partners' investment in Facebook, deals worth hundreds of millions, and potentially billions, of dollars each (Cassidy, 2006). As for the humble email, the "forward" and "reply all" buttons and the electronic address book are invaluable tools for viral email messaging. Carlton Draught's very funny "Big Ad" (www.bigad.com.au) received one million page hits within two weeks of being launched online, thanks to friends telling friends about it (Lees, 2005). Across all these consumer-controlled electronic media, the quality and content of the messages determine how widely information is transmitted.

It is interesting to note the evolution of tracking technologies for digital marketplaces, and of consumer-based promotional initiatives in particular. In November 2000, David Holtzman launched Opion.com, a buzz-tracking website that evaluated online chatter in chat rooms, bulletin boards, newsgroups and websites, looking for trends that would affect various markets. Opion attempted to predict, among other things, box office receipts, election results, and Wall Street swoops and wobbles (Wakefield, 2001). Subsequent shifts in the marketplace, most notably the explosion of consumer-based initiatives, have caused the field of online analysis and trend prediction to expand enormously; as of February 2006, Opion no longer existed, having been rolled, in a series of acquisitions, into a new venture called Nielsen BuzzMetrics. BuzzMetrics's client list includes Nokia, Target, Proctor & Gamble, Sony, pharmaceutical firms, HBO, and Microsoft, and they promise to "help companies gain market feedback and understand how consumers talk about important issues, advocate products and spread information ... by combining superb brand and consumer expertise, proprietary datamining technology, and Nielsen's unrivaled experience in media measurement and client service" (www.nielsenbuzzmetrics.com).

Another web-based initiative that has contributed enormously to the electronic consumer-based marketing revolution is the advent of weblogs (aka, "blogs"), which started as little more than electronic journals or diaries and have evolved into serious means of niche/mass communication. They are primarily personal accounts focused on a particular theme (e.g., the blogger's take on politics, favourite sports, or day-to-day activities) and provide primary and secondary information along with the blogger's commentary related to these items. Furthermore, blogs are usually designed to encourage readers to provide their own commentary on either the subject matter or the blogger's (or other readers') reactions to the subject matter. Often, bloggers will dissect – while naming names – their employers, favourite new products, brands they love and hate, and bad service encounters. Because blogging is such a new medium, there are relatively few rules governing its use, and most use is considered protected under the First Amendment.

Firms are trying to protect themselves and their brands from blog abuse through various means. For example, in 2004 Delta Airlines fired Ellen Simonetti (aka, Queen of Sky) after she posted "inappropriate" photos of herself in uniform on her blog (queenofsky.journalspace.com). In the photos, Simonetti is fully clothed in her Delta flight attendant's uniform, onboard an otherwise empty airplane, posing in ways that emphasize her body as she performs work-related tasks (e.g., serving drinks, putting luggage in an overhead bin). The photos are more silly than sexy, but Delta found them offensive and out of keeping with its corporate image and policies. Simonetti has fought back by maintaining her blog (which includes the photos in question and an audio file of the phone conversation in which her supervisor fired her), hiring a press agent, and writing a roman à clef.

Jonah Peretti became an Information Age celebrity of sorts in 2001 when he published an email exchange he had had with Nike over the term "sweatshop" on his blog (www.shey.net/niked.html). The satirical David-and-Goliath story rocketed through cyberspace and was shortly picked up by media outlets worldwide, including such ideologically diverse media outlets as *The Wall Street Journal, The Nation, USA Today,* and *The Village Voice*. Nike's response to the blogging itself was minimal (as was Delta's in the Simonetti case), but Peretti has achieved a modicum of lasting fame among those he terms "the Bored at Work Network (BWN)" by posting content at www.contagiousmedia.org and www.eyebeam.com. He writes, "This low-budget, bottom-up approach makes it possible to create a global cascade that begins with a small group of friends and extends to the set of CNN or the *Today* show. These Contagious Media Experiments suggest new opportunities for artists and activists in the networked age" (www.contagiousmedia.org). Though Peretti may not like it, the notion of contagious media is also at the heart of all consumer-based promotions, especially in its evolving electronic forms.

With Podcasting and Skypecasting, consumers remain in control of the audio files that they receive, and the sender may be either the firm or another consumer. The target audiences for Pod- and Skypecasts are self-selected and usually very engaged with either the sender or the subject matter. A small sample of available Podcasts includes music (the first use of the medium), interviews with video game designers, wine and beer reviews, travel and tourism guides, and NASCAR updates (see, e.g., www.podcastalley.com).

Consumer-generated media

Firms were using their customers' creative energies as a way to generate official marketing materials long before the advent of the Internet. *The Prize Winner of Defiance, Ohio: How My Mother Raised 10 Kids on 25 Words or Less* (Ryan, 2001) details the story of a Midwestern housewife whose amateur ad jingle-writing skills kept her family afloat during the 1950s and 1960s. The Pillsbury Bake-Off® Contest debuted in New York City in 1949 and has been inspiring amateur chefs to take a shot at the grand prize, in 2006 worth $1 million and a kitchen full of stainless steel appliances (www.pillsbury.com). Jones Soda began distributing its "alternative beverages" in 1996, using consumer-submitted photographs for all its marketing and packaging materials, including bottle labels. They also encourage users to send in quotes and flavor suggestions (www.jonessoda.com). While those whose input is chosen don't win money or prizes, the number of photos submitted to the website indicates that the glory of winning a bottle label is almost as compelling as a million dollars. Other firms that have adopted similar consumer-generated campaigns include Converse, MasterCard, Chevrolet, L'Oreal and Sony.

The Internet has fostered an explosion of consumer-generated promotions, thanks to the ease with which users can create and distribute material. Online, consumers' creating and posting brand- and product-related creative output is pervasive. In 2003, 44% of wired Americans reported having created and/or posted content online (Lenhart et al., 2004). Often, consumers create their own amateur online advertisements simply because they love or hate a particular product. If they get picked up and disseminated through blogs and email, these ads can achieve a massive amount of exposure (Kahney, 2004). For an interesting contrast between iPod users, see George Masters's digital love letter to his "Tiny Machine" (available at www.imediaconnection.com), versus the Neistat Brothers' expose of the "iPod's Dirty Secret" (i.e., its short-lived, non-replaceable battery, available at www.ipodsdirtysecret.com).

Key features distinguishing different consumer-based promotional techniques

Seven attributes distinguish consumer-based promotions. Each method is ranked along these dimensions in Table 5.5.1.

Consumer commitment

The level of interest in either the brand or the promotional medium that is required for Consumer 1 to participate in a consumer-based campaign. For instance, driving a car bearing a commercial auto wrap requires a very high level of commitment from the owner/driver, while forwarding an email recommendation (e.g., a movie review) to a friend requires significantly less commitment. Some consumer-based promotional techniques are so creatively compelling, such as designing an advertisement (e.g., Converse), or so entertaining (e.g., The "Big Ad"), or offer great potential for reward, such as having one's artwork selected in a contest to be used as a product label (e.g., Jones Soda), that consumers will participate in a peer-to-peer promotional campaign even though their commitment to the brand itself is negligible.

Consumer risk

Risk includes a variety of dimensions, including legal, physical, emotional, and economic risk (or a loss of privacy) (Conchar et al., 2004). Opportunity costs also fall into this category. Consumer 1 assumes a certain amount of risk by participating in consumer-based promotions. The permanent tattooing of a brand logo entails considerable risk; sending a paper postcard entails relatively little. Sending an electronic postcard opens the sender to receiving unwanted email from the host website, and is, therefore, somewhat riskier. Risk is where the majority of public-policy concerns regarding consumer-based promotions come into play.

Visibility

Visibility describes the number of potential recipients of the marketing message. In other words, how many Consumer 2s will each Consumer 1 be able to reach? Auto-wrapping companies require monthly odometer checks to ensure maximum visibility of their marketing messages. A sticker on a student's backpack will be seen by significantly fewer people.

Ease of use

Ease refers to the amount of effort required for Consumer 1 to transmit the marketing message to Consumer 2. A bumper sticker is easy to use, a postcard is a little harder, maintaining a weblog is harder still, and designing a website requires yet more time and effort. However, electronic media such as blog hosting websites are becoming increasingly user-friendly.

Initiation

The party that initiates a consumer-based promotional campaign may be the brand's corporate parent, the consumer, or a hybrid of the two. Hybridized forms generally start as consumer-initiated, but then marketing managers seek to influence or adopt the method. For example, the idea of promotional graffiti sprang from graffiti used for artistic or political expression. In other cases, brand-initiated peer-to-peer promotions might coexist with independent consumer-initiated forms in the same medium, such as official websites, fansites, and anti-fansites all dedicated to a particular brand.

Who pays?

Sometimes, Consumer 1 pays for the privilege of basking in a brand's cachet (e.g., buying a "brand-name" product for conspicuous use). Sometimes, the brand's owner pays Consumer 1 to deliver its marketing message (e.g., autowrappers pay drivers a monthly stipend). Most often, the brand will pay to create and launch the consumer-based campaign, including researchers', consultants' and recruiters' fees, but not actually pay consumers themselves to participate.

Recruitment methods

There are a variety of means for recruiting participants. Sometimes, the brand owner actively works to attract Consumer 1 (e.g., handing out band-logo temporary tattoos at a music festival). Some owners "seed" the street with marketing messages to attract Consumer 1 passively (e.g., placing free, well-stocked postcard kiosks in trendy restaurants and bars). Sometimes, Consumer 2 is a likely target for conversion into a Consumer 1 (e.g., encouraging online consumers to forward web sites to friends by placing an easy-to-use button at the bottom of a webpage).

Multilevel marketing systems such as Amway and Mary Kay are not included in this table, even though these methods rely upon consumer-driven, word-of-mouth marketing. These methods are omitted because participants in such systems are functioning not only as communicators of promotional messages, but also as direct sellers and distributors for the products, and recruiters for new salespeople (www.amway.com).

IMPLICATIONS FOR MANAGERS AND RESEARCHERS

Why do consumer-based promotions work?

In analysing the effectiveness of peer-to-peer promotional techniques, a key question to answer is: Do consumer-based promotions change consumers' attitudes through central or peripheral channels of perception (Petty and Cacioppo, 1986)? In other words, do consumers really notice the brands that they are marketing to each other, or are they buying and using them without realizing jut how valuable their participation in the process actually is? Based on the variety of techniques currently in use, we argue that advertisers believe that it can be either, or both, depending on the message, the product, Consumer 1, Consumer 2, the environment, and other mediating factors.

When consumer-based promotion works primarily at the peripheral level, it indicates the following chain of events. First, there is an apparent nonchalance on the part of Consumer 1, and this results in lowered anti-marketing perceptual filtering by Consumer 2. These lowered defences lead to an increased penetration of marketing messages (i.e., awareness of logos and brands). Firms' adoption and use of peripheral-based techniques (e.g., simply affixing an identifiable logo to all the firm's materials) seems to follow this "It can't hurt" strategy.

Another explanation, for situations in which conspicuous consumption and status-seeking are important (Veblen and Mills, 2000; O'Shaughnessy, 1987), is that consumer-based promotion operates through a central cognitive route. That is, consumers routinely take notice of each other on a conscious level. Because there is a reflexive relationship between consumption choices and communities, what we wear, drive, and otherwise consume convey social and utilitarian meanings about ourselves to other people (Arnould et al., 2004). Consumers' intense observation of others' consumption choices triggers metacognition and/or metaperception.

Metacognition is the process of thinking about thinking, either about what is happening inside one's own head, or inside others' (Jost et al., 1998; Petty et al., 2002). When consumers ask themselves if they are making the right decisions, or coming to the correct conclusions; when they wonder if they have all the facts; when they wonder if the salesperson is really giving good advice or merely trying to make a sale, they are engaging in metacognition. In all stages of the consumption process, from pre-purchase search to post-purchase evaluation, people generate beliefs and then challenge and validate them through metacognition (Kruglanski, 1989, 1990).

A hypothetical example of process is illustrated when an established shoe manufacturer introduces a new type of skateboard shoes. A teenage boy, Jason, sees the new brand and thinks it looks cool, but is reluctant to buy it because it might be too trendy and not acceptable among real skaters. Later, he notices that a classmate, Nick, who is a skater and one of the cool kids at school, is wearing the shoe. Jason's original opinion about the shoe's street cachet (its coolness) is validated. At the same time, his evaluation of the shoes as useful skate equipment increases. In this way, Jason learns to trust his own opinion about what is cool (and what isn't). He recognizes that his initial assessments of the shoes' qualities are valid, based on their convergence with the beliefs and behaviours of others around him.

Through metaperception, people pay attention to what others think about them (Laing et al., 1966). In the preceding example, Nick, the cool skater kid, could use Jason's imitation of his footwear to reinforce his belief that other people think he is cool. Furthermore, Jason could observe the way others treated him, following his purchase of the new shoes, and adjust his behaviours (including purchase behaviours) to generate positive reactions from other people.

From a postmodern perspective, both metacognition and metaperception play important roles in consumer choices. As stated earlier, we as consumers synthesize public identities through a mix-and-match process of consumption. During the process, we step outside of ourselves to gauge other people's perceptions of us. We wonder if we are making wise, socially acceptable consumption choices. As social animals, we behave in accordance with images we are trying to portray to others (Firat and Venkatesh, 1993; Albright et al., 2001). Consumer-based promotional techniques rely on these established cognitive and behavioural principles in order to heighten both brand awareness and brand equity. Brands are only meaningful if consumers adopt and use them.

AN AGENDA FOR FUTURE RESEARCH

What is the relative effectiveness of various consumer-based promotional techniques? A systematic content analysis of peer-to-peer techniques would reveal ways in which they have been able to harness consumer power to disseminate information. Are the "sexier" methods, such as creating and distributing personalized electronic advertisements, better at raising overall awareness of the brand than more traditional variants of word-of-mouth (e.g., postcards), or even of plain old word-of-mouth itself?

Are certain *methods* more effective at generating sales than others? For example, does eating from "gift" dishes have a more lasting impact on children than playing with branded toys? Is there a significant relationship between its features (e.g., risk, initiation) and the overall effectiveness of a consumer-based promotional campaign? Are there interaction effects between features?

Are some *brands* more successful than others when they are associated with consumer-based promotional campaigns? What brands and products are most suitable for such methods? Are there any brands for which consumer-based promotions would be ineffective, or even detrimental, to their overall objectives?

How do *consumer* responses vary across the methods shown in Table 5.5.1? Does the success of a peer-to-peer campaign depend on the ages of the participants? Kindergarteners demonstrate an amazing level of brand literacy. Does this come from traditional advertising, from mere exposure, from acculturation or from consumer-based promotions (including honest old-fashioned word-of-mouth)? To what extent are adult identities shaped by lifelong patterns of consumption and self-brand identification?

What is the role of brands in creating consumption communities? Many theories (e.g., those relating to information processing, choice behaviour, self-concept formation) need to be re-examined and potentially modified in an age of commercialization and commodification of the consumer. The creation of personal identities and multifaceted lifestyles are topics of particular interest to managers and marketing scholars.

It is important to understand the cognitive processes stimulated by consumer-based promotions. Is peripheral exposure (in the form of branded items) enough to influence consumer decision-making, or does it merely add to the advertising "noise" that these peer-to-peer techniques are trying to break through? How aware are consumers of our conspicuous consumption choices? How aware are we of others' choices?

How do consumer-based promotional methods influence the relationship between consumers and corporations? Do consumers appreciate the more personal approach that consumer-based methods seem to offer, or do they rebel against the commodification of formerly private spaces? Anti-corporate and anti-consumption behaviours and attitudes are just starting to be identified and tested, and they present new perspectives for studying consumer behaviour (Austin et al., 2005; Zavestoski, 2002). Research may uncover both latent and overt resistance to consumer-based promotions. Consumer resistance to traditional means and media of commercial persuasion lies at the heart of these peer-to-peer techniques. If there were no resistance, there would be little need for advertisers to experiment with consumer-based promotions.

There is a distinct group of consumers who are concerned with "McDonaldization," i.e., western capitalism's apparent effects on global economics, politics, cultures and the environment (Ritzer, 1996). Some consumer-based techniques, namely tattooing and graffiti, have attracted similarly negative attention from consumer and environmental advocates. What sort of regulation is necessary to protect consumer-marketers who choose to participate, knowingly or not, in these campaigns? Are children, teens, or other segments of the population especially vulnerable to risks presented by peer-to-peer methods, and therefore in need of special protections?

SUMMARY

The promotional methods discussed here are constantly evolving in tandem with technological and socio-cultural changes. By its nature, consumer-based promotion is a topic that seems well suited for interdisciplinary inquiry. Among the fields that have potential to contribute are social psychology, mass communication, perception and cognition, business administration, marketing, information systems and others.

Some peer-to-peer promotional techniques (e.g., postcards) have been around for years in various forms, but their full commercial potential is presently expanding, as is the overall menu of consumer-based marketing opportunities. Their use is accelerating partly due to a paradigm shift in the marketplace, as firms are realizing that their own customers are potentially great allies for communicating key messages.

The ultimate impact of consumer-based promotional techniques depends on the direction and strength of consumers' connections to the brand. Consumers' creativity, insights, and energy are crucial to pass along brand messages to others, but there is no guarantee that one consumer's excitement about any viral promotional technique, or about the brand itself, will be contagious in others. The quality, content, novelty, and entertainment value of the marketing messages themselves determine how widely and quickly information is transmitted among consumers, and smart brand managers will take these variables into consideration in any consumer-based promotions that they propose.

Consumer-based promotional techniques rely on established cognitive and behavioural principles in order to heighten both brand awareness and brand equity. They operate through both active and passive consumer processing mechanisms, though why they actually work, and how effective they actually are, are still largely unexplored in the academic literature. Their longevity and proliferation in the marketplace indicate that managers intuit that they are effective for communicating brand messages, even in the absence of hard evidence that they work. What we do know is that brands are only meaningful if consumers believe in their meanings; through their use and contagious adoption, these meanings are reinforced even as they evolve.

REFERENCES

Albright, L., C. Forest and K. Reiseter (2001), "Acting, Behaving, And The Selfless Basis Of Metaperception," *Journal of Personality and Social Psychology*, 81 (5), 910–21.

Arias, J.T. and L.B. Acebron (2001), "Postmodern Approaches In Business-To-Business Marketing And Marketing Research," *The Journal of Business & Industrial Marketing*, 16, 7–20.

Arnould, E.J., L.L. Price and G.M. Zinkhan (2004), *Consumers*, New York: McGraw-Hill Higher Education.

Arnould, E.J. and C.J. Thompson (2005), "Consumer Culture Theory (Cct): Twenty Years Of Research," *Journal of Consumer Research*, 31 (4), 868–82.

Aubert-Gamet, V. and B. Cove (1997), "Exit, Voice, Loyalty And Twist: Consumer Research In Search Of The Subject," *Workshop on Interpretive Consumer Research*, Oxford, April 10–12.

Austin, C.G., C.O. Peters and C. Plouffe (2005), "Anti-Commercial Consumer Rebellion: Conceptualisation And Measurement," *Journal of Targeting, Measurement and Analysis for Marketing*, 14 (1), 62–78.

Belk, R. (1988), "Possessions And The Extended Self," *Journal of Consumer Research*, 15 (2), 139–68.

Bosman, J. (2006), "Chevy Tries a Write-Your-Own-Ad Approach, and the Potshots Fly," *The New York Times*, April 4, C1.

Bourdieu, P. (1984), *Distinction: A Social Critique of the Judgement of Taste*. Cambridge, MA: Harvard University Press.

Carl, W.J. (2006), "What's All the Buzz About? Everyday Communication and the Relational Basis of Word-of-Mouth and Buzz Marketing Practices." *Management Communication Quarterly*, 19 (4), 601–34.

Cassidy, J. (2006), "Me Media," *The New Yorker*, May 15, 50–59.

Close, A.G. and G.M. Zinkhan (2005), "Market Resistance," *Working paper*, University of Georgia.

Conchar, M.P., G.M. Zinkhan, C.O. Peters and S. Olavarrieta (2004), "An Antegrated Framework for the Conceptualization of Consumers' Perceived-Risk Processing," *Journal of the Academy of Marketing Science*, 32 (4), 418–36.

Dittmar, H. (1992), *The Social Psychology of Material Possessions: To Have is to Be*. Hemel Hempstead: Harvester Wheatheaf.

Doster, G.L. (1991), *From Abbeville to Zebulon: Early Post Card Views of Georgia*, Athens: University of Georgia Press.

Dunn, J. (2001), "The Secret Life Of Boys," *Rolling Stone*. July 5, 106.

Dye, R. (2000), "The Buzz on Buzz," *Harvard Business Review*, November–December, 139–46.

Elliott, R. and K. Wattanasuwan (1998), *International Journal of Advertising*, 17 (2), 131–44.

Firat, A.F. and A. Venkatesh (1993), "Postmodernity: The Age Of Marketing," *International Journal of Research in Marketing*, 10, 238.

Firat, A. and A. Venkatesh, (1995), "Liberatory Postmodernism and the Reenchantment of Consumption," *Journal of Consumer Research*, 22 (3), 239–67.

Fournier, S. (1998), "Consumers And Their Brands: Developing Relationship Theory In Consumer Research," *Journal of Consumer Research*, 24 (4), 343–73.

Gabriel, Y. and T. Lang (1995), *The Unmanageable Consumer: Contemporary Consumption and its Fragmentations*. London: SAGE Publications.

Giddens, A. (1991), *Modernity and Self-Identity: Self and Society in the Late Modern Age*. Cambridge: Polity Press.

Gladwell, M. (2000), *The Tipping Point: How Little Things Can Make a Big Difference*, New York: Little, Brown.

Godin, S. (1999), *Permission Marketing: Turning Strangers into Friends, and Friends into Customers*, New York: Simon & Schuster.

Gonnerman, J. (1999), "Sidewalk Politics: Graffiti Campaign Demands 'No More Prisons,'" *The Village Voice*, November 24, permalink at http://www.villagevoice.com/news/9947,gonnerman,10352,5.html.

Hafner, K. (2006), "VC Nation; Wary of a New Web Idea that Rings Old," *The New York Times*, March 24, C6.

Harris, S. (2000), "'Nader Traders' May Have Affected Outcome In Florida," CNN.com, November 17.

Hill, S. and G. Rifkin (1999), *Radical Marketing: From Harvard to Harley, Lessons from Ten That Broke the Rules and Made it Big*, New York: HarperBusiness.

Holt, D. (2002), "Why Do Brands Cause Trouble? A Dialectical Theory of Consumer Culture and Branding," *Journal of Consumer Research*, 29 (1), 70–90.

Huba, J. (2006), "Chevy Tahoe Campaign: Not CGM," customerevangelists.typepad.com, March 16.

Irvine, M. (1998), "The Postmodern, Postmodernism, Postmodernity: Approaches to Pomo," www.georgetown.edu/irvinemj/technoculture/pomo.html.

Jost, J.T., A.W. Kruglanski and T.O. Nelson (1998), "Social Metacognition: An Expansionist Review," *Personality and Social Psychology Review*, 2, 137–54.

Kahney, L. (2004), "Home-Brew iPod Ad Opens Eyes," www.wired.com, December 13.

Kenigsberg, A. (2001), "Peace, Love and Marketing: Sidewalk-Graffiti Ads Mark Another Step Forward For The Commercial Colonization Of Public Spaces," *Mother Jones*, July 20, permalink at http://www.motherjones.com/news/feature/2001/07/ibm.html.

Kozinets, R. (2002), "Can Consumers Escape the Market? Emancipatory Illuminations from Burning Man," *Journal of Consumer Research*, 29 (1), 20–38.

Kozinets, R.V., J.F. Sherry, D. Storm, A. Duhachek, K. Nuttavuthisit and B. DeBerry-Spence (2002), "Themed Flagship Brand Stores in the New Millennium: Theory, Practice, Prospects," *Journal of Retailing*, 78, 17–29.

Kruglanski, A.W. (1989), *Lay Epistemics and Human Knowledge: Cognitive and Motivational Bases*. New York: Plenum Press.

Kruglanski, A.W. (1990), "Lay Epistemic Theory In Social-Cognitive Psychology," *Psychological Inquiry*, 1, 181–97.

Laing, R.D., H. Phillipson and A.R. Lee (1966), *Interpersonal Perception: A Theory and a Method of Research*. New York: Springer.

Lascu, D.N. and G.M. Zinkhan (1999), "Consumer Conformity: Review And Applications For Marketing Theory And Practice," *Journal of Marketing Theory and Practice*, 7 (3), 1–12.

Lazarsfeld, P.F., B.R. Berleson and H. Gaudet (1944), *The People's Choice*. New York: Columbia University Press.

Lees, N. (2005), "Big Ad Hits One Millionth Viewer," www.AdNews.com.au, 29 July.

Lenhart, A., J. Horrigan and D. Fallows (2004), "Content Creation Online," *Pew Internet and American Life Project*, February 29.

Muniz, Jr., A.M. and T.C. O'Guinn (2001), "Brand Community," *Journal of Consumer Research*, 27 (4), 412–32.

Niccolai, J. (2001), "IBM's Graffiti Ads Run Afoul Of City Officials," CNN.com, April 19.

O'Shaughnessy, J. (1987), *Why People Buy*. Oxford: Oxford University Press.

Petty, R.E. and J.T. Cacioppo (1986), *Communication And Persuasion: Central And Peripheral Routes To Attitude Change*. New York: Springer-Verlag.

Petty, R.E., P. Brinol and Z.L. Tormala (2002), "Thought Confidence As A Determinant Of Persuasion: The Self-Validation Hypothesis," *Journal of Personality and Social Psychology*, 82 (5), 722–41.

Perez, J.C. (2005), "Q&A: Vint Cerf On Google's Challenges, Aspirations," www.computerworld.com, November 25.

Phelps, J.E., R. Lewis, L. Mobilio, D. Perry and N. Raman, (2004), "Viral Marketing or Electronic Word-of-Mouth Advertising: Examining Consumer Responses and Motivations to Pass Along Email," *Journal of Advertising Research*, December, 333–48.

Pitt, L., P. Berthon, R. Watson and G.M. Zinkhan (2002), "The Internet and the Birth of Real Consumer Power," *Business Horizon*, 45 (4), 7–14.

Ramirez, R. (1999), "Value Co-production: Intellectual Origins and Implications for Practice and Research," *Strategic Management Journal,* 20 (1), 49–65.

Ritzer, G. (1996), *The McDonaldization of Society.* Thousand Oaks CA: Pine Forge Press.

Robinson, F. (2001), "Tattoos Used As Advertisement Not Welcome," *The Times-Picayune* (New Orleans), April 1.

Rosen, E. (2000), *The Anatomy of Buzz: How to Create Word-of-Mouth Marketing,* New York: Doubleday.

Rubin, A. (2001), "Tattoos Used As Ads Have Drawn NBA's Ire." *New York Daily News,* April 1, 80.

Rumbo, J. (2002), "Consumer Resistance in a World of Advertising Clutter: The Case of *Adbusters,*" *Psychology & Marketing,* 19 (2), 127–48.

Ryan, T. (2001), *The Prize Winner of Defiance, Ohio: How My Mother Raised 10 Kids on 25 Words or Less,* New York: Touchstone.

Sirgy, M.J. (1982), "Self-Concept In Consumer-Behavior: A Critical Review," *Journal of Consumer Research,* 9 (3), 287–300.

Thomas, M.J. (1997), "Consumer Market Research: Does It Have Validity? Some postmodern thoughts," *Marketing Intelligence and Planning,* 15 (2), 54–9.

Thompson, J.B. (1995), *The Media and Modernity: A Social Theory of the Media,* Cambridge: Polity.

Trist, E.L. (1973), "Task And Contextual Environments For New Personal Values," in *Towards a Social Ecology: Contextual Appreciations of the Future in the Present, eds.* F. Emery and E. L. Trist, Plenum, London, 182–9.

Veblen, T. and C.W. Mills (2000), *The Theory of Leisure Class,* New Brunswick: Transaction Publishers.

Wakefield, J. (2001), "Catching A Buzz: New Internet Traffic Watchers Aim To Elevate Marketing To A Science," *Scientific American,* November, 30–2.

Walker, R. (2006), "Faux Logo," *The New York Times Magazine,* May 14, 24.

Watson, J. (2003), "Nike Swooshes In On Converse," www.Forbes.com, July 9.

Watson, R.T., P. Berthon, L.F. Pitt and G.M. Zinkhan (2000), *Electronic Commerce: The Strategic Perspective,* Fort Worth: Dryden Press.

Wells, M. (1999), "Hey, Is That An Advertisement On Your Arm? From Tattoos To ATMs, Ads Pop Up In New Places," *USA Today,* July 23, B12.

Wutz, L.E. (2000), "New Girl Scout Ads Send Wrong Message," *The Buffalo News,* November 6, B5.

Zaret, E. (2000), "How the Net Can Transform Voting," www.MSNBC.com, November 7.

Zavestoski, S. (2002), "Guest Editorial: Anticonsumption Attitudes," *Psychology and Marketing,* 19 (2), 121–6.

WEBSITES

en.wikipedia.org/wiki/Converse
queenofsky.journalspace.com
www.amway.com
www.autowraps.com
www.bigad.com.au
www.bzzagent.com
www.contagiousmedia.org
www.imediaconnection.com/content/4900.asp
www.ipodsdirtysecret.com
www.jonessoda.com
www.nielsenbuzzmetrics.com
www.pillsbury.com/bakeoff/default.aspx
www.platial.com
www.podcastalley.com
www.shey.net/niked.html
www.thespecspot.com
www.voteswap.com
www.zillow.com

Communication and New Product Adoption

Donald R. Lehmann and Dina Mayzlin

Although both advertising and new products have been the subject of considerable research, work directly relating the two is relatively scarce. Therefore, this chapter begins by first briefly delineating the new product adoption process and how advertising can influence it. In addition, this chapter focuses on a relatively understudied area of social interactions (such as word of mouth marketing) and the firm's influence on these processes. In this sense, this chapter is a companion to Chapter 5.5, which discusses the evolution of peer-peer media. We discuss how both new product adoption and advertisers' influence on this process can be modeled quantitatively.

While advertisers can influence the consumer's actions through advertising, consumer decisions are often impacted by everyday social interactions: conversations with friends and neighbors, posts in an online community, entries in Web logs (blogs) as well as by what celebrities wear. Following Godes et al. (2006), we define a social interaction

broadly as the contact of one consumer with another that may result in a change of valuation of a product or a service. This definition includes face-to-face contacts and technology-aided interactions (whether they take place in an online chat room or over the mobile phone), as well as observational learning (watching what car the neighbors are driving). Other factors, such as information clutter, have also contributed to a decrease in the effectiveness of traditional advertising and to an increase in the importance of social interaction (Berry and Keller, 2004).

This chapter is organized in the following manner. The next section addresses consumer new product decisions and motivation to engage in word of mouth. We then discuss how the overall market behaves. The following section addresses the impact of both advertising and social interactions on consumer decisions. Then we deal with ways in which a firm can manage its advertising, and the final section discusses the management of social interactions.

CONSUMER NEW PRODUCT DECISIONS

New product adoption is either done independently (by an innovator), in response to the adoption of others (by an imitator), or some combination of the two. The three subsections address the factors that drive the consumer's decision to adopt, the word of mouth generation process, and, finally, adoption at the aggregate level and the Bass model, which is flexible enough to combine both the effects of advertising and social effects.

The new product adoption process

When customers consider a new product, they can follow either a deliberative (first gather information, then weigh pros and cons, and only then make a decision) or instinctive ("I want it," purchase, then evaluate) process. For customers who follow a deliberative process, the specific attributes considered vary across products. Nonetheless, the attributes generally fall into six broad categories (Rogers, 1983):

1. *Relative Advantage*

This captures the benefits the product has vs current alternatives, i.e., why it is a better mousetrap. It is often useful to divide these into functional, economic and psychological (e.g., "I want to be first to see independent movies") factors.

2. *(In)compatibility*

This factor relates to the potential dislocation caused by adopting a new product. It encompasses a variety of aspects including physical space ("where can I store a new watercraft?"), skill based ("how can I figure out how to use it?"), and routine based (I always apply the product once a year). In general the more severe the dislocation, the greater is the resistance to adopting an innovation.

3. *Risk*

Categories of risk include performance, financial, physical and psycho-social (e.g., "how will I be perceived by others if I use this product.")

4. *Complexity*

Complexity can have implications for ease of use, and likelihood of breaking down.

5. *Observability/communicability*

The ability succinctly to (a) identify, (b) communicate, and (c) assess the effectiveness of a new product.

6. *Trialability/divisibility*

The ability to try out the innovation at low risk and cost. The seller can use samples, free trials, no question returns policies, etc. to induce trial.

While all six dimensions are relevant, the first three generally drive decisions with the others operating through the first three (Holak and Lehmann, 1990). Thus the advertiser of a new product needs to consider the relevance of all six aspects, including the reduction of risk, especially psychological and social.

The adoption of the product by others makes many products more attractive, i.e., there is network externality. The externality effect can be rational due to a direct network effect. For example, a financial analyst prefers to use Microsoft Word since her co-workers use it, while an engineer prefers Latex since it has been adopted by her colleagues. For products where direct network effects are a major issue, it is important to achieve scale quickly since the product's attractiveness is proportional to the size of its client base. This can be done either through advertising or word of mouth as elaborated in the final sections of this chapter.

Another interesting set of products are those where indirect network effects are involved. For example, the popularity of the Sony Playstation console depends on the attractiveness of the games that are designed for the system. In such situations, advertisers often choose to focus promotion on the game, which then results in a boost of console sales.

Social considerations may be important. An early adopter who considers himself to be a technological maven "must have" the latest gizmo simply because it will enhance his reputation as an expert. Moreover, late adopters who observe their better informed peers using a certain product are more likely to adopt it since they consider the risk to be lower. The social motive to obtain a new product can be either positive (e.g., "I want to be the first in my group to have a new product") or negative (e.g., "I am afraid not have the new product") based, similar to promotion versus prevention focus (Higgins, 1998), suggesting that a new product managers needs to penetrate certain segments in order to spur wider adoption.

What motivates consumers to engage in word of mouth

"Product evangelists" are consumers who passionately spread the gospel of the product. Firms may be able to convert consumers into evangelists with the use of incentives. Thus, there are two fundamental motivations behind the spread of word of mouth: *intrinsic* motivation (an inherent desire to promote a product) and *extrinsic* motivation (a desire due to incentives set up by the firm). Differences in the consumer's desire to communicate may be due to the loyalty to the product as well as expertise and the social network of the "buzzer." Accordingly consumers may be segmented as, for example, opinion leaders, early adopters, market mavens and "connectors." Understanding their motivations is essential for a firm that is either trying to orchestrate a word of mouth campaign or wants to estimate the extent of "natural" word of mouth.

Extrinsic motivation includes monetary and product incentives (prizes, product samples) as well as social ones (e.g., the most successful "buzzer" is publicly singled out on a firm's web site). Incentive campaigns may backfire due to, for example, negative press if the firm's tactics are seen as deceptive. For example, Ralph Nader's group, Commercial Alert, sent a letter to FTC in October of 2005 complaining that "There is evidence that some of these companies are perpetuating large-scale deception upon consumers by deploying buzz marketers who fail to disclose that they have been enlisted to promote products."[1] Even if the practice is within acceptable standards, the campaign may be ineffective because consumers can ignore information that they perceive to be biased. This discounting effect has been demonstrated by Verlegh (2004) – that is, the natural credibility of word of mouth may be compromised if it is known that the word of mouth is "manufactured."

Negative word of mouth is more powerful than positive word of mouth (Anderson, 1998). Some factors may suppress the transmission of negative information. Wojnicki and Godes (2004) show that category experts seem to pass along positive news more than negative. The same is not true of novices. This finding may be due to the negative effect that a negative experience has on the expert's reputation. For example, status as a movie buff may be questioned if friends discover that the expert chose to watch a terrible film. Loyal opinion leaders may primarily generate impactful word of mouth for a firm (Godes and Mayzlin, 2004).

The preponderance of positive reviews and conversations may also be due to self-selection: when consumers research products before they purchase them, they are relatively happy with the outcomes or at least say they are to reduce dissonance. A third reason is due to "gaming" of reviews: firms have incentives to post positive reviews about their own products. Nonetheless firms should worry about negative reviews. In fact, due to the preponderance of positive word of mouth, negative word of mouth may be especially impactful. As many advertisers recognize already, research has shown that negative information may appear *more credible* than positive information (see Chevalier and Mayzlin, 2006).

The adoption process: Market level

While it is important to understand consumer behavior at the individual level, market level response matters more to advertisers. Are there common patterns in adoption across different product categories and/or countries? Can these patterns be influenced by marketers and in what ways?

We first address the issue of common patterns. For the most part first purchases follow one of the three patterns shown in Figure 5.6.1. Pattern A occurs for minor extensions and "search" goods where decisions to purchase are made fairly easily. The classic example is movies, where most large budget movies (but not so called sleeper movies) have their largest box office on the opening weekend and decline thereafter (e.g., Lehmann and Weinberg, 2000). Unsurprisingly the main focus of advertising is then to increase initial sales (e.g., opening weekend box office revenue).

Pattern B is the pattern shown in most textbooks. While several functions can capture this shape, by far the most widely used model of this type is due to Bass (1969). Therefore we use it as the basis of the discussion in parts of this chapter. The Bass model suggests the "hazard" (probability) of adopting, given a potential customer has not yet adopted, has two components: one due to innovation (i.e., adopting on their own) and one due to imitation (i.e., adopting because of the influence of others, aka word of mouth). Mathematically this is expressed as:

$$H(t) = p + q\frac{F(t)}{m}$$

where

$H(t)$ = probability of adoption
p = coefficient of innovation
q = coefficient of imitation
$F(t)$ = cumulative adoptions up to time t
and m = market potential (the saturation level)

Sales at t is then the probability of adopting times the number of potential adopters who have not yet adopted:

$$S(t) = H(t)[m - F(t)]$$
$$= \left(p + q\frac{F(t)}{m}\right)(m - F(t))$$
$$= pm + (q - p)F(t) - \frac{q}{m}F(t)^2$$

This form is quite flexible. For example, by setting $q = 0$ (assuming no word of mouth effect), the model captures shape A, i.e., sales decline each period.

Pattern C is a variation on Pattern B with a low p lending to a long lead-time (Kohli et al., 1999); i.e., time to take-off (Agarwal and Bayus, 2001; Golder and Tellis, 1997). There can be many causes of the delay

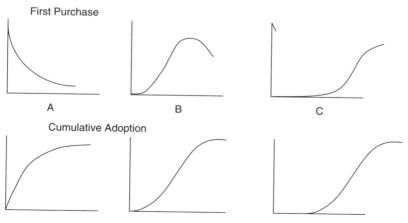

Figure 5.6.1 Adoption patterns

including low quality of initial products, high prices and issues with suppliers and retailers (e.g., getting shelf space) as well as lack of information availability, and being "ahead of its time."

Advertising's influence on the process can be modeled using a multiplier of the "natural" hazard rate as in the extended Bass model (Bass et al., 1994):

$$H(t) = \left(p + q\frac{F(t)}{m}\right)X(t)$$

where $X(t) =$ function of marketing activities at time t. For example, advertising spending with a diminishing marginal impact on sales can be captured as $X(t) = a + \log(Adv)$ or $X(t) = a + b\sqrt{Adv}$.

The effect of advertising can also be captured by assuming it directly impacts the model parameters p, q, and m as well as the "dead" (lead) time before takeoff. In some cases the impact of advertising may be primarily on the coefficient of innovation, i.e., on the likelihood that an individual will hear about a new product and/or be motivated to buy it on their own. In such cases, we can assume $p = a + b \log(Adv)$ or a similar form which again assumes diminishing effects of advertising. On the other hand, advertising might both re-enforce and encourage word of mouth communication. In that case the implication is that q is a function of advertising, i.e., $q = k_0 + k_1$ (Advertising), effectively creating an interaction effect between advertising and past adopters (aka the installed customer base) on the purchase likelihood.

THE IMPACT OF COMMUNICATION ON THE ADOPTION OF NEW PRODUCTS

Here we summarize research that deals with the effect of advertising as well as social interactions on consumer adoption decisions. The three subsections discuss the impact of advertising on new product purchase decisions, the ability of advertising to defend against new product competition, and finally the impact of social interactions on consumer behavior.

The impact of advertising on consumer decisions

Several studies have examined the factors behind successful new products (e.g., Cooper, 1994; DiBenedetto, 1999; Montoya-Weiss and Calantone, 1994; Henard and Szymanski, 2001; Goldenberg et al., 2001). Although product features are usually seen as most critical (e.g., Cooper, 1994), advertising strategy has also been shown to be related to new product profitability (DiBenedetto, 1999). More broadly, marketing competence (e.g., market orientation) and effort in general has been shown to be associated with successful new products (Henard and Szymanski, 2001).

Dodson and Muller (1978) extended Bass (1969) by modeling purchase probability as an explicit function of advertising which generates both awareness and relative product (brand) preference. Nakanishi (1973) modeled the impact of advertising and promotion on new product introductions over time and considered both initial and repeat purchases. Horsky and Simon (1983) extended this model to analytically derive optimal advertising expenditures. Eliashberg et al. (2000) empirically examined the impact of advertising on consideration in the context of movies.

A basic question asked by consumers about new products is "what is it," i.e., "what category does it belong to?." The way customers process information depends on how well a product fits an existing category (Ozanne et al., 1992). Moreau et al. (2003) showed that advertising can influence the category a new product is associated with and hence the expectations for various attributes (e.g., the quality of pictures in a digital camera).

A logical impact of advertising is to speed up the diffusion process. Van den Bulte (2000) studied the diffusion of 31 household durables and found penetration varied based on purchasing power, demographics, and competition and competing standards, but did not assess the impact of advertising. More recently, Chakravarti and Xie (2008) explored the impact of competing standards and the effectiveness of comparative versus non-comparative ads. Their experimental results suggest that comparative ads are more effective when there are competing standards and non-comparative more effective when there are not.

Because of its significance in terms of both dollars and impact on life, considerable work has focused on pharmaceuticals, in particular, direct to consumer (DTC) advertising (Mintzes et al., 2002) and detailing. Narayanan et al. (2005) found that marketing communications have an additional impact early in a product life cycle through their ability to provide more accurate and certain quality information.

In addition, researchers have attempted to measure the effect of advertising on purchases, i.e., "advertising elasticity" – the marginal impact of advertising on the amount spent. The diminishing effect of advertising is widely accepted (Simon and Arndt, 1980). A classic paper by Parsons (1975) showed that advertising elasticity declined over the life cycle. This is an important result since most studies of advertising elasticity have found that on average they are small. Assmus et al. (1984) found an average elasticity of 0.2 in a meta analysis. Others have found smaller ones (e.g., Riskey, 1997; Sethuraman and Tellis, 1991).

Manchanda et al. (2006) developed a model and tested it on data from a particular web site. The results suggest that multiple exposures of banner ads have a positive impact on repeat purchases and produce an average elasticity in the 0.02 to 0.05 range, somewhat smaller than the 0.1 found by Sethuraman and Tellis (1991). Importantly their results also suggest there is substantial heterogeneity in response to banner ads.

Expanding usage is an important objective of advertising (Wansink and Ray, 1996). Often this is part of the maturation of a product. Bayus (1988) showed that while advertising could shorten the replacement cycle for color TVs, a 50% increase in spending was required

to get a shift (acceleration) of 11 months. Multiple color TVs, etc. have evolved as the norm and greatly enhanced the product's potential and sales. Because our focus is on new products, we do not discuss such issues further here. Still it is worth noting that many extended (and unintended) uses are developed by customers and firms often benefit from observing and then promoting such uses.

Defending against new products

The discussion thus far has been from the perspective of a firm selling a new product. In reality the number of firms faced with the problem of responding to a new product is greater than the number of new products introduced.

Hauser and Shugan's (1980) "defender" model concentrates on two elements of the marketing mix: product and price. Their model shows it may be optimal (if counter-intuitive) to raise price in the face of some new entrants as well as to cut advertising spending. Expanding the notion of defensive reaction further, Bell and Carpenter (1992) suggest it may be optimal to respond to competitive threats by utilizing different elements of the mix, e.g., by raising advertising in response to a new entrant. Some empirical evidence suggests this is not an effective strategy (Thomas, 1999) while others suggest it is (e.g., Geroski, 1995). Thomas (1999) showed that in the ready-to-eat cereal market, incumbents do increase advertising to limit the impact of new entry, especially when there is a major new entrant.

The impact of social interactions on new product adoption

Researchers have used Usenet forums to measure word of mouth for TV shows (Godes and Mayzlin, 2004) and for purposes of an ethnographic study (Kozinets, 2002), online user book reviews to study the effect of online ratings on sales in Amazon and Barnes and Noble (Chevalier and Mayzlin, 2006), online user movie ratings to forecast movie revenues

(Dellarocas et al., 2004), and the Hollywood Stock Exchange as a proxy for word of mouth (Elberse and Eliashberg, 2003). In addition to academic research, there has been a joint industry-academia effort to come up with a set of metrics supported by the Word of Mouth Marketing Association.[2]

ADVERTISING MANAGEMENT

This section adds some notes to the discussion of advertising practice in other chapters of this Handbook in the context of new product introduction and diffusion. Specifically we consider strategy, targeting, copy and expenditure.

Determinants of ad strategy

While every new product is to some extent unique, new products can be described in terms of a few key attributes. Here we focus on three: product newness, the nature of the need served by the product, and the use of brand name.

Product newness: Products can be described in terms of how new they are, ranging from incremental to radical/really new. In general, really new products are more difficult to sell because they raise issues of compatibility and risk.

Nature of the need: One useful classification of needs is between active, latent and passive. When consumers are seeking a solution (product), the needs are active. By contrast, latent needs must be stimulated, albeit this can sometimes be done reasonably easily, e.g., by communicating the product benefit(s). Finally, passive needs are needs customers are unaware they have (e.g., email before it became widespread) and for which simply stating the intended benefits is inadequate to generate purchase. Unsurprisingly, passive needs (which typically are targeted by really new products) are the most difficult to sell.

Brand name: An established brand name attached can be helpful depending on the brand's reputation and how well the new product fits (matches) that reputation.

Unknown names bear the additional burden of skepticism about the maker's quality and likelihood of remaining in business, i.e., they involve greater risk. Unsurprisingly both the amount of effort and the nature of the advertising task varies depending on the reputation (or lack thereof) of the parent brand.

Targeting

Incremental innovations typically target existing brand segments. For example, when Apple–Cinnamon Cheerios were introduced, there was little point in focusing on non-cereal eaters or those who want low sugar products. For really new products, on the other hand, the source of demand may be unclear. For example, when digital photography was introduced, one could have targeted traditional film camera users or computer–savvy individuals for whom the digital technology (e.g., using a printer to get hard copies, sorting and editing) was familiar. New products may target the relatively small group of innovators and hope they will inspire adoption in the broader population, or begin with the broader "imitator" population and try to overcome their natural resistance.

In general, choosing a narrow category limits potential for the new product but speeds adoption as long as the target is well chosen (i.e., one where the product has strong appeal to the limited target audience). By contrast, choosing a broader target gives a higher upside but is likely to be accompanied by slower adoption and, at least initially, lower satisfaction and repeat rates. For example, Moreau et al. (2003) found that, in the case of digital photography, minor change in copy (i.e., from "picture your world" to "scan your world") changed the reference category from film based cameras to computer devices. This in turn impacted expected quality (higher for film-based) and which customers (traditional photographers vs. computer users) found it more appealing. The research also found that when it was positioned as "really new," i.e., as computer based, experts in traditional photography were less interested in buying it.

Copy

Lee and O'Connor (2003) examined the roles of pre-announcements and copy appeal (emotional vs. functional). Based on surveys of product managers, it appears that functional ads work when a product has a clear advantage as long as it is easy to adopt but are inferior to emotional ones when incompatibility (adoption difficulty) is high. One key impact of advertising is risk reduction (Byzalov and Shachar, 2004). Others include information dissemination and prestige/image building (Ackerberg, 2001). Kopalle and Lehmann (2006) examined whether overstating quality helps or retards new product diffusion and suggest an optimal level of "hype" exists which depends on factors such as firm reputation and customer satisfaction. Chandy et al. (2003) discuss how appeals should change over a product life cycle.

Expenditure

Researchers have long sought to improve the productivity of advertising (Nerlove and Arrow, 1962). In general, we know advertising is more effective for new products, e.g., Batra et al. (1995), Eastlack and Rao (1989) and Lodish et al. (1995). Studies also suggest advertising elasticity may be in the 0.2–0.3 range for new products but drop to close to zero (0.01–0.03) for mature ones (Assmus et al., 1984; Riskey, 1997). Models capturing advertising spending effects include those of Kalish (1985) and Mesak and Clark (1998) as well as the extended Bass model (Bass et al., 1994). See Tellis (2007) for an overview.

Assume the Bass diffusion model captures the diffusion process as a means of modeling customer acquisition. Once acquired, the value of a customer depends mainly on their usage (u) and retention (r) rates (see Gupta and Lehmann, 2004). Consequently the value of a new product can be computed via a spreadsheet as in Table 5.6.1. The value of advertising is the increase in revenue it causes by altering key parameters (m, p, q, u, or r) minus its cost.

Implementing this approach is, of course, a non-trivial task. Concept and copy tests can be used to assess changes in p and m versus control (e.g., by asking consumers whether they would buy it this year and they would like to have one in the future and then calibrating the responses in terms of actual behavior). Even better, planned or natural experiments can be employed.

Impacts on q, u, and r are more difficult to access. Therefore a decision-calculus style approach may be useful which relies on the subjective inputs of managers (Little, 1979). Essentially this entails obtaining managerial assessments of the expected changes in p, etc. due to a particular advertising strategy when empirical results are unavailable. Alternatively, for a set of values of the other parameters (e.g., q, m, u and r), one can calculate the change in p required to breakeven on the ad campaign and subjectively access whether this is reasonable to expect to occur.

Another focus of research is the pattern of spending, i.e., pulsing versus level (Zielske, 1979, 1986).

For new products a major decision is whether to advertise before the product is available, potentially building excitement and word of mouth, but also giving competition more time to react and running the risk

Table 5.6.1 A template for evaluating advertising spending for new products

Year	Customers acquired (sales)	Usage rate	Retention rate	Long run customer value
1	pm	u_i	r_i	$s(1)u_i(p-vc)\dfrac{1}{1+d-r}$
2	$p(m-pm)+qp(1-p)m$	u_2	r_2	$s(2)u_2(p-vc)\dfrac{1}{(1+d-r)(1+d)}$
3	$\left[p+\dfrac{q[s(1)+s(2)]}{m}\right][m-s(1)-s(2)]$	u_3	r_3	$s(3)u_3(p-vc)\dfrac{1}{(1+d-r)(1+d)^2}$

that customers and hence channels will be frustrated by the non-availability, or delay most spending until the product or service is actually available.

A pre-launch blitz is common for movies (Eliashberg et al., 2000). Mahajan and Muller (1986) examined the impact of spending patterns, i.e., level vs. pulsed. Which is better depends on, among other things, the relation between advertising and recall.

Mesak and Clark (1998) studied a new communication service and found advertising impacts innovation and, consequently, its impact (elasticity) decreases over time. Recent support for front end loading advertising expenditures is provided by Narayanan et al. (2005) in the context of pharmaceuticals. Less spending is needed for a brand extension than a new brand (Pitta and Katsanes, 1995). More broadly, Tellefson and Takada (1999) linked media availability (a necessary condition for traditional advertising) to new product diffusion rates, in particular the p (innovation) coefficient in the Bass model.

SOCIAL INTERACTIONS

Godes et al. (2004) suggest four roles that a firm can play in social interactions: (1) Observer: The firm here acts as an information-collector; (2) Moderator: The firm *facilitates* communication between users and non-users or between users of the product; (3) Mediator: The firm *manages* the communication; and (4) Participant: The firm *creates* word of mouth (see Figure 5.6.2 below for illustration). In the next section, we define and illustrate each role in more detail.

The firm as observer

As mentioned earlier, much can be learned from monitoring word of mouth through either surveys or online communities.[3] However, there are a number of decisions that a firm needs to make before embarking on such an endeavour:

1. How should a firm select the universe of communities (blogs) to monitor? Ideally, the set

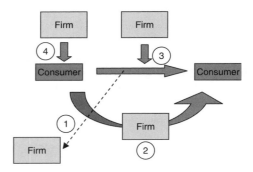

Figure 5.6.2   Four WOM-management strategies
Source: Adapted from Godes et al. (2005).

would be wide enough to present a clear picture of overall word of mouth. On the other hand, the set would be focused enough to make analysis manageable.

2. The type of analysis should depend on the goal of the project. If the objective is to obtain mainly qualitative research, a detailed content analysis may be required. For example, ConAgra got an early warning from the Internet that the low carbohydrate craze was fading.[4] However, if the firm is looking for more generalizable measures of word of mouth, a wider sampling is probably necessary, which would make content analysis difficult. (Instead, measures such as counts or dispersion of conversations may be used.)

The firm as moderator

Fostering consumer conversations can be facilitated by including a consumer review section on a website. Chevalier and Mayzlin (2006) demonstrate that user reviews matter in the sales of a particular book for Amazon and BN.com. However, they stop short of concluding that enabling customers to post reviews is a profitable strategy for Amazon since it is possible that reviews improve "matching" of books to customers but do not increase Amazon's total book sales.

Another form of moderation is the creation of customer recommendation programs. Some pass along campaigns have no obvious incentives while others either pay the participants for recruiting members or have less direct incentives. For an interesting recent example, see http://www.gothookedup.com. Sprint involved participants in previewing the phone and services of a Sprint Power Vision network and passing the phone on to another eligible participant. The incentives were twofold: (1) participants in the longest chain received the phone and (2) Sprint donated money to charity as more people registered foe the contest.

One challenge of these programs is for the firm to figure out which customers to target for participation. That is, should the firm target its loyal customers, opinion leaders, etc? Even in the case of simply providing a forum for consumer interaction, the firm often has to make an investment to encourage discussion. Many forums online have very few posts. The popularity of a forum is influenced by the popularity of the site or its products. However, a start-up has to consider issues such as creating the mass that would enable a lively discussion as well as maintaining the quality of discussions to ensure that the forums are not flooded by biased or inappropriate messages.

The firm as mediator

In this role, the firm decides how the information is disseminated. This is in contrast to an online review site or a member recommendation program where the firm has little control over either the message or its recipients. For example, consider a campaign that is directed by a buzz agency. As part of the campaign, the firm may encourage the consumer to contact certain segments of the consumer population. For example, PETA (people for the ethical treatment of animals) features a number of "missions" on their web site (www.peta2.com) that promote the organization's agenda. One mission encourages readers to lobby their baseball parks to feature vegetarian hot dogs. Other missions are similarly specific on whom to target as part of the campaign.

The firm as participant

Finally, firms can take an active role in directly communicating with consumers.

Such campaigns may occur either anonymously or the firm may reveal its identity. Such campaigns may be effective, but the topic does not appear to have been the subject of formal research. Two questions are whether these campaigns generate incremental word of mouth and whether they are able to affect sales.

Some creative campaigns utilize social interactions, e.g., the campaign organized by Kayem Foods to promote Al Fresco chicken sausage.[5] The campaign, conducted by BzzAgent, included encouraging the participants (buzz agents) to serve the sausage at family cookouts and to ask stores to carry them. While BzzAgent's approach is to target ordinary consumers for its campaigns, a rival M80 focuses on "superfans:" those consumers who are extremely passionate and persuasive about the product.[6] For example, in 2003 the company successfully promoted a DVD of a recently canceled Fox show "Family Guy." As part of the campaign, Fox discovered that a large part of the fan base believed that the show was canceled prematurely. Fox eventually brought the show back.

As the examples above illustrate, there are several controversial issues concerning the effectiveness of these campaigns. First, it is not clear whether such campaigns remain effective if consumers realize that word of mouth may be biased. Mayzlin (2006) used game theory to demonstrate that word of mouth may still be persuasive even if consumers are aware that word of mouth may in fact be biased if the amount of unbiased word of mouth is large enough, Dellarocas (2004) finds that manipulation of online forums can either increase or decrease the information value of a forum to consumers.

Second, while some companies target ordinary consumers, others try to target "unusual" consumers: opinion leaders, superfans, etc. Godes and Mayzlin (2004) partially address this issue in a study of a campaign in which a national firm created word of mouth through two populations: loyal customers and non-loyal customers. Surprisingly, they found that it is the non-loyal (or less loyal) customers who create the word of mouth that are most effective at driving sales. They hypothesize that this is due to the fact that loyal customers may have already talked to the members of their social network about the product prior to the start of the campaign. This hypothesis suggests that the members of the non-loyals' social network may be less aware of the product and thus represent a more effective group for targeting. They also find that for non-loyal customers, agents with a wide social network are most effective at creating this kind of word of mouth.

SUMMARY

This chapter summarized research on marketing of new products. We discussed two types of marketing activities: traditional advertising and management of social interactions after considering the process of new product adoption and what motivates consumers to engage in word of mouth. Consumer behavior can be either analysed on the individual (e.g., when is an opinion leader motivated to talk about a restaurant that she loves) or the aggregate level (e.g., the adoption pattern may involve a steep take-off or a peak followed by a rapid descent). In addition, we discussed how advertising and word of mouth impacts consumer decisions. Finally, we outlined how a firm can take an active role in managing its advertising programs as well as how it can manage social interactions.

Our main findings were:

- New product adoption may be either deliberate by six types of attributes, or instinctive.
- Consumers may be segmented according to their propensity for word of mouth for that category.
- Negative word of mouth is often more powerful than positive.
- At the aggregate level, adoption typically follows the Bass S-shaped growth curve, which eventually declines.
- Customer assessment of new products of existing brands is strongly influenced by their fit to the brand's current categories.
- Selecting a narrow category as a frame of reference limits potential but speeds adoption.

- Advertising is more efficient for new products and also for brand extensions relative to new brands.
- A firm can play one of four roles in social interaction with customers, i.e., word of mouth involvement, which vary by the extent of its participation.

NOTES

1 http://www.commercialalert.org/buzzmarketing.pdf
2 http://www.womma.org/research.htm
3 For an example of a firm that specializes in such measurement, see http://www.nielsenbuzzmetrics.com
4 "Blog Buzz Helps Companies Catch Trends in the Making," Steven Levigston, washingtonpost.com, March 3, 2006, A01.
5 "The Hidden (In Plain Sight) Persuaders," Rob Walker, nytimes.com, Dec 5, 2004.
6 "Taking the Fans' Word For It," Charles, Duhigg, latimes.com, March 15, 2006.

REFERENCES

Aaker, D.A. and K.L. Keller (1990), "Consumer Evaluations of Brand Extensions," *Journal of Marketing*, 54, January, 27–41.

Ackerberg, D. (2001), "Empirically Distinguishing Informative and Prestige Effects of Advertising," *RAND Journal of Economics*, 32, 2, 316–33.

Agarwal, R. and B. Bayus (2002), "The Market Evolution and Sales Takeoff of Product Innovations," *Management Science*, 48, August, 1024–52.

Allenby, G. and D.M. Hanssens (2005), "Advertising Response," *MSI Reports*, 5, 1–8.

Anderson, E.W. (1998), "Customer Satisfaction and Word of Mouth," *Journal of Service Research*, 1 (1), 5–17.

Assmus, G., J.U. Farley, and D.R. Lehmann (1984), "How Advertising Affects Sales: Meta-Analysis of Econometric Results," *Journal of Marketing Research*, 21, February, 65–74.

Banerjee, A. (1992), "A Simple Model of Herd Behavior," *Quarterly Journal of Economics*, 110, 797–817.

Bass, F.M., T.V. Krishnan, and D.C. Jain (1994), "Why the Bass Model Fits Without Decision Variables," *Marketing Science*, 13, 3, Summer, 203–23.

Batra, R., D.R. Lehmann, J. Burke, and J. Pae (1995), "When Does Advertising Have an Impact? A Study of Tracking Data," *Journal of Advertising Research*, 35, September/October, 19–32.

Bayus, B.L. (1987), "Forecasting Sales of New Contingent Products: An Application to the Compact Disc Market," *Journal of Product Innovation Management*, 4, 243–55.

Bayus, B.L. (1997), "Speed-to-Market and New Product Performance Trade-offs," *Journal of Product Innovation Management*, 14, 485–97.

Bayus, B.L. (1988), "Accelerating the Durable Replacement Cycle with Marketing Mix Variables," *Journal of Product Innovation Management*, 5, 216–26.

Berry, J. and Keller, E. (2004), *The Influentials: One American in Ten Tells the Other Nine How to Vote, Where to Eat, and What to Buy,* New York: The Free Press.

Bell, S.S. and G.S. Carpenter (1992), "Optimal Multiple-Objective Strategies," *Marketing Letters*, 383–93.

Biyalogorsky, E., E. Gerstner, and B. Libai (2001), "Customer Referral Management: Optimal Reward Programs," *Marketing Science*, 20, 82–95.

Bikhchandani, S.D., D. Hirshleifer, and I. Welch (1991), "A Theory of Fads, Fashions, Custom and Cultural Change as Information Cascades," *Journal of Political Economy*, 100, 992–1026.

Bolton, L., J. Machin, and J. Lilie (2005), Consumer Research in a New Media World: Analyzing Bulletin Board Content. Marketing Science Institute Fall Board of Trustees Meeting and Conference on Connecting with Customers in a Complex World, Chicago.

Bronnenberg, B.J. and C.F. Mela (2004), "Market Roll-Out and Retailer Adoption for New Brands," *Marketing Science*, 23, 4, Fall, 500–18.

Brooks, Jr., R.C. (1957), "Word of Mouth" Advertising in Selling New Products," *Journal of Marketing*, 22, 2, October, 154–61.

Byzalov, D. and R. Shachar (2004), "The Risk Reduction Role of Advertising," *Quantitative Marketing and Economics*, 2, 4, 283–320.

Chakravarti, A. and J. Xie (2008), "Standards Competition and Effectiveness of Advertising Formats in New Product Introduction," Conditionally accepted for publication at *Journal of Marketing Research*.

Chandy, R., G.J. Tellis, D. MacInnis, and P. Thaivanich (2001), "What to Say When: Advertising Appeals in Evolving Markets," *Journal of Marketing Research*, 38, 4 (November), 399–414.

Chen, Y. and J. Xie (2004), "Online Consumer Review: A New Element of Marketing Communications Mix," *SSRN working paper series*, Available at SSRN: http://ssrn.com/abstract=618782.

Chen, Y. and J. Xie (2005), "Third-Party Product Review and Firm Marketing Strategy," *Marketing Science*, 24 (2), 218–40.

Chen, Y. and M. Shi (2004), "The Design and Implications of Customer Recommendation Programs," *NYU Working Paper*.

Chevalier, J. and D. Mayzlin (2006), "The Effect of Word of Mouth on Sales: Online Book Reviews," *Journal of Marketing Research*, 43, 3, 345–54.

Cooper, R.G. (1994), "New Products: The Factors that Drive Success," *International Marketing Review*, 11, 1, 60–76.

Das, S., A. Martínez-Jerez, and P. Tufano (2005), "eInformation: A Clinical Study of Investor Discussion and Sentiment," *Financial Management*, 34, 3.

Das, S. and M. Chen (2004), "Yahoo! for Amazon: Sentiment Extraction from Small Talk on the Web," *Santa Clara University Working Paper*.

Dellarocas, C. (2006), "Strategic Manipulation of Internet Opinion Forums: Implications for Consumers and Firms," *Management Science*, 52, 10, 1577–93.

Dellarocas, C., N. Awad, X. Zhang (2004), "Exploring the Value of Online Reviews to Organizations: Implications for Revenue Forecasting and Planning," *MIT Working Paper*.

Di Benedetto, and C. Anthony (1999), "Identifying the Key Success Factors in New Product Launch," *Journal of Product Innovation Management*, 16, 530–44.

Dodson, J.A. and E. Muller (1978), "Models of New Product Diffusion through Advertising and Word-of-Mouth," *Management Science*, 24, November, 1589–97.

Docker, E. and S. Jorgensen (1988), "Optimal Advertising Policies for Diffusion Models of New Product Innovation in Monopolistic Situations," *Management Science*, 34, 1, January, 119–30.

Eastlack, J.O. and A.G. Rao (1989), "Advertising Experiments at Campbell Soup Company," *Marketing Science*, 8, Winter, 57–71.

Elberse, A. and J. Eliashberg (2003), "Demand and Supply Dynamics for Sequentially Released Products in International Markets: The Case of Motion Pictures," *Marketing Science*, 22, 3 (Summer), 329–354.

Eliashberg, J., J.-J. Jonker, M.S. Sawhney, and B. Wierenga (2000), "MOVIEMOD: An Implementable Decision-Support System for Prerelease Market Evaluation of Motion Pictures," *Marketing Science*, 19, 3, Summer, 226–43.

Erdem, T. and B. Sun (2002), "An Empirical Investigation of the Spillover Effects Advertising and Sales Promotions in Umbrella Branding," *Journal of Marketing Research*, November, 408–20.

Foster, A. and M. Rosenzweig (1995), "Learning by doing and learning from others: Human capital and technical change in agriculture," *Journal of Political Economy*, 103 (6), 1176–210.

Garber, T., J. Goldenberg, B. Libai, and E. Muller (2004), "From Density to Destiny: Using Spatial Analysis for Early Prediction of New Product Success," *Marketing Science*, 22 (3), 419–28.

Geroski, P.A. (1995), "What do we know about entry?" *International Journal of Industrial Organization*, 13, 421–40.

Gladwell (2000), "*The Tipping Point*," Little, Brown and Company.

Godes, D. and D. Mayzlin (2004), "Using Online Conversations to Measure Word of Mouth Communication," *Marketing Science*, 23 (4), 545–60.

Godes, D. and D. Mayzlin (2004), "Firm-Created Word of Mouth Communication: A Quasi-Experiment," *Harvard Business School Working Paper*.

Godes, D., D. Mayzlin, Y. Chen, S. Das, C. Dellarocas, B. Pfeiffer, B. Libai, S. Sen, M. Shi, and P. Verlegh (2005), "The Firm's Management of Social Interactions," *Marketing Letters*, 16 (3/4), 415–28.

Goldenberg, J., B. Libai, and E. Muller (2004). "The Chilling Effect of Network Externalities on New Product Growth," *Tel-Aviv University Working Paper*.

Golder, P.N. and G.J. Tellis (1997), "Will It Ever Fly? Modeling the Takeoff of Really New Consumer Durables," *Marketing Science*, 16, 3, 256–70.

Golder, P.N. and G.J. Tellis (1998), "Beyond Diffusion: An Affordability Model of the Growth of New Consumer Durables," *Journal of Forecasting*, 17, 259–80.

Gould, J.P. (1970), "Diffusion Processes and Optimal Advertising Policy," *Microeconomic Foundations of Employment and Inflation Theory*, eds. E.S. Phelps et al. W.W. Norton, New York, 338–67.

Granovetter, M. (1973), "The Strength of Weak Ties," *American Journal of Sociology*, 78 (6): 1360–80.

Gupta, S. and D.R. Lehmann (2002), "Customers as Assets," *Journal of Interactive Marketing*, 17, Winter, 1–16.

Hauser, J., G.J. Tellis, and A. Griffin (2004), *Research on Innovation: A Review And Agenda for Marketing Science*, 111–152.

Henard, D.H. and D.M. Szymanski (2001), "Why Some New Products Are More Successful Than Others," *Journal of Marketing Research*, 38, 3, 362–75.

Higgins, E.T. (1998), "Promotion and Prevention: Regulatory Focuses as a Mathematical Principle," *Advances in Experimental Psychology*, 46, 1–46.

Hirschey, M. (1982), "Intangible Capital Aspects of Advertising and R&D Expenditures," *Journal of Industrial Economics*, 30, June, 375–90.

Holak, S.L. and D.R. Lehmann (1990), "Purchase Intentions and the Dimensions of Innovation: An Exploratory Model," *Journal of Product Innovation Management*, 7, March, 59–73.

Holak, S.L. (1988), "Determinants of Innovative Durables Adoption," *The Journal of Product Innovation Management*, 5, 50–69.

Horsky, D. and L.S. Simon (1983), "Advertising and the Diffusion of New Products," *Marketing Science*, 2, 1, Winter, 1–17.

Joshi, A. and D.M. Hanssens (2004), "Advertising Spending and Market Capitalization," *MSI Reports*, 2, 79–95.

Kalish, S. (1985), "A New Product Adoption Model with Price, Advertising, and Uncertainty," *Management Science*, 31, December, 1569–85.

Kaul, A. and D.R. Wittink (1995), "Empirical Generalizations About the Impact of Advertising on Price Sensitivity and Price," *Marketing Science*, 14:3, G151–60.

Kohli, R., D.R. Lehmann, and J.H. Pae (1999), "The Extent and Impact of Incubation Time in New Product Diffusion," *The Journal of Product Innovation Management*, 16, March, 134–44.

Kopalle, P.K. and D.R. Lehmann (1995), "The Effects of Advertised and Observed Quality on Expectations about New Product Quality," *Journal of Marketing Research*, 32, August, 280–90.

Kopalle, P.K. and D.R. Lehmann (2006), "Optimal Quality and Advertised Quality When Entering a Market: The Impact of Satisfaction," *Marketing Science*, 25, Winter, 8–17.

Kozinets, R.V. (2002, February), "The Field behind the Screen: Using Netnography for Marketing Research in Online Communities," *Journal of Marketing Research*, 39, 61–72.

Lee, Y. and G. Colarelli O'Connor (2003) "The Impact of Communication Strategy on Launching New Products: The Moderating Rose of Product Innovativeness," *Journal of Product Innovation Management*, 20, 4–21.

Lehmann, D.R. and C.B. Weinberg (2000), "Sales Through Sequential Distribution Channels: An Application to Movies and Videos," *Journal of Marketing*, 64, July, 18–33.

Leone, R.P. and R.L. Schultz (1980), "A Study of Marketing Generalizations," *Journal of Marketing*, 44, Winter, 10–18.

Little, J.D.C. (1979), "Decision Support Systems for Managers," *Journal of Marketing*, 43, Summer, 9–26.

Lodish, L.M., M. Abraham, S. Kalmenson, J. Livelsberger, B. Lubetkin, B. Richardson, and M.E. Stevens (1995), "How T.V. Advertising Works: A Meta-Analysis of 389 Real World Split Cable T.V. Advertising Experiments," *Journal of Marketing Research*, 32, May, 125–39.

Mahajan, V. and E. Muller (1986), "Advertising Pulsing Policies for Generating Awareness for New Products," *Marketing Science*, 5, 2, Spring, 89–106.

Mahajan, V., E. Muller, and R.K. Srivastava (1990), "Determination of Adopter Categories by Using Innovation Diffusion Models," *Journal of Marketing Research*, 27, February, 37–50.

Mahajan, V., E. Muller, and F.M. Bass (1995), "Diffusion of New Products: Empirical Generalizations and Managerial Uses," *Marketing Science*, 14, 3, Part 2 of 2: Special Issue.

Manchanda, P., J.-P. Dube, K.Y. Gog, and P. Chintagunta (2006), "The Effect of Banner Advertising on Internet Purchasing," *Journal of Marketing Research*, 43, February, 98–108.

Mayzlin, D. (2006), "Promotional Chat on the Internet," *Marketing Science*, 25 (2), March–April, 155–63.

McFadden, D.L. and K.E. Train (1996), "Consumers' Evaluation of New Products: Learning from Self and Others," *Journal of Political Economy*, 104, 4, 683–703.

Mesak, H.I. and J.W. Clark (1998), *Monopolist Optimum Pricing and Advertising Policies for Diffusion Models of New Product Innovations*, John Wiley & Sons, Ltd.

Monahan, G.E. (1984), "A Pure Birth Mode of Optimal Advertising with Word-of-Mouth," *Marketing Science*, 3, Spring, 169–78.

Montoya-Weiss, M. and R. Calantone (1994), "Determinants of New Product Performance: A Review and Meta-Analysis," *Journal of Product Innovation Management*, 11, September, 397–417.

Moreau, C.P., D.R. Lehmann, and A.P. Markman (2001), "Entrenched Knowledge Structures and Consumer Response to New Products," *Journal of Marketing Research*, 38, February, 14–29.

Nakanishi, M. (1973), "Advertising and Promotion Effects on Consumer Response to New Products," *Journal of Marketing Research*, 10, 3, August, 242–9.

Narayanan, S., P. Manchanda, and P.K. Chintagunta (2005)," Temporal Differences in the Role of Marketing Communication in New Product Categories," *Journal of Marketing Research*, 62, August, 278–90.

Nerlove, M. and K.J. Arrow (1962), "Optimal Advertising Policy under Dynamic Conditions," *Economica*, 29 (114), 129–42.

Ozanne, J.L., M. Brucks, and D. Grewal (1992), "A Study of Information Search Behavior during the Categorization of New Products," *Journal of Consumer Research*, 18, March, 452–63.

Pauwels, K., J. Silva-Risso, S. Srinivasan, and D.M. Hanssens (2004), "New Products, Sales Promotions, and Firm Value: The Case of the Automobile Industry," *Journal of Marketing*, 68, October, 142–56.

Parsons, L.J. (1975), "The Product Life Cycle and Time-Varying Advertising Elasticities," *Journal of Marketing Research*, 12, November, 476–80.

Pitta, D.A. and L.P. Katsanis (1995), "Understanding Brand Equity for Successful Brand Extension," *The Journal of Consumer Marketing*, 12, 4, 51–64.

Putsis, W., S. Balasubramanian, E. Kaplan, and S. Sen (1997), "Mixing Behaviour in Cross-Country Diffusion," *Marketing Science*, 16, 354–69.

Riskey, D.R. (1997), "How TV Advertising Works: An Industry Response," *Journal of Marketing Research*, 34, May, 292–3.

Rogers, E.M. (2003), *Diffusion of Innovations*, New York: Simon and Schuster

Rosen, E. (2000), *The Anatomy of buzz*, New York: Doubleday.

Sasieni, M.W. (1971), "Optimal Advertising Expenditure," *Management Science*, 18, December, 64–72.

Sethuraman, R. and G.J. Tellis (1991), "An Analysis of the Tradeoff between Advertising and Price Discounting," *Journal of Marketing Research*, 28, May, 160–74.

Shankar, V. and B.L. Bayus (2001), "Network Effects and Competition: An Empirical analysis of the Home Video Game Industry," College Park, Md.: University of Maryland, *Working Paper*.

Simon, H. and K.-H. Sebastian (1987), "Diffusion and Advertising: The German Telephone Campaign,*" *Management Science*, 33, 4, 451–66.

Simon, J.L. and J. Arndt (1980), "The Shape of the Advertising Response Function," *Journal of Advertising Research*, 11–28.

Srinivasan, R., G.L. Lilien, and A. Rangaswamy (2004), "First In, First Out? The Effects of Network Externalities on Pioneer Survival," *Journal of Marketing*, 68, January, 41–55.

Sultan, F., J.U. Farley, and D.R. Lehmann (1990), "A Meta-Analysis of Applications of Diffusion Models," *Journal of Marketing Research*, 27, February, 70–7.

Sun, B., J. Xie, and H.H. Cao (2004), "Produce Strategy for Innovators in Markets with Network Effects," *Marketing Science*, 23, 2, 243–54.

Tellefsen, T. and H. Takada (1999), "The Relationship Between Mass Media Availability and the Multicountry Diffusion of Consumer Products," *Journal of International Marketing*, 7, 77–96.

Tellis, G.J. (2007), "Effectiveness in Contemporary Markets," in *The SAGE Handbook of Advertising*, eds. G.J. Tellis and T. Ambler, London: Sage.

Tellis, G.J. (1998), "Advertising Exposure, Loyalty and Brand Purchase: A Two-Stage Model of Choice," *Journal of Marketing Research*, 25, May, 134–44.

Tellis, G.J. (1988), *Advertising and Sales Promotion Strategy*, Reading, MA: Addison-Wesley.

Thomas, L.A. (1999), "Incumbent firm's response to entry: Price, advertising, and new product introduction," *International Journal of Industrial Organization*, 17, August, 527–55.

Thomas, T. and H. Takada (1999), "The Relationship Between Mass Media Availability and the Multi-country Diffusion of Consumer Products," *Journal of International Marketing*, 7, 1, 77–95.

Thomke, S. and E. von Hipple (2002), "Customers as Innovators: A New Way to Create Value," *Harvard Business Review*, 80, 4, April, 74–81.

Thompson, G.L. and J.T. Teng (1984), "Optimal Pricing and Advertising Policies for New Product Oligopoly Models," *Marketing Science*, 3, Spring, 148–68.

Vakratsas, D. and T. Ambler (1999), "How Advertising Works: What Do We Really Know?" *Journal of Marketing*, 63, January, 26–43.

Van den Bulte, C. (2000), "New Product Diffusion Acceleration: Measurement and Analysis," *Marketing Science*, 19, 4, Fall, 366–80.

Verlegh, P.W.J., C. Verkerk, M.A. Tuk, and A. Smidts (2004), "Customers or Sellers? The Role of Persuasion Knowledge in Customer Referral." *Advances in Consumer Research*, 31, 304–5.

Vidale, M.L. and H.B. Wolfe (1957), "An Operations Research Study of Sales Response to Advertising," *Operations Research*, 5, June, 370–81.

von Hipple, E. (1986), "Lead Users: A Source of Novel Product Concepts," *Management Science*, 32, 7, 791–805.

Wansink, B. and M.L. Ray (1996), "Advertising Strategies to Increase Usage Frequency," *Journal of Marketing*, 60, 1, January, 31–46.

Wojnicki, A. and D. Godes (2004), "Word of Mouth as Impression Management," *HBS Working Paper*.

Zelske, H.A. (1979), "Optimal Advertising Policy with the Contagion Model," *Journal of Optim. Theory Appl.*, 29, December, 615–27.

Zelske, H.A. (1986), Comment on "Advertising Pulsing Policies for Generating Awareness for New Products," *Marketing Science*, 5, 2, Spring, 109.

Zinkhan, G.M., C.G. Austin, and J.H. Song (2007), "Peer-to-Peer Media Opportunities," in *The SAGE Handbook of Advertising*, eds. G.J. Tellis and T. Ambler, London: Sage Publications.

The Advertising Environment

Advertising Regulation

Jef I. Richards and Ross D. Petty

Near the end of this past century, the Catholic Church's study of advertising and its role in society concluded:

> "There is nothing intrinsically good or intrinsically evil about advertising. It is a tool, an instrument: it can be used well, and it can be used badly. If it can have, and sometimes does have, beneficial results such as those just described, it also can, and often does, have a negative, harmful impact on individuals and society."
>
> (Foley et al., 1997)

Shortly thereafter, the Court of Appeals for the District of Columbia Circuit affirmed the Federal Trade Commission's (FTC) order for corrective advertising, to cure lingering effects of harmful advertisements. The FTC ordered the maker of Doan's Pills to include a disclosure in its advertising for one year, until it had expended $8 million. This was the average amount it spent annually over an eight year period to persuade consumers that Doan's Pills was a superior product for relief of back pain over other pain relief products. There was no substantiation to support this superiority claim (*Novartis Corp. v. FTC*, 2000).

This sort of misleading and unsubstantiated claim in commercial advertising is the primary focus of advertising regulation throughout the world and the main focus of this chapter. This regulation of commercial deceptiveness not only protects consumers from being misled, but also bolsters advertising's credibility. Greater advertising credibility can lead to less resistance to ads and greater belief of their claims, resulting in more effective marketing communications. In this way, both consumers and advertisers benefit from regulating advertising deceptiveness.

However, advertising regulation includes much more than dealing with deceptiveness. The next section describes four domains of advertising regulation. It is followed by a discussion of freedom of speech concerns and the regulation of political advertising. The third section examines regulation of deceptiveness in detail followed by a discussion of fairness concerns in advertising regulation. We conclude with a summary of the chapter. While this chapter focuses on advertising regulation in the United States, the European Community (EC) approach also is discussed since Europe is evolving to become the largest single consumer market as measured by worldwide sales.

SCOPE OF ADVERTISING REGULATION

While most advertising regulation throughout the world addresses problems with deceptive advertising, advertising also can be the target of regulators when the advertisements are not the problem. Rather, the regulation is seen to hold promise as a solution for social ills like lung cancer (Petty, 1999; Richards, 1996), obesity (Seiders and Petty, 2004) or even racial discrimination (Petty et al., 2003). The forms and purposes of regulation are numerous and varied. Municipalities, for example, have used local ordinances to beautify communities through elimination or restriction of commercial signage (e.g., Marbin and Journey, 1991). Similarly, many laws seek to curtail unwanted telemarketing (Smolla, 2005) or unsolicited email or fax ads (Zitter, 2004). Laws, too, are used to protect children from ads that might injure or take advantage of them (Curran and Richards, 2000). Laws even are used to force some companies to finance ads that are not in their own best interests (*Johanns v. Livestock Marketing Assn.*, 2005).

The domains of advertising regulation can be roughly categorized as entailing:

(1) *Persuasive effects on purchase behaviour.* Deceiving someone into buying a product or taking advantage of them at a moment of weakness, such as convincing a recently mugged person to buy an alarm system, are examples of problems at which governmental intervention may be directed. Selling illegal products or services, such as cigarettes to minors, also would fall under this heading.

(2) *Persuasive effects beyond purchase behaviour.* Advertising not only urges purchase, it encourages consumption which may contribute to materialism, excess smoking or drinking, racial or gender stereotyping, among other things. These effects potentially reach far beyond the sales transaction. Regulations, then, are crafted to prevent advertising from causing or encouraging some consequential behaviour.

(3) *Intrusive effects.* Many criticisms of advertising have nothing to do with the ad's message,

but with the form or the location where it is placed. In these situations the effects are "content-neutral," because the message content is virtually irrelevant. Billboards frequently are banned or restricted, not because of their message, but because they are aesthetically unpleasing. Unsolicited email, fax, too, are restricted because they are intrusive. These regulations, including privacy laws, protect our personal environment.

(4) *Effects on political behaviour.* Advertising for political candidates, and concerning political causes, also is subject to regulation. Some laws are designed to insure one party (or cause) gains no unfair advantage over another by using advertising. Some ensure more information to the electorate. Whatever the intent, however, it is the political – as opposed to commercial – nature of the advertising that distinguishes these effects from those above.

Advertisements can, of course, have effects in more than one category, but the stated purpose for a regulation generally arises from just one of these types. Ultimately, the legitimacy of a regulation often is determined by its purpose.

US First Amendment

In the United States, the principal limit on government's ability to regulate both political and commercial advertising is the guarantee of free speech written into the First Amendment of the US Constitution. Some other countries have similar protections of free speech, but may apply them differently than the US. Still others have no explicit guarantee of free speech at all.

For the first century and a half after the First Amendment was ratified, advertising never received serious consideration for protection as "speech" under that provision. Courts recognized the Amendment as designed to protect the expression of political ideas and protest against the government. Yet even such advertising for political purposes, by a political candidate or by anyone supporting/criticizing the government, is subject to legal limitations. There are laws on the books to restrict everything from anonymously contributing money to political ad campaigns to using an outdated photograph of a candidate in an ad, and more (Richman, 1998; Richards and Caywood, 1991). But because these laws affect the most highly valued speech, US courts look very closely before enforcing them.

One recent attempt to fence in advertising by political candidates is the McCain-Feingold bill (*Bipartisan Campaign Reform Act, 2001*). Most provisions of that law were declared Constitutional by the Supreme Court (*McConnell v. Federal Election Commission*, 2003), ensuring its enforceability. It largely prohibits corporations and unions from paying for "issue ads" immediately preceding an election. This illustrates that the Constitution does not entirely prohibit regulation of political speech, considered the "core" value of First Amendment protection (*FEC v. National Conservative PAC*, 1985), but commercial ads always were subject to even more regulation.

Not until 1976, in *Virginia State Board of Pharmacy v. Virginia Citizens Consumer Council*, did the Supreme Court finally declare commercial speech, defined as that which does no more than propose a commercial transaction (*Pittsburgh Press v. Pittsburgh Commission on Human Relations*, 1973), to be constitutionally protected. But in the years that followed, the judiciary struggled with this new constitutional status, recognizing the need to both protect advertising *and* prevent deception and other negative ad effects (Richards, 1997). To provide judges, and legislatures, some guidance as to when a regulation would be allowed and when it would tread on free speech rights, *Central Hudson Gas & Electric v. Public Service Commission of New York* (1980) established a four-part test:

Step 1. Is the speech concerning a lawful activity and not misleading?
Step 2. Does the government have a substantial interest in regulating it?
Step 3. Does the regulation directly advance that interest?
Step 4. Is the regulation more extensive than necessary?

If the speech is misleading or promotes illegal activity, clearly it can be regulated or even prohibited. Otherwise, to be constitutional the regulation must meet all of steps 2–4. This same test is used today, except that the fourth step was later refined to mean that the regulation must be "narrowly tailored" to be a reasonable fit to the interest being protected (*S.U.N.Y. v. Fox*, 1989).

So, for example, if a city passed a law banning advertising signs in homeowners' yards, that law must pass the four-step test. Unless the law targeted only deceptive ads, or ads for illegal products/services, the first step would yield a "yes." Consequently, the second step would ask the government's purpose. If the purpose were simply that the mayor did not like the signs, it probably would fail the test as being "not substantial." But if the signs are distracting drivers, causing accidents, the purpose being to prevent those accidents is likely a substantial interest, so it would pass that step. The third step, then, would ask whether banning the signs *will* prevent accidents. If "yes," it would pass again. If "no," it would fail the test. Finally, if only certain types of signs, such as those with naked models on them, are causing accidents, banning *all* signs would not be "narrowly tailored," causing the law to fail the test. All of these determinations, ultimately, would be made by a court.

The *Central Hudson* test proved somewhat variable in its results from case to case, and for years the extent to which commercial speech received speech-of-the-second-class status under the First Amendment was unclear. But this finally was clarified in *44 Liquormart v. Rhode Island* (1996), when the Supreme Court introduced a new – and still current – way to look at commercial speech cases.

In that decision, the Court explained the lesser protection for commercial speech as being limited to ensuring "fair bargaining." Prohibition of deceptive claims, for example, is all about assuring a level playing field in the commercial bargaining process. Conversely, where laws are designed to achieve some goal other than fair dealing, such as reducing tobacco consumption or removing billboard eyesores from the public right-of-way, the affected speech deserves protection on a par with more highly valued expression. This decision indicated commercial speech would receive less protection than other speech *only* where the government's substantial interest involved the *Persuasive Effects on Purchase Behaviour* category mentioned earlier. The second and third categories would be judged by the stricter standards accorded most forms of speech. The fourth category, though, involves political speech rather than commercial speech. Thus, while the First Amendment stands as a tall hurdle to much regulation, clearly its call for "no law abridging the freedom of speech" is not interpreted as a total prohibition on legal restraints.

Deceptiveness

The first part of the *Central* Hudson test denies First Amendment protection to misleading (also called deceptive) commercial speech. Numerous guidelines in the US and throughout the world help advertisers avoid deceptiveness in advertising. Most are published by self-regulatory groups such as the National Advertising Division (NAD) of the Council of Better Business Bureaus (CBBB) in the US, the Advertising Standards Authority in the UK, or the International Chamber of Commerce. The FTC also publishes *guidelines*, providing mere guidance, as well as *rules* that have the force of law. Otherwise, deceptiveness in advertising is regulated through specific case-by-case challenges to particular ads.

These challenges to deceptive advertising can be examined in five stages: (1) how advertising challenges are brought, (2) what message is conveyed to consumers, (3) what is the likelihood the message will mislead consumers, (4) the accuracy of the advertising claims, and (5) what remedy, if any, is appropriate (cf. Petty and Kopp, 1995; Petty, 1997). Each of these stages is discussed in turn below.

Challenging deceptive advertising

Advertising is policed for deception through industry self-regulation, government regulation, or private lawsuits (most commonly by competitors, but sometimes by consumers or consumer organizations). In the US, advertising legal challenges arise from all three sources. Media also can play an important role, through self-regulation, screening out ads that might mislead consumers. Twenty years ago the major US television networks reviewed about 50 000 advertisements and received challenges to less than 100 of those advertisements. More recent figures are not available, but in the late 1980s networks cut the number of people employed to scrutinize ads for problems (Gordon, 1988). Some individual television stations (Rotfeld et al., 1990) and magazines also review advertising before accepting it (Rotfeld and Parsons, 1989).

The primary mechanism for industry *self*-regulation in the US is the NAD of the CBBB. It receives about 200 advertising complaints each year and opens about half that number into formal cases (Boddewyn, 1988). These cases can be appealed to the National Advertising Review Board, also a part of the CBBB, but that rarely happens. Rarer still, if the advertiser does not comply with its ruling, the NAD can refer the case to the appropriate government authority. This happened for the first time in 1992 (*Sunshine Makers, Inc.*, 1992).

The Federal Trade Commission is the main source of formal US *legal* regulation of advertising. It opens about 50 advertising investigations and issues 10–15 orders annually. It can try advertising cases administratively, before its own Administrative Law judges, or it can seek injunction in federal district court (Petty, 1992). In addition, state attorneys general also have attempted to regulate advertising in recent years (Richards, 1991).

Also, competitors sue one another for misleading advertising under the Lanham Act – the trademark protection law – at least as frequently as the FTC brings cases (Petty, 1992: 58, 98–99). Thus, private lawsuits by competitors are the third source of US advertising regulation. Rarely do consumers sue to challenge advertising in the US, and when they do they are relegated to state, rather than federal, courts.

Outside the United States, the EC adopted its directive on misleading advertising in 1984 (Council Directive, 1984), requiring member states to adopt its provisions into national law. It requires laws to challenge misleading advertising before either a court or an administrative authority by "persons or organizations regarded under national law as having a legitimate interest in" prohibiting misleading advertising. The United Kingdom insisted that the directive also recognize the validity of self-regulation. The UK's Advertising Standards Authority (ASA) is the largest, most active, and best financed self-regulatory system in the world, and is supported by the government. Its authority is derived from the British Code of Advertising Practices (Baudot, 1989: 116–26; Boddewyn, 1988: 267–94). Consistent with the directive, ASA decisions can be appealed to a court for review (Newell, 1989). Legal actions in Great Britain generally follow only after self-regulatory solutions are sought. A similar process is followed in Ireland (Boddewyn, 1985).

Italy, Belgium and Switzerland likewise have active industry self-regulation (Maxeiner and Schothofer, 1992). Italian law allows competitors (not consumers) to sue privately, but courts seldom find advertising to be misleading. So self-regulation handles about 80% of all advertising disputes (Schricker, 1990: 631–6). In the Netherlands both private lawsuits and industry self-regulation are active arbiters of advertising challenges. But like the UK, the Dutch self-regulatory body can be overruled by the courts (Dommering, 1992: 269).

Scandinavian countries actually have displaced industry self-regulation with a consumer ombudsman who functions much like the US FTC by receiving advertising complaints, attempting to resolve them, and litigating if necessary. Many of its guidelines were based on prior industry self-regulation, so industry supports and cooperates with the ombudsman (Boddewyn, 1985).

In contrast, Germany, Austria, and Spain base ad regulation on private lawsuits by competitors and consumer organizations. Indeed, advertising litigation is more prevalent in Germany than in any other country, but roughly 90% of these disputes end in a settlement between the parties (Maxeiner and Shotthofer, 1992: 170). The German Weberat is the primary self-regulatory body, and it complements the legal system by focusing on questions of taste and opinion, rather than deceptiveness (Horn et al., 1982: 284–7; Grimes, 1971: 1778–93).

France, Luxembourg, and Belgium also allow recognized consumer organizations to bring lawsuits challenging advertising. These three countries and the rest of Western Europe generally fall somewhere in between the two extremes of Italy and Germany, with a more even balance of private lawsuits, self-regulation, and some government regulation (Petty, 1997).

In all countries, the advertiser can be held liable for its advertising. In the US, the FTC also pursues advertising *agencies* that were active participants in creating the ads and knew or should have known of the legal problems. Similarly, under the US Lanham Act, advertising agencies may be sued, though it is rare. In Europe, ad agencies may be sued in Belgium (in lieu of an advertiser located in another country), Denmark, Ireland, Italy, France (if negligent), Germany, Austria, Portugal, Switzerland, and the UK. In Germany, Ireland, Italy, Switzerland, and the UK, the magazine, TV station, etc., also may be held liable (Maxeiner and Schotthofer, 1992). In the US, agencies can be held liable but media generally are not, although the FTC has started encouraging media to take more responsibility for the ads they publish (Galloway et al., 2005).

Message conveyed to consumers

To find an advertisement misleading, it must first be "interpreted" to determine what message is communicated to consumers. For explicit claims, the regulator need only look at the advertisement itself. However, such literal interpretation may miss messages that are implied (Preston and Richards, 1986).

For example, when newspaper ads proclaimed "Hertz has more new cars than Avis has cars," the trial court interpreted the ads literally and counted the cars owned by each company. It found the ad to be literally false and ordered a permanent injunction and required Hertz to place corrective notices in the same newspapers where the ad ran. In contrast, the court of appeals recognized that the message conveyed to consumers was that Hertz had more cars available for rent than Avis. This interpretation was found true since Avis was in the process of selling a large number of cars that it still owned, and they were no longer available for rent. The court dismissed the complaint.

In the US, *implied* deceptive claims can be condemned even if the literal statements in the advertising are true. A variety of methods are used by all these authorities to "interpret" the ad to determine what message is conveyed, from simply looking at the ad and drawing conclusions to conducting consumer surveys or having marketing experts evaluate them (Petty, 1992; Richards, 1990: 31–4).

The 1984 EC Directive on Misleading Advertising is silent on interpretation and the regulation of implied claims (Council Directive, 1984). Not surprisingly, most European countries also do not explicitly address these issues. Most simply have the judge or other authority examine the advertisement and apply their personal judgement to interpret it. However, the newly adopted Directive Concerning Unfair Business to Consumer Commercial Practices that Member States must enact into law by early 2008, declares:

> A commercial practice shall also be regarded as misleading if, in its factual context, taking account of all its features and circumstances, it causes or is likely to cause the average consumer to take a transactional decision that he would not have taken otherwise ... (Directive 2005/29/EC)

That language closely mirrors the policy followed by the US FTC. At present, Germany and the US are the only countries that routinely use consumer research to help determine the meaning of advertising.

Two varieties of implied claims that illustrate the need to look beyond the explicit are omissions of material (i.e., important) information and visual claims. In the US

the FTC pursues omissions more readily than courts under the Lanham Act (Petty, 1992). And state attorneys general are more likely than the FTC to find omissions and require additional disclosures (Beales, 1991). Many EC countries also regulate misleading omissions (Petty, 1997), so it is not surprising that the new Unfairness Directive condemns the omission of material information that the average consumer needs to make an informed decision in the marketplace.

Advertising messages communicated visually are perhaps more difficult to address than omissions of fact. Advertisers are skilled at using visual imagery, while lawyers, regulators, and judges who review advertising challenges are trained to analyze words more than images. But visual content certainly can deceive, so it is regulated in some cases (Richards and Zakia, 1981). For example, the FTC and the Texas State Attorney General both challenged Volvo advertisements as deceptive for showing a "monster" truck rolling over a line of cars, all of which were crushed except the surreptitiously re-enforced Volvo. In contrast, the FTC refused to pursue animated visual claims by Perrier that, arguably, falsely told consumers Perrier water was unprocessed, by showing historical figures such as Napoleon dipping a cup into an unrefined natural spring and drinking the Perrier water (Petty, 1993).

Germany occasionally has condemned visually misleading advertising. Similarly France challenged the advertising of TANG drink mix that showed an empty orange peel, a glass of TANG surrounded by green leaves, and the slogan: "the taste of fresh squeezed oranges." This advertising was found to falsely claim TANG contained orange juice, despite a fine print listing of TANG's artificial ingredients (Baudot, 1989: 136–7). French courts also condemned an ad for a legal advisor shown wearing a robe, creating the impression the advisor was an attorney (Maxeiner and Schotthofer, 1992: 125).

Likelihood of misleading consumers

After determining the messages perceived by consumers, regulators must decide whether those messages are likely to mislead. Ivan Preston (1982) uses the word "deceptiveness" to refer to the *potential* to mislead consumers, as distinguished from *actual* deception. The FTC is empowered to regulate ads even when no one is yet deceived; it need not wait until someone gets hurt. For example, in the Volvo and Perrier cases, above, the FTC apparently believed consumers would be misled by the Volvo demonstration, but not by the animated Perrier demonstration.

For more than six decades the FTC's standard was described as requiring only that a representation have a "capacity or tendency to deceive" (*FTC v. Sterling Drug, Inc.*, 1963). But during the Reagan Administration, the new *Policy Statement on Deception* fundamentally changed that standard, declaring the representation must be "likely" to deceive (Cliffdale, 1984). This effectively shifted the standard from a *possibility* ads would deceive, to a *probability* they would deceive. In addition, the old standard required evidence of a capacity or tendency to deceive almost anyone, including "the ignorant, the unthinking and the credulous" (*Aronberg v. FTC*, 1942). But over time the FTC stopped going so far as to protect the feebleminded, and the *Policy Statement* stated the Commission would only protect consumers "acting reasonably under the circumstances" (Cliffdale, 1984). These changes appear to reduce the level of consumer protection.

The US State Attorneys General tend to apply the old "capacity or tendency" standard (Beales 1991). The US Lanham Act follows that general approach, without going so far as to protect truly gullible consumers. This is the same standard now recognized in most of Europe.

Yet another question that must be answered is whether that deceptive advertising claim is "material" (i.e., important) to consumers. For example, the FTC charged Kraft with deceiving people about the calcium content of its cheese, compared to milk and imitation cheese slices. Kraft argued since its product is a good source of calcium, the relative amount of calcium per slice was not material to consumers' purchase decisions. Kraft,

however, lost that argument (*Kraft Inc. v. FTC*, 1992). Similarly, Doan's Pills, mentioned earlier, unsuccessfully argued the claim of superior back pain relief was immaterial to consumers given the truthfulness that the product was an effective pain reliever (*Novartis Corp. v. FTC*, 2000).

Materiality also received a new definition in the *Policy Statement on Deception*, changing from "the natural and probable result of the challenged practices it to cause one to do that which he would not otherwise do" (*Bockenstette v. FTC*, 1943) to "information that is important to consumers, and, hence, likely to affect their choice of, or conduct regarding, a product" (Cliffdale, 1984). So a deceptive claim is material, if it affects product-related behaviour, such as where consumers shop, even if it does not ultimately change the consumers' purchase decisions. But in most cases the FTC assumes that if a claim is used in an ad it must be designed to affect consumer decisions, and hence is material (Richards and Preston, 1992). Similarly, under the Lanham Act, the likelihood of deceiving consumers is presumed (Petty, 1992: 96–7).

The 1984 European Community Directive on Misleading Advertising also adopts a deceptiveness standard. It defines misleading advertising as that which deceives or is likely to deceive persons to whom it is addressed or whom it reaches and which by reason of its deceptive nature, is likely to affect their economic behaviour or which, for those reasons, injures or is likely to injure a competitor.

The new Unfairness Directive seems to narrow this definition to that which causes, or is likely to cause the average consumers to make a different *transactional* decision, as opposed to shopping at a different store.

The US, Belgium, France, Greece, Ireland, Italy also recognize the defence of "puffing" – claims of quality too vague to be relied upon by consumers. Puffing occurs when advertisers obviously exaggerate, state opinions, or make vague quality claims such as that a product is "best." For example, in France a competitor challenged Samsonite luggage advertising that showed a pair of bulldozers "playing" with a suitcase that was shown undamaged. The lower court found the commercial misleading because many suitcases had been used and damaged during the filming of the commercial. The court of appeals held that the average consumer would recognize this as exaggeration, and not take it as literal truth (Rijkens and Miracle, 1986: 150). Denmark, Portugal, and Germany do not recognize this defence, and France requires that superlatives be verified (Maxeiner and Schotthofer, 1992). A claim not believed by consumers is unlikely to play a material role in their purchase behaviour. More information on puffing and its ethical implications can be found in Chapter 6.2.

Accuracy of the advertising claims

Once the conveyed meaning of an ad is determined, it is compared to the reality of the product (or service) attribute or characteristic. Historically, challengers had the burden of proving falsity, rather than advertisers needing to prove the truth of their claims. This rule is still applied in the US for Lanham Act cases, but beginning in the 1970s for the FTC, state attorneys general, and NAD, as well as in Europe under the 1984 Directive, the burden has shifted. In order to clarify this change and describe what is reasonable substantiation, given the wide variety of possible products and claims, the FTC wrote a policy statement regarding advertising sub-stantiation (Thompson Medical Co., 1984).

There are a few important principles of this policy. Most important, the advertiser must have evidence of the claim's accuracy *before* the claim is made. If an advertiser is charged with deceptive advertising and has no such evidence in hand, the advertiser is liable even if subsequent evidence proves the claim was accurate. Additionally, if the advertiser led consumers to believe a claim is based on a specific type of evidence (e.g., "According to tests by an independent laboratory. ..."), the advertiser must have that exact evidence. In all other situations the advertiser must have *at least* a "reasonable basis" for believing the claim to be true. In deciding what is reasonable, the FTC will look at several factors including, among other things, what type of product is involved and what experts in that field consider reasonable forms of proof (Thompson Medical Co., 1984).

Remedies

Once a problem with advertising is found, a solution is needed. Self-regulation throughout the world has no legal authority to impose a remedy, but many such systems are buttressed by the threat of formal legal action if a self-regulatory recommendation is not followed. The typical remedy requested by self-regulation is to stop or modify the ad to eliminate the problem.

In the US, the normal FTC and Lanham Act remedy also requires stopping or modifying the advertisement. Something like 85% of deceptive advertising cases at the FTC end with consent order, whereby the advertiser *voluntarily* agrees to change its advertising (Richards and Preston, 1987). Unlike industry self-regulation, such consent orders have the force of law and advertisers can be fined for violating them, just like any other FTC order. Those orders also may "fence-in" the advertiser, to prohibit similar types of claims for similar types of products in the future.

The consent order ends a case while it is still in process, before any final decision is reached about a claim's deceptiveness. For cases where a decision actually is reached by the FTC commissioners, though, there really are only three possible outcomes. The oldest and most common is the Cease and Desist Order, which merely requires the advertiser to stop making the claim. This remedy stops the damage but can allow advertisers to keep any ill-gotten gains (Ward, 1992). Another remedy especially useful where deceptiveness arises from a material omission in the ad is Affirmative Disclosure, requiring information be added to future advertising (Richards and Preston, 1992). The third option is Corrective Advertising, a form of affirmative disclosure designed to correct deceptive beliefs held by consumers resulting from a long history of using a deceptive claim (Wilkie et al., 1984). This third approach, though, is rarely used.

Because FTC advertising adjudications may last several years, the FTC Act was amended in the mid-1970s so the agency could obtain court-ordered injunctions in advertising cases *where violations are clear cut*. That new clause, known as Section 13(b), allowed the FTC to effectively surrender jurisdiction to a court, and the courts interpreted this as inviting them to fashion their own remedies (Ward, 1992). So in addition to preliminary (before the full adjudication) and permanent injunctions, courts ordered other outcomes such as consumer redress, requiring advertisers to repay customers for losses caused by the ad. This has become a powerful fourth remedial option for especially egregious cases of deceptive advertising.

The principal remedy in Lanham Act cases is a preliminary injunction. In order to obtain a preliminary injunction, the plaintiff has a higher burden than the FTC, and must prove that: (1) the plaintiff likely will win the lawsuit because the advertising is false, (2) the defendant's advertising is likely to cause or has caused injury to the plaintiff, and (3) the plaintiff's injury without the injunction is likely to be higher than the defendant's injury with the injunction (balancing of the hardships). Courts in Lanham Act cases rarely order damages (monetary compensation), which must be proven with specificity. State attorneys general, by contrast, may obtain an injunction and often recover costs of their investigation (McKinney and Caton, 1990–1).

The 1984 EC Directive on Misleading Advertising similarly calls for injunctions. It permits interim injunctions while the case outcome is pending. It also authorizes requiring the advertiser to publish the decision in appropriate cases; essentially a form of corrective advertising. Not surprisingly, the primary formal remedy in most European countries is an injunction. When self-regulation is ignored in the UK, its Director of Fair Trading is authorized to seek an injunction. In Germany, approximately 80% of misleading advertising cases include an injunction during the trial, which often becomes permanent (Schricker, 1990: 630).

Most European countries also have a provision allowing the advertiser to simply publish a retraction (called rectification in the Netherlands) but this remedy is rarely used. Plaintiffs also may request that a court's decision be published at the advertiser's expense. Most European countries allow for the awarding of money for damages if they can be proven, but such awards also are rare in advertising cases (Maxeiner and Shotthofer, 1992), Germany allows consumer groups to sue for damages, but it requires proof of intentional or negligent misconduct (Grimes, 1971: 1791). Finally, a few countries invoke *criminal* penalties, at least on occasion. In Great Britain, fines are typically ordered (and possible jail time) for explicitly false advertising claims. Similarly, France and Greece can impose jail time or criminal penalties (Maxeiner and Shotthofer, 1992). In the US the FTC Act does not permit criminal penalties, though there are occasions where criminal penalties may arise under a separate set of laws concerning mail fraud. Also, some states do have criminal laws on the books, but these rarely are applied.

Unfairness

While the substantial majority of advertising challenges involve deceptiveness, advertising regulation also addresses persuasive effects beyond product purchase and the intrusiveness of advertising. Both the FTC and Europe generally address such issues as "unfair." The breadth of this authority is illustrated by the European 1979 revision to the proposed directive concerning unfair and misleading advertising, defining unfair advertising as that which:

(a) casts discredit on another person by reference to his nationality, origin, private life or good name; or

(b) injures or is likely to injure the commercial reputation of another person by false statements or defamatory comments concerning his firm, goods, or services; or

(c) abuses or manifestly arouses sentiments of fear; or

(d) promotes discrimination on grounds of sex, race or religion; or

(e)   abuses the trust, credulity or lack of experience of a consumer, or influences or is likely to influence a consumer or the pubic in general in any other improper manner

This language was based on the International Chamber of Commerce advertising code followed by most self-regulatory bodies in Europe (http://www.itcilo.it/english/actrav/telearn/global/ilo/guide/iccadv.htm). However, this part of the proposal was not adopted in the new Unfairness Directive. Rather the directive condemns misleading and aggressive practices that are contrary to professional diligence and likely to change transactional decisions such as harassing, threatening, or coercive behaviour.

In contrast to this specific listing of a few concerns, the modern US approach is largely captured by a 1994 amendment to the FTC Act, defining unfairness as:

(1)   the act or practice causes or is likely to cause substantial injury to consumers,
(2)   which is not reasonably avoidable by consumers themselves, and
(3)   is not outweighed by countervailing benefits to consumers or to competition (Federal Trade Commission, 2005).

As in Europe, unfairness has proven controversial in the US. For decades the FTC applied a relatively sweeping definition of "unfair" as "immoral, unethical, oppressive, or unscrupulous" acts (Statement of Basis, 1964). Virtually any ad disliked by commissioners might fit within one of those descriptors. For this reason, some businesses suggested the FTC held far too much power.

The new definition reflects a fundamental shift in approach, incorporating a cost–benefit analysis (e.g., Schechter, 1989). Under this standard even an ad that causes actual injury to consumers cannot be regulated as unfair if other considerations outweigh that "cost." So, for example, if a particular marketing practice created a more competitive market and benefited the market as a whole, the fact that a few consumers would be hurt might not justify stopping the practice.

Persuasive effects on purchase behaviour

Most persuasiveness concerns dealing with unfairness are aimed at curbing advertisers' ability to take advantage of vulnerable consumers, like children (Curran and Richards, 2000). In *FTC v. Keppel & Bro.* (1934), the Supreme Court upheld the FTC's decision that using a lottery to sell candy unfairly encouraged gambling among children, who were ill equipped to understand the nature of odds. More recently, the FTC adopted its "900-Number" Industry Rule banning 900-Number service directed at children under the age of twelve, presumably because children may not comprehend the associated charges, running up large bills.

On the other side of the pond, Article 16 of the European *Directive Concerning Television Broadcasting* (1989) requires that television advertising not:

(a)   directly exhort minors to buy a product or a service by exploiting their inexperience or credulity;
(b)   directly encourage minors to persuade their parents or others to purchase the goods or services being advertised;
(c)   exploit the special trust minors place in parents, teachers or other persons

Even before this was adopted, self-regulation in most European countries applied similar rules to protect children. French law also limits the use of children as endorsers in ads, prohibits the use of heroes to sell to children, and bans ads that extol a product as a status symbol (Maxeiner and Schotthofer, 1992).

Other vulnerable groups, like the elderly, also can raise unfairness issues. In the early 1970s the FTC pursued a few cases where the exploitation of emotional desires and weaknesses were alleged to be unfair practices. For example, in *Arthur Murray Studio of Washington* (1971) salespeople pressured elderly widows to purchase exorbitant numbers of dance lessons, using high pressure sales tactics and preying on their loneliness. The FTC declared this unfair. For additional discussion of advertising to vulnerable audiences, (see Chapter 6.4).

Unfairness can reach beyond inherently vulnerable groups, however. For example, in *J.B. Williams Co.* (1972), an FTC Consent Order prohibited Vivarin, an over-the-counter stimulant, from advertising that use of any such product would solve an individual's marital, sexual, or personality problems, or improve their personality, physical appearance, marriage, or sex life. Sometimes cases also involve unfair omissions of information. In *International Harvester Inc.* (1984), tractor ads did not mention safety, but the FTC found that failing to disclose information on a dangerous safety problem was unfair because consumers could not avoid the problem without such knowledge.

The new European Unfairness Directive condemns harassing or coercing consumers into purchase, making an inaccurate claim about risks to the consumer's personal security, or threatening that the salesperson will lose his job if the consumer does not buy. Austria, Germany, the Netherlands, and Greece prohibit using psychological pressure to buy, such as using gratitude for a free gift or the exploitation of emotions like compassion, fear, or superstition. Several European countries also ban solicitations that are considered too aggressive or surprising or invasive of consumers' privacy (Maxeiner and Schotthofer, 1992). The Unfairness Directive establishes a minimum level of protection, allowing these more stringent protections to continue. A discussion of the ethics of inappropriate persuasion appears in Chapter 6.2.

Persuasive effects beyond purchase

Persuasiveness concerns beyond purchase cover a variety of issues: social equality, unsafe product behaviour depicted in advertising, and fair competition through comparative advertising. Though arguably within its authority, the first of those really never has been addressed by the FTC (Petty et al., 2003), but the US Equal Credit Opportunity Act and the Fair Housing Act prohibit racially discriminatory advertising for credit and housing, respectively. In Europe, the Television Broadcast Directive prohibits discriminatory advertising generally for that medium.

The Directive likewise bans advertisements that unreasonably show minors in dangerous situations. Similarly, Denmark, Ireland, the UK (self-regulatory) and the Netherlands require that advertising not cause physical or mental harm to children. The Netherlands expands this concept with specific regulation of sweets, banning promotion of: excessive consumption, meal replacement, and ridicule of those who do not eat sweets. Children's ads even must remind the audience to brush teeth after eating sweets. Portugal requires advertisements to mention safety precautions (Maxeiner and Schotthofer, 1992). Perhaps the most obvious example of safety concerns are the restrictions on tobacco and alcohol advertisements in most developed countries.

The FTC also has been concerned with depictions of unsafe product use behaviour (Petty, 1995). In *Mentholatum Co.* (1980), the Commission prohibited showing people wearing dentures for prolonged periods of time, contrary to product instructions. While that case concerned adults mimicking behaviour in ads, other cases involve mimicry by children, such as unsafe bicycle riding, using adult appliances, and eating wild nuts and berries (Petty, 1995).

Finally, comparative advertising has given rise to concerns in most countries. The US long has permitted comparative claims, and in the 1970s the FTC contacted the major television networks to persuade them to allow naming competitor products in advertising. It was felt this would lead to greater information for consumer decision-making. So the FTC rarely challenges such claims, but they constitute a majority of Lanham Act and NAD cases (Petty, 1992).

With some resistance the EC has come to allow comparison advertising, but with more restrictions than the US. Like the US, the EC prohibits comparisons that are misleading, unsubstantiated, or confusing about the source of the products. In addition, the EC requires that they concern essential elements of comparable products that are fairly chosen, and that they not be denigrating or unduly negative. The US merely requires that comparisons not be disparaging or falsely negative (Spink and Petty, 1998).

Intrusive effects

Regulations are a common recourse for limiting advertising intrusions into peoples' lives, and this has become even more common in the wake of new technologies. For example, a recent FTC decision entailed a company using misspelled domain names to hijack consumers browsing the Internet, then effectively forcing consumers to view web pages for adult entertainment, etc. (*FTC v. Zuccarini*, 2002). The FTC also has addressed other forms of intrusive advertising like the Telemarketing Sales Rule (2005), which prohibits not only deceptiveness but also bans automatically dialed calls to cell phones and telephone harassment (Petty, 2000). The newly added Do-Not-Call Registry allows consumers to avoid the intrusive telemarketing calls by placing their telephone numbers on the Registry (Smolla, 2005).

Other recent rules related to intrusiveness include the Children's Online Privacy Protection Rule (2005), derived from the Children's Online Privacy Protection Act of 1998, rules regarding Privacy of Consumer Financial Information (2005) in accordance with the Gramm-Leach-Bliley Act, and Rules Implementing the CAN-SPAM Act of 2003 (2005). Each of the statutes behind those rules guaranteed important privacy rights, but left the FTC to determine the specifics. Those rules fill in the details. When companies announce a privacy policy, the FTC also has targeted violations of that policy.

The EC Unfairness Directive condemns persistent and unwanted solicitations by any remote media. This includes automatic calling devices and fax machines under the Distance Selling Directive (Directive 97/7/EC), and e-mail under the Privacy and Electronic Communications Directive (Directive 2002/58/EC), without prior consent or the ability to object easily and without cost.

Many other agencies are involved with intrusiveness issues. Local agencies often are concerned with ads that intrude on the sanctity of public areas. Not long ago, for instance,

the Buildings Department in New York City ordered a 15-story ad removed from the historic Flatiron building, calling it a safety hazard (Lueck, 2005), and several years earlier in Palm Harbor, Florida, an 8-foot wooden flamingo advertising a carpet cleaning service was ordered removed because it represented "visual clutter" (Marbin and Journey, 1991). The ethics of privacy are addressed in Chapter 6.2.

SUMMARY

The law is constantly, but slowly, changing and adapting to new social realities, political dynamics, and new methods of advertising. This chapter has focused on fundamental advertising law concepts that form the basis for this evolution. Many regulatory agencies have some authority over advertising for specific industries. The US alone has the Food and Drug Administration, the Federal Communications Commission, the Postal Service and the Securities and Exchange Commission, among others. Furthermore, there are *many* federal laws other than the FTC Act that in some way involve advertising regulation. Less likely to spring to mind when thinking about ad regulation, are products sector-related such as the Plant Variety Protection Act (1980) which prohibits certain ad claims in the sale of plant materials. More obvious are those like Copyright Law (2005), which protects creative advertising materials from being closely copied without permission, and the Trademark Law (2005), which prohibits the registration of deceptive trademarks and prevents the use of marks confusingly similar to existing marks.

Most advertising laws and regulations are intended to protect either consumers or businesses, or both. While the FTC's original mission was to protect businesses from unfair methods of competition, two of its very first cases involved consumer deception. The commissioners quickly realized that business tactics aimed at cheating consumers usually have the consequential effect of cheating competitors (*Clarence N. Yagle*, 1916).

They were wise enough then to realise that business interests and consumer interests are inextricably commingled.

Since then the two interests were treated as discrete, and even as being two opposing ends of a continuum, although public policy swings over time to favour one interest or the other. For example, in the early 1980s, under the Reagan Administration, the prevailing school of economic thought was replaced by the introduction of "Chicago School" economists into the FTC (Richards, 1991). These economists felt that in a well-intentioned effort to *protect* consumers it was possible to over-regulate businesses, which could lead to reducing competition and the free flow of information, thereby ultimately *harming* consumers.

Advertising regulation covers much more than dealing with deceptiveness. The other three domains of advertising regulation are:

- *Persuasive effects beyond purchase behaviour.* Advertising not only urges purchase, it encourages consumption which may contribute to materialism, excess smoking or drinking, racial or gender stereotyping, among other things.
- *Intrusive effects.* Billboards frequently are banned or restricted, not because of their message, but because they are aesthetically unpleasing. Unsolicited e-mail and fax are restricted because they are intrusive.
- *Effects on political behaviour.* Advertising for political candidates, and concerning political causes, also are subject to regulation. Some laws are designed to insure one party (or cause) gains no unfair advantage over another by using advertising. Some ensure more information to the electorate. Whatever the intent, however, it is the political – as opposed to commercial – nature of the advertising that distinguishes these effects from those above.

While this chapter has focused on advertising regulation in the United States, the European Community (EC) approach has also been discussed and advertising regulation worldwide is evolving in similar ways.

Although some of their attempts to deregulate arguably went too far, they called attention to the interrelatedness of consumer and business interests. While they shone the light on over-regulation as a threat to consumers, a corollary to this is that under-regulation, while outwardly appearing to favour business interests, can be equally dangerous to business interests. The trick, of course, is finding the optimal level of regulation, to serve the best interests of society as a whole. Clearly, some regulations go too far and some not far enough. But because there are dangers in excessive regulation, and because the US has a First Amendment limiting government interference with speech, regulation alone cannot address every potential problem of advertising. Therefore, ethics and morality, or perhaps just a long-term view of corporate reputation, should rule where the law is powerless to stop abuses of the power and influence of marketing communication.

REFERENCES

Aronberg v. FTC, 132 F.2d 165 (7th Cir. 1942).

Arthur Murray Studio of Washington (1971), 78 F.T.C. 401, *affirmed*, 458 F.2d 622 (5th Cir. 1972).

Baudot, B.S. (1989), *International Advertising Handbook*. Lexington, MA: Lexington Books.

Beales, H.J. (1991), "What State Regulators Should Learn From FTC Experience in Regulating Advertising," *Journal of Public Policy & Marketing*, 10(1), 101–17.

Bipartisan Campaign Reform Act of 2001, S.27, 107th Cong. Section 214 (2001).

Bockenstette v. FTC, 134 F.2d 369, 371 (10th Cir. 1943).

Boddewyn, J.J. (1985), "The Swedish Consumer Ombudsman System of Advertising Self-Regulation," *Journal of Consumer Affairs*, 19(1), 140–62.

Boddewyn, J.J., (1988), *Advertising, Self-Regulation and Outside Participation*, Westport Cn.: Quorum Books.

Central Hudson Gas & Electric v. Public Service Commission of New York, 447 US 557 (1980).

Children's Online Privacy Protection Rule, 16 C.F.R. Part 312 (2005).

Clarence N. Yagle, 1 F.T.C. 13 (1916).

Cliffdale, 103 F.T.C. 110, 174 (1984).

Copyright Law, 17 USC. 101, et seq. (2005).

Council Directive 84/450/EEC of 10 September 1984 relating to the approximation of the laws, regulations and administrative provisions of the Member States concerning misleading advertising. Available at http://www.bild.net/dir84450EEC.htm.

Curran, C.M., and J.I. Richards (2000), "The Regulation of Children's Advertising in the US," *International Journal of Advertising & Marketing to Children*, 2(2), 139–54.

Curran, C.M., and J.I. Richards (2004), "Public Privacy And Politics," *Journal of Consumer Marketing*, 21(1), 7–9.

Directive 2002/58/EC of the European Parliament and of the Council of 12 July 2002 concerning the processing of personal data and the protection of privacy in the electronic communications sector.

Directive 2005/29/EC of the European Parliament and of the Council Concerning Unfair Business-to-Consumer Commercial Practices in the Internal Market. Available at: http://register.consilium.eu.int/pdf/en/05/st03/st03616.en05.pdf

Directive 97/7/EC of the European Parliament and of the Council of 20 May 1997 on the protection of consumers in respect of distance contracts.

Directive Concerning Television Broadcasting, 89/552, 3 Oct. 1989, *Official Journal* L 298/23.

Dommering, E. (1992), "Unlawful Publication Under Dutch And European Law – Defamation, Libel, And Advertising," *Media Law And Practice*, 13(4), 262–70.

Drumwright, M.E. (2007), "Advertising Ethics: A Multi-level Theory Approach," in *The SAGE Handbook of Advertising*, eds. G.J. Tellis and T. Ambler, London: Sage Publications.

FEC v. National Conservative PAC, 470 US 480 (1985).

Federal Trade Commission Act, section 5, 15 USC.S. § 45 (2005).

Foley, J.P., and the Pontifical Council for Social Communications (1997), *The Catholic Church's Handbook on Ethics in Advertising*. Vatican City, February 22.

44 Liquormart v. Rhode Island, 517 US 484 (1996).

FTC v. Keppel & Bro. (1934), 291 US 304.

FTC v. Sterling Drug, Inc., 317 F.2d 669 (2d Cir. 1963).

FTC v. Zuccarini (d/b/a Cupcake Party), No. CIV. A. 01-CV-4854, 2002 WL 1378421 (E.D. Pa. April 9, 2002).

Galloway, C.S., H.J. Rotfeld, and J.I. Richards (2005), "Holding Media Responsible for Deceptive Weight-loss Advertising," *West Virginia Law Review*, 107(2), 353–84.

Gordon, R.L. (1988), "Networks Hit for Ad Clearance Cuts," *Advertising Age*, 59(37), 6.

Grimes, W.S. (1971), "Control of Advertising in the United States and Germany: Volkswagen has a Better Idea," *Harvard Law Review*, 84(8), 1769–1800.

Horn, N., H. Kotz, and H.G. Leser (1982), *German Private and Commercial Law: An Introduction,* Oxford: Clarendon Press.

International Harvestor Co., 104 F.T.C. 949 (1984).

J.B. Williams Co. (1972), 81 F.T.C. 238.

Johanns v. Livestock Marketing Assn., 125 S.Ct. 2055 (2005), Docket No. 03-1164.

Kraft Inc. v. FTC (1992), 970 F.2d 311, *cert. denied*, 61 USL.W. 2091.

Lueck, T.J. (2005), "15-Story Ad on Flatiron Building Must Go, the City Says," *The New York Times*, April 8, B3.

Marbin, C.A., and M. Journey (1991), "Signs Of Change In The Air," *St. Petersburg Times*, June 17, 1.

Maxeiner, J.R., and P. Schotthofer (eds.) (1992), *Advertising Law in Europe and North America*. Deventer, Netherlands: Kluwer Law and Taxation Publishers.

McConnell v. Federal Election Commission, 124 S. Ct. 619 (2003).

McKinney, L.C., and D.J. Caton (1990–1), "What to do When the Attorney General Calls: State Regulation of National Advertising," *DePaul Business Law Journal*, 3(1), 119–65.

Mentholatum Co., 96 F.T.C. 757 (1980).

Newell, C.S. (1989), "Advertising Standards in Court," *New Law Journal*, (September) 1161–2.

Novartis Corp. v. FTC (2000), 223 F.3d 783 (D.C. Cir.).

Petty, R.D. (1992), *The Impact of Advertising Law on Business and Public Policy*. Westport Conn.: Quorum Books.

Petty, R.D. (1993), "Joe Camel and the Commission: The Real Legal Issues," *Journal of Public Policy & Marketing*, 12(2), 276–81.

Petty, R.D. (1995), "Regulating Product Safety: The Information Role of the US Federal Trade Commission," *Journal of Consumer Policy*, 18(4), 387–415.

Petty, R.D. (1997), "Advertising Law in the US and EU," *Journal of Public Policy & Marketing*, 16(1), 2–13.

Petty, R.D. (1999), "Tobacco Marketing Restrictions in the Multi-state Attorneys General Settlement: Is This Good Public Policy?" *Journal of Public Policy & Marketing*, 18(2), 244–57.

Petty, R.D. (2000) "Marketing Without Consent: Consumer Choice and Costs, Privacy and Public Policy," *Journal of Public Policy & Marketing*, 19(1), 42–53.

Petty, R.D., A.-M.G. Harris, T. Broaddus and W.M. Boyd III (2003), "Regulating Target Marketing and Other Race-Based Advertising Practices," *Michigan Journal of Race & Law*, 8, 335–94.

Petty, R.D., and R.J. Kopp (1995), "Advertising Challenges: A Strategic Framework and Current

Review," *Journal of Advertising Research*, 35(2), 41–55.

Pittsburgh Press v. Pittsburgh Commission on Human Relations, 413 US 376 (1973).

Plant Variety Protection Act, Pub. L. No. 96-574 (1980) (codified at 7 USC. 2321).

Preston, I.L. (1975). *The Great American Blow-Up: Puffery in Advertising and Selling*. Madison, WI: University of Wisconsin Press.

Preston, I.L. (1982), "The Difference Between Deceptiveness and Deception, and Why It Should Matter to Lawyers, Researchers, and Advertisers," *1982 Proceedings of the American Academy of Advertising*, 81.

Preston, I.L., and J.I. Richards (1986), "Consumer Miscomprehension as a Challenge to FTC Prosecutions of Deceptive Advertising," *John Marshall Law Review*, 19, 605–35.

Privacy of Consumer Financial Information, 16 C.F.R. Part 313 (2005).

Richards, J.I. (1990), *Deceptive Advertising: Behavioural Study of a Legal Concept*. Hillsdale, NJ: Lawrence Erlbaum Associates.

Richards, J.I. (1991), "FTC or NAAG: Who Will Win the Territorial Battle?" *Journal of Public Policy & Marketing*, 10(1), 118–32.

Richards, J.I. (1996), "Politicizing Cigarette Advertising," *Catholic University Law Review*, 45(4), 1147–212.

Richards, J.I. (1997), "Is 44 Liquormart a Turning Point?" *Journal of Public Policy and Marketing*, 16 (1), 156–62.

Richards, J.I., and C.L. Caywood (1991), "Symbolic Speech in Political Advertising: Encroaching Legal Barriers," in *Television and Political Advertising, Volume II; Signs, Codes, and Myths*, ed. F. Biocca, Hillsdale, NJ: Lawrence Erlbaum Associates, 231–56.

Richards, J.I., and I.L. Preston (1987), "Quantitative Research: A Dispute Resolution Process for FTC Advertising Regulation," *Oklahoma Law Review*, 40, 593–619.

Richards, J.I., and I.L. Preston (1992), "Proving and Disproving Materiality of Deceptive Advertising Claims," *Journal of Public Policy & Marketing*, 11(2), 45–56.

Richards, J.I., and R.D. Zakia (1981), "Pictures: An Advertiser's Expressway Through FTC Regulation," *Georgia Law Review*, 16, 77–134.

Richman, E. (1998), "Deception in Political Advertising: The Clash Between the First Amendment and Defamation Law," *Cardozo Arts & Entertainment Law Journal*, 16, 667–705.

Rijkens, R., and G.E. Miracle (1986), *European Regulation of Advertising*. Amsterdam, North Holland Co.

Rotfeld, H.J., and P.R. Parsons (1989), "Self-Regulation and Magazine Advertising," *Journal of Advertising*, 18(4), 33–40.

Rotfeld, H.J., A.M. Abernathy and P.R. Parsons (1990), "Self-Regulation and Television Advertising," *Journal of Advertising*, 19(4), 18–26.

Rules Implementing the CAN-SPAM Act of 2003, 16 C.F.R. Part 316 (2005).

Schechter, R.E. (1989), "The Death of the Gullible Consumer: Towards a More Sensible Definition of Deception at the FTC," *Illinois Law Review*, 1989, 571–623.

Schricker, G. (1990), "Law and Practice Relating to Misleading Advertising in the Member States of the EC," *International Review of Industrial Property and Copyright Law*, 21(5), 620–44.

Seiders, K., and R.D. Petty (2004), "Obesity and the Role of Food Marketing: A Policy Analysis of Issues and Remedies," *Journal of Public Policy & Marketing*, 23(2), 153–69.

Smolla, R.A. (2005), "The 'Do-Not-Call List' Controversy: A Parable of Privacy and Speech," *Creighton Law Review*, 38, 743–60.

Spink, P., and R. Petty (1998), "Comparative Advertising in the European Union," *International and Comparative Law Quarterly*, 47(October), 855–76.

Statement of Basis and Purpose of Trade Regulation, Unfair or Deceptive Advertising and Labeling of Cigarettes in Relation to the Health Hazards of Smoking, 29 Fed. Reg. 8325, 8355 (1964).

Sunshine Makers, Inc. (1992), National Advertising Division Case Report dated March 16.

S.U.N.Y. v. Fox, 492 US469 (1989).

Telemarketing Sales Rule, 16 C.F.R. Part 310 (2005).

Thompson Medical Co., 104 F.T.C. 648, 839 (1984).

Trademark Law, 15 USC. 1051, et seq. (2005).

Virginia State Board of Pharmacy v. Virginia Citizens Consumer Council, 425 US 748 (1976).

Ward, P.C. (1992), "Restitution for Consumers Under the Federal Trade Commission Act: Good Intentions or Congressional Intentions?" *American University Law Review*, 41, 1139–97.

Wilkie, W.L., D.L. McNeill, and M.B. Mazis (1984), "Marketing's 'Scarlet Letter': The Theory and Practice of Corrective Advertising," *Journal of Marketing*, 48(2), 11–31.

Zitter, A. (2004), "Good Laws for Junk Fax? Government Regulation of Unsolicited Solicitations," *Fordham Law Review*, 72, 2767–822.

Advertising Ethics: A Multi-level Theory Approach

Minette E. Drumwright

Advertising ethics. Just saying the phrase evokes many different responses. Some smirk and ask if it isn't an oxymoron – even "the ultimate oxymoron?" (Beltramini, 2003) Others insist that advertising is among the most ethical of professions because of close regulation. A common reaction is a desire simply to avoid the topic. Delving into ethical questions is hard for any profession. It raises complex and perplexing issues, and many prefer to let sleeping dogs lie. Avoidance, however, is probably never a good strategy; in a post-Enron, post-WorldCom world, it surely is not.

Advertising pushes the boundaries of what is familiar and acceptable. In such an environment, making ethical judgments can be particularly difficult. Concomitantly, scholarship about ethics in advertising faces difficulties ranging from making normative judgments to defining the object and scope of an investigation. Ethics is now considered a mainstream topic in the advertising literature (Hyman et al., 1994), but the amount of academic research on it has not been commensurate with its importance (Drumwright and Murphy, 2004). The scope of advertising

ethics is so broad and encompassing that research is thin and inconclusive in important areas, and some issues have received far greater treatment than others.

Historically, the topic of ethics in advertising has been examined largely through a bipolar approach – a micro-macro divide. The "macro" perspective focuses on advertising's effects on society; the "micro" perspective focuses at a more individual level–individual consumers, individual advertising practitioners, individual ads or campaigns, and specific advertising practices. I propose a third level: the "meso." The term is borrowed from organizational science (House et al., 1995). The meso level, between the micro and macro levels, is the level of the organization or groups of organizations – whether agencies, clients, or media. It has largely been ignored. Neglect of the meso level is particularly problematic because the organizational culture of advertising agencies has a strong influence on the moral[1] sensitivity of individual advertising practitioners (Drumwright and Murphy, 2004; Keith et al., 2003). Moreover, solutions to some macro level ethical problems to which advertising contributes require the collaborative efforts of organizations or groups of organizations (Brenkert, 1998; Bishop, 2000).

This chapter presents ethical issues in the context of a multilevel framework of micro, meso, and macro and concludes with a discussion of approaches to discriminating between ethical and unethical behavior and a summary. Before turning to the multilevel framework, it is important to confront a major problem, the law–ethics distinction that often blocks or impedes engagement with ethical issues.

THE LAW–ETHICS DISTINCTION

There is often confusion between law and ethics. Frequently the two are mistakenly equated. Other professions also confuse these two topics, but the problem seems especially acute in advertising.[2] Laws are ultimately a reflection of ethical judgments, and we often make illegal what we consider most unethical. A fundamental mistake, however, is to assume that because something is legal, it is ethical, or if something is unethical, it will be made illegal (Drumwright, 1993). Advertising law is a subset of the domain of advertising ethics.[3] It does not and cannot encompass all of advertising ethics. Nor do professional codes complete the task. In many professions, industry codes set higher standards than law, but advertising industry codes, such as those of the American Advertising Federation and the American Association of Advertising Agencies, are less helpful. They generally restate the law and focus largely on avoiding deception and staying free of fraud. Advertising practitioners can conclude that if something is not explicitly against a code, then it must be ethical. Ethical considerations may lead to laws or codes, but ethical judgment is also about making decisions in areas that are not currently regulated. Cunningham (1999: 500) defined advertising ethics as "what is right and good in the conduct of the advertising function. It is concerned with questions of what ought to be done, not just what legally must be done." Preston (1994: 128) observed that for advertisers who believe that the law is sufficient, "ethics never really starts."

Reliance on the law is problematic from several perspectives beyond the fact that writers in ethics generally view the law as the "floor," the moral minimum. Another problem is that law is often reactive. It is slow to be instituted, and it often takes effect only after a problem has become egregious. Even practices that are ethically egregious may not be codified in law for any of a variety of reasons. A problem may not be well enough understood to inspire legislation, or a legislative solution may not be available. For example, the First Amendment precludes law from dealing with some ethical problems that arise from advertising. Legislation to solve one problem may create another equally or more troubling problem. And of course, political interests often outweigh ethical judgments.

Many of the ethical judgments about advertising that have been codified in law involve manifestations of truthfulness – avoiding deception and staying free of fraud. They set parameters around what advertisers can and cannot do. They involve such questions as, "What are advertisers' rights? What can they do and what must they do to avoid deception and fraud?" The discourse around these issues is based on two fundamental assumptions: (1) that advertising is worthwhile from economic and social perspectives and (2) that advertisers have the right to persuade. When the discourse turns from law to ethics, it begins to question the assumptions. It is not about the rights of advertisers; it is about their responsibilities – what advertisers should do. The discourses – law and ethics – are often based on different sets of assumptions, approaches, and research paradigms. As such, the participants typically appear to be talking past each other and do not inform each other as much as they might (Drumwright, 1993). Participants in the legal discourse often fail to raise the broader questions, while participants in the ethical discourse often have difficulty bringing their discussion to the practical level of empirical investigation. This is, at least to some degree, a manifestation of the micro-macro divide and the paucity of integrating meso-level research.

THE MULTILEVEL FRAMEWORK

We now return to the multilevel framework that encompasses micro, meso, and macro levels. The framework enables us to think about ethical issues in advertising in an integrative manner and allows us to borrow insights outside of advertising and ethics per se. Management scholars have argued that multilevel approaches "begin to bridge the micro-macro divide, integrating the micro domain's focus on individuals with the macro domain's focus on organizations, environment, and strategy" (Klein et al., 1999: 243). The three levels are often interdependent and overlapping. The point is not to precisely categorize each issue at the correct level but to consider issues at different levels, since they often raise different problems and prompt us to ask different research questions.

Micro-level ethical issues

Effects on individuals are traditionally at the core of advertising research. Not surprisingly, much of the work done on advertising ethics falls in this vein. Like advertising research more generally, this work draws on psychology more than other social sciences and on experimental paradigms that examine the short term effects of specific stimuli, and there is more empirical research at the micro level than at the macro level. Micro-level research can be grouped according to questions about the message, the product, the target audience, the media, or the behavior of the advertising practitioner.

Is the message unethical because of inappropriate persuasion?

Perhaps the most prevalent issue related to advertising content involves the information versus persuasion distinction. Does the ad merely inform with facts, or does it use persuasive messages – for example, emotional appeals, self expressive benefits, and/or visual

representation – that may be harmful in some way?

Some philosophers such as Santilli (1983) have asserted that all informative advertising is ethical, and all persuasive advertising is unethical. Persuasive ads are objectionable because they can undermine the rational cognitive processes by which people determine what their needs really are. As such, advertising actually creates desires (e.g., Galbraith, 1958, 1967; Braybrooke, 1969), and consumers act on desires that are not really their own when they buy persuasively advertised products or services. The most common criticism involves the negative effect that advertising can have on individual autonomy, which is the "ability of an individual to recognize (and neutralize) the manipulative power of advertising" (Nwachukwu et al., 1997: 108). For example, Hyman and Tansey (1990) found fault with "psychoactive ads" that use emotion to play on the anxiety and fears of consumers in ways that can be harmful.

Others have argued that advertising does not violate consumer autonomy in any relevant way (e.g., Arrington, 1982; Bishop, 2000; Sneddon, 2001). In an analysis of image ads, Bishop (2000) argued that consumers have choice regarding whether they are exposed to most image ads, that they can accept or reject the creation of symbols and images in the ad, and that they do have choice in buying the product. Although Bishop acknowledged that image ads can create desires, he argued that the desires created are not compulsive, unconscious, irrational, or not truly the desires of the consumer. As such, autonomy of desire is not violated. Bishop's analysis is representative of the typical defence of advertising – "that consumers knowingly interpret visual or text-based messages, selectively choose meanings and resist rhetorical persuasion" (Borgerson and Schroeder, 2005: 258). Some argue that this defence is in sync with what consumers believe because "it does not feel like one is being jerked around and parted from one's money like a puppet," and as such, "advertising is implausibly seen as a threat to autonomous choice" (Sneddon, 2001: 15). In contrast, Pollay (1986: 23) referred to this perception as the "myth of immunity from persuasion."

The stance against persuasion at the micro level is problematic for several reasons. First, it sometimes can be difficult to make a distinction between information and per- suasion in an ad. Most, if not all, advertising messages appear to combine information and persuasion. Second, we often want persuasion regarding advertisements of social causes, such as prevention of drinking and driving, drug abuse, and AIDS. Should advertisers of social causes be denied persuasion as a tool? Few ethicists would say "yes." For less noble causes, one must ask, what is wrong with persuasion? Is it harmful because of its medium, the mass media? Are other forms of persuasion – for example, personal selling, telemarketing, or direct mail – wrong? That all persuasion is not bad does not invalidate concerns about inappropriate persuasion.

Is a message with puffery unethical?

Another potential accusation of persuasive ads is that they create false or misleading promises. Ads that create false or misleading promises are generally illegal and are dealt with in depth in Chapter 6.1. Some scholars, however, assert that puffery, which is legal, makes misleading promises (e.g., Preston, 1975, 1994; Prosser, 1971). Puffery is defined as "advertising or other sales presentations that praise the product or service with subjec- tive opinions, superlatives, or exaggerations, vaguely and generally, stating no specific facts" (Preston, 1975: 17). Prosser (1971: 723) asserted that "the 'puffing' rule amounts to a seller's privilege to lie his head off, so long as he says nothing specific …." Preston (1975: 29) referred to puffery as "soft core" deception and asserted that its "continued existence in the mass media shows that advertisers think it effective with a substantial portion of the public in obtaining reliance and altering purchase decisions." Others have dif- ferent views. Bishop (2000) argued that image ads do not create false or misleading promises because they do not make specific product claims and implied claims are discounted by

consumers as puffery. He also asserted that some implied claims (e.g., wearing a certain brand of jeans will make one sexier) could be self-fulfilling prophecies.

Puffery is generally acceptable under the law. Richards (1990) argued that scholars such as Preston use an overly broad, colloquial defi- nition of puffery and that the legal definition of puffery is narrower and precludes deception. The key legal distinction is between falsity and deception. Deception is a characteristic that is subjectively interpreted as injurious to consumers and, as such, is illegal. In contrast, falsity is an objective characteristic that may or may not be deceptive and illegal. The legal question regarding puffery is not whether it is false, but whether or not it is deceptive.

The Federal Trade Commission (FTC) and the courts view puffery as not decep- tive on three grounds (Stern and Eovaldi, 1984). First, they assume that reasonable consumers do not rely on positive expres- sions of praise by the seller in making purchases. Second, because these positive expressions of praise are not likely to be relied on by reasonable consumers, they do not have the capacity to deceive. Third, there is not an objective way to establish that general statements of praise are false.[4]

Is an ad message unethical if the sponsor is not clearly identified?

Ads that are designed to look like editorial material fall into this category, but increas- ingly popular *nontraditional* approaches such as product placement in films and buzz advertising fall into this category as well. For example, when Ford introduced the Focus, they recruited opinion leaders in key markets to drive and talk up the car without revealing that the company supplied it (Murphy et al., 2005). Do consumers have a right to know the sponsor of an advertisement or of marketing communications more broadly? In political advertising, regulators have decided that viewers have a right to know the sponsor of an ad.[5] Nebenzahl and Jaffe (1998) asserted that consumer autonomy is lessened when vital information about paid sponsorship is withheld. They recounted that the right to be informed is among the basic consumer rights that were adopted by President Kennedy and the Congress in 1962.[6] They asserted that the right to be informed includes the right to know if a message is sponsored.

When is an ad with a controversial message unethical?

Answering this question often involves making the difficult distinction between "pushing the edge of the envelope" appropriately versus being unduly offensive, in poor taste, or even harmful. Researchers have investigated consumers' perceptions of ad messages that are considered controversial, such as sexual appeals, fear appeals, and political messages. For example, a majority of respondents in Treise et al.'s (1994) study believed that there is too much sex in current advertising and that nudity is not appropriate for general interest magazines. Maciejewski (2004) found that female Gen Y respondents (individuals born between 1977 and 1994) were more likely to view the use of the sexual appeals as unethical than male Gen Y respondents. Both male and female Gen Y respondents appeared to be permissive of fear appeals. Forty-three percent of the consumers whom Triff et al. (1987) surveyed believed political advertising misrepresented the political candidates that they publicized. Tinkham and Weaver-Lariscy (1994) found that ethical judgments of political ads were salient and contributed significantly to global evaluations of political commercials. However, they found that an unethical political ad could also have a positive impact, if it tapped positive emotional feelings of the hedonic type. Questions have been raised regarding the ethics of negativity in political advertising both because of its increasing prevalence (West, 1993; Lau and Sigelman, 1998) and data that demonstrate that it disenfranchises voters, which can lead to low voter turnout and involvement (Ansolabhere and Iyergar, 1995). While prior research has shown that negative information about candidates is more influential than positive information

(Klein 1991, 1996), Klein and Ahluwalia (2005) recently have demonstrated that this is the case only when voters dislike the candidate.

Identifying potentially controversial ads that significant groups of consumers find offensive before they appear in the mass media has proven difficult. Recognizing this problem, Bush and Bush (1994) introduced "the narrative paradigm" as a tool to identify aspects of an ad that convey an underlying meaning that will be problematic to audience segments before the ads appear. In addition, techniques for scanning and evaluating media and public discourse to identify emerging social issues and attitude shifts could be helpful, if applied to ethics. Some advertising agencies provide "futurist" services such as these for their clients.

How do consumers make ethical judgments about ads?

Some empirical research investigates the manner in which consumers' perceptions of advertising ethics varies based on their personal perspectives on moral philosophy. For example, Triese et al. (1994) investigated the manner in which consumers' ethical judgments varied as a function of their stances on relativism and idealism. Relativism was defined as the degree to which ethical judgments are context bound and subjective versus universal. Idealism was defined as the degree to which consumers believe that acts should be judged as right or wrong irrespective of the outcomes versus the degree to which acts should be assessed as right or wrong based on their outcomes (pragmatism). Triese et al.'s (1994) results suggested that relativists were more tolerant of many controversial advertising practices and more likely to grant latitude to advertisers. Idealists were more likely to object to practices targeting children and to cigarette ads. Using Triese et al.'s approach, Maciejewski (2004) found that Gen Y respondents' stances on moral philosophy affected their perceptions of sex appeals but not of fear appeals. Although descriptive in nature, work in this vein draws upon a compelling theoretical base in moral philosophy.

Are ads unethical because of the product?

Is the client's product or service dangerous or problematic in some way? Some approaches to determining the morality of advertising hinge on the worthiness of the product rather than on the characteristics of the message, the media, or any behavior of the advertiser (e.g., Leiser, 1979). Ads for cigarettes, alcohol, gambling, or guns could be deemed unethical on these grounds, and marketing in each of these product categories has been subject to a high degree of controversy (Davidson, 2003). Nwachukwu et al.'s findings (1997) suggested that consumers make moral assessments on the basis of the product advertised. Respondents perceived ads for harmful products (e.g., cigarettes, alcohol) as less ethical than ads for nonharmful products (e.g., baby formula, athletic shoes). Likewise, advertising practitioners who refuse to work on tobacco or alcohol accounts are making decisions on these grounds. Determining morality based on the product's worthiness involves making what are often difficult judgments about the harmfulness of certain products and services. For example, are sugared cereals problematic enough to be considered harmful? What about high fat fast food or diet pills?

Some ads may be deemed ethical based on the usefulness of the product. For example, Leiser (1979) asserted that moral ads are those about products and services that are essential and useful, while immoral ads are about those things that people do not need. Such an approach requires determining what the genuine needs of various individuals really are. Do people really need designer clothes or expensive jewelry? Does everyone need the same thing? Are financial planning and nursing home insurance needed by some people and not by others?

The difficulties of determining the morality of an ad based on the product are at least three-fold: (1) how to determine which products are problematic enough to be considered harmful, (2) how advertisers (or anyone) can determine the genuine needs of various individuals or groups, and (3) how a message can be confined to the people who need it.

Others such as Santilli (1983) have argued that morality should be determined by the truthfulness of the message rather than by the worthiness of the product. They make a distinction between moral problems with making and selling a product as opposed to informing the public of the product, and in their view, advertising practitioners are not responsible for decisions regarding whether products should be made or sold.

Is it unethical to target certain groups?

If we assume that targeting vulnerable groups is unethical, then we have to examine the characteristics of the individuals in the target segment and raise normative questions about the appropriateness of targeting them.[7] For example, should a state lottery target people in low income neighborhoods, who can be more easily lured with the prospects of winning megabucks, or should the target be affluent professionals for whom the expense of a lottery ticket is trivial? Should a company with high fat, high sugar products target young children, who are unable to think critically about the commercial messages they see on television, or young adults, who have the ability and knowledge to understand the risks of their products? Should a cigarette company target nonsmokers, or should it target existing smokers? It is important to recognize that vulnerable groups who were not the intended or primary target of advertising can also be affected by advertising because of the inability to limit the reach of mass media. These issues are dealt with in Chapter 6.4. Here, suffice it to say that some people assert that advertising is harmful and immoral, even if truthful, when those receiving the message are unable to respond in a normal, mature manner. As such, ethical issues related to targeting typically involve assessing consumer sovereignty, which is "the level of knowledge and sophistication of the target market of an advertisement" (Nwachukwu et al., 1997: 108). The logic underlying consumer sovereignty is that knowledgeable, sophisticated consumers are autonomous and thus can distinguish between their own genuine needs and those needs created by advertising.

Smith (1993: 30) recommended a three-part test for assessing consumer sovereignty, which he asserted is based on "the promise of marketing ideology: promoting as first priority the interests of the consumer." First, the capability of the consumer must be assessed for vulnerabilities that would compromise sovereignty (e.g., young children's deficiencies related to reasoning and cognitive processing). Second, the quality and availability of information must be examined to determine if it is sufficient for the consumer to judge whether her expectations will be fulfilled upon purchase. Third, the test involves determining whether the consumer has choice and the opportunity to switch to an alternative supplier, which involves examining the level of competition and the "switching costs." Consumer sovereignty is product specific in that a consumer may be sovereign with respect to one product and not another, and it can be affected by the amount of information provided by an advertiser (Nwachukwu et al., 1997). As such, assessing the ethics of targeting a specific market segment involves understanding potential interactions among the target, the product, and the ad content.

Do ads, because of media characteristics, invade privacy?

Can consumers opt out of exposure to advertising? Is advertising "creep" through newly discovered media inundating consumers? Is new technology enabling advertisers to access and share consumer information in ways that consumers would not choose or condone? Accusations of intrusiveness and issues of privacy come into play. Determining whether consumers have a choice regarding whether they are exposed to advertising is an important factor in assessing accusations of intrusiveness and invasion of privacy. The characteristics of various media must be considered. For example, consumers generally can opt out of exposure to print advertising. Outdoor ads, which have been criticized for polluting the environment, are more difficult to avoid, but they comprise only six to seven percent of

total mass media expenditures (Bishop, 2000). Technological advances provide consumers with products that enable them to screen or skip broadcast ads. However, Hyman and Tansey (1990) argued that people viewing an ad often do not suspect that it will have images that they find intolerable until it is too late to avoid them. They recommended that advertisers introduce potentially problematic broadcast ads with an announcement to give viewers time to decide if they want to opt out. They also urged advertisers to use media with well defined audiences rather than a mass audience so that they can create ads with themes that are acceptable to specific audiences. New media and new technologies often create powerful "double edged swords." They often enable tighter targeting, providing consumers with more relevant information and lessening aggravation and waste, and as such, can make targeting practices more ethical. However, they also enable the collection and use of consumer data – data mining and data sharing – in ways that are beyond the consumers' control and that can violate consumer privacy. The continuing advent of new forms of nontraditional media and new technologies will keep issues of privacy on the agenda.

Is the behavior of advertising practitioners unethical?

The role and behavior of advertising practitioners themselves raise skepticism and mistrust among the public. In polls assessing consumer trust, advertising practitioners typically duke it out with used car salesmen for last place (e.g., Steel, 1998). In recent scandals, individual advertising practitioners in venerable agencies have been convicted for the likes of bid rigging, inflated billing, cash kickbacks, and excessive gift giving (e.g., Edwards, 2004a, 2004b, 2005a, 2005b).

Relatively few studies have examined the views of advertising practitioners. Of those that exist, most have used scenarios to assess the perceptions of respondents regarding the ethics of certain behaviors and practices (e.g., Davis, 1994; Ferrell et al., 1983; James et al., 1994; Pratt and James,

1994; Moon and Franke, 2000). These studies are helpful in identifying behaviors that are generally accepted or condemned and in revealing differences in groups' or individuals' perceptions. For example, in Pratt and James's (1994) study, the most criticized practice involved the use of outdated research findings to make an agency's campaign appear more effective than was indicated by new research results. Moon and Franke (2000) found that Korean advertising practitioners were more ethically sensitive in their reactions to the scenarios, on average, than American advertising practitioners. James et al. (1994) used scenarios to identify differences in the reactions of students versus practitioners. For example, students were more likely to apply deontological approaches (i.e., duty-based thinking) to ethical decision-making than practitioners. Deontological approaches are often contrasted with teleological or outcome based approaches.

A small body of work has surveyed advertising practitioners to ascertain perceived ethical problems. Rotzoll and Christians (1980: 429) reported that most of their respondents encountered ethical issues at work and that "most of the responses show a lively interest in doing the right thing." They ascertained that the major areas of ethical concern involved the content and creation of advertising messages and the agency/client relationship. Hunt and Chonko (1987) reported that most of their respondents reported ethical problems in their daily work, and more than half of them encountered problems involving treating clients fairly or creating honest, non-misleading, socially desirable advertisements. Hunt et al. (1989) found that advertising agency personnel, in comparison to other marketing professionals, "perceived their companies to have the highest ethical values" (p. 84).

Drumwright and Murphy's (2004) findings from in-depth interviews with advertising practitioners were not nearly so encouraging. They found that within their sample of the advertising community, significant numbers of practitioners either did not see ethical dilemmas that arose or their vision was shortsighted – a condition they referred to as "moral myopia." When ethical issues were recognized, there was little communication about them – a condition they called "moral muteness." Often rationalizations were the culprits that prevented advertising practitioners from seeing or talking about ethical issues. The authors categorized common reasons and rationalizations underlying moral muteness and moral myopia. Some advertising practitioners did see and talk about ethical issues. The ethically sensitive advertising practitioners did not differ from the others in any systematic way in terms of age, seniority level, gender, job assignment, or background. What did seem to matter was the context in which the advertising practitioners were working.

Wilkins and Coleman's findings (2005) regarding the ethical reasoning of advertising practitioners also provide reason for concern. Wilkins and Coleman administered a web-based survey to a nonrandom sample of advertising practitioners using the Defining Issues Test, a set of scenarios presenting ethical dilemmas that were developed by psychologists in the 1970s and have been administered to 20 000 people in different professions. They found that advertising practitioners demonstrated considerably lower ethical reasoning than journalists, lower than most other professions tested, and lower than US adults in general. Advertising practitioners used lower moral reasoning when the dilemmas were about advertising than when they dealt with other professions. Wilkins and Coleman argued "that advertising practitioners are capable of reasoning at a higher stage of moral development, but when asked to do so in a professional setting, they suspend moral judgment to focus on the financial implications of their decisions, specifically the financial implications for themselves and the client" (2005: 119). Working longer in the advertising industry was negatively correlated with moral reasoning, a finding that raises troubling questions related to industry socialization.

The dominant paradigm of micro-level research involves a consumer information processing model in which advertising is viewed as a conduit of information. Much micro-level work has been descriptive as opposed to normative, as has been the case for research in marketing ethics more generally (Dunfee et al., 1999). To advance, research cannot be solely descriptive and must engage normative questions. Relatedly, consumer perceptions cannot be the sole determinant of ethicality.

Macro-level ethical issues

Macro-level criticisms of advertising focus on the aggregate effects of advertising. They are sometimes referred to as "advertising's unintended social consequences, the social by-products of the exhortations to 'buy products" (Pollay, 1986: 19). Macro-level criticisms of advertising are a major part of the social and economic criticisms focused on the marketing system (Wilke and Moore, 1999).[8] However, there is little empirical work on macro-level concerns. Scholarship consists mostly of commentary and debate.[9] It typically raises a variety of far reaching societal concerns rather than focusing on answering a single question. Mirroring the literature, we will not focus on specific questions but on the broader concerns.

It is important to emphasize that macro-level criticisms usually do not focus on an individual ad or campaign but on the collective impact of many ads and campaigns. Whatever the ethics of a single advertisement for liquor or cigarettes that targets inner-city African Americans, the aggregate number of advertisements for liquor or cigarettes targeting inner-city blacks might be problematic. As an example, in Baltimore 76% of the billboards in low income neighborhoods advertise alcohol and cigarettes as compared to 20% in middle and upper income neighborhoods (Brenkert, 1998). While intimately related to micro-level criticisms of individual ads and campaigns, macro-level criticisms raise a different sort of issue.

Although there have been a myriad of social criticisms of advertising, many of them fall into three categories: (1) encouraging excessive materialism, (2) creating, or at least reinforcing, problematic stereotypes, and (3) creating false values and the resulting problematic behavior. The charges related to excessive materialism revolve around negative effects from elevating consumption over other social values, socializing individuals as consumers rather than as citizens, and using goods to fulfil social needs such as friendship and love. Examples of the harmful effects of materialism include inducing a work-spend treadmill, a general dissatisfaction with one's life, and a state of "affluenza," which is sickness from affluence (de Graff et al., 2001).[10] The charges related to stereotypes revolve around the manner in which advertising portrayals can selectively reinforce stereotypes, whether for sexes, races, ages, occupations, or any other group in a way that is harmful to that group. For example, in a comprehensive study of gender roles in television advertising around the world, Furnham (1999: 434) found that ads "typically show men as authoritative and knowledgeable, whereas women are confined at home." Taylor et al. (2005) found that portrayals of Asian Americans in magazine advertising conform to the stereotypes of them as the "model minority" – successful, hard-working, serious, and technologically savvy. The authors highlighted the manner in which even positive stereotypes do a disservice to a group as a whole and harm group members. Often, the most marginalized and vulnerable groups are the focus of the stereotyping. The specific harms of stereotyping typically involve damage to the self-esteem of group members and/or undermining their opportunities in addition to reinforcing and perpetuating the stereotypes among the entire audience. The accusations related to false values and the resulting problematic behavior are many and varied. For example, advertising allegedly promotes values that contribute to ecological problems (e.g., waste, pollution, over-consumption of natural resources), nutritional problems (e.g., over-consumption of high sugar, high fat, high caffeine products), self-image problems (e.g., idealized conceptions of female beauty), taste and decency problems (e.g., sexualized images, near nude images), and other harmful behaviors (e.g., idealized images of smoking or drinking). Macro-level criticisms are dealt with in Chapter 6.5 and Chapter 6.6.

Debate and commentary regarding advertising's aggregate effects have a long history and cut across academic disciplines (e.g., Bishop, 1949; Galbraith, 1958, 1967; Leiser, 1979; Pontifical Council for Social Communication, 1997; Waide, 1987). Pollay (1986) typified these writings by scholars from fields other than advertising and marketing as "a major indictment of advertising" (p. 31), which he characterized as "shocking" in its "veritable absence of perceived positive influence" of advertising (p. 19).[11] In contrast, advertising practitioners have difficulty taking macro-level criticisms seriously. Drumwright and Murphy (2004) found that the advertising practitioners in their sample were least likely to recognize ethical issues at the societal level. Common defences among practitioners and academics alike are that advertising does not create values – it merely reflects them – and that the real culprits are other parties – for example, peers, parents, regulators, media (Lantos, 1987). Because macro-level criticisms often involve subjective judgments (e.g., what are false values?), some authors merely admonish advertising practitioners to adhere to their own sense of decency (e.g., Bishop, 2000), which is a micro-level response to a macro-level issue. It is the aggregate effect that is problematic. If one individual changes, while commendable, it may not address the problem. Phillips (1997) argued that criticisms of advertising related to materialism are really criticisms of capitalism for which advertising gets blamed. Often, macro-level criticisms are met with micro-level defences such as advertising's role in providing information. Responding to macro-level criticisms with micro-level defences typically ends in a stalemate.

Accusations of harm done by advertising in the aggregate hinge not only on advertising's pervasiveness, persuasiveness, and intrusiveness but also on its lack of a social conscious or a sense of responsibility to society. Historian David Potter (1954: 177) asserted that "though it wields an immense social influence, comparable to the influence of religion and learning, it [advertising] has no social goals and no social responsibility for what it does with its influence, so long as it refrains from palpable violations of truth and decency." In addition, consumers have little education or training in understanding advertising's social, cultural, or pedagogical role or in interpreting and resisting advertising's influence as a representational system (Borgerson and Schroeder, 2005).

Macro-level criticisms often are premised on acknowledging that advertising can act as a "representational system that produces meaning outside the realm of the promoted product or service" (Borgerson and Schroeder, 2005: 257). As such, macro-level criticisms often hinge the "gross imbalance of the images presented" in advertising (Bishop, 2000: 381). Marketing communication's ubiquity does not necessarily improve one's capacity to engage in reflective analysis of it as a representational system (Schroeder, 2002).

The difficulties of dealing with macro-level criticisms are legion. First, it is difficult to imagine having any perceptible impact on macro-level social problems from the micro-level of an individual practitioner; we will deal with this difficulty in the next section on meso-level concerns. Second, macro-level criticisms are difficult to research. As Pollay observed, "… our research paradigms are at quite a loss in dealing with the fundamental questions in the macro market's evolution" (1986: 32). For example, since the alleged macro-level effects occur over time and are not typically directly observable, longitudinal effects must be captured, and appropriate measures are difficult and perplexing. But beyond that, there is the daunting difficulty of researching environmental issues from within the environment in which all individuals are already "treated." Pollay (1986) called for drawing on greatly expanded research approaches that draw from other disciplines such as history, literary criticism, sociology, and anthropology, to name a few. As an example, Ahuvia (1998: 143) advocated and demonstrated a "doubly integrated" approach to social criticism that combines literary analysis with the use of empirical data and also integrates the system by which ads are produced with the way they are comprehended. Schroeder and Borgerson (1998) used an interpretive method drawing from social psychology, feminist theory, and art history to analyze contemporary images of gender. Borgerson and Schroeder (2002) examined visual representations in ads from an interdisciplinary perspective that drew on ethics, visual studies, and critical race theory.

In part because they are difficult to research, macro-level criticisms are among the most contentious and controversial issues in society. There often is not a general consensus about whether a problem exists, or if it does exist, whether business has a responsibility to deal with it.[12] For example, some people claim that advertising's commercial effects on culture are positive and lead to increased prosperity, while others argue that they lead to "affluenza" (de Graff et al., 2001). Friedman (1970) argued that the social responsibility of a business is simply and only to create profits for its shareholders and jobs for its workers–not to solve society's problems. In contrast, others (e.g., Donaldson and Dunfee, 1995; Quinn and Jones, 1995) argued that corporations are responsible for multiple stakeholders, including society. Furthermore, the fact that society allows corporations to exist implies a social contract that imposes obligations on companies to consider society's interests in their actions.

Advocates of corporate ethics and corporate social responsibility have long argued that companies should be concerned with a "triple bottom line." In addition to the traditional, financial bottom line, responsible and ethical businesses should also be concerned with a social bottom line, which focuses on stakeholder relationships with the immediate community, and an environmental bottom line, which involves assessing the business's impact on the natural environment. Now some experts propose a quadruple bottom line.[13] The fourth dimension is cultural, which assesses a firm's influence and impact on the culture or cultures within which it operates, and puts macro-level issues on the agenda of socially responsible firms in an increased way. Given the prevalence of macro-level criticisms, the cultural bottom line seems especially relevant for firms operating in the advertising industry.

Meso-level ethical issues

During the past several years, the trade press has been abuzz with reports of scandals among venerable agencies and their organizational partners. An understanding of ethics at the meso level – the level of the organization and of groups of organizations – is critical to encouraging ethical decision making at the individual level and to finding ethical solutions to macro-level problems. Murphy (1998b: 318) referred to the primary players in the advertising industry – agencies, clients, and media – as "the unholy trinity" because of the opportunity that they have to "pass the buck" to the other players, causing ethical behavior to sink to the lowest common denominator. Unfortunately, there is a paucity of research at the meso level.

At the level of the organization, issues related to organizational climate, culture, systems, policies and procedures that encourage individuals to be ethically sensitive come into focus. In a study of how advertising practitioners view ethics, Drumwright and Murphy (2004) found that organizational context had a tremendous influence on the ethical sensitivity of individuals. In fact, it seemed to be the differentiating factor between advertising practitioners who were ethically sensitive and those who were "morally mute" and "morally myopic." In a study using scenario analysis, Keith et al. (2002) found that an advertising agency's ethical culture – especially the ethical behavior of peers – affected the comfort level and the ethical behavior of students who are potential employees. Yet, there is a dearth of advertising literature that addresses these organizational topics that encourage ethical sensitivity. As compared to other businesses, advertising agencies appear to be underdeveloped with respect to organizational codes of ethics and explicit policies and procedures that encourage ethical sensitivity. Pratt and James (1994) reported that advertising practitioners in their survey reported that they perceived strong reluctance on the part of their ad agencies to institute policies, either written or oral, that would proscribe unethical conduct. In a book of exemplary ethics statements, Murphy (1998a) featured only two codes from advertising agencies. Advertising agencies appear to be less concerned with the potential for perverse effects due to organizational and industry incentive systems. For example, there is little work on whether a powerful client's advertising revenues shape media programming and influence news coverage in undue ways. Historically, advertising agencies have been compensated on the basis of the media time that they buy for their clients, which has the potential to bias the recommendations made to clients. However, ethical problems with incentive systems have not been a major topic in advertising management research. It certainly appears to have been a major issue to clients, who have recently insisted on different approaches to agency compensation. Ethical leadership and ethical training are other organizational topics that warrant more investigation. How can leaders encourage and reinforce ethical leadership in an advertising agency, and what types of training programs are most effective in equipping advertising practitioners with the capabilities and skills needed for ethical decision-making?

At the level of the advertising industry, ethics codes provide a form of self regulation. The most prominent are those of the Better Business Bureau (http://www.bbb.org/membership/codeofad.asp), the Better Business Bureau's Children's Advertising Review Unit (www.caru.org/guidelines/guidelines.pdf), the American Association of Advertising Agencies (http://www.aaaa.org/eweb/upload/inside/standards.pdf), and the American Advertising Federation (http://www.aaf.org/about/principles.html). Self-regulation – the development of norms and responsibility for self monitoring – is one of the primary criteria for a profession, and

as such, codes play an important role in the process of creating and maintaining a "profession" (Advertising Faculty, 2000; Shaver, 2003). Yet, advertising industry codes deal primarily with micro-level concerns. They are largely a reflection of laws and primarily revolve around avoiding deception and staying free from fraud. As such, they do not deal with meso or macro-level concerns, and they pose some of the same problems as the law in that one could assume that if a behavior is not forbidden in an industry code, it must be ethical. Shaver (2003) asserted that codes require "a minimum level of ethical reasoning – the advertising practitioner must examine the decision or choice to be made and decide whether it fits into one of the established guidelines or rules" (p. 296). In addition, advertising industry codes typically are stated in terms of "negative absolutes" or practices that advertisers should not engage in. They might be more effective and inspirational if they were stated in terms of "positive absolutes" or meritorious duties that advertisers should do (Murphy et al., 2005). Awareness of industry codes is often low, and unlike self-regulation in professions such as law or medicine in which professionals' licenses can be revoked, self-regulation in advertising often imposes no real penalty (Shaver, 2003).

The most comprehensive mechanism for advertising self-regulation is the National Advertising Review Council (NARC), which was established in 1971 by the Council of Better Business Bureaus, the American Association of Advertising Agencies, the American Advertising Federation, and the Association of National Advertisers. It has two operating arms: the National Advertising Division (NAD) of the Council of Better Business Bureaus and the National Advertising Review Board (NARB). The NAD monitors advertising practice and reviews complaints. When a complaint is valid, the NAD contacts the advertiser and requests modification or discontinuation of the ad. If the NAD and the advertiser reach an impasse, either party has the right to review by an NARB panel, whose decision is binding.

Do groups of organizations have a collective responsibility for the cumulative consequences of their actions? Brenkert (1998: 13) asserted that a group of businesses can have a collective responsibility if they can communicate and act together even if they do "not have a formal decision making structure." He cited industry associations and joint lobbying efforts as evidence that a group of businesses can communicate and act together. Brenkert argued that malt liquor advertisers that targeted inner-city blacks had a collective responsibility for the harms that their collective actions imposed upon blacks. Likewise, Bishop (2002) argued that the fashion industry had such a responsibility in as much as the images it created had the potential to harm the self-esteem of groups of women consumers.

One could argue that advertising agencies are merely doing their clients' bidding, and that the clients, not the advertising agencies, bear the responsibility for collective action of the type that Brenkert recommended. This perspective reduces the advertising agency to the roles of craftsmen or implementers rather than trusted business advisors and professional counselors. If advertising agencies are to claim the roles that they desire both as trusted business advisors and as professionals, they cannot relinquish professional responsibility along these lines. Professionalizing the advertising industry through ethics education and training is one approach to affecting meso-level concerns.

Determining what is ethical

In an area as contentious as ethics, advertising practitioners and scholars would certainly benefit from a set of principles that discriminate between ethical and unethical behavior. However, agreement on such a set of principles goes to the heart of what we consider ethical, and that will probably always be under contention. That said, a few authors have proposed batteries of questions that advertising practitioners should address when contemplating whether an action is ethical. One approach is to elicit questions based on the issues specific to advertising such as those discussed in this chapter, while another approach is to fashion questions or tests based on comprehensive ethical theories. As an example of the specific approach, Garrett (1961) presented a battery of questions that deal with topics such as ad content (e.g., Is the information in the ad truthful?), the psychological effects of advertising (e.g., Does the ad seriously disturb the existing psychological position of the person without sufficient reason?), and social consumption (e.g., Does the ad and the product advertised lead to a waste of natural resources?) Murphy et al. (2005) adapted Garrett's list and proposed that advertising agencies and their clients develop their own checklist of ethical questions for their mutual consideration. While it is important to be systematic in asking questions, the checklist approach has shortcomings. For example, it does not tell one how to make ethical judgments; it only suggests what one should think about. As an example of the ethical theories approach, Murphy et al. (2005) proposed a set of eight questions based on ethical theories that are intended to provide tests regarding the ethics of an action. For example, will major damages to people or organizations result from the action (the consequences test)? Is the action contrary to widely accepted moral obligations (e.g., duties of fidelity, duties of gratitude, duties of justice, etc. [the duties test])? Does the action enhance the ideal of a moral community, and is it consonant with what the marketing organization wants to be (the virtues test)? Does the action leave another person or group less well off (the justice test)? While it is helpful to consider how ethical theories would play out in a specific situation, how does one know which test to draw upon in any given situation, and what should one do when there are conflicts between tests or even within a test? How would one apply a given test, and how would it translate into action? For example, what exactly does it mean to be virtuous or just in advertising? Which duties are the most important? Certainly, this is an area that is ripe for further research and reflection.

Issues and methods of assessing fairness in behavioral economics may provide a helpful paradigm.[14] For example, Kahneman et al. (1986a, 1986b) conducted experiments to identify the criteria that people use in their fairness judgments and the specific pricing and compensation tactics that they perceive to be unfair. Similar studies could be conducted to determine what consumers view as fair, virtuous, or meritorious in advertising. Note that Kahneman et al. (1986a, 1986b) found that the manner in which a tactic was framed made significant differences in perceptions of fairness, indicating that perceptual biases may influence consumers' perceptions. While consumer perceptions can certainly inform managers regarding the impact of advertising tactics, one has to wonder if consumer perceptions are sufficient to illuminate the ethics that should guide managerial action.

SUMMARY

Advertising pushes the boundaries of what is familiar and acceptable. Making ethical judgments can be difficult, and a common desire is to avoid the topic or rationalize. A confusion between law and ethics impedes engagement with ethical issues, often leading advertising practitioners to assume that if something is legal that it is ethical or that if something is not illegal it must be ethical. Law is a subset of ethics, and ethics often involves making decisions in areas that are not regulated.

Ethics in advertising has been investigated through a bipolar approach. The "micro" perspective focuses at a more individual level– individual consumers, individual advertising practitioners, individual ads or campaigns, and specific advertising practices. Micro-level research can be grouped according to questions about the message, the target audience, the media, or the behavior of advertising practitioners. The "macro" perspective focuses on the aggregate effects of advertising on society. Criticisms generally fall into three categories: (1) encouraging excessive materialism, (2) creating or reinforcing problematic

stereotypes, and (3) creating false values. This paper proposes a meso level. It is the level of the organization or groups of organizations – agencies, clients, or media. Issues related to organizational climate, culture, systems, and policies come into focus at the meso level as do industry level approaches such as self-regulatory codes and other collective actions of groups of organizations. This paper argues that research must incorporate an awareness of all three levels – the micro, meso, and macro. For example, the micro-level decisions of individuals influence the ethical sensitivity of the organizational culture at the meso level. In turn, meso-level issues such as organizational culture create a context that affects the moral sensitivity of individual advertising practitioners and their micro-level decisions about individual ads. It is often insufficient to determine the morality of an ad or an advertising campaign by looking only at the micro-level of a single campaign. A campaign must be assessed in terms of the collective effects of similar campaigns targeting the same group or groups. It is often insufficient to consider only an information processing model of research in which advertising is viewed as a conduit for information. Advertising must also be examined as a visual and nonverbal form that is part of a larger representational system. The Meso-level collaboration of organizations or groups of organizations typically is needed to affect macro-level criticisms of advertising.

Practitioners, scholars, critics, and ethicists will continue to disagree about what constitutes unethical behavior, when the line is crossed, where responsibility lies, and how to study ethics in advertising. Disagreement is not the problem. Avoidance of the topic is.

ACKNOWLEDGMENTS

The author thanks Tim Ambler, Janet Dukerich, Mary Gentile, Patrick Murphy, H.W. Perry, Jr., Jef Richards, and Gerald Tellis for their helpful comments.

NOTES

1 I use the term "moral" as a synonym for "ethical." This interpretation is slightly different from some of the moral philosophical accounts, which define morality as more of a systemwide practice and ethics to be more individually focused (DeGeorge, 1999: 19).

2 In a study of how advertising professors define ethics, Tucker and Stout (1999) found that the majority referred to legal analysis and stressed the rewards and punishments associated with adherence to the rules, rather than the intellectual process of reasoning and ethical analysis. The authors stated that "frequent references to legalistic analysis could suggest that advertising instructors draw more on law and policy studies in their teaching than from the ethics branch of philosophy" (p. 114).

3 Advertising law and regulation are dealt with in depth in Chapter 6.1.

4 For a fuller discussion of the defence of puffery, see Stern and Eovaldi (1984), pp. 375–7.

5 One can question whether providing the name of the sponsor of some political ads (e.g., MoveOn.org, Swift Vets and POWs for Truth) provides consumers with the information that they need to evaluate the ad.

6 On March 16, 1962, President Kennedy delivered a message to Congress on protecting consumers' interests in which he outlined the Consumers' Bill of Rights: the right to safety, the right to be informed, the right to choose, and the right to be heard. These rights were given the force of law in the Privacy Act of 1974 (Churchill, 1995: 65).

7 The March 2005 issue of *Journal of Macromarketing* is a special issue on vulnerable consumers.

8 Four of the eight classic social and economic debates concerning the marketing system that Wilke and Moore (1999: 215) identified were focused on advertising.

9 See the classic debate between Pollay (1986) and Holbrook (1987).

10 deGraff et al., (2001: 2) define "affluenza" as a painful, contagious, socially transmitted condition of overload, debt, anxiety, and waste resulting from the dogged pursuit of more.

11 Pollay (1986) provides an excellent review of the criticisms of advertising by scholars outside of marketing and advertising.

12 See Baker (1999) for an examination of five models for justifying persuasive commercial communication that vary dramatically in their assumptions regarding the motivations, roles, and responsibilities of business and the behaviors that can be justified as ethical.

13 This information is based on a telephone interview with Paula Ivey, president and founder of The CSR Group, a consulting firm that specializes in corporate social responsibility and corporate ethics.

14 Murphy et al. (2005: 179) characterized fairness as a meritorious duty. As such, it is one of a number of duties that a deontological or duty based approach to ethical analysis could encompass. Duty based theories were one of four groups of comprehensive ethical theories discussed by Murphy et al.

REFERENCES

Advertising Faculty (2000), "Thoughts about the Future of Advertising Education," White Paper by the Department of Advertising Faculty, College of Communication, the University of Texas at Austin, http://www.ciadvertising.org/studies/reports/future/future2.html.

Ahuvia, A.C. (1998), "Social Criticism of Advertising: On the Role of Literary Theory and the Use of Data," *Journal of Advertising*, 27 (Spring), 143–63.

Ansolabhere, S. and S. Iyengar (1995), *Going Negative: How Attack Ads Shrink and Polarize the Electorate*, New York: The Free Press.

Arrington, R.L. (1982), "Advertising and Behavior Control," *Journal of Business Ethics*, 1 (February), 3–12.

Baker, S. (1999), "Five Baselines for Justification in Persuasion," *Journal of Mass Media Ethics*, 14 (No. 2) 69–81.

Beltramini, R.F. (2003), "Advertising Ethics: The Ultimate Oxymoron?" *Journal of Business Ethics*, 48 (December), 215–16.

Bishop, F.P. (1949), *The Ethics of Advertising*. Bedford Square: Robert Hale Limited.

Bishop, J.D. (2000), "Is Self-Identity Image Advertising Ethical?" *Business Ethics Quarterly*, 10 (2), 371–98.

Bonifield, C. and C. Cole (2007), "Advertising to Vulnerable Segments," in *The SAGE Handbook of Advertising*, eds. G.J. Tellis and T. Ambler, London: Sage Publications.

Borgerson, J.L. and J.E. Schroeder (2002), "Ethical Issues of Global Marketing: Avoiding Bad Faith in Visual Representation," *European Journal of Marketing*, 36 (5/6), 570–94.

Borgerson, J.L. and J.E. Schroeder (2005), "Identity in Marketing Communications: An Ethics of Visual Representation," in *Marketing Communication: New Approaches, Technologies, and Styles*, ed. A.J. Kimmel, New York: Oxford University Press.

Braybrooke, D. (1969), "Skepticism of Wants, and Certain Subversive Effects of Corporations on American Values," in *Human Values and Economic*

Policy, ed. S. Hook, New York: New York University Press, 502–8.

Brenkert, G.G. (1998), "Marketing to Inner-city Blacks: Powermaster and Moral Responsibility," *Business Ethics Quarterly*, 8 (January), 1–18.

Bush, A.J. and V.D. Bush (1994), "The Narrative Paradigm as a Perspective for Improving Ethical Evaluations of Advertisements," *Journal of Advertising*, 23 (September), 31–42.

Churchill, G.A., Jr. (1995), *Marketing Research: Methodological Foundations*, 6th ed., Fort Worth, TX: The Dryden Press.

Cunningham, P.H. (1999), "Ethics of Advertising," in *The Advertising Business*, ed. J.P. Jones, Thousand Oaks: Sage Publications Inc., 499–513.

Davidson, K. (2003), *Selling Sin: The Marketing of Socially Unacceptable Products*. 2nd ed., Westport, CT: Quorum Books.

Davis, J.J. (1994), "Ethics in Advertising Decision-making: Implications for Reducing the Incidence of Deceptive Advertising," *The Journal of Consumer Affairs*, 28 (Winter), 380–402.

DeGeorge, R.T. (1999), *Business Ethics*, 5th ed., Upper Saddle River, NJ: Prentice Hall.

de Graff, J., D. Wann, and T.H. Naylor (2001), *Affluenza: The All-Consuming Epidemic*. San Francisco: Berrett-Koehler Publishers, Inc.

Donaldson, T. and T.W. Dunfee (1995), "Integrative Social Contracts Theory: A Communitarian Conception of Ethics," *Economics and Philosophy*, 11 (April), 252–84.

Drumwright, M.E. (1993), "Ethical Issues in Advertising and Sales Promotion," in *Ethics in Marketing*, eds. N. Craig Smith and John A. Quelch, Homewood, IL: Irwin.

Drumwright, M.E. and P.E. Murphy (2004), "How Advertising Practitioners View Ethics: Moral Muteness, Moral Myopia, and Moral Imagination," *Journal of Advertising*, 33 (Summer), 7–24.

Dunfee, T.W., N.C. Smith, and W.T. Ross, Jr., (1999), "Social Contracts and Marketing Ethics," *Journal of Marketing*, 63 (July), 14–32.

Edwards, J. (2004a), "Taken for a Ride," *BrandWeek*, Nov. 1.

Edwards, J. (2004b), "Shades of Grey: Inside an Agency Scandal," *BrandWeek*, Nov. 8.

Edwards, J. (2005a), "News Analysis: Greater Client Scrutiny Seen After Ogilvy Trial," *BrandWeek*, Feb. 28.

Edwards, J. (2005b), "Legal: Messner, Vetere Implicated in Alleged Kickback Scam," *BrandWeek*, April 7, 2005.

Ferrell, O.C., M. Zey-Ferrell, and D. Krugman (1983), "Comparisons of Predictors of Ethical and Unethical Behaviors Among Corporate and Advertising Agency Managers," *Journal of Macromarketing*, 3 (Spring), 19–27.

Friedman, M. (1970), "The Social Responsibility of Business is to Increase its Profits," *The New York Times Magazine*, Sept. 13.

Furnham, A. (1999), "Sex Role Stereotyping in Television Commercials: A Review and Comparison of Fourteen Studies Done in Five Continents Over 25 Years," *Sex Roles*, 41 (September), 413–37.

Galbraith, J.K. (1958), *The Affluent Society*. Boston: Houghton Mifflin.

Galbraith, J.K. (1967), *The New Industrial State*. Boston: Houghton Mifflin.

Garrett, T.J. (1961), *An Introduction to Some Ethical Problems of Modern Advertising*. Rome: Gregorian University Press.

Holbrook, M.B. (1987), "Mirror, Mirror on the Wall, What's Unfair in the Reflections on Advertising?" *Journal of Marketing*, 51 (July), 95–103.

House, R., D.M. Rousseau, and M. Thomas-Hunt (1995), "The Meso Paradigm: A Framework for the Integration of Micro and Macro Organizational Behavior," *Research in Organizational Behavior*, 17, 71–114.

Hunt, S.D. and L.B. Chonko (1987), "Ethical Problems of Advertising Agency Executives," *Journal of Advertising*, 16 (4), 16–24.

Hunt, S., V.R. Wood, and L.B. Chonko (1989), "Corporate Ethical Values and Organizational Commitment in Marketing," *Journal of Marketing*, 53 (July), 79–90.

Hyman, M.R. and R. Tansey (1990), "The Ethics of Psychoactive Ads," *Journal of Business Ethics*, 9 (February), 105–14.

Hyman, M.R., R. Tansley, and J.W. Clark (1994), "Research on Advertising Ethics: Past, Present, and Future," *Journal of Advertising*, 23 (September), 5–15.

James, E.L., C.B. Pratt, and T.V. Smith (1994), "Advertising Ethics: Practitioner and Student Perspectives," *Journal of Mass Media Ethics*, 9 (2), 69–83.

Kahneman, D., J.L. Knetsch, and R. Thaler (1986a), "Fairness as a Constraint on Profit Seeking: Entitlements in the Market," *American Economic Review*, 76 (September), 728–41.

Kahneman, D., J.L. Knetsch, and R. Thaler (1986b), "Fairness and the Assumptions of Economics," *Journal of Business*, 59 (4), S285–300.

Keith, N.K., C.E. Pettijohn, and M.S. Burnett (2003), "An Empirical Evaluation of the Effect of Peer and Managerial Ethical Behaviors and the Ethical Predispositions of Prospective Advertising Employees," *Journal of Business Ethics*, 48 (December), 251–65.

Klein, J.G. (1991), "Negativity Effects in Impression Formation: A Test in the Political Arena," *Personality and Social Psychology Bulletin*, 17 (August), 412–17.

Klein, J.G. (1996), "Negativity Impressions of Presidential Candidates Revisited: The 1992 Election," *Personality and Social Psychology Bulletin*, 22 (March), 289–96.

Klein, J.G. and R. Ahluwalia (2005), "Negativity in the Evaluation of Political Candidates," *Journal of Marketing*, 69 (January), 131–42.

Klein, K.J., H. Tosi, and A.A. Cannella, Jr. (1999), "Mulitlevel Theory Building: Benefits, Barriers, and New Developments," *Academy of Management Review*, 24 (April), 243–8.

Lantos, Geoffrey P. (1987), "Advertising: Looking Glass or Molder of the Masses?" *Journal of Public Policy and Marketing*, 6 (No. 1), 104–28.

Lau, R.R. and L. Sigelman (1998), *The Effectiveness of Negative Political Advertisements: A Literature Review*. Washington, D.C.: American University, Center for Congressional and Presidential Studies, Campaign Management Institute.

Leiser, B. (1979), "Beyond Fraud and Deception: The Moral Uses of Advertising," in *Ethical Issues in Business*, eds. T. Donaldson and P. Werhane, Englewood Cliffs, N J: Prentice-Hall, 59–66.

Maciejewski, J.J. (2004), "Is the Use of Sexual and Fear Appeals Ethical? A Moral Evaluation by Generation Y College Students," *Journal of Current Issues and Research in Advertising*, 26 (Fall), 97–105.

Moon, Y.S. and G.R. Franke (2000), "Cultural Influences on Agency Practitioners' Ethical Perceptions: A Comparison of Korea and the U.S.," *Journal of Advertising*, 29 (Spring), 51–65.

Murphy, P.E. (1998a), *Eighty Exemplary Ethics Statements*. Notre Dame, Indiana: University of Notre Dame Press.

Murphy, P.E. (1998b), "Ethics in Advertising: Review, Analysis, and Suggestions," *Journal of Public Policy and Marketing*, 17 (Fall), 316–19.

Murphy, P.E. and G.R. Laczniak (1992), "Traditional Ethical Issues Facing Marketing Researchers," *Marketing Research*, 4 (March), 8–21.

Murphy, P.E.,G.R. Laczniak, N.E. Bowie, and T.A. Klein (2005), *Ethical Marketing*. Upper Saddle River, New Jersey: Pearson Education.

Nebenzahl, I.D. and E.D. Jaffe (1998), "Ethical Dimensions of Advertising Executions," *Journal of Business Ethics*, 17 (May), 805–15.

Nwachukwu, S.L.S., S.J. Vitell, Jr., F.W. Gilbert, and J.H. Barnes (1997), "Ethics and Social Responsibility in Marketing: An Examination of the Ethical Evaluation of Advertising Strategies," *Journal of Business Research*, 39 (June), 107–18.

O'Guinn (2007), "Advertising, Consumption and Welfare," in *The SAGE Handbook of Advertising*, eds. G.J. Tellis and T. Ambler, London: Sage Publications.

Phillips, B.J. (1997), "In Defense of Advertising: A Social Perspective," *Journal of Business Ethics*, 16 (February), 109–18.

Pollay, R.W. (1986), "The Distorted Mirror: Reflections on the Unintended Consequences of Advertising," *Journal of Marketing*, 50 (April), 18–36.

Pontifical Council for Social Communications (1997), *Ethics in Advertising*. Vatican City: Vatican Documents.

Potter, D.M. (1954), *People of Plenty*. Chicago: University of Chicago Press.

Pratt, C.B. and E.L. James (1994), "Advertising Ethics: A Contextual Response Based on Classical Ethical Theory," *Journal of Business Ethics*, 13 (June), 455–568.

Preston, I. (1975), *The Great American Blow-Up: Puffery in Advertising and Selling*. Madison, WI: University of Wisconsin Press.

Preston, I. (1994), *The Tangled Web They Weave*. Madison, WI: The University of Wisconsin Press.

Prosser, W. (1971), *Handbook of the Law of Torts*, 5th ed., St. Paul, MN: West Publishing.

Quinn, D.P. and T.M. Jones (1995), "An Agent Morality View of Business Policy," *Academy of Management Review*, 20 (January), 22–44.

Richards, J.I. (1990), "A 'New and Improved' View of Puffery," *Journal of Public Policy and Marketing*, 9 (No. 2), 73–84.

Richards, J.I. and R.D. Petty (2007), "Advertising Regulation," in *The SAGE Handbook of Advertising*, eds. G.J. Tellis and T. Ambler, London: Sage Publications.

Rotzoll, K.B. and C.G. Christians (1980), "Advertising Agency Practitioners' Perceptions of Ethical Decisions," *Journalism Quarterly*, 57 (Autumn), 425–31.

Santilli, P.C. (1983), "The Informative and Persuasive Functions of Advertising: A Moral Appraisal," *Journal of Business Ethics*, 2 (February), 27–33.

Schroeder, J.E. (2002), *Visual Consumption*. London: Routledge.

Schroeder, J.E. and J.L. Borgerson (1998), "Marketing Images of Gender: A Visual Analysis," *Consumption, Markets and Culture*, 2 (2), 161–201.

Shaver, D. (2003), "Toward an Analytical Structure for Evaluating the Ethical Content of Decisions by Advertising Professionals," *Journal of Business Ethics*, 48 (December), 291–300.

Smith, N.C. (1993), "Ethics and the Marketing Manager," in *Ethics in Marketing*, eds. N.C. Smith and J.A. Quelch, Homewood, IL: Richard D. Irwin, Inc.

Sneddon, A. (2001), "Advertising and Deep Autonomy," *Journal of Business Ethics*, 33 (September), 15–28.

Steel, J. (1998), *Truth, Lies, and Advertising: The Art of Account Planning*, New York: Wiley.

Stern, L.W. and T.L. Eovaldi (1984), *Legal Aspects of Marketing Strategy: Antitrust and Consumer Protection Issues.* Englewood Cliffs, N.J.: Prentice Hall.

Taylor, C.R., S. Landreth, and H.-K. Bang (2005), "Asian Americans in Magazine Advertising: Portrayals of the 'Model Minority,' " *Journal of Macromarketing*, 25 (December), 163–74.

Tinkham, S.F. and R.A. Waver-Larisay (1994), "Ethical Judgments of Political Television Commercials as Predictors of Attitude Toward the Ad," *Journal of Advertising*, 23 (September), 43–57.

Treise, D., M.F. Weigold, J. Conna, and H. Garrison (1994), "Ethics in Advertising: Ideological Correlates of Consumer Perceptions," *Journal of Advertising*, 23 (September), 59–70.

Triff, M., D.B. Benningfield, and J.H. Murphy (1987), "Advertising Ethics: A Study of Public Attitudes and Perceptions," *Proceedings of the 1987 Conference of the American Academy of Advertising*, R50–4.

Tucker, E.M. and D.A. Stout, "Teaching Ethics: The Moral Development of Educators," *Journal of Mass Media Ethics*, 14 (No. 2), 107–18.

Waide, J. (1987), "The Making of Self and World in Advertising," *Journal of Business Ethics*, 6 (February), 73–9.

West, D. (1993), *Air Wars: Television Advertising in Election Campaigns, 1953–1992.* Washington, D.C.: Congressional Quarterly.

Wilkie, W.L. and E.S. Moore (1999), "Marketing's Contributions to Society," *Journal of Marketing*, 63 (Special Issue October), 198–218.

Wilkie, W.L. and E.S. Moore (2007), "Advertising Performance in a Market System," in *The SAGE Handbook of Advertising*, eds. G.J. Tellis and T. Ambler, London: Sage Publications.

Wilkins, L. and R. Coleman (2005), *The Moral Media: How Journalists Reason About Ethics.* Mahwah, New Jersey: Lawrence Erlbaum Associates.

Advertising Across Cultures

Susan P. Douglas and C. Samuel Craig

Advertising is a pervasive and persuasive component of society. Designed by firms wishing to sell goods and services, its manifestations are present in nearly all aspects of daily life as a constant reminder of commerce in society. Through the social roles it portrays, the language used and the values it reflects, it both echoes and fashions the cognitions and attitudes that underlie behaviour, not only in the market place, but in all forms of social expression. In addition to being an ever present business activity, it is an important component of culture. It mirrors the patterns of day-to-day life and the norms which govern social interaction. It communicates and reinforces the values which govern social behaviour and at the same time provides a showcase for the material artifacts which are a product of that culture.

Typically, advertising reflects conventions and appeals that are central to a particular culture or context. Consequently, advertisements created in a particular culture often show a high degree of congruity with cultural norms and mores. However, each culture has its own distinctive features, tastes, values, and behaviour patterns. Consequently, advertising created in one country typically differs from that in other countries. Where advertisers create campaigns spanning more than one country, they need to understand and account for these differences. Ads must be modified or adapted to eliminate cultural elements that are likely to be ineffective or inappropriate in other cultures. Further, appeals and conventions appropriate for the other cultures can enhance the ads' effectiveness.

This chapter examines cross-cultural advertising, which is defined as advertising that takes place in more than one culture. First, the nature and role of culture in advertising are examined, including the extent to which advertising reflects the value orientations of society, its material artifacts as well as the language used in relation to products and services. Next, studies that have examined advertising in different countries or cultural contexts are reviewed. These include studies that have examined the societal values reflected in advertising, how gender roles are portrayed and celebrities or children used as well as rational versus emotional appeals or visual components. After drawing implications for managers, particularly in terms of ability to use standardized appeals and suggesting some directions for future research, we summarize the chapter.

CULTURE AND ADVERTISING

Perhaps the most widely accepted definition of culture is the one given by E.B. Tylor (1881) who described culture as, "that complex whole which includes knowledge, belief, art, morals, law, custom and any other capabilities acquired by man as a member of society." This was later synthesized by Heskovitz (1955) as the "manmade" part of the environment, i.e., what distinguishes humans from other species. Cultural boundaries typically, but not always, correspond to the political boundaries that define countries.

The majority of studies that examine cross-cultural advertising look at the type and content of advertising that appears in two or more countries. The majority of advertising campaigns are designed and launched on a national basis. The media infrastructure is typically established on a national basis with major media such as TV, newspapers, magazine, and radio providing national coverage. Even in countries with linguistic subdivisions, such as Belgium or Canada, there are typically media with national coverage. Sub-cultures, such as ethnic, sociodemographic or other groupings exist within countries and often have their own distinctive interests, consumption and purchasing behaviour patterns.

To the extent that different subcultures speak different languages, embrace different norms, or pursue different interests, advertising campaigns targeted at them should reflect these differences. The relevant cultural entity or unit for developing advertising strategy thus becomes the subculture rather than the culture. For example, in the US advertisers have found in certain cases it is more effective to develop specific appeals and advertising targeted to Hispanic consumers (Kerrigan, 2002; McDonald, 2001; Koslow et al., 1994).

While a number of studies examine advertising for different cultural groups within a country, the emphasis in this chapter is on cross-country groups. Essentially, such studies consider the different themes and appeals that are used in different countries

and how these reflect different societal values, mores, and beliefs. They examine the way people are portrayed in advertising, gender roles in ads, use of celebrity endorsers, and advertising executions such as humour or the use of visual appeals. Thus, the primary focus is on examining how the content of advertising differs across contexts.

Underlying the contextual differences are fundamental differences in the cultural context in which advertising takes place. While culture has many manifestations it has typically been viewed as having three main dimensions (Sojka and Tansuhaj, 1995): values and beliefs, material artifacts, and communications. Advertising reflects these values and beliefs and at the same time is an important and pervasive form of communication in a society. These dimensions are evident to varying degrees, as advertising is a form of communication in a particular culture often selling material artifacts. At the same time how these artifacts are portrayed reflects the underlying values and beliefs of that culture.

Advertising is created in a particular culture by individuals who are part of the culture. The creators of the advertising are guided by their values and beliefs. Further, they use communication conventions and incorporate material artifacts that are part of the dominant local culture. The advertising is then directed at inhabitants of a particular culture who in turn interpret the content. Consumers interpret the advertising based on their values and beliefs. They also respond to the communication conventions and the material artifacts portrayed in the ads. These relationships are shown in Figure 6.3.1. To expand on this framework for viewing cross-cultural advertising, each of these different dimensions is examined.

Culture as value orientation

Cultural orientation, typically characterized in terms of Individualism/Collectivism has been a key theme in cross-cultural psychology and social psychology (Triandis, 1995; Oysermann et al., 2002). In marketing, cultural orientation has been studied primarily

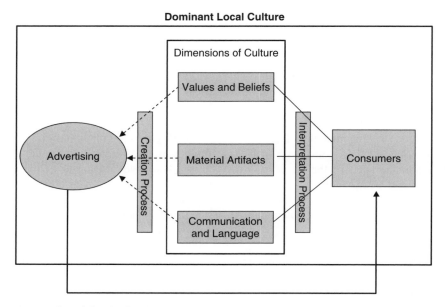

Figure 6.3.1   Advertising is shaped by local culture

in relation to marketing communications and cognitive processes. Differences have been found between individualist and collectivist societies in relation to the influence of consensus information on product evaluation (Aaker and Maheswaran, 1997), information content in advertising (Hong et al., 1987) emotional appeals in advertising (Aaker and Williams, 1998) and in the accessibility or diagnosticity of persuasion appeals (Aaker, 2000). These studies suggest the existence of major differences in the salience of appeals between individualist and collectivist societies (i.e., importance of the individual relative to the group).

Advertising also reflects the value orientations of society. Lifestyles, mores, and ideals are all depicted in the scenarios used by advertisers to display their products and services. For example, in the US the importance attached to cleanliness and hygiene is reflected in detergent commercials which stress the pride in a cleaner wash, while commercials for deodorant and mouthwash promise instant social acceptance. At the same time, it has been argued that US commercials aptly reflect the materialistic values of US society (Belk and Pollay, 1985).

The extent to which advertising reflects societal values may, however, vary from country to country. In Japan, for example, the primary purpose of advertising is to entertain. Consequently, in many commercials there is little or no "selling" as is typical in the US (Green et al., 1975). Rather commercials reflect a mood or emphasize visual images and often the only connection with the advertiser or the product or service being advertised is the display of the advertiser's name at the end of the commercial. The viewer is then left to make the association between the positive feeling created by the commercial and the advertiser's product.

Culture as material artifact

Each culture has its own vision of the world and set of culturally constituted meanings that provide understanding and rules for its members that may be unintelligible to others. Cultural categories of time, space, nature, and person are identified as the fundamental coordinates of meaning that organize the phenomenal world (McCracken, 1986; Applebaum and Jordt, 1996). Advertising provides one mechanism through which viewers or readers interpret the meaning of consumer goods (Tse et al., 1989; Belk and Pollay, 1985).

Advertising also reflects the lifestyles, mores, and rituals of society which are depicted in the scenarios used in commercials. In particular "slice of life" commercials reflect the day-to-day life and habits of individuals in a culture or sub culture and provide a picture of the customs, manners of inter-acting, and behaviours which characterize a particular culture. Insofar as products and brands are embedded in the cultural fabric of society, their role as cultural icons is also reflected in advertising (Chapter 1.4). The clothing worn by an individual symbolizes the owner's position in that society and may depict membership of a particular grouping. Similarly, food consumption patterns depicted in advertising form part of the ritual of daily life and punctuate daily rhythms. Advertising mirrors these consumption phenomena and displays the role of products in the cultural fabric of a society.

Culture as communication

Advertising is one form of communication within a society and provides a commercially motivated means of interpreting material artifacts and the meanings consumers ascribe to them (Chapter 2.5). Closely related to this is the meaning and implications of language as an interpretation of culture. Language has many facets that relate to the meaning of consumer products. Linguistic structure plays an important role in the formation of cognitive processes such as perception and hence judge-ment and choice (Schmitt and Zhang, 1998) as well as in brand recall and recognition (Schmitt et al., 1994) and the encoding and recall of information (Tavassoli, 1999). Equally, foreign language and loanwords can help in establishing the identity of a local (indigenous) product (Sherry and Camargo, 1987). Use of a minority subculture's lan-guage in advertising (Koslow et al., 1994) has also been found to impact consumer response.

The language used in advertising reflects the terms used in relation to products and services and helps to shed light on how they are used in day-to-day life as well as their significance in a social setting. The terms used provide an added richness and help to explain the meaning that products and services have for individuals. They help to understand and explicate their functional use in everyday life as well as to interpret their symbolic use in interchange between individuals. Differences in the significance which individuals or groups of individuals may attach to them are also clarified. Language may also have a different significance and role depending on the advertising medium. In print media the informational content of the message may be more clearly evident and play a more significant role than in TV or radio. In TV and radio the emotional content of the message may be more apparent resulting in emphasis on appeals to feelings and the senses.

CONTENT OF CROSS-CULTURAL ADVERTISING

Numerous studies have compared advertising in different cultural contexts, often the US versus another country, though a few have examined multiple countries. These studies can be classified in terms of the three main dimensions of culture: societal values, material artifacts and communication. Studies examining the societal values reflected in advertising look at broad macro-cultural val-ues such as individualism-collectivism as well as more specific values such as humour (Han and Shavitt, 1998; Cho et al., 1999; Zhang and Neelankavil, 1997; Weinberger and Spotts, 1989; Alden et al., 1993). Advertising selling products naturally includes material artifacts since products are the main focus of many ads. Other studies include gender role portrayals and the use of celebrities and children in cross-cultural advertising. A primary interest in many of the studies of communication structure in cross-cultural advertising is the use of rational versus emotional appeals as well as the manner in which different visual components are utilized. In sum, these studies

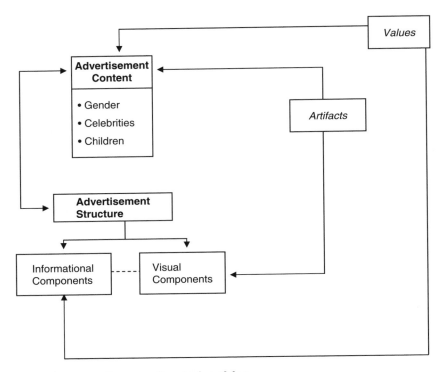

Figure 6.3.2   Elements of cross-cultural advertising

deal either with the content of ads or their structure (see Figure 6.3.2).

Influence of value orientation on cross-cultural advertising

Cross-cultural advertising and societal values

Various studies have examined the type of advertising appeals used in individualistic versus collectivistic societies (Han and Shavitt, 1998; Cho et al., 1999; Zhang and Neelankavil, 1997). One study (Han and Shavitt, 1998) compared the types of persuasive appeals used in magazine advertisement in the US and South Korea. Advertisements in the US, an individualistic society, employed appeals focused on individual benefits and preferences, personal success and independence to a greater extent than advertisements in Korea, a collectivistic society. Korean advertisements, on the other hand, emphasized in-group benefits, harmony and family integrity to a greater extent.

US advertisements emphasizing individualistic benefits were also found to be more persuasive and ads emphasizing family or in-group benefits less persuasive than in Korea.

Similarly, another study comparing US and Korean commercials (Cho et al., 1999) found that individualism appeals were more dominant in US commercials, but collectivism appeals did not appear to be more prevalent in Korean commercials. No significant differences were observed with regard to future versus past orientation or relationship to nature, as had been hypothesized, suggesting a greater movement in Korea toward Western appeals and values.

The same tendency was found in a study of advertising appeals in the US and China (Zhang and Neelankavil, 1997). Overall, US subjects were found to prefer an individualistic appeal and Chinese subjects a collectivistic appeal. Although in China, an individualistic appeal was found to be more effective for a personal product (a razor), than for a less personal product (a camera). Again, this may suggest that individualistic appeals are gaining ground in China as its economy grows and the level of economic development increases.

Humour in cross-cultural advertising

Use of humour in advertising differs significantly across countries. Used primarily as an executional device, it reflects underlying values which pervade society. Consistent with the greater reliance on a soft sell and more importance attached to entertainment in British advertising, humour is more commonly used in the UK than in other countries. Weinberger and Spotts (1989), for example, compared use of humour in television advertising in the UK and the US and found it to be more prevalent in the UK. This confirmed previous studies (Lannon, 1986; Nevett, 1992) that UK advertisers use humour more and in a different way from their counterparts in the US.

Another study comparing the use of humour in television advertising in four national cultures, South Korea, Germany, Thailand and the United States found differences between the four countries as well as some similarities (Alden et al., 1993). Despite the diversity of national cultures, they were found to share certain universal structures underlying the use of humour, and in particular the use of incongruent contrasts between expected and unexpected situations and of incongruity resolution. However, the specific content of humourous advertising differed.

Thus, there appears to be substantial evidence that advertising in different cultures is fashioned by the broad underlying values of society reflecting how these mold and influence societal interactions. At the same time, the set of academic studies that have been reviewed explore collectivism, individualism, and humour. However, there are clearly many other societal values that dictate appropriate or inappropriate themes. Some of these are obvious such as the avoidance of sex to sell products in countries with strong moral values. But, there are also subtle differences which if not taken into account will cause the advertising to be less effective. For example,

in comparing brand personality dimensions in Spain and the US, Aaker et al. (2001) found a number of dimensions common to both countries as well as one unique to Spain (Passion) and two unique to the US (Competence and Ruggedness).

Material artifacts and the portrayal of people in cross-cultural advertising

Gender roles in cross-cultural advertising

Another area which has attracted considerable attention in cross-cultural advertising is the extent to which people are featured in commercials and how they are portrayed. A study comparing portrayal of sex roles in television advertising in Australia, Mexico and the US found significant differences in the way the sexes were portrayed in all three countries (Gilly, 1988). In all countries, stereotyping was prevalent. In the US and Mexico, women were consistently less likely to be portrayed as employed than men and equally no women were portrayed in occupations that could be classified as professional/high level executive. Women were, however, portrayed in these roles in Australia. Equally, in the US and Mexico women were more likely to be portrayed in roles that defined them in relation to others such as spouse, parent or housewife than in Australia. Overall, Australian commercials exhibited the fewest differences between men and women suggesting that Australian ads are more egalitarian in terms of sex roles than US and Mexican ads.

An analysis of gender roles in Chinese and US TV commercials also demonstrated stereotyping. In both countries advertising portrayed more men in occupational roles and more women in non-occupational roles and depicted more men in recreational activities and more women in decorative situations. However, Chinese TV advertising was found to reinforce stereotypes even more than US TV advertising. Men, for example, played relaxing roles more often, but family roles less often in Chinese commercials.

A comparison of the portrayal of women in TV commercials in the US and Japan revealed some similarities and difference in roles considered appropriate for women. In both the US and Japan more men than women are likely to appear in working roles as high level business executives and blue collar workers. In addition, in the US, although men are as likely as women to appear in a family setting and in a recreational role, women are more likely than men to appear in a decorative role. In Japan women are also more likely to appear in a decorative role, but less likely to appear in a recreational role.

Examination of the content of women's fashion and beauty magazines in Singapore, Taiwan and the US (Frith et al., 2005) revealed a significant difference in the sexual portrayal of women in the three countries. The Asian ads featured a higher proportion of cosmetic and facial beauty products while the US ads were dominated by clothing. This suggests that beauty in the US may be constructed more in terms of the body whereas in Singapore and Taiwan, the defining factor is a pretty face.

Celebrities in cross-cultural advertising

Another area in which significant differences have been found in cross-cultural advertising is in the use of celebrities. Ads using celebrities are particularly prevalent in Asian countries such as Japan and South Korea where their use or endorsement of the product helps to give the brand "face." This appears to be linked to the tendency to place greater emphasis on status appeals reflecting the heightened efficacy of group-related appeals characteristics of a collectivistic society. A study of US and Korean print advertising (Cutler et al., 1995) found that Korean ads placed greater emphasis on celebrities who were significantly more likely to appear in Korean ads than in US ads (32.3% versus 8.5%). At the same time the use of a status appeal was considerably higher in Korean ads, particularly in the case of durable goods. This appears to reflect the Confucian philosophy, dominant in Korea, which emphasizes the class concept and different roles being appropriate for different classes of people.

Aspiration for respect, class, and status are very strong in Korean society and consequently provide natural appeals for promoting products in Korea. This was further confirmed in another study (Choi et al., 2005) in which Korean TV commercials were found to make significantly greater use of celebrities, especially male celebrities, than US commercials, particularly in relation to products characterized as low involvement thinking products.

Children in cross-cultural advertising

A number of studies have also examined similarities and differences in advertising targeted at children in different countries. Here as might be expected greater differences were found between TV commercials in the US and collectivist Asian cultures such as China and South Korea than between the US and other European countries, notably the UK.

One study of TV commercials directed toward children in the US and the UK found substantial similarities (Furnham et al., 1997) In both cases, males (52% in the US and 28% in the UK) were more numerous than females (40% in the US and 21% in the UK) with males generally portraying more central and authoritative roles and more often being used in voice-overs. This was true even though the advertisements were targeted more at girls than at boys. This appears to relate to the perception that males provide better spokespeople and are perceived as having more expertise than females.

A comparison of children's television commercials from China and the United States showed a substantial number of differences (Ji and McNeal, 2001). The Chinese commercials tended for the most part to reflect traditional Chinese cultural values. They were, for example, more likely to include informational content to avoid ambiguity reflecting high uncertainty avoidance in China. They were also less likely than US commercials to reflect fun/happiness/entertainment appeals consistent with China's tradition of collectivism and emphasis on group rather than individual hedonistic values. Somewhat surprisingly, in view of China's higher power distance and respect for older people as authority figures, US commercials were more likely to use adult spokespersons and adult voice-overs. This may, however, reflect the increasing importance attached to children with the one child policy, thus changing the traditional status of older people. Thus in general, compared with US commercials, Chinese commercials still reflect China's traditional culture. However, there is some evidence that this may be changing to reflect the new social reality of one child per family, as mirrored in minimal usage of adults as spokespersons and in voice-overs.

Not surprisingly, the way people are portrayed in advertising differs across cultures reflecting underlying differences in social roles and norms. People play a key role in selling products in advertisements as they help to infuse life into the mundane situations in which products and services are used. They provide a palpable reality for products apart from the solely functional attributes. Advertisers wishing to sell products in particular countries need to incorporate portrayals that are consistent with the prevailing norms.

Structure of communication in cross-cultural advertising

Information content of cross-cultural advertising

In comparing the content of advertising in different cultures, the amount and nature of information contained in the ads have received considerable attention. This has in some cases been related to the cultural environment of the country, i.e., collectivist versus individualistic cultures and high versus low context cultures. Since in low context cultures information is contained in the message rather than the context, rational appeals are more likely to be used in low context cultures and emotional appeals are more likely to occur frequently in high context cultures. This does, however, appear to vary depending on the particular product type. Some products, for example, functional products such as electrical goods or equipment, are more susceptible to rational

appeals than status or emotive products such as clothing or personal products.

A study (Taylor et al., 1997) comparing the effectiveness of TV commercials in the US and South Korea confirmed the importance of the cultural context in affecting information content. In this study, an experiment was conducted varying the level of information content in 20 matched commercials (10 high, 10 low information content) shown in each country. Since Korea is a high context country, it was hypothesized that Koreans would react more positively to TV commercials with low levels of information content. Conversely US consumers (a low context country) were expected to respond more positively to commercials with high levels of information content than to those with low content. The results largely confirmed that US and Korean subjects reacted differently to high versus low information commercials, confirming the importance of cultural context in influencing the effectiveness of advertising.

A comparison of service advertising in the US and Hong Kong (Tai and Chan, 2001) showed significantly more use of information cues in Hong Kong than in the US. Hong Kong ads also showed greater use of price cues reflecting a close relationship between price and concern for status characteristics of a high power distance society. Content cues were also more prevalent in Hong Kong ads reflecting the concern to protect group interests and eliminate uncertainty in buying decisions in Hong Kong, a high uncertainty avoidance society.

Several studies have been undertaken comparing advertising in the US and the UK. These typically find that UK commercials contain less information than US commercials (Nevett, 1992; Weinberger and Spotts, 1989). Weinberger and Spotts (1989) compared information content in US and UK advertising using the Foote Cone and Belding planning matrix. This showed a higher percentage of informative ads in the US (64.5% compared with 53.6% in the UK) though no significant differences were observed across the planning matrix. As expected, more informational cues were observed in relation to rational decisions than emotional decisions, supporting the thesis that the amount of information contained in ads is proportionate to the decision-making situation. This tends to lend credence to the belief that US ads are more "hard sell" than in the UK.

Nevett (1992) suggests that use of a softer sell is more acceptable in the UK as consumers are more interested in entertainment rather than learning about new brands. He points out that British TV advertising draws on a shared cultural experience, making frequent use of features inherent in British culture such as the persistence of class divisions and a tolerance for eccentricity. It often employs understated humour relying more heavily than US advertising on visual cues. As a result, UK advertising is able to establish a strong cultural relationship with its audience and achieve a high degree of social acceptance. It has, for example, been argued that the most marked difference between US and British advertising is the higher entertainment quotient of British ads (Bernstein, 1986).

A comparison of print advertisements in the US and France based on content and expression also found significant differences in the use of emotional appeals as also the amount of information cues (Biswas et al., 1992). French advertisements used more emotional appeals than US ads; while US ads used more information cues than did French ads. In particular, consistent with stereotyping and the perception that France is more sexually liberated; sex appeals were used more frequently in French ads than in US ads. Humour was also used differently with US ads making greater use of puns and satire, while the French ads relied to a greater extent on jokes.

While many studies focus on contrasting differences between the US and other countries, particularly Asian countries, emphasizing differences between collectivist as opposed to individualistic cultures, a longitudinal study of ads from Hong Kong, the People's Republic of China and Taiwan (PRC) revealed distinctive consumer cultures in each of these three countries (Tse et al., 1989). PRC ads emphasized utilitarian appeals, promised

a better life and focused on states of being as a key consumption theme, reflecting the relatively less developed state of consumption in that country. Hong Kong ads, on the other hand, stressed a hedonistic life style emphasizing luxury, promising easier Western life styles and focusing on doing as a main consumption theme. This reflected their higher living standard and greater openness to the West. Taiwan, where living standards were not as high as in Hong Kong, but were closer to those in the PRC fell between the two, but appeared to be converging toward Hong Kong in their emphasis on a more materialistic hedonistic life style.

Visual components of cross-cultural advertising

Visual components of advertising have also been found to differ across culture. In particular the significance and meaning of colours differs across cultures as well as the association of colours in different cultures, which can make them more or less appropriate in a given advertising context. A study of colour in US and Taiwanese advertising in business magazines (Huang, 1993) found, for example, that US ads used more brown and less yellow than Taiwanese ads. This may be due at least in part to the fact that yellow is considered by the Chinese to be the colour of royalty and is a favorite colour.

Another study contrasted the visual components of print advertising in five countries, the US, the UK, France, Korea, and India (Cutler et al., 1992). Differences were observed in the absolute size of the visuals with French ads having the largest size though this difference was not substantial. Countries spending more on advertising also made more use of colour advertising. As expected, the US was a larger user of photographs, though the differences between the US, the UK and Korea were not large.

Differences in the use of art and text in advertising from country to country appear in some cases to reflect the ability to express different types of messages using text or art. Examination of Japanese advertising reveals, for example, extensive use of mood and emotional appeals (Hong et al., 1987; Hudson and Watkins, 1988). This is in part due to the dilemma faced by copywriters in that the Japanese language is sparse in terms that are neutral with regard to status differences. For example, use of the imperative commonly used in US commercials is inappropriate as its use is restricted to superiors giving commands to social inferiors. As a result greater reliance is placed on visual images and themes which appeal to the emotions and rely on building atmosphere. Analysis of these suggest that some of the most dominant themes relate to eroticism and violence, which may reflect deep-seated emotions largely masked by the formal interactions and social behaviour characteristics of Japanese society.

Values, beliefs and material artifacts are all embodied in how and what people communicate in a society. Advertisements reflect spoken and written conventions, colloquialisms, and visual imagery. However, the way in which people communicate varies from one society to another. Some societies prefer more rational presentation of messages or more information content. This dictates how messages should be structured for maximum effectiveness as well as the nature of the content. These elements of communication are among the most complex and nuanced aspects of advertising. Yet, most studies have looked at one or two variables at a time. In reality, there are a multitude of interacting factors that should be examined in order to understand the full complexity of how and what advertising messages communicate.

MANAGERIAL IMPLICATIONS

A decision that managers face is whether to standardize strategies across cultures or adapt to each location. The increasing globalization of the marketplace has caused advertisers to seek to develop a more holistic approach targeting the entire world. Brands can thus be positioned relative to the emerging global consumer culture rather than being associated with a local specific consumer culture or

associated with a specific foreign culture (Alden et al., 1999). This objective is, however, rendered more complex due to the cultural differences across countries and also the differences in advertising conventions. Not surprisingly, an examination of issues related to standardized advertising (van Raaij, 1996) concluded that standardization was often in conflict with differences in cultures around the world.

As a result managers need to pay substantial attention to cultural factors when they develop advertising strategies. This should go beyond the broad issue of whether to standardize or adapt strategy to considering questions of execution and the role of cultural factors in advertising implementation. Even where some common theme can be identified, the campaign is likely to be more effective if there are differences in execution, for example, the way people are portrayed in advertising, use of local role models and symbols, or the use of humour.

While differences are observed within individualistic and collectivist cultures, for example, between horizontal individualism in Sweden and vertical individualism in the US, individualism-collectivism is perhaps the most basic dimension of cultural variability identified in cross-cultural research. Its importance in influencing the effectiveness of different appeals is clearly indicated in the preceding review. In high individualism countries such as the US, Australia, the UK and Canada managers need to consider the importance of tailoring appeals to the independent self and use themes that emphasize self-reliance, achievement, and autonomy and center around the individual. Conversely, in countries high in collectivism such as China, South Korea, Guatemala, Ecuador and Venezuela, managers need to emphasize appeals that center around the group and family and focus on concepts of harmony and blending in and integrating with others.

Cultures also differ on other dimensions identified by Hofstede (2001) and these differences need to be taken into consideration in designing advertising appeals. Countries high on uncertainty avoidance are likely to be more responsive to appeals reflecting security and a stable environment while egalitarian appeals reflecting equality and absence of class differences in society are likely to be more effective in countries low on Power Distance.

Another important dimension on which countries differ is high context and low context. In high context countries such as Japan, South Korea, and China, information is contained in the context of the message rather than the message itself. In low context countries such as the United States and the United Kingdom, information is contained explicitly in the message itself. In many respects these differences overlap those of individualism/collectivism in that individualistic countries tend to be low context and collectivistic countries tend to be high context. This distinction has, however, important implications for information content in advertising. In low context cultures, managers need to pay greater attention to the provision of informational content in advertising, whereas in low context cultures such as Japan, emotional appeals emphasizing visual content are likely to be more effective.

Given the range of differences observed across cultures, it is prudent for any firm contemplating an advertising campaign that spans more than one country to rely on local advertising agencies that are knowledgeable about the local culture and know best how to communicate effectively. For major advertising campaigns that are being coordinated by large global advertising agencies, agencies have local offices or affiliates in each country to help ensure that the ads are appropriate. This type of oversight and consultation will help create ads that conform to local cultural norms and communicate effectively. There is one final caveat. The results of academic research studies discussed in this chapter are biased toward showing differences. Not that the reported research studies themselves are flawed, but rather research studies that find no differences between countries are unlikely to be accepted for publication in peer reviewed journals. Thus, research that found no differences is less likely to appear in the literature,

creating an impression that differences predominate. While there are profound and systematic differences, as many of the reported studies indicate, there are also important similarities in advertising across countries.

DIRECTIONS FOR FUTURE RESEARCH

Overall, the studies reviewed in this chapter deal with the underlying cultural values of a particular society, portray artifacts as part of the ads content and employ a particular language and communications conventions. The individual findings of various studies combine to suggest that there are important differences between ads appearing in different parts of the world. However, with the exception of themes evident in collectivist versus individualistic societies, it is hard to identify consistent findings that help establish clear rules for cross-cultural advertising. The clearest finding is that ads are different reflecting difference in the values of the cultures in which they appear.

Considerable additional research is needed in order to better understand the role of cultural factors in advertising in a broader ranges of cultures. To date, most research focuses on comparing advertising in the United States with that in other countries, particularly in Asia such as South Korea, China, Taiwan, and Hong Kong, and to a lesser extent in Europe. Research is needed to examine advertising appeals used in countries in Latin America and in the Middle East to see how these differ with those in other countries.

In essence, previous research consists of a patchwork of studies often focusing on comparing ads in different countries and relating these to macro-environmental characteristics such as societal values – individualism/collectivism, high versus low context, etc. Going forward, the most fruitful area for additional research is continued focus on the role of values in shaping advertising. Values are the most central element of a culture and influence, to varying degrees, all its aspects. Further research is needed to probe understanding of the role of values in influencing the composition and appearance of ads and the mechanisms by which social values affect the success of these ads. This is particularly critical as cultures become more intertwined and elements of one culture, for example, individualism begins to creep into another, for example, collectivist cultures (see Craig and Douglas, 2006).

Further, the majority of the studies have examined differences in the content of the ads in different countries. However, the studies have not taken the next step to see whether this translates into more effective advertising. The implicit assumption has been that if a particular practice is more prevalent, it must be more effective. This assumption needs to be verified. Rather than descriptive studies comparing ads and relating these to environmental characteristics such as values, more experimental studies need to be conducted, examining the effectiveness of using different types of ads, for example, different appeals, use of celebrities, information content, etc.

In addition, attention has primarily been focused on differences in advertising in different countries. More emphasis might be placed on examining common elements in themes and in execution. While managers need to be sensitive to differences, it is also important to identify common elements which can aid managers in improving the cost efficiency of their advertising campaigns and in achieving potential synergies across different markets.

Finally, attitudes toward the use of foreign or global images and icons might be further investigated. Most attention has been focused on responsiveness to local role models, scenarios and images. As, however, markets become increasingly integrated world wide, attitudes toward foreign images may be changing and interest in global images may be increasing. More emphasis needs to be placed on examining visual effects which are more readily transferable across cultures than information content.

Better understanding of these images and effects will help in adapting advertising campaigns to the changes taking place in the global marketplace.

SUMMARY

- Cross-cultural advertising is defined as advertising that takes place in more than one culture.
- Culture is generally viewed as having three dimensions – values and beliefs, material artifacts, and communications. It has a profound influence on advertising and the way it is portrayed and interpreted in different contexts.
- The values and beliefs which are the core of a culture (e.g., individualist versus collectivist societies) are reflected in the themes and appeals used in advertising. The material artifacts of a culture (e.g., gender roles, use of celebrities) are portrayed in the scenarios depicted in TV, radio, billboards, posters, on the Internet, and in print advertising. At the same time the communication and language used in advertising (e.g., informational versus emotional appeals) mirrors the way in which individuals interact and respond to each other. These all vary from country to country.
- This relationship is not unidirectional – advertising exerts some influence on culture, as elements of advertising slogans or images become incorporated more broadly into normal discourse.
- While it is clear that business and marketing activities are becoming increasingly global, it is far less evident whether a common advertising theme is likely to be effective in diverse cultures. It would seem that standardization is generally in conflict with differences in cultures around the world, and that advertising themes (or at least their executions) must adapt and respond to cultural differences.
- Research consistently finds that advertising across countries should reflect the fundamental underlying cultural differences between those countries and their different expectations from advertising, for example, the US expects more information and less entertainment than the UK.
- With this range of differences observed across cultures, firms attempting cross-country advertising should rely on local advertising agencies or offices that are knowledgeable about the local culture.

REFERENCES

Aaker, J.L. (2000), "Accessibility or Diagnosticity? Disentangling the Influence of Culture on Persuasion Processes and Attitudes," *Journal of Consumer Research*, 26, 4, 340–57.

Aaker, J.L. and D. Maheswaran (1997), "The Effect of Cultural Orientation on Persuasion," *Journal of Consumer Research,* 24, 3, 315–28.

Aaker, J.L. and P. Williams (1998), "Empathy versus Pride: The Influence of Emotional Appeals across Cultures," *Journal of Consumer Research,* 25, 3, 241–61.

Aaker, J.L., V.B. Martinez, and J. Garolera (2001), "Consumption Symbols as Carriers of Culture, A Study of Japanese and Spanish Brand Personality Constructs," *Journal of Personality and Social Psychology,* 81, 3, 492–508.

Alden, D.L., J. Benedict, E.M. Steenkamp, and R. Batra (1999), "Brand Positioning through Advertising in Asia, North America and Europe: The Role of Global Consumer Culture," *Journal of Marketing,* 63, 1, 75–87.

Alden, D.L., W.D. Hoyer, and C. Lee (1993), "Identifying Global and Culture-Specific Dimensions of Humor in Advertising: A Multinational Analysis," *Journal of Marketing,* 52, 2, 64–75.

Applebaum, K. and I. Jordt (1996), "Notes Towards an Application of McCracken's Cultural Categories for Cross-Cultural Consumer Research," *Journal of Consumer Research,* 23, 3, 204–17.

Belk, R.W. and R.W. Pollay (1985), "Materialism and Status Appeals in Japanese and U.S. Print Advertising," *International Marketing Review,* 2, 12, 38–47.

Bernstein, D. (1986), "The Television Commercial: An Essay," in *British Television Advertising: The First 30 Years,* ed. H. Brain, 251–86.

Biswas, A., J.E. Olsen, and V. Carlet (1992), "A Comparison of Print Advertisements from the United States and France," *Journal of Advertising,* 21, 4, 73–82.

Carrier, J. (1991), "Gifts in a World of Commodities: The Ideology of the Perfect Gift in American Society," *Social Analysis,* 29, 1, 19–37.

Cho, B., U. Kwon, J.W. Gentry, S. Ju, and F. Krupp (1999), "Cultural Values Reflected in Theme and Execution: A Comparative Study of U.S. and Korean Television Commercials," *Journal of Advertising,* 28, 4, 59–73.

Choi, S.M., W.-N. Lee, and H.-J. Kim (2005), "Lessons From the Rich and Famous: A Cross-Cultural Comparison of Celebrity Endorsement in Advertising," *Journal of Advertising,* 34, 2, 85.

Craig, C.S. and S.P. Douglas (2006), "Beyond National Culture: Implications of Cultural Dynamics for Consumer Research," *International Marketing Review ,* 23, 3, 327–42.

Cutler, B.D., R.G. Javalgi, and D. Lee (1995), "The Portrayal of People in Magazine Advertisements: The United States and Korea," *Journal of International Consumer Marketing,* 8, 2, 45–58.

Cutler, B.D., R.G. Javalgi, and M.K. Erramilli (1992), "The Visual Components of Print Advertising: A Five-Country Cross-Cultural Analysis," *European Journal of Marketing,* 26, 2, 7–20.

Frith, K., P. Shaw, and H. Cheng (2005), "The Construction of Beauty: A Cross-Cultural Analysis of Women's Magazine Advertising," *Journal of Communication,* 55, 1, 56–70.

Furnham, A., S. Abramsky, and B. Gunter (1997), "A Cross-Cultural Content Analysis of Children's Television Advertisements," *Sex Roles,* 37, 1/2, 91.

Gilly, M.C. (1988), "Sex Roles in Advertising: A Comparison of Television Advertisements in Australia, Mexico, and the United States," *Journal of Marketing,* 52, 2, 75–85.

Green, R.T., W.H. Cunningham, and I.C.M. Cunningham (1975), "The Effectiveness of Standardized Global Advertising," *Journal of Advertising,* 4, 3, 25–30.

Han, S.-P. and S. Shavitt (1998), "Persuasion and Culture: Advertising Appeals in Individualistic and Collectivistic Societies," *Journal of Experimental Social Psychology,* 30, 326–50.

Herskovits, M.J. (1955), *Cultural Dynamics,* New York: Alfred A. Knopf.

Hofstede, G. (2001), *Culture's Consequences: Comparing Values, Behaviors, Institutions and Organizations Across Cultures,* Thousand Oaks, CA: Sage.

Hong, J.W., A. Muderrisoglu, and G.M. Zinkham (1987), "Cultural Differences and Advertising Expression: A Comparative Content Analysis of Japanese and US Magazine Advertising," *Journal of Advertising,* 1, 16, 55–86.

Huang, J.-H. (1993), "Color in U.S. and Taiwanese Industrial Advertising," *Industrial Marketing Management,* 22, 195–8.

Ji, M.F. and J.U. McNeal (2001), "How Chinese Children's Commercials Differ From Those of the United States: A Content Analysis," *Journal of Advertising,* 30, 3, 79–92.

Joy, A. (2001), "Gift-giving in Hong Kong and the Continuum of Social Ties," *Journal of Consumer Research,* 28, 2, 239–56.

Keller, K.L. (2007), "Advertising and Brand Equity," in *The SAGE Handbook of Advertising,* eds. Gerard J. Tellis and Tim Ambler, London: Sage Publications.

Kerrigan, J. (2002), "Playing to Hispanics Garners Rewards," *Marketing News,* July 22.

Koslow, S., P.M. Shamdasani, and E.E. Touchstone (1994), "Exploring Language Effects in Ethnic Advertising: A Sociolinguistic Perspective," *Journal of Consumer Research,* 20, 575–85.

Krober, A.L. and C. Kluckholn (1952), "Culture: A Critical Review of Concepts and Definitions," *Papers of the Peabody Museum of American Archeology and Ethnology,* 47 (1), 1–223, Cambridge, MA: Harvard University.

Lannon, J. (1986), "New Techniques for Understanding Consumer Reactions to Advertising," *Journal of Advertising Research,* 26, 4, 6–9.

McCracken, G. (1986), "Culture and Consumption: A Theoretical Account of the Structure and Movement of the Cultural Meaning of Consumer Goods," *Journal of Consumer Research,* 13, 1, 71–84.

McDonald, M. (2001), " Madison Avenue's New Latin Beat," *US News and World Report,* June 4th.

Mehta, R. and R.W. Belk (1991), "Artifacts, Identity and Transition: Favorite Possessions of Indians and Indian Immigrants to the United States," *Journal of Consumer Research,* 17, 4, 398–411.

Nevett, T. (1992), "Differences Between American and British Television Advertising: Explanations and Implications," *Journal of Advertising,* 21, 4, 61–71.

Oysermann, D., H. Coon, and M. Kemmelmeier (2002), "Rethinking Individualism and Collectivism: Evaluation of Theoretical Assumptions and Meta-Analyses," *Psychological Bulletin,* 128, 1, 3–72.

Schmitt, B.H., Y. Pan, and N.T. Tavassoli (1994), "Language and Consumer Memory: The Impact of Linguistic Differences Between Chinese and English," *Journal of Consumer Research,* 21, 3, 419–31.

Schmitt, B. and S. Zang (1998), "Language, Structure and Categorization: A Study of Classifiers in Consumer Cognition, Judgment and Choice," *Journal of Consumer Research,* 25, 2, 108–22.

Sherry, J.F. and E.G. Carmago (1987), "'May Your Life Be Marvelous': English Language Labeling and the Semiotics of Japanese Promotion," *Journal of Consumer Research,* 14, 3, 174–88.

Sojka, J.Z. and P. Tansuhaj (1995), "Cross-Cultural Research: A Twenty-Year Review," *Advances in Consumer Research,* 22, 461–74.

Tai, S.H.C. and R.Y.K. Chan (2001), "Cross-Cultural Studies on the Information Content of Service Advertising," *The Journal of Services Marketing,* 15, 6/7, 547–62.

Tavassoli, N. (1999), "Temporal and Associative Memory in Chinese and English," *Journal of Consumer Research,* 26, 2, 170–81.

Taylor, C.R., G.E. Miracle, and R.D. Wilson (1997), "The Impact of Information Level on the Effectiveness of U.S. and Korean Television Commercials," *Journal of Advertising,* 26, 1, 1–18.

Triandis, H.C. (1995), *Individualism and Collectivism,* Boulder, CO: Westview Press.

Tse, D.K., R.W. Belk, and N. Zhou (1989), "Becoming a Consumer Society: A Longitudinal and Cross-Cultural Content Analysis of Print Ads from Hong Kong, the People's Republic of China, and Taiwan," *Journal of Consumer Research,* 15, 4, 457–72.

Tylor, E.B. (1881), *Anthropology: An Introduction to the Study of Man and Civilization.* New York: D. Appleton.

van Raaij, W.F. (1996), "Globalization of Marketing Communication?" *Journal of Economic Psychology,* 18, 259–70.

Weinberger, M.G. and H.E. Spotts (1989), "A Situational View of Information Content in TV Advertising in the U.S. and U.K," *Journal of Marketing,* 53, 1, 89–94.

Zaltman, G. and D. MacCaba (2007), "Metaphor in Advertising," in *The SAGE Handbook of Advertising,* eds. G.J. Tellis and T. Ambler, London: Sage Publications.

Zhang, Y., and J.P. Neelankavil (1997), "The Influence of Culture on Advertising Effectiveness in China and the USA: A Cross-Cultural Study," *European Journal of Marketing,* 31, 2, 134–49.

Advertising to Vulnerable Segments

Carolyn Bonifield and Catherine Cole

In a special issue of the *Journal of Advertising*, entitled Perspectives on Advertising Research, Professor Terry Shimp responded to a question about the direction he would like to see the field of advertising research take in the future in the following way: "I personally would like to see much more research that examines the potential deleterious effects of advertising practice. For example, we know little about how advertising affects the moral development of children, how it influences the desire for products such as tobacco, how it influences purchase decisions by vulnerable consumers (e.g., elderly consumers' purchasing of direct to consumer, or DTC products) or how it affects relations between parents and children" (Carlson et al., 2005: 138). This chapter addresses some of these problems by reviewing recent research on advertising effects on vulnerable consumers.

Specifically, we have two objectives: to clarify the definitions and measures of consumer vulnerability, and to discuss factors which influence vulnerability in two specific consumer groups (older adults and children). These objectives guide the outline of our

chapter. First, we clarify how the literature defines and measures vulnerability. Then we discuss factors which influence vulnerability in older adults, which is followed by a section on children and teenagers. We summarize the literature about older consumers in Table 6.4.1 and about children in Table 6.4.2. For each group, we separate empirically supported propositions from future research directions. In the general discussion, we discuss how advertisers can adapt to target market vulnerability as well as how public policy can address the needs of these markets. We also discuss areas for future research.

VULNERABILITY

Consumers become vulnerable because of uncontrollable conditions related to physical, cognitive, motivational or social characteristics. Specifically, vulnerability refers to "those who are more susceptible to economic, physical or psychological harm in or as a result of economic transactions because of characteristics that limit their

Table 6.4.1   Propositions and future research directions for research on older adults

Dependent variable	Propositions	Future research directions
Recall	Older consumers recall different executional elements of commercials than younger consumers. Older adults recall emotional advertising as well as, but recall informational advertising less well, than younger adults. Age differences in recall of advertising are greater for television than for print. Increasing repetitions of commercials increases older adults' recall of advertising messages, but makes them more vulnerable to the truth effect.	Are there age differences in recall of other advertising elements such as warnings? Are there age differences in the recall of emotional and informational advertising elements?
Comprehension	Age differences in comprehension increase on tasks which utilize memory capacity (speech) and decrease on tasks which put smaller demands on memory capacity (written text). In print, putting important information in a standard place reduces age differences in comprehension. In print, age differences for comprehension are smaller for direct assertions than implied claims.	
Persuasion	Older adults employ heuristic instead of systematic processing more often, even when relying on systematic processing would be more appropriate.	Can older adults be taught to employ more systematic processing of advertising? Are there age and/or cohort differences in the level, currency, accessibility, and willingness to use persuasion knowledge?
Coping strategies	Older adults are more likely than younger adults to (a) look for product information in different places, (b) delegate decisions, and (c) avoid decisions.	What other coping mechanisms do older adults employ?

Table 6.4.2   Propositions and future research directions for research on children and teenagers

Dependent variable	Propositions	Future research directions
Recall	The size of age differences in recall depends on the age of the children and presence of cues, so that those under 7 recall the least, those between 7 and 11 recall as well as older children if cues are present, and those 12 and over recall as well as adults. Low levels of knowledge may explain differences in recall among different aged children.	Are there age differences in recall of specific advertising elements? If so, can advertisers design ads that affect recall of specific advertising elements, especially among cued and limited processors? Can consumer education improve recall of advertising?
Comprehension	By age five, most, but not all children are able to distinguish between advertising and programming. By about age eight, most children begin to understand the persuasive intent of advertising.	Does children's comprehension of specific claims vary in the four developmental stages identified by Piaget?
Persuasion	Children develop persuasion knowledge as they age. Children's emotions may override persuasion knowledge.	Are there age differences in the level, currency, and accessibility of persuasion knowledge? Can consumer education increase persuasion knowledge more quickly?
Coping strategies		What coping mechanisms do children employ?

ability to maximize their utility and well being" (Smith and Cooper-Martin, 1997: 4). According to Morgan et al. (1995), although the most strongly established legal definitions of vulnerable consumers incorporate only people with physical sensitivities to harm-causing products (e.g., allergies to dyes), two federal laws, the Americans with Disabilities Act (1990) and the Fair Debt Collection Practices Act (1968) expanded the definition of vulnerable populations to include people with impaired physical competency, mental competency and/or sophistication.

Recently, Baker et al. (2005: 134) point out that vulnerability arises from the "*interaction* of individual states, individual characteristics, and external conditions within a context where consumption goals may be hindered and the experience affects personal and social perceptions of self." This definition of vulnerability enhances the discussion because it shifts the focus away from vulnerability as an inherent characteristic of a social group to vulnerability as a state which can arise as a result of various interactions. In our analysis, we emphasize two segments, older adults and children, where demographic and environmental variables may be especially likely to combine to render these consumers vulnerable.

Vulnerability can be assessed on several dimensions. One is the accuracy of memory. If certain populations – such as older adults or children – selectively recall certain types of advertising information, then they may be vulnerable if they act on inaccurate beliefs, which are stored in memory. Another related measure of vulnerability is accurate comprehension of product benefits and risks. Finally, we also consider a third measure of vulnerability as the ability to resist the persuasive message, or consumer skepticism. To protect themselves against persuasion attempts, consumers build up a repertoire of persuasion knowledge, which is knowledge about persuasion tactics and methods of resisting persuasion attempts (Friestad and Wright, 1994; Campbell and Kirmani, 2000). If certain consumers (e.g., the very young) lack adequate levels of persuasion knowledge

or if consumers cannot always quickly access their knowledge (e.g., elderly adults receiving high pressure telemarketing communications), then they may be vulnerable.

OLDER ADULTS

Demographic trends point to a large, wealthy, and healthy mature market (American Association of Retired Persons, 2005). Today, there are approximately 34.9 million Americans over the age of 65, but by 2010 one in seven Americans will be 65 or older as the Baby Boom generation ages. The oldest baby boomers turned 60 on January 1, 2006. Europe is seeing similar demographic trends. For example, between 1995 and 2015, the 20–29 age group will decrease by 11 million, while the 50–64 age group will increase by 16.5 million (Carrigan and Szmigin, 2003).

This means that the amount of marketing and advertising targeted to the older market will increase. Vulnerability to advertising may arise in older consumers when their considerable knowledge and experience cannot compensate for age-associated changes in cognitive abilities. In this section, we examine how ageing and advertising characteristics interact to affect memory, comprehension, and reactions to persuasion attempts.

Memory

Although there is widespread agreement that ageing negatively affects performance on many memory tasks, there are unresolved issues about why, when, and the extent to which age-related differences in memory occur (Craik et al., 1995). Older adults' ability to recall information depends on the characteristics of the information, the medium of communication, how often it is repeated and even the way recall is assessed. For example, one analysis of a large commercial advertising research database found that older consumers tended to recall different executional elements than their younger counterparts. Memory-enhancing elements include advertising characteristics such as an "actor playing an ordinary person" and "product results being demonstrated" (Phillips and Stanton, 2004).

Recent research shows that memory for emotional information is preserved with age so that as people age, they increasingly recall and prefer persuasive messages with emotional rather than rational (Williams and Drolet, 2005) or knowledge-related appeals (Fung and Carstensen, 2003). Future research should investigate whether age differences in recall of emotional material extend to particular elements of advertising. For example, are older adults less likely to recall the informational risks than the emotional benefits presented in direct-to-consumer pharmaceutical advertising?

In another study, younger adults recalled more in the television medium than they recalled in the print medium, but older adults did not realize the learning benefits of television. As a result, age differences were larger in television (Cole and Houston, 1987). Repetition of advertising messages increases older adults' recall of advertising claims (Cole et al., 1995), but runs the risk of alienating young people (Singh and Cole, 1993) and of making older adults more vulnerable to the truth effect (the tendency for adults to give higher truth ratings to previously presented statements than to similar new statements) (Law et al., 1998). An interesting extension of this research reports that repeatedly identifying a claim as false helped older adults remember it as false in the short term, but made them more likely to remember it as true after a three day delay. In contrast, younger adults' memories for truth benefited from repeated warnings after both short and long delays (Skurnik et al., 2005).

Comprehension

The literature suggests that the size of age differences in comprehension of advertising information will depend on how the advertising is presented. For example, models of speech processing indicate that language comprehension depends on the ability to interpret relatively small chunks of information within a limited capacity working memory. Because working memory capacity is often more limited among elderly adults, the size of the age differences in comprehension often depends on how much memory capacity is needed to understand. For example, age differences in comprehension for speech, but not for print, are often observed (e.g., Cohen, 1988).

An exception to this rule may occur when the printed information is very complex with similar information mixed together, such as that found on a nutritional label or with complex claims, such as pragmatic implications. A series of studies investigated how age differences in selective attention might affect older adults' ability to comprehend and use printed nutritional information contained on product labels (Cole and Gaeth, 1990). In the experiments, subjects had to select a cereal that met certain criteria. Some subjects learned to circle the relevant information on the nutritional label with a red pen before they made a decision. Both older and younger adults benefited from the perception aid. However, older consumers remained less able to make good nutritional choices than younger consumers even after being encouraged to focus on the relevant information. In another experiment, the investigators boxed the relevant information and placed it in a separate location on the label. This time, subjects with moderate, but not severe, disembedding deficiencies were helped but the field independent subjects gained little from the aid. This study suggests that to facilitate communication with older consumers, complicated information in print materials should be placed in the same spot on all print advertising.

A study investigated whether or not there are age differences in abilities to judge truthfulness of direct and pragmatic claims in print advertising (Gaeth and Heath, 1987). Participants viewed a series of ads that included such statements as "Brimstone tires will increase the safety of your winter driving" (a direct assertion) or "Have a safe winter. Drive on Brimstone tires" (a pragmatic implication). Then, in the case of the Brimstone ad, viewers were asked if the following statement has to be true: Brimstone tires will increase the safety of your winter driving. Results suggested that there are no age differences when consumers judge statement truthfulness from memory because everyone did poorly. However, young adults were more likely than older adults to correctly judge the truthfulness of implied claims when the advertisements were available during assessment.

Persuasion

Across time, older adults build up a knowledge system that they can deploy to resist persuasion attempts. Some argue that knowledge systems become increasingly selective and domain-specific with age, so that older adults can draw on this rich knowledge system to make better decisions. For example, Kovalchik et al. (2005) report that older subjects did somewhat better than younger subjects on a 20-item multiple choice trivia test. More important from a persuasion knowledge perspective, however, older subjects in the study were better calibrated (knew better what they knew and did not know) than younger subjects.

However, an American Association of Retired Persons (hereafter referred to as AARP) survey suggests that older adults lack knowledge in important areas such as their rights as consumers. For example, older consumers (those over the age of 65) are much less likely than consumers under the age of 65 to know that individuals have several days to cancel purchases made from door-to-door salespeople (36% versus 53%) and that consumers are not able to cancel purchases made by credit card over the telephone (19% versus 28%) (cited in Lee and Geistfeld, 1999). Additionally, rapid changes in technology may mean that some older consumers' persuasion knowledge is outdated. Recently, Dave Nahmias (2004), Deputy Assistant Attorney General, US Department of Justice, identified increases in online fraud often targeted to older users. This fraudulent activity includes identify theft, "phishing" schemes in which criminals set

up emails and websites designed to look like those of legitimate companies and financial institutions, non-delivery of merchandise, and investment fraud. It is unclear whether age and/or cohort effects underlie age differences in the currency of persuasion knowledge.

With older adults, a question arises about their willingness to use their persuasion knowledge (Langenderfer and Shimp, 2001). Since the early 1970s, marketing research has reported that older consumers are often reluctant to complain about or to be rude to salespeople (LaForge, 1989). LaForge (1989) offers as an explanation the theory of "learned helplessness," which suggests that after repeated punishment or failure, people become more passive and continue to remain so even after the environment changes to make success possible. In the case of older adults, they may learn this helplessness from prior experiences in eras when businesses did not respond to complaints. Also, their feelings of helplessness may increase as physical disabilities make them aware of their own limitations. However, it is unclear how much of this learned helplessness is a cohort effect. For example, the ageing baby boomers who are accustomed to getting results by complaining may not experience the same reticence to complain as earlier elderly cohorts (Kaplan, 2005).

Because ageing may affect how people process advertising information, it may also affect how they access existing persuasion knowledge. As a result, older adults in some circumstances may encounter problems accessing and using their persuasion knowledge. Recent empirical work indicates that when cognitive capacity is constrained, consumers are less likely to use persuasion knowledge to resist selling efforts (Campbell and Kirmani, 2000). Because as people age, their cognitive capacity often becomes more constrained, one would predict decreased ability to use existing persuasion knowledge as consumers age (Aditya, 2001).

Regarding persuasion, mature consumers tend to favor heuristic processing and rely less on careful deliberate processing of information. Hess et al. (2001) have proposed a resource allocation hypothesis, which states that because older adults have limited cognitive resources, they tend to employ heuristic information processing strategies in order to conserve their mental energy for important tasks. However, this hypothesis also suggests that older adults can, when necessary, employ deliberative information processing and decision making (a production deficiency). The frontal ageing hypothesis suggests that age-related changes in frontal systems can favor heuristic type decision making (see Denburg et al., 2005, for a discussion). This would tend to suggest that because of age-related changes in the frontal lobe of the brain, some older adults are unable to employ deliberative decision making (a processing deficiency). As a result, older adults will be more likely to be persuaded by advertising elements that are predicted to be persuasive in low elaboration conditions by the Elaboration Likelihood Model (e.g., source attractiveness) (Petty and Cacioppo, 1986). According to Langenderfer and Shimp (2001), this tendency to favour low elaboration processing makes older adults more vulnerable to scams because they do not carefully evaluate the offer.

Coping strategies

Aware that age-associated changes in information processing abilities may increase their vulnerability, older consumers may search for information in different places than younger consumers. For example, when making investment decisions, older consumers, compared to younger consumers, are more likely to use television media and less likely to use the Internet for information about investments (Lin and Lee, 2004). Research also points to a tendency for older adults to avoid making complex or difficult decisions by postponing or delegating them. In medical decision making, older adults are more likely than younger adults to indicate that they would leave medical decisions up to others (Finucane et al., 2002). In other everyday decisions, older adults preferred avoidant strategies, but younger adults preferred problem-focused action (Blanchard-Fields

et al., 2004). A recent report (Kirmani and Campbell, 2004) adds to this literature by finding that middle aged informants (30–60 years old) used a broader variety of coping strategies in response to persuasion attempts than younger, inexperienced consumers (18–23 year olds) and older respondents (60–75 year olds).

CHILDREN AND TEENAGERS

In this section, we review literature discussing how advertising and consumer characteristics interact to affect memory, comprehension, and persuasion effects in children and teenagers.

Memory

The literature suggests that accuracy of recall in children and teenagers depends on both age and level of knowledge. Roedder (1981) categorized children into three distinct segments based on how they acquire, encode, organize, and retrieve information. Strategic processors, the oldest segment who are aged 12 and older, spontaneously use several strategies for storing and retrieving information from memory, including verbal labeling, rehearsal, and retrieval cues as a guide for memory search. Cued processors, the middle segment who are aged seven to 11, use strategies similar to strategic processors to enhance information storage and retrieval, but need prompts or cues to help them employ these strategies. Limited processors, who are the youngest segment (under seven), have difficulty using storage and retrieval strategies, even with the use of prompts and cues because their processing skills are not fully developed. As a result, young children are unable to effectively encode information, that is, put thoughts, ideas, or information into a symbolic form and understand the intended message, nor are they able to use strategies such as semantic encoding, imagery, rehearsal, and organizational strategies to store information in memory or to use retrieval cues to aid in retrieving stored information (Ashcraft et al., 1976; Bach and Underwood,

1970; Bray et al., 1977; Jusczyk et al., 1975; Ornstein and Corsale, 1979).

Beyond the limitations of children's cognitive development, children also have considerably less knowledge than do adults, which in turn impacts their ability to learn and to problem-solve. We know that individual's prior knowledge influences their categorization of new objects and concepts and correspondingly, their encoding, comprehension, and storage of new information. Lindberg (1980) suggests that children's lack of experience and knowledge impacts their ability to use memory strategies such as organizational strategies. Ackerman (1982) finds that children's ability to use retrieval cues is negatively impacted, due to undeveloped knowledge structures.

Comprehension

Two questions about children's comprehension arise in the literature: when do children understand the difference between advertising and programming, and when do children understand the persuasive intent of advertising. A common psychological model of children views them as progressing through a series of cognitive and emotional developmental stages that affects their ability to comprehend the world around them. The most well known and influential of these theories, Jean Piaget's theory of intellectual development, categorizes children's cognitive abilities and experiences into four major stages: sensorimotor (birth to two years), pre-operational (two years to seven years), concrete operational (seven years to 11 years), and formal operational (11 years and above) (Ginsburg and Opper, 1988). According to Piaget's framework, children's cognitive abilities differ widely at each of these four stages. During the sensorimotor stage, children, who are learning about the environment, demonstrate the ability to classify or assign meaning to objects. At the preoperational stage, children focus on the perceptual properties of stimuli, but they tend to focus on a single dimension. In addition, they begin to develop symbolic thought. At the concrete operational stage, children can think about several dimensions of a stimulus concurrently, more abstractly, and in a more meaningful way. At the formal operational stage, children are capable of more complex thought patterns.

Palmer and McDowell (1979) showed videotapes to kindergartners and first graders and asked the children to identify what they had viewed. The children correctly identified commercials approximately half of the time. Blosser and Roberts (1985) found that only one in ten children under age five correctly identified ads, but by age five to six, the percentage increased to 62%, and by age ten and above, 100% of the children correctly identified the ads. Although the literature is mixed, much literature concludes that by age five, most, but not all, children are able to make this distinction.

However, children's ability to describe the difference between programs and commercials is rudimentary; descriptions of ads generally are that they are shorter or funnier, and commercials are generally viewed as entertaining and unbiased. Butter et al. (1981) found that when separators (e.g., "the XYZ program will return after this message") were inserted between programs and commercials that 70% of children aged four and 90% of children aged five correctly identified all of the commercials. However, although they were able to distinguish between programs and commercials, this did not translate into understanding the actual difference between the two in terms of purpose and intent; children at this point are generally unaware of the persuasive intent of advertising.

Most of the research suggests that children begin to understand the persuasive intent of advertising by about eight years of age. One influential study (Robertson and Rossiter, 1974) asked children "What is a commercial?" and "What does a commercial try to get you to do?" and found that 53% of children ages six and seven, 87% of children ages eight and nine, and 99% of children ages ten and 11 understood the persuasive intent of ads. Other studies have found similar results

(Blosser and Roberts, 1985; Ward et al., 1977). In the area of Internet advertising, the results thus far are less clear. One study found that fourth- and fifth-grade children did not have a sophisticated understanding of the persuasive intent of advertising, and primarily viewed websites as informative rather than commercial (Morrison, 2004). Interestingly, Henke (1999) studied whether children ages nine through 11 were able to identify the persuasive intent of advertising on the web, and found that only 13% of the participants thought the purpose of their favourite website was to advertise.

Persuasion

An important question is whether children have the awareness and capabilities to defend themselves against highly persuasive advertising. Research suggests that ads directed to children are effective in creating purchase requests (Schor, 2004). A study by Robinson (2001) in which third and fourth graders watched less television for a period of 6 months found that those children whose television viewing time declined made 70% fewer toy requests than those whose television viewing did not decline. Another study found that children who watched more television requested a greater number of items from Santa Claus (Pine, 2002). A comparison group of children from Sweden, where advertising to children is not permitted, asked for significantly fewer items (Pine, 2002).

Children around the age of eight become aware of the use of deception in advertising (Robertson and Rossiter, 1974; Ward et al., 1977). Ward et al. (1977) found that 50% of kindergartners believe that advertising never or only sometimes is truthful, while 88% of third graders and 97% of sixth graders believed that advertising is never or only sometimes truthful. In the same study, Ward et al. (1977) found that while kindergartners did not have an understanding of why advertising is at times untruthful, the third and sixth graders attributed the reason for lying to persuasive intent. Bever et al. (1975) talked with children ages five through 12 and found

that many of the children ages nine and ten indicated that they could not really evaluate advertising and that "you don't really know what's true until you've tried the product" (p. 114). Moreover, while seven- to ten-year-old children were "particularly hostile toward misleading advertising" and believed that deceptive practices are immoral, the 11- and 12-year-old children were less bothered about adult deceptions and somewhat cynical about social and economic misrepresentation. Boush et al. (1994) studied sixth through eighth graders' skepticism toward advertising and their beliefs about the persuasive tactics that advertisers use. They found that the level of skepticism toward advertising claims was high, and was positively related to having a more adult understanding of advertising tactics.

While at around age eight, children appear to both have some understanding of the persuasive intent of advertising as well as doubts about the truthfulness of advertising, it is unclear whether this knowledge functions as a cognitive defense against advertising. Christenson (1982) found that children's cognitive defenses have little effect on evaluations and preferences for advertised products. Ross et al. (1984) conducted two studies of boys ages eight to 14 using celebrity endorsements and found that although the eight to ten-year olds were more reliant on the endorser's advice than the 11- to 14-year-old children, that the two age groups were not differentially affected by the ads. They concluded that children's understanding about advertising intent and techniques and cynicism about ads has almost no influence on product preference after viewing. Roedder John (1999) offers two explanations for this disconnect, including the possibility that an understanding of advertising's persuasive intent is overridden by a child's desire and enthusiasm for a particular product or that children's advertising knowledge acts as a cognitive defense only when that knowledge is accessed during commercial viewing. The latter is likely related to children's general difficulty in retrieving stored information (Brucks et al., 1988).

GENERAL DISCUSSION

What are the possible consequences of target market vulnerability to unfair or deceptive advertising? One possibility is that advertising managers will adapt their advertising to the abilities of the target market, either because of ethical considerations (as discussed in Chapter 6.2) or because of competitive pressures from the marketplace. Competition in a free market mitigates the ability of firms to rampantly exploit consumers' vulnerability. In addition, policy makers may also intervene to prohibit unfair or deceptive practices. Finally, consumers themselves may develop strategies to cope with persuasive messages. Because there is a dearth of literature on consumer coping strategies, we discuss it in the future research section, but address manager adaptation and regulation here.

Adaptation by advertising managers

Advertisers need to carefully consider how to design advertising that will effectively communicate with vulnerable populations, but they also need to recognize that it is unlikely that controversies over advertising to vulnerable groups will diminish. Thus, companies should develop their own set of guidelines, rather than relying either on industry groups or waiting for government regulations to tighten. As companies develop these policies, they should recognize that many groups outside of the vulnerable target market actively monitor advertising (e.g., adult children of older consumers, parents of children, physicians, teachers, AARP). As a result, companies should incorporate these support people into panels when formulating policy and pretest possible advertisements on both the target audience and the support personnel.

Advertising for culturally sensitive products

As discussed in Chapter 6.2, advertising for some products, such as cigarettes and alcohol, raises ethical concerns because there is evidence that this advertising influences the initiation and use of these products (cigarettes: Andrews and Franke, 1991; alcoholic beverages: Ellickson, 2005; Smart, 1988). This is an area that has drawn particular concern in the area of advertising to children. However, some alcohol advertisers are taking proactive steps. In Europe, Diageo, which has often been blamed for promoting underage and binge drinking with its portfolio of sweet and easy-to-drink flavoured beverages, recently launched two television ads illustrating how excessive drinking can ruin an evening. The company also claims to have stopped researching the under-21 market in some countries (Unsigned, 2006).

Because cultural definitions of controversial products can shift across time, firms need to scan the environment continuously. For example, in the United States, firms who appear to have ignored warning signs that the growing talk over childhood obesity would result in litigation, and took few proactive actions with respect to their products and advertising practices (such as Kellogg Company and Nickelodeon parent Viacom Inc.) have been threatened with a $2 billion lawsuit from the Center for Science in the Public Interest and the Campaign for a Commercial-Free Childhood. In contrast, some companies, such as Kraft Foods, have taken a proactive stance. In January 2005, Kraft Foods announced it would shift the majority of its $800 million ad budget to brands that qualify for their Sensible Solutions label, which are Kraft brands that provide essential nutrients or reduced sugars, calories or fat. In September 2005, Kraft added their own websites to the list of marketing vehicles in which it will only promote products meeting their nutrition standards when targeting children ages six to 11 years old. Although Kraft has received praise from some critics for their new policies, some nutrition experts believe that the moves don't go nearly far enough to address the issue (Advertising Age, 2005).

In the United Kingdom, the UK Food Standards Agency commissioned the Hastings Study to examine whether or not food promotion to children affects food knowledge, preferences, and behaviour. Ambler (2004) reviewed both the findings of the Hastings Study and studies commissioned by the UK Advertising Association through its Food Advertising Unit. Ambler finds that food advertising tends to affect brand knowledge, preferences, and behaviours, not category knowledge, preferences, and behaviours. He suggests that the governmental agency should work with food manufacturers to identify ways that these industries can help alleviate child obesity problems, such as developing new products, revising codes of practice, and targeting educational ads to especially vulnerable groups.

In Europe, soft-drink marketers have pledged to stop marketing to children under 12 years old and to limit soft-drink sales in schools, in an effort to prevent European Union legislation. Some countries in Europe have already legislated in the area of advertising to children. Parts of Scandinavia ban advertising to children altogether. In France, a new law requires food marketers to either add a health message to ads for any manufactured food or beverage except water, or pay a tax equivalent to 1.5% of their annual ad budget for a national institute to do campaigns to promote healthier eating (Advertising Age, 2006).

The message from around the world is the same: products which may not be viewed as controversial in one era can become controversial in another time period. Firms need to be proactive in identifying how to advertise these controversial products to vulnerable populations.

Industry guidelines

Industry associations can also establish voluntary guidelines. For example, in August (2005), responding to increased criticism, the pharmaceutical industry announced a set of voluntary guidelines aimed at governing the way drugs are advertised to consumers (Dooren, 2005; Richardson and Luchsinger, 2005). In 1997, regulations of the Food and Drug Administration were liberalized to allow for increasing advertising of pharmaceutical products directly to customers through television, radio, print, the Internet, and other media. On the one hand, such advertising increases awareness about diseases and helps people become better informed about treatments available for relief from bothersome conditions. Opponents of this advertising include physicians who deal with misinformed consumers, and consumer groups who think the advertising can seduce vulnerable groups such as the elderly with one-sided messages that overemphasize the benefits and underemphasize risks, costs, and alternative therapies.

Recently, the National Advertising Review Council (NARC), the advertising industry's self-regulatory body run by the Council of Better Business Bureaus, announced that it will expand its panel of academic experts to help set standards for reviewing ads. In addition, its Children's Advertising Review Unit (CARU) will take a closer look into several controversial areas such as product placement and the use of cartoon characters in ads (Advertising Age, 2005). According to NARC's President and CEO, James Guthrie, these actions are in response to concerns expressed at a recent joint FTC and Department of Health and Human Services workshop that looked into the role marketing plays in the childhood obesity crisis (Advertising Age, 2005).

However, many advocacy organizations and experts view these corporate and industry actions with skepticism and suspicion. Gary Ruskin, director of one such group called Commercial Alert, stated that "Advertisers are very afraid that they will be held responsible for producing an epidemic of marketing-related diseases in our kids," and called the changes a "stream of verbiage that tries to cloak doing nothing." Susan Linn, a Harvard psychologist who found the Campaign for a Commercial-Free Childhood, compares the ad industry to the tobacco industries of the 1980s and 1990s, stating that the government and not the corporations should be the "guardians of public health" (Advertising Age, 2005). Senator Tom Harkin, D-Iowa, warns that Congress will take action if advertisers don't act to limit marketing to children and states that any voluntary industry plan that relies on CARU and voluntary compliance "is a non-starter," stating that CARU, in his opinion, has no real independence and no sanction authority (Advertising Age, 2005).

Policy adaptation

Consumer education

If the targeted consumers' knowledge is inadequate, education programs might succeed in increasing the vulnerable populations' level of persuasion knowledge. For example, Lee and Geistfeld (1999) suggest that consumer education about telemarketing fraud be conducted over the telephone because older isolated adults, who are often especially vulnerable to telemarketing fraud, are favorably disposed to the social interactions generated by telephone conversations. Gaeth and Heath (1987) developed an interactive training program to reduce susceptibility to misleading advertising without increasing consumer suspicion of advertising claims. They found that the training: (1) reduced susceptibility to misleading statements in both young adults and older adults; (2) equated misleadingness between older trained adults and younger untrained adults; but (3) reduced the younger adult's ability to discriminate between non-misleading and potentially misleading claims. The Skurnik et al. paper (2005) cited earlier also suggests that regulatory efforts to correct false advertising will have different effects on older and younger adults.

Legislation

As discussed in Chapter 6.1, advertising regulations can protect societal interests and enhance advertising credibility by limiting deceptive and unfair advertising. Both the FTC (Federal Trade Commission – US) and the ASA (Advertising Standards Authority – England) consider how the advertising practice in question affects the targeted consumer to be a critical element in judging unfairness and deception (Aditya, 2001). For example, the FTC announced reviews of direct to consumer (DTC) pharmaceutical product advertising because of concerns about deceptive and unfair advertising (Mathews, 2005).

As discussed in Chapter 6.1, much criticism and subsequent regulation has been leveled against marketing aimed specifically at children. As noted, the European *Directive Concerning Television Broadcasting* (1989) imposed restrictions on advertising directed to children in Europe. In the US, in 1979, the Federal Trade Commission (FTC) held hearings on proposed regulatory changes in the area of advertising to children. An FTC report recommended banning all television advertising for any product directed at or seen by audiences comprised largely of children under age eight because they are too young to understand the selling intent of advertising (FTC Staff Report, 1978). After intense debate in which the advertising industry and several companies argued strongly against it based primarily on advertisers' right of free speech under the First Amendment, the FTC proposal was defeated. However, Congress approved the Children's Television Act in 1990, which specifically limits the amount of commercial time in children's programming to 10.5 minutes per hour on weekends and 12 minutes per hour on weekdays.

FUTURE RESEARCH

We list possible research topics in Tables 6.4.1 and 6.4.2. One important area for future research relates to coping strategies. Kirmani and Campbell (2004) suggest that research on coping strategies examine multiple dimensions of coping strategies including types, variety, timing (before, after or during persuasion attempt), sequencing (early in, in the middle of, or near the end of persuasion presentations), and assertiveness versus aggressiveness. Most likely, coping strategies vary by target market. For example, older adults may adjust the way they gather information, while the parents of children may adjust their children's shopping habits.

Another important future research area relates to persuasion knowledge, which helps protect consumers against persuasion attempts. In vulnerable groups, we need to understand how it develops and changes across time, and the external factors (such as social pressure and overwhelming emotions) which affect consumers' willingness to deploy it. For example, among older adults, cohort differences, not age differences, may underlie age differences in the level, currency, accessibility, and willingness to use persuasion knowledge. Among children, emotions may override their persuasion knowledge.

Another direction for future research is to examine how vulnerable populations recall and comprehend the different components of advertisements. For example, do age differences in recall extend to specific elements of the advertisement? If older adults remember emotional benefits as well as younger adults, but remember information about risks more poorly than younger adults, there is the potential for advertisers to exploit this vulnerability. In children, cues embedded in the advertising could influence recall of specific advertising elements, especially among cued and limited processors. Among children, age differences in comprehension of different types of claims may emerge. For example, understanding about product risks may vary depending on which of the four Piaget development stages characterizes the child's cognitive abilities. Such research might also provide new insights into how elements of the advertisement work together.

SUMMARY

- This chapter clarified the definitions and measures of consumer vulnerability, the factors which influence vulnerability, how advertisers can allow for target market vulnerability and how public policy can address the needs of these markets.
- Two age groups were examined – older adults and children.
- People move in and out of vulnerability because vulnerability is not an inherent trait of an individual but arises from the interaction between the individual and his or her environmental context.

- Vulnerability is multidimensional and should be assessed with multiple measures including recall accuracy, message comprehension, and reactions to persuasion attempts.
- Vulnerability to advertising may arise in older consumers when their knowledge and experience cannot compensate for age-associated changes in cognitive abilities. Therefore, any form of advertising which puts large demands on working memory increases older adults' vulnerability.
- Older consumers tend to favor heuristic processing and rely less on careful deliberate processing of information. Time pressure also exacerbates vulnerability in older adults.
- Older adults often lack knowledge regarding their rights as consumers, and changes in technology may also mean that their knowledge is outdated.
- Older consumers tend to search for information in different places than younger consumers. They also tend to avoid making complex or difficult decisions by postponing or delegating them.
- Regarding coping strategies, older adults build a complex knowledge system which they can deploy to cope with persuasive efforts.
- Children have considerably less knowledge than adults, thus impacting their ability to learn and to problem-solve, or to use memory strategies such as organizational strategies. They are also unable to effectively encode, store or retrieve information.
- Recall of advertising information is likely to vary according to the age of the child.
- The age of the child has a dramatic impact on vulnerability. For young children, advertisements that are not clearly separated from television programming and that encourage immediate emotional responses may exploit vulnerability.
- Researchers have found that at about the age of five, children can distinguish between advertising and programming, but they do not understand the persuasive intent of advertising until about the age of eight.
- Other research shows that ads directed to children are effective in creating purchase requests, and that television viewing is positively related to the number of toys a child will request, thus highlighting the persuasive effects of advertising on this young segment. However, when children become teenagers, their skepticism toward advertising grows as they gain a more adult understanding of advertising tactics.
- Either because of ethical considerations or competitive pressures, target market vulnerability may lead to advertisers adapting their advertising to the abilities of the target market. Guidelines may

be imposed by the firm itself, by industry groups, or government regulation.

REFERENCES

Ackerman, B.F. (1982), "Retrieval Variability: The Inefficient Use of Retrieval Cues by Young Children," *Journal of Experimental Child Psychology*, 33 (June), 413–28.

Aditya, R. (2001), "The Psychology of Deception in Marketing: A Conceptual Framework for Research and Practice," *Psychology & Marketing*, 18 (Jul), 735–60.

Advertising Age, "CARU Targets Product Placement and Cartoon Ads," September 16, 2005, available at http://www.advertisingage.com.

Advertising Age, "Children See Less TV Food Advertising in 2004 than in 1977," July 14, 2005, available at http://www.advertisingage.com.

Advertising Age, "Europe Stops School Soft-Drink Marketing," January 31, 2006, available at http://www.advertisingage.com.

Advertising Age, "Kraft Web Sites to Only Tout Healthier Foods," September 15, 2005, available at http://www.advertisingage.com.

Ambler, T. (2004), "Does the UK Promotion of Food and Drink to Children Contribute to Their Obesity?" Centre for Marketing *Working Paper, No.04-901*, London Business School, Regent's Park, London.

American Association of Retired Persons (2005), The State of 50+ America, Washington, D.C. 20049, Consumer Affairs, American Association of Retired Persons, 1909 K Street NW, Washington, D.C. 20049.

Andrews, R.L. and G.R. Franke (1991), "The Determinants of Cigarette Consumption: A Meta-Analysis," *Journal of Public Policy and Marketing*, 10 (Spring), 81–100.

Ashcraft, M.H., G. Kellas, and D. Keller (1976), "Retrieval Processes in Fifth Graders and Adults," *Journal of Experimental Child Psychology*, 21 (April), 264–76.

Bach, M.J.J. and B.J. Underwood (1970), "Developmental Changes in Memory Attributes," *Journal of Educational Psychology*, 61 (August), 292–6.

Baker, S.M., J. Gentry, and T. Rittenburg (2005), "Building Understanding of the Domain of Consumer Vulnerability," *Journal of Macromarketing*, 25 (December), 128–39.

Bever, T.G., M.L. Smith, B. Bengen, and T.G. Johnson (1975), "Young Viewers' Troubling Response to TV Ads," *Harvard Business Review*, 53 (November–December), 109–20.

Blanchard-Fields, F., R. Stein, and T.L. Watson (2004), "Age Differences in Emotion-Regulation Strategies in Handling Everyday Problems," *Journals of Gerontology Series B-Psychological & Sciences Social Sciences*, 59 (6), 261–9.

Blosser, B.J. and D.F. Roberts (1985), "Age Differences in Children's Perceptions of Message Intent: Responses to TV News, Commercials, Educational Spots, and Public Service Announcements," *Communication Research*, 12 (October), 455–84.

Boush, D.M., M. Friestad, and G.M. Rose (1994), "Adolescent Skepticism Toward TV Advertising and Knowledge of Advertiser Tactics," *Journal of Consumer Research*, 21 (1), 165–75.

Bray, N.W., E.M. Justice, R.P. Ferguson, and D.L. Simon (1977), "Developmental Changes in the Effect of Instructions on Production-Deficient Children," *Child Development*, 48 (September), 1019–26.

Brucks, M., G.M. Armstrong, and M.E. Goldberg (1988), "Children's Use of Cognitive Defenses Against Television Advertising: A Cognitive Response Approach," *Journal of Consumer Research*, 14 (March), 471–82.

Butter, E.J., P.M. Popovich, R.H. Stackhouse, and R.K. Garner (1981), "Discrimination of Television Programs and Commercials by Preschool Children," *Journal of Advertising Research*, 21 (April), 53–6.

Campbell, M.C. and A. Kirmani (2000), "Consumers' Use of Persuasion Knowledge: The Effects of Accessibility and Cognitive Capacity on Perceptions of an Influence Agent," *Journal of Consumer Research*, 10, 69–83.

Carlson, L., S.J. Grove, and M.R. Stafford (2005), "Perspectives on Advertising Research: Views from Winners of the American Academy of Advertising Outstanding Contribution to Research Award," *Journal of Advertising*, 34 (Summer), 117–49.

Carrigan, M. and I. Szmigin (2003), "Regulating Ageism in UK Advertising: An Industry Perspective," *Marketing Intelligence & Planning*, 21 (4/5), 198–205.

Christenson, P.G. (1982), "Children's Perceptions of TV Commercials and Products: The Effects of PSAs," *Communication Research*, 9 (October), 491–524.

Cohen, G. (1988), "Age Differences in Memory for Texts: Production Deficiencies or Processing Limitations, in *Language, Memory and Aging*, eds. L. Light and D. Burke, New York: Cambridge University Press, 171–90.

Cole, C., N. Castellano, and D. Schum (1995), "Quantitative and Qualitative Differences in Older and Younger Consumers' Recall of Radio Advertising," in *Advances in Consumer Research*, eds. F. Kardes and M. Sujan, Provo, Utah: Association for Consumer Research, 22, 617–21.

Cole, C.A. and G. Gaeth (1990), "Cognitive and Age-Related Differences in the Ability to Use Nutritional Information in a Complex Environment," *Journal of Marketing Research*, 17, 175–84.

Cole, C.A. and M.J. Houston (1987), "Encoding and Media Effects on Consumer Learning Deficiencies in the Elderly," *Journal of Marketing Research*, 24, 55–63.

Craik, F., I.M. Norman, D. Anderson, S.A. Kerr, and K.Z. Li (1995), "Memory Changes in Normal Aging," in *Handbook of Memory Disorders*, eds. A.D. Baddeley, B.A. Wilson, and F.N. Watts, 211–41. New York: Wiley.

Denburg, N.L., D.T. Tranel, and A. Bechara (2005), "The Ability to Decide Advantageously Declines Prematurely in Some Older Persons," *Neuropsychologia*, 43 (7), 1099–106.

Dooren, J. (2005), "Drug Industry Creates Voluntary Ad Guidelines," *Wall Street Journal (Eastern edition)*. New York, NY: Aug 3, 2005, D.4.

Drumwright, M.E. (2007), "Advertising Ethics: A Multi-level Theory Approach," in *The SAGE Handbook of Advertising*, eds. G.J. Tellis and T. Ambler, London: Sage Publications.

Ellickson, P.L. (2005), "Does Alcohol Advertising Promote Adolescent Drinking? Results from a Longitudinal Assessment," *Addiction*, 100 (2), 235–46.

Finucane, M., P. Slovic, J.H. Hibbard, E. Peters, C.K. Mertz, and D.G. MacGregor (2002), "Aging and Decision-Making Competence: An Analysis of Comprehension and Consistency Skills in Older versus Younger Adults Considering Health-Plan Options," *Journal of Behavioral Decision Making*, 15 (2), 141–64.

FTC Staff Report on Advertising to Children (Washington, D.C.: Government Printing Office, 1978).

Friestad, M.A. and P. Wright (1994), "The Persuasion Knowledge Model: How People Cope with Persuasion Attempts," *Journal of Consumer Research*, 21, 1–31.

Fung, H.H. and L.L. Carstensen (2003), "Sending Memorable Messages to the Old: Age Differences in Preferences and Memory for Advertisements," *Journal of Personality and Social Psychology*, 85, 163–78.

Gaeth, G.A. and T.B. Heath (1987), "The Cognitive Processing of Misleading Advertising in Young and Old Adults," *Journal of Consumer Research*, 14, 43–54.

Ginsburg, H.P. and S. Opper (1988), *Piaget's Theory of Intellectual Development*. Englewood Cliffs, NJ: Prentice-Hall.

Henke, L.L. (1999), "Children, Advertising, and the Internet: An Exploratory Study," in *Advertising*

and the World Wide Web, eds. D.W. Schumann and E. Thorson, Mahwah, NJ: Lawrence Erlbaum Associates.

Hess, T., D.C. Rosenberg, and S.J. Waters (2001), "Motivation and Representational Processes in Adulthood: The Effects of Social Accountability and Information Relevance," *Psychology and Aging*, 16 (4), 629–42.

Jusczyk, P.W., D.G. Kemler, and E.A. Bubis (1975), "A Developmental Comparison of Two Types of Visual Mnemonics," *Journal of Experimental Child Psychology*, 20 (October), 327–40.

Kaplan, D. (2005), "Look Who's Turning 60: A New Age for Boomers," *The Houston Chronicle*, August 21, 2005, Section A, p. 1.

Kirmani, A. and M. Campbell (2004), "Goal Seeker and Persuasion Sentry: How Consumer Targets Respond to Interpersonal Marketing Persuasion," *Journal of Consumer Research*, 31 (3), 573–83.

Kovalchik, S., C. Camerer, D. Grether, C. Plot, and J. Allman (2005), "Aging and Decision Making: A Comparison between Neurologically Health Elderly and Young Individuals," *Journal of Economic Behavior and Organization*, 58 (September), 79–94.

LaForge, M. (1989), "Learned Helplessness as an Explanation of Elderly Consumer Complaint Behavior," *Journal of Business Ethics*, 359–66.

Langenderfer, J. and T. Shimp (2001), "Consumer Vulnerability to Scams, Swindles and Fraud: A New Theory of Visceral Influences on Persuasion," *Psychology and Marketing*, 18 (7), 763–83.

Law, S., S.A. Hawkins, and F.I.M. Craik (1998), "Repetition-induced belief in the elderly: Rehabilitating age-related memory deficits," *Journal of Consumer Research*, 25 (September), 91–107.

Lee, J. and L. Geistfeld (1999), "Elderly Consumers' Receptiveness to Telemarketing Fraud," *Journal of Public Policy and Marketing*, 18 (Fall), 208–17.

Lin, Q.C. and J. Lee (2004), "Consumer Information Search When Making Investment Decisions," *Financial Services Review*, 13, 319–32.

Lindberg, M.A. (1980), "Is Knowledge Base Development a Necessary and Sufficient Condition for Memory Development?" *Journal of Experimental Child Psychology*, 30 (February), 401–10.

Mathews, A. (2005), "FDA to Review Drug Marketing To Consumers," *Wall Street Journal*, August 2: B1

Morgan, F.W., D.K. Schuler and J. Stoltman (1995), "A Framework for Examining Legal Status of Vulnerable Consumers," *Journal of Public Policy and Marketing*, 14 (2), 267–77.

Morrison, K.L. (2004), "Children Reading Commercial Messages on the Internet: Web Sites that Merge Education, Information, Entertainment, and

Advertising," *Dissertation Abstracts International, Section A: Humanities and Social Sciences*, 64 (11-A), 3957.

Nahmias, Deputy Assistant Attorney General, Criminal Division, U.S. Department of Justice, Testimony before Senate Special Aging Committee, March 23, 2004.

Ornstein, P.A. and K. Corsale (1979), "Organizational Factors in Children's Memory," in *Memory Organization and Structure*, ed. C. Richard Puff, New York: Academic Press.

Palmer, E.L. and C.N. McDowell (1979), "Program/ Commercial Separators in Children's Television Programming," *Journal of Communication*, 29, 197–201.

Petty, R.E. and J. Cacioppo (1986), *Communication and Persuasion: Central and Peripheral Routes to Attitude Change*, New York: Springer.

Phillips, D. and J. Stanton (2004), "Age-Related Differences in Advertising: Recall and Persuasion," *Journal of Targeting, Measurement and Analysis for Marketing*, 13 (1), 7–21.

Phillips, L.W. and B. Sternthal (1977), "Age Differences in Information Processing: A Perspective on the Aged Consumer," *Journal of Marketing Research*, 19 (November), 444–57.

Pine, K.J. (2002), "Dear Santa: The Effects of Television Advertising on Young Children," *International Journal of Behavioral Development*, 26 (6), 529–39.

Richards, J.I. and R.D. Petty (2007), "Advertising Regulation," in *The SAGE Handbook of Advertising*, eds. G.J. Tellis and T. Ambler, London: Sage Publications.

Richardson, L. and V. Luchsinger (2005), "Direct-To-Customer Advertising of Pharmacuetical Products: Issue Analysis and Direct-To-Consumer Promotion," *Journal of American Academy of Business*, 7 (September), 100–4.

Robertson, T.S. and J.R. Rossiter (1974), "Children and Commercial Persuasion: An Attribution Theory Analysis," *Journal of Consumer Research*, 1 (June), 13–20.

Robinson, T.N. (2001), "Effects of Reducing Television Viewing on Children's Requests for Toys: A Randomized Controlled Trial," *Journal of*

Developmental and Behavioral Pediatrics, 22 (3), 179–84.

Roedder, D.L. (1981), "Age Differences in Children's Responses to Television Advertising: An Information Processing Approach," *Journal of Consumer Research*, 8 (September), 144–53.

Roedder, D. (1999), "Consumer Socialization of Children: A Retrospective Look at Twenty-Five Years of Research," *Journal of Consumer Research*, 26 (December), 183–213.

Ross, R.P., T. Campbell, J.C. Wright, A.C. Huston, M.L. Rice, and P. Turk (1984), "When Celebrities Talk, Children Listen: An Experimental Analysis of Children's Responses to TV Ads with Celebrity Endorsement," *Journal of Applied Developmental Psychology*, 5 (July–September), 185–202.

Schor, J.B. (2004), *Born to Buy: The Commercialized Child and the New Consumer Culture*, New York, NY: Scribner.

Singh, S. and C.A. Cole (1993), "The Effects of Length, Content, and Repetition on Television Commercial Effectiveness," *Journal of Marketing Research*, 30 (1), 91–105.

Skurnik, I., C. Yoon, D. Park, and N. Schwarz (2005), "How Warnings about False Claims Become Recommendations," *Journal of Consumer Research*, 31 (March), 713–24.

Smart, R.G. (1988), "Does Alcohol Advertising Affect Overall Consumption? A Review of Empirical Studies," *Journal of Studies on Alcohol*, 49 (4), 314–23.

Smith, N.C. and E. Cooper-Martin (1997), "Ethics and Target Marketing: The Role of Product Harm and Consumer Vulnerability," *Journal of Marketing*, 61, (July), 1–20.

Unsigned (2006) "Alcohol-Ready to-Drink: Diageo Banks on Quinn's," *Marketing Week*, London: 9 (March), 28.

Ward, S., D.B. Wackman, and E. Wartella (1977), *How Children Learn to Buy*, Beverly Hills, CA: Sage.

Williams, P. and A. Drolet (2005), "Age-Related Differences in Responses to Emotional Advertisements," *Journal of Consumer Research*, 32 (December), 343–54.

Advertising, Consumption and Welfare

Thomas C. O'Guinn

The central question of this chapter is what is advertising's role in consumption and collective welfare? What have been the effects of advertising on our collective well-being? Obviously, these are big questions. Perhaps not quite as obvious is the fact that the answers are so few, so small, and so qualified.

After opening up the questions that need answers, and some background history, this chapter addresses the central issue of wants, needs and materialism. Does advertising simply convert wants into needs? Is advertising an agent of social stasis, particularly where race and gender are concerned. Is advertising the thing that really made capitalism safe once and for all from revolutionary impulses? Is this made worse by the third person effect? Before the concluding summary, I review whether the case against advertising has been overstated and it is little more than noisy wallpaper.

SOME QUESTIONS TO BE ANSWERED

What are the social effects of advertising? What constitutes the social welfare in which

we are interested? For example, was our material abundance brought to us, at least in part, by advertising and the market capitalism it helps drive? Is the unequal distribution of that abundance a side effect of advertising? Are our homes and lives filled with so many things because of advertising? Are so many of our daily activities and even our language consumption centered because of the cumulative force of ubiquitous consuming messages? Are we more uncaring, selfish, carnal, vacuous, materialistic, fatter, thinner, smokers, drinkers, gamblers, over-spent and over-worked because of advertising? Or, are we generally better informed, more materially comfortable, healthier, freer, and happier? Are we better off, or have we been harmed? In sum, how have we fared after more than a century of modern advertising?

Ultimately, these are near-impossible questions. Those who seek to specify advertising's precise causal contribution to some particular behavioral outcome such as increased childhood obesity prevalence assume a level and extent of scientific inquiry that is more wish than fulfillment. The bigger and deeper questions are much tougher still. To actually offer definitive answers to questions regarding the role of materiality in human existence, existential fulfillment and the marketplace is to do what world religions, philosophers, artists, writers, and the daily experience and pondering of billions of human beings have not yet done. Yet, their collective thoughts, their "naive theories" reveal an acceptance of contradiction, paradox, exception, and nuance that are typically absent in academic theories.

Addressing the question of advertising's impact on the general social condition is also significantly hampered by the way in which these questions have typically been approached. Because advertising is simultaneously so many things, several academic disciplines make contact with it. But they do so sporadically, casually, and with too little meaningful engagement with one another. Interdisciplinary discourse on advertising is regrettably rare, ignorance of other literatures far too common. For example, promising literatures on advertising exist in the humanities but remain largely unknown to social scientists, even though they may be purchased in just about any bookstore in North America or Europe or checked out from any public library. Even more discouraging is the oft encountered attitude among some behavioral scientists that their "narrow-by-design" mode of inquiry makes a certain level of ignorance preferable, a good thing. Those in the humanities are almost (but not quite) as unaware of what has been produced on the other side of the great divide by behavioural scientists. Across the board there is also a too often hubristic underlying sentiment that it is "only advertising," how hard could it be to study. The bias of deeming advertising as "low culture" is often conflated with an assumption of phenomenological simplicity. This is a truly depressing situation; broader reading habits and less moral certitude are strongly encouraged.

Where macro-questions regarding advertising are concerned the application of behavioral science has either been too occasional and restricted, or it just isn't the right tool set in the first place. Although it shouldn't need saying, let me say it anyway: advertising is neither molecule nor protozoa. Advertising is an object of study that is hardly an object at all, but a multi-layered and historically determined institution. Social psychologists routinely mistake stimulus material for ads; although some argue that they actually realize this and are really interested only in mental "process," not generalization to real world advertising.

Even more to the point, just exactly what type of experiment(s) would one design to answer such big (social level) questions anyway? For the most part the big questions, certainly the ones about well-being and social welfare, are about the effects of years, decades, even lifetimes of acquiring, modifying, accommodating, negotiating, accepting and sometimes rejecting the consumption-related communication practices of a consumer society. How would these effects be detectable in experimental settings? How do you manipulate socialization? Where do you find the control group? When the big questions are chopped down to a far less meaningful series of small and disconnected ones, lengthy and tortuously specific literature reviews end with the accurate, but entirely predictable, "*it depends*." Of course it does.

At the other end of the spectrum, critical theorists write about advertising sans data. Meaning is located in texts (ads) that are apparent only to the critical eye and result in the pre-determined conclusion (with various added twists and turns for critical club members): advertising is a hegemonic force of market capitalism and consumers possess little or no agency, and are ultimately victims. If consumers act upon information contained in ads they do so according to marketer's directives and blithely bend to the will of the system's incredibly clever and universally successful protection of capital. All this is said to occur under the nose of an utterly unenlightened mass public. Who says academics don't practice religion?

Of course, the really big questions are as much philosophical and political as they are empirical. So, why should we be surprised that the everyday practice of behavioural science or the anti-science of critical thought could or would produce meaningful and stable answers: Because, on rare occasions, they do. There are a few meaningful findings, good arguments, and evidence to be assembled from these diverse literatures. You have to look long and hard, but there are some things we can reasonably (although rarely unambiguously) extract from the literature. Still, for many of the questions there are simply no clear answer to be had: we simply don't know, and pretending otherwise does no one any good.

A LITTLE HISTORY

One thing is certain: the question of advertising's impact on social well-being and consumption with no sense of history is an empty one. All assessments of human welfare are set in time and are relative to social standards we have known in the past or come to expect of the future. It is the case that what advertising means now is significantly determined by its history. Advertisements are not simply fixed "information" sitting forever on a page to be processed by a computer-as-analogue mind, equally fixed in time outside of social context. This fact is doubly important when asking how it (advertising) has affected the general social welfare.

Modern advertising emerged in the mid to late 1800s (Fox, 1985; Wicke, 1988); it came into full bloom in the early twentieth century. Its rise corresponds to the fading of the Victorian era and the rise of the modern consumer. What we now call advertising is a product of modernity (Fox, 1985; Marchand, 1985; Lears, 1994; Wicke, 1988), and modernity is more than an epoch. It is a philosophy completely consistent with the ends of advertising and consumption: faith in never-ending progress, the promise of urbanism, science and technology, choice and plentitude. When we talk of advertising's impact on the general social condition we are talking about its impact inseparable from modernity and its advance … and, very significantly here, inseparable from the counter-balancing academic *critique* of modernity that was fomenting at the very same moment. The entire discourse surrounding advertising, consumption and welfare cannot be separated from an on-going conversation about the *appropriate* role of material things, self, pleasure, authenticity, and *morality* in the context of advancing modernity and its close relationship to market capitalism. Advertising and social welfare debates have never existed outside that broader discourse; to argue otherwise is either historically unaware, naive, or disingenuous. Despite protests to the contrary, most writings and pronouncements on advertising and welfare are really, when you get right down to it, about who should have what or how much, what pleasure should or should not be derived from having these things, who will be in control of that pleasure's allocation and distribution, who was unfairly influenced to acquire these things, which things are real and authentic, and who shall be charged with surveillance and sanctioning of the whole process.

Advertising, born on the cusp of waning Victorian morality and nascent modernity, was an awkward thing most properly associated with carnivals, sideshows and over-promised spectacle (Fox, 1985; Lears, 1981). It was not, however, out of place. This crude advertising fit the harsh realities of a harsh world quite well, a world with few of the things now assumed as minimal standards of daily life, an un-regulated and wide open market, and an aggressive style of capitalism that took few prisoners. This is a period in which none other than Thomas Alva Edison filmed and exhibited the public electrocution of an elephant (Jowett, 1976). This is the P.T. Barnum age. Advertising's early reputation for hyperbole and spectacle was deserved (Fox, 1985; Lears, 1994; Marchand, 1985). In the US, early advertising was completely un-regulated: it was not uncommon for ads to claim to cure cancer, paralysis, and all sorts of human ills. Until 1906, American marketers didn't even have to reveal the contents of their products. You could pretty much sell anything you wanted and say anything about it that you cared to, true or not (Fox, 1985).

At the very same moment early advertising was advancing, social thought in the US and Europe was developing around an essential critique of market capitalism. This is the period in which the shift to modernity, driven by early mass consumerism, is seen as the death of legitimate community, the source of anomie, and a litany of other social ills (Lasch, 1991). The foundational social thought flowing from this period rests on a basic critique of modern capitalism, and advertising is one of modernity's very visible agents. To be fair, early advertising didn't help its own cause; its often tawdry nature and sometimes bad behavior made an easy target. So, from its very beginning advertising is cast negatively in academe's morality infused view. Later, when advertising matured, was more regulated and better behaved, finer distinctions did not catch up; old grudges and biases lingered. Babies went out with bathwater. This early view of bad advertising became the received view for decades of social theorists (Twitchell, 1999). In fact, advertising has never escaped the essentialist assumptions that fell forward from this period. The world changed, advertising changed, but the essential assumptions of social thought regarding advertising never fully did. It made too good a story, a story resonant with a central meta-narrative of the rise of consumer culture as paradise lost. No matter how it behaved, advertising would pretty much be seen in a negative light by social theorists from this point forward.

Modern advertising is "invented" because brands became the building blocks of modern market capitalism. In the late nineteenth century, brands replaced many unmarked commodities. While there were branded products prior to this period, it is during the last two decades of the nineteenth century that the ubiquitous branding we know today began. Between 1875 and 1900, a flood of branded products replaced unbranded commodities. Soap, previously sold by weight from a generally unbranded cake, becomes Ivory (1882) and Sapolio (circa 1875). Beer, previously drawn from an unnamed keg, becomes Budweiser (1891) and Pabst (1873). All across the spectrum of goods and services, existing commodities became brands, as did the flood of new things designed for the modern marketplace. The mass market promised lower priced, uniform, and higher quality goods. These things came in the form of brands.

It was a necessity of modern market capitalism to create and promote brands. Consider the economics. Commodities (beer, soap) have elastic demand functions. If there is no distinction between soaps, all soaps are completely interchangeable. The set of acceptable substitutes is large and the demand is price elastic; price increases are met with decreases in demand. But when soap became Ivory in 1882, all that changed. Procter and Gamble began to impart different, additional, and particular meanings to the previously unmarked commodity. Due to the new marketplace meanings of Ivory brand soap (purity in particular); there were far fewer acceptable substitutes at any given price. Ivory's demand function became more inelastic. Ivory delivered more value through purity, packaging, and all the other bundle of meanings that the modern Ivory brand communicated, and it delivered more profit than mere soap: consumers began to demand the soap that floats (O'Guinn and Muniz, 2005).

Brands made good economic sense, and modern market capitalism became reliant on branding. It is no coincidence that this period is also known as the birth of the modern advertising industry and the rapid growth of mass market magazines. Advertising expenditures increased tenfold between 1864 and 1900 (Fox, 1985). Magazine circulations produced a similar arc. Mass media flourished as a means to project national brands into national consciousness. The word "mass" here is not insignificant. Advertising is, as was the media that carried it, for the masses, another sin for which it has never been completely forgiven (Marchand, 1985; Twitchell, 1999; O'Guinn and Muniz, 2004).

Over its history, advertising has often leveraged existing social concerns and imparted social meaning to brands in attempts to sell things. For example, Ivory would claim purity during a period when purity was of vital concern to Americans. The average life expectancy in the US in 1900 was 49.2 years; infant mortality was twice what it would be just 25 years later (Sullivan, 1926). A concerned public pushed Congress to pass the Pure Food and Drug Act in 1906. Purity was more than a word; it was, at that time, one of the few things the public believed might prevent them, or their children, from dying young. So, Ivory floats. Its purity was demonstrated by a market logic. No one really had to understand the physical mechanism that related purity to floating. Social context gave meaning to Ivory's branding, its advertising claim, its marketplace logic, and the meaning of a bar of soap that floated. Ivory *meant* something, something socially agreed upon, and something important. It was pure, $99^{44/100}$ pure. Ivory was no longer a commodity; its set of acceptable substitutes shriveled. The same mechanisms of meaning were applied to countless other branded goods and services.

Do not, however, get the impression that this was all ad-hype; it was not. It is very possible that advertiser's efforts to promote cleanliness and hygienic practices may have actually saved a good many lives. Media and demographic analysis indicate that advertising was a significant vector for public health practices in early modernity, admittedly for a profit motive, but with an undeniably positive outcome: saved lives (O'Guinn and Swicegood, 2008). Ivory was actually pure. Unlike other soaps of this period, Ivory neither went rancid nor burned the skin with lye. By separating (early usage segmentation) soap for the bath from soap to wash the floor, Ivory and a few other competitors promoted modern washing and bathing practices. These practices saved lives while they made profits for companies.

There are other positive outcomes as well. Too often we too easily dismiss the demise of drudgery that the world of modern goods yielded. Although it makes comfortable theorists uncomfortable, the modern world of goods made life a lot easier for a great many, particularly during the early days of the twentieth century. Even the "underclass" upon whose backs this progress was supposedly strapped had real positive changes in daily existence in the reduction of very real drudgery. And these changes for the good, like it or not, came from an advancing consumer society pushed along by modern advertising.

Advertising discovered many of its rhetorical forms by the beginning of World War II (Fox, 1985; Marchand, 1985). One of those forms was to artfully leverage social concerns, anxieties, dislocations, and other conflicts in mass society (Frank, 1997; Lears, 1994; Marchand, 1985). In times of rapid social change there are no shortages of anxieties. Shifting social roles and expectations produce anxiety, and these same social shifts provide opportunities for advertisers. Advertisers often offer their goods and services as remedies or "therapies" for the trials and tribulations of modern living (Lears, 1981; Marchand, 1985). This "therapeutic ethos" has been a staple of the advertising industry for well over a century (Lears, 1981). It is an exceptionally efficient rhetorical strategy (O'Guinn, 2008). Market economies require ever expanding demand, and without the cycle of problem–solution–new problem–new solution, market economies would have a hard time sustaining growth. The exact nature of the problems and solutions vary with time and circumstance, but the basic mechanism does not. Consumers sometimes accept and sometimes reject the specific appeals of advertisers, but the general strategy endures. Social change has been good for the advertising industry and modern market capitalism.

Significant advertising regulation did not occur in the US until the Wheeler-Lea Amendment to the FTC charter in 1938. This was precipitated by the generally anti-business spirit of the Great Depression and advertising's overall tawdriness and occasional misbehavior during the same period (Marchand, 1985). It was not until the 1960s that a second round of significant reform occurs. From this point forward most everyone accepts that "special audiences" such as children deserve some protection from advertising abuses. This is significant in that we now officially codify the belief that advertising can be powerful enough to be harmful to some. Public attitudes toward advertising have remained ambivalent to generally negative (Calfee, 1997).

Over the last 30 or 40 years advertising has continued to grow in dollars, minutes, space and clicks, but the public's view of advertising has not changed appreciably. It is still regarded as essentially self interested and occasionally dishonest, but paradoxically providing "valuable information" (Calfee, 1997). Advertising's own history coupled with a long-standing cultural ambivalence toward the intersection of money, the marketplace, wealth and mass consumption, has as much to do with these conflicting attitudes as anything. Critics also allege more specific harms: advertising is responsible for millions of smoking related deaths, drunk-driving carnage, and obesity, just to name a few. Defenders of the institution claim there is little hard evidence to support such claims (e.g., Calfee, 1997; Luick and Waterston, 1996). Most recently, Thomas Frank (1997) asserts that advertising is now a force that makes meaningful social movement virtually impossible. According to Frank, advertising has turned revolutionary language into hip ad-speak, and thus neutralized it.

Running counter to this, others scholars have offered support of advertising on various fronts, including being a generally good source of product information (Schudson, 1984), a contributor to the general prosperity of market economies and their citizens, and even a force of limited liberation (Twitchell, 1999; Chambers, 2007). Yet, it is fair to say that strong academic supporters of advertising are scarce (Rotzoll et al., 1986) .

WANTS, NEEDS, MATERIALISM

A familiar chant in the critical modernist mantra is that advertising turns what would otherwise be mere wants into needs. According to this fable once wants become needs; consumers become lemmings, resistance is difficult, if not impossible. Underlying this very familiar myth is the assumption that if left alone by advertising consumers would behave rationally and consume only the things they truly need, or at least a much smaller set of things, and only things good for them (as determined by cultural elites, and other would-be parent figures). This claim is problematic on several fronts. First, the very idea that advertising turns "wants" into "needs" is to believe that there is some small set of "true" or "real" needs distinct from the less true (and less "real") wants. Schudson (1984) and Twitchell (1999) among others have held that this is simply wrong. The difference between wants and needs is either non-existent, much slipperier than typically thought, and is entirely socially constructed, highly variable, and determined by relative social, not absolute material standards. To buy into this simple model one would of necessity have to believe in some Eden like myth in which pre-modern (and pre-advertising) societies behaved in a thoroughly rational and utilitarian way and (although contradictory with the first two attributes) altruistic manner. How could this be? It can't. The human record consists of no place where materiality and meaning are strangers. Goods have always had social meaning, often important ones. As Schudson (1984) notes, there is no record anywhere of a society that did not have a very special place for things, there has never been a society without luxuries. This begs the question: just exactly what is materialism, and why is it supposed to be such a modern malady? This would require a separate chapter.

But what of matters-of-degree; has advertising pushed consumption more to the center of the human experience? That is a much more reasonable question. Is it possible that advertising, *en masse*, has less direct, but still significant macro effects, and some of these push materiality more to the fore of contemporary human existence? These effects may be missed by the brute force of economic or cross-sectional survey analysis or by the typical social psychology experiments with middle class college sophomores. But are they still there, just less detectable, more subtle? For example, O'Guinn and Shrum (1997) demonstrated that a simple measure of hours of television viewed per week significantly affected consumer's perceptions of what other people had and consumed, particularly people outside their own social milieu. This was true even when stratification variables income, education and age were accounted for, and most significantly as these mediated visions interacted with actual direct experience. Most of their dependent measures came directly from television program content, not advertising. But, was the world as revealed by programming content all that different from that constructed by TV ads? Probably not, and it is certainly less likely today as programming and advertising merge (Donaton, 2004). It thus seems likely that advertising is one of many cultural agents providing the mental materials by which consumers construct their social worlds, worlds of aspiration, and expectation, and of consumption norms. So in this way advertising is resonant with a mediated mental world that is consumption friendly and consumption rich, and provides easily accessible images of aspirational target lives.

Advertising is the wallpaper of a consumer society, but how much impact it really has, apart from that resonance, is a particularly elusive answer. Even decades of longitudinal empirical study would still be overmatched by the vagaries of shifting cultural sands, and the multitudes of interaction forces. It certainly makes sense that a primary agent of consumer society (advertising) helped locate modern consumption near its center. Yet, it just as certainly had a great deal of help from other social forces and a generally eager group of consumers (Twitchell, 1999; Muniz and O'Guinn, 2005).

AGENT OF SOCIAL STASIS: THE PROBLEMS OF RACE AND GENDER

A common criticism of advertising is that it acts to protect the existing social order: keeping things as they are, and people in "their place." According to this charge, advertising is an agent of social stasis, a defender of inequity, particularly in terms of race and gender.

While not dismissing the claim at all, the evidence for it is, at best, equivocal. Over the long haul, the advertising industry and its clients have benefited far more from social change than by protecting the status quo. It is when society moves beneath consumer's feet that new anxieties and problems arise and new opportunities for advertisers are created (Marchand, 1985; Frank, 1997; Holt, 2004; O'Guinn, 2007). Advertisers have a vested interest in social change; it is generally good for business. And given advertising's modernist impulse it has generally favoured change over stasis. The 1950s may be the only good counter example (Friedan, 1963; Briens, 1992), and even there the case may be a bit over-stated. After all, advertisers benefited greatly by the emergence of the "teen" market, the birth of rock-and-roll, cultural rebel icons such as Elvis Presley and James Dean, and the sexual restlessness of the late 1950s (Halberstam, 1993; Heath and Potter, 2005).

Race: In terms of race, it is simply unarguable that US advertising for two thirds of the twentieth century employed racial stereotypes and presented an overly white world (Fox, 1985). While a separate black press and advertising industry existed, "mainstream" American advertising was very white until the mid to late 1960s. Up until this time people of colour were largely relegated to servants and trade characters, if they were represented at all. To put it in context, while the sixties white suburban flower children were celebrating free love and mind expansion, Madison Avenue was still afraid to put a black person in an ad in a non-servant role. Brand managers were sometimes terrified of their brand becoming the "negro brand" (Fox, 1985; Chamber, 2007); Pepsi is a good example of a brand where racial overlays were of significant concern to a major brand (Smithsonian Oral History Archives). Since the late 1960s things have changed, but the advertising industry is still considered to be one of the whitest in America, and debates about racial representations in advertising have not gone away (Sanders, 2006). In fact the issue has been prominent in the trade press (e.g., *Advertising Age*) in this very year.

Now, to the social welfare question: what have been the effects of these representations? While content analyses have yielded valuable statistics regarding relative representation and prominence of various ethnic minorities in ads (e.g., Seiter, 1994) *meaningful, long-term* effects of this content have not been significantly demonstrated. We simply do not have the longitudinal studies to know what effect years of stereotyping or critical absence has had on racial attitudes, assumptions, self image, social expectation, and prejudice. Again, the problem is not with science per se, but the simple dearth of long-term studies with measures sensitive enough to pick up meaningful effects. Laboratory studies demonstrating treatment effects of various racial representations are very valuable in terms of processing effects, as small scale cross-sectional surveys are alerting us to likely long-term effects (see Williams et al., 2004), but are by their nature inadequate to assess the larger long-term effects of such representations on the general social welfare. It is certainly intuitive to believe that these larger social welfare effects exist.

Some recent socio-historical work has offered a different and more nuanced argument. Chambers (2007) argues that advertising actually served a libratory role where race is concerned. The argument goes something like this: by not picturing blacks in ads, the absence became visible, noticeable, so much so that it helped define a meaningful civil rights front. Out of sight had been out of mind. When getting people of colour on television (including advertising) and into magazine advertising became a civil rights objective, advertising became more important in the context of race, and more pressure was brought to bear. Chamber's argument is supported by work by Hale (1999) and to a lesser extent by Cohen (2003). It should be abundantly clear that in many ways the black civil rights movement of the twentieth century was fought on battlegrounds

of consumption: lunch counters, busses, theaters, housing, and retail. The "Don't Buy Where You Can't Work" protests in New York's Harlem and Chicago of the 1930s demonstrated the power of the consumer sphere for civil rights (Greenberg, 1999). Given that we are a consumer society, denial of access to consumption venues or second class treatment within those venues, makes these the front lines.

Chambers (2007) argues that advertising can be an effective instrument of shared everyday-ness, and thus normalization of race relations. He believes that it was seeing black people washing clothes, brushing their teeth, drinking sodas, and putting their children to bed that made the ordinary visible and demystified the "other." Then, and sometimes now, ads were one of our only glimpses into the "backstage" (Goffman, 1959) lives of "the other," in this case black American consumers. In a segregated world para-social interaction through media and advertising let us glimpse inside what was otherwise cut off to us: aspects of the mundane and everyday life of otherwise marginalized people (Gates, 1994). O'Guinn and Shrum (1997) have empirically shown how people use television to form consumption worlds in their heads that they never directly encounter. Certainly something similar must have happened with advertising in the early days of integration. When someone is missing or hidden from view they can be constructed in all sorts of ways, when they are there and visible, then the ordinary has to be dealt with. Advertising provided this opportunity.

Yet, there are still plenty of concerns with racial representations in advertising and its presumed effects. To the extent that stereotyped and skewed social representations still exist, the body of socialization theory, taken as a whole, would predict negative effects on self concept, bias, and a restriction of the mental world we as consumers construct around others and ourselves (O'Guinn and Faber, 1991).

Gender: The social welfare question of advertising and gender is similar to the racial one but hardly identical. The vast majority of critiques of gender and advertising involve representations of white women and are focused on issues of beauty and objectification. From advertising's very beginning women accounted for a sizeable majority of consumer purchases. The industry has talked openly about this for over a century; Marchand (1985) and Fox (1985) extensively quote major industry figures in the trade press. This is hardly a secret or a controversy (Fox, 1985; Laermans, 1993; Lears, 1981; Marchand, 1985; Schudson, 1984). Put simply, advertising is more about women than it is about men. Men, as Marchand (1985) has shown were so peripheral that they were largely undifferentiated as targets. It was not until the late 1950s or early 1960s that we see men, even at home, without being dressed in a business suit. In other words, according to the visual rhetoric of advertising, men were just visual clichés, a guy in a suit: dad, the provider. Mom ran the house, raised the kids, took care of the home, and bought most of the things that came into the home. Women's representations were, despite the stereotypes, more varied, had more lines colored in. What effect has all this had? What is advertising's contribution to the social welfare of women . . . and men?

It is also an empirical reality that early twentieth century advertising targeted women with several strategies that are widely seen as problematic (Fox, 1985; Leiss et al., 2005; Marchand, 1985; Schudson, 1984; Sheehan, 2004). For example, women were commonly pitted against other women for the grand prize: the well-to-do husband in the "beauty contest of life" (Marchand, 1985). Mothers are told to take care of their daughter's looks from day one . . . begin the beauty regimen in infancy. Women were warned about being left behind by their more modern (and working) husbands. Clearly, some not-insignificant-number of ads attempted to use feelings of responsibility and guilt in a myriad of ways: anxiety over their housekeeping and cooking abilities, their attractiveness and their social graces (Friedan, 1963; Marchand, 1985; O'Guinn, 2007). The existence, prevalence, and revealed strategy of these ads are hardly

a matter of controversy. One need only go to any of the major published histories (Fox, 1985; Marchand, 1985; Scott, 2004), or better yet to the data themselves, the actual ads to observe this (O'Guinn, 2008). The extant data are anything but equivocal.

However, the question at hand, the effects question, is a more complex one ... a much more difficult one. Where does representation meet significant social effect? A core feminist criticism of advertising is that advertising yielded unrealistic expectations of beauty and attached all manner of social anxiety to various gender role enactments (Courtney and Whipple, 1983; Friedan, 1963; Sheehan, 2004). Women in most ads are not of modal proportion or weight, and advertising often plays on women's anxieties in the pursuit of marketplace goals; put benignly; it offers solutions to gender related problems. Advertising points to and exacerbates these problems, while minimizing others (O'Guinn et al., 2004). Of course, the problems are rarely created out of whole cloth, but from existing social fabric. Even the problems that are more "ad-created" would not seem like problems at all unless they had some attachment, no matter how remote, to an underlying social dynamic and anxiety. Leveraging women's social anxiety is one of the oldest advertising strategies around (Lears, 1981, 1994; Fox, 1985; Marchand, 1985).

What are the effects of repeated exposure to these gendered representations? Again, if we rely on the social science we have a very hard time getting from x to y. Think of the enormity of the problem. Careful longitudinal research is required for this and for reasons we know all too well (like getting tenure), it rarely gets done. Certainly, there are survey and experimental studies suggestive of negative consequences (e.g., Richins, 1995), but taken as a whole the case cannot be made definitively. One can either say that this is merely a failure of method, or one can argue that advertising is a relatively weak force in terms of overall gender socialization.

It seems to me, however, that it is more likely than not, based on socialization theory and on what we do know of long-term media effects in general, that the effects of advertising on gender stereotypes and self esteem are non-zero. For example, advertising, until just recently, rarely showed women eating, and when it did, it was often presented as "guilty pleasure" (Bordo, 1993). Men in ads, on the other hand, are much freer to yield to their appetites, appetites of all sorts. Does repeated exposure to these different gender representations with respect to food, which are likely essentially consistent with real world differences in food behavior, have an impact on normative beliefs about women and eating? They probably do, but again, it has not been demonstrated empirically? The truth is we just don't know what the long-term exposure to this type of advertising representations produce (Percy and Lautman, 1994), although we can theorize and speculate. If all the published consumer socialization and social reality effects research is valid, then we have to believe that, at a minimum, these representations along with others become part of assumed norms, of constructed, and relied upon assumptions about the world, and the attractiveness, desirability, and happiness of those people "out there." But just as certainly it is not a simple causal relationship. One should also note the stance of Scott (2004) who asserts that advertising from time to time has actually been a force for liberation where gender is concerned. She believes that advertising has actually pushed women toward a form of lipstick feminism and has often been surprisingly progressive in its treatment of alternative lifestyles, and sometimes legitimately liberating. Hers is the conventional view, but significantly points out the polemic, anti-empirical, simplistic and ahistorical nature of the "standard" feminist critique of advertising.

SOCIAL CONTROL

One of the more important books to be written on advertising is Thomas Frank's 1997 *Conquest of Cool*. The book advances a general cultural theory of advertising, and has been received by many as a significant advance in theorizing modern advertising. It asserts that advertising emerged from the 1960s Cultural Revolution fundamentally changed in that from that time forward, most if not all, revolutionary impulses are played out in a consumption motif. Advertising played a significant role in this shift. According to his reasoning, this makes advertising powerful and capitalism safe. People act out revolutionary impulses by buying the revolutionary-approved accoutrements, revolutionary utterances become hip ad copy, but structurally nothing is challenged because now nothing is outside the ad-commercial-sway, not even politics. Because advertising so completely appropriated the language and look of revolution, youth and cool, consumer culture and market capitalism are now immune to serious threat. Frank views the sixties as the tipping point, a point at which advertising completed its appropriation of everything important culturally, including its enemies. "Youth has won (Frank, 1997: 235; quoting Steir, 1967); advertising has won." In the 1960s advertising began to market the safe accessories, the props, the set dressing of revolution ("John Lennon glasses," "Hippie Ponchos," etc.) and learned that as long as you speak the language and project the look of revolution, revolution (even anti-capitalist revolution, as long as it doesn't go too far) is good business. It's a strategy of giving the kids what they want because we all know that someday soon they will have a mortgage, so let them play revolutionary now; they will work for us later.

Frank makes good points, and his evidence is sometimes convincing. But with Frank, as is true with most all critically inspired commentators, the parable can have only one end, one moral: resistance through the marketplace is illusory; all commercial utterances regarding popular resistance are really marketing strategy; hegemony is all. How rhetorically convenient is this? How does one counter argue such a stance? If you do, as Twitchell (1999) suggests, you are dismissed as just "not getting it." Frank precludes even the possibility that consumers are *meaningfully* aware of the difference between an ad slogan and a cry for social justice, or that they make important distinctions between purely fashion politics and purposefully self-aware political action. More fundamentally troubling is the essential critical blind spot: that there can be meaningful discourse and resistance within the commercial sphere, that the merger of market and politics is neither new nor futile. Frank's thesis is itself wrapped in hip nihilism; the idea of market populism is repulsive to the hip advisers (see Holt, 2004), to the politically hip, and the selfproclaimed above-it-all critic.

While I can readily accept the argument that radical sentiments are often (too often) reduced to fashion, and that often, maybe even very often consumers are primarily interested in the fashion and delude themselves softly into thinking that wearing the symbol of revolution is the same thing as revolution, I do not think that most consumers are that unaware most of the time. It is also the case that fashion is sometimes as meaningful as politics; sometimes fashion is politics, real politics. Further, consumers appear to have a more sophisticated and self aware view of these two domains and their boundaries than Frank admits. Also, Frank may, like so many, over-estimate the 60s influence. Due to shear demographic weight, its inhabitants' self absorbed legacy often noted self absorbed nature (cite), and an increasingly tiresome question: were the sixties revolution or mere fashion, the appeal lingers. But the sixties are over, and advertising during the next half century has been far more variable on more dimensions than Frank acknowledges. His argument could be more nuanced, his history less sweeping, and his analysis of the actual ads more systematic, empirical and fine-grained. Further, the critical stance, particularly where advertising is concerned, is hardly courageous on a college campus (or for that matter most any place), nor anything new. Helping people believe that they are more enlightened, informed and generally "in-on" what advertisers are doing to the less intelligent and informed is simply good business, which is, ironically, consistent with Frank's thesis.

It does not, however, seem to me that advertising has done-in meaningful politics, not even radical politics. If anything it seems that brands are becoming more politicized, as well as public opinion regarding the corporate culture of brands. When activists want to protest US policy on foreign soil they now look for a McDonalds instead of an embassy. Wal-Mart has become a bona fide political issue in American politics. This politization of brands certainly seems more meaningful than the kind of play-revolutionary hipster Frank describes (O'Guinn and Muniz, 2004). It needs more attention.

THIRD PERSONS

One of the most robust findings in communication research is the "third person" effect (Davidson, 1983; Gunther and Thorson, 1992). It has been demonstrated in scores of papers, and in many content domains. It is a very real effect. It says that individuals will believe that others (third persons) are much more affected by media (including advertising) than they themselves are. Even more revealing is that the effect is its strongest in an up-to-down SES context: the effect is greatest when people of higher education and higher income are asked to estimate the effect of advertising on those with less education and income. The more educated and affluent believe that advertising affects them relatively little, but is very powerful for those less educated and less affluent. These consumers are often coded as "the information poor." Some consider this term and its underlying philosophy patronizing. No matter how noble the motives, a group of more educated and wealthier (typically white) people assuming that they are less susceptible to advertising by virtue of their education, wealth and other places in relative strata hierarchies, simply begs the change of elitism, paternalism and patronization.

The third person effect is highly significant in the general social welfare question. How do we negotiate this question when the tendency for the highly educated (academics, policy makers) is to believe that the "under-class" and other "vulnerable consumers" are the most significantly affected, and they themselves are relatively immune? How do we address these stratification-based personal immunity myths? Is this a place where well-done social science could contribute? Yes.

NOISY WALLPAPER

As Figure 6.5.1 indicates one of the issues of advertising and social welfare is addressed by simply looking at just how much of it there is. A recent *Advertising Age* editorial as well as other volumes (see Donaton, 2004) termed this a "death spiral of disrespect." Some, including prominent CEOs, actually believe it possible that advertising will simply kill itself off from overexposure (Donaton, 2004). In the meantime, what should we make of the sheer volume of advertising? Does it adversely affect us, or is it just a mild annoyance?

One of the great advertising personages of all time was Howard Gossage. Creator of many famous campaigns he also more or less invented socially aware advertising. Besides being Marshall McLuhan's publicist, Gossage did things like help launch what was then a new environmental organization called the Sierra Club. He helped campaign against a government plan to flood parts of the Grand Canyon. One of the government's

sillier arguments in support of the proposal was that with the canyon partially flooded boaters could get a better view of the beautiful canyon walls. Gossage created an ad that said that by applying the same logic, we should flood the Sistine Chapel to get a better look at the ceiling. In some part due to his effort, the project went no further.

One of Gossage's biggest concerns about advertising was just how much of it there was, and when he wrote this in the 1960s, there was roughly one third of what there is now. In his famous essay entitled "Is Advertising Worth Saving" he said:

> Yes, if we can learn to look at advertising not as a means for filling so much space and time but as a technique for solving problems. And this will not be possible until we destroy the commission system and start predicating our work on what is to be earned rather than on what has to be spent. (Gossage,1995: 11)

Well, the simple 15% commission system died about 20 years ago (O'Guinn et al., 2004). Before it died it was simple ... a flat 15% commission on media buying. The more ads an agency advised a client to buy, the more money the agency made. Not surprisingly, agencies seldom advised less advertising. Gossage was right, a very simple reason there is so much advertising was a simple "15% more money for me" system. Now that it is gone, agencies more commonly wring their

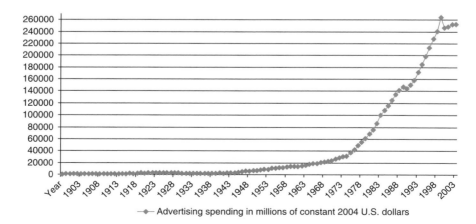

—◆— Advertising spending in millions of constant 2004 U.S. dollars

Figure 6.5.1   Total U. S. advertising spending 1900–2004

hands about "the end of advertising." But there is still a lot of it and more and more of it is appearing in alternative (e.g., branded entertainment, placement, promotion) and other "below the line" forms (*Advertising Age* 2005; O'Guinn et al., 2004).

To me and to Gossage one of the biggest problems of advertising is its sheer volume, its ubiquity. It is everywhere. Ironically, this may have decreased advertising's power and actually produced fewer sales (see Donaton, 2004; and Section 3 of this volume). Advertising has become background noise, maybe easier to tune out, and this is not just the opinion of cultural critics, but also of CEOs, one of their often stated reasons for leaving traditional advertising behind (Donaton, 2004).

But does advertising still present a significant social ecological problem beyond clutter? Although theory, intuition and cross-sectional research (e.g., O'Guinn and Shrum, 1997) point in the direction of social-construction effects, the production of normative beliefs about what others possess and desire. But to really nail this down will require several longitudinal studies over the life-course. If we had included even a few good measures on surveys such as the General Social Survey even a decade ago, we would have some better data at this point. It is my view that in addition to committing to long-term empirical inquiry we must also open ourselves to other forms of evidence and other approaches. Good histories and extended engagement field work offer promise (see Chapters 3–7, this volume). Ritson and Elliot's (1999) foundational ethnography of British adolescents showing how advertising copy and commercial logic infuses everyday reality is a great example. Creative data-mining and meta-analysis of existing longitudinal data could also yield meaningful findings. Commercial environmental background effects remain important in the social welfare question.

British economists Luik and Waterson (1995) conclude that advertising is a generally weak force in the marketplace. They may be right, but it may be advertising's ubiquity that yield individually small but collectively significant background effects, effects that color our daily perceptions of consumer reality and quality of life. Generally speaking, the social science data come down on the side of the defenders of advertising (Calfee, 1997). Yet, we should not be too quick to see null effects as a conclusion of no effects. The very things that makes advertising so intriguing, its multifacets, layers, generally weak effects, and its amoebic nature, are the very qualities that researchers avoid, those that make the research inconvenient. To really see the effects of advertising on society empirically will happen only after the capture and summation of many small and individually weak effects that may add up over time to something very significant ... or not. But one thing is certain, until we try, and quit doing business as usual, we will never know.

We should also remember that criticizing advertising takes no social courage at all, quite the contrary. To invoke the memory of millions of parents: *just because it's cool, doesn't make it right.* Much of the criticism is, in fact, a well rehearsed chant, an unexamined bias, and a form of requisite cultural capital. Knowing that to criticize advertising is fashionable is like knowing that the sky is blue. Yet, its critics, both academic orthodox and lay pat themselves so much on the back for their "bravery" as to certainly be at risk of elbow injuries. This is, as philosophers Heath and Potter (2004) note, is not only hypocritical, but based on the meta-myth of counter-culture to begin with, the self-congratulatory mythology that by criticizing consumer society and its trapping, one is taking a brave, enlightened and even revolutionary stand. They argue that nothing could be further from the truth; this is merely a comfortable illusion, and a profitable one for the cultural studies industry and all the Neiman-Marxists who profit so handsomely from it (Twitchell, 1999).

SUMMARY

To come full circle, these questions of advertising's interaction with its social context are as much political and philosophical as they are empirical. I have tried to address some of the more stubborn and important ones. First, I do not see compelling evidence that advertising as a singular social agent has made humans any more materialistic than before. Humans were materialistic (again, whatever that means) long before advertising's very recent appearance on this planet. Materiality has always been central to human existence; it always will be, with or without advertising. The causal order is reversed; humans are not materialistic because of advertising; humans have advertising because we are materialistic. Humans like material things: collect them, horde them, share them, ritualize them, worship them, and otherwise make them special, and have been doing so centuries before advertising existed.

Secondly, advertising's role as a social agent is, however, more troubling, the scholarship more mixed. Advertising may, as Fox (1985) suggests, have been out in front of (leading) society only during the 1920s, when it acted as an "an apostle of modernity" (Marchand, 1985), but rarely since. Advertising has lagged behind on many important social trends, but were happy to catch the cultural wave when it looked profitable. When waves of change occur, advertising is more than happy to ride them and take advantage of the turbulence. But, it rarely produces the waves. Advertising is happy to be safely revolutionary when there is money to be made in revolutionary rhetoric, otherwise it's happy to sit and wait on the beach.

Obviously, humans struggle with pleasure and the social sanctions against it; its relationship with things and consumption practices has a long history (Schudson, 1984; Twitchell, 1999). It is no accident that advertising began to flourish as Victorian morality, a system not so friendly to public displays of consumption and hedonism, faded (Marchand, 1985). Nor was it an accident that Madison Avenue had a well-publicized affair with neo-Freudians in the frightened and repressed 1950s, a time of belief in hidden persuaders, subliminal advertising, mind control, the power of repressed sexual desire and all things unconscious

(Fox, 1985). Just below the surface of the on-going advertising discourse are always questions about the rightness and wrongness of desire and having, power and control. We should never pretend that questions regarding social welfare and advertising are absent a moral component whether in the form of classical social theory or elite editorial.

Advertising, as a part of a larger affluent consumer culture, probably has contributed to the social construction of a world of things, and consumption-centred solutions. It is hard to imagine consumer culture without advertising. Advertising helped train consumers in the 1920s and 1930s to expect stylistic changes, model years, the ensemble, and other aspects which lead to the institutionalization of planned obsolescence (Marchand, 1985). Advertising repackaged social movement on top of social movement in order to sell stuff (March, 1985; Frank, 1997; Fox, 1985; Scott, 2004; Holt, 2004; Twitchell, 1999; O'Guinn et al., 2004; O'Guinn and Muniz, 2004; Lasch, 1991). The historical record is abundant with evidence.

Still, advertising, in my view, as part of an advancing consumer culture has contributed positively as well. It has, on balance, been a good source of consumer information. It has represented a world of material aspirations for over a century, and some of that resulted in more people demanding consumer comforts from their societies. Some of those demands were impossible under the planned economies of that era. I truly believe it helped produce a proliferation of market democracies, flawed certainly, but democracies none the less. The ideas of plentitude and choice are not easily contained within the marketplace; they have a tendency to spread. True, advertising has brought this new world unequally to its inhabitants, or at least to a world well acquainted with material inequality. Further, it has not always been good to those upon whom it tried to leverage anxiety; it undoubtedly made some people feel bad, some very bad. Yet, it brought a more honest and open acknowledgment of our relationship with things and an honest striving for a better material existence, and that isn't all bad.

REFERENCES

Advertising Age (2004), "A Death Spiral of Disrespect," April 15.

Advertising Age (2005), "100 Leading National Advertisers," adage.com.

Bordo, S. (1993), "Hunger as Ideology," in *The Consumer Society Reader*, eds. J.B. Schor and D.B. Holt, New York: New Press, 2000, 99–114.

Brienes, W. (1992), "Sexual Puzzles," in *Young, White, and Miserable: Growing Up Female in the Fifties*, Boston: Beacon, 47–83.

Calfee, J. (1997), *Fear of Persuasion: A New Perspective on Advertising and Regulation*, Monnaz, Switzerland: Agora.

Chambers, J. (2006), *Black Men in Gray Flannel Suits*, Philadelphia: University of Pennsylvania Press.

Cohen, L. (2003), *A Consumer's Republic: The Politics of Mass Consumption in Post War America*, New York; Knopf.

Courtney, A. and T. Whipple (1983), *Sex Stereotyping in Advertising*, Lexington, MA: Lexington.

Davison, W.P. (1983), "The Third-Person Effect In Communication," *Public Opinion Quarterly*, (Spring), 47 (1), 1–15.

Donaton, S. (2004), *Madison and Vine: Why the Entertainment and Advertising Industries Must Converge to Survive*, New York: McGraw-Hill.

Fox, S. (1985), *The Mirror Makers: A History of American Advertising and Its Creators*, New York: Vintage.

Frank, T. (1997), *The Conquest of Cool: Business Culture, Counterculture, and the Rise of Hip Consumerism*, Chicago: University of Chicago Press.

Friedan, B. (1963), "The Sexual Sell," in *The Feminine Mystique*, New York: W.W. Norton, 206–32.

Gates, H.L. Jr. (1994), "Prime Time," in *Colored People: A Memoir*, New York: Knopf, 17–28.

Goffman, E. (1959), *The Presentation of Self in Everyday Life*, New York: Anchor.

Gossage, H. (1995), "Is Advertising Worth Saving?" in *The Book of Gossage*, eds. K.B. Rotzoll, J. Graham, and B. Mussey, Chicago: The Copy Workshop.

Greenberg, C. (1999), "Don't Buy Where You Can't Work," in *Consumer Society in American History: A Reader*, ed. Lawrence B. Glickman, Ithaca: Cornell University Press, 241–73.

Gunther, A.C. and E. Thorson (1992), "Perceived Persuasive Effects Of Product Commercials And Public Service Announcements: Third-Person Effects In New Domains," *Communication Research*, 19 (5), (October), 574–97.

Halberstam, D. (1993), *The Fifties*, New York: Villard, 496–507.

Hale, E.G. (1999), *Making Whiteness: The Culture of Segregation in the South: 1890–1940*, New York: Vintage.

Heath, J. and A. Potter (2004), *Nation of Rebels: Why Counterculture Became Counter Culture*, New York: Harper.

Holt, D.B. (2004), *How Brands Become Icons: The Principles of Cultural Branding*, Cambridge, MA: Harvard Business School Press.

Jowett, G. (1976), *Film: The Democratic Art*, New York: Little, Brown.

Laermans, R. (1993), "Learning to Consume: Early Department Stores and the Shaping of the Modern Consumer Culture (1880–1914)," *Theory, Culture and Society*, Newbury Park, California: Sage, 79–102.

Lasch, C. (1991), *The True and Only Heaven: Progress and Its Critics*, New York: Norton.

Lears, T.J.J. (1983), "From Salvation to Self-Realization: Advertising and the Therapeutic Roots of the Consumer Culture, 1880–1930," in *The Culture of Consumption: Critical Essays in American History, 1880–1980*, eds. R.W. Fox and T.J. Jackson Lears, New York: Pantheon Books, 1983, 3–38.

Lears, J. (1994), *Fables of Abundance: A Cultural History of Advertising in America*, New York: Basic Books.

Leiss, W., S. Kline, S. Jhally and J. Botterill (2005), *Social Communication in Advertising: Consumption in the Mediated Marketplace*, 3rd ed., London: Routledge.

Luik, J.C. and M.J. Waterson (1996), *Advertising and Markets: A Collection of Seminal Papers*, Oxfordshire, UK: NTC.

Marchand, R. (1985), *Advertising: The American Dream*, Berkeley: University of California Press.

Muñiz, A.M., Jr. and T.C. O'Guinn (2005), "Marketing Communications in a World of Consumption and Brand Communities," in *Marketing Communication: New Approaches, Technologies, and Styles*, ed. A.J. Kimmel, London: Oxford University Press.

O'Guinn, T.C. (2001), "Community, Ideology, and Societal Marketing," in *Marketing, Corporate Social Initiatives, and the Bottom Line*, eds. L. Aksoy and K. Elliot, Cambridge, MA: Marketing Science Institute, Report No. 01-106, 7–8.

O'Guinn, T.C. (2004), "Hail, Hail Materialism," in *Advances in Consumer Research*, eds. B. Kahn and M.F. Luce, (v. 31), Provo, UT: Association for Consumer Research, 236.

O'Guinn, T.C. (2008), *Brand Communication Strategies*, Cincinnati: South-Western, in preparation.

O'Guinn, T.C. and A.M. Muñiz, Jr. (2004), "The Polit-Brand and Blows Against the Empire: The

Collectively Approved Brands of the New-New Left," in *Advances in Consumer Research*, eds. B. Kahn and M.F. Luce, (v. 31), Provo, UT: Association for Consumer Research 100.

O'Guinn, T.C. and A.M. Muñiz, Jr. (2004), "The Polit-Brand and Blows Against the Empire," paper presented to *Association for Consumer Research Annual Conference*, Toronto, ON.

O'Guinn, T.C. and A.M. Muñiz, Jr. (2005), "Consumption Communities," in *Inside Consumption: Frontiers of Research on Consumer Motives, Goals, and Desires*, eds. D.G. Mick and S. Ratneshwar, New York: Routledge, 252–72.

O'Guinn, T.C. and C.G. Swicegood (2008), "*Advertising as a Vector of Germ Theory: 1890–1920*," unpublished manuscript, University of Wisconsin-Madison.

O'Guinn, T.C. and L.J. Shrum (1997), "The Role of Television in the Construction of Consumer Reality," *Journal of Consumer Research*, March, 278–94.

O'Guinn, T.C. and R.J. Faber (1991), "Mass Communication Theory and Research," chapter in *Handbook of Consumer Behavior Theory and Research*, eds. H.H. Kassarjian and T.S. Robertson, Englewood Cliffs, NJ: Prentice Hall, 349–400.

Percy, L. and M.R. Lautman (1994), "Advertising, Weight Loss, and Eating Disorders," in *Attention, Attitude and Affect in Response to Advertising*, eds. E.M. Clark, T.C. Brock and D.W. Stewart, Hilldale, NJ: Lawrence Erlbaum.

Richins, M. (1995), "Social Comparison, Advertising and Consumer Discontent," *American Behavioral Scientist*, 38 (Feb.), 593–607.

Ritson, M. and R. Elliot (1999), "Social Uses of Advertising: An Ethnographic Study of Adolescent Advertising Audiences," *Journal of Consumer Research*, 26 (3), 260–77.

Rotzoll, K.B., J. Haefner and C. Sandage (1986), *Advertising in Contemporary Society: Perspectives Toward Understanding*, Cincinnati; South-Western.

Sanders, L. (2006), "NYC TO SUBPOENA AD AGENCY EXECS IN DIVERSITY PROBE: Industry's Minority-Hiring Practices Called a City 'Embarrassment'," *Advertising Age*, March 6.

Schudson, M. (1984), "*An Anthropology of Goods*" in *Advertising the Uneasy Persuasion*," New York: Basic Books, 129–46.

Scott, L.M. (2004), *Fresh Lipstick: Redressing Fashion and Feminism*, New York: Palgrave.

Seiter, E. (1994), "Different Children, Different Dreams: Racial Representation in Advertising," in *Gender, Race and Class in Media: A Text-Reader*, eds. G. Dines and J.M. Humez, Thousand Oaks, CA: Sage, 99–108.

Sheehan, K. (2004), *Controversies in Contemporary Advertising*, Thousand Oaks, California: Sage.

Smithsonian Oral History Collection, "Ku Klux Klan Handbill, The Pepsi-Cola Papers," Series 2; Box 13, National Museum of American History, Smithsonian Institution, Washington, D.C.

Sullivan, M. (1926), "Immense Decrease in the Death Rate," in *Visions of Technology: A Century of Debate About Machines, Systems and the Human World*, ed. Richard Rhodes, New York: Touchstone, 88–9.

Twitchell, J.B. (1999), "The Liberating Role of Consumption," in *Lead Us Into Temptation: The Triumph of American Materialism*, New York: Columbia University Press, 271–86.

Wicke, J. (1988), *Advertising Fictions, Literature, Advertisement, and Social Reading*. New York: Columbia University Press.

Williams, J.D., W.-N. Lee and C.P. Haugtvedt (2004), *Diversity in Advertising: Broadening the Scope of Research Directions*, Mahwah, NJ: Lawrence Erlbaum.

Advertisings' Performance in a Market System

William L. Wilkie and Elizabeth S. Moore

Most of the chapters in this volume have approached advertising from a managerial perspective, serving a firm's goals through effective communications with its target audiences. This chapter moves beyond the single firm to the more aggregate analysis embodied in the broad question, *"How does advertising impact society?"* This leads to issues concerning capitalist market systems and social and economic impacts. As other chapters in this volume focus on advertising's social effects on citizens (Chapter 6.5) and how governments choose to regulate advertising in society (Chapter 6.1), we only briefly touch on these topics. Instead, our focus is on socioeconomic benefits advertising can bring to consumers in market-based systems, as well as debates about economic problems it may also cause. However, advertising does not operate in isolation: it is important to begin by appreciating that advertising is an integral component of the larger field of Marketing. We begin, therefore, with two perspectives on marketing and advertising, namely that of the individual and the system as a whole.

We then review the economic debates on advertising seen as persuasion, as information

and as something more. For example, advertising can add social prestige in addition to any persuasion or information. We see advertising as giving rise to four societal questions: impacts on prices, the fostering of innovation, the creation of demand and roles for governments. The consumer movement has long been concerned with the asymmetric power of advertising, its intrusiveness and the advertising of dangerous products (e.g., tobacco), and such as tobacco, and/or to vulnerable groups (e.g., children). These remain unresolved but require consideration. Before summarizing the chapter, we look to the future and to the Internet in particular.

A LARGER VIEW: THE AGGREGATE MARKETING SYSTEM

Each year an astonishing amount of money is spent on advertising aimed at consumers around the world, over a quarter of a trillion dollars in the United States alone (O'Guinn et al., 2006). Almost every business firm advertises, as do many non-profits.

Advertising is a major industry in its own right, accounting for 3% of the gross domestic product in the United States. It is also carried out as an inherent part of the larger field of marketing.

In order to capture the totality of marketing in an entire society, Wilkie and Moore (1999) proposed the concept of an "Aggregate Marketing System", a huge, powerful, yet intricate complex operating to serve the needs of its host society.[1] The Aggregate Marketing System is different for each society: it is an adaptive human and technological institution that reflects the idiosyncrasies of the people, their culture, geography, socio-political decisions, and those economic opportunities and constraints that are unique to each society. Wilkie and Moore (1999) focused their original article on the Aggregate Marketing System of the United States, as an extensively developed capitalist-based market system. We continue with this analytical focus here: most of our analyses of advertising will pertain to other societies as well, though adjustments may be needed in certain areas.

The three primary sets of actors within an Aggregate Marketing System are: (1) marketers; (2) consumers; and (3) government entities whose public policy decisions are meant to facilitate the maximal operations of that system for the benefit of the host society. The fact that each actor brings a unique perspective to the marketplace is a central issue for market-based systems. Viewed in this manner we must consider the goals and interests of all three parties in an Aggregate Marketing System, not simply the advertiser alone.

Marketers and consumers are active on a daily basis, each approaching the marketplace in order to make transactions. Marketers know that consumers can be highly responsive to different marketing programs: this leads to the fact that, within a market-based system, it is consumers' responsiveness to offerings that actually drives supply allocations and directs future resources. Thus, *competition is the main driving force in the system.* Marketers search for effective marketing mixes to drive sales, profits, and growth, and advertising can

be a valuable tool in this process for each competing firm.

From a societal perspective, a key task for advertising in the Aggregate Marketing System is to contribute to a competitive marketing process that is as flexible and adaptive as possible. This not only can best serve current consumer needs, but can also create a welcoming context for new innovations and efficiencies in the future (Vaile et al., 1952). Thus the Aggregate Marketing System relies upon adaptive adjustment by its marketers over time. As customers respond favorably or unfavorably to marketers' efforts, adjustments are made: more favoured goods and services are produced, and less of disfavoured items. New competitors are attracted to areas of opportunity, prices are often adjusted downward through competition and/or production efficiencies, and new buyers join in the consumption of the favored offerings: some markets grow while others whither away. Furthermore, not all marketing operations are successful: The effort to bring dynamism to consumption can lead to excesses, failures, and sometimes unforeseen costs. However, across time, the dynamic elements of the Aggregate Marketing System in the United States and elsewhere have brought dramatic and positive changes to the daily lives of their societies' members.

ADVERTISING'S KEY BENEFITS IN AN AGGREGATE MARKETING SYSTEM

Advertising is an inseparable part of the Aggregate Marketing System, working to supplement other marketing activities to ensure effective system operations. Figure 6.6.1 abstracts advertising's key benefits: (1) to individual consumers, and (2) to the operations of the aggregate system.

Key benefits to individual consumers

In theory, consumers attempt to maximize personal satisfaction, and this is only possible with knowledge of product alternatives' abilities to deliver desired benefits

I. <u>Benefits to Individual Consumers:</u>

- *Provision of Information*
  - re: Product Knowledge and Use
  - re: New Products and Services
  - re: Prices and Specials

- *Decision-Making Enhancements*
  - Assists with Shopping Patronage Decisions
  - Lowers Search Costs

- *Subsidizes Media and Events*
  - News and Editorial
  - Entertainment and Sports

- *Provides Entertainment Itself*

II. <u>Benefits to the Aggregate System:</u>

- *Enlarges Market Demand*
  - Reduced Unit Distribution Costs
  - Eases Entry by New Competitors
  - Lowered Prices through Competition

- *Assists the Success of New, Improved Products*

- *Fosters the Diffusion of Innovations Across Society*

Figure 6.6.1   Societal benefits from advertising

(Sandage, 1989). As indicated in Figure 6.6.1, a primary benefit of advertising is its provision of information to help consumers better understand products, learn about new offerings, and alert them to prices available.[2] Advertising also enhances consumer decisions by reducing search costs, assisting in the choice of stores and brands, and reducing downside risk and effort in the process. Further, advertising's role in subsidising media (e.g., free television, websites, magazines and newspapers) provides viewers with substantially more news, editorial, and entertainment than would be the case without advertising's support. Finally, advertising often provides enjoyment to consumers through its own creative devices, as with humorous and/or musical campaigns. It should be noted that American consumers also recognize most of these benefits as well (and express some reservations about taste and excess), as shown in Bauer and Greyser's (1968) classic study of advertising in America and in a subsequent analysis by Pollay and Mittal (1993).

Key benefits to aggregate market systems

Advertising contributes to market growth

Beyond benefits to individuals, advertising also can bring significant benefits to economic systems in which it is freely employed. As indicated in Figure 6.6.1, a primary benefit is that advertising can be a major contributor to growth in market demand. This benefits marketers with growing revenues, and also in achieving economies of scale to lower production costs for future periods. In this regard, further indirect benefits of category growth include (a) the reduction of unit distribution costs, (b) the attraction of new entrants to bring new competitive offerings to a category, and (c) the ensuing likelihood of price reductions through competition.

Advertising assists new product successes

Of significant importance to the dynamic of marketplace competition is the fact that advertising is often a key contributor in the successful introduction of new products and services. In an extensive recent review of the academic literature on advertising's effects, Stewart and Kamins (2002) conclude that advertising is an effective tool for making consumers aware of new products, and in stimulating their interest in experiencing them. This anticipated interest at the consumer level is a significant motivator for wholesalers and retailers to agree to carry, and perhaps even feature, new products. When this occurs on a broad level, the maker can attain economies of scale, achieve cost reductions, and emerge as a real competitor in the marketplace. This process stimulates existing competitors to improve their offerings to meet or beat the new entrant, perhaps to compete with lowered prices as well, and to likely to use further advertising to communicate to consumers that these improved offerings are now available. Recent research also discusses why advertising is especially impactful for new products. For example, Chandy et al. (2001) conclude that in young markets advertising is an effective tool for reaching large numbers of consumers who were previously unaware of a product and its benefits, in contrast to well-established products where there is little new information to be learned.[3]

Advertising helps bring innovation to its society

A final key benefit of advertising is that it is often a major factor in the successful commercialization of innovative products and services that can bring real improvements to the quality of life in a society. This point is difficult to discern on a day-to-day basis, but strikingly apparent if we step back one hundred years or more, and examine progress in the US and elsewhere. For example, the sheer energy and size of productivity gains brought by the Industrial Revolution clearly held the potential to change the day-to-day life of American society (e.g., the 20 years from 1880 to 1900 alone saw the invention of electricity, aluminium, the steam engine, automobile, telephone, phonograph, rechargeable battery, tractor, cellulose film, and various types of electric motors (Desmond, 1986). The need for advertising arose in conjunction with building mass markets and delivering the new and worthwhile innovations that could ease and enhance the lives of consumers fortunate to possess them. In this regard the development of specialized advertising, with pictures, in printed catalogues by Montgomery Ward and Sears Roebuck provided many citizens, including those in rural locales not served by retail stores, to learn about, then order and use, many of the new products emerging from growing manufacturers of the time (see Tellis, 1998, for an historical look at advertising's growth in the United States). Consider, for example, the implications of the availability of electricity alone, and the many new appliances that have been invented, then developed and delivered to citizens – refrigerators, freezers, clothes washers and dryers, vacuum cleaners, microwave ovens, music systems, television sets, air conditioners, automatic dishwashers, computers, and so forth – all with the use of advertising to inform and motivate purchases on a mass market basis. Today, with the advent of mass media such as television, and now the Internet, advertisers have increased their

capacities to bring innovations to the attention of increasingly global audiences.

ECONOMIC DEBATES ON ADVERTISING: INFORMATION, PERSUASION, OR MORE?[4]

Despite the recognized potentials for advertising to enhance society, economists, social theorists and public policy makers have long been interested in understanding its potential harms as well – in assessing the extent to which advertising overall is actually enhancing the lives of the citizens of the society. A number of questions have been raised in the economic realm such as: Is there too much advertising, such that some is wasting society's resources? Does advertising assist market entry, or is it stifling competition by creating barriers to entry? Does advertising always help consumers to make better purchase decisions, or is some advertising actually misdirecting consumers in their resource allocation decisions? In this section we briefly review three basic economic views on advertising.

Explicit attention to both positive and negative economic effects of advertising began about one hundred years ago when Marshall (1890, 1919) posited that advertising can play both a *constructive role* that is positive (through informing consumers that products exist, some of their qualities, and where they can be found), and a *combative role* that can be socially wasteful (through repetitive efforts to redistribute purchases from rival firms to the advertiser). Chamberlin (1933) then formalized an economic analysis of advertising by incorporating it into his theory of monopolistic competition. Here advertising is viewed as a tool to assist in creating product differentiation in two ways: (1) information provision and (2) altering consumers' tastes or desires. Depending on which of these two properties is emphasized, advertising can be seen to have either positive or negative impacts. These early insights led to the development of several schools of thought that came to quite different conclusions about advertising effects on competition (broadened consumer welfare considerations are reflected through an acceptance that consumers will accrue greater benefits when the marketplace is competitive).

The "advertising as persuasion" school

This first school of thought began in the late 1920s and early 1930s, strongly influenced by Chamberlin's analysis and spearheaded by two female economists, Braithwaite (1928) and Robinson (1933).[5] While recognizing that advertising provides information to consumers, here stress is placed on advertising's strong persuasive powers (in fact, the root Latin term for *advertising* means *to turn*). Advertising is seen as a form of persuasion, holding a power to shape consumer preferences, create differentiation among brands and help establish brand loyalties for heavily advertised products. In turn this leads to consumers being willing to pay higher prices for their preferred brands, thereby lessening the funds available for other purchases and in the aggregate lessening consumer welfare.

Beyond this, the persuasive power of advertising was seen as having potentials to hinder the workings of competition in the marketplace (this stream of thought thus became known in some circles as the "Market Power School"). Due to advertising-induced brand loyalties consumers would consider fewer substitutes and become less price-sensitive in their purchasing decisions, thus making it more difficult for new products to enter and succeed in a market. Competitively, moreover, a new competitor could be required to invest high advertising costs merely to receive notice among the existing advertising stimuli already in the marketplace. In this sense advertising by leading brands could be seen as a barrier to entry for any smaller firms wishing to offer new benefits and/or lower prices. Among longer-term outcomes of concern to the advertising as persuasion school of thought were:

- An increasing industry concentration (i.e., fewer firms actively competing in a marketplace,

with subsequent reductions in benefits from competition).
- Higher profits to large advertisers.
- Higher prices for consumers.

Beneficial effects from advertising are also acknowledged, so it was not assumed that advertising's effects are *necessarily* a problem. However vigilance was urged, to discern situations harmful to consumer welfare and calling for government antitrust actions.

The "advertising as information" school

While the advertising as persuasion school was long associated with academics from Harvard, much of the thinking of the advertising as information school was driven by the University of Chicago, well-known for its emphasis on the value of competitive markets and flaws of government regulation. Also stemming from Chamberlin's original work on monopolistic competition in the 1930s, this stream of thinking began to coalesce in the early 1960s with the work of Ozga (1960), Stigler (1961), and Telser (1964). Emphasis here is on the information that advertising offers to consumers, and the role that this plays in the operation of free markets. It is stressed that consumers are free to choose to buy or not, and information is instrumental in helping them make this choice. Further, consumers are thought to be highly skeptical of advertising, and thus likely to dismiss any unsubstantiated claims they encounter. And because products are profitable only if consumers provide repeat sales, advertisers have an incentive to be truthful. Because of repurchase potentials, competing sellers have incentives to maintain product quality, to innovate, and to advertise prices and other information as well, since advertising can signal a seller's commitment to quality and customer satisfaction. Thus advertising here is seen to be working to improve markets by reducing monopoly power, increasing price sensitivity among consumers, and lowering price levels in the competitive marketplace.

Advertising's secondary effects are also seen to promote public welfare, as when a firm's ability to communicate new discoveries via advertising provides an incentive to invest in further research and product improvements. Calfee (1997), for example, relates that public health officials had been trying for several years, without success, to encourage consumers to increase fiber in their diets. Then, in the mid-1980s, Kellogg's, in conjunction with the National Cancer Institute, began to stress the benefits of a high fibre diet in its advertising for All-Bran cereal. When sales of the brand increased, competitors took notice and adjusted their advertising as well. Across the industry advertising increasingly began to speak to the benefits of specific nutrients and vitamins, as well as the dangers of high-cholesterol, high-fat and high-sugar diets. This advertising attention and the positive consumer response to it stimulated popular media to increasingly cover health and diet issues. More firms then increased their research and development in this direction, leading to improved products available for consumers to ingest. Did this impact consumer welfare? According to a Federal Trade Commission study, consumers' awareness of dietary steps to reduce risks of cancer increased significantly over that period (Ippolito and Mathios, 1990). The use of advertising to provide essential health information has also occurred in other industries, including dental hygiene and pharmaceuticals, where firms have introduced medicines to alleviate such conditions as depression, hypertension or elevated cholesterol (Wilkie and Moore, 2002).

What about economic *problems* from advertising? The advertising as information school is generally optimistic on these issues, centering on the assumption that markets naturally tend toward efficiency, and that market imperfections are generally temporary and self-correcting in nature (Gundlach, 2001). Advertising is seen as a driver of the system through its capacity to deliver information in the marketplace, and interference with such free flows through government regulation has traditionally been a concern to this school of thought.

The complementary view

The two schools as presented appear extreme, in that two apparently opposing properties of advertising are stressed. A third view then emerged that worked toward integrating the two properties of information and persuasion, though proceeding from a different theoretical base (Bagwell, 2005). Building on Chicago-school thinking, the complementary view extended a framework to allow welfare analysis of apparently persuasive advertising, but without having to assert that information is indirectly provided. Grounded in Stigler and Becker's (1977) theoretical work on consumer utility, advertising here is seen as an input to the household production function, with the potential to raise the perceived value of a product even if the advertising is uninformative in the traditional sense ("Social prestige" would represent one such case, wherein the presence of a firm's advertising can influence the utility a consumer obtains from consumption of a particular good).

In summary, these theoretical streams of thought set the stage for addressing several key societal questions about advertising, including: (1) whether advertising raises or lowers prices, (2) whether advertising accelerates or inhibits product entry and innovation, and (3) whether advertising in fact causes markets to grow. In the following sections key findings on these issues are summarized.

ADVERTISING'S PERFORMANCE ON KEY SOCIETAL QUESTIONS

Does advertising raise or lower prices?

Beyond serving as a possible barrier to entry, the effect of advertising on prices is also raised by noting that advertising is an additional cost for a business, that such a cost must be recaptured, and that higher prices could represent the way this is accomplished. Further, it has been noted that firms with substantial advertising spending budgets often charge retailers a price premium above unadvertised brands, and in turn these brands sell for higher prices to consumers than unpromoted products (Aaker, 1991). However, it is also the case that in the early stages of the brand or product life cycle, advertising's capacity to drive sales can lower per-unit production and distribution costs, and thus potentially contribute to lower market prices in the category. Considerable work on this issue has been undertaken by marketing scholars, yielding fruitful concepts and findings.

Finding I: Advertising Does Not Operate In Isolation: The Behavior Of Distribution Channels, Competition, And Consumers All Help To Determine What Happens To Price Levels.

For example, Robert Steiner (1973) provided substantial insights on this issue by noting that the power of advertising could allow a manufacturer to charge more to wholesalers and retailers, but that to predict consumer price levels it is necessary to take into account the dynamics of competition, retailer strategies, and consumer behavior in order to appreciate how advertising actually works in a marketplace. Steiner (a toy company president who turned to public policy economics later in his career) used the toy industry's experience to illustrate how increased advertising in his industry led to considerable sales growth, decreased markups by the distribution channels, and generally decreased price levels for consumers in the US and Canada. Those brands that were most heavily advertised, moreover, had lower retail markups that those with less advertising (Steiner, 1973). This line of thinking was further developed by Farris and his associates (e.g., Farris and Albion, 1980; Abela and Farris, 2001), who also argue that even in mature markets advertising may help some firms gain economies of scale, and may also enable private labels and generics to succeed (by communicating the essential value of a product category). At the same time, in-store competition between these private labels and

advertised brands acts as a form of price control, reducing the ability of the advertised brands to raise prices beyond limits. They also point out that if advertising were not available, alternative and more costly communication methods such as sales promotion, direct marketing or retail salespersons would need to be used, and presumably prices would rise (Abela and Farris, 2001).

Finding II: All Advertising Is Not Equal: Advertising With Different Purposes Can Have Different Impacts.

Consumers' price sensitivity can also be impacted by advertising, and serves as a useful indicator of price movements that are stimulated by advertising in a marketplace (i.e., as price sensitivity increases, prices decline). Kaul and Wittink (1995) offer key insights on the nature of these effects. In brief, they examined 18 relevant empirical studies, some of which showed advertising to decrease price sensitivity (as would be the case if consumers are willing to pay more for the brand to which they have become loyal), and some of which showed advertising to increase price sensitivity (as when consumers shop for lower prices in the marketplace). They then explored the studies in detail, searching for reasons why these mixed results may have occurred. Their search led to the following three "empirical generalizations" about advertising's impact on price:

- An increase in price advertising (e.g., local advertising featuring price information) leads to higher price sensitivity among consumers.
- The use of price advertising leads to lower prices in a marketplace.
- An increase in nonprice advertising (e.g., most national brand ads aimed at increasing brand preference) leads to lower price sensitivity among consumers.

Thus the answer depends on the type of advertising that is being discussed.

Finding III: Manufacturer's Advertising And Retail Price Promotions Work Together, Supporting The "Advertising As Information" View That Advertising Serves To Lower Prices Consumers Pay.

Sethuraman and Tellis (2002) point out that in the US approximately 25% of grocery purchases are bought on deal by consumers, amounting to $100 billion each year. Also, as sales promotions were increasing over the past 20 years, national brand advertising was decreasing as a proportion of brand budgets. Does this suggest that promotions and advertising are viewed as substitutes (wherein the use of advertising suppresses the use of price promotions), or as complements (wherein more advertising implies more price promotion)?[6] Following development of a game theoretic model, the authors conclude that empirical testing is required, since results will depend on whether advertising is operating to increase brand loyalty and reduce response to price promotions (the persuasion school), or is informative enough to increase response to price promotions (the information school). Their empirical analysis covered 82 grocery product categories, and found (1) a positive correlation (+0.69) between advertising expenditure and the frequency of retail discounts, and (2) a positive correlation (+0.31) between advertising expenditure and size of retail discounts. Both results are due to higher advertising being associated with higher promotional price activity, which is supportive of the information school's view of advertising's impacts on prices.

That said, we might still ask whether at some point the level of advertising in a product category is too high, such that societal resources are wasted and all production, distribution, and communication economies have been exhausted. Research has found a number of situations where individual advertisers appear to be overspending, sometimes as a defensive competitive posture (e.g., Albion and Farris, 1981; Tellis, 2004).

Additional issues regarding societal impacts

Advertising fostering innovation
As noted earlier, advertising encourages new product development by providing an efficient way to inform potential buyers about new offerings and the benefits they present. In fact, innovation requires significant investments in research and development that might be difficult to justify if advertising could not be used to communicate the existence of the innovation efficiently (Aaker, 1982). There are, however, some pockets of concern as well. For example, what exactly is an "innovation?" If a new product offering is really not a meaningful improvement, or is priced higher than its benefits warrant, is its advertising actually a positive societal force? Albion and Farris (1981), in examining the fact that industries with large advertising expenditures also have many brands, reported that there is some validity to the charge that firms are using brand proliferation and large advertising budgets to occupy all market niches. This is particularly likely in those markets in which consumer involvement is low, many product attributes are hidden, and slight variations in preferences exist (e.g., breakfast cereals, laundry detergents). However in the long run real product innovation is essential, and advertising alone is unlikely to gain market penetration for "me-too" offerings.

Advertising and the creation of demand
Questions about advertising's impact on the overall demand for products and services have been studied and debated by economists for many years (see e.g., Borden, 1942). These issues are not straightforward: consider, for example, that positive correlations between aggregate demand and advertising expenditures often exist, but the direction of causality is not clear, as advertising will often increase *in response* to a growing market, rather than leading the growth itself. When Baby Boomers came of age the consumption of cigarettes and soft drinks increased substantially: was this due to increased advertising, however, or to a very large group of new potential consumers becoming teenagers and young adults? This example illustrates some of the measurement challenges faced in attempting to disentangle advertising effects at an aggregate level.

Based on their recent review of empirical evidence that takes causality into account,

Stewart and Kamins (2002) report two important conclusions:

1. Advertising does accelerate the growth of new markets in total, and of new competitive entries in those markets as well.
2. With respect to mature markets, however, there is little causal evidence that advertising increases primary demand.

The mature market result is a generalization, and exceptions can exist, as when new product uses are promoted, when product categories with low levels of awareness and usage are made more salient to consumers, or when reminder advertising stimulates consumers' use occasions, such as with soft drinks (Albion and Farris, 1981). Overall, however, circumstances in which advertising increases the overall size of mature markets are limited.

Societal roles for government and advertising

An area of serious concerns to societies with market-based systems is exactly how much government regulation should occur, and in what manners. As this is the topic of Richards and Petty (2007), we will only briefly comment here. With respect to advertising, economists have tended to focus on the impacts government regulation can have on the flow of information in the marketplace. Advertising restrictions have been imposed in a number of markets over the years, including cigarettes, prescription drugs, eyeglasses, advertising by professionals, and specific health claims. Ideally, government regulation should help to correct informational market failures and protect consumers: public policy makers have a variety of possible remedies at their disposal to do so (e.g., Mazis et al., 1981).

Apart from specific remedies, one general economic analysis issue concerns the costs versus benefits of government regulations. Calfee (1997), one of the leading advertising economists of the Information School, posits that government regulation can be costly in that it can suppress the free flow of information and disrupt the natural operations of the market system. There is, moreover, evidence that when restraints to information flow have been lifted, markets have been enhanced. For example, consumer prices dropped substantially when the Federal Government moved to eliminate legal barriers to eyeglass advertising in some states (Wilkie, 1994). Currently, another policy decision under examination involves the current freedoms accorded to direct-to-consumer (DTC) advertising of prescription drugs, which are less than ten years old in the United States. Removal of these restrictions led to an explosion of DTC advertising, to the point that in only a few years it shot to the third largest category for television advertising, behind only fast food and automobiles. Is this a good or bad experiment, however? The US and New Zealand are the *only* nations in the world that allow DTC advertising: if this is in fact a good policy, should not other nations be adopting it as well? This is one of the questions in need of further study by marketing academics (Farris and Wilkie, 2005).

VIEWS OF THE CONSUMER MOVEMENT ON ADVERTISING

The Aggregate Marketing System consists of three sets of actors, two of which – marketers and public policymakers – we have discussed thus far. Many interests of the third sector, consumers (citizens) are covered in Chapter 6.5 in terms of advertising and social issues. Here, we delve into some views of the consumer movement that concern economic analyses. It should be noted that the "consumer movement" is highly variegated, with national lobbying organizations such as the Consumer Federation of America as well as thousands of local groups that focus on single issues such as the environment or cooperative buying. It is not generally antagonistic to the marketing system itself. Instead its efforts are geared to serving consumers' interests, rather than marketers' interests, when trade-offs occur.

A serious concern with the asymmetric power of advertising

A root belief sustaining the consumer movement is that *economic imperfections persist within the marketing system*, particularly as related to product information and pricing (Maynes, 1997). Specifically, an asymmetry of resources works to the advantage of business firms relative to consumers, and that this pervades a market economy. With respect to advertising, specific concern is expressed that consumers are at a disadvantage in part because of the dispersed nature of consumer activities (across all the products and services they purchase) relative to the focused attention a firm places on each specific product and service sold. Further, while advances in technology have brought great benefits, they have also created much more complex decisions for consumers. Imperfections in the informational environment can thus be attributed to the character of an affluent society and modern markets rather than the actions of specific marketers. Moreover, the challenge to consumers is exacerbated by the fact that correlations between price and actual quality may be rather low, suggesting that consumers can be losing purchasing power when this is the case (e.g., Sproles, 1977).

In contrast to the arguments advanced by the "advertising as information" proponents discussed earlier (e.g., Calfee, 1997), advocates of this view disagree with the notion that heavy levels of competitive advertising will trigger sufficient self-correcting market mechanisms. Advertising by necessity provides information in bits and pieces as individual competitors advance their brands, thus the onus necessarily falls to consumers to integrate available information from multiple sources, with multiple styles, and available at multiple times. Furthermore, particular deficiencies – which can be social, economic, or personal – that limit consumers' abilities to make effective decisions are also of concern to the consumer movement, as are (at times) perceived underrepresentation of the consumer interest in government and a perceived ineffectiveness of certain regulatory agencies.

Debates about advertising

Inside the consumer movement there are also some *continuing open questions* that receive discussion, but with little or no prospects for resolution as the consumer advocate community is itself not united on these issues (nor, interestingly, is the community of marketers). Familiar examples include the promotion of dangerous products (e.g., cigarettes, alcohol, guns), advertising to vulnerable groups (e.g., children), and problems of increasing marketplace encroachment (e.g., intrusiveness of advertising), some of which are discussed in more depth in Richards and Petty (2007) and O'Guinn (2007).

INTO THE FUTURE: EMERGING ISSUES AND THE EVOLUTION OF ADVERTISING

The inherent challenges for advertising continue

A persistent issue that receives continuing consideration is: How far should advertising go in trying to persuade consumers to purchase a product? Within the broad question of limits to persuasion are two more specific issues: information disclosure and advertising intrusiveness.

Information disclosure

Throughout this chapter "full information" has been repeated as one of the fundamental assumptions of a market system, and for every advertiser "how much information to provide?" is a decision to be made as a natural part of business operations. *From a societal perspective, however, it is also important to recognize that while advertising is a prominent source of information provision, it is by no means the only one* (e.g., Wilkie, 1997). Marketers possess many other tools with which to also disseminate product information to consumers, including packaging, product labels, in-store displays, brochures, owners manuals, guarantees and warranties, toll free telephone lines, retail salesperson, and websites. Advertising can be used to direct consumers to more detailed sources of information, as well as other independent sources (e.g., encouraging consumers to consult their physician). Finally, marketers are not the sole source of product information in our system. Public policy makers, consumer advocates, independent rating organizations, and consumer themselves through word-of-mouth are also important disseminator groups.

Finally, the topic of information disclosure cannot be fully understood without recognizing the fact that consumers' use of information is imperfect. Consumers may fail to attend to particular information, or miscomprehend aspects of what they read in the print media (Jacoby and Hoyer, 1987). Given time constraints inherent in broadcast media, advertisers are limited in the amount and complexity of information they can communicate to consumers in these venues. Competing demands in a consumer's life or limited product knowledge may also lead to a greater reliance on simplifying rules or heuristics than might otherwise be optimal (e.g., Alba and Hutchinson, 1987). Thus, the challenges that advertisers face in deciding how much information to provide and how it should best be communicated are significant, and likely to escalate as media clutter, the topic of the next section, continues to increase.

Intrusiveness: The challenge of "advertising clutter"

From a societal perspective, when aggregated across brands, across product categories and across marketers, there is a tremendous accumulation of advertising messages in our marketing system. The advent of new media is further providing an array of clever new outlets, Internet banner ads, product placements, buzz marketing for ad placements, further increasing the amount of advertising in our world. As noted, critics are quick to point to the intrusiveness of advertising, and "information overload" is a term that has worked its way into the consumer literature.

This enormous aggregation of advertising is a characteristic of the system in that it is the result of millions of individual marketers choosing their best tools with which to compete with one another to gain attention and consumer patronage. The state of "ad clutter" is paradoxical, in that the same time an advertiser is contributing to it, he or she is also having to find ways to cut through the noise so as to reach the target audience efficiently, and this has become more difficult to do as media clutter has increased. One recent addition to planning in this area has arisen in "integrated marketing communications" (IMC), which encourages the coordinated use of multiple media to meet an advertiser's communication goals (e.g., Naik and Raman, 2003).

The Internet revolution brings new options

Technology, growth, and globalization are changing the consumer marketplace and bringing new opportunities and new problems. The Internet, for example, has brought a dramatic increase in product information for those consumers who can take advantage of it, with numerous tools to facilitate information gathering and evaluation that are increasingly independent of the marketers who produce the products and services that are being assessed. The Internet thus holds promise for redressing some of the informational asymmetry issues just discussed. For example, "intelligent agents" are software tools designed to facilitate decision making by allowing consumers to search for specific types of information, store search results, and construct information displays (Coupey, 2005). Similarly, a "shopping bot" is an intelligent agent that scouts the Internet on behalf of consumers who specify their search criteria (Turban et al., 2004). Some specialize in product categories (e.g., autobytel.com, bankrate.com) while others cover a range of products (e.g., mysimon.com).[7] Such agents can significantly enhance search for making brand comparisons, though they do require time to use and cognitive effort to process information (Montgomery et al., 2004). With respect to the topic of advertising, it is also worth noting that these independent information agents are themselves primarily supported by advertising revenue.

Based on the potentials of these new technologies, some prominent marketing scholars have begun to call for fundamental strategic shifts in how individual firms interact with customers and prospects. Glen Urban (2005) of MIT, for example, forecasts that the successful firm of the future will choose to become a "customer advocate" by providing consumers with honest and complete information, including that the best option is not a product of that firm, but that of a competitor (e.g., a recent advertising campaign by Progressive Insurance represents a version of this approach). In response, Urban forecasts that appreciative customers will reward the "advocating" firm with loyalty and patronage (in part because the firm will have had to become much more sensitive to finding ways to truly satisfy their clients). Whether or not matters change to this extent, the new world of the Internet will clearly impact advertising's economic roles and performance in the coming years.

SUMMARY

This chapter has covered a range of topics related to the performance of advertising as an aggregate activity within a society. Advertising needs to be understood at a number of different levels from the individual to the system as a whole. In particular social and economic aspects are interwoven. We have noted size and breadth of advertising, but also that it is commonly employed as one of a number of tools within marketing, suggesting that its complementary functions are also important to recognize. We have introduced the concept of the "Aggregate Marketing System" to bring analysis to the societal level. The Aggregate Marketing System is different for each society: it is an adaptive human and technological institution that reflects the idiosyncrasies of the people, their culture, geography, socio-political decisions, and those economic opportunities and constraints that are unique to each society. We have noted that economic dimensions are significant to this analysis, and have reviewed a number of more detailed issues in this domain. In particular, we examine advertising's impact on prices, its roles in fostering innovation and in creating demand.

Advertising can be a major contributor to growth in market demand. This benefits marketers with growing revenues, and also in achieving economies of scale to lower production costs for future periods. In this regard, further indirect benefits of category growth include (a) the reduction of unit distribution costs, (b) the attraction of new entrants to bring new competitive offerings to a category, and (c) the ensuing likelihood of price reductions through competition. This is borne out by more detailed work showing how ads and promotions work together (to lower price). However, different ads have different objectives and some advertising for high quality goods does indeed support higher prices.

In this chapter, consideration was given to the consumer movement's concerns with the asymmetric power of advertising, its intrusiveness, the advertising of dangerous, products (e.g., tobacco) and advertising to vulnerable groups (e.g., children). These remain unresolved but are matters which need to be taken very seriously.

A consistent theme throughout this chapter is that advertising should not be viewed in isolation: advertising does provide information but it is not the only source. The increasing variety of media and volume of advertising is exacerbating problems of intrusiveness and clutter ("information overload"). This is paradoxical in the sense that advertisers are creating the problem, but are also having to work to find solutions. The Internet adds intriguing dimensions to the analysis. It both adds to the difficulties and offers potential solutions as customers become more active in communication partnerships.

In summary, while not perfect, advertising is seen to brings benefits and dynamism to market-based systems, connecting buyers and sellers across the sprawling marketplace, and helping to forge better standards of living for those societies employing it.

NOTES

1 Interested readers can obtain copies of the article "Marketing's Contributions to Society," (Wilkie and Moore, 1999) and an associated article, "Scholarly Research in Marketing: Exploring the >4 Eras of Thought Development" (Wilkie and Moore, 2003) by downloading from http://web2.business.nd.edu/Faculty/wilkie.html.

2 Advertising exists in many forms beyond products and services, of course, and offers potential societal benefits in each of these – e.g., employment ads and public service advertising. In this chapter we focus, however, on products and services.

3 Consistent with this reasoning, the authors go on to show that argument-based appeals and expert sources in advertising are more effective in newer markets, (relative to emotional appeals, which tend to be more effective in mature markets).

4 Discussion in this section has benefited especially from Bagwell's (2005) extensive review of the economic analysis of advertising, as well as earlier works by Albion and Farris (1981), Farris and Albion (1989), and Calfee (1997).

5 Later contributors to development of this perspective include Kaldor (1950), Bain (1956), Galbraith (1958, 1967), and Comanor and Wilson (1967, 1974).

6 The costs and benefits of retail price promotions have been extensively studied following the advent of retail scanner data. See, for example, Blattberg and Neslin, 1990; Mela et al., 1997; and Sethuraman and Tellis, 1991.

7 Various intelligent agents exist, some helping with search, comparison and purchase (e.g., cnet.com), others crawl the web to find the cheapest price. An example of the latter is mysimon.com.

REFERENCES

Aaker, D.A. (1982), "The Social and Economic Effects of Advertising," in *Consumerism – Search for the Consumer Interest*, 4th ed., eds. D.A. Aaker and G.S. Day, New York, NY: Free Press, 190–209.

Aaker, D.A. (1991), *Managing Brand Equity*, New York, NY: Free Press.

Abela, A.V. and P.W. Farris (2001), "Advertising and Competition," in *Handbook of Marketing and Society*, eds. P.N. Bloom and G.T. Gundlach, Thousand Oaks, CA: Sage, 184–205.

Alba, J.W. and J.W. Hutchinson (1987), "Dimensions of Consumer Expertise," *Journal of Consumer Research*, 13 (March), 411–54.

Albion, M.S. and P.W. Farris (1981), *The Advertising Controversy – Evidence on the Economic Effects of Advertising*, Boston, MA: Auburn House.

Bauer, R.A. and S.A. Greyser (1968), *Advertising in America: The Consumer View*. Boston, MA: Research Division, Harvard Business School.

Bagwell, K. (2005), *The Economic Analysis of Advertising*, Monograph, Columbia University, Accessed at: http://www.columbia.edu/%7Ekwb8/papers.html (August).

Bain, J.S. (1956), *Barriers to New Competition: Their Character and Consequences in Manufacturing Industries*, Cambridge, MA: Harvard University Press.

Blattberg, R.C. and S.A. Neslin (1990), *Sales Promotion: Concepts, Methods, and Strategies,* Englewood Cliffs, NJ: Prentice Hall.

Borden, N.H. (1942), "Findings of the Harvard Study on the Economic Effects of Advertising," *Journal of Marketing*, 6 (April), 89–99.

Braithwaite, D. (1928), "The Economic Effects of Advertising," *Economic Journal*, 38, 16–37.

Calfee, J.E. (1997), *Fear of Persuasion – A New Perspective on Advertising and Regulation*, La Vergne, TN: AEI Press.

Chamberlin, E. (1933), *The Theory of Monopolistic Competition*, Cambridge, MA: Harvard University Press.

Chandy, R.K., G.J. Tellis, D.J. MacInnis and P. Thaivanich (2001), "What to Say When: Advertising Appeals in Evolving Markets," *Journal of Marketing Research*, 38 (November), 399–414.

Comanor, W.S. and T.A. Wilson (1967), "Advertising, Market Structure and Performance," *The Review of Economics and Statistics*, 49, 423–40.

Comanor, W.S. and T.A. Wilson (1974), *Advertising and Market Power*, Cambridge, MA: Harvard University Press.

Coupey, E. (2005), *Digital Business: Concepts and Strategy*, 2nd ed., Upper Saddle River, NJ: Pearson/Prentice Hall.

Desmond, K. (1986), *A Timetable of Inventions and Discoveries*, New York, NY: M. Evans & Co.

Farris, P.W. and M.S. Albion (1980), "The Impact of Advertising on the Price of Consumer Products," *Journal of Marketing*, 44 (Summer), 17–35.

Farris, P.W. and M.S. Albion (1989), The Impact of Advertising on the Price of Consumer Products, in *Advertising in Society*, eds. R. Hovland and G.B. Wilcox, Lincolnwood, IL: NTC Books, 298–333.

Farris, P.W., M.S. Albion and W.L. Wilkie (2005), "Marketing Scholars' Roles in the Policy Arena: An Opportunity for Discourse on Direct-to-Consumer Advertising," *Journal of Public Policy & Marketing*, 24 (Spring), 3–6.

Galbraith, J.K. (1958), *The Affluent Society,* Boston, MA: Houghton-Mifflin.

Galbraith, J. K. (1967), *The New Industrial State,* Boston, MA: Houghton-Mifflin.

Gundlach, G.T. (2001), "Marketing and Modern Antitrust Thought," in *Handbook of Marketing and Society,* eds. P.N. Bloom and G.T. Gundlach, Thousand Oaks, CA: Sage, 34–50.

Ippolito, P.M. and A.D. Mathios (1990), "Information, Advertising and Health Choices: A Study of the Cereal Market," *RAND Journal of Economics,* 21 (Autumn), 459–80.

Jacoby, J. and W.D. Hoyer (1987), *The Comprehension and Miscomprehension of Print Communications: An Investigation of Mass Media Magazines,* New York, NY: Advertising Educational Foundation.

Kaldor, N.V. (1950), "The Economic Aspects of Advertising," *Review of Economic Studies,* 18, 1–27.

Kaul, A. and D.R. Wittink (1995), "Empirical Generalizations about the Impact of Advertising on Price Sensitivity and Price," *Marketing Science,* 14 (3), G151–60.

Marshall, A. (1890), *Principles of Economics,* London: MacMillan and Company.

Marshall, A. (1919), *Industry and Trade: A Study of Industrial Technique and Business Organization and of Their Influences on the Conditions of Various Classes and Nations,* London: MacMillan and Company.

Maynes, E.S. (1997), "Consumer Problems in Market Economies," in *Encyclopedia of the Consumer Movement,* ed. S. Brobeck, Santa Barbara, CA: ABC-CLIO, 158–64.

Mazis, M.B., R. Staelin, H. Beales and S. Salop (1981), "A Framework for Evaluating Consumer Information Regulation," *Journal of Marketing,* 45 (Winter), 11–21.

Mela, C.F., S. Gupta and D.R. Lehmann (1997), "The Long-Term Impact of Promotions and Advertising on Consumer Brand Choice," *Journal of Marketing Research,* 34 (May), 248–61.

Montgomery, A.L., K. Hosanagar, R. Krishnan and K.B. Clay (2004), "Designing a Better Shopbot," *Management Science,* 50 (February), 189–206.

Naik, P.A. and K. Raman (2003), "Understanding the Impact of Synergy in Multimedia Communications," *Journal of Marketing Research,* 60 (November), 375–88.

O'Guinn, T.C., C.T. Allen and R.J. Semenik (2006), *Advertising and Integrated Brand Promotion,* 4th ed., Thomson South-Western.

O' Guinn, T.C. (2007), "Advertising, Consumption and Welfare," in *The SAGE Handbook of Advertising,* eds. G.J. Tellis and T. Ambler, London: Sage Publications.

Ozga, S.A. (1960), "Imperfect Markets Through Lack of Knowledge," *Quarterly Journal of Economics,* 74, 29–52.

Pollay, R.W. and B. Mittal (1993), "Here's the Beef: Factors, Determinants, and Segments in Consumer Criticism of Advertising," *Journal of Marketing,* 57 (July), 99–114.

Richards, J.I. and R.D. Petty (2007), "Advertising Regulation," in *The SAGE Handbook of Advertising,* eds. G.J. Tellis and T. Ambler, London: Sage Publications.

Robinson, J. (1933), *Economics of Imperfect Competition,* London: MacMillan and Company.

Sandage, C.H. (1989), "Some Institutional Aspects of Advertising," in *Advertising in Society,* eds. R. Hovland and G.B. Wilcox, Lincolnwood, IL: NTC Books, 3–26.

Sethuraman, R. and G. Tellis (1991), "An Analysis of the Tradeoff between Advertising and Price Discounting," *Journal of Marketing Research,* 28 (May), 160–74.

Sethuraman, R. and G. Tellis (2002), "Does Manufacturer Advertising Suppress or Stimulate Retail Price Promotions? Analytical Model and Empirical Analysis," *Journal of Retailing,* 78, 253–63.

Sproles, G.B. (1977), "New Evidence on Price and Product Quality," *Journal of Consumer Affairs,* 11 (Summer), 63–77.

Steiner, R.L. (1973), "Does Advertising Lower Prices?" *Journal of Marketing,* 37 (October), 19–26.

Stewart, D.W. and M.A. Kamins (2002), "Marketing Communications," in *Handbook of Marketing,* eds. B.A. Weitz and R. Wensley, Thousand Oaks, CA: Sage, 282–309.

Stigler, G.J. (1961), "The Economics of Information," *Journal of Political Economy,* 69, 213–225.

Stigler, G.J. and G.S. Becker (1977), "De Gustibus Non Est Disputandum," *American Economic Review,* 67 (March), 76–90.

Tellis, G.J. (1998), *Advertising and Sales Promotion Strategy.* Reading, MA: Addison-Wesley, Inc.

Tellis, G.J. (2004), *Effective Advertising – Understanding When, How, and Why Advertising Works,* Thousand Oaks, CA: Sage.

Telser, L.G. (1964), "Advertising and Competition," *Journal of Political Economy,* 72, 537–62.

Turban, E., D. King, J. Lee and D. Viehland (2004), *Electronic Commerce: A Managerial Perspective,* Upper Saddle River, NJ: Pearson/Prentice-Hall.

Urban, G.L. (2005), "Customer Advocacy: A New Era in Marketing?," *Journal of Public Policy & Marketing,* 24 (Spring), 155–9.

Vaile, R.S., E.T. Grether and R. Cox (1952), *Marketing in the American Economy,* New York, NY: Ronald Press Co.

Wilkie, W.L. (1994), *Consumer Behavior*, 3rd ed., New York, NY: Wiley.

Wilkie, W.L. (1997), "Information Dissemination," in *Encyclopedia of the Consumer Movement*, ed. S. Brobeck, Santa Barbara, CA: ABC-CLIO, 321–30.

Wilkie, W.L. and E.S. Moore (1999), "Marketing's Contributions to Society," *Journal of Marketing*, 63 (Special Issue), 198–218.

Wilkie, W.L. and E.S. Moore (2002), "Observations on the Social Value of Pharmaceutical Marketing," *Journal of Pharmaceutical Marketing & Management*, 15 (1), 5–14.

Wilkie, W.L. and E.S. Moore (2003), "Scholarly Research in Marketing: Exploring the "4 Eras" of Thought Development," *Journal of Public Policy & Marketing*, 22 (Fall), 116–46.

Index

Jan18/08